OXFORD STUDIES IN MEDIEVAL
EUROPEAN HISTORY

General Editors

JOHN H. ARNOLD   PATRICK J. GEARY

JOHN WATTS

On Hospitals

Welfare, Law, and Christianity in
Western Europe, 400–1320

SETHINA WATSON

OXFORD
UNIVERSITY PRESS

OXFORD
UNIVERSITY PRESS

Great Clarendon Street, Oxford, OX2 6DP,
United Kingdom

Oxford University Press is a department of the University of Oxford.
It furthers the University's objective of excellence in research, scholarship,
and education by publishing worldwide. Oxford is a registered trade mark of
Oxford University Press in the UK and in certain other countries

First Edition published in 2020

Impression: 1

Published in the United States of America by Oxford University Press
198 Madison Avenue, New York, NY 10016, United States of America

British Library Cataloguing in Publication Data
Data available

Library of Congress Control Number: 2019955809

ISBN 978-0-19-884753-3

Printed and bound by
CPI Group (UK) Ltd, Croydon, CR0 4YY

To my parents

Acknowledgements

I am grateful to many people who have sustained both the project and its author over the years.

This study has been something of a detour, from a longer project on English hospitals, and it is possible that it could only have been written at York. The students and the culture of co-teaching at the Centre for Medieval Studies, and especially colleagues in Literature, Art History, and Archaeology have taught this historian much about reading and looking, and about place. Fellow medievalists in the history department, Pete Biller, Katy Cubitt, Mary Garrison, Jeremy Goldberg, Guy Halsall, Tom Johnson, Harry Munt, Mark Ormrod, Sarah Rees Jones, Lucy Sackville, Craig Taylor, and Pragya Vohra, have each at some point (or many) offered support, counsel, and just the right reference. Conversations with doctoral students kept ideas bubbling through busy terms. The history department has offered consistent support, in many forms, and the University's Anniversary Lectureship in 2008/9 provided precious time to sketch out early questions. Without Pete Biller, Elizabeth Tyler, Mark Jenner, and Simon Ditchfield, friends and colleagues from whom I have learned so much, this would have been a very different—and far poorer—book.

Many years ago, Ian Forrest and I began a conversation that continues to this day, and which became the seeds of Social Church. To him, and to the many folks of Social Church, I owe particular thanks. Among them, Frances Andrews, Lucy Donkin, Emilia Jamroziak, Sarah Hamilton, Nick Karn, Rob Lutton, Tom Pickles, Theo Riches, Catherine Rider, Rebecca Rist, and Simon Yarrow offered encouragement, suggestions, and stimulating questions, during the course of this project. Judy Frost made me think harder (and better) about monasteries and kept me going in the difficult stretches. Jocelyn Wogan-Browne and Howard Robinson provided a place to think, and inspiration, when I most needed it; without them, this book could not have been written.

This was a book that willed itself into being. It pulled the author along, somewhat in fear but more fundamentally in wonder. At many points I would have stumbled if not for the expertise, advice, and encouragement of many scholars. There would be no book without Pete Biller and Kathleen Cushing, who read an early version when the ideas were but a (long) article. At later stages, others took the time to read chapters, or parts of chapters, offering an expert eye and generous advice: Peter Clarke (Chapter 7), Jinty Nelson (Chapters 4 and 6); Eric Knibbs (on Pseudo-Isidore), Ian Forrest (Introduction), and Mayke De Jong, whose comments on the whole of Part II helped a new arrival to the early middle ages find focus. The case for Courson's council of Reims was first set out at the Lateran IV Octocentennial Conference in Rome in 2015, and I am grateful to Pascal Montaubin, Brenda Bolton, Adam Davis, and Danica Summerlin for discussion in its wake. Annette Kehnel and Herwig Weigl generously answered queries. Maureen Jurkowski helped in many collegial ways with multi-tasking. Henrietta Leyser read the whole manuscript and offered characteristically sage counsel. The mistakes that remain are my own.

Particular thanks are due to the readers for OUP (Adam Davis, Peregrine Horden, and a third, anonymous reader, who helped me to think better about law). Their rigorous, perceptive, and generous advice helped reframe the book and its main arguments. John Arnold offered sound advice at all points in the process; he and the other editors of the series and, at OUP, Stephanie Ireland and Cathryn Steele, have been a wonderful editorial team. Eric Wolever, Hollie Morgan, Tom Powles, and Lauren Stokeld assisted in checking references and Laura Napram with the index. The final product would have been far less clear without the critical eyes of Tim Ayers, Joseph Spooner (Chapters 1–6) and Elizabeth Tyler (Chapters 7–9), the best of readers.

Others have helped me along the way. To my teachers – Susan Sharpling, Phil Niles, Benedicta Ward, Benjamin Thompson, Sally Mapstone, and Lesley Smith – I owe a special debt. The collegiality and learning of Lesley Abrams, Martin Conway, Lyndal Roper, and Simon Skinner at Balliol college continue to inspire me. Friends have made the burden lighter, and life far brighter. They include Elisabeth and Al Dutton, Anna Gedrich, Torrey Clark, Jeff Feldstein and Beth Tieman, Heather Hilleren, Nat and Charles Blundell, Kai Esbensen, Eric Hall, Eric Resler, Emma Cavell, Katy Beebe, Giles Gasper, Richard Dobson, and Diana Robbins. My family have walked this path with me for too many years to count. To the Ayers family, to Hannah and Mike, Boyd and Lincoln, and to Martha: thank you.

Finally, there are two people without whom this book could not have been written. Henrietta Leyser supervised my doctorate (a very different kind of project), so many years ago. It was the lessons I learnt from her then, and the model of her scholarship, that helped me chart ways forward when things seemed most daunting. Tim Ayers has stood beside me every step of the way, encouraging, advising, and sustaining me. Without him, the project would have foundered before it reached the ninth century.

It is dedicated to my parents, John and Marigold Watson, with thanks and love.

Contents

List of Figures and Table

Abbreviations

Alex III	P. D. Clarke and A. J. Duggan, eds, *Pope Alexander III (1159–81): The Art of Survival* (Aldershot, 2010)
Ann. reg. Franc.	*Annales regni Francorum inde ab a. 741 usque ad a. 829*, ed. F. Kurze, MGH *SS rer. Germ.* VI (Hanover, 1895)
ASBHH	*Annales de la Société Belge d'Histoire des Hôpitaux*
Ben. rule	Benedictine rule, cited from *The Rule of Saint Benedict*, ed. and tr. B. L. Venarde (Cambridge, MA, 2011)
BL	London, British Library
BMCL	*Bulletin of Medieval Canon Law* NS
BnF	Paris, Bibliothèque nationale de France
Boshof, 'Armenfürsorge'	E. Boshof, 'Armenfürsorge im Frühmittelalter: Xenodochium, matricula, hospitale pauperum', *Vierteljahrschrift für Sozial- und Wirtschaftsgeschichte* 71:2 (1984), 153–74
Brodman, *CRME*	J. W. Brodman, *Charity and Religion in Medieval Europe* (Washington, DC, 2009)
C&S	*Councils and Synods: with Other Documents Relating to the English Church* I: *AD 871–1204*, ed. D. Whitelock, M. Brett, and C. N. L. Brooke, 2 vols (Oxford, 1981) II: *AD 1205–1313*, ed. F. M. Powicke and C. R. Cheney, 2 vols (Oxford, 1964)
Caron, '*pia fundatio*'	P. G. Caron, 'L'evoluzione dalla *quarta pauperum* alla *pia fundatio* a scopo ospedaliero', *Il Diritto Ecclesiastico* 73 (1962), 137–59
COGD	*Conciliorum oecumenicorum generaliumque decreta*, ed. G. Alberigo, A. Melloni, et al., Corpus Christianorum, 2 vols (Turnhout, 2006–13) I: *The Oecumenical Councils: From Nicaea I to Nicaea II (325–787)* II: *The General Councils of Latin Christendom: From Constantinople IV to Pavia-Siena (869–1424)*
CCCM	Corpus Christianorum Continuatio Medievalis
CCEMA	L. Kéry, *Canonical Collections of the Early Middle Ages (ca. 400–1140): A Bibliographical Guide to the Manuscripts and Literature* (Washington, DC, 2013)
CCRL	D. Johnston, ed., *The Cambridge Companion to Roman Law* (Cambridge, 2015)
CCSL 148, 148A	Corpus Christianorum Series Latina: 148: *Concilia Galliae A.314–A.506*, ed. C. Munier (Turnholt, 1963) 148A: *Concilia Galliae A.511–A.695*, ed. Charles De Clercq (Turnhout, 1963)

CDL I, II	*Codice diplomatico longobardo*, I and II, ed. L. Schiaparelli, Fonti per la Storia d'Italia 62–3 (Rome, 1929–33)
Ch. Heir	P. Godman and R. Collins, eds, *Charlemagne's Heir: New Perspectives on the Reign of Louis the Pious (814–840)* (Oxford, 1990)
Chron. Maj.	Matthew Paris, *Chronica Majora*, ed. H. R. Luard, 7 vols (London, 1872–83)
CICMA	C. M. Radding and A. Ciaralli, *The Corpus Iuris Civilis in the Middle Ages: Manuscripts and Transmission from the Sixth Century to the Juristic Revival* (Leiden, 2007)
Cod.	*Codex Iustinianus*, ed. P. Krüger, 13th ed., Corpus Iuris Civilis II (Berlin, 1963)
1–5 Comp	Compilationes 1, 2, 3, 4, 5, as examined in *QCA*
CPR	*Calendar of Patent Rolls of Henry III*, ed. H.C. Maxwell Lyte, 6 vols (London, 1901–13)
CS	*Die Canones—sammlungen zwischen Gratian und Bernhard von Pavia*, ed. E. Friedberg (Leipzig, 1897; repr. Graz, 1958)
C.Th.	Codex Theodosianus, using the edition *Theodosiani libri xvi cum constitutionibus sirmondianis et leges novellae ad Theodosianum pertinentes*, ed. T. Mommsen and P. M. Meyer, I (Berlin, 1905)
DEC	*Decrees of the Ecumenical Councils*, ed. N. P. Tanner, II (Washington, DC, 1990)
De Spiegeler, *Liège*	P. De Spiegeler, *Les hôpitaux et l'assistance à Liège (X^e–XVe siècles): Aspects institutionnels et sociaux* (Paris, 1987)
Dickson, 'Courson'	M. and C. Dickson, 'Le cardinal Robert de Courson: Sa vie', *Archives: D'Histoire Doctrinale et Littéraire du Moyen Age* 9 (1934), 53–142
EHP	M. Mollat, ed., *Études sur l'histoire de la pauvreté (Moyen Age–XVIe siècle)*, 2 vols (Paris, 1974)
EHR	*English Historical Review*
EME	*Early Medieval Europe*
Europ. Spitalwesen	M. Scheutz, A. Sommerlechner, H. Weigl, and A. S. Weiß, eds, *Europäisches Spitalwesen: Institutionelle Fürsorge in Mittelalter und Früher Neuzeit/ Hospitals and Institutional Care in Medieval and Early Modern Europe*, Mitteilungen des Instituts für Österreichische Geschichtsforschung, Ergänzungsband 51 (Vienna, 2008)
Fondations	J. Dufour and H. Platelle, eds, *Fondations et œuvres charitables au Moyen Age* (Paris, 1999)
Frank, 'Hospitalreformen'	T. Frank, 'Spätmittelalterliche Hospitalreformen und Kanonistik', *Reti Medievali Rivista* 11 (2010), 1–40
Gesta Aldrici	'Gesta domni Aldrici Cenomannicae urbis episcopi', in *Geschichte des Bistums Le Mans von der Spätantike bis zur Karolingerzeit: Actus pontificum Cenomannis in urbe degentium und Gesta Aldrici*, ed. M. Weidemann, I (Mainz, 2000)

Gratian	*Decretum magistri Gratiani*, ed. E. Friedberg, Corpus Iuris Canonici I (Leipzig, 1879)
Greg. Epp.	*Gregorii I papae Registrum epistolarum*, ed. P. Ewald and L. Hartmann, MGH *Epp.* I–II (Berlin, 1887–91); tr. J. R. C. Martyn, *The Letters of Gregory the Great*, 3 vols (Toronto, 2004)
Hartmann, *Synoden*	W. Hartmann, *Die Synoden der Karolingerzeit im Frankenreich und in Italien*, Konziliengeschichte A: Darstellungen (Paderborn, 1989)
HDC	J. Imbert, *Les hopitaux en droit canonique (du décret de Gratien à la sécularisation de l'administration de l'Hôtel–Dieu de Paris en 1505)*, L'Eglise et l'Etat au Moyen Age 8 (Paris, 1947)
HHF	J. Imbert, ed., *Histoire des hôpitaux en France* (Toulouse, 1982)
HMCL	W. Hartmann and K. Pennington, eds, *The History of Medieval Canon Law in the Classical Period, 1140–1234: From Gratian to the Decretals of Pope Gregory IX* (Washington, DC, 2008)
HMMA	P. Montaubin and J. Schwerdroffer, eds, *Hôpitaux et maladreries au Moyen Age: Espace et environnement* (Amiens, 2004)
Itin. Fid.	R. Helmholz and R. Zimmermann, eds, *Itinera Fiduciae: Trust and Treuhand in Historical Perspective*, Comparative Studies in Continental and Anglo-American Legal History 19 (Berlin, 1988)
JE, JK, JL	*Regesta pontificum romanorum ab condita ecclesia ad annum post Christum natum MCXCVIII*, ed. P. Jaffé, rev. S. Loewenfeld, F. Kaltenbrunner and P. Ewald, 2nd ed., 2 vols (Leipzig, 1885–88; repr. Graz, 1956)
JEC	*Journal of Ecclesiastical History*
JMH	*Journal of Medieval History*
Kaiser, *Epit. Iul.*	W. Kaiser, *Die Epitome Iuliani: Beiträge zum römischen Recht im frühen Mittelalter und zum byzantinischen Rechtsunterricht*, Studien zur Europäischen Rechtsgeschichte 175 (Frankfurt, 2004)
Liber Pont.	*Liber pontificalis*, ed. L. Duchesne, *Le Liber pontificalis: Texte, introduction et commentaire*, 2 vols (Paris 1886–92)
Mansi	*Sacrorum conciliorum nova et amplissima collectio*, ed. G. D. Mansi, 31 vols (Venice, 1758–98), repr. and cont. L. Petit and I. B. Martin, 60 vols (Paris, 1901–27)
MGH	Monumenta Germaniae Historica
Cap. I, II, NS	I–II: Capitularia. Legum Sectio II: *Capitularia Regum Francorum*, ed. A. Boretius and V. Krause, 2 vols (Hannover, 1883–97) NS: Capitularia. Legum Sectio II (new series) *Collectio Capitularium Ansegisi/Die Kapitulariensammlung des Ansegis*, ed. Gerhard Schmitz (Hanover, 1996)

Cap. episc. I–IV:	*Capitula episcoporum,* ed. P. Brommer, R. Pokorny, and M. Stratmann, 4 vols (Hannover, 1984–2005)
Conc.	Concilia. Legum Sectio III I: *Concilia aevi Merovingici,* ed. F. Maassen (Hanover, 1893) II.i–ii: *Concilia aevi Karolini,* 2 vols, ed. A. Werminghoff (Hanover and Leipzig, 1896) III: *Concilia aevi Karolini 843–859,* ed. W. Hartmann (Hanover, 1984) IV: *Concilia aevi Karolini 860–874,* ed. W. Hartmann (Hanover, 1998)
Epp. III–V:	*Epistolae Merovingici et Karolini aevi* I–III, ed. E. Dümmler (Berlin, 1892–9)
Leges IV:	*Leges Langobardorum,* ed. G. H. Pertz (Hanover, 1868)
SS	*Scriptores (in folio),* 39 vols (Hanover, 1826–2009)
SS rer. Germ.	*Scriptores rerum Germanicarum in usum scholarum separatim editi,* 81 vols (Hanover, 1871–2016)
SS rer. Lang	*Scriptores rerum Langobardicarum et Italicarum saec. VI–IX,* ed. G. Waitz (Hanover, 1878)
SS rer. Merov.	*Scriptores rerum Merovingicarum,* ed. B. Krusche and W. Levison, 7 vols (Hanover, 1885–1987)
Mordek, *Studien*	H. Mordek, *Studien zur fränkischen Herrschergesetzgebung: Aufsätze über Kapitularien und Kapulariensammlungen* (Frankfurt am Main, 2000)
MPM	J. W. Baldwin, *Masters, Princes and Merchants: The Social Views of Peter the Chanter and his Circle,* 2 vols (Princeton, 1970)
MS Blankenburg	Wolfenbüttel, Herzog August Bibliothek, MS Blankenburg 130
N.Marc.	*Novellae Marciani* in *Theodosiani libri xvi cum constitutionibus sirmondianis et leges novellae ad Theodosianum pertinentes,* ed. T. Mommsen and P. M. Meyer, II (Berlin, 1905), 179–96
Nov.	Justinian's Novella, cited from *Novellae,* ed. R. Schöll and W. Kroll, 6th ed., Corpus Iuris Civilis III (Berlin, 1959)
PL	*Patrologiae Cursus Completus, seu bibliotheca universalis omnium ss. Patrum doctorum, scriptorumque ecclesiasticorum,* Series Latina, ed. J. –P. Migne, 221 vols (Paris, 1844–64)
PLEMA	D. Jasper and H. Fuhrmann, eds, *Papal Letters in the Early Middle Ages* (Washington, DC, 2001)
Potthast	A. Potthast, ed., *Regesta Pontificum Romanorum,* 2 vols (Berlin, 1874–5)
PPEMA	W. Davies and P. Fouracre, eds, *Property and Power in the Early Middle Ages* (Cambridge, 2010)
QCA	*Quinque Compilationes Antiquae,* ed. E. Friedberg (Leipzig, 1882; repr. Graz, 1956)
Relig. Franks	R. Meens et al, eds, *Religious Franks: Religion and Power in the Frankish Kingdoms: Studies in Honour of Mayke de Jong* (Manchester, 2017)

Schönfeld, 'Xenod.'	Walther Schönfeld, 'Die Xenodochien in Italien und Frankreich im frühen Mittelalter', *ZRG* 43 *Kan. Abt.* 12 (1922), 1–54
Statuts	L. Le Grand, *Statuts d'hôtels-dieu et de léproseries: Recueil de textes du XIIe au XIVe siècle* (Paris, 1901)
TRHS	*Transactions of the Royal Historical Society*
VC	Visigothic Code, cited from *Lex Visigothorum*, ed. K. Zeumer, MGH LL. nat. Germ. I (Hannover, 1902)
X	*Liber extravagantium decretalium*, ed. E. Freidberg, Corpus Iuris Canonici II (Leipzig, 1881)
Wood, *Prop. Ch.*	S. Wood, *The Proprietary Church in the Medieval West* (Oxford, 2006)
ZRG Kan. Abt.	*Zeitschrift der Savigny-Stiftung für Rechtsgeschichte (Kanonistische Abteilung)*

All other references in the footnotes are given, as far as possible, in short form. Full titles are provided in the bibliography.

PART I

CANON LAW AND THE REVOLUTION IN CHARITY (1150–1250)

1

Introduction

The Sheep and the Goats

This is a book about the church in the world. It glimpses the messy, determined variety of human *caritas* through the eyes of law-makers. More specifically, it explores the limits of the church's jurisdictional claims over Christian practices, in an arena of activity that lay within the concerns of churchmen but beyond the claim of canon law. Here, canonists bumped up against the creative energies of men and women of all walks of life. And, here, law-makers' ambition was defined by its limits. Over the course of a millennium, the boundary between what law-makers could and could not do shifted slightly, although it was always defined more by what could not be done. It also marked out a legal borderland that maintained certain characteristics. It was a place where pastoral concern, and human entreaty, found no certain answer, and no general right of action in law. And, without canonical authority as a guide, it was a place of controversy and invention. Here, activists, dreamers, and forgers played, imagining new, often fleeting, law. The divide was not between clerics and laity, for while churchmen usually crafted the responses, both parties sat on either side, with laity calling for regulation, especially over clerics, and popes and canonists counselling caution. It was a place where ideals stretched beyond what was legally possible or, more to the point, permissible.

Our subject is welfare houses: the variety of facilities that cared for the needy and that were known by various, often overlapping, names such as xenodochia, hospitals, leprosaria, *maisons-dieu*, and almshouses. Along with churches and monasteries, welfare institutions arose as one of the three great types of Christian foundations from the earliest centuries of the church. Churches, monasteries, and welfare foundations were monuments to the church's highest ideals, as well as the places where these ideals were most intensively lived out: where Christian service was performed, paths to salvation charted, and social obligations made manifest. In practice, the lines between the three were blurred: monasteries had a church, for example, and a hospital might be attached to a monastery, or served by clerics or communities of religious. But, in law, the terms were clear. Churches were *ecclesiae* (or, early on, *oratoria*), consecrated places for worship; monasteries housed monks and nuns and so were defined by the communities (convents) of religious, who had permanently left the world; and welfare institutions were ... xenodochia.

On Hospitals: Welfare, Law, and Christianity in Western Europe, 400–1320. Sethina Watson, Oxford University Press (2020). © Sethina Watson.
DOI: 10.1093/oso/9780198847533.001.0001

For almost a century, historians have embraced a particular model of welfare institutions in medieval law. According to this model, they were an ecclesiastical form that belonged ultimately to the Church and so fell under canon law. Welfare houses were answerable to the bishop and should be governed according to a religious rule, in imitation of monasteries. The body of law that had defined them was the *Corpus iuris civilis*, promulgated under the Emperor Justinian in the 530s and observed by the Western church thereafter. By the thirteenth century, canon law recognized two types of hospital: those with chapels and so regulated by the bishop; and those without, and so not. Law in theory might not necessarily be observed in practice, but it did establish what hospitals *should* be in Western Christendom.

This study offers the first concerted investigation of welfare institutions in canon (and other) law across the middle ages, from the fourth to the fourteenth century. It rejects each component of our long-held model. It offers a new definition of hospitals in law, of their legal genesis in the West, and of the relationship between Roman and canon law in the formation of hospitals and so, ultimately, the underpinnings of charities, social welfare institutions, and charitable trusts. Yet the definition is only part of a larger picture, and a more interesting problem. For to understand the place of hospitals in the church, we must look differently at law itself, at the activity of law-makers, and at the relationships between the legal remit of the church and Christian practice. Here we find a new story of hospitals and of the centrality of welfare in Western Christianity.

A Confusion of Hospitals

The term 'hospital' refers to a dizzying array of charitable facilities.[1] They arose in the Eastern Empire in the mid-fourth century, in the early decades of Roman Christianity (and after Constantine had moved the capital of the empire east, to Constantinople/Byzantium). In fact, these facilities were a response to the challenge posed by the conversion of a state to Christianity: how could a religion

---

[1] What follows is a story of medieval Christian welfare in the West: other societies and religious groups developed their own, often similar, models of charity. On Byzantium in cross-cultural context, P. Horden, 'The Invention of the Hospital', in S. F. Johnson, ed., *The Oxford Handbook of Late Antiquity* (Oxford, 2012); P. Horden, 'The Earliest Hospitals', *Journal of Interdisciplinary History* 35:3 (2005), and, more widely, Z. Chitwood, 'Endowment Studies', *Endowment Studies* 1 (2017); P. Hennigan, *The Birth of a Legal Institution* (Leiden, 2004), 52–70; M. Borgolte, 'Foundations "for the Salvation of the Soul"', *Medieval Worlds* 1 (2015). Pre-Christian (Greek) institutions, which included *xenones*, are treated in D. J. Constantelos, *Byzantine Philanthropy and Social Welfare* (New Brunswick, NJ, 1968), 6–11; and early Christian almsgiving by R. Finn, *Almsgiving in the Later Roman Empire* (Oxford, 2006). For Jewish and Islamic charity, albeit in a later period, M. R. Cohen, *Poverty and Charity in the Jewish Community of Medieval Egypt* (Princeton, 2005); A. Ragab, *The Medieval Islamic Hospital* (Cambridge, 2015).

requiring its adherents to reject the currencies of the world be a religion of empire? As the work of Peter Brown has revealed, wealth and poverty were at the centre of the problem, and fundamental to its answer. A call to embrace society's neediest and most abject sounded forth. This duty of care helped make sense of the hierarchical structures of society and, especially, of the obligations attendant on wealth and leadership.[2] In answer, there developed a range of institutions, dedicated to the welfare of the desperate and powerless in Byzantium and its provinces. They had a clear typology, serving different categories of the needy: foundlings (*brephotrophia*), orphans (*orphanotrophia*), the poor (*ptochotrophia*), the sick (*nosocomia*), the traveller (*xenodochia*), and the elderly (*gerontocomia*). Codified in the legislation of the Byzantine Emperor Justinian, each institution was both a monument to the (shared) values of Christian community and to the (personal) sacrifice of those who gave of their wealth to create them and of themselves to minister there.

The picture that emerged in the West was very different. The first welfare facilities arrived in the 390s, firmly in the Greek model. They are known from the letters of Jerome, who celebrated the wealthy founders who had surrendered themselves (and their worldly assets) to serve the poor: Pammachius and his wife, Paulina, who established a *xenodochium* at the port on the mouth of the Tiber to provide rest for embarking travellers, and Fabiola, a wealthy Roman widow and 'the first person to establish a *nosokomeion*, in which she would gather and tend to those unfortunates from the streets, wasted by sickness and starving'.[3] Yet welfare in the West was not to develop along Greek lines. The formal typology of Byzantine institutions did not take root; what arose instead was a more miscellaneous collection of places, smaller and more chaotic.[4] They were generically known as *xenodochia*, the term that would always be preferred in canon law, although it was gradually replaced in practice by *hospitales*. From the eighth century, a meandering assortment of terms—among them, *xenodochium, hospitale, domus, habitaculum, mensa*, and *ptochium*—referred to a wide range of facilities tending to human welfare. They were established near towns or churches, on main routes and Alpine passes. They fed the poor, sheltered pilgrims or the sick, accommodated widows, orphans, and the aged poor, or the weak, blind, or lame, and in various combinations. In Francia, an Irish religious order operated *hospitalia Scottorum* to serve pilgrims to Rome; canons and canonesses

---

[2] P. Brown, *Through the Eye of a Needle* (Princeton, 2012); P. Brown, *Poverty and Leadership in the Later Roman Empire* (Hanover, NH, 2002). The Eastern tradition is considered in Chapter 5.

[3] Jerome, *Epist.* 77.6: 'et prima omnium nosocomeion instituit, in quo aegrotantes colligeret de plateis, et consumpta languoribus atque inedia miserorum membra foveret', and 77.10 (*PL* 22, col. 694, 697); E. Hubert, 'Hôpitaux et espace urbain', in *HMMA* 115–16; R. Santangeli Valenzani, 'Pellegrini, Senatori e Papi', *Rivista dell'Istituto Nazionale d'Archeologia* 19/20 (1996/7), 204–10.

[4] The account here differs slightly from early studies, which tend to assume an ideal of Byzantine typology and wonder how far it was followed in practice. For this work, and for these facilities in the West, see Part II.

established *hospitalia* and *receptacula* under the Aachen rule (816); and bishops might maintain two *hospitalia*, one for paupers, another for nobles. We know most about facilities attached to a church, because theirs are the archives that weathered best the next thousand years. But everywhere laity were setting up these facilities, sometimes entrusting them to local clerics or monasteries, sometimes (and more often than we now can see) to their own heirs.

The great era of hospital foundation in the West was the twelfth and thirteenth centuries. An unprecedented boom, an 'efflorescence' of foundations between *c*.1150 and *c*.1250 is famously celebrated by historians as a 'Charitable Revolution'.[5] It began in the eleventh century with leper-houses and hostels for pilgrims, then hospitals, *hôtels-dieu*, and *domus dei* to serve the destitute and the sick poor, aged, or invalid. In the twelfth century, hospitals inspired new religious orders, too. International orders, dedicated to serving pilgrims on the frontiers of Christian expansion, quickly also became military orders, most famously the Knights of St John of Jerusalem (the Hospitallers), the Teutonic Knights, and the Order of Santiago.[6] Smaller congregations of religious ran local networks of hospitals, often in the mountain passes and on pilgrim routes to Rome, Jerusalem, and Santiago de Compostela; they included the orders of Roncevaux, St James of Altopascio, the Holy Spirit of St Saxia, with its great hospital in Rome, as well as that of St Anthony of Vienne, dedicated to sufferers of ergotism.[7] The Trinitarians, a hospitaller order dedicated to the ransom of captives, reinforce the capaciousness of the term 'hospital' in the middle ages: as places dedicated to charitable service, broadly conceived in Christian terms.[8]

Meanwhile, outside the religious orders, and in towns and on roads across Europe, local charities boomed and in even greater numbers. Each one was a one-off foundation, with a particular charitable charge and accorded particular arrangements by which it was overseen. The scale of the phenomenon was vast, with leper-houses alone running into the thousands across Europe;[9] cathedral

---

[5] 'la révolution de la charité', A. Vauchez, 'Assistance et charité en occident, XIIIe–XVe siècles', in V. B. Bagnoli, ed., *Domanda e consumi* (Florence, 1978), 152. *Efflorescence* is the term of P. Bonenfant, *Hôpitaux et bienfaisance publique dans les anciens Pays-Bas* (Brussels, 1965), 24; M. Mollat preferred *floraison*, 'Floraison des fondations hospitalières (XIIe–XIIIe siècles)', in *HHF*.

[6] Introductions to the military orders include H. Nicholson, *The Knights Hospitaller* (Woodbridge, 2001); Brodman, *CRME* 90–114; D. Marcombe, *Leper Knights* (Woodbridge, 2003); and the essays in M. Barber, ed., *The Military Orders* (Aldershot, 1994).

[7] G. Jugnot, 'Deux fondations augustiniennes en faveur des pèlerins', in M.-H. Vicaire, ed., *Assistance et charité*, Cahiers de Fanjeaux 13 (Toulouse, 1978); A. Meyer, 'Organisierter Bettel und andere Finanzgeschäfte des Hospitals von Altopascio', in Drossbach, ed., *Mittelalter und früher Neuzeit*; G. Drossbach, *Christliche caritasals Rechtsinstitut: Hospital und Orden von Santo Spirito in Sassia* (Paderborn, 2005), and Drossbach, 'Hospitäler in Patrimonium Petri', in *Europ. Spitalwesen*; D. Le Blévec, 'L'ordre canonial et hospitalier des Antonins', in *Le Monde des chanoines*, Cahiers de Fanjeaux 24 (Toulouse, 1989). And see the wide-ranging discussion in Brodman, *CRME* 115–77.

[8] G. Cipollone, ed., *La liberazione dei 'captivi' tra Cristianità e Islam* (Vatican City, 2000).

[9] In 1227, Louis VIII left a bequest to the 2,000 leproseries of his realm. Recent studies have identified 517 leproseries in the diocese of Sens and 320 in England: F.-O. Touati, *Archives de la lèpre* (Paris, 1996), 9, 32; C. Rawcliffe, *Leprosy in Medieval England* (Woodbridge, 2006), 106. The

chapters and bishops oversaw their own facilities for the poor, pilgrim and sick, as did kings, aristocrats, cities, and abbeys. By the thirteenth century, there were also houses for the blind, the weak, aged or blind priests, young scholars, and Jewish converts, and soon *maisons-dieu* and almshouses for the 'noble' poor. They could be tiny habitations for two or three or, by the late thirteenth century, complex institutions for hundreds.[10] Many hospitals accommodated thirteen needy men or women, an apostolic number that represented Christ and his apostles. Some were run by religious, others by clerics or lay brothers and sisters, by a priest or lay administrator, even by married couples.[11] The full range of moneyed society was represented as founders and overseers, creating royal, baronial, episcopal, capitular, monastic, civic, seigneurial, burghal, and clerical houses.[12] If this account seems bewildering in its variety, that is, in essence, the point. For what characterized welfare in the West was the persistence of its variety and the constant innovation of new kinds, new formats, and new purposes. Indeed, the phenomenon lacks any formal typology, and even terminology: there is no basic term for them as a group, although canon lawyers used 'xenodochia'.

A problem of language persists to this day. The term 'hospital', from *hospes* meaning guest, was never fixed (or even limited to) what it originally described: that is, a hostel to receive travellers. The term 'hospital' is liable to cause confusion today because it has been appropriated by modern medicine and calls to mind an industrial-medical complex. This was not its medieval meaning, although bodily, spiritual, and emotional care were fundamental to many such places, and even medical care to an elite few. But 'hospital' was a problematic term for medieval law-makers, too, because of its constantly evolving meanings. Under canon law, the new religious orders of hospitallers confused the issue, since they were not

---

diocese of Liège had thirty-four welfare houses, twenty-five of them established between 1175 and 1300, De Spiegeler, 'Les structures hospitalières', in *HMMA* 101–2. These numbers are the tip of a lost iceberg, since many are known by a single reference and chance survival.

[10] In 1287, St Leonard's, York, had an infirmary for 229 men and women, a school of nineteen boys under two masters, a children's home (*domus puerorum*) with twenty-three orphans, and a wider staff of a warden, thirteen chaplains, eleven lay brothers, seventeen sisters, seventeen pages, and seventy-six servants and officials: P. H. Cullum, 'St Leonard's Hospital, York, in 1287', in D. Smith, ed., *The Church in Medieval York* (York, 1999), 21.

[11] On the latter, S. Framer, 'The Leper in the Master Bedroom', in R. Voaden and D. Wolfthal, eds, *Framing the Family* (Tempe, AZ, 2005), 91–4. See, e.g., Sabelia, who in 1202 married John the *hospitalarius* of a hospital attached to a Benedictine priory and joined him there to serve the poor (J. H. Mundy, 'Hospitals and Leproseries in Toulouse', in Mundy et al., eds, *Essays in Medieval Life and Thought* (New York, 1965), 194, 197n., 198). For a vivid later picture, which extends beyond the walls of the hospitals, D. J. Osheim, 'Conversion, Conversi, and the Christian Life in Late Medieval Tuscany', Speculum 58:2 (1983).

[12] On patterns of foundation, Brodman, *CRME* 45–88, stressing the numerical superiority of lay foundations; De Spiegeler, 'Les structures hospitalières', 101–2; S. Sweetinburgh, *The Role of the Hospital in Medieval England* (Dublin, 2004), 29–32. Localities could buck general trends: e.g. Florence saw enthusiastic foundation between 1250 and 1349, J. Henderson, *The Renaissance Hospital* (London, 2006), 14. N. Orme and M. Webster, *The English Hospital 1070–1570* (London, 1995), remains an excellent introduction to the subject.

'hospitals' (*xenodochia*) in law but congregations or chapters of *regulares*; that is, regular religious. Canon law clung to 'xenodochium' to distinguish local welfare facilities from these *regulares*, in part because the antiquated term could be fixed in law. Meanwhile, the term 'hospital' roamed free in the world. It could be used as a generic label for welfare houses, but it was also a specific, if constantly evolving, subcategory of houses, for pilgrims and travellers and, soon, for the poor and then the sick poor. The cohort of welfare foundations were gathered by contemporaries under the often-interchangeable labels 'hospitals' or 'xenodochia', a practice that is adopted in this study.

With the rise of social history, the study of hospitals has seen its own *efflorescence*. A vibrant field, focused on the later middle ages, draws together urban, religious, medical, social, and cultural historians, art historians, and archaeologists.[13] Unlike monasteries, hospitals rarely produced chronicles or hagiography and so must be approached through bitty administrative documents, in dense or scattered archives.[14] As a result, major studies are deeply archival, focusing on one house or region and often on a city with a hospital (and its large archive) at its centre.[15] They are local studies, and that is the point. They take us into the challenges of daily life, of urban development and local administration, especially *c*.1250–*c*.1450, when the documentary trail is most revealing. Studies in this period tease out the activities of benefactors and provincial authorities, as well as the routines inside the houses, to explore charity and the nature of care, and to shed light on devotion, social policy, and government in action. A particular draw to historians is the glimpse that hospitals afford of human experiences that are so often hidden from the record: of encounters with the poor, the incapacitated, and the marginalized, that is, with the most vulnerable of society. The houses themselves emerge as indisputably local institutions, rooted in their immediate environment, at the intersection of faith and politics, ideals and practice. Each house or city has its own cache of documentary material—charters, statutes, rules, and accounts—and this is distinctive in its variety. From this material, each house has

---

[13] The many initiatives and agendas are laid out in S. Watson, 'Hospitals in the Middle Ages', in P. E. Szarmach, ed., *Oxford Bibliographies in Medieval Studies* (New York, 2017).

[14] On the range of documentary material, Touati, *Archives de la lèpre*; S. Watson, 'The Origins of the English Hospital', *TRHS* 6th ser. 16 (2006); and M. Scheutz et al., eds, *Quellen zur europäischen Spitalgeschichte* (Vienna, 2010).

[15] Major contributions include G. Maréchal, *De sociale en politieke gebondenheid van het Brugse hospitaalwezen* (Kortrijk-Heule, 1978); J. Caille, *Hôpitaux et charité publique à Narbonne* (Toulouse, 1978); A. Saint-Denis, *L'Hôtel-Dieu de Laon 1150–1300* (Nancy, 1983); De Spiegeler, *Liège*; M. Rubin, *Charity and Community in Medieval Cambridge* (Cambridge, 1987); F.-O. Touati, *Maladie et société au Moyen Age: La leper, les lépreux et les léproseries dans la province ecclésiastique de Sens* (Brussels, 1998); J. W. Brodman, *Charity and Welfare: Hospitals and the Poor in Medieval Catalonia* (Philadelphia, PA, 1998); C. Rawcliffe, *Medicine for the Soul: The Life, Death and Resurrection of an English Medieval Hospital* (Stroud, 1999); D. Le Blévec, *La part du pauvre: L'assistance dans les pays du Bas-Rhône*, 2 vols (Paris, 2000); P. Montaubin, 'Origine et mise en place des hôpitaux cathédraux', in M.-C. Dinet-Lecomte, ed., *Les hôpitaux, enjeux de pouvoir: France du Nord et Belgique (IVe–XXe siècle)* (Lille, 2008), 13–46; Henderson, *Renaissance Hospital*.

its own tale to tell, especially of the way that it navigated its own path between material care and spiritual devotion, as well as between the lay and the clerical. Yet as our picture of welfare grows ever richer and more diverse, it has become more difficult to stand back and say what 'hospitals' were and what they were not.[16] We can recognize their huge variety but less so what unites them.

If it is agreed that hospitals, including leper-houses, were by definition ecclesiastical; it is also agreed that this model was not observed on the ground.[17] Of course, there were straightforwardly ecclesiastical hospitals, under a rule and answerable to the bishop or his agent, but many, even most, did not fit this framework. Even leper-houses, potentially the most 'ecclesiastical' of forms, might not attract the attention of clerical authorities.[18] The question of regulation is perhaps the most confusing. The new military and hospitaller orders adopted papally approved rules, but most welfare houses were outside such formal orders. From the thirteenth century, local authorities took a growing interest in regulating these independent hospitals, but what was done, when, and by whom followed no set path. As a result, large hospitals, especially cathedral *hôtels-dieu*, might receive episcopal or capitular statutes, and these might include vows, devotional routines, and behavioural regulations, yet even these texts are peculiarly individual, laying down duties, devotional and administrative routines, staffing, and government specific to that house.[19] Some received brief customs from a monastic custodian, others regulations or statutes from towns or lay patrons.[20] Many houses were simply managed according to a charter or long-held practice; authorities were most concerned that a house simply do what it had been established to do, according to the terms of its foundation.[21] Most confounding is the range of

---

[16] This can be seen most clearly in essay collections, whose richness rests on the very different local pictures painted by the individual studies. *HMMA; Fondations;* S. le Clech-Charton, ed., *Les établissements hospitaliers en France du Moyen Age au XIXᵉ siècle* (Dijon, 2010); N. Bulst and K. H. Speiß, eds, *Sozialgeschichte mittelalterlicher Hospitäler* (Ostfildern, 2007).

[17] Among the many statements that the hospital as a form belonged to the Church: J. Gaudemet, *Le gouvernement de l'église à l'époque classique IIᵉ partie: Le gouvernement local* (Paris, 1979), 126–7; J. Hourlier, *L'âge classique (1140–1378): Les religieux* (Paris, 1974), 146–7; Caron, '*pia fundatio*', esp. pp. 144–5; M. Mollat, 'Dans la perspective de l'Au-delà', in *HHF* 92; De Spiegeler, *Liège*, 105–6; Orme and Webster, *English Hospital*, 32, 37–9; Brodman, *CRME* 46–7, 77, 85–8, and references below.

[18] See Chapter 2. When Juette de Huy went to live with the lepers of Huy in *c.*1181, the site consisted of a simple dwelling (*mansio*) beside a derelict church (Hugh of Floreffe, *De B. Juetta sive Jutta, vidua reclusa* in *Acta Sanctorum*, II, 152). In Toulouse only two of seven known leper-houses seem to have had a church or chapel (Mundy, 'Hospitals and Leproseries', 201).

[19] On the idiosyncrasy of thirteenth-century statutes: A. Saunier, 'La trame hospitalière médiévale', in *HMMA* 208–11; G. Drossbach, 'Das Hospital—eine kirchenrechtliche Institution? (ca. 1150–ca. 1350)', *ZRG* 118 Kan. Abt. 87 (2001), 518–19; J. Avril, 'Le statut des maisons-dieu', in *Actes du 110ᵉ Congrès National des Sociétés savantes* (Paris, 1987); Watson, 'Origins', 82–3; Montaubin, 'Hôpitaux cathédraux', 26–30. And see the texts in *Statuts*.

[20] A catalogue is given for England in S. Watson, 'The Statutes and Constitutional Documents of English Hospitals to 1300' (D.Phil. dissertation, University of Oxford, 2004), 300–58.

[21] Watson, 'Origins', examines this principle, which is basic to the histories of most houses. On varieties of government: De Spiegeler, *Liège*, 105–32; Mollat, 'L'Au-delà', 92–5; Henderson, *Renaissance Hospital*, 7–25, 28–31; K. Goudriaan, 'Early Hospital Development in the Provinces of Holland, Zealand and Utrecht', in his *Piety in Practice and Print* (Hilversum, 2016), 51–3.

jurisdictions under which houses might sit. For while bishops supervised some, and cathedrals, monasteries, or religious orders others, many were in the hands of laity, be they the Crown, local lords, town authorities, or lay guilds or confraternities. These often failed to recognize any supervisory authority in the bishop who, in turn, did not seem interested in asserting his claims over them.[22] Most mysteriously, there was no clear division between those under ecclesiastical authority or in lay hands. The former can be difficult to categorize as 'religious', the latter not particularly 'secular'.[23] Jurisdictions were mutable, regulations came and went. Welfare houses seem to have lived by their own rules. We just don't know why or even what they were.

Since 1947, it has been routine to note, with some resignation, the gulf between theory and practice. As Nicholas Orme and Margaret Webster observed, 'the doctrine that hospitals belonged to the ecclesiastical sphere often meant less than a practice which dictated quite the opposite'.[24] The failure of hospitals to submit to ecclesiastical jurisdiction is blamed on medieval churchmen: bishops were lax or indifferent, incapable of exercising their legal responsibilities;[25] and canonists, buried in their books, produced legislation that was feeble and ill-adapted to the world in which bishops lived.[26] The legal model, as historians have defined it, is now believed to be purely theoretical, the problem one of uptake and enforcement. So the model itself has been simply set aside.

This has had defining consequences for the study of welfare in the middle ages. First, it leaves their status as ecclesiastical foundations unresolved. Studies note,

---

[22] Brodman, CRME 82–3, 87–8; Orme and Webster, English Hospital, 32–4. There are even cases of bishops, like those in Liège, handing houses over to lay authorities (De Spiegeler, Liège, 111, 115–21). By contrast, the bishop of Rouen (1248–75) worked to assert an ecclesiastical jurisdiction over hospitals in his diocese and place communities under rules, A. J. Davis, The Holy Bureaucrat (Ithaca, NY, 2006), 80–2.

[23] The hospitals of St Alexius and St John the Baptist, Exeter, were founded by citizens of Exeter. They were both civic, since the citizens maintained the hospitals and civic officials appointed their priors, and religious. In c.1240, when the two were united, one of the lay refounders 'entering the fraternity of the hospital was made master of its brothers and sisters', clearly a form of conversion. To add to the confusion, in 1244 the bishop and the citizens exchanged hospitals, effecting a permutacio fundatorem, with the now-united hospital of St John and St Alexius entrusted to the bishops, the leper-house to the town. Up until that point the bishop had played no role in the business of St John's. S. Watson, 'Sources for English Hospitals', in M. Scheutz et al., eds, Quellen, 78–83.

[24] Orme and Webster, English Hospital, 35. This was clear from the earliest social histories: 'Au total, la suprématie de l'archevêque sur les hôpitaux de Narbonne nous paraît, en réalité, extrêmement théorique. La révérence due à cette haute autorité ecclésiastique ne lui laisse guère plus qu'un vague droit de visite que nous voyons s'exercer en 1404, non pas tant sur les établissements hospitaliers eux-mêmes d'ailleurs, que sur les chapelles qui y sont adjointes', Caille, Narbonne, 62. For a recent statement, Goudriaan, 'Early Hospital Development', 55–6.

[25] Mundy, 'Hospitals and Leproseries', 194n.; Montaubin, 'Hôpitaux cathédraux', 23; B. Resl, 'Hospitals in Medieval England', in Europ. Spitalwesen, 46.

[26] HDC 115n.; De Spiegeler, Liège, 106.

time and again, the peculiar position of welfare houses 'between church and world', two tectonic plates between which hospitals sat, awkwardly and seemingly forgotten.[27] A central theme of scholarship remains the tension between, or shifting mix of, secular and religious. This can be elucidated but not explained, except as a failing by churchmen: try as clerics might, these houses fell through the cracks.[28] Hospitals were of the church and of the world, but is unclear how those lines were drawn, and even what lines there were. The term 'quasi-religious' captures scholarly puzzlement as much as medieval status. It also becomes a go-to answer; so, for example, in the absence of an alternative, post-1100 historians have tended to view hospitals as arranged according to a monastic template, as a conventual community according to a rule.[29] Second, we lack principles or even basic terms with which to define welfare houses. When leading scholars gathered in Vienna to launch a comparative study of hospitals across Europe, their first task was to agree a definition for the objects of study. The group provided a clear taxonomy for the early modern period but stalled for the middle ages. Here, they could offer only a '"minimum common denominator"...of care associated with a building to which persons were admitted temporarily or long-term'; even the source material, they admitted, provided no organizing language for these houses.[30] Even if we know one when we see it, historians lack defining terms for what we study. What may be inconvenient when bringing locality to life becomes a road-block to thinking comparatively, and especially across borders.

Finally, it is not surprising, then, that an understanding of welfare houses themselves has suffered from this confusion. As the Viennese attempt illustrates, definitions are not merely feeble, they make the houses themselves seem inconsequential.[31] Our eyes see one thing—the *efflorescence* of welfare, at the heart of medieval society and Christian devotion; our explanations paint a different picture. The apparent failure of canonists, popes, and bishops to confront the

---

[27] An issue most engagingly articulated by Drossbach, 'Das Hospital', esp. p. 510.

[28] The problem has been eloquently laid out by J. W. Brodman: 'Not only did ecclesiastical authorities fail to impose the religious life upon all hospitals, they also failed to impose any consistent governance upon them. Again, this was not for absence of effort...Charity thus developed as a partnership between clergy and laymen, between Church and State, between the public sphere and the private. This mixed character denied it a conventional identity as purely clerical, as in the case of monks and friars, or purely laic, as with penitential confraternities or municipally operated hospitals. The hierarchy was certainly uncomfortable with this ambiguity, as witnessed by its efforts to absorb the practitioners of charity into a more traditional mold.' Brodman, *CRME* 282, 285, the conclusion to his chapter on hospitals, 'Between Two Worlds: An Elusive Paradigm'.

[29] Thoughtful examples include Le Blévec, 'Fondations et œuvres', 7–11; De Spiegeler, *Liège*, 105–6; Orme and Webster, *English Hospital*, 69–75; Rubin, 'Development and Change'; Drossbach, 'Das Hospital'.

[30] M. Scheutz et al., 'Einleitung', in *Europ. Spitalwesen*, 13, 17.

[31] It has been noticed how similar is this definition to my own, of 'a site, a designated form of alms and an endowment...to supply those alms': Resl, 'Hospitals', 44; Watson, 'Origins', 87.

issue suggests that welfare houses were side-line concerns, even nuisances to the church: a messy practice that was not important enough to sort out. It is not surprising, then, that studies of medieval Christianity tend to offer the houses as an afterthought or even set them aside, as muddled, minor, and even vaguely comic.[32]

What if the problem was not one of medieval enforcement, but of modern understanding? Perhaps the failure was not of medieval Christians to conform to theory, or churchmen to care, but of modern eyes to grasp what underpinned a millennium of practice. Perhaps there was a reason why bishops, canonists, and popes (including even Alexander III and Innocent III) seem so comfortable with all this apparent disorder.

Our legal model fails to account for the diversities of form, administration, and supervision that we find across Europe. It cannot even say why, across all this local variety, there remains an odd consistency in the fact and nature of that variety. For in Barcelona, York, Liège, Arles, Cologne, and Florence, in oddly similar ways, founders dictated the terms of their welfare facilities, while a panoply of authorities, ecclesiastical and lay, regulated hospitals as they saw fit, concocting regulations that were specific to that house, be these statutes, regulations, customs, or a simple directive in a charter, and in observance of the terms of foundation.

So much is known of the messy variety on the ground, it is time to look at the thinkers.

On Canon Law (a European Question)

The question of hospitals in law is among the oldest fields of ecclesiastical scholarship. It has preoccupied French, Italian, and German scholars for a century, although the questions have yet to penetrate English-language scholarship.[33] Few have left a mark on the conceptual frameworks, and none have displaced, or even updated the model of hospitals in law, which was settled seventy years ago. Because this model has never been critically examined, it requires unpicking in some detail now.

---

[32] They are noticed only around the edge of the medieval church: J. H. Lynch and P. C. Adamo, *The Medieval Church*, 2nd ed. (London, 2014), 231–2; M. Rubin, ed., *Medieval Christianity in Practice* (Princeton, 2009), 212–13, in the chapter by B. Resl, 'Bequests for the Poor'; J. Arnold, ed., *The Oxford Handbook of Medieval Christianity* (Oxford, 2014), largely in the chapter, 'Civic Religion', by N. Terpstra.

[33] But see, Rubin, *Charity and Community*, 103–4, who noticed Imbert's model (tenet 4) and, in so doing, caught my imagination many years ago. Recent efforts to define legal personality are treated in Chapter 2.

Orthodoxies

The model is composed of the following tenets:

1. that law for hospitals was laid down under the East Roman Emperor Justinian, as part of the *Corpus iuris civilis*, and adopted wholesale in the West in the early middle ages (Schönfeld/Imbert);
2. that, in accordance with that legislation, hospitals were under the bishop: ecclesiastical forms and so directed under canon law (Schönfeld/Imbert);
3. that the church launched a policy to place hospitals under religious rules at councils in Paris in 1212 and Rouen in 1214 (Le Grand);
4. and that the late medieval church defined two types of hospitals: (i) religious or public houses, with chapels (*loci religiosi* or *hospitalia publica*) and (ii) secular or private hospitals, without (*hospitalia privata* or *simplices*) (Imbert).

The model is a fusion of disparate arguments laid down by three scholars (two French, one German), working between 1890 and 1947. They did not critically engage with one another and, in fact, disagree on core principles. Their work, and the agendas behind it, needs to be exposed in order to understand why the model fails and to reveal grand narratives that continue to structure (and segregate) hospital scholarship.

If the modern study of welfare houses has an epicentre, it is France. This is due to two men who, together, consolidated our main reform model. The first was Léon Le Grand who, in the 1890s, gathered and edited statutes for French hospitals. He found a diverse corpus of texts and behind them a movement to place *les religieux hospitaliers* under written (Augustinian) rules. These, he argued, were the fruit of councils at Paris (1212) and Rouen (1214) under Robert de Courson, which required that rules be provided to leper-houses and *maisons-dieu*.[34] His reform model was quickly adopted in France.[35] In the 1970s it was

---

[34] *Statuts*, pp. ix–xxv, and his earlier articles: 'Les maisons-dieu: Leurs statuts au XIIIᵉ siècle', *Revue des Questions Historiques* 60 (1896), 111–17, 132; 'Les maisons-dieu: leur régime intérieur au moyen âge', *Revue des Questions Historiques* 63 (1898), 101. The passage deserves quoting at length: 'Ce qui prouve bien d'ailleurs que la rédaction des règles hospitalières était à l'ordre du jour dans le monde religieux, dès le début du XIIIᵉ siècle, c'est que les conciles de Paris and de Rouen, tenus en 1212 et 1214 sous la présidence du légat du pape, Robert de Courson, au sujet de la discipline ecclésiastique, firent entrer dans leur programme de réformes l'établissement d'une règle pour toutes les Maisons-Dieu et les léproseries dont les ressources comportaient la présence d'une congrégation religieuse. Les évêques réunis dans ces deux conciles provinciaux fixèrent les principes fondamentaux sur lesquels devaient reposer ces statuts ... Au bout de quelques années, les prescriptions des conciles de Paris et de Rouen commencèrent à porter leurs fruits.' *Statuts*, pp. xi–xiii.

[35] See D.-L. MacKay, *Les hôpitaux et la charité à Paris au XIIIᵉ siècle* (Paris, 1923), 34–50. It was also translated into Spanish, N. Guglielmi, 'Modos de marginalidad en la Edad Media', *Anales de Historia Antigua y Medieval* 16 (1971).

embraced by Michel Mollat, whose poverty seminar in Paris inspired a new generation to take up the study of the poor and charity, a study that placed the great urban institutions of the later middle ages at its centre.[36] Mollat embraced Le Grand's reform model and became its modern evangelist, assuming, in addition, that the Paris agenda was taken up by Innocent III at his Fourth Lateran Council in 1215.[37] It has become routine to note that, in obedience to Paris (1212) and Rouen (1214), hospitals found security under the Church, where they were organized into autonomous communities under the Augustinian rule. So unquestioned is Le Grand's model that Courson's hospital reform has never actually been studied. Even Le Grand had relied only on Philippe Labbe's edition of the Parisian decrees, whose wrong date for the council he copied;[38] in fact, the Paris council took place not in 1212, but 1213.[39]

Jean Imbert's, *Les hôpitaux en droit canonique (du décret de Gratien à la sécularisation de l'administration de l'Hôtel-Dieu de Paris en 1505)* ('Hospitals in Canon Law (from Gratian's Decretum to the Secularization of the Administration of the Hôtel-Dieu of Paris in 1505)'), published in 1947, remains the authoritative study of hospitals in law. Despite its title, it dismissed hospitals in classical canon law in two pages, as constituting merely 'two ancient texts' in Gratian's *Decretum*, 'manifestly inadequate' for such a vast topic.[40] Finding no secular French legislation before the sixteenth century and no canon law of substance, Imbert believed the middle ages to be an era that observed 'ancient traditions' rather than new law.[41] His study drew largely on French administrative sources, especially charters and rules, and on late medieval commentators.[42] The scale of Imbert's lack of interest in canon law itself was revealed in a basic error: it was not Gratian's *Decretum* (1139×1151) that contained the two texts but Gregory IX's *Decretals*, also known as the *Liber extra* (1234)—and one of the texts was not so ancient.

---

[36] On the seminar, Rubin, *Charity and Community*, 3–4; for its early fruit, *EHP*.

[37] Mollat, 'Floraison', 56–7; M. Mollat, 'Hospitalité et assistance au début du XIIIe siècle', in D. Flood, ed., *Poverty in the Middle Ages* (1975), 40.

[38] *Statuts*, p. xii; *Sacrosancta concilia*, ed. P. Labbe and G. Cossartii, XIII (Venice, 1730), cols 819ff., 865ff. Mansi also places Paris in 1212, Mansi XXII. 835–6, 913. Both editions rely on Labbe's original edition of 1672.

[39] The correct date has been known to scholars of Innocent III: J. C. Moore, *Pope Innocent III (1160/1–1216)* (Leiden, 2003), 220; *MPM* I. 20. But 1212 remains the date in hospital scholarship: B. Tabuteau, 'De l'expérience érémitique à la normalisation monastique', in *Fondations*, 93; A. J. Davis, 'Preaching in Thirteenth-Century Hospitals', *JMH* 36:1 (2010), 77; Touati, *Maladie et société*, 403, 659; A. Rigon, 'Schole, confraternite e ospedali', in G. Andenna, ed., *Pensiero e sperimentazioni istituzionali nella 'Societas Christiana' (1046–1250)* (Milan, 2007), 426; A. Sommerlechner, 'Spitäler in Nord- und Mittelitalien', in *Europ. Spitalwesen*, 116; and Watson, 'Origins', 81. Montaubin, 'Hôpitaux cathédraux', 28, and Brodman, *CRME* 78–9, avoid the trap.

[40] 'Deux textes anciens sont reproduits au Décret de Gratien,... notoirement insuffisants pour une matière aussi vaste que la législation hospitalière... les établissements hospitaliers se développeront à l'époque même où la législation est inexistante, pendant les XIIe et XIIIe siècles.' *HDC* 55–6.

[41] 'Comment pouvons-nous expliquer cette absence de textes sur un sujet aussi important?... Sans doute, jugeait-on inutile de réglementer une matière où les traditions anciennes donnaient toute satisfaction.' *HDC* 55.

[42] The latter were largely commentators on *Quia contingit* (1317).

Even the only canon law dedicated to welfare houses, the Council of Vienne's *Quia contingit* (1312), which circulated from 1317 in a collection of law known as the Clementines, did not pique his interest.[43] Instead, seeking an answer for his 'ancient traditions', Imbert surveyed Roman and Carolingian precedents for charities, which he set out in a preliminary section to the book.[44] If this has proven to be his most influential contribution, it is also his weakest. Imbert was not a medievalist, so he turned to a 1922 study, by the German historian Walther Schönfeld, which offered a neat answer to the question of 'ancient traditions', in Justinian's sixth-century *Corpus iuris civilis*. On these grounds, Imbert advanced his two most influential conclusions: that canon law, and so Western Christendom, defined hospitals according to (Justinian's) Roman law, and that, in accordance with that legislation, hospitals were under the bishop's authority.

Yet the case is more fragile than it seems. Imbert and Schönfeld shared the conviction that hospitals were governed by Justinianic law,[45] but the two scholars held contradictory views as to the place of that law in the West. Noting that 'xenodochia arose in the Roman Empire and under the rule of its law', as ecclesiastical institutions subject to the bishop,[46] Schönfeld rather simplistically equated Roman law with canon law, and so the (Eastern) Roman Empire with the (Western) church of Rome. He then used the *Corpus iuris civilis* to provide the ecclesiastical model for hospitals. His article, still an authoritative account of hospitals in the early medieval West, surveyed a wide range of legal and documentary material and found a gulf between Justinianic law and what appeared in practice. Most fundamentally, lay patrons failed to hand over the supervision of xenodochia to a bishop. Schönfeld saw this not as a difference between East and West, or Roman and canon law, but as the erosion of Roman (church) law by Germanic (lay) practice. And he found it early, in the seventh and eighth centuries, 'a kind of legal earthquake' as the *Volk* overthrew the shackles of Roman law.[47] Although mid-ninth-century papal councils tried to reassert the Roman ideal of an ecclesiastical form (this was Schönfeld's interpretation of Carolingian legislation), their efforts proved futile. Imbert ignored Schönfeld's Germanic arguments and, with them, the latter's whole model of Roman law. To Imbert, a scholar of

---

[43] He noticed it briefly, in a late discussion of administrators; *HDC* 233–5.

[44] 'Titre préliminaire': *HDC* 9–54.

[45] The principle that hospitals (as *xenodochia* and *piae causae*) were, in law, Justinianic, pre-dates Schönfeld, whose 'Xenod.', provides references in his footnotes. It remains the bedrock of the field.

[46] Schönfeld, 'Xenod.', 23, 38: 'Die Xenodochien sind im römischen Reich und unter der Herrschaft seines Rechts aufgekommen.'

[47] Schönfeld, 'Xenod.', 35–49, with 19, 23–30 on Roman law: 'So ist der Stiftungsgedanke als Rechtsbegriff mit dem römischen Kirchenrecht hochgekommen und, soweit dieses durchbrochen ist, mit ihm dahingegangen. Die auf das Recht am Grund und Boden gestützte potestas des Stifters und seiner Genossen hat sich gegen ihn erhoben, eine Art juristisches Erdbeben in verschlungen.' (p. 41). The idea of a *Volksrecht*, and *Volksgeist*, rested on a longer—and more complex—German tradition; C. Kletzer, 'Custom and Positivity: The Hegel-Savigny Controversy', in A. Perreau-Saussine and J. B. Murphy, *The Nature of Customary Law* (Cambridge, 2007).

Roman law in the eighteenth century, it seemed natural that Justinian's laws provided the ancient form that he was seeking, that pre-dated the canonists. To Imbert, the early date of Justinian's law, and its presumed continuity across the centuries, also explained the meagre Carolingian legislation. In so doing, Imbert ignored Schönfeld's copious evidence that Roman law, and especially any super-visory authority by the bishop, was missing in practice.

So did the Justinianic form continue (Imbert), or was it overthrown by the laity (Schönfeld) in the eighth century? The historical case that hospitals rested on Roman law in the West hinges on one piece of evidence: a chapter from *novel 7*, incorporated by Abbot Ansegis of St Wandrille into his 827 collection of royal capitularies. This was Imbert's smoking gun, the proof that the West had imported 'wholesale' Justinian's law and, with it, the legal personality and typology of those institutions.[48] It was on this basis that Imbert used the *Corpus iuris civilis* to define welfare institutions in the West.[49] But in 1956 Imbert retracted his claims about Ansegis:[50] he had trusted an 'overconfident editor', who had published the chapter as law promulgated by Louis the Pious.[51] Imbert admitted that Ansegis's chapter was no genuine decree but foreign material, inserted as a pious fraud by the abbot; in so doing, he removed the plank on which his Justinianic model rested. At the time Imbert offered no new legal definition for Carolingian hos-pitals, but the problem haunted him for forty-five years.[52] His retraction went unnoticed by the field.

It continues to be held that welfare houses followed 'the Eastern model', whose institutional forms and law were imported into the West and reinforced via Frankish and papal councils.[53] The idea that welfare institutions were defined in

---

[48] Imbert did not mince his words: 'Ainsi définis dans leur structure juridique, ces établissements ressemblent singulièrement à ceux que nous avons vus régis par le droit de Justinien. La législation orientale parait avoir passé en bloc, en ce qui concerne notre matière, dans les pays occidentaux: du VIe au XIe siècle, les établissements hospitaliers obéissent aux mêmes règles de fondation et d'administra-tion, en Grèce et en France.' *HDC* 44–5.

[49] Indeed, *novel 123* was the basis for his much-cited assertion that hospitals rested under episcopal authority.

[50] J. Imbert, 'Le droit romain dans les textes juridiques carolingiens', in *Studi in onore di Pietro de Francisci*, III (Milan, 1956), 65–6. He had been taken to task in F. L. Ganshof's review, in *L'Antiquité Classique* 18:1 (1949), 214–15.

[51] Alfred Boretius included it in his 1883 edition of Carolingian royal capitularies, dividing it into two as no. 153, '*Capitula e lege romana excerpta, 826?*' (MGH, *Cap.* I, 310), believing that it was promulgated by the emperor or in a council and ascribing a date from the fact that the chapter followed Louis's *Admonitio* (825) in Ansegis's collection.

[52] It was the subject of his last essay: J. Imbert, 'Les conciles et les hôpitaux (IXe siècle)', in *Fondations*. Published posthumously, many sections were left unfinished and one, *Quid novi?* unstarted (p. 43). The essay took xenodochia as ecclesiastical institutions and credited Louis the Pious with initiating legislation on the matter. Imbert saw the Carolingian bishops, epitomized by the council of Meaux-Paris (845/6), asserting an ancient episcopal jurisdiction by threatening as 'murderers of the poor' those who harmed hospitals (pp. 39–42, 44–6, esp. p. 42). Others have dismissed Ansegis's chapter as 'a thoughtless or boastful borrowing' but not questioned the early primacy of Justinian's law in the West; Schönfeld, 'Xenod.', 19; Boshof, 'Armenfürsorge', 153–4.

[53] F. Merzbacher, 'Das Spital im Kanonischen Recht bis zum Tridentinum', *Archiv für Katholisches Kirchenrecht* 148 (1979), 74–8; Caron, '*pia fundatio*', 140–1; E. N. Rocca, *Il diritto ospedaliero nei suoi*

the West by Justinian's corpus has yet to be challenged. For legal historians, what hospitals were, how they were run, their rights and duties, and their supervision, have been sought as a matter of practice in the wide array of legislative texts issued under Justinian's name between 529 and 534, and especially the Codex, Institutes, and Novels.

Imbert's original contribution was his argument that later canon law recognized *la doctrine* of two types of hospitals: *locus religiosus/publicus*, a greater 'religious place', under the bishop; and *hospitale simplex/privatus*, a lesser 'private hospital', without chapel or cemetery. This he distilled from late-medieval commentators on the Clementines (that is, on *Quia contingit* of 1317), who consistently cited the principle that 'anyone can make a hospital, without the bishop's permission' (on what grounds has never been established).[54] It sat uncomfortably with their other statement in law, that 'hospitals are religious and belong to the bishop'.[55] In an attempt to clarify what canonists had not, Imbert proposed his two types and gave them names.

Imbert's two types were undone the very year his book was published, and by Imbert himself, in an article that set out to explore the 'doctrine' in practice, in Northern France and Belgium. To do so, Imbert had to change that doctrine to recognize the municipal activity of the region, so he silently dropped the 'private hospital' and divided the first type into two: *loci religiosi*, under ecclesiastical authority and usually established by cathedral chapter or monastery; and the more numerous *loci publici*, under secular authority, in which the bishop had no right.[56] But, even then, Imbert found that most hospitals were of a third category, which he termed *hôpitaux mixtes*: part public, or secular, but with religious features. This was an unstable form, he argued, because it depended on an unsustainable cooperation between ecclesiastical and secular authorities. Yet he found that the houses themselves did not submit to even this typology, forcing Imbert to wonder 'whether canonical rules were flouted or simply by-passed?'[57] Neither of his doctrines were observed in practice. Imbert concluded that his two original types were largely identical in practice, except for the identity of the

---

lineamenti storici (Milan, 1956), 35–41, 49; M. Mollat, *Les pauvres au Moyen Age* (Paris, 1978), 31; Frank, 'Hospitalreformen', 6, 10; T. Sternberg, *Orientalium more secutus: Räume und Institutionen der Caritas des 5. bis 7. Jahrhunderts in Gallien* (Münster, 1991), 155–7; H. Coing, 'Remarks on the History of Foundations', *Minerva* 19:2 (1981), 273; E. Patlagean, 'La pauvreté Byzantine au VIᵉ siècle', in *EHP* 77; W. Ullmann, 'Public Welfare and Social Legislation in the Early Medieval Councils', *Studies in Church History* 7 (1971), 9. A more analytical approach is taken by H. Siems, 'Von den *piae causae* zu den Xenodochien', in *Itin. Fid.* 60ff.

[54] 'hospitalis domus potest edificari sine licentia episcopi', the phrase is Johannes Andreae's, although Imbert noted earlier iterations by Innocent IV and Hostiensis; *HDC* 55–6, 67–73.

[55] From the title to (X 3.36.3): 'Ut religiosae domus suos episcopos sint subiectae'.

[56] J. Imbert, 'Le régime juridique des établissements hospitaliers du Nord de la France', *Revue du Nord* 29 (1947), 196–7.

[57] 'Les règles canoniques ont-elles été bafouées ou simplement tournées?', Imbert, 'régime juridique', 197–8, 201.

supervising authority. This second retraction has also passed unnoticed, and the 'two types', *locus religiosus* and *hospitale simplex*, has continued to serve as the definition in canon law.[58]

The doctrine of 'two types' is thus modern and repudiated by its creator. It is unsurprising, therefore, that its alleged originators, the late medieval canonists and commentators, failed to embrace, or even acknowledge it. In fact, among these commentators there is little consistency in terminology and no agreement as to the meaning of, or boundary between, ecclesiastical and non-ecclesiastical hospitals: indeed canonists did not even seem interested in the difference.[59] A canonist like William de Monte Lauduno could even observe that non-ecclesiastical hospitals might have a priest and oratory approved by the bishop over which the bishop had no right of inspection.[60] At this point it may be observed that the canonists actually do agree in theory with the picture that Imbert found in practice in his article: that there were no 'types' of hospitals, just different supervising authorities, lay as well as ecclesiastical.

This long-standing model is thus composed of contradictory parts, resting on failed or unexamined evidence. Its definitions of legal personality (tenets 1, 2, and 4) no longer stand, by their originator's own admission. When it comes to the legal personality of welfare houses, what we have is lore rather than law. As a result, the field has diverged along separate paths. Following Imbert, legal historians look to Justinian's *Corpus* for an enduring definition of hospitals. In contrast, ecclesiastical and social historians, working with hospitals on the ground after 1100, follow Le Grand and look to Courson's councils for a vision of reform.[61]

Nationalisms

To understand why this faulty model has endured for so long, we need to recognize national frameworks that were established by these early scholars and which continue to shape hospital scholarship.

We start with Le Grand, whose interest in hospitals was also very much of *his* day. A programme to secularize French hospitals was reaching an ugly climax in France in the 1890s, as reformers sought to introduce medically trained staff from nursing schools, in imitation of hospitals in Britain, the United States, and Switzerland. In France, where hospitals remained untouched by Protestant Reformation, controversy centred on the religious congregations of sisters who

---

[58] Caron, '*pia fundatio*', 152–5, esp. 152; De Spiegeler, *Liège*, 105; Rubin, *Charity and Community*, 103–4; Brodman, *CRME* 244–6.

[59] This was noticed (with some surprise) in Frank's perceptive article, 'Hospitalreformen', 34, 39.

[60] Frank, 'Hospitalreformen', 27–8.

[61] The separation appears even in Imbert's work, where Courson's councils appear near the end of his study, as having 'triggered' the drafting of statutes across France; *HDC* 268–70.

tended the sick and whose expulsion was the main obstacle to reformers' ambitions.[62] The restructuring was 'rapide et brutale' and the debates were polemical. In 1901, the year Le Grand published his edition, the municipal council of Reims declared religious vows a renunciation of what made us human, and Catholic congregations a 'passive submission to...foreigners' that jeopardized the very existence of the nation: 'there is no possible *entente* between the church and civil society, or reconciliation between the tyranny of dogma and free evolution of reason'.[63] In response, traditionalists argued that vowed sisters embodied the highest ideals of service, and that religious rules were the basis of effective administration and of the very stability of hospitals. It is no coincidence that Le Grand's first publications celebrated the religious administration of medieval hospitals (1891) and the beguines of medieval Paris (1893).[64] His work offered a historical perspective and an attempt to reframe the debate, from one of dogma versus reason, or foreign versus nation, to the enduring character of France, with religion at its core. For Le Grand, the introduction of religious rules by the Paris council had been the definitive reform of French hospitals. And this reform— hatched at the *hôtel-dieu* at Montdidier, formulated by bishops at Paris, and rolled out across the country via Courson's six councils—was wholly French.[65] Le Grand's work was an argument in defence of religious hospitals and for their French origins. The security of hospitals under the Church, and their characterization as autonomous communities under rules that were fashioned by native reformers, were issues of immediate significance to this founder of the field.

Beyond France, other pioneering works laid down their own national visions. In England, Rotha Mary Clay produced *The Mediaeval Hospitals of England* (1909). The self-educated daughter of a vicar, Clay's commitment to social work saw her live and work among Bristol's poor for almost fifty years.[66] It also propelled her into the archives in search of its medieval past. *Mediaeval Hospitals* aimed to root modern social work in an English tradition that stretched

---

[62] On the controversy: Y. Marec, 'Le création de l'école d'infirmières de Rouen en 1900', in Dinet-Lecomte, ed., *Les hôpitaux*; K. Schultheiss, 'The Secularization of Hospital Nursing in France, 1880–1914', *French History* 12:3 (1998). The fight was personal as well as ideological, since sisters were from local families who had supported their vocation as a life of religious service.

[63] 'Le Conseil considérant qu'en prononçant les vœux de célibat, d'obéissance et de pauvreté, les membres des diverses congrégations renoncent aux attributs essentiels de la personne humaine et que leur exemple ne pourrait se généraliser sans compromettre l'existence même de toute nation, qu'en vivant en commun, courbés sous la même règle, soumis passivement à l'autorité de chefs la plupart du temps étrangers, ils constituent des associations dangereuses pour l'état qu'ils menacent dans ses prérogatives essentielles [...], considérant qu'il n'y a pas d'entente possible entre l'église et la société civile, de conciliation entre la tyrannie du dogme et la libre évolution de la raison.' From the deliberations of the municipal council, 24 November 1901, in J. Lalouette, 'Une laïcisation hospitalière menée tambour battant', in Dinet-Lecomte, ed., *Les hôpitaux*, 251, and quotation on p. 248.

[64] Le Grand, 'Régime intérieur'; Le Grand, 'Les béguines de Paris', *Mémoires de la Société de l'Histoire de Paris* 20 (1893).

[65] *Statuts*, pp. xi, xiii, xvi.

[66] N. Orme, 'Clay, Rotha Mary (1878–1961)', *Oxford Dictionary of National Biography* (2004).

back a thousand years, in her own words: 'to secure a fuller recognition of the widespread activity of the Church of England in former days... [a vision which] proves that clergy and laity were battling bravely with social problems'.[67] Her study focused on the nature and administration of care, as medieval welfare expanded to embrace new categories of recipients, from wayfarers and lepers to the 'feeble and destitute' and pensioners. Here, regulations (chapter 9: 'The Constitution') and staffing (chapter 10: 'The Household and its Members') made only a brief appearance, and in non-Le Grandian terms. Instead, the study offered a chronology of hospital types and thematic discussion of their dwellings, funding, and administration. The study offered little law, only passing reference to a few English decrees, notably the parliamentary acts of 1410 and 1414. Clay offered an English programme of philanthropy, nestled within an English Christianity, and propelled not by clerical injunction but moral conscience. Clay's hospitals had regulations *ab initio*.[68] The challenge faced by English bishops was how to maintain them in the face of fading ideals and concomitant mal-administration, a failure to care that led inexorably towards the Reformation. Their early ideals were in 1909 a clarion call to return to social work.

In Germany a very different vision was laid out, by two students of Ulrich Stutz, the legal historian who was also a nationalist and monarchist. Writing in 1922, Schönfeld was at the forefront of a movement in German legal philosophy that rejected Roman law as 'alien from the people, selfish, individualistic, liberal, commercial, rational . . , and certainly "un-German"'.[69] Under the National Socialists, whose party Schönfeld soon joined, this virulent attack intensified, driving Roman legal scholars into exile. The opposition between German law (native, human, of the people and the soil) and Roman law (foreign, intellectual, and individualistic) was the political basis of his interest. (Writing in the aftermath of war, Imbert was alive to Schönfeld's nationalist arguments, which may be why he ignored the 'legal earthquake' of the *Volk* so completely.[70]) The successor, chronologically and philosophically, to Schönfeld was Siegfried Reicke, who

---

[67] R. M. Clay, *The Mediaeval Hospitals of England* (London, 1909), pp. xvii–xviii.

[68] She presumed that the earliest houses were under a rule, adopted from a monastic custodian or provided by the bishop (when politely asked), and 'there was apparently a definite Anglican Rule'; Clay, *Mediaeval Hospitals*, 29, 34, 212, and esp. p. 126.

[69] The language is that of M. Stolleis, *The Law under the Swastika*, tr. T. Dunlap (Chicago, 1998), 59, where pp. 58–60 discusses the movement more widely. Also, A. Carrino, 'From the Criticism of Neo-Kantianism to Neo-Hegelianism', in E. Pattaro and C. Roversi, eds, *Legal Philosophy in the Twentieth Century: The Civil Law World*, I (Berlin, 2016), 204–7.

[70] On Imbert's early career, J.-L. Harouel, 'Un grand savant et administrateur: Jean Imbert (1919–1999)', *Tijdschrift voor rechtsgeschiedenis* 78:1 (2000); and Schönfeld's subseqent career, F.-R. Hausmann, *'Deutsche Geisteswissenschaft' im zweiten Weltkrieg* (Dresden, 1998), 232–9, 263–4, places Schönfeld's subsequent career in context. Imbert picked the wrong side of Schönfeld's theory/practice conflict. Setting aside the ideological nationalism, Schönfeld's observations of lay activity stand up better than his appropriation of Justinian's legislation as church law in the medieval west. See my Chapters 5 and 6.

located his own small earthquake in the German towns of the later middle ages.[71] His monumental study, *Das deutsche Spital und sein Recht im Mittelalter* ('The German Hospital and its Law in the Middle Ages'), his habilitation thesis, was the launch in 1932 of what would be a starry career under the Third Reich.[72] The son of the city archivist at Nuremberg, Reicke, like Clay, also used archives to map a local tradition, although where Clay's tended to the bucolic and social, Reicke's was urban and governmental. Reicke saw hospitals as originally religious institutions, once firmly in the grip of the (Roman Catholic) Church, under monasteries and houses of canons and then, in the twelfth century, also religious confraternities, and especially military and hospitaller orders. From the thirteenth century, a process of municipalization (*Kommunalisierung*) brought them under lay administrators and into the hands of town magistrates: the 'ecclesiastical hospital' (*das kirchliche Spital*) gave way to the 'civic hospital' (*das bürgerliche Spital*), although the latter still was very much a house of God.[73]

Reicke's discussion of *Spitalrecht* was one of German custom and innovation, expressed through hospital statutes, royal privileges, and city ordinances.[74] It is a subtle and complex case, rightly influential; it is also a story of Germanization that sets aside canon law.[75] It might be compared to another model, this one Italian. Emilio Nasalli Rocca, writing a decade after the Second World War, explored the origins of 'the great Italian hospital tradition'. These were rooted in the Roman legal tradition (that is, Justinian's laws), but only began to bloom in the late-

---

[71] Stutz was the inspiration behind both hospital studies and generously shared his own findings with his protégés (Schönfeld, 'Xenod.', 1n.). Reicke studied under Stutz at Berlin and married Stutz's daughter. For Reicke's early years, see M. Heckel, 'Siegfried Reicke †', *ZRG* 89 Kan. Abt. 53 (1972), whose biographical detail ends abruptly at 1933. On Stutz, M. Grüttner, 'Der Lehrkörper 1918–1932', in M. Grüttner, ed., *Die Berliner Universität zwischen den Weltkriegen* (Berlin, 2012), 154–5.

[72] S. Reicke, *Das deutsche Spital und sein Recht im Mittelalter, Erster Teil: Geschichte und Gestalt, Zweiter Teil: Das deutsche Spitalrecht*, 2 vols (Stuttgart, 1932). Reicke rose quickly under the new regime, becoming Professor of German and Canon Law in Königsberg (1933) then Marburg (1936), and Professor for Jurisprudence at Berlin (1941–45). He assumed an early leadership role in academic initiatives of the regime, speaking at the League of National Socialist German Jurists in Dec. 1934 and directing the legal historians for the Aktion Ritterbusch, the 'war effort by the Humanities', a job he did particularly effectively; Hausmann, '*Deutsche Geisteswissenschaft*', 69–76, 188–9, 196–7, 263; Stolleis, *Law under the Swastika*, 50, where pp. 40–69 offer the wider context of this difficult time.

[73] Reicke, *Das deutsche Spital*, esp. I. 198. The process of municipalization has been further nuanced for Germany by Jürgen Sydow, and reinterpreted for English towns by Miri Rubin: J. Sydow, 'Kanonistische Fragen zur Geschichte des Spitals', *Historiches Jahrbuch* 83 (1964); J. Sydow, 'Spital und Stadt in Kanonistik und Verfassungsgeschichte', in H. Patze, ed., *Der deutsche Territorialstaat im 14. Jahrhundert* (Sigmaringen, 1970–1); M. Rubin, 'Development and Change', in L. Granshaw and R. Porter, eds, *The Hospital in History* (London, 1989).

[74] As Reicke reflected in his inaugural address at Berlin in 1942: 'Von Landschaft zu Landschaft, von Stadt zu Stadt fortschreitend versuchte ich, die rechtliche Ordnung dieser Institution auf deutschem Boden in ihren mannigfachen Ausprägungen und Wandlungen, die in den Städten durch den Prozeß allmählicher Verbürgerlichung gekennzeichnet sind, aufzuzeigen. Es ergab sich hierbei, wie stark diese aus dem Schoß der Kirche geborene Einrichtung in ihrer Gestalt und Auswirkung deutsch-rechtlich Züge angenommen hat.' 'Antrittsrede des Hrn. Reicke', in *Jahrbuch der Preußischen Akademie der Wissenschaften: Jahrgang 1942* (Berlin, 1943), 164, and the reply, 165–6.

[75] He offers only brief notices in a discussion of lepers and a footnote on *Quia contingit*; Reicke, *Das deutsche Spital*, II. 253 and 179n.

medieval Italian city states, where great hospitals emerged. Rocca's was a long story of the rise of ambitious and carefully designed institutions that would eventually aspire to the 'total assistance' of the people.[76] The point here is not that these foundational studies should be discarded. Many were remarkable works of archival scholarship, and the core frameworks that they established—of religious regulation (Le Grand), social work (Clay), municipalization (Reicke), and industrial care (Rocca)—remain relevant. And there *were* regional patterns to the form, foundation, and supervision of hospitals.[77]

The point, rather, is in three parts. First, these studies, generated at moments of national stress, laid down visions of an ideal *national* past that spoke to that present, and their agendas produced conflicting master narratives. In the early twentieth century, medieval welfare (the interplay of social order and religion) was swept up into a nation's long story of the place of religion in the state. So, Le Grand, confronting a *secularisation brutale*, argued for religion as a native, reforming force in French society; Reicke, under the Weimar Republic (a system of government, nationalists thought, which had been imposed by foreign design), saw the German *Volk* take charge of their own government and destiny. Unable to look beyond the English Channel, Clay saw religion as a cultural activity that was local, individual, and helpful (and very English); while Rocca saw the church and the civic authorities work side by side to care for the people of Italy.[78] Their visions embody national ideals at a moment of political contest; yet as the bedrock of each national field, too easily divided by language, their frameworks have constructed national ways of thinking, from approaches and agendas, to languages for and models of change. Even studies that reach across borders are subject to the gravitational pull of their own national conversation.[79]

Second, the conflict between these master narratives is concentrated on the period 1150 to 1300, the great era of hospital foundation, and on the nature of change at this time. It was then that Reicke's municipalities seized church hospitals as civic, Le Grand's churchmen captured hospitals for the church, Rocca's Renaissance citizens began to build a state for the people, and Clay's local idealism waxes then begins to wane. It is not only grand narratives that are in conflict. The very idea of what hospitals were, where they came from, and how and why they changed is also in conflict. Was the church asserting its authority by bringing hospitals under episcopal oversight (Le Grand), or finding its ancient control

---

[76] Rocca, *Il diritto osped.* 34–94, esp. p. 93. On the *Corpus iuris civilis*, underpinning medieval law, ibid. 34–50, esp. pp. 46 and 49.

[77] See the essays in *Europ. Spitalwesen.*

[78] Few of us are immune to such forces. I began this book in 2012, thinking about canon law as an umbrella (European) law; I write in Brexit Britain, with a heightened sense of the question of Europeanness.

[79] This makes the work of scholars who cross borders intellectually, such as Miri Rubin, Gisela Drossbach, and Thomas Frank, particularly valuable. Belgian scholarship has proven particularly fertile, in part because it can engage with both the German and French traditions.

eroded by civic claims or the growing autonomy of the welfare houses themselves (Reicke)?[80] Whole definitional questions fall between the cracks. We discover how wide these cracks are when reaching beyond national borders. So, what had attracted Le Grand to the Paris council of 1213—the regional nature of its hospital reform—ensures that the model fails on a European stage. The challenge thus has been to explain how Courson's reforms were broadcast across the church universal: some offer Lateran IV (1215) as the vehicle; others simply suggest that Paris and Rouen required a programme of hospital regulation that reached across France and beyond.[81] Courson's Paris council is still seen as the moment when the submission of hospitals to religious rules became church policy. The trouble is that there is no evidence that it did.

Third, canon law was intentionally written out of each national paradigm, as something foreign. Le Grand turned to the Paris council because it seemed French (fortunately, the name of Robert de Courson, an Englishman, sounds French), Clay found people with no need of Rome, Reicke's *Volk* seized native control from the (alien) Roman church, and Rocca saw Roman law underpinning efforts of both church and cities. Each defined a national arena that in turn rejected canon law for its international character. This is why the errors in our legal model have passed unnoticed for seventy years. Without a sense of the international view and activity of canon law, it is difficult to talk across borders and so to explore the place of welfare in the Western church, at the heart of Christian practice.[82] Canon law has the potential to offer new keys for thinking comparatively about regions. When, how far, and even whether legal ideas shaped practice in a city or diocese offers a means to identify regional cultures in an international framework and also to tap into local and international networks through which ideas might have spread. Of course, canon law also had a geography—a subtitle for this book might

[80] For opposing positions, see D. Le Blévec, 'Fondations et œuvres charitables au moyen âge', in *Fondations*, 8–9, 21; Mollat, *Les pauvres*, 183–7; Montaubin, 'Hôpitaux cathédraux', 23, 26, 35; F.-O. Touati, 'Un dossier à rouvrir: L'assistance au Moyen Age', in *Fondations*, 28–33; Maréchal, *Brugse hospitaalwezen*; Rocca, *Il diritto osped.* 54, 58; *Statuts*, pp. x–xvi, xxiv. Some suggest that both paradigms might be true; Brodman, *CRME* 47, 68–71, 77, 82–4; De Spiegeler, *Liège*, 105–6, 117–18; Drossbach, 'Das Hospital', esp. pp. 513, 516.

[81] For Lateran IV: Mollat, 'Floraison', 56; Touati, *Maladie et société*, 422; G. B. Risse, *Mending Bodies, Saving Souls* (Oxford, 1999), 151–2. For its French impact, Montaubin, 'Hôpitaux cathédraux', 28; J. W. Brodman, 'Religion and Discipline in the Hospitals of Thirteenth-Century France', in B. S. Bowers, ed., *The Medieval Hospital and Medical Practice* (Aldershot, 2007), 124–6, 132. For Belgium: De Spiegeler, *Liège*, 112; W. De Keyzer, 'L'évolution interne des léproseries', in B. Tabuteau, ed., *Lépreux et sociabilité du Moyen Age aux temps modernes* (Rouen, 2000), 13. Drossbach, 'Das Hospital', 515, 521, sees the profusion of hospital statutes in Germany as evidence 'daß die Bestimmungen des Pariser Konzils umgesetzt wurden', as does M. Uhrmacher, 'Die Verbreitung von Leprosorien', in *HMMA* 165.

[82] Such comparative study promises to reshape the field. Early efforts have worked to digest scholarship or evidence from different countries, presenting cases side by side. Major contributions are *Europ. Spitalwesen*; M. Scheutz et al., eds, *Quellen*; G. Drossbach, ed., *Mittelalter und früher Neuzeit: Frankreich, Deutschland und Italien* (Oldenbourg, 2007), esp. its introductory survey by Drossbach, Frank, and Touati. And, for Eastern Europe, K. Brunner, ed., *Special Issue: Themenschwerpunkt Europäische Spitäler* 115:3–4 (2007).

be 'many roads lead to Pavia and quite a few others to Reims'—and most of the efforts that emerge sprang from local, even personal initiative. But each of them aimed to define hospitals as Christian forms, within the church universal, and so to a degree within a European frame.

Having been set aside, medieval canon law has yet to reveal these definitions. We lack knowledge of what law existed, and when, as well as the legal framework through which hospitals were interpreted at any given time in the middle ages. This has implications not only for our understanding of the church and the laity, the relationship between religion and social institutions, and a long history of social welfare, but for the development of charity law (for here, at its base, is a social history of the development of charity, trusts, and social institutions).[83] Canon law explores what hospitals were in the eyes of the church, or at least in the eyes of the popes, bishops, abbots, canonists, and clerics who tried to articulate these claims. It takes us to the heart of the question of hospitals 'between church and world'. How far *was* a 'hospital' an ecclesiastical form? What was that form, and how did it change over a millennium? More curiously, why did canonists and popes tolerate the messiness of welfare so readily? What efforts they made in law bear witness to the forces, legal and political, for order and so the direction of change across a period. To understand welfare houses in their world, we must understand their place in law. Across a millennium, *ptochia*, *xenodochia*, hospitals, leper-houses, *domus dei*, and almshouses inspired new law and were altered in turn as law changed around them. They were of church and world: law offers a framework to explain how, and why.

On Xenodochia, 1100–1320

The ongoing confusion is ultimately due to canon law itself. The situation for those communities in military and hospitaller orders was clear. Like other new orders of the twelfth century, they submitted to a papally approved rule and their vowed members, as well as their buildings and property, were governed by canon law on the regular religious, or *regulares*. Most hospitals, however, were not part of these orders. These were 'xenodochia', local welfare facilities, and they are the subject of this study. These places were rarely mentioned in canon law: only the *Liber extra* (1234) included a statement *De xenodochiis* ('On the matter of hospitals'), and this was the antiquated sentence that Imbert so swiftly dismissed. Only the Council of Vienne (1312) acted decisively, issuing *Quia contingit* (1317),

---

[83] R. H. Helmholz, 'The Law of Charity and the English Ecclesiastical Courts', in P. Hoskin et al., eds, *The Foundations of Medieval Ecclesiastical History* (Woodbridge, 2005), concludes 'that the medieval canon law possessed no text or other locus that could serve as the point of departure for the creation of a law of charity', esp. on the subject of charitable institutions (p. 123, and see, too, 113–14).

which has been called 'the Magna Carta of hospital organisation'.[84] This was the only substantial legislation for welfare houses, although its aims remain confusing (it is still unclear what this decisive council actually decided to do). For the first millennium of welfare houses, we have only bitty and contradictory statements in law, even for the period 1140 to 1300, the era when canonists worked so hard to define the full range of Christian principles and practices. That this absence in law had meaning, that can be read, and that the distinctiveness of each statement provides a window into a moment of welfare and law-making, are two of the underlying arguments (and approaches) of this book.

It is clear, however, that contemporaries did know what a xenodochium was, in law as well as in practice. We can glimpse a reference in Northampton in 1200, when the priory of St Andrew provided a plot of land to Peter fitzHerbert and his son to build 'a certain house for the reception of pilgrims and paupers', a hospital. The priory did so on condition:

> that [the house] be established in this form: namely that in that place in the future no college be made, whether of monks or canons or Templars or Hospitallers or nuns, and that the house itself at no time be changed into a church or into the form of a church *nor transcend the form of a xenodochium*.[85]

(Emphasis added)

The priory's charter did not spell out what that form was, but it did make clear that a xenodochium was neither a church (*ecclesia*) nor a body (*collegium*) of religious and, indeed, that it was a more circumscribed form than either of them.[86] St Andrew's priory was a centre of legal learning in the late twelfth century. They understood that 'the form of a xenodochium' was recognized in legal terms and could be guaranteed in law.[87] What did they mean, and to what were they referring?

---

[84] 'als die Magna Charta der mittelalterlichen Spitalsorganisation': W. M. Plöchl, *Geschichte des Kirchenrechts*, II (Vienna/Munich, 1955), 458; cited in Merzbacher, 'Das Spital', 86.

[85] '...domum quandam in susceptionem peregrinorum et pauperum in loco nostro...sub hac forma construi: scilicet quod in loco prenominato nullum inposterum fiet collegium sive de monachis sive de canonicis sive de templariis sive de hospitelariis sive de monialibus; ita est quod domus ipsa nullis temporibus in ecclesiam vel in formam ecclesie commutabitur nec formam xenodochii excedet.' BL Cotton Vespasian E XVII, fol. 33v, ed. Watson, 'Sources for English Hospitals', in M. Scheutz et al., eds, *Quellen*, 73–7.

[86] The term 'collegium' seems also to reflect their legal learning, and an awareness of the use of Roman law by canonists in the later twelfth century (see Chapter 7).

[87] Northampton had preceded Oxford as a centre of scholarship in the late twelfth century, and especially law. It left its mark on the priory, which held a recension of the Bamberg group, an early systematic collection of decretals from the 1180s; C. Duggan, 'The Making of the New Case Law', in *HMCL*. For the Northampton law schools: P. Stein, 'Vacarius and the Civil Law', in C. Brooke et al., eds, *Church and Government in the Middle Ages* (Cambridge, 1976), 131–3; but cf. P. Landau, 'The Origins of Legal Science in England', in M. Brett and K. G. Cushing, eds, *Readers, Texts and Compilers in the Earlier Middle Ages* (Farnham, 2009), 173.

Approach and Structure

What follows offers the first dedicated study of welfare institutions in Western law and the first concerted investigation of the full range of legal material for hospitals, from the late antique through the high middle ages. The chapters establish, for the first time, a Western legal model for the hospital, one that takes us beyond canon law and into vulgar Roman law, Justinian's Code and Novels, as well as Carolingian capitularies. In so doing, it illuminates how and why hospitals were legally distinct from monasteries and identifies their peculiar place, just beyond the reach of canon law. It establishes the legal principles that defined hospitals and the small legal innovations, from time to time, that could have such large effects. The place of welfare in law, and in Christianity itself, prevented even the most assertive churchmen from claiming hospitals as an ecclesiastical form. And here was the great conundrum behind their work: how to engage with a Christian foundation over which the church had no basic claim?

To chart this conceptual wrangle, and the activity in law that it produced, this study leaves behind the activity of the streets and even in the courts, to focus on the intellectual challenge of comprehending and articulating law. It puts the creators and refiners of law front and centre: the councils, popes, canonists, commentators, and compilers of legal collections, who struggled to engage with a subject for which they often had no language and little legal tradition. While new legal principles and instruments are identified, they are not followed out into the charters of individual houses to explore how law was put into practice. Such efforts require dedicated studies, each focused on a locality, moment, or network.[88] The world of welfare is everywhere around, and within, the legal thinking, and many actual houses will be noticed; but to pretend that an official package of legal thought was created, enacted, and obeyed would be misleading.

Across a thousand years, the world of welfare was changing relentlessly, and so too was law. Seismic shifts in the political shape (and jurisdictional claim) of the church redefined who spoke for its people and rights, and the terms on which they spoke. Until the twelfth century, this was usually a question of regional leadership and claims to act. Meanwhile, relations with secular powers could open up, distract, or hothouse church claims. The structures by which problems were articulated and decisions made shaped in turn the priorities and agendas of lawmakers, as well as who it was who formulated law.[89] This included centres of

---

[88] This book interrupted one such study, on the charters and statutes of English hospitals, c.1100–1307, to which I plan to return. On the importance and the problems of teasing out relationships between (written) law and (customary) practice, A. Rio, 'Introduction', in A. Rio, ed., *Law, Custom, and Justice in Late Antiquity and the Early Middle Ages* (London, 2011).

[89] An important collection of essays, which think in more complex terms about the creation, use, and reuse of law, is C. Rolker, ed., *New Discourses in Medieval Canon Law Research: Challenging the Master Narrative* (Leiden, 2019), which arrived just as this book was going to press.

learning, be they monastery, episcopal see, papal curia, or royal palace, and the rise of the schools in the twelfth century. And finally, and especially, the means by which law was disseminated and written—the constantly changing conceptual and material mechanisms of law—framed not only the shape, reach, and languages of law, but the possibilities of innovation. It is perhaps not surprising that statements on xenodochia—by definition pioneering—so often appear at the forefront of new vistas and new technologies of law. Here is where the daring could push the boundaries.

To move across a millennium, then, chapters must navigate changing cultures of law-making. At the heart of the study lies the problem, medieval and modern, of how to think about welfare houses. For us, just as the councils and canonists of an earlier era, it is the challenge of comprehending what was done but not said. The challenge works on two levels. The first requires us to pause, now and then, to untangle scholarly orthodoxies. These have grown up around the early historiography, they rest on old and unspoken assumptions and contain fundamental contradictions, laid down by long national traditions. Only by unpicking these knots can we open up the material to new interpretations. The second and principle task, then, is to apprehend the disparate, sporadic, and often contradictory statements in law and to understand the thinking—immediate and structural—behind them. To do so, chapters must first recognize the endeavour of law-making at that moment and so the ways in which legal ideas were made. This is both a matter of the evidence that survives (and the nature in which it survives) and a question of how to approach law at a particular time; both owe a debt to the legal historians who have charted complex manuscript traditions and, more recently, offered conceptual keys for understanding the practices by which records were made. The diverse material, and the distinctive legal environments that produced it, construct fundamentally different challenges and these, in turn, frame the approach of each chapter. At times, the work must be highly technical. Throughout, the question is less what law-makers thought than how they thought and to what ends.

Despite this diversity, the analysis is sustained by three underlying claims. First, that the forces that produced a statement on hospitals were deliberate, original, and very much of their moment. Because there was no canon law of hospitals, no statement was inherited. The very act of addressing welfare houses was extraordinary and the intrusion of an alien object into a familiar arena. Second, that any statement in law was itself an argument, one that had to be authored for its audience. Its manufacturer wove the text from threads that had, or could be made to have, meaning to that audience; this allows for close readings to untangle these threads which, when followed, reveal unexpected agendas. And third, that the act itself was designed to address a phenomenon that was pressingly contemporary. The concern often reflected wider pressures faced by bishops, or alarm at particular circumstances, but the shape of the answer was crafted by the law-makers.

This is not a top-down story of law as something that fashioned its world, but a study of how law-makers observed a phenomenon that was bigger than law.

The structure of this book is analytical, not chronological. This is, in part, an argument against developmental teleology. The latter is not a philosophical stance, but a historical argument: there was no package of law for law-makers to inherit. Like the historian today, a canonist who took an interest in hospitals was confronted with an overarching silence, punctuated by scraps of contradictory and confusing legal chatter. We can best understand the originality and seriousness of their work, and the nature of their research, when we appreciate the blank page from which they started. But, in larger part, the structure is analytically necessary. The problem itself is fundamentally a high medieval problem: of the absence of canon law (Part I). The answer is early medieval: of the legal roots and development of welfare houses in the West (Part II). The implications can then be drawn out in the work of canonists of later centuries (Part III). In the first two parts, each chapter creates a key that opens up the next until, finally, we can unlock the late-antique tradition and the inheritance of Roman law in Chapter 5, via material that is otherwise silent as to welfare foundations in the West. To aid the reader, dates have been provided as far as possible in the titles and headings.

Chapter 2 begins by looking at the Lateran councils, to redefine the problem of canon law as one of absence, teasing out its implications for reading legal material. The contours of a long tradition sends us back to the early middle ages, for Part II. Chapter 3 unpicks the early medieval model for the origins of law in the West (a Frankish model) and the work of the councils of Orléans in 549 and Aachen (816), with its rule for canons and canonesses. Chapter 4 looks at Carolingian Lombardy to identify, for the first time, the only sustained attempt to create law for xenodochia, and the institutional model it reflected. Armed with this model, Chapter 5 rethinks the Roman law tradition and, with it, the relationship between East and West regarding welfare, examining Ansegis's activity, Justinian's collection of laws, and the emergence of a Western model, rooted in the testamentary traditions of provincial Roman law. Chapter 6 follows the implications of this model into the ninth century, to observe a series of efforts to create rights of action and, within these, the growing role undertaken by bishops, via initiatives in Lombardy, Rome, and Francia, in particular at the councils of Olona (825), Rome (826), and Meaux-Paris (845/6), behind which we observe the Pseudo-Isidorians. Part III returns to the classical era of canon law, to observe the efforts of law-makers as they prowled the borderlands of law. Chapter 7 examines the frustrated silence of decretists and the creative labour of decretalists to carve out small statements in law, among them a new legal category, of 'religious house'. Chapter 8 moves into the streets of Flanders and Artois to unearth the hospital reform behind Robert de Courson's decree and the forgotten council of Reims (1213) that gave it voice. And, finally, Chapter 9 turns to *Quia contingit* (1317) to make sense of the Magna Carta of hospitals. Along the way, and through the eyes of law-makers eager to respond to their world, we observe hospitals of the Irish brothers, Alpine hostels and small charities of Lombardy, the struggles of leper-houses, a hospital network under the Cruciferi, beguine life, and a new instrument in law, hatched in 1186, to bring security to lay and clerical foundations.

This study contributes to three fields of history. To the history of hospitals, it offers a new legal definition of the hospital. It identifies a distinctively Western model, rooted in provincial Roman law and embraced in church law. It unravels long-held models regarding the place of hospitals in medieval Christianity and the nature of change, revealing a form that was legally distinct from monasteries. It uncovers a wealth of new material, identifying new legislation and legal initiatives in every period: from late-antique frameworks to Carolingian capitularies, coun-cils to canonical collections, decretals, and commentaries. In so doing, it offers a new compendium of law and a wider legal framework in which welfare facilities operated and through which they can be studied. What emerges is a new history of the hospital that is also, and fundamentally, a European history.

To the history of law, it offers an unusual lens through which to view canon law. Canon law was never a fixed artefact nor a baton of settled knowledge, passed down the generations: until well into the thirteenth century. It was constantly recomposed or—more to the point—someone was always trying to make new sense of an unwieldy inheritance.[90] But canon law rested on central claims. Even, and perhaps especially, its pioneers and radical actors had to engage with the traditions and rights of action that made up those claims. This is a study of what happened when there was no legal inheritance, nor even an authority through which to act. It is canon law without the canon. Here, at the fringes of law, the desperate might dare to work and crusaders, agitators, and forgers played. Their need to author new text can reveal unexpected agendas. These shed light on councils familiar—Orléans (549), Meaux-Paris (845/6), Aachen (816), Lateran II (1139), Lateran III (1179) and IV (1215), Vienne (1311/2)—and forgotten: Olona (825), Reims (1213). And we see surprising new sides of major figures, including Abbot Ansegis of St Wandrille, Abbot Wala of Corbie, the Pseudo-Isidorian forgers, Pope Alexander III, Bernard of Pavia, and Robert de Courson.

To the history of Christianity, it offers a new picture of welfare, at the heart of Christianity across a millennium. The place of welfare houses, at the edge of law, has for too long encouraged the idea that welfare itself was peripheral to popes and canonists, and so, by implication, to those who designed the priorities of the church. When the efforts of law-makers are revealed to be not the fruit of ignorance and lack of interest but, in contrast, creative attempts to reach beyond their legal (if not their pastoral) jurisdiction, the picture is transformed. We

---

[90] Among the many penetrating studies that illuminate these processes of reconstitution and reinvention, see the essays in D. Jasper and H. Fuhrmann, eds, *Papal Letters in the Early Middle Ages* (Washington, DC, 2001); Brett and Cushing, eds, *Readers, Texts and Compilers*; HMCL; U.-R. Blumenthal, A. Winroth, and P. Landau, eds, *Canon Law, Religion and Politics* (Washington, DC, 2012); Rolker, ed., *New Discourses in Medieval Canon Law Research*; as well as Wood, *Prop. Ch.*

notice the ambitions of churchmen in different periods, the restrictions they faced, and the ingenious paths they tried to craft around them. And, most particularly, we discover a Christian foundation that could belong not to the church but to the people.

This is a book about the limits of the church's legal claim over the activity of Christians. On the edge of what was permissible and even, briefly, just beyond that limit, law-makers were active and innovative, but they could not stake a general claim over a vast field of Christian practice. As a result, the scale of what was happening, why it was happening, and how it mattered, remained unspoken in their work. So it is important, before launching into their world of the implicit, to acknowledge the phenomenon itself: not the vast, creative, enterprise of foundation, as laid out above; but what was behind it. For what was at stake was salvation itself. Judgement day was an image that confronted every medieval Christian when they entered a church, often literally, in stone, mosaic, and painting, and always conceptually, for that would be the moment when salvation was decided. Core medieval ideas—of the sheep and the goats, as well as of the corporal works of mercy—came from one Bible passage: Matthew 24–5, where the coming of Christ as the king was laid out. It culminated in the Last Judgement, when Christ would assume his throne and separate the sheep from the goats; that is, the saved from the damned (Matt. 25:31–45). At this moment, Christ would explain to the saved why they were chosen, saying, 'For I was hungry, and you gave me to eat; I was thirsty, and you gave me to drink; I was a stranger, and you took me in; Naked, and you covered me; sick, and you visited me: I was in prison, and you came to me.' The righteous, confused, would have no memory of doing this and would ask when they did such things, repeating the list of actions, to be told that 'as long as you did it to one of these my least brethren, you did it to me'. He would then identify the damned, repeating the list in the negative 'For I was hungry, and you gave me not to eat...' and they, confused, would ask, 'when did we see thee hungry...and did not minister to thee?' and receive the same answer, in the negative. The full list of corporal works of mercy was repeated four times.[91] The whole dialogue of judgement day was one of welfare. In tending to the least, to those who suffered most acutely.

Human charity, *caritas*, the act of ministering to the bodily needs of fellow Christians, and attending to the very least in society, was what marked the saved from the damned. This obligation was never at the edge of Christianity. While it was exhorted by the church, and required in church law of clerics and religious, the endeavour to tend to Christ by tending to the wretched lay out there, in the world. It was the obligation of every Christian who sought salvation. And it was the performance of these acts of human care, that distinguished sheep from goat, saved from damned.

---

[91] The list would become known as the Seven Corporal Works of Mercy, when burying the dead was added.

2

Reading around the Edges

Welfare Houses and the General Councils, 1139–1274

The historical problem of hospitals in canon law is centred on the late twelfth and early thirteenth centuries. For the period of the charitable revolution, *c.*1150–*c.*1250, coincides almost exactly with another, legal revolution: the consolidation of what has been called classical canon law.[1] Fuelled by local demand to resolve questions of practice and law, by a more far-reaching papacy, and by the rise of the schools, bishops, popes, canonists, as well as laity and religious, sought to clarify and codify Christian life. These efforts produced what became authoritative compendia of law, an endeavour initiated with Gratian's *Decretum*—whose title, *Concordia discordantium canonum*, literally 'the harmonizing of discordant canons', reveals the scale and nature of the challenge—and consolidated by Gregory IX's *Decretales* (1234), also known as the *Liber extra*. It was an endeavour marked, too, by general councils, especially Lateran III (1179) and IV (1215) under popes Alexander III and Innocent III, often regarded as the most legally ambitious popes of the era.

If the problem of hospitals in canon law has a focus, it is this era and these two councils. For historians have tended to see Lateran III and Lateran IV as the great engines of reform on the ground, defining and driving the major programmes of Christian renewal. It is natural then that historians have looked to these councils to understand the place of welfare houses in the church and in Christian life. The councils' reluctance to address them has been interpreted as a sign of neglect, by a church indifferent to activity on the streets. This chapter sets out to redefine the problem of hospitals in canon law, which rests on a basic misconception of what we see (or, rather, have failed to see) when looking at law. It then uses the Lateran councils to give shape to a new challenge: reading absence in law.

---

[1] P. D. Clarke, *The Interdict in the Thirteenth Century* (Oxford, 2007), 4–12, offers a clear introduction to its development, *c.*1140 to *c.*1325. See also B. Tierney, 'Canon Law and Church Institutions', in P. Linehan, ed., *Proc. of the Seventh Int'l Congress of Medieval Canon Law* (Vatican City, 1988), 49. My Chapter 7 addresses the canonists.

On Hospitals: Welfare, Law, and Christianity in Western Europe, 400–1320. Sethina Watson, Oxford University Press (2020). © Sethina Watson.
DOI: 10.1093/oso/9780198847533.001.0001

Giving Shape to Absence in Canon Law (*c*.1150–*c*.1260)

The oddity of hospitals in canon law is most readily revealed when we look at monasteries. These had a straightforward definition in law, which had been laid down at the council of Chalcedon in 451. The council ruled that a monastery could only be built with the *conscientia* (knowledge, approval, participation) of the bishop (c. 4).[2] Once consecrated by the bishop, a monastery was to remain a monastery and never be transformed back into a worldly dwelling, and its possessions were secured to that monastery; anyone who tolerated such a reversion or dispossession was to be subject to ecclesiastical censure (c. 24). The bishop had a duty to oversee the monastery, and its monks were subject to him; they, in turn, were to live apart from the world, dedicated to fasting and prayer, and not to leave the monastery or attend to business except at the bishop's urging (c. 4). Thus in 451, the status of a monastery's site, its people, property, supervision, and defence were established in the official view of the church. In law monasteries were consecrated sites, wholly ecclesiastical institutions, created under and subject to the bishop. They housed communities who were dedicated to a life of prayer and whose house and possessions were protected by canonical sanction.

Chalcedon would be the basis of all church law that followed. It established ecclesiastical jurisdiction, over monasteries and monks, as well as churches and priests. In consequence, the supervision of monastic life was a fundamental obligation of prelacy and so of church government. It is hard to find a council, and near-impossible to find a collection of law, that did not have something to say about monastic life. In practice, monastic life changed constantly: between the fifth and twelfth centuries there were periods when episcopal authority lost out to lay power and when security of monastic possessions was lost; monasteries adopted rules, and formulated new rules; international orders arose, with networks of daughter houses; and houses and whole orders were granted exception from diocesan oversight and subjected directly to a mother house or to the papacy. These changes brought conflict and required new law, as did shifting expectations of the life that religious should lead. By the twelfth century, the accumulation of law on monastic life was vast. Gratian alone dedicated five whole books (*Causae*) of his *Decretum* to the subject of monks, monasteries, and abbots, tackling relationships between monks and parish churches (Causa 16) and between a monastery and a bishop (C. 18), as well as converts, especially clerics (C. 19), regretful priests (C. 17), and child oblates (C. 20). Each book was broken down

---

[2] (c. 4) 'placuit nullum quidem usquam aedificare aut constituere monasterium vel oratorii domum praeter conscientiam civitatis episcopi, monachos vero per unamquamque civitatem aut regionem subiectos esse episcopo'. (c. 24) 'QUOD NON LICEAT MONASTERIA QUAE CONSECRATA SUNT, DIVERSORIA SAECULARIA FIERI. Quae semel ex voluntate episcopi dedicata sunt monasteria, manere monasteria et res quae ad ea pertinent, monasteriis reservari nec posse ea ultra fieri saecularia habitacula. Qui vero hoc fieri permiserint, canonum correptionibus subiacebunt.' *COGD* I. 140, 148.

into questions, answered with examples (chapters) of law: 'whether monks may celebrate divine office for the laity and give them penance and baptise' (C.16 q.1) has sixty-eight chapters of law, including a restatement of Chalcedon (c. 4) at chapter 12.[3] Yet the definition established at Chalcedon endured. It remained the yardstick by which questions of ecclesiastical jurisdiction were measured and, as a result, its rulings reverberate through the coming chapters.

There was no such definition for hospitals, and no compendium of law. Legal historians have tended to ignore Robert de Courson's decree at the council of Paris (1213), because it did not circulate as canon law: it was not issued via a papal council or decretal, nor copied into any canonical collection. This has left studies with the same 'insufficient' corpus that Imbert had scorned: two chapters in the *Liber extra* (1234), and *Quia contingit* (1317), that disappointing 'Magna Carta of hospital organisation'. The latter is usually overlooked.[4] One of the *Liber extra* chapters has been entirely ignored (X 3.36.4); the other (X 3.36.3), just twenty words long, noticed simply as a statement that hospitals belonged to the bishop. The origins and meaning of both *Liber extra* chapters remain unclear: they are now commonly said to be thirteenth-century creations, although one (X 3.36.3) has also been attributed to Eugenius III (1145–53).[5]

This absence of canon law has meant that legal and legal/institutional historians have had to look to the *longue durée* for a definition of what a hospital was in law. Most draw a direct line from Justinian's Byzantium through the late middle ages, although many studies progress from pagan hospitality to the early modern or modern hospital.[6] Almost inevitably, such an approach constructs a developmental teleology. Diffuse texts across a wide geography and over a millennium are treated as a unified body of law and a single, evolving endeavour, and for law the account rests on Justinian's *Corpus iuris civilis*. Because it fits uncomfortably into this long story, it has been easy to skip over the small corpus of canon law of 1100–1300 and, with it, the world it addresses. The charitable revolution, and its range of local houses, can easily be lost. In addition, over the *longue durée* 'religion' and 'medicine', and 'church' and 'secular', have sometimes become

---

[3] Chalcedon (c. 4) is also cited in C.18 q.2 cc.9–10 and underpins C.18 q.2 c.12. The volume of his monastic material fuelled theories that Gratian himself was a monk, although recent work has tended to argue that he taught law at Bologna then became bishop of Chiusi: A. Winroth, 'Where Gratian Slept', *ZRG Kan. Abt.* 99 (2013); J. T. Noonan, 'Gratian Slept Here', *Traditio* 35 (1979).

[4] Brian Tierney saw *Quia contingit* as 'the foundation of hospital law' and, finding no interest among canonists before this date, restricted his brief comments on hospitals to this canon and its commentators; B. Tierney, *Medieval Poor Law* (Berkeley, CA, 1959), 85–7. But see, now, the exploration of reformist discourses in Clementine commentaries, *c.*1320–*c.*1440, Frank, 'Hospitalreformen', 5 n.

[5] *HDC* 55–6, 68, 115 n.; Drossbach, 'Das Hospital', 514; Frank, 'Hospitalreformen', 11. Merzbacher, 'Das Spital', 83–4, repeats Imbert's error.

[6] *HDC*; Rocca, *Il diritto osped.* 34–94; Risse, *Mending Bodies*. For recent studies across the *longue durée*, J. Henderson et al., eds, *The Impact of Hospitals 400–1500* (Bern, 2007).

conflicting binaries,[7] and the late medieval hospital a prototype for the modern hospital.[8] Messier, more 'medieval' visions of welfare, and even the great era of hospitals in the twelfth and thirteenth centuries, have become a blip in this longer march of secular-medical progress.[9]

Three important studies reveal the difficulty of defining hospitals in law in the era of charitable revolution. Two of them rest on Justinian and an inventive use of Gratian. Friedrich Merzbacher selected four texts from Gratian's *Decretum* that urged bishops to care for the poor, sick, and orphaned. Here he sought and found an echo of Justinian's law. On the basis of the latter, he argued that hospitals were, and had been from the late antique period, works of piety and charity: Christian institutions, subordinate to the bishop.[10] Pier Giovanni Caron also saw hospitals as arising out of an early moral and legal duty that required bishops to allocate income from their estates to hospitality and care for the poor; over time, these assets became detached from episcopal estates, an independencè recognized in law by Justinian. Caron found here the 'long evolution' of *hospitalitas* into 'the hospital', a new type of institution that was defined in law by twelfth-century decretists in their glosses to Gratian.[11] Lacking twelfth-century laws on hospitals, Merzbacher and Caron both looked to episcopal duties, but stressed different ones. As a result, they selected different chapters from Gratian. The result was two idiosyncratic assortments of laws, whose main similarity to each other is that any relationship to hospitals is purely conjectural.

In contrast, Gisela Drossbach returned to Imbert's small corpus of canon law to argue, against Imbert's quick dismissal, that it in fact constituted a visionary intervention by the church.[12] She suggested that hospitals had failed to attract the attention of Gratian and his commentators, the decretists, because in the

---

[7] Frank, 'Hospitalreformen', 6. It should be stressed that medical historians themselves challenge easy assumptions about medical progress and, with them, the definition of interventive care: faith, liturgy, emotions, medicine, art, music, and human comfort played a role in creating restorative spaces or routines. This has been a particularly fertile area in English-language scholarship, esp. P. Horden, 'A Non-Natural Environment', in Bowers, ed., *Medieval Hospital*; Horden, 'Religion as Medicine', in P. Biller and J. Ziegler, eds, *Religion and Medicine in the Middle Ages* (York, 2001); C. Rawcliffe, 'Christ the Physician Walks the Wards', in M. P. Davies and A. Prescott, eds, *London and the Kingdom* (Donington, 2008) and *Medicine for the Soul*; Henderson, *Renaissance Hospital*.

[8] In such long histories, legal or medical, the breach is overcome through a model that is implicitly medical, moving from Byzantium via the Hospitallers to the Renaissance: T. S. Miller, 'The Knights of Saint John and the Hospitals of the Latin West', *Speculum* 53:4 (1978); Risse, *Mending Bodies*, 117–65; Merzbacher, 'Das Spital', 82–3. A recent challenge to any simple model of institutional progress is offered in Horden, 'Earliest Hospitals'.

[9] Of course, historians who focus on either the early or the late middle ages offer dedicatedly medieval visions: Touati, *Maladie et société*; Rawcliffe, *Medicine for the Soul*; and Horden, above, n. 7. On the growth of liturgical and other activities in later hospitals, Rubin, 'Development and Change'.

[10] Merzbacher, 'Das Spital', 84–5, resting on D.82 c.1; D.86 c.6; D.87 c.2; C.12 q.2 c.71.

[11] Caron, '*pia fundatio*', esp. 137, 142–5, 156. And see Frank, 'Hospitalreformen', 10–11.

[12] Drossbach, 'Das Hospital', 510–22, esp. 512 n.11, 515. This innovative study recognizes currents of change across the period and relates them to law; it also attempts to reconcile Germanic and French traditions of reform, relating *Kommunalisierung* to de Courson's Parisian decree via *Quia contingit* (pp. 517–20).

mid-twelfth century hospitals still rested securely under episcopal oversight. When in the late twelfth century independent hospitals arose, the church responded first at Courson's Paris council, requiring that hospital communities follow a rule, then in 1234, when Gregory IX subordinated them to the bishop and provided to them the same legal protections as monasteries (X 3.36.3). Defined finally in canon law, hospitals could be organized according to a rule and a religious purpose, which was hospital service. This monastic model was consolidated in 1317 by *Quia contingit*.[13]

On the face of it, these forays offer contradictory models and share little common ground. Was the hospital a steady institutional form under the bishop (Merzbacher), an ecclesiastical form given the status of an independent institution by twelfth-century decretists (Caron), or one that went rogue at this moment, to be captured by thirteenth-century clerics (Drossbach)? Were hospitals being made into a monastic form (Drossbach), or were they extra-monastic institutions that were securely episcopal (Merzbacher) or released finally into the world (Caron)? Their pictures are irreconcilable, but, underneath, all three were navigating the same problem: what law to use? No matter how perceptive, each model collapses because it cannot be rooted in legislation. A corpus of laws must first be devised. Early medievalists tend to use decrees on clerical hospitality and the *cura pauperum*, later medievalists monastic models and monastic decrees. Beyond these basic horizons, each corpus is different. Either the links between the laws themselves and to hospitals must be invented, or, in Drossbach's more carefully framed corpus, laws must be made to stretch beyond their reach, for neither the *Liber extra* texts, nor *Quia contingit* mentions rules for hospitals—only Courson's councils do that.[14] To build the definition of hospitals in law, historians have had to invent continuities and even legislation. Absence of law has been silently treated as the problem to be overcome. In fact, it is the phenomenon that defines hospitals in law.

In theory, there were both the means and the motive to create law, as classical canon law took shape. Security under the church (the presumed reason for its lack of concern) would be no reason not to legislate:[15] monastic houses had a clear and ecclesiastical form, a fact that encouraged detailed decrees regarding their organization, observance, and oversight. From the mid-twelfth century, canonists also

---

[13] 'Das Spital sollte nicht nur eine wie auch immer qualifizierte kirchliche Institution sein, sondern eine monastische. Insbesondere sollte das Hospital in Organisations- und Lebensform der des Klosters angepaßt werden...In Anlehnung an die Definition eines Klosters sehe ich das Hospital als Organisationsform, das Gelübde als Verpflichtung auf eine innere Ordnung, die Spitalregel oder Statuten als normative Verhaltensstruktur, den Spitaldienst als geistige Zielsetzung'; Drossbach, 'Das Hospital', 514–16, 521, with quotation at p. 516.

[14] Of course, *religious* orders of hospitallers were monastic under canon law, as *regulares*. One such example was the Holy Spirit in Saxia, for which see Drossbach, *Christliche caritas*. The chapters that follow find monasteries to be a more helpful contrast to xenodochia.

[15] Orme and Webster, *English Hospital*, 37–9, suggest that hospitals attracted little attention because they were small, traditional houses, securely under the bishop; also, Drossbach, 'Das Hospital', 512–14.

worked to unravel a tangle of customs that had built up over centuries through an interplay of secular and ecclesiastical law. In their writings, as Stephan Kuttner observed, 'such important legal aspects of the Church's institutional life as benefices, monastic exemptions, or the internal organization of cathedral chapters... emerge into the broad daylight of the written law'.[16] The volume of legal material, often in the form of decretals, was especially large in cases where boundaries needed to be delineated—when temporal and spiritual interests might collide, such as marriage, usury, or patronage.[17] Prelates and law-makers worked to impose a rational order on Christian institutions. Why not xenodochia?

In practice, there was every reason to address them. The efflorescence of new foundations saw constant innovation in their forms, duties, and government, but a paucity of law to guide founders, patrons, custodians, and bishops. Such eagerness to found new facilities created disputes from the earliest years. In Angers a series of conflicts ran through the twelfth century, drawing in bishop and pope, when lay ambitions for a *domus elemosinaria* were frustrated by the monks of St Nicholas, only to be realized eighty years later in 1206 with a papal resolution.[18] In Ypres, controversies over a leper-house and hospital continued from at least 1186 until 1217 and involved the cathedral chapter, bishop, archbishop, three popes, papal judges delegate, a papal legate, the town government, the count, and repeated threats *sub excommunicatione iam lata*.[19] Welfare houses were neither uncontroversial nor securely under ecclesiastical oversight. Disputes focused on rights of access to spiritual service, as well as on jurisdiction over the hospital, and the *cura* of hospital staff over both household and visitors. It also mattered to clerics and local laity that hospitals worked and how they worked, making administration a growing issue of concern from the later twelfth century. Many of these controversies were laid at the feet of bishops

---

[16] S. Kuttner, 'Some Considerations on the Role of Secular Law and Institutions', in *Scritti di sociologia e politica in onore di Luigi Sturzo*, II (Bologna, 1953), 357.

[17] C. Duggan, 'English Secular Magnates in the Decretal Collections', in S. Chodorow, ed., *Proc. of the Eighth Int'l Congress of Medieval Canon Law* (Vatican City, 1992); *Papal Decretals Relating to the Diocese of Lincoln*, ed. and tr. W. Holtzmann and E. W. Kemp (Lincoln, 1954); P. Landau, *Jus patronatus* (Cologne, 1975).

[18] J.-M. Bienvenu, 'Fondations charitables laïques au XIIᵉ siècle: Anjou', in *EHP* 566–7. For an early dispute in Cologne: J. P. Huffman, 'Potens et Pauper: Charity and Authority in Jurisdictional Disputes', in R. C. Figueira, ed., *Plenitude of Power* (Aldershot, 2006), 115–16. The papacy dealt with hospitals as a matter of routine. Its *Liber censuum* of 1192 records over seventy hospitals and almshouses among its 'ecclesie, vel monasteria, hospitalia, seu domus helemosinarie'; *Liber censuum de l'Eglise romaine*, ed. P. Fabre and L. Duchesne, 3 vols (Paris, 1889–1952), I. 2.

[19] *Les cartulaires de la prévôté de Saint-Martin à Ypres*, ed. E. Feys and A. Nelis, 2 vols (Bruges, 1880–4), II. nos. 39–42, 53, 64, 68, 77–8, 81, 84, 89–90. In 1207, the cathedral secured papal confirmation of an agreement that revealed how authorities could be pulled into such controversies. The agreement was 'cum scabinis et fratribus hospitalis in foro Yprensi constructi, super capella et capellano, que a bone memorie C[elestino] papa predecessore nostro in vestre prejudicium ecclesie postulabant, mediante venerabili fratre nostro Morinensi episcopo inistis, sicut sine pravitate provide facta est.' (ibid., no. 64). A similar range of participants can be found in 'controversia quae super hospitali domo... diutius agitata est' through the late 1130s near Florence; *PL* 179, cols 625–6.

and papal judges delegate, who increasingly found themselves on the front line of protracted local disputes regarding xenodochia.[20] Yet, for some reason, they were not armed with explicit law.

In an era marked by the church's determination to address Christian life in its many forms, the legal silence regarding welfare houses, maintained so consistently, was no accident. The general councils offer a chance to give shape to that absence in law, and absence itself becomes the key to its reading.

The General Councils: Excavating What has been Hidden

In response to papal calls, prelates from across western Europe convened at the Lateran palace and church in Rome in 1123, 1139, 1179, and 1215, and then in Lyons in 1245 and 1274.[21] Here, disputes were resolved, matters of dogma clarified, and new law promulgated for the health and reform of the church. A belief that the church enacted reforms for hospitals, and that the papacy brought these houses securely under ecclesiastical management, rests on these councils, and on two in particular: Lateran IV, which is said to have taken up Courson's reforms at Paris (1213) and required hospitals to adopt a rule; and Lateran III, which is credited with bringing leper-houses, finally, under the church. In each case, there is a conviction that the council acted, but no consensus as to *how* it acted. This is because the actions cannot be anchored in decrees: the councils are said to act but cannot be found to have done so. The legislation deserves reading.

The Odd Case of Lateran IV (1215)

Perhaps no council enjoys a greater reputation than Innocent III's Fourth Lateran council. It dealt definitively with religious orders, old and new, as well as lay Christians and pastoral care.[22] It is easy to imagine the council acting for hospitals,

---

[20] Among the many examples, De Spiegeler, *Liège*, 105–43; J. Avril, 'Le IIIe concile du Latran et les communautés de lépreux', *Revue Mabillon* 60 (1981); and n. 18–19.

[21] These were part of a much longer and wider pattern of conciliar activity: D. Summerlin, 'Papal Councils', in A. Larson and K. Sisson, eds, *Companion to the Medieval Papacy* (Leiden, 2016).

[22] The literature is vast. For introductions see A. García y García, 'The Fourth Lateran Council and the Canonists', in *HMCL*; R. Foreville, *Latran I, II, III et Latran IV* (Paris, 1965); M. Gibbs and J. Lang, *Bishops and Reform 1215–1272* (Oxford, 1934); P. B. Pixton, *The German Episcopacy and the Implementation of the Decrees of the Fourth Lateran Council* (Leiden, 1994); A. Reeves, *Religious Education in Thirteenth-Century England* (Leiden, 2015). The octocentenary of the council has produced much new scholarship, among its early fruits: A. A. Larson and A. Massironi, eds, *The Fourth Lateran Council and the Development of Canon Law and the* ius commune (Turnhout, 2018).

and particularly easy to imagine that it adopted Courson's hospital reform, because Innocent made use of a number of the Parisian decrees.[23] However, Lateran IV did not pick up, promulgate, adapt, or even notice the hospital decree; in fact, it offered no canon on hospitals.

It seems that Michel Mollat was the first to claim that Lateran IV had required hospitals to adopt rules. He offered no details, but his statement has become a commonplace and broad claims have been made for the council's activity and impact. Most often studies gesture vaguely towards the council.[24] Those who cite actual legislation point to canon 13, which forbade anyone henceforth to devise a new form of religious life (*nova religio*), requiring those who wished to devote themselves to a religious life (*ad religionem converti*) to adopt one that was already approved, and those wishing to found a religious house (*religiosam domum de novo fundare*) to adopt an approved rule and institution; a monk, it added, must not belong to multiple monasteries, nor an abbot rule over more than one.[25] Canon 13 was part of a wider effort to bring greater uniformity to religious life; here, to those who had left the world and submitted to a recognized rule.[26] It followed a long canon that organized heads of independent monasteries into provincial chapters so that 'diligent work be carried out for reform of the order and observance of their rule'.[27] This swept up those Benedictine and Augustinian houses that were not already in a congregation of houses, as many of the new orders were. Now, in the Cistercian manner, heads of such houses were to meet every three years to harmonize customs and appoint visitors to correct every house. Canon 13 was part of this wider restraint on religious life. As such, it encompassed religious hospitaller orders, such as the Hospitallers of St John, the Trinitarians, the Order of the Holy Spirit in Saxia,

---

[23] *MPM* I. 20–1; Moore, *Innocent III*, 220–1, 225; Foreville, *Latran I–IV*, 294–7. The influence of Paris (1213) can best be traced in the footnotes of *COGD* II. 163–204, from which the canons are cited here.

[24] Mollat, 'Hospitalité', 40; Risse, *Mending Bodies*, 151–2; F.-F.-O. Touati, '"Aime et fais ce que tu veux": Les chanoines réguliers et la révolution de charité au Moyen Age', in M. Parisse, ed., *Les Chanoines réguliers* (Saint Étienne, 2009), 205. Orme and Webster, *English Hospital*, 73–4, suggest that Lateran IV reinforced a pattern of individual rules.

[25] *COGD* II. 175 n., where the final sentence is linked to part II, c. 8, 17 of Paris (1213) (Mansi XXII. 827–8, 830). This relationship is faint: that an abbot presides over one monastery interpolates the sense, if not the language or detail, of c. 17, while c. 8 (based on Chalcedon, c. 10) forbade a monk from moving community in hope of promotion.

[26] Foreville, *Latran I–IV*, 294–7. The Lateran decree was adapted at Lyons II (1274) to address the profusion of mendicant orders of recent decades; *COGD* II. 354, c. 28. On the council's efforts, G. Constable, 'The Fourth Lateran Council's Constitutions on Monasticism', in Larson and Massironi, eds, *Fourth Lateran Council*, 147–57; and on the relationship between rule (of St Benedict or St Augustine) and institutes (of a specific order), see J. Dubois, 'Les ordres religieux au XIIe siècle selon la curie romaine', *Revue bénédictine* 78 (1968).

[27] (c. 12) 'in quo diligens habeatur tractatus de reformatione ordinis et observantia regulari'. It established a system of corporate governance with directives to carry this out.

and St Anthony of Vienne.[28] All but the latter had had their ways of life confirmed before 1215.[29]

The canon made no reference to *hospitales* or *xenodochia*. More significantly, it was not recognized as affecting them by those who glossed the decree, by canonists addressing hospitals, or by bishops enacting Lateran reforms. In England, Lateran IV was adopted with particular energy. Bishops took up its programme in their synodal statutes, and, in obedience to canon 12, provincial chapters were established for Benedictine and Augustinian monasteries.[30] Yet no synodal legislation, papal letter, or episcopal charter suggests that canon 13 was interpreted as applying to local hospitals.[31] Most significant is the gulf between the canons' purpose and the practice for hospitals: canon 12 sought to harmonize customs in independent monasteries, and canon 13 brought an end to the innovation of new forms of religious life. They thus prescribed the opposite of what they are credited with creating among hospitals, since the 'quasi-religious' statutes for local hospitals emerged haphazardly and are confounding in their diversity.[32] In the century after Lateran IV standardized the regular religious under papally approved rules, many hospitals across Europe were presented with individually crafted, inventive, and heterogeneous sets of regulations.

This lack of explicit laws did not leave welfare houses untouched by reform. Canons on clerics and monastic life reinforced an expanding culture of diocesan regulation;[33] others reinforced the supervisory powers of bishops, including the right to grant permission for chapels, oversee elections, and appoint or remove

---

[28] On these orders: A. Luttrell, 'The Earliest Hospitallers', in B. Z. Kedar et al., eds, *Montjoie: Studies in Crusade History* (Aldershot, 1997); essays in H. Nicholson, ed., *The Military Orders*, II (Aldershot, 1998); G. Cipollone, 'Les Trinitaires', in *Fondations*; Drossbach, *Christliche caritas*; and Chapter 1 nn. 5, 6.

[29] The century-old Antonines received their monastic vows from Pope Honorius III in 1217, probably in answer to this canon. Le Blévec, 'L'ordre . . . des Antonins'.

[30] Gibbs and Lang, *Bishops and Reform*, 94–179; *C&S* II. 52–154; *Documents Illustrating the Activities of the General and Provincial Chapters*, ed. W. A. Pantin, 3 vols (1931–7); *Chapters of the Augustinian Canons*, ed. H. E. Salter (London, 1922).

[31] The exception suggests the rule. Richard Poore's synodal statutes, Salisbury I (1217×1221), c. 100: 'Quoniam religionum nimia diversitas gravem in ecclesia dei confusionem induct, precipimus quod qui volunt domum hospitalem vel scenodochium fundare de novo regulam et institutionem de nobis accipiant secundum quam religiose et regulariter vivant.' (*C&S* II. 92). To do so it adapted the Lateran phrase, *qui voluerit religiosam de novo fundare, regulam et institutionem accipiat de religionibus approbatis*, omitting all that canon's references to *religionem* as a noun, often translated as 'religious order', gesturing more vaguely to 'religiously'. Given the context, Poore's term *regulariter* seems to mean 'in accordance with what is laid down by the bishop', since his statute seems to be setting up more flexible local arrangements, as provided by the bishop. Poore's was the most significant assertion of episcopal control over hospitals by an English bishop, the only one to require a rule, yet it stepped carefully away from Innocent's provisions for *regulares*. For context, see my Chapter 8.

[32] The Augustinian rule did influence many statutes, especially in France, yet the nature of that influence could vary significantly. Most hospitals did not follow such a rule: Saunier, 'La trame hospitalière', 218–19; Montaubin, 'Hôpitaux cathédraux', 26–30; Drossbach, 'Das Hospital', 519; Watson, 'Origins', 82–3.

[33] See e.g. Davis, *Holy Bureaucrat, passim*, with pp. 80–2 for hospitals.

clerics in parish churches or as heads of churches.[34] Along with stronger administrative machinery in the diocese, they developed a bishop's ability to intervene,
and on a wider range of issues. This affected many welfare houses by the late
twelfth century, especially when negotiating rights to spiritual services. It is
important to note, however, that no Lateran or Lyons canon suggested that
bishops should oversee hospitals. Indeed, none explicitly addressed welfare
houses.

Hospitals were only named twice in general councils of the era. Among his
many faults, Frederick II was reproached by the council of Lyons I (1245) for a
failure to build 'churches, monasteries, hospitals, and other pious places'.[35]
Lateran IV did mention hospitals, in what is essentially an appendix or attachment
to a canon. Canon 62 on the care of saints' relics required that alms collectors
obtain a written papal or episcopal licence and, as a template for bishops, it
provided a sample letter, whose second half exhorts that:

> Because *their own resources are not sufficient to maintain the brothers and the*
> *destitute people* who flock to such a hospital, we admonish and exhort every one
> of you in the Lord, and enjoin upon you for the remission of your sins, to *provide*
> *pious alms and the pleasing assistance of charity to them from the goods* that God
> has bestowed on you, so that *their lack may be met through your aid* and that,
> through these and other good deeds performed through God's inspiration, you
> may reach joy everlasting.[36]   (Emphasis added)

This statement enjoined Christians to give of their own goods to alleviate the
material lack of those who were without, in hospitals. The language marked by
italics will become familiar in Part III, echoing wider definitions for hospitals. At
this point in our analysis, it appears to be an incidental notice. What matters now
is not merely that it said nothing of regulation or supervision but that, inserted
crudely into a canon on relics, it made a wholly different case. It admonished
Christians to care materially for those who went without. And, in providing this
admonition in a template to copy, it was literally putting words into bishops'
mouths. It not only directed bishops to champion hospitals, but laid out a model
for how a hospital should be maintained: to meet their (material) lack through aid.

---

[34] Many were ancient rights, elaborated in new detail, such as those reinforcing diocesan power in
the face of exempt religious (Lateran III, c. 9). On the canons more generally: A. J. Duggan, 'Conciliar
Law 1123–1215', in *HMCL*. For the exercise of episcopal rights, De Spiegeler, *Liège*, 105–7.

[35] 'nec ecclesias nec monasteria nec hospitalia seu alia pia loca cernitur construxisse.' *COGD* II. 221.

[36] (c. 62) 'Cum igitur *ad sustentationem fratrum et egenorum* ad tale confluentium hospitale, *proprie*
non suppetant facultates, universitatem vestram monemus et exhortamur in domino atque in remis-
sionem vobis iniungimus peccatorum, quatenus *de bonis* a Deo vobis collatis, *pias eleemosynas et grata*
eis caritatis subsidia erogetis, ut *per subventionem vestram ipsorum inopie consulatur*, et vos per hec et
alia bona que domino inspirante feceritis ad eterna possitis gaudia pervenire.'; cf. Brodman, 'Religion
and Discipline', 125, which links it with c. 22, on physicians.

One archbishop, at least, took up the call.[37] It suggests that the attachment may be more carefully crafted than at first appears. Its approach echoes that of a more cunning decree, thirty-five years earlier.

Cum dicat Apostolus at Lateran III (1179)

Alexander III's council of 1179 did engage with charitable houses. Its canon 23, *Cum dicat Apostolus*, granted groups of lepers living together the right to have a church, cemetery, and priest and released them from the obligation to pay tithes on their gardens and animals.[38] It is most famous for its statement that lepers 'cannot dwell with the healthy or gather with others at churches', and so is discussed alongside the Old Testament command that a leper, defiled and unclean, must dwell alone 'outside the camp' (Lev. 13: 46).[39] *Cum dicat Apostolus* has a long and still intractable place in history, as the moment when the medieval church enacted the law of Moses. It is still often said that Lateran III commanded the removal of lepers from society, as dead to the world.[40] This is despite the authoritative work by François-Olivier Touati and Carole Rawcliffe, in particular, that has subjected the very notion of exclusion to sustained attack. They have revealed the multivalent roles played by leprosy in the medieval imagination and revealed how those afflicted with leprosy might be integrated into the devotional and economic life of town and court.[41]

This reappraisal has yet to affect the interpretation of Lateran III. In England, the council is seen to be providing amenities for leper-houses, but in response to

---

[37] The phrasing was adopted by Archbishop Walter de Gray in indulgences in 1228, including one to support the hospital of Royston (Herts.): York, Borthwick Institute, Archbishops Reg. 1A, mem. 9 (nos. 116, 118).

[38] For the council, R. Foreville and J. Rousset de Pina, *Du premier Concile du Latran à l'avènement d'Innocent III* (Paris, 1944), 156–76; J. Longère, ed., *Le troisième concile de Latran (1179)* (Paris, 1982); and Danica Summerlin's work, below.

[39] A formulation most influentially laid out by R. I. Moore, *The Formation of a Persecuting Society* (Oxford, 2007), 54–5, 180–3; R. Gilchrist, *Contemplation and Action* (London, 1995), 39–40; and J. Richards, *Sex, Dissidence and Damnation* (London, 1990), 10, 152–6. Even nuanced interpretations can present segregation as the canon's main purpose: Sweetinburgh, *Role of the Hospital*, 31; Marcombe, *Leper Knights*, 140.

[40] An extreme view of the council's activity persists in literary studies. To take one recent example: 'Lateran III declared the afflicted as already "deceased", and prescribed a religious ritual, the *Separatio Leprosorium* [sic], during which the Office of the Dead was read over the patient.' C. M. Boeckl, *Images of Leprosy: Disease, Religion and Politics in European Art* (Kirksville, MO, 2011), 48. It rests on errors in S. N. Brody, *The Disease of the Soul* (Ithaca, NY, 1974), 64–5. Such beliefs have been held by historians until recently, e.g. K. P. Jankrift, 'Vieillir parmi les morts "vivants"', in Tabuteau, ed., *Lépreux et Sociabilité* (Rouen, 2000).

[41] Touati, *Maladie et société*, 102–9, 274–80; C. Rawcliffe, *Leprosy in Medieval England* (Woodbridge, 2006), 29–34, 72–3, 110–11. See also E. Brenner, *Leprosy and Charity in Medieval Rouen* (Woodbridge, 2015). The authors discover a growing fear of contagion in later centuries, and especially the fourteenth.

(and after affirming) Mosaic law.[42] It remains an act of segregation, perhaps no longer instigating separation but reinforcing an existing state. Discussion of the canon has been brief, concerned to relate the council to wider practice rather than to explore the canon's legal character. Joseph Avril's ground-breaking 1981 study of French leper-houses, c.1150–c.1250, remains the only concerted investigation of the canon's effects. Drawing on a wealth of documentary evidence, Avril drew a picture of local diversity and some turmoil, but also of an increasing drive to fashion leper-houses along monastic lines. He credited this impetus to Lateran III, and suggested that the council forged a religious character for leper-houses, as ecclesiastical sites, organized on ecclesiastical models.[43] In his footsteps, French scholars have recognized Lateran III as the defining moment jurisdictionally, when the church claimed general authority over leper-houses, and legally, when the church began to legislate for hospitals.[44] Avril offered *Cum dicat Apostolus* as a watershed in canon law for hospitals, forming the basis of subsequent hospital legislation, and notably *Quia contingit*. This, as shall be seen, was not the case. The canon was exceptional, and its character and legal origins deserve examination.

We start with a basic observation: *Cum dicat Apostolus* is no Levitican injunction. The language that a leper, unclean, must dwell 'outside the camp' can be found often in contemporary writings, usually as a metaphor for sin, heresy, or excommunication. Alexander III used its imagery when writing about excommunication, but he never referred to lepers themselves in those terms.[45] Indeed, as will be seen, he spoke very differently of those afflicted with the disease. His canon makes no use of Leviticus, nor any Old Testament language. In fact, its appeal is resolutely New Testament and from its opening phrase: 'Even though the apostle [Paul] commands...' It is worth looking closely at its language and structure (as will be the pattern herein; the apparatus is mine):

[i. DEPRIVATION] Even though the apostle commands that more abundant dignity be accorded to our frailer members [1 Cor. 12: 22–3], there are certain people, seeking their own interests and not those of Jesus Christ [Phil. 2: 21], who

---

[42] Rawcliffe, *Leprosy*, 258–60; Brodman, *CRME* 78; and influential earlier statements in Rubin, *Charity and Community*, 115; Orme and Webster, *English Hospital*, 27, 39; also, F. Bériac, *Histoire des Lépreux au Moyen Age* (Paris, 1988), 161, 180–1; cf. C. Rawcliffe, 'Learning to Love the Leper', *Anglo-Norman Studies* 23 (2001), 237.

[43] Avril, 'Le IIIe concile du Latran', 36–43, 52–3, 61, 65.

[44] N. Bériou and F.-O. Touati, *Voluntate dei leprosus* (Spoleto, 1991), 6–7; Touati, 'Dossier', 28. De Spiegeler, *Liège*, 106–7, followed this interpretation, but found little evidence that it did in practice, concluding that 'l'application du décret ne fut ni immédiate ni uniforme'. The great modern study of leprosy in this period does not re-examine Lateran III, seeing the council as reinforcing ongoing trends: Touati, *Maladie et société*, esp. 330, 340–2.

[45] *PL* 200, col. 707 (echoing Num. 5: 4): 'Excommunicatio enim ad modum leprae, quae totum corpus corrumpit, totum hominem contaminat et deturpat. Leprosi namque, sicut in Testamento Veteri legitur, extra castra abjiciebantur.' Such language is also absent from Alexander's 1181 statement that Baldwin IV, king of Jerusalem, was too badly afflicted with leprosy to rule, *PL* 200, cols 1294–6. On the papal judgement against Baldwin, see Rawcliffe, *Leprosy*, 54–5.

go against this and do not allow lepers, unable to dwell with the healthy or gather with others at churches, to have churches and cemeteries or be tended by the ministry of their own priest.

[ii. PERMISSION] Since this is known to be far removed from Christian piety, in accordance with apostolic kindness, we decree that wherever such a number [of lepers] have gathered together [Matt. 18: 20] under a common way of life and have the means to build a church for themselves with a cemetery and rejoice in their own priest, that they be allowed to have [this] without any dispute.

[iii. PROTECTION] Nevertheless, let them take care not to harm in any way the parochial rights of long-standing churches. For we do not wish what is granted to them from piety to result in harm to others.

[iv. CONCESSION] We also declare that they should not be forced to pay tithes from their gardens or farming of their animals.[46]

The canon uses biblical language at three points. Paul is employed twice in its opening justification: to establish a duty to weaker members of the Christian community and to condemn those who fail to do this. Through Paul, attending to lepers is not merely opposed to selfishness, but equated with serving Christ. Finally, with echoes of Matthew 18: 20 ('where two or three have gathered in my name, I am there among them') groups should be permitted a church, cemetery, and priest. Their very act of congregation has brought Christ among them.

Even the canon's famous phrase—of lepers 'who are unable to dwell with the healthy or gather with others at churches'—is distinctly un-Levitican. As others have pointed out, it is not prescription but description, of a state wrought through custom, albeit one informed by biblical teaching.[47] Yet Alexander's language suggests not a recognition of Mosaic law, but its rejection. Entirely absent is any language of Leviticus and Numbers, where the leper was 'defiled', 'separated', 'polluted and unclean', to 'dwell alone without the camp', and to 'be cast from the

---

[46] c. 23 (X 3.48.2): '[i] Cum dicat apostolus [1 Cor. 12: 22–3], abundantiorem honorem membris infirmioribus deferendum, econtra quidam, quae sua sunt, non quae Iesu Christi, quaerentes, [Phil. 2: 21] leprosis qui cum sanis habitare non possunt vel ad ecclesias cum aliis convenire, ecclesias et coemeteria non permittunt habere nec proprii iuvari ministerio sacerdotis. [ii] Quod quia procul a pietate christiana esse dignoscitur, de benignitate apostolica constituimus, ut* ubicumque tot simul sub communi vita fuerint congregati [Matt. 18: 20], qui ecclesiam, cum coemeterio sibi construere et proprio valeant gaudere presbytero, sine contradictione aliqua permittantur habere. [iii] Caveant tamen ut iniuriosi veteribus ecclesiis de iure parochiali nequaquam exsistant. Quod enim eis pro pietate conceditur, ad aliorum iniuriam nolumus redundare. [iv] Statuimus etiam ut de hortis et nutrimentis animalium suorum decimas tribuere non cogantur.' COGD II. 143–4; DEC 222–3. Truncated versions begin at *, with Statuimus quoque ut, D. Summerlin, 'Three Manuscripts Containing the Canons of 1179', BMCL 30 (2013), 30–2, 33 n.

[47] Rawcliffe, Leprosy, 257; Bériou and Touati, Voluntate, 13–14. On customs regarding lepers: S. Lefevre, 'Les lépreux à Saint-Lazare de Paris', in Santé, médecine et assistance au Moyen Age (Paris, 1987), 400.

camp lest he contaminate it'.[48] On the contrary, the council now 'decree[s] in accordance with apostolic kindness' and condemns those who fail as going 'against' apostolic commandment and Christ himself. Only the word 'dwell' (*habitare*) is similar, but even here the Levitican leper (in the singular), who must live banished and alone (*solus habitabit*), sits in contrast to this canon's many lepers 'gathered together' under a 'common' way of life and with means to provide for themselves. In an era when Levitican verses tripped off the pens of clerics, their absence seems knowing, a means of recognizing local custom but undermining its biblical (and thus legal) authority. *Cum dicat Apostolus* was not constructing defilement or banishment, but countering it—theologically, by over-writing removal with New Testament obligation; socially, by recognizing groups of lepers as Christian communities; and legally, by investing them with rights.

We can go further, for this well-known clause sets up not a moral scourge of leprosy, but a specific disability visited upon lepers, 'who are unable (*non possunt*) to dwell with the healthy or gather with others at churches'. Because of this inability, they are deprived of basic spiritual services. Their deprivation provides the justification for the canon, which acts pastorally to reinstate what has been denied. Its very structure is framed around disability:[49] establishing the lepers' deprivation [i], remedying this lack [ii], protecting the parish from harm [iii], then offering a concession to help bolster their common foodstocks [iv]. The disabled person is the locus of this law: the place where need meets action.

Cum dicat Apostolus did not address hospitals in general, nor even speak of leper-houses. In fact, it fails to specify any type of house, or mention a site at all. Physical places are oddly absent from its text, appearing only as centres that denied access to lepers. Instead, the canon attaches the right to have a church, cemetery, and priest to a group of people: lepers, 'wherever so many have gathered together under a common way of life', or, as repeated in a canon of the council of Westminster (1200), 'wherever so many have gathered together'.[50] Communities

---

[48] Contrast sections [i] and [ii] to Lev. 13: 44–6: 'quicumque ergo *maculatus* fuerit lepra et *separatus* ad arbitrium sacerdotis, habebit vestimenta dissuta, caput nudum, os veste contectum, *contaminatum ac sordidum* se clamabit. Omni tempore quo leprosus est et immundus, *solus habitabit extra castra*.' Or, similarly, to Num. 5: 2–4: 'praecipe filiis Israhel, ut *ejiciant de castris* omnem leprosum, et qui semine fluit, pollutusque est super mortuo: tam masculum quam feminam *ejicite de castris*, ne contaminent ea cum habitaverint vobiscum. Feceruntque ita filii Israel, et *ejecerunt eos extra castra*, sicut locutus erat Dominus Moysi.' (author's italics)

[49] In thinking about disability, I am stressing not the effects of leprosy on a human body but its consequences for those afflicted among the social body. Cultural responses constructed specific social and religious disabilities, and it is the spiritual manifestations of these that the canon seeks to remedy. Thinking in terms of disability highlights how removal from the healthy engendered an effective (if unjust) excommunication and suggests the degree to which law-makers were working here to craft a place for lepers as members of the Christian community, with access to its rites (sacraments) and rights (marriage). In this, I have been inspired especially by conversations with Chris Baswell and Edward Wheatley. For an introduction to the challenges in thinking about disability and impairment, see J. R. Eyler, 'Introduction', in Eyler, ed., *Disability in the Middle Ages* (Aldershot, 2010), 2–8.

[50] *C&S* I. 1068, discussed in n. 69.

under the privilege *religiosam vitam eligentes* ('choosing a religious life') already possessed such privileges.[51] Here, Lateran III was reaching beyond this group, to a wider array of communities who lived upon shared resources, perhaps under limited or contingent vows, and found themselves denied access as lay Christians to a parish church.[52] Such living required resources: a means of sustenance, including the cultivation of gardens and animals (from whose tithes they were now exempt), and thus a site and endowment. This combination of community and site could only refer to leper-houses, a fact confirmed by papal privileges that secured these rights to specific communities.[53] Yet nowhere is place mentioned in the canon. Its legal rationale is constructed in decidedly human terms, and the right is attached to people, not because of where they were (a leper-house), but where they could not be (other churches). Leper-houses are absent, both in name and as destinations. Missing as geographical sites, they are missing also as places in law. Alexander's target could only have been leper-houses, but his canon addressed a human and pastoral issue: it was working hard to forge rights for a subject that it did not mention.

This particular law originated at Lateran III and so is one of 'the novelties' for which the council has been recognized.[54] There are no conciliar precedents. Raymonde Foreville has argued that many of the canons originated in Alexandrine decretals, so might this be the case for *Cum dicat Apostolus*?[55] No earlier decretal can be identified, nor a conceptual statement of its principles. But there may have been an indirect prompt, from Richard of Dover, archbishop of Canterbury. He had asked his suffragans to enquire into abuses in their dioceses

---

[51] I see no sign that the decree was working to cultivate regular life in leper-houses (its repetition at Westminster even omitted *sub communi vita* to speak of *tot simul fuerint congregati*). It is missing language directed at religious that was used so readily at this time, e.g. at Hubert Walter's legatine council at York (1195): 'Exigit professio religiose sanctitatis ut monachi et canonici regulares et moniales religiose et regulariter conversentur' (*C&S* I. 1050). On the privilege, J. E. Sayers, *Papal Government and England* (Cambridge, 1984), 121–2. Its use for hospitals and leper-houses awaits study.

[52] De Keyzer stresses the lesser status of such 'convents' of lepers, under *des vœux simples* while they resided in the house partaking in a *vita communis* that 'implique la cohabitation sous un même toit, la participation aux mêmes exercices, l'uniformité de la nourriture, des vêtements et du mobilier, enfin la mise en commun de tous les gains individuels'; De Keyzer, 'L'évolution interne', 15–16. See also A. Uyttebrouck, 'Hôpitaux pour lépreux', *ASBHH* 10 (1972), 10, 27. Living from a common fund did not necessarily mean living under vows, as the customary arrangements for the lepers of St Mary Magdalene, Reading (Berks.), in the early thirteenth century make clear: *Reading Abbey Cartularies*, ed. B. R. Kemp, 2 vols (London, 1986–7), I. no. 221.

[53] Freedom from tithes of provender appear in papal charters to leper-houses and, occasionally, to other hospitals and small priories, e.g. *Papsturkunden in England*, ed. W. Holtzmann, 3 vols (Göttingen, 1930–52), III. nos. 334, 349, 400.

[54] Peter the Chanter, for one, was concerned that Lateran III's new rules would create transgressors where before there had been none, Peter the Chanter, *Verbum abbreviatum*, ed. M. Boutry (Turnhout, 2004), 519–27, esp. 522; Foreville and Rousset de Pina, *Du premier Concile*, 173, 176.

[55] Foreville, *Latran I–IV*, 152; Summerlin, 'Three Manuscripts', 22–3. Of Alexander's privileges to leper-houses for a chapel or cemetery, Bériac writes vaguely that '[a]près deux décennies ou plus de tâtonnement, ces dispositions trouvent une codification solennelle au IIIe concile de Latran', in her *Histoire des lépreux*, 161. The privileges are discussed below.

and from their responses drafted thirty-seven propositions for deliberation at his Westminster council of 1175, among them was a brief statement, 'That from this time forward lepers must not associate with the healthy'.[56] This statement was not one of the twenty-two decrees enacted, but it was one of eight propositions sent by that council to the papal curia.[57] These prompted a series of rulings (decretals) in reply, seven of them straight-forward responses. For the eighth, on lepers, proposition and decretal are so different that their very association has been questioned.[58]

The decretal, *Pervenit* (X 4.8.1), became a fundamental statement on lepers in canon law.[59] Alexander had been informed that men or women, assailed by leprosy, were 'by general custom separated from the communion of men and removed to isolated places outside cities and towns', and that their wives or husbands did not go with them. Alexander now commanded that the latter follow their afflicted spouse and minister to them in conjugal affection, or live chastely, and he enjoined bishops to exhort and then punish any who refused.[60] *Pervenit* (1176) affirmed the indissolubility of marriage and found its way into the *Breviarium extravagantium* and from there into *Liber extra*'s book 4 (on marriage), under the title 'on the marital union of lepers'.[61] At first glance, the decretal

---

[56] 'Leprosi inter sanos amodo non conversentur', *C&S* I. 981, no. 34.

[57] The council took particular care as to the authority of its decrees: all were based upon canonical or biblical precedents, except for one, *tam regia quam nostra freti auctoritate* (c. 9), on presentation to benefices (*C&S* I. 967–8). The enquiries were revealed by M. Cheney, 'The Council of Westminster 1175', in D. Baker, ed., *Sources and Methods of Ecclesiastical History* (1975). For recent comment: *C&S* I. 968–70; A. J. Duggan, 'The Role of Episcopal Consultation', in B. C. Brasington and K. G. Cushing, eds, *Bishops, Texts and the Use of Canon Law* (Aldershot, 2008), 198–200. It has been suggested that the canons were the work of Gérard Pucelle, a trained lawyer: A. J. Duggan, 'Making Law or Not? The Function of Papal Decretals', in P. Erdő and S. Szuromi, eds, *Proc. of the Thirteenth Int'l Congress of Medieval Canon Law* (Vatican City, 2010), 43–55; Summerlin, 'Westminster', 132–3.

[58] Cheney, 'Westminster', 67. *C&S* I. 970 n., judged the association 'likely', the difference reflecting modification by the Westminster council.

[59] *Pervenit* (JL 13794) made its way quickly into decretal collections, among them *Parisiensis I* (c. 3); *Collectio Cantabrigiensis* (c. 82); *Appendix concilii Lateranensis* (37.2), and thence 1 Comp. 4.8.1 (in CS, p. 53). Dates of collections and commentaries herein have been drawn from K. Pennington et al., 'Medieval and Early Modern Jurists: A Bio–Bibliographical Listing', http://faculty.cua.edu/pennington/biobibl.htm [Aug. 2014]. The full decretal can be found in BnF lat. 587, fol. 133r: see S. Chodorow, 'A Group of Decretals by Alexander III', in 'Three Notes on Decretal Letters', *BMCL* (1973), 52 n.

[60] (X 4.8.1) '*Pervenit* ad nos, quod, quum hi, qui leprae morbum incurrunt, de consuetudine generali a communione hominum separentur, et extra civitates et villas ad loca solitaria transferantur, nec uxores viros, nec viri uxores suas taliter aegrotantes sequuntur, sed sine ipsis manere praesumunt. Quoniam igitur, quum vir et uxor una caro sint, non debet alter sine altero esse diutius, fraternitati tuae per apostolica scripta praecipiendo mandamus, quatenus, ut uxores viros, et viri uxores, qui leprae morbum incurrunt, sequantur, et eis coniugali affectione ministrent, sollicitis exhortationibus inducere non postponas. Si vero ad hoc induci non poterunt, eis arctius iniungas, ut uterque altero vivente continentiam servet. Quodsi mandatum tuum servare contempserint, vinculo excommunicationis adstringas.'

[61] Alexander's decretals on marriage (but not *Pervenit*) are addressed in C. Donohue Jr, 'The Dating of Alexander the Third's Marriage Decretals', *ZRG Kan. Abt.* 68 (1982); A. J. Duggan, 'Master of the Decretals', in *Alex III*, 387–409. For Alexander's statements on married lepers, and the tangled arguments among canonists that resulted, see P. Landau, 'Die Leprakranken im mittelalterlichen kanonischen Recht', in D. Schwab et al., eds, *Staat, Kirche, Wissenschaft* (Berlin, 1989), 569–74.

seems unrelated to Richard's original proposition that there be a lawful right henceforth (*amodo*) to remove lepers from society. Its terms are wholly different, even to the degree that Richard spoke of 'lepers' and Alexander of 'those struck with the disease of leprosy'. It is possible that the verb Richard used for 'associate' (*conversari*) came about because the original controversy at Canterbury had concerned a healthy and an ill spouse, but this seems unlikely given the proposition's silence on the subject of marriage. It seems rather that marriage was introduced in the papal response, after papal question as to the nature of the custom of separation. The response rested on a principle established in an earlier Alexandrine decretal that a woman struck with leprosy could not be separated from her husband.[62] This was now redeployed in *Pervenit* not only to reject *non conversari*, but to uphold association in the most intimate terms; it then enjoined bishops to ensure that continued association. Whereas the other decretals had upheld Westminster's original propositions, *Pervenit* reacted against the very principle of this proposition and in a most profound way.

Pervenit and *Cum dicat Apostolus* may appear to be unrelated statements of law, but underlying similarities suggest an association. They were issued by Alexander within a few years of each other. Like the Lateran canon, *Pervenit* countered (Old Testament) customs of separation with (New Testament) apostolic injunction, in defence of Christian rights. Here Alexander used Christ's statement on marriage: 'now they are not two, but one flesh (*una caro*); what therefore God has joined together (*coniunxit*), let no one separate (*separet*)' (Matt. 19: 6). As would Lateran III, it avoided Levitican language when referring to the custom of removal, although it did speak of 'lonely places' and the afflicted person as 'separated' from the communion of men.[63] The choice serves to highlight the unlawfulness of separating those joined by God. The two rulings offer increasingly strong statements against the custom of segregation, which a later canonist would call wicked (*mala consuetudo*).[64] As would Lateran III, *Pervenit* upheld the Christian personhood of those with leprosy. It talked of 'lonely places', but also ignored the subject of leper-houses. An English query instigated the statement in law of *Pervenit* (1176/7),[65] and perhaps helped inspire *Cum dicat Apostolus* (1179), but the approach in law, and the principles it embraced, were those of the papal curia.

---

[62] JL 13773, already in *Parisiensis II* (1177×1179), 87.1 (*CS*, p. 44), for whose date, C. Duggan, 'Decretal Collections', 270–1. For the decretal, Landau, 'Die Leprakranken', 570.

[63] E.g. it avoided language of corruption and preferred *transferantur* to *abiiciebantur*.

[64] Bernhard of Parma, cited in Landau, 'Die Leprakranken', 574 n. Landau argues more generally that canon law took a keen interest in lepers, effecting a general improvement in their status (pp. 567, 569–70).

[65] English clergy seem to have had a particular concern regarding the status of lepers in law, as can be seen from the wide diffusion of *Pervenit* among decretal collections (*CS*, p. 53) and other inquiries, e.g. as to a parish rector struck with leprosy (1183×84); *Papal Decretals rel. to Lincoln*, ed. Holtzmann and Kemp, no. 21.

It has become clear in recent years that the Lateran canons were neither promulgated nor received as definitive legislation. As Danica Summerlin has revealed, they were dispersed via 'chaotic' texts, lacking fixed content or structure, and implemented haphazardly from the 1190s, as a new generation of *magistri* brought university learning to bear on local problems.[66] Among them, *Cum dicat Apostolus* stands out in its ready use. It can be found explicitly in papal and episcopal grants of privileges to leper-houses and implicitly, in wider efforts to establish chapels and cemeteries for leper-houses.[67] In practice, prelates understood that its object was leper-houses and, furthermore, that it charged churchmen not merely to attend to these places, but to champion their rights under the church. In concept, however, the reception of *Cum dicat Apostolus* was neither immediate nor straightforward. Although it found wide dissemination among the Lateran III canons, as an individual decree it attracted little attention.[68] It was not picked out by provincial synods; only Archbishop Hubert Walter's council of Westminster II (1200) repeated it, an echo of the earlier Westminster council's concerns regarding lepers.[69] Several early English collections of decretals also reveal this local interest in the status of lepers as afflicted individuals, but not in *Cum dicat Apostolus* and leper communities. Over time, a growing corpus of decretal collections made no mention of leper-houses and were to show little interest in lepers beyond *Pervenit*'s contribution to the indissolubility of marriage.[70] When *Cum dicat Apostolus* was finally used in legal collections, it was

---

[66] D. Summerlin, 'The Reception and Authority of Conciliar Canons', *ZRG Kan. Abt.* 100 (2014), identifies over 50 manuscripts with 44 sequences; Summerlin, 'Using the Canons of the Third Lateran Council of 1179', in P. Carmassi and G. Drossbach, eds, *Rechtshandschriften des deutschen Mittelalters* (Wiesbaden, 2015).

[67] E.g. Avril, 'Le IIIᵉ concile du Latran', 22–4; Touati, *Maladie et société*, 394–7; Rawcliffe, *Leprosy*, 258; and Summerlin, 'Using the Canons', 254–6, for a long-running dispute involving a privilege awarded by Richard, archbishop of Canterbury.

[68] Variations between Lateran III versions are minor, and concentrated in the opening justification: William of Newburgh's *Historia Regum Anglicanum*, for example, names the apostle as Paul and explains simply that *proprii non permittunt iuvari ministerio sacerdotis*: Cambridge, Corpus Christi College, MS 262, fol. 50v. The decree found its way swiftly into decretal collections, in the list of Lateran canons attached to *Parisiensis I* (11), *Bambergensis* (56, 21), in *CS*, pp. 52, 115; Summerlin, 'Three Manuscripts', 30–2, 33 n.

[69] *C&S* I. 1068, in a truncated version, from * and omitting 'sub communi vita' and 'de iure parochiali'. Summerlin makes clear that Westminster II was unusual in its dissemination of ten Lateran canons, a selection drawn from decretal collections (and from Canterbury's *Appendix concilii Lateranensis* family), because, she suggests, they spoke particularly to local conditions, D. Summerlin, 'Hubert Walter's Council of Westminster', in M. H. Eichbauer and D. Summerlin, eds, *Canon Law and Administration* (Leiden, 2018), 130–8; Summerlin, 'Using the Canons'. Other councils, including Rouen (1190), Montpellier (1195), and Paris (1208) did not repeat the decree: *Concilia Rothomagensis provincial*, ed. G. Bessin, 2 vols (Rouen, 1717), I. 94–8; Mansi XXII. 939–50; O. Pontal, ed., *Les statuts synodaux francais du XIIIᵉ siècle*, I (Paris, 1971), 150 ff.

[70] 1 Comp. 4.8.1 = X 4.8.1. The Canterbury *Collectio Claudiana* (1185×88) copied the latter half (from *ut ubicumque*) under the title DE PRIVILEGIIS ET IMMUNITATE LEPROSORUM (BL, Cotton MS Claudius A IV, fol. 202v). The exceptions are the *Appendix concilii Lateranensis* (37) and *Parisiensis II* (87), which both did include a section, 'DE LEPROSIS', with four chapters, the former including *Pervenit* (*CS*, pp. 44, 79; Landau, 'Die Leprakranken', 567, 571). On the decretalists, S. Kuttner and E. Rathbone, 'Anglo-Norman Canonists', *Traditio* 7 (1951).

under the heading 'On the distribution of ecclesiastical benefices', which recognized not leper-houses or lepers but the challenge of maintaining a benefice adequate to support a priest.[71] Ultimately, it found its place under the title 'On building and repairing churches'. It was incorporated in full under this title into Bernard of Pavia's *Breviarium extravagantium* (1 Comp. 3.35.1) of *c*.1190, from where it was copied into the *Liber extra* (X 3.48.2).[72] *Cum dicat Apostolus* failed to establish any presence for leper-houses in law.

If its legal reception was muted, its use by the papal curia was vigorous. In his study of the province of Sens, Touati noted 'a clear turning-point... quantitative and qualitative' in papal policy towards leper-houses in the aftermath of Lateran III and especially under Lucius III (1181–5).[73] In fact, we can detect a change in papal engagement from at least the late 1160s. From this time, the language of disability develops within papal letters to construct a disadvantaged group (lepers) rather than an insufficient place (leper-houses). Privileges established rights for *infirmi fratres*, *infirmi*, and *leprosi* to secure an oratory, chaplain, and consecrated burial ground, and to retain tithes of food.[74] Because the lepers were without a priest, Alexander declared, many died without confession or last rites, while others carried their dead across half a league for burial.[75] In these privileges, Alexander was developing a legal weapon to support lepers in leper-houses and, as would *Cum dicat Apostolus*, it addressed people, acting to provide spiritual care to those deprived.

This was no mere rhetoric, for Alexander cared personally about the issue. In February 1176—around the time he received the archbishop of Canterbury's proposition 'That from this time forward lepers not associate with the healthy'—Alexander was dedicating the chapel and house of the lepers in Veroli, 'with our own hands, though unworthy'. His privilege to them, *dilecti in domino filii*, speaks in moving terms of a duty to cherish those afflicted with an incurable disease in their distress and misery, to show them great humanity, and

---

[71] Avril, 'Le IIIe concile du Latran', 36. The canon was also ignored by moral theologians and only noticed by two Victorines in 1215 (Longère, 'L'influence de Latran III sur quelques ouvrages de théologie morale', in Longère, ed., *Le troisième concile*); they were probably reacting to Courson's reforms in 1213/4.

[72] X 3.48.2, DE ECCLESIIS AEDIFICANDIS VEL REPARANDIS, where the chapter is titled *Leprosi permitti debent, sine praeiudicio antiquarum parochiarum, habere ecclesiam propriam et presbyterum, nec tenentur solvere decimas de hortis vel nutrimentis animalium*. The title is taken from 1 Comp. 3.35.1.

[73] Touati, *Maladie et société*, 393–6, with quotation at p. 393. See, too, Avril, 'Le IIIe concile du Latran', *passim*.

[74] The privilege to retain tithes was often awarded to groups of lepers, and before 1179. In 1167×69, Alexander rebuked three religious houses in Cambrai for seizing such tithes 'cum eis sicut caeteris infirmis a Romana Ecclesia sit indultum ut nemini de his quas praediximus decimas exsolvere teneantur.' *PL* 200, cols 516–17, also 515–16, 753, 934, 936–7, 961–2, 1155, 1190; Avril, 'Le IIIe concile du Latran', 33–4, 42–3.

[75] E.g. in 1171/2: 'Audivimus autem quod infirmi de Sparnaco saepe pro defectu capellani gravia incurrunt pericula, et sine viatici participatione decedunt', *PL* 200, col. 830, also 558, 979.

to inspire others to offer compassion and support.[76] Such activity was a feature of his age. Across Europe prelates and patrons worked to equip leper-houses with incomes and spiritual care; indeed, it was the difficulty of this process, and the disputes with local churches that it could engender, that saw the canon so readily adopted in localities. Even Alexander's affective concern was not unusual in the twelfth century. Compassion for lepers was widely promoted as a Christian virtue, and close human contact recognized as a mark of peculiar piety, even sanctity.[77] What is notable is that these themes—the governmental and the compassionate— were brought together in the actions of Alexander himself and, in turn, in his canon. It sought to provide a new tool for prelates, but also a new configuration of what the afflicted suffered and of the Christian duty towards them.

Cum dicat Apostolus was the only canon in a papal council of the twelfth and thirteenth centuries to be directed at any kind of welfare house. In both its drafting under Alexander III and its ready uptake in localities it reveals the eagerness of churchmen to cultivate such houses. As within *Pervenit* three years earlier, the canon was informed by human and pastoral concerns. Compassion was built into its language, theology, and legal argument. It also acted governmentally, to establish explicit rights and to furnish a patron or prelate with a new arsenal of papal directive, Christian entreaty, and leverage of clerical assistance. There is no question its target was leper-houses: only an endowed house could support such a group from common means. It extended the privileges held by communities that had assumed a religious life (*religiosam vitam eligentibus*) to a wider class of houses that maintained lepers *sub communi vita degentibus* ('dwelling—or passing time—under a common way of life').[78] The houses themselves, not an ecclesiastical community therein, were its target.

If *Cum dicat Apostolus* worked to protect leper-houses without saying so, its silence contrasts with the language of contemporary charters. Historians of leprosy have noticed a change in terminology in the later twelfth century, from people (*leprosi*) to place (*domus leprosorum*), evidence they suggest of a gradual institutionalization, as informal groups gained privileges, possessions, and

---

[76] 'Eos quos dominus incurabili morbo afflixit et continuis cruciatibus flagellauit, oculo debemus benigniori respicere et in suis angustiis et miseriis pastorali sollicitudine confouere, ut quanto eis maiorem humanitatem exhibuerimus, tanto alios ad ipsorum compassionem et subsidium amplius inuitemus.... domum uestram et capellam, quam propriis manibus licet inmeritis dedicauimus', , 'Papsturkunden in Campanien', ed. P. Kehr, in *Nachrichten von der Königl. Gesellschaft der Wissenschaften zu Göttingen: Phil.-hist. Klasse* (Göttingen, 1900), no. 18. On Alexander's activity in the region, see B. Bolton, 'The Absentee Lord? Alexander III and the Patrimony', in *Alex III*, 176–9. Bolton suggests that his local work inspired *Cum dicat Apostolus*.

[77] C. Peyroux, 'The Leper's Kiss', in S. Farmer and B. H. Rosenwein, eds, *Monks and Nuns, Saints and Outcasts* (London, 2000); Rawcliffe, 'Learning to Love the Leper'.

[78] This suggests that we should be cautious in reading papal protections to houses *sub communi vita* as a mark of religious life, as e.g. *Bibliotheca Topographica Britannica*, ed. J. Nichols, 8 vols (London, 1780–90), I. 235; *Cartulaire de l'abbaye de Saint-Corneille de Compiègne*, ed. É.-É. Morel, III (Paris, 1977), 45; Sayers, *Papal Government*, 104.

recognition.[79] Such a shift can also be found in Alexander's privileges, which from the 1170s increasingly name (and confirm) the sites of individual communities as *domus infirmorum*.[80] The curia had embraced the terminology of place in practice, but left places unnamed in law. In fact, *Cum dicat Apostolus* went to considerable efforts to avoid the very subject it addressed: its basis for action was the deprivation of sufferers as Christians, first established and then answered by the canon; its injunction to act was directed at all Christians, and especially local prelates.[81] It acted to address leper-houses by acting on the Christian community in general. This was not an act of jurisdiction, but a call to the faithful in service to Christ. The canon did not bring, or seek to bring, leper-houses under the church,[82] nor did it envisage a change in their internal arrangement. It did not say anything about the lepers themselves, except as an object of Christian compassion.

Alexander III was a bold law-maker, and Innocent III was perhaps the most ambitious pope of his era. Each took an energetic interest in welfare, promoting and founding hospitals and leper-houses, as well as hospital orders.[83] Their efforts at Lateran III and IV reinforce this picture, suggesting a desire to use the councils as pulpits—legal and exhortatory—to develop a sense of ecclesiastical responsibility for such places. Their efforts were not directed at the facilities, but reached around these places to Christians more generally, enjoining them to relieve want, to clerics to promote this. Their response speaks, in part, to the role of charity at the heart of Christian community: only when embraced by individuals were the communal values of *caritas* most powerfully made manifest.

These popes' failure to mention the facilities themselves extends beyond their great councils: of their copious decretals, a more direct and less exhortatory medium, none set out law for hospitals. Why not address the houses explicitly? Such a silence in law, so consistently held, suggests a structural challenge. And that their efforts were so carefully crafted suggests an attempt to address places on which they had no right to act. How to account for this?

---

[79] Bériac, *Histoire des lépreux*, 155–60; M. Satchell, 'The Emergence of Leper Houses in Medieval England' (D.Phil. dissertation, University of Oxford, 1998), 113–48; De Keyzer, 'évolution interne'. But compare Touati, *Maladie et société*, 330, which counters Bonenfant's Belgian picture of 'groupements disparates et anarchiques' with more orderly communities of Sens (discussing Bonenfant, 'Hôpitaux et bienfaisance', 25).

[80] *PL* 200, cols 961–2, 1009–10, with even earlier letters at cols 180–1, 435.

[81] Its language, castigating those who 'seek the things that are their own; not the things that are Jesus Christ's' (Phil. 2: 21), is also directed against cardinals, bishops, and archdeacons in the council's canon 5, on procurations during visitations.

[82] Local houses remained under assorted, and often private, jurisdictions: Avril, 'Le IIIᵉ concile du Latran', 43–63; Satchell, 'Leper Houses', 251–399.

[83] On Alexander, see Chapter 7; on Innocent, Drossbach, *Christliche caritas*, 41–88; B. Bolton, 'Hearts Not Purses?', in E. Albu, ed., *Through the Eye of a Needle* (Kirksville, MO, 1994); *PL* 214, cols 903–6; *PL* 215, cols 83–4, 272–5, 355–61. Early in his pontificate, Innocent authored a dedicated treatise on alms, *Libellus de Eleemosyna*, ed. S. Fioramonti as *Elogio della carità* (Vatican City, 2001).

The wider activity of general councils offers a key, for they issued many decrees to regulate religious life.[84] In addition to those above, Lateran I affirmed episcopal authority over monks, while Lateran II prohibited intimate association with wives, and Lateran III prohibited monks from being received into monasteries for money. Lateran III issued decrees for the communities themselves, regulating appointment of officers, duties of abbots, and removal of priors, and required that monks be posted in groups outside their monastery. Monks were also forbidden to possess their own money, and any unconfessed transgressor was to be buried away from his brethren. As we have seen, Lateran IV organized the heads of independent monasteries into congregations and required new religious, and founders of monasteries, to adopt an existing rule. There is a theme: the legislation was directed at the monks, nuns, priors, and abbots, and copious directives were sent to archbishops, bishops, archdeacons, and priests. Like *Cum dicat Apostolus*, they regulated people not place.

The church universal had no jurisdictional claim over the residents or sojourners in a hospital, and so legal jurisdiction over the places themselves, unless the community had joined a religious order. Those without religious communities eluded the church's claim. In the following chapters we shall watch the reach of this jurisdiction gently ebb and flow. Nevertheless, in the long history of welfare institutions, the silence in canon law was never so tightly observed as it was during the twelfth century, when the claims of church and kingdom were especially contested, even over clerics (culminating most violently, and exceptionally, in the murder of Thomas Becket). At the point when bishops, in practice, most needed new law for so many, and such a variety of new facilities, the church was most constrained in its ability to act. The studious care by Alexander III and Innocent III to address these places indirectly, by exhorting others to act, reinforces their significance and their unusual status. To adopt the phrases in Innocent's letter, these were Christian entities in need of resources to supply the lack of those who were without. They are defined by their very materiality. It was not until the thirteenth century that 'religious house' (*domus religiosa*) emerged as a category in law. As we shall see in Part III, it was a category crafted especially for hospitals.

Lateran II (1139) and False Nuns

Given these conclusions—that law-makers addressed people by right or duty of ecclesiastical *cura*, but could not address hospitals as places—might there be other

---

[84] Lateran I, c. 16, 19–22; Lateran II, c. 7–9, 11, 26–7; Lateran III, c. 9, 10, 16; Lateran IV, c. 12–13, 59–61, 64.

canons that addressed welfare houses in a similarly sly manner? One emerges that has not previously been associated with hospitals.

Canon 26 of Lateran II acted against false nuns—women who wished to be regarded as nuns (*sanctimoniales*), but did not follow the approved rules of Benedict, Basil, or Augustine. The council bemoaned that 'when they should be living according to a rule in monasteries and be in a church and a common refectory or dormitory [such women] have built themselves their own refuges (*receptacula*) and private dwellings where, under the cover of hospitality, they shamelessly receive guests indiscriminately and those who are not at all religious'.[85] The canon had several wider contexts. Most fundamentally, the drive to cloister female communities in monasteries and under an approved rule was not new.[86] In addition, this was a period marked by its search for new forms of religious life, when men and women, in imitation of the *vita apostolica*, gathered in informal communities. Many priories were built around such groups of women between the 1140s and 1160s.[87] Canon 26 was part of wider efforts to limit the scandals that might accompany this experimentation, and especially arising from contact between religious women and men.[88] It had a broad context, but apparently a particular target in hospitals. *Receptaculum* was the term used for *hospitale*, 'where paupers may be gathered', in the rule for canons and canonesses, promulgated at the council of Aachen (816) and since then widely disseminated.[89] In the Lateran canon, the women were explicitly not attending church services but otherwise engaged in hospitality and the indiscriminate reception of guests. Among the targets of the Lateran canon were women who were not dedicating themselves to a life of communal prayer, but engaged in charitable service. Legarda, widow of William of Apulia, offers one such example in England.

---

[85] (c. 26) 'Ad haec perniciosam et detestabilem consuetudinem…Cum enim, iuxta regulam degentes in coenobiis, tam in ecclesia quam in refectorio atque dormitorio communiter esse debeant, propria sibi aedificant receptacula et privata domicilia, in quibus sub hospitalitatis velamine passim hospites et minus religiosos contra sacros canones et bonos mores suscipere nullatenus erubescunt…hoc tam inhonestum detestandumque flagitium, ne ulterius fiat, omnimodis prohibemus et sub poena anathematis interdicimus.' COGD II. 112, tr. DEC 203, here with minor adaptations.

[86] It is a running theme among reformers. Caesarius of Arles had defined *sanctimoniales* as those who entered a monastery, submitted to a rule, and surrendered their possessions, while Carolingian reformers worked to organize nuns into regular monasteries: E. Magnou-Nortier, 'Formes féminines de vie consacrée', in E. Privat, ed., *La Femme dans la vie religieuse du Languedoc* (Toulouse, 1988), 200–2; E. Makowski, 'A Pernicious Sort of Woman' (Washington, DC, 2005), 14–18. For a 'campaign for the "Benedictinization"' of women's communities in the early twelfth century, see S. Vanderputten, 'Female Monasticism', *French Historical Studies* 36:3 (2013).

[87] For the problems faced by women in creating new forms of religious life, see M. de Fontette, *Les religieuses à l'âge classique du droit canon* (Paris, 1967), 9–18, 27–37; S. Thompson, *Women Religious* (Oxford, 1991); Thompson, 'The Problem of the Cistercian Nuns', in D. Baker, ed., *Medieval Women* (Oxford, 1978); S. K. Elkins, *Holy Women of Twelfth-Century England* (Chapel Hill, NC, 1988), 19, 49–50, 65–6, 71–5.

[88] The next canon prohibited nuns from joining canons and monks in choir (Lateran II, c. 27).

[89] (c. 141) 'ubi pauperes colligantur', MGH *Conc.* II.i. 416, and an imperial letter, II.i. 460. A possible context might be offered by, J. Ziegler, 'Secular Canonesses as Antecedents of the Beguines', *Studies in Medieval and Renaissance History* NS 13 (1992), 124–9.

In 1144, she was called 'nun' (*monialis*) and recorded with her associates 'serving the sick' at the leper-house of St Mary Magdalene in Norwich.[90]

The canon hints at a longer association between hospitals and informal religious service by women.[91] This can be found widely in the decades around 1200, especially with the rise of beguines in Flanders and Northern France, in houses variably termed beguinages or hospitals.[92] A similar association may also be found at the council of Vienne (1311/2), whose 'Magna Carta for hospital organisation' (c. 17) immediately followed the canon prohibiting beguines, women 'who promise obedience to nobody, neither renounce possessions nor profess any approved rule, [and who] are not religious at all, although they wear a habit said to be that of the beguines' (c. 16).[93] The prohibition excluded those faithful women (*fideles mulieres*) who, whether they promised chastity or not, led a life of penance, serving God, in their own *hospitia* (a private lodging, especially a town-house). However tenuous, the connection between Lateran II and Vienne, almost two centuries apart, is the use of law to reinforce boundaries between approved and illicit religious service by women. They acted to distinguish *regulares* from other women, including those *fideles mulieres*, sworn to chastity and Christian service. In each case, it was the women not the places that were the subject of the canons.

In requiring devout women to embrace a monastic life, the 1139 canon also reinforced a boundary between monastic houses and xenodochia. In practice, such boundaries were being eroded where the charitable revolution—and its call to charitable service—met the quest to live out the *vita apostolica*. The line drawn at Lateran II did not end this confusion, nor did it temper impulses by men and

[90] Thomas of Monmouth, *The Life and Miracles of St William of Norwich*, ed. A. Jessop and M. R. James (Cambridge, 1896), 31–2: 'cum suis, que pro dei amore apud sanctam Mariam Magdalenam manet infirmis seruiens talibusque obsequiis anime sue salutem mendicans ... monialis illa.'

[91] The tension between women's efforts to forge devotional lives serving the needy and ecclesiastical efforts to enclose them in cloisters has been stressed from the thirteenth century, with an eye towards the papal bull *Periculoso* (1298). For 'la charité féminine' and these later efforts, see D. Le Blévec, 'Le rôle des femmes dans l'assistance et la charité', in E. Privat, ed., *La femme dans la vie religieuse du Languedoc* (Toulouse, 1988); R. Cossar, 'Lay Woman in the Hospitals of Late Medieval Bergamo', *Florilegium* 21 (2004); E. Makowski, *Canon Law and Cloistered Women* (Washington, DC, 1997), 21–42.

[92] W. Simons, *Cities of Ladies* (Philadelphia, 2001), 35–60. For efforts by women to lead religious lives through charity, see C. Neel, 'The Origins of the Beguines', in J. M. Bennet et al., eds, *Sisters and Workers in the Middle Ages* (Chicago, 1976); B. M. Bolton, 'Mulieres Sanctae', in D. Baker, ed., *Sanctity and Secularity: The Church and the World* (Oxford, 1973); J. Dor, L. Johnson, and J. Wogan-Browne, eds, *New Trends in Feminine Spirituality* (Turnhout, 1999). A. E. Lester, *Creating Cistercian Nuns* (New York, 2011), 117–46, explores care of lepers and hospitals by Cistercian convents in Champagne.

[93] (c. 16) 'Cum de quibusdam mulieribus, beguinabus vulgariter nuncupatis, quae, cum nulli promittant oboedientiam nec propriis renuncient, neque profiteantur aliquam regulam approbatam, religiosae nequaquam exsistunt, quanquam habitum, qui beguinarum dicitur, deferant.' This, in turn, followed a canon (15) that required more intensive oversight of nunneries, including of 'women vulgarly called secular canonesses, who lead a life like that of secular canons, neither renouncing private property nor making any profession', and now to be subject to a rule ('mulieres quae vulgo dicuntur canonicae saeculares et, ut saeculares canonici, vitam ducunt, non renunciantes proprio nec professionem aliquam facientes'); *COGD* II. 427–8. The term 'secular canonesses' also harks back to the Aachen rule, with its *receptacula*.

women to forge religious lives dedicated to charity. But the act of the council is suggestive. It reveals the priorities of prelates, not simply to draw a line, but to draw this particular line: targeted not at hospital service itself, but at women whose religious life, the (male) council believed, should be fully *regularis*, and cloistered, centred around church, and in community.

And while we must be cautious of the reach of Lateran II's exhortations, it may be possible to glimpse its effects in several localities. The notorious 'ambiguity' between hospitals and priories, and a sense that one form could migrate into another, is first seen in a tendency of hospitals to become nunneries, especially in the mid-twelfth century.[94] It suggests that, in some cases at least, there may have been a guiding hand—or a directing command to the women—behind the change.[95] It is possible that the uptake was particularly strong in England, whose bishops proved eager to digest and implement laws in the second half of the twelfth century. There, at least, vague references to *moniales* serving in hospitals in the early twelfth century soon disappear.[96] What matters here is the principle that was laid down at Lateran II: that women who identified as nuns should transform the place where they lived into a monastic house, or enter an existing convent. A hospital (*receptaculum*) was no place for nuns to live. In calling for *moniales* to be in a convent, under a rule, Lateran II reinforced the jurisdictional boundaries between convents—under the church—and xenodochia, as places of Christian service in the world. Here we see welfare houses as places where new devotional and religious lives were being forged; in the gendered eyes of these councils, such spaces were too worldly for the religious innovations of women.

The Lateran councils established no reform agendas nor claim of governance over welfare houses. They offered no directives for the houses themselves; in fact, they issued no canon that explicitly mentioned these houses. Yet their outward silence obscures sustained and creative activity. Lateran II, III, and IV each responded to the boom in welfare houses, and from its earliest decades. Here, representatives of the church universal acted first, in 1139, to protect the integrity of religious life,

---

[94] On the ambiguity, D. Knowles and R. N. Hadcock, *Medieval Religious Houses*, 2nd ed. (London, 1971), 288–9; Thompson, *Women Religious*, ch. 3. For hospitals becoming priories of men, *c.*1230, see J. C. Dickinson, *The Origins of the Austin Canons* (London, 1950), 145; S. Watson, 'A Mother's Past and her Children's Futures', in C. Leyser and L. Smith, eds, *Motherhood, Religion, and Society* (Farnham, 2011).

[95] Possible candidates in England might include Carrow (Norf.), St Bartholomew's (Newcastle), and Hutton Lowcross (Yorks.): Thompson, *Women Religious*, 43, 49, 52, 218; W. Dugdale, *Monasticon Anglicanum*, 6 vols (London, 1846), V. 507–8; *Durham Episcopal Charters, 1071–1152*, ed. H. S. Offler (1964), 131–2.

[96] There were informal groups of 'nuns' connected with charity, near the great abbeys at Bury St Edmunds, Evesham, and St Albans in the late eleventh and early twelfth century, and *moniales* at Alkmonkton (Derbs.) in 1155/6, Woodstock (Oxon.) in 1181/2, and St James, Westminster, in 1183/4, where there were also leper-houses (Thompson, *Women Religious*, 47; Satchell, 'Leper Houses', 239). A 1341 visitation in Ripon (Yorks.) recalled 'sororibus in dicto hospitali, quasi religiose viventibus', in the early years of the hospital, *Memorials of the Church of Ripon*, I, Surtees Society 84 (1882), 224.

where prelates perceived the greatest threat to order. The (male) law-makers fixed their anxieties on nuns' bodies and the scandals that might arise from the open welcome of hospitality, a metaphor as much as an opportunity for sexual access. In 1179, Lateran III acted to ensure that leper-houses were used to serve and not deprive vulnerable members of the Christian community. It extended a privilege *sub communi vita degentibus*, with freedom from tithes of food and animals, to leper-houses that fed their residents from common stocks, and whose resources permitted a church, chaplain, and cemetery. And in 1215, Lateran IV led a call to alms to every Christian, to give of what they had to those without, in hospitals. Here were new tools that local prelates and founders might wield, to shepherd the profusion of houses and to reinforce existing houses. And these were not simply technical exercises. They reveal the importance of welfare as a Christian pursuit, cultivated by the church. In giving language to the obligation to care for those without, Innocent III was echoing what Alexander III had done when the latter used the language of the New Testament to overwrite segregation with human embrace, calling on prelates and the faithful to act. In its new language, and its remapping of human relationships, it offered a new cosmology of Christian obligation.

At this point, what matters was the formal silence of the general councils, even when they were determined to act. It reveals that the absence of welfare houses in law was no accident, and no manifestation of neglect. Only by recognizing what could not be done in law can we appreciate the character of each council's response. On one hand, their actions were very much of their moment. Each canon was alive to the challenges presented by contemporary foundations and to address the issue each pope or council had to confect a statement in law. To do so, they sought out a familiar reference point or template through which to speak, be that the canons' rule (Lateran II), the New Testament (Lateran III), or an indulgence (Lateran IV). Their creations allow us to view welfare houses, or more precisely an agenda regarding welfare, through the eyes of the author. On the other hand, the councils inherited a concept of welfare facilities. Their awareness of this form is revealed in the way that each council danced around the facilities. Across eighty years we find a consistent restraint, observed even by the era's two most ambitious popes, and an ongoing sense of the limits of action. In the long twelfth century, general councils acted on people, not places. For hospitals, the councils had to reach around the places to those over whom they had a claim: nuns, bishops, and the community of the faithful. What was it they were reaching around? The absence of hospitals in law had a shape, whose bounds were carefully walked. It was a model not articulated in canon law, but somehow it was known.

To understand the hospital in law, we must discover what it was that the twelfth century inherited. The answer lies in the early middle ages, where we shall discover the legal origins of hospitals in the West. The place to start is the early medieval model as it has long been understood, and this takes us to Francia.

PART II
A WESTERN MODEL (400–900)

3

The Question of Francia (400–816)

Early medieval hospitals are more mysterious than their later counterparts. This is partly an issue of documentation, since references to them tend to be fleeting. With no house archives, and often only a single mention or charter, there is little scope to explore the facilities themselves. It is not surprising, then, that studies have focused on quantitative over qualitative analysis, often by surveying the scattered documentary references in an attempt to give shape to the broad, if untidy picture they present.[1] But part of their mystery is also, and perhaps fundamentally, a question of law. For here, once again there is a complete disconnect between theory (our model) and practice (documentation). Our account of its early law is organized, institutional, and transnational, while the facilities themselves seem chaotically varied. To question early medieval law is to question the very origins of hospitals. And, in this story, it has always been believed, Francia and Louis the Pious were central.

It is clear, at least, that councils in the early medieval West were eager to address hospitals. Decrees survive from the sixth century, and in relatively large numbers after c.780. They usually refer to 'xenodochia', from the Greek *xenodochion*, a place for lodging strangers,[2] although during the eighth century, the Latin-derived *hospitales* or *hospitalia* (from *hospes*, guest or stranger) gained wider use.[3] Contemporaries stressed that the two were synonyms. Alcuin, for example, wrote in 796 from Francia to a new archbishop of York, exhorting him to consider 'where you might direct that *xenodochia*, that is *hospitales*, be created, in which poor people and pilgrims might every day be received and from our material

---

[1] See this chapter, nn. 15–16. A second approach has been to chart geographical distribution, Sternberg, *Orientalium more secutus*; Hubert, 'Hôpitaux et espace urbain'; Santangeli Valenzani, 'Pellegrini'; J. le Maho, 'Hospices et xenodochia du diocèse de Rouen', in *Fondations*; M. Mollat, 'Les premiers hôpitaux', in *HHF* 18–24.

[2] M. Anderson, 'Mistranslations of Josephus', *EME* 25:2 (2017), 151–3, explores the fourth-century origins of the term.

[3] The term is often said to have been introduced by the Irish *hospitalia Scottorum* in the late eighth century (Boshof, 'Armenfürsorge', 159, 163; *HDC* 48; L. Gougaud, *Les Chrétientés celtiques* (Paris, 1911), 166–8). Yet it can be found in Italy by 724, where a Luccan will provided for a certain house *qui ospitale vocatur* (*CDL* I. no. 34). In c.790 Pope Hadrian wrote to Charlemagne of the 'monasterium … qui positus est in Calligata, una cum hospitals [sic], qui per calles Alpium siti sunt, pro peregrinorum susceptione' (*Codex Carolinus*, ed. W. Gundlach, MGH *Epp.* III (Berlin, 1892), 623). For early papal uses of *hospitale*, see F. R. Stasolla, 'A proposito delle strutture assistenziali ecclesiastiche', *Archivio della Società romana di storia patria* 121 (1998), 7, 14, 22.

On Hospitals: Welfare, Law, and Christianity in Western Europe, 400–1320. Sethina Watson, Oxford University Press (2020). © Sethina Watson. DOI: 10.1093/oso/9780198847533.001.0001

goods find relief'.[4] In the ninth century, the terms could be used interchangeably. While *xenodochium* seems to have been preferred at times for a facility for the poor, and *hospitalis* for travellers, both were also generic labels for welfare facilities and might encompass a variety of charitable functions.[5] Over time, *hospitalis/ hospitale* would replace its Greek precursor, but *xenodochium* remained the preferred term until the twelfth century and was clearly in common use until then.

The volume of early legislation is due to the character of early medieval councils. Since the Gallic council of Agde (506), called by the Visigothic king Alaric II and convened under Bishop Caesarius of Arles, ecclesiastical law had developed alongside royal authority and law-giving.[6] It was increasingly under princely authority that councils were called, business organized, and acts disseminated and enforced. The movement reached its zenith under Charlemagne (768–814) and his son, Louis the Pious (814–40), whose royal councils had grown out of the practice of convening church councils.[7] These did not limit their reach to secular matters. Embracing the image of Old Testament kings, Carolingian rulers sought to bring order to religion, cultivate faith, and unify the realm, and they saw law as the tool by which this should be done.[8] Major reforms of the church, including the *Admonitio generalis* (789), emerged from convocations under royal authority.

While it is possible, then, to speak of 'secular' and 'church' law in this period, it is often uncomfortable to do so, and more helpful to think, initially at least, in terms of legal activity, albeit with a more imperial or ecclesiastical thrust at various

---

[4] 'Consideret quoque tua diligentissima in elemosinis pietas, ubi xenodochia, id est hospitalia fieri iubeas, in quibus sit cotidiana pauperum et peregrinorum susceptio; et ex nostris substantiis habeant solatia.' Alcuin, *Epistolae*, ed. E. Dümmler, MGH *Epp*. IV (Berlin, 1895), 169. On Alcuin's ideals of episcopacy, shaped by his experience in Francia, S. Coates, 'The Bishop as Benefactor and Civic Patron', *Speculum* 71:3 (1996).

[5] The council of Quierzy in 858: (c. 10) 'xenodochiorium, id est hospitalium' (MGH *Conc*. III. 418). A ninth-century note on the flyleaf of St Gall, Stiftsbibliothek MS Cod. Sang. 196, includes 'xenodochia' among a list of Greek terms for charities, labelling the group 'types of hospitals (*gen[era] hospitalorum*)'. It has been suggested that the terms reflect two institutional forms, with pilgrim *hospitalia* gradually replacing *xenodochia* for the poor by the twelfth century (*HDC* 49–50; H. W. Dey, 'Diaconiae, xenodochia, hospitalia', *EME* 16 (2008), 410–11; Stasolla, 'Proposito', 7–8). Such distinctions should be treated with caution. *Hospitalis* was one of a range of terms, reflecting new fashions in care that had grown out of and were layered onto existing forms. Both itinerant poor and pilgrims were to be welcomed (e.g. MGH *Cap*. I. 96, c. 27).

[6] In 506, Alaric also promulgated the *Breviarium Alaricianum*, a digest of Roman laws for his Roman subjects, W. E. Klingshirn, *Caesarius of Arles* (Cambridge, 2004), 95–104. On the interplay between ecclesiastical and Roman law, I. Wood, 'Disputes in Late Fifth- and Sixth-Century Gaul', in W. Davies and P. Fouracre, eds, *The Settlement of Disputes* (Cambridge, 1986), 19–22; J. L. Nelson, 'Law and its Applications', in Noble and Smith, eds, *Early Medieval Christianities*, 299–302, 307–9; P. Wormald, 'Lex Scripta and Verbum Regis', in his *Legal Culture in the Early Medieval West* (London, 1999), 25–35. T. S. Brown, 'Louis the Pious and the Papacy', in *Ch. Heir*, sheds light on the complex dance between emperor and pope in Ravenna.

[7] H. Mordek, 'Fränkische Kapitularien', in Mordek, *Studien*, 7–15.

[8] R. McKitterick, *The Frankish Church* (London, 1977), 1–44; J. Barrow, 'Ideas and Applications of Reform', in Noble and Smith, eds, *Early Medieval Christianities*; M. de Jong, 'Charlemagne's Church', in J. Story, ed., *Charlemagne: Empire and Society* (Manchester, 2005).

times. Xenodochia were a matter of concern for many such convocations. Indeed, given the amount of business relating to them, it is surprising that the corpus has not been investigated. The oversight has been brought about by approaches that have distracted the field. This chapter unpicks these approaches and questions the place of Francia in the development of law for hospitals, re-examining the two councils usually cited as the basis of Western law for hospitals: Orléans (549) and Aachen (816). The next chapter turns to the main corpus of Carolingian decrees, which are in fact from Lombardy. Roman law and its presumed conduit, Abbot Ansegis of Saint-Wandrille, are treated in Chapter 5, and efforts to develop systems of oversight in Chapter 6.

Approaches to East and West

As we noticed in chapter two, it has been difficult to imagine the legal form of xenodochia without subsuming it within a larger teleology: the birth of the medical hospital. In this drama the early medieval West plays only a walk-on part and, usually, provides a comic interlude with little impact on the plot. Historians have agreed that Justinian's law was adopted without adaptation in the West but, beyond that fact, each has told their own story of the emergence of the hospital.[9] In these long stories, early Western councils have simply been conduits between the charitable movements of the (Greek) East and the charitable awakening of the twelfth century. There has also been little consensus as to which councils were significant, although studies have tended to embrace two basic, if not mutually exclusive, approaches.

The first approach, the long story, has told of the rise of the hospital, tracing its emergence as an institution from late antique Byzantium and through the late middle ages, often into the early modern era.[10] It has seen the first hospitals as institutional manifestations of new social ideals—hospitality and care for the poor—that were promoted by a newly Christianized empire in the East and enjoined particularly upon bishops, from whose labours hospitals first arose.[11] These Byzantine institutions were given legal form by Justinian and moved to the West, where in the twelfth century the hospital gained new life and complexity as

[9] National historiographies tend to draw on Schönfeld, 'Xenod.' (German), Caron, 'pia fundatio' (Italian), or, Imbert, HDC (French). The latter shaped the well-distilled discussion in Brodman, CRME 48–50. On the long teleology, 15–17, 33–5.

[10] HDC 11–54; Rocca, Il diritto osped.; Boshof, 'Armenfürsorge', 153–74; Caron, 'pia fundatio'; Merzbacher, 'Das Spital'; H. Coing, 'Remarks on the History of Foundations', Minerva 19:2 (1981). To give the broad shape, and reveal underlying assumptions, what follows paints a necessarily simplistic picture; the specific contributions of the works cited are teased out in other sections.

[11] A sophisticated treatment is Brown, Eye of a Needle, where hospitals make only a brief appearance. They are recognized in Brown, Poverty and Leadership, 33–5, as an example of the new mix of a Christian exhortation to love the poor with classical notions of euergesia, the civic virtue of making gifts for the public good.

an institution and its course of development began. This teleology has often, explicitly or implicitly, looked forward to the medical establishments of the modern age. In this long story, the early medieval West was a period of developmental pause, so the narrative challenge has been how the hospital survived to reach the twelfth century.

Within this approach, authors have gravitated towards two different storylines and, with them, two different Frankish councils, depending upon whether their interest begins in the East (with bishops) or the West (under St Benedict); that is, whether they are telling the story of law or physical survival. Those looking back from the twelfth century, for the origins of welfare in practice, have looked to monastic communities, whose rules obliged them to be hospitable, citing the sixth-century rule of St Benedict of Nursia and the council of Aachen (816), which promulgated rules for canons and canonesses.[12] Those looking forward from the late antique East seek an ongoing legal framework in the West and have looked to sixth-century councils, especially that of Orléans (549). In its threats of anathema against *necatores pauperum* ('murderers/assassins/slayers of the poor'), they have seen a rhetorical formulation to protect hospitals and define 'the hospital' in law: as church property under the authority of the bishop.[13] The two storylines have often interwoven, offering monastic rules as the inspiration for hospital foundation and *necatores pauperum* as the mechanism by which they were defined as institutions in law. Although some stress the agency of bishops, others monastic rules, the underlying legal story has been similar.[14] A new type of institution was created by churchmen, often in their own precincts, out of a Christian duty of hospitality or to the poor. It was made an autonomous institution in law under Justinian, as part of the patrimony of the church. The basis of its legal form was the bishop's duty of care and, as a result, that form was ecclesiastical. Subsequent councils in the West then acted to reinforce, in practice, the bishop's right to oversee hospitals.

The second approach, the documentary study, has focused on forms of charity between the sixth and ninth centuries, placing xenodochia alongside *diaconiae*

---

[12] As does Merzbacher, 'Das Spital'. This can morph into a Western-origin story, W. Witters, 'Pauvres et pauvreté dans les coutumiers monastiques', in *EHP*; K. B. Wolf, *The Poverty of Riches* (Oxford, 2003), 138 n. 14. The case has also been made that Eastern hospitals arose from monastic duties of care, A. T. Crislip, *Christian Monasticism and the Transformation of Health Care* (Ann Arbor, MI, 2005), but see Horden, 'Invention of the Hospital', 720–2.

[13] Its most well-formulated statement is Boshof, 'Armenfürsorge', 154–8. The versatility of *necator pauperum* can be seen in Imbert's work, which saw it first as the expression of Justinianic principles (*HDC* 40) and, later, as a Merovingian framework redeployed by the Carolingians, Imbert, 'Les conciles', 42.

[14] Schönfeld, 'Xenod.', 23, 38; *HDC* 40, 52–3; Stasolla, 'Proposito', 44; W. Ullmann, 'Public Welfare and Social Legislation', *Studies in Church History* 7 (1971), 10; Coing, 'History of Foundations'; Brodman, *CRME* 48. Cf. Boshof, 'Armenfürsorge', 161.

and *matriculae*, the diocesan church's institutions of poor relief.[15] It has looked to charters, letters, rules, and inventories, to uncover a pattern of activity by laity, monastic communities, and clerics.[16] The picture of hospital foundation that emerged has clear geographical contours, arriving from Byzantium in Rome in 397, and being centred in Francia during the fifth to seventh centuries, and Lombardy from the early eighth century. The houses are believed to have had a clear institutional-legal form, 'according to the Eastern model', as set out in Justinian's legislation,[17] although the Byzantine typology of charities cannot be found in the documentary evidence.[18] Because the decrees of Western councils are believed to have propounded this ineffectual Byzantine model, they have tended to be dismissed as 'useless', as 'not reflect[ing] reality', and so 'an uncertain guide to the realities of caritative practice'.[19]

From a legal perspective, both approaches struggle with the same challenge: how to characterize the relationship between East and West. The West is seen to have (poorly) adopted the form of the Byzantine hospital, but more certainly clung to its law—and between these two poles lies confusion. The question among legal historians has been whether hospitals had a legal personality, which they have answered with a resounding yes, because hospitals could hold and administer property.[20] A secondary question, asked of councils, has been how hard they worked to impose Byzantine law across the Frankish Empire.[21] Here, Walter

---

[15] Dey, '*Diaconiae*'; Boshof, 'Armenfürsorge'; Mollat, *Les pauvres*, 55–7; Ullmann, 'Public Welfare', 6–12. For *matriculae*, Rouche, 'Matricule'; Sternberg, *Orientalium more secutus*, 192–3; A. E. Jones, *Social Mobility in Late Antique Gaul* (Cambridge, 2009), 219–22, 226.

[16] Stasolla, 'Proposito'; Boshof, 'Armenfürsorge'; HDC 36–54; Schönfeld, 'Xenod.'; Siems, '*Piae causae*'.

[17] Sternberg, *Orientalium more secutus*, 190–2. The phrase appears in the seventh-century *Passion of Praejectus*, a bishop who 'took the trouble to build a *xenodochium* on his own property, following Eastern custom, in a place called Columbarius. He charged physicians and vigorous men with its care, requiring that twenty sick persons be always cared for there and receive allowances of food until they gain their strength, at which point their place should be given to heal another.' ('Xenodochium quoque in propriis rebus, orientalium more secutus, in loco qui Columbarius dicitur fabricare curavit. Medicos vel strenuos viros, qui hanc curam gererent, ordinavit, ita tamen, ut semper ibidem XX egroti mederentur, ut stipendia cibi acciperent, postquam vero convalescerent, aliis locum curandi darent.') *Passio Praeiecti episcopi et martyris Averni*, ed. B. Krusch, MGH SS rer. Merov. V (Hanover, 1905), 235. The account uses 'xenodochium', the generic Western term for welfare facilities, but the facility takes the form of a *nosocomium*, a medical facility for the sick found in the East. In establishing such a facility, Praejectus was following an Eastern tradition, and the *Passio* suggests that he was consciously doing so, aware that it was exotic.

[18] On typologies, Boshof, 'Armenfürsorge', 153–4; Stasolla, 'Proposito'.

[19] Quotations from HDC 10; Boshof, 'Armenfürsorge', 154; Brodman, CRME 50. Several later councils, notably Rome (853) and Quierzy (858), can be cited to suggest policies regarding hospital management.

[20] Early medievalists were responding to claims by Hans Liermann, among others, that hospitals in the West lacked legal personality. A preoccupation to prove the fact of legal personality has prevented more penetrating questions, of the substance, character, or continuities of personality in law (Siems, '*Piae causae*', 57–9, who asks how far Justinian's legislation for *piae causae* was adopted, and even developed, for xenodochia in the early medieval, and largely Merovingian West).

[21] Imbert, Rocca, Stasolla see them as passive reflections, Schönfeld, Mertzbacher, Caron, and Boshof as active agents, inculcating a programme in the West.

Ullmann's positivist picture has proven influential: in the very number of conciliar decrees he saw a policy by Frankish bishops to create hospitals and to promulgate a framework for their organization and support. It was a framework laid down by Justinian, cultivated at Aachen (816), given 'heightened protection' by classifying abusers as 'murderers of the poor', and finally demonstrated by Ansegis's 'collection of laws'.[22]

There is one other common theme: a sense that the early medieval story must be a Frankish story. If Carolingian councils acted, it was surely at the behest of Charlemagne or Louis the Pious, who have both been envisioned as reaching out to the East for dossiers of law, to furnish the West with a Byzantine model.[23] Lacking examples of Frankish legislation, a corpus has been fleshed out using conciliar injunctions that clerics be hospitable, and care for pilgrims and the poor. And it relies on the councils of Orléans (549) and Aachen (816).

Two Councils, Two Pursuits

The story of the early medieval West hinges on Orléans (549) and Aachen (816) because these were the *only* Frankish councils to address hospitals in any substantial fashion. They are exceptional and, as such, they offer extraordinary windows into two moments when Frankish councils, 250 years apart, did act regarding hospitals. For all these reasons, they deserve investigation now.

The Council of Orléans (549) and *Necatores Pauperum*

Summoned by King Childebert I, the council of Orléans in 549 was a huge affair, with fifty bishops and many other ecclesiastics, the largest council of its era.[24] It was the first Frankish council to mention xenodochia, issuing not one but two decrees. A first, brief decree (canon 13) protected the property and possessions of churches, monasteries, and xenodochia, banning violators from entering a church as 'murderers of the poor'.[25] It is the second, longer decree (canon 15) that has

---

[22] Ullmann, 'Public Welfare', 9–11. For its enduring influence, F.-O. Touati, 'La géographie hospitalière médiévale (Orient–Occident, IVe–XVIe siècles)', in *HMMA* 12.

[23] Touati, 'Géographie hospitalière', 10–11; Imbert, 'Les conciles', 44. Ullmann, 'Public Welfare', tells a different, but equally Frankish story.

[24] Halford, *Frankish Councils*, app. A. On Childebert's councils, Mordek, 'Fränkische Kapitularien', 8–10; O. Pontal, *Histoire des conciles mérovingiens* (Paris, 1989), 101–33.

[25] (c. 13) 'Ne cui liceat res uel facultates ecclesiis aut monasteriis uel exenodochiis pro quacumque elemosina cum iustitia deligatas retentare, alienare adque subtrahere. Quod quisque fecerit, tanquam necator pauperum antiquorum canonum sententiis constrictus ab ecclesiae liminibus excludatur, quamdiu ab ipso ea, quae sunt ablata uel retenta, reddantur.' CCSL 148A, p. 152.

attracted attention, although oddly, it has not been examined in depth. It deserves laying out here in full:

> Concerning the xenodochium specifically that the most pious king Childebert and his wife Queen Ultrogotha, with the Lord's inspiration, have established in the city of Lyons, the arrangements for whose institution (*ordo institutionis*) and the account of whose disbursements (*expensae rationem*) we have confirmed at the request of the same [king and queen] with a subscription below in our own hands, it has seemed good to us, joined together into one, to decree with an authority to be enduring by the contemplation of God:
>
> [i] that (*ut*)—whatever has been or will be bestowed on the aforesaid xenodochium, of any kind of thing or person, either through the gift of the abovesaid rulers or through alms of whomsoever of the faithful—the bishop (*antestis*) of the church of Lyons take for himself or transfer to the right of his church nothing from there at any time.
>
> [ii] that (*ut*) the priests who succeed one another with the passage of time, mindful of eternal retribution, do not merely diminish anything of the same xenodochium's inheritance or of its customary rights or legal arrangements, but endeavour that the permanence of the xenodochium itself suffer in no part any loss or diminution.
>
> [iii] that (*ut*) its superintendents (*praepositi*), ever active and God-fearing, be put in place by those who are departing and that the responsibility for the sick and the number and reception of pilgrims continue always with inviolable permanence in accordance with the arrangements (*institutio*) put in place.
>
> But if anyone (*si quis*) at any time, a person of whatever office or category, should attempt to act against this our decree (*constitutionem*), or remove anything from the customary rights or inheritance of the same xenodochium, so that the xenodochium (God forbid!) should cease to be, he should be struck with an irrevocable anathema as a murderer of the poor.[26]

[26] (c. 15) 'De exenodocio uero, quod piisimus rex Childeberthus uel iugalis sua Vulthrogotho regina in Lugdunensi urbe inspirante Domino condiderunt, cuius institutionis ordinem uel expensae rationem petentibus ipsis manuum nostrarum suscriptione firmauimus, uisum est pro Dei contemplacione iunctis nobis in unum permansura auctoritate decernere, [i] ut, quidquid praefato exenodocio aut per supra dictorum regum oblationem aut per quorumcumque fidelium elemosinam conlatum aut conferendum est in quibuscumque rebus adque corporibus, nihil exinde ad se quolibet tempore antestis ecclesiae Lugdunensis reuocet aut ad ius ecclesiae transferat, [ii] ut succedentes sibi per temporum ordinem sacerdotes non solum aut de facultate exenodocii ipsius aut de consuetudine uel institutione nil minuant, sed dent operam, qualiter rei ipsius stabilitas in nullam partem detrimentum aut deminutionem aliquam patiatur, providentes intuitu retributionis aeternae, [iii] ut praepositi semper strenui ac Deum timentes decedentibus instituantur et cura aegrotantium ac numerus uel exceptio peregrinorum secundum inditam institutionem inuiolabili semper stabilitate permaneat. Quod si quis quolibet tempore, cuiuslibet potestatis aut ordinis persona, contra hanc constitutionem nostram uenire timptauerit aut aliquid de consuetudine uel facultate exenodocii ipsius abstulerit, ut exenodotium, quod auertat Deus, esse desinat, ut necator pauperum inreuocabili anathemate feriatur.' CCSL 148A, p. 153.

In canon 15, the council confirms the royal foundation of a hospital in Lyons, its endowments, and the arrangements put in place for its administration,[27] and it reveals the scale of the foundation, which had its own priests and so, by implication, a chapel. The council added three commands, forbidding that the bishop remove any of its property, requiring its priests to preserve the arrangements and resources as had been set up, and giving directives concerning the appointment and duties of its superintendents. The act concludes with a threat of anathema upon any who act against the council's decree or endanger the house.

Orléans (549) has been seen as the moment when Frankish councils 'took up the question of hospitals', securing them under the bishop and as church property,[28] and the anathema of canon 15 (with its *necator pauperum*) the 'propagandistically very effective' means by which this was done.[29] Yet the canon does not bear out such interpretations. First, it did not act to secure hospitals under a bishop. Its first command [i], protected this xenodochium against the local bishop. That he might turn a greedy eye upon the facility implies that a bishop might make (or even have) a claim over the house; but this canon granted him—and recognized in him—no rights or responsibilities, it offered only an injunction *not* to despoil the house. At [iii] it even provided that the appointment of a new head of the xenodochium belonged to its outgoing superintendent, an act designed to protect the facility against external authorities including, given the context, the bishop. Secondly, it was aimed at one specific hospital, Childebert and Ultrogotha's foundation at Lyons. It staked no claim to include other houses, nor (as will be seen) did contemporaries interpret it in this way.

This was simply an act of royal foundation, singled out for special recognition. Such places are distinguished, Barbara Rosenwein argues, not by their form but by their location.[30] If so, we should seek the inspiration for its foundation, and thus the activity at the council, in the location of this particular house: Lyons. This puts the council, and its use by the king, in a different light. For in 534 Childebert had annexed part of the kingdom of Burgundy that included Lyons. It was a major ecclesiastical centre, whose bishop laid claim to the title, 'Primate of Gaul'.[31] In 549, the archbishop of Lyons was Sardo or Sacerdos (544–52), a royal counsellor who was also, it turns out, conducting Childebert's council at Orléans.[32] It is

---

[27] Sternberg, *Orientalium more secutus*, 203–7, on the hospital's site and its status as an ecclesiastical institution.

[28] Merzbacher, 'Das Spital', 79; Caron, '*pia fundatio*', 138; Schönfeld, 'Xenod.', 31, reflecting a wider consensus. But see now Siems, '*Piae causae*', 79, which sees in this decree an admission that a hospital's goods were not simply vulnerable but violable.

[29] The phrase is Boshof, 'Armenfürsorge', 157: 'Zweckbestimmung propagandistisch recht wirksam zum Schutz ihres ständig wachsenden Besitzes einsetzen ließ.'

[30] B. H. Rosenwein, *Negotiating Space* (New York, 1999), 51, 57–8; Rosenwein, 'Property Transfers', 568–9.

[31] B. K. Young, 'Autun and the Civitas Aeduorum', in T. S. Burns and J. W. Eadie, eds, *Urban Centers and Rural Contexts* (East Lansing, MI, 2001), 37.

[32] J. Gadille, Le diocèse de Lyon (Paris, 1983), 25–6.

unlikely, then, that the protections were directed at him. More likely, they were to guarantee the permanent independence of the royal xenodochium in the newly acquired city, a lavish gift to establish a public royal presence in the town.[33] The great national council of Orléans was the perfect political opportunity to proclaim its creation.

There is another problem with reading canon 15 as law for hospitals. What is copied there is a confirmation by the bishops of a new foundation. It is a public statement, and a decree of sorts, but its language and structure suggest a charter. After a few words of introduction in the council's record, the act seems to begin at 'quod piisimus rex', with the bishops issuing their confirmation 'at the request of the same [king and queen]', an act which they have attested 'in our own hands' at its base. The latter statement is incongruous in a conciliar canon but in keeping for a charter.[34] The anathema clause at the end was therefore no new tool of law, nor even an act of law, but an element of charter diplomatic: a *si quis* clause. These penalty clauses threatened sanctions, often in the form of a curse, against anyone who contravened the arrangements in the deed.[35] At Orléans the bishops gave weight to their curse by using a phrase that was already on their lips: *necator pauperum*, which the council also used in canons 13 and 16. Canon 15 seems to be a rare survival of a charter copied into the council acts.[36]

The wider argument that sixth-century councils devised law for hospitals through *necator pauperum* rests on Orléans's canon 15. If we look further afield, to other councils, it emerges that Orléans was not merely the first council to address hospitals in the West, it was the only Merovingian council to do so. How far, then, can *necator pauperum* offer a legal formula to define hospitals? A preceding canon (13) at Orléans not only used this phrase, but is the only canon in any church council to insert 'xenodochia' beside 'churches and monasteries' into church law on these latter. The actions at Orléans become all the more curious, as does its use of *necator pauperum*.

---

[33] F. Curta, 'Merovingian and Carolingian Gift Giving', *Speculum* 81 (2006), 698, sees aristocratic gift-giving as a kind of 'surrogate warfare…to overwhelm and thus to dominate'. Childebert's *xenodochium* was a very different kind of gift but perhaps, similarly, a manifestation of political strategy and lavish display.

[34] For the latter, H. Mordek, 'Karolingische Kapitularien', in Mordek, *Überlieferung und Geltung normativer Texte* (Sigmaringen, 1986), 30.

[35] For early sixth-century examples, *Die Urkunden der Merowinger*, ed. T. Kölzer et al., 2 vols (Hanover, 2001), I. 17, 25. For the *si quis* clause in later centuries, J. A. Bowman, 'Do Neo-Romans Curse?', *Viator* 28 (1997), 8–20. For anathema, C. Vogel, 'Les sanctions infligées aux laïcs et aux clercs', *Revue de droit canonique* 2 (1952); R. E. Reynolds, 'Rites of Separation and Reconciliation', in *Segni e riti nella Chiesa* (Spoleto, 1987); L. Little, *Benedictine Maledictions* (Ithaca, NY, 1993), 30–3.

[36] For the few examples, G. I. Halfond, *The Archaeology of Frankish Church Councils* (Leiden, 2010), 12. A later charter, a forgery, claimed that the council of bishops at Orléans in 511 had confirmed a royal gift to the monastery at St Hilaire at Poitiers, repeating its threat of anathema: 'Si quis … et huius sancti concilii auctoritate atque praesentium episcoporum omnium anathematis vinculo ligatum ac nostre maiestatis reum se sentiat.' (*Urkunden der Merowinger*, I. 28.)

The phrase 'murderers of the poor' was a popular one in Gallic and Merovingian councils. Its origins have been the source of some confusion, but can be identified in southern Gaul in the fifth century.[37] It first appears in an early variant, *necatores egentium* (murderers of the destitute), at the council of Vaison-la-Romaine, near Avignon, in 442, when it was used to castigate heirs who failed to hand over post-mortem bequests to churches, thereby defrauding the dead of their vow and the poor of sustenance.[38] Vaison's canon rested on Jerome's letter to Nepotian concerning the clerical life, which it quoted in its final line that 'it is theft to steal from a friend, sacrilege to defraud the church'.[39] The council's phrase *necator egentium* may have been inspired by this letter, which characterized the keeping of such gifts as 'the most manifest of crimes'. The council at Vaison deployed Jerome's language to defend bequests to churches, defining a crime by creating a name for its perpetrators, *necator egentium*. The phrase was part of a wider vocabulary developed at this time to defend gifts of property to the church, and perhaps to override a Roman legal tradition that protected the rights of heirs against alienation of their patrimony.[40] It was also a part of a wider response to the difficult question of why the church could own property and how it might justify in law episcopal claims to administer, secure, and hold property in perpetual tenure.[41]

---

[37] To Rosenwein it had a 'biblical feel', while Mollat ascribed it to St Ambrose (Rosenwein, *Negotiating Space*, 142 n., and 42–6 for its sixth-century uses; Mollat, *Les pauvres*, 34, 54); I can find evidence for neither. M. E. Moore, 'Christian Antiquity, Patristics and Frankish Canon Law', *Millennium: Jahrbuch* 7 (2010), 321, notices its first appearance at Vaison-la-Romaine.

[38] CCSL 148, pp. 97–8: (c. 4) 'Qui oblationes defunctorum fidelium detinent et ecclesiae tradere demorantur, ut infideles sunt ab ecclesia abiiciendi, quia usque ad exinanitionem fidei peruenire certum est hanc pietatis diuinae exacerbationem, qua et fideles de corpore recedentes uotorum suorum plenitudine et pauperes collatu alimoniae et necessaria sustentatione fraudantur. Tales enim quasi egentium necatores nec credentes iudicium Dei habendi sunt unius quoque patrum in hoc, quam scriptis suis inseruit, congruente sententia qua ait: *Amico quidpiam rapere furtum est, ecclesiam fraudare sacrilegium.*'

[39] 'Amico quippiam rapere furtum est, ecclesiam fraudare sacrilegium est. accepisse pauperibus erogandum et esurientibus plurimis vel cautum esse velle vel timidum aut, quod apertissimi sceleris est, aliquid inde subtrahere, omnium praedonum crudelitatem superat. ego fame torqueor et tu iudicas quantum ventri meo satis sit? aut divide statim quod acceperis aut, si timidus dispensator es, dimitte largitorem ut sua ipse distribuat.' Jerome, *Ad Nepotianum* (ep. 52), at c. 16 (2, 3), ed. A. Cain, *Jerome and the Monastic Clergy* (Leiden, 2013), 54–6, 262–3.

[40] E. Magnou-Nortier, 'The Enemies of the Peace: Reflections on a Vocabulary', in T. Head and R. Landes, eds, *The Peace of God* (Ithaca, NY, 1992), 58–9, whose study looks at the endurance of a rhetoric against *invasores, depraedatores, raptores, oppressores*, and its influence on the Peace of God movement. For measures to protect church property at the council of Orléans in 511, see Halford, *Frankish Councils*, 110–13.

[41] The right of the early church to retain property as a legal (and perpetual) person was articulated most influentially by the fifth-century Julianus Pomerius, who defined church property as 'the offerings of the faithful, the penitential payments of sinners, and the patrimony of the poor', administered by prelates on behalf of the poor (a category that included secular and regular clergy); D. Ganz, 'The Ideology of Sharing', in W. Davies and P. Fouracre, eds, *Property and Power in the Early Middle Ages* (Cambridge, 1995), 26. In the words of Julian: 'Non ut possessores, sed ut procuratores facultates ecclesiae possidebant. Et idcirco scientes nihil aliud esse res ecclesiae, nisi vota fidelium, pretia peccatorum, et patrimonia pauperum; non eas vindicaverunt in usos suos, ut proprias, sed ut commendatas pauperibus diviserunt.' *De vita contemplativa* 2.9 (*PL* 59, col. 454).

The phrase was also a striking inversion of a familiar injunction 'to love the poor', which called on bishops to be *amatores pauperum*.[42] Vaison's *necator egentium* was thus primed to catch the imagination of contemporaries.[43] It had the potential to be a powerful rhetorical weapon, if someone should choose to wield it. That someone was Caesarius of Arles, to whom we owe its wide dissemination, as well as its transformation into *necator pauperum*, a phrase first used at his council of Agde (506). Caesarius repurposed Vaison's decree, translating a simple (human) failure to act—that is, to hand over bequests—into an institutional context: addressing clerics and laity, and defining both the forms of gift (as offerings by kin, grants, and bequests from wills) and their recipients (churches and monasteries).[44] By substituting *pauperum* for *egentium* the council embraced a wider meaning for the 'poor', one that called to mind clerics and religious. What had been a crime of character at Vaison, depriving deceased donors and the hungry poor, became at Agde a failure to fulfil a legal obligation whose potential victims were institutions and whose transgressors now faced an institutional response, in exclusion from the church. Caesarius's concern was to protect church property and devise protections for monasteries, in particular.[45] After Agde, the phrase disappeared, only to be revived at Orléans (549). The threat of exclusion for *necatores pauperum* was then used often until 650, as it had been at Agde, to protect church property against a variety of malefactors. In fact, it was most frequently directed against churchmen, especially clerics or abbots who had allowed their own benefices to deteriorate.[46] But no other Merovingian council would use the term in relation to xenodochia.

The phrase *necator pauperum* had been rediscovered by the council of Orléans and was deliberately deployed by it. It occurs three times, in a group of canons

---

[42] On *amator pauperum*, Brown, *Poverty and Leadership*, ch. 1. Brown touches briefly on *necatores pauperum* as an innovation of sixth-century councils, in his 'From *Patriae Amator* to *Amator Pauperum*', in D. T. Rodgers et al., eds, *Cultures in Motion* (Princeton, 2014), 102.

[43] Vaison's canon appeared in redacted form in the *Statuta ecclesiae antiqua*, a late fifth-century confabulation of canons: (c. 86) '*Qui oblationes defunctorum* aut negant *ecclesiis* aut cum difficultate reddunt, tanquam *egentium necatores* excommunicentur' [author's italics mark the words in Vaison's decree]. The collection masqueraded under a false attribution to the fourth council of Carthage in 398, its canons 86–9 adapted from Vaison's canons 4, 3, 5, and 7. It was created by a reformer and cleric in southern Gaul, perhaps Gennade de Marseille, between 476 and 485: *Les Statuta ecclesiae antiqua*, ed. C. Munier (Paris, 1960), 94–5, with discussion of its origins at pp. 209–36.

[44] CCSL 148, p. 194: (c. 4) 'Clerici etiam uel saeculares, qui oblationes parentum aut donatas aut testamentis relictas retinere perstiterint, aut id quod ipsi donauerint ecclesiis uel monasteriis crediderint auferendum, sicut synodus sancta constituit, uelut necatores pauperum, quousque reddant, ab ecclesiis excludantur.' The decree's structure and use of excommunication suggests that it used the version in *Statuta ecclesiae antiqua*. For the council, and Caesarius's influence on its decrees, Klingshirn, *Caesarius of Arles*, 97–104.

[45] He was soon to make a plea to Pope Symmachus to permit the use of church goods to endow monasteries but was disappointed in his response; Klingshirn, *Caesarius of Arles*, 127–8.

[46] Rosenwein, *Negotiating Space*, 45–6; M. E. Moore, *A Sacred Kingdom* (Washington, DC, 2011), 321–3.

(13–17) concerning church property. These seem to constitute a corpus of material, crafted to serve an agenda. To take them one by one:

> Canon 13 retools the Agde canon, adding 'xenodochia' to its 'churches and
> monasteries' and changing its focus. For, where Agde addressed the removal
> (*auferre*) of parental or testamentary bequests, Orléans now addressed the
> retention, alienation, or removal (*retentare, alienare adque subtrahere*) of assets
> and inheritances (*res uel facultates*) from these institutions. 'Bound by the
> judgement of ancient canons', it includes the threat of excommunication as
> 'murderers of the poor'.[47] The revised decree now defends the property of
> institutions.
>
> Canon 14 commands that no bishop, cleric, or person of any station take
> possession of (*accipere*) the property of another church. Those who do are to
> be expelled from the communion of the altar and from the charity of all brothers
> and sons until what is taken is returned.
>
> Canon 15 follows on from the preceding, with its charter to protect the posses-
> sions and arrangements of the Lyons hospital.
>
> Canon 16 in familiar terms, if new language, forbids grantors or heirs from
> withdrawing any gifts made 'to priests, churches *or any kind of holy place*',[48]
> depriving them of communion as a murderer of the poor.
>
> Canon 17 outlines a process by which 'a bishop or administrator of the church'
> might be accused and complaints addressed.[49]

The canons' concerns are familiar. Canons 13, 14, and 16—aimed especially at
bishops, priests, and administrators—defended the property of ecclesiastical institutions from seizure or subtraction. Canon 17 established a system whereby
redress from the bishop and other administrators could be sought. Together,
they enforce or adapt existing protections for the property of churches and
monasteries and, in two cases, stretch the boundaries of that protection to include
xenodochia (canon 13) and, more generically, 'other kinds of holy places' (canon
16). The themes are those of the confirmation of Childebert and Ultrogotha's great
foundation in Lyons, which sits conceptually (and literally) at the centre of this
activity, as canon 15. Threading through this corpus is the threat of anathema as
'murderer of the poor' for those who seize property; it is part of a whole package of
law to protect Childebert's foundation.

Given the importance of this task and the creative effort it engendered, it is
interesting what the council did not do in law. It did not extend to xenodochia

---

[47] Adapting *Statuta ecclesiae antiqua*, c. 86 (above, n. 43).

[48] 'sacerdotibus aut eclesiis *aut quibuslibet locis sanctis*' (author's italics).

[49] 'si quaecumque persona contra episcopum uel actores aeclesiae'. The canons are CCSL 148A,
pp. 152–5.

well-established church laws for monasteries; those, for example, that prohibited churches or monasteries from returning to secular uses, or that placed them under the diocesan. In fact, it did little to specify the legal standing of xenodochia, or even directly address these houses. Xenodochia are conspicuously absent from most of these decrees, yet considerable effort was poured into creating implicit relationships. The group of canons bolstered the injunctions in the Lyons confirmation, whose threat of 'murderer of the poor' created a direct link. It did not add xenodochia to the canon 14, which protected a church's property from the bishop and other clerics; instead, the opening phrase of the Lyons act (*De exenodochio vero...*) linked the royal foundation to the preceding decree, as if it were a specific example of that canon. The king and queen (or their archbishop) were using the public authority of the council to protect their foundation, and the council responded with a sustained effort of legal creativity. They formulated a series of conciliar pronouncements around a central objective: to protect the assets of the royal xenodochium from the bishop and its own administrators. This was stressed in the confirmation (c. 15) and by its accompanying decrees. The only normative statement that it made for xenodochia, the only canon to which it added the term 'xenodochia', was canon 13, which forbade their possessions from being withdrawn.

The council of Orléans (549) offers an early window onto the politics behind the creation of a major welfare foundation, and one with a clear ecclesiastical component. Bishops feature prominently, both as the greatest potential threat to the house, in the form of future diocesans, and as its best protection, as prelates acting in chorus at the royal council, in service to royal plans. But it cannot be said that the council either in intention or consequence forged law for hospitals, nor that it placed xenodochia under episcopal jurisdiction. Its efforts were not an expression of the phenomena so often said to define hospitals in law, the *cura pauperum*: of episcopal patrimony, and the duty that bishops be hospitable and charitable to the poor. These elements were ideologically in conversation and they did inform the sense of duty, as well as the responses, of churchmen at this council—but they did not unite in law at this moment to define hospitals.

In focusing on these elements, it has been easy to miss what *did* concern Childebert's council, and how it used its authority. The Christian call to protect hospitals echoes through the council and is given voice for the Lyons xenodochium in the threat against 'murderers of the poor'. Yet the concern of the Lyons charter (c. 15) was to preserve two elements: the xenodochium's endowment, at (i) and (ii); and the arrangements for its administration, its *institutio* (ii), which included its management and the service owed to the sick and pilgrims (iii).[50]

---

[50] That 'cura aegrotantium ac numerus uel exceptio peregrinorum secundum inditam institutionem inuiolabili semper stabilitate permaneat' suggests that more detailed arrangements had been put in place (*institutio*) than are captured in the bishops' *consuetudo*.

Endowment and *institutio* were linked at the opening, when the council confirmed the founding arrangements (*institutionis ordo*) and disbursements (*expensae ratio*). These were to continue 'in inviolable steadfastness', no bishop or priest was to disrupt or diminish them, and the superintendent was charged to maintain them. The council's work emerges as an extraordinarily determined effort to capture and secure the arrangements laid down by the king and queen.[51]

The vivid condemnations of *necatores pauperum* served a specific purpose in 549. They were not indicative of wider work by sixth-century councils. The only general decree from Orléans regarding xenodochia, to protect their property, was never to be repeated. When the only other Merovingian council to mention xenodochia acted, a century later in *c.*650, it did so in terms now familiar, to protect the property of parish churches, xenodochia, and monasteries against incursions by the bishop or archdeacon.[52] The phrase 'murderers of the poor' did not reappear in relation to hospitals until the 840s, when Frankish bishops reached back to the early councils, in search of ancient and thunderous threats.[53] Only when churchmen were trying to wrestle property from royal hands was this 'propagandistically effective' malediction embraced once again.

The Aachen Rules for Canons and Canonesses (816)

Our second council was convened three centuries later, in 816, at the high-water mark of Carolingian rule. The council of Aachen (Aix-la-Chapelle) was summoned by Louis the Pious to regulate religious life in fulfilment of his father's

---

[51] The rarity of such conciliar confirmations for foundations and the elaborate treatment in the surrounding canons suggest a particularly determined use of the Orléans council. Cf. Halford, *Frankish Councils*, 12–13.

[52] At Chalon, 647×653: (c. 7) 'Vt defuncto presbytero uel abbate nihil ab episcopo auferatur uel archidiacono uel a quemcumque de rebus parrochiae, exinodotie uel monasterii aliquid debeat minuere. Quod qui fecerit, iuxta statuta canonum debeat cohercere.' (CCSL 148A, p. 304). This time it was at the death of a priest or abbot, and so a moment of institutional interregnum.

[53] For their efforts, see my Chapter 6. The Pseudo-Isidorians discovered the phrase, likely from the late eighth-century *Collectio Dacheriana*, which included the decrees from Vaison (442) and Agde (506) (ed. J.-L. D'Achery, *Spicilegium sive collectio veterum*, I (Paris, 1723), 539; CCEMA 87–92). In later years, the decrees from *Statuta ecclesiae antiqua*, Vaison (442), and Agde (506) were included together in Gratian's *Decretum*, C.13 q.2 c.9–11. Before this moment, I can find the phrase *necator pauperum* for hospitals only in the will of 616 of Bertrand, bishop of Le Mans, in establishing a *matricula et sinodotii* at Pontlieue, a suburb of Le Mans. He entrusted this to a nearby abbot's care, concluding his instructions with a threat: 'Quod si in aliquo...et si de praedicta locella quicumque aliquid retraxerit, tanquam necatur pauperum, ante conspectu divino judicetur.' (*Das Testament des Bischofs Berthramn*, ed. M. Weidemann (Mainz, 1986), 26; on the will, Wood, 'Disputes', 13–14). The will contains many grants to religious foundations, but this is its only use of *necator pauperum*. Le Mans has been identified as a centre of forgery, with Pseudo-Isidorian links (W. Goffart, *The Le Mans Forgeries* (Cambridge, MA, 1966), which notes the significance of Bertrand and his testament to the forgers, pp. 174–7, 196–8, 263–4). The will is recognized as authentic although, in this context, its use of *necator pauperum* is suspicious. It may be another modification by the copier, as Goffart suggests the addition of the term 'episcopus' might be (*Forgeries*, 196).

intentions (Charlemagne had died in 814). The council did not issue decrees regarding hospitals. Instead, over a series of meetings until 819, the council confirmed the Benedictine Rule for monks and nuns, and promulgated a new rule each for canons and canonesses, to unite each under a common way of life.[54] The authorship of the new rules is a matter of some disagreement, and there is little evidence, but they were revised between sessions of the council, making use of the imperial library.[55] The rule for canons, the *Institutio canonicorum* (hereafter *IC*), has 145 prescriptions, the first (and longer) portion of these drawn from patristic writings and containing canonical quotations, largely from the *Dionysio Hadriana*, a collection of church laws solicited by Charlemagne from the pope.[56] At chapter 114 this gives way to the *Regula canonicorum*, provisions for community life, which has often been compared to an earlier rule for canons, written c.755 by Archbishop Chrodegang for his cathedral clergy at Metz.[57] The Aachen rule laid out the duties—corporate, moral, and liturgical—required of the canons, as well as the buildings to support their corporate life, such as cloister, dormitory, and refectory.

One of its last chapters (141) was titled 'To whom the stipends of the poor must be committed'.[58] This required the dignitaries (*praelati*) of a major church to build

---

[54] For simplicity and clarity, I use the term 'canonesses' here. The rule itself, *Institutio sanctimonialium*, did not use the term, even though it has been credited with establishing it (e.g. J. Ziegler, 'Secular Canonesses', 121, 123). It spoke instead of *sanctimoniales canonice degentes* ('consecrated women living canonically') under an *abbatissa*, laying out *qualiter eisdem sanctimonialibus infra claustra monasterii vivendum* (MGH *Conc.* II.i, 313). The term can be found in a chapter title of Charlemagne's 802 council, *Ut abbatissae canonicae et sanctimoniales canonice secundum canones vivant*, and the council of Chalon (813), whose directions were preparations for *IS*, as *sanctimoniales...quae se canonicas vocant* (MGH *Cap.* I. 103 (c. 34); *Conc.* II.i, 284 (c.53)). An early manuscript does offer *IS* under the title *Incipit regula et modus vivendi sanctimonialium que vocatur canonicae* (Munich, BSB, CLM 14431, fol. 7v; MGH *Conc.* II.i, 422 n.).

[55] Recent work suggests authorship by committee, J. Barrow, *The Clergy in the Medieval World* (Cambridge, 2015), 82; J. Bertram, *The Chrodegang Rules* (Aldershot, 2005), 93–4. The prologue states that the emperor directed the assembly to create a new form of life and gave them access to his collection of sacred texts to do so (MGH, *Conc.* II.i, 312–13). For the council, Hartmann, *Synoden*, 156–60.

[56] R. Kramer, *Rethinking Authority* (Amsterdam, 2019), 93–121, considers the authorities drawn upon, in the form of *florilegia*, and their significance to the rule's episcopal authors.

[57] For the two rules and the development of canonical life, Bertram, *Chrodegang Rules*, 84–9; Barrow, *Clergy*, 75–85; B. Langefeld, *The Old English Version of the Enlarged Rule of Chrodegang* (Frankfurt, 2004), 8–15. As with other studies of the *IC*, these mention neither hospitals nor chapter 141. The hospital chapter in the women's rule has never been examined, to my knowledge.

[58] 'CUI COMMITTI DEBEANT STIPENDIA PAUPERUM. [i. ARENGA/RATIONALE FOR ACTION] Evangelicis atque apostolicis instruimur documentis in colligendis hospitibus ante omnia operam dare debere, ut merito de nobis a Domino dicatur: *Hospes fui, et collegistis me* [Matt. 25: 35], et caetera. [ii. PROVISION] Proinde oportet, ut praelati ecclesiae praecedentium patrum exempla sectantes aliquod praeparent receptaculum, ubi pauperes colligantur et de rebus ecclesiae tantum ibidem deputent, unde sumptus necessarios iuxta possibilitatem rerum habere valeant, exceptis decimis, quae de ecclesiae villis ibidem conferuntur. Sed et canonici tam de frugibus quam etiam de omnibus elemosinarum oblationibus in usus pauperum decimas libentissime ad ipsum conferant hospitale. [iii. MANAGEMENT & SUPERVISION] Et boni testimonii frater constituatur, qui hospites et peregrinos adventantes utpote Christum in membris suis suscipiat eisque necessaria libenter pro viribus administret, qui etiam ea, quae in usus pauperum cedere debent, nequaquam in suos usus reflectat, ne cum

a hostel (*receptaculum*) 'where paupers should be gathered' and to provide for their needs, as far as possible, from the church's possessions.[59] The canons were also exhorted as individuals to give willingly to that same hospital (*ad ipsum hospitale*), a tenth of any income from harvests and from offerings they received. This *hospitale pauperum* was to be administered by a trustworthy canon, who must receive travellers and pilgrims as if they were Christ himself, guard the goods for the poor, and never seize them for his own purposes.[60] The canons were to serve there regularly, at the very least washing the feet of the poor each Lent;[61] so that they could do this, the hospital was to be conveniently sited near their church. Finally, should the canon-administrator fail in his charge, he should be removed and judged most severely by his superiors.

This moment has so often been portrayed as a turning-point in hospital law, but to do so, proponents must paint as a conciliar canon what was, in fact, a chapter of a religious rule. Although of average length for a chapter in this rule, chapter 141 is far longer than the contemporary decrees that we will meet in the following chapters, making it one of the most vivid Carolingian statements on the administration and use of hospitals (and the reason why it has so often been cited). The rule itself was influential: it survives in over one hundred Frankish manuscripts and it was actively used to reform cathedral chapters from the early ninth century and with renewed zeal in the eleventh century.[62] When the rule was

---

Iuda loculos Domini furante [John 12: 6] sententiam damnationis excipiat. Sed et praeletorum debet vigilare industria, ne eum, cui hospitale pauperum committitur, res pauperibus deputatas in aliquo minuere aut his quasi beneficiario munere concessis sinant uti, quod a praelatis quibusdam curam pauperum parvipendentibus fieri comperimus. [iv. CANONS' MINISTRATIONS] Clerici namque, si aliis temporibus nequeunt, saltim quadragesimae tempore pedes pauperum in competenti lavent hospitali iuxta illud evangelicum: *Si ego Dominus et magister lavi vobis pedes, quanto magis vos debetis alter alterius lavare pedes* [John 13: 14], et caetera. Quapropter expedit, ut in competenti loco hospitale sit pauperum, ubi perfacilis ad illud veniendi conventus fieri possit fratrum. [v. PUNISHING ABUSE] Quodsi is, cui hospitale commissum est, curam pauperum neglexerit eorumque res in suos usus retorserit, quamquam divina ultione dignus sit, severius tamen quam caeteri delinquentes a praepositis iudicandus et a ministerio removendus est, nec inmerito, quippe qui et pretia peccatorum et alimenta pauperum et thesaurum caelo recondendum suis, quod fas non fuit, aptavit usibus.' MGH *Conc.* II.i, 416–17, tr. Bertram, *Chrodegang Rules*, 166–7. The editorial insertions are my own. The title appears in early manuscripts, such as Cologny, Fondation Martin Bodmer, Cod. Bodmer 68, fol. 148v.

[59] Barrow, *Clergy in the Medieval World*, 83, discusses terms for the *praelati*. The hostel and hospital appear to be the same place in the rule for canons. They are different sites in the rule for canonesses.
[60] Its imagery was inspired by the Rule of St Benedict (c. 53, On receiving guests), but not its provisions. The Benedictine rule required that a guesthouse (*cella hospitum*) be administered under a God-fearing brother and set out the procedure for receiving guests. Its themes were obedience, humility, and ritual; it made no mention of the administration of resources.
[61] The term used is *clerici*, but it is clear from the use of *clerici* elsewhere that it refers to the canons. For the interchangeability of *clerici* and *canonici*, G. Constable, 'Monks and Canons in Carolingian Gaul', in A. C. Murray, ed., *After Rome's Fall* (Toronto, 1998), 328. The version in Mansi adds: 'Et boni testimonii *de ipsa congregatione* frater constituatur' (Mansi XIV. 242; Bertram, *Chrodegang Rules*, 124).
[62] For the rule, J. Barrow, 'Review Article: Chrodegang, his Rule and its Successors', *EME* 14.2 (2006), 203–4; Barrow, *Clergy*, 83–5. A revised eleventh-century rule for canons, integrating elements from the Aachen rule into Chrodegang of Metz's *Regula canonicorum*, included the hospital chapter (Bertram, *Chrodegang Rules*, 206, c. 45).

created, an imperial letter gave bishops one year to enact it locally before envoys (*missi*) would be dispatched to confirm that they had done so and that the necessary buildings and resources had been arranged, specifying, in particular, that 'houses be equipped as hostels (*receptacula*) for the poor'.[63] In its wake, many hospitals were established in Germany, France, and the Low Countries by or for cathedral chapters.[64] Because they were attached to such stable communities, many survived the dislocations of the coming centuries, making the Aachen rule perhaps the most significant—and certainly the most enduring—initiative to create and maintain hospitals. But does this make it a turning point in hospital law?

Examination of the text suggests that the drafters at Aachen took a particular interest in hospitals as a symbol of community. Chapter 141 appears to be their creation and has no known textual antecedents. The equivalent chapter in Chrodegang's rule was directed to *matricularii*, the registered poor who received pensions from the cathedral and other churches while living in various places (*in loca sua*), including what was clearly an almshouse. It made no mention of their material support, or the administration of resources; instead, it focused on these pensioners and their obligation to gather regularly at the cathedral for confession, preaching, and morning offices.[65] The Aachen rule laid out a very different system of poor relief. Alms were not to be directed to individuals but to the *hospitale pauperum*, a corporate facility to aid nameless poor. To the Aachen drafters, devising a common life for clerics, hospitals provided a means by which clerical alms could be communally and openly dispensed. Their interest was not in hospitals as institutions, but in systematizing clerical almsgiving. Chapter 141 was reinventing the *cura pauperum* for a community, as a communal facility that each canon helped to maintain, and where he was to serve the poor publicly, at least ritually through the maundy.

In both the rule for canons and the rule for canonesses, the hospital chapter was conceived in terms of the greater religious community. In the *IC* it is placed among the chapters (cc. 138–44) on the offices or custodial duties to which canons were to be appointed. Coming after a prelate, prior, and cellarer, it established an administrator without name but with a clear portfolio, to keep and dispense to the poor the alms of the church and its canons. In its very structure, the chapter established how the canons as a community should undertake: [i] the biblical

---

[63] 'quoniam … perquirere iubebimus … quis in claustris canonicorum et ceteris habitationibus construendis et in necessariis stipendiis eis tribuendis et in domibus ad receptacula pauperum praeparandis sanctioni nostrae paruerit', MGH *Conc.*, II.i, 460. On the circulation of the rule, F. L. Ganshof, *Recherches sur les capitulaires* (1958), 63.

[64] Bonenfant, *Hôpitaux et beinfaisance*, 11–12; Montaubin, 'Hôpitaux cathédraux', 17–19.

[65] Bertram, *Chrodegang Rules*, 49–50, c. 34: '*DE MATRICULARIIS UT LECTIONEM DIVINAM AUDIANT, VENIANT IN STATUTA ECCLESIA IN DOMO*'. On its significance as the final chapter of Chrodegang's rule, as 'a marvellous turning outward from the cathedral Chapter to the wider world of the *civitas* of Metz', see M. A. Claussen, *The Reform of the Frankish Church* (Cambridge, 2004), 111.

imperative to welcome strangers; [ii] a system of material support for the poor; [iii] its administration by an accountable canon; [iv] a duty to wash the feet of the poor and [v] to punish a miscreant administrator. The officers of the church were not to allow the hospital's resources to be diminished or concede it as a benefice as 'we know has been done by certain prelates'.[66] This was a managerial decree, aimed at the officers.

The equivalent chapter in the rule for canonesses, *Institutio sanctimonialium* (*IS*), was conceived in wholly different terms. This was not an office for one of the canonesses. Instead, it appears as the final chapter of the rule, entitled 'That a hospital for the poor should be outside the women's monastery'.[67] The opening stated simply that hospitality was an obligation, giving a theological definition of church property, from Julianus Pomerius, as the offerings from the faithful, the penitential payments of sinners, and the patrimony of the poor.[68] The personal act of welcoming that was so central to the *IC* and the Benedictine rule (and from Matt. 25, 'I was a stranger and you welcomed me') has disappeared, to be replaced by a duty in concept if not in practice. This distance between the canonesses and the hospital's work was reinforced in the rest of the chapter. The *hospitale pauperum* was to be outside the monastery gate, beside the church where the priest and his ministers officiated, and it was to be administered by a trustworthy

---

[66] On the granting of estates as *beneficia*, P. Fouracre, *The Age of Charles Martel* (London, 2000), 139–43; Fouracre, 'The Use of the Term *Beneficium*', in W. Davies and P. Fouracre, eds, *The Languages of Gift* (Cambridge, 2010), 70–4; also, Halfond, *Frankish Church Councils*, 121–6; Wood, *Prop. Ch.*, 247–51, 270–1; G. Constable, 'Nona et decima: An Aspect of Carolingian Economy', *Speculum* 35 (1960). A vivid picture of the uses (and dissipation) of *beneficia* by military followers of bishops and abbots is painted in C. West, 'Lordship in Ninth-Century Francia', *Past and Present* 226:1 (2005), 12–13, 19–20.

[67] (c. 38) 'UT HOSPITALE PAUPERUM EXTRA MONASTERIUM PUELLARUM. [i. ARENGA] Quia sanctarum scripturarum auctoritatibus liquido demonstratur, quod *hospitalitas* modis omnibus sit diligenda, et res ecclesiae oblationes sint fidelium, praetia peccatorum, patrimonia pauperum: [ii. LOCATION AND MANAGEMENT OF *HOSPITALE*] quamquam ad portam monasterii locus talis sit rite habendus, in quo *adventantes* quique *suscipi*antur, oportet tamen, ut extra, iuxta ecclesiam scilicet, in qua presbiteri cum ministris suis divinum explent officium, sit *hospitale pauperum*, cui etiam praesit talis, qui et avaritiam oderit et hospitalitatem diligat. [iii. PROVISION] Et *exceptis decimis, quae de ecclesiae villis ibidem conferuntur, de rebus ecclesiae*, prout facultas subpetit, eidem *deput*etur hospitali, *unde* pauperes ibidem recreentur et foveantur. *Sed et de oblationibus*, quae a fidelibus sanctimonialibus deferuntur, decimae dentur ad eorundem sustentationem pauperum. [iv. CUSTODIAN] Is namque, cui hospitale committitur, nequaquam res *pauperum* in suos usus retorqueat, *ne cum Iuda loculos Domini furante sententiam damnationis excipiat.* [v. LOCATION, USE AND FOOT-WASHING AT *RECEPTACULUM*] Sit etiam intra monasterium *receptaculum, ubi* viduae et pauperculae tantummodo recipiantur et alantur, et si non possint alio, *saltim quadragesimae tempore* sancti Domini adimplentes praeceptum earum *lavent pedes iuxta illud: Si ego Dominus et magister vester lavi vobis pedes, quanto magis vos debetis alter alterius lavare pedes.*' MGH *Conc.* II.i, 455–6. Author's italics mark the language found in *IC*.

[68] From his *De vita contemplativa* 2.9 (*PL* 59, col. 454), for which see n. 41 of this chapter. Pomerius appears in the *IC* as *Prosperus*, in discussions of property and stipends, and his three-fold definition of church property opens its chapter 116: 'QUID SINT RES ECCLESIAE' (MGH *Conc.* II.i, 398, 400, 402). J. Timmermann, 'Julianus Pomerius's Carolingian Audience', *Comitatus* 45 (2014), explores his misidentification as Prosper of Aquitaine and its role in the *IC*, pp. 1–2, 28–30; J. Devisse, 'L'influence de Julien Pomère', *Revue d'histoire de l'Église de France* 56:157 (1970), notices the *IC* on p. 293 as 'le seul moment où la pensée globale de Pomère ait réellement influencé le clergé carolingien'.

THE QUESTION OF FRANCIA 77

male agent. There was to be a second facility inside the monastic compound, a hostel (*receptaculum*) to harbour and feed widows and poor girls. It was here that the canonesses were to perform the maundy, in accordance with biblical injunction. The two-facility design speaks to the fears of the (male) Aachen drafters about female communities. The *hospitale pauperum*, run by a male agent, kept strangers and men outside an enclosure, where the canonesses were to dwell, while the *receptaculum* preserved the moral reputation of all resident women, including the widows and the girls being educated by the community, by keeping them inside.[69] Meanwhile the canonesses could practice foot-washing—a ritual whose practice had once been challenged for nuns, because of its clerical associations and its intimacy[70]—on this group of approved women and away from public view. The design was to preserve the integrity of the women's enclosure. This was the statement that Lateran II echoed, when it commanded so-called nuns to leave the *receptaculum*, submit to a rule and cloistration, and spend their time in church.[71]

At the core of the *IC* was the preservation and correct administration of payments (*stipendia*) to the poor. While this was also a concern in *IS*, it remained secondary to the desire to prevent contact with men. Both rules defined ritual encounters between members of the community and paupers through foot-washing. The timing of this ('at least during Lent') made clear that it was a ceremonial linking of convent and hospital.[72] Lastly, the two facilities in the women's rule (hospital and hostel) help to make sense of the *IC*, where the canons were instructed to build a *receptaculum*, to which 'same hospital' they were to contribute income. The confusing change of terms may be a deliberate attempt to link the arrangements for men with those for the women. The desire to cloister the women produced a markedly different institutional arrangement in the *IS* and the effort to accommodate this difference reveals a great deal about the nature and role of hospitals, in the eyes of the rule-makers. For behind their differences, both arrangements were designed to achieve the same two goals: to dedicate funds to corporate facilities for the support of pilgrims and paupers, and to foster a ritual connection between the community and paupers through foot-washing.[73]

The drafters at Aachen built hospitals inventively into their rules. As the emperor's letter makes clear, *receptacula* were public markers that a community

---

[69] Nuns were not permitted to school boys, S. F. Wemple, *Women in Frankish Society* (Philadelphia, 1981), 167–9. There may be an echo of *matriculae* here, which had at times also been within cloisters and where widows were often pensioned; Rouche, 'Matricule', 90, 92, who argues that *matriculae* were absorbed into *xenodochia* during the seventh century (101–2, 104).

[70] The concerns were dismissed in 751 by Pope Zacharius; Wemple, *Women in Frankish Society*, 166, 291.

[71] See p. 53–4.

[72] The Benedictine rule (c. 53) required daily foot-washing to honour guests.

[73] Kramer, *Rethinking Authority*, 104, suggests that 'social cohesion' was a central preoccupation of the *IC*.

had embraced the imperial vision of a *vita communis*. Yet to consider this a 'hospital reform' might be going too far.[74] The two chapters were not crafted as legislation with a public reach, and they did not act (or seek to act) on the many xenodochia that dotted roads, towns, and mountain passes. They addressed a small, if important, group of clerics and religious women. The priority of the *IC* and *IS*, and so of their hospital chapters, was to establish well-ordered communities in a common life, where property could be held individually but charity dispensed corporately and a clear moral, ritual, and administrative order imposed. They sought not to reform hospitals but to *deploy* them. And, in so doing, they reveal two important ideas. First, to the drafters of the rules, how readily these versatile facilities could be reimagined to serve a wider vision, in this case an imperial reform of religious life. Second, the significance of hospitals as a symbol of community that was visible to all, as a publicly recognized ideal and agent of Christian service, and a marker of moral and political order.

The councils of Orléans (549) and Aachen (816) laid out the most detailed visions of hospitals to survive from the early middle ages, and especially as to their systems of administration. They preserve two moments when xenodochia became objects of a public conversation, and secular and ecclesiastical leaders agreed a course of action. At these two moments, 250 years apart, Frankish activity heaves into view. They reveal two very different uses of welfare, although in both these are royal visions: one, grand and highly political, in which charity was both an expression of Christian piety and a marker of rule; the other, one of many means by which to effect a common life, and particularly to make manifest, in the town and open to all-comers, a new religious order and imperial vision. The two reveal the potential scale and significance of institutional welfare. The importance of their public statements suggest that welfare foundations were widely familiar, their Christian meaning clear. At the same time, their wholly different visions reveal how readily welfare could be reimagined and accommodated to different uses.

As instances of 'law', these two texts are significant in three ways. First, that neither acted on xenodochia as a category of institution; neither can be said to lay down law that defined hospitals. Yet, second, that they nevertheless reflect similar ideas of form, centuries apart: one that focuses on endowment or income, on defining systems for the administration of that income, and for safeguarding that administration. Taking a wider view, gender also emerges as a recurrent theme, with prelates keen to separate women from the act (if not the ideal) of charity, while celebrating and even requiring personal contact for men. Third, that the

---

[74] '[l]'application de la réforme hospitalière de 816', Montaubin's, 'Hôpitaux cathédraux', 19, which offers the most compelling picture for its implications in cathedral communities, across the province of Reims. Also, De Spiegeler, *Liège*, 37; HDC 40.

language and terms of each directive was different; even the obligations imposed varied, although each had been specifically laid out.

Orléans (549) and Aachen (816) were the only two Frankish assemblies to engage with the question of welfare houses in late antique Gaul, Merovingian Francia, and through the reigns of Charlemagne and Louis the Pious. It was not until 845/6 that a northern French council would direct its concern towards hospitals. Yet elsewhere in the Carolingian empire, a movement to address hospitals was taking shape, slowly in the decades after 780. Several generations later, this would inspire papal policy and, eventually, Frankish bishops into action. We turn now to Lombardy to see how this movement arose and what it reveals about the character of welfare houses, and their place in law.

4

Carolingian Lombardy (780–860)

It was in Lombardy, in the 780s, that assemblies began to address xenodochia. Over the next eighty years, until *c*.860, emerge records of deliberations regarding the preservation and, eventually, management of these facilities. This Lombard tradition ran in parallel to the Frankish activity of the previous and following chapters, although both reflect a burst of imaginative activity *c*.813–825, and an intensification of episcopal interest mid-century. The North Italian councils have left over thirty resolutions on xenodochia, a level of activity never to be repeated in the middle ages. Together, they form a unique dossier of governmental statements—royal, episcopal, and even papal—concerning these houses. Remarkably, this corpus has never been identified and so its councils never examined for what they might reveal about Carolingian approaches to welfare houses.[1] (Assuming that the legal model for hospitals was Justinianic, historians have not searched for a model in Western law.) The present chapter sets aside the East to investigate xenodochia as they are reflected in these texts. It reveals a conversation forged in Lombardy and Italian in character, but fundamentally Carolingian. For the precipitating act was Charlemagne's conquest of Pavia in 774, when Lombardy was brought under Carolingian rule.

The statements may have appeared in Lombardy but they were the fruit of Carolingian initiatives that had brought to Italy a new kind of council, and a new kind of record. The Carolingian pursuit of Christian imperial government iden-tified empire and church closely, one with the other.[2] Theirs was a shared vision, and an ambitious one: at its height, the Frankish palace sought not merely a comprehensive *emendatio* of religious life, but a unified ordering of the morals, customs, and institutions of the church. Although there remained differences between the activities of ecclesiastical synods and royal assemblies, too firm a distinction should not be drawn.[3] Either might address secular business as well as

---

[1] Several late Italian councils have been noticed, as illustrations of wider Frankish activity and a Justinianic model: *HDC* 44–5; Imbert, 'Les conciles', 44–7; Schönfeld, 'Xenod.', 23–30. Boshof, 'Armenfürsorge', 161–3, offers a brief survey that is sensitive to regional variation.

[2] For recent work in English: McKitterick, *Frankish Church*, 1–64; De Jong, 'Charlemagne's Church', and De Jong, 'The State of the Church', in W. Pohl and V. Wieser, eds, *Der frühmittelalterliche Staat* (Vienna, 2009); J. L. Nelson, 'The Voice of Charlemagne', in R. Gameson and H. Leyser, eds, *Belief and Culture* (Oxford, 2001); J. L. Nelson, 'Legislation and Consensus', in P. Wormald, ed., *Ideal and Reality* (Oxford, 1983); Kramer, *Rethinking Authority*, 37–40.

[3] 'Staatliche und kirchliche Gesetzgebund sind bei den Franken von Beginn an untrennbar mitei-nander verbunden': Mordek, 'Karolingische Kapitularien', 29. Assemblies are the focus of renewed interest: L. Roach, *Kingship and Consent in Anglo-Saxon England* (Cambridge, 2013), esp. 5–24;

On Hospitals: Welfare, Law, and Christianity in Western Europe, 400–1320. Sethina Watson, Oxford University Press (2020). © Sethina Watson. DOI: 10.1093/oso/9780198847533.001.0001

the duties of bishops, priests, and monks; both drew from secular and church law, and even patristic authors.[4] Gatherings drew from a small corps of Carolingian elite, who had common concerns and shared ideals, while decrees picked up, echoed, or reinforced those of other synods or assemblies and called upon the same local authorities, ecclesiastical and secular, to act.[5] Royal assemblies were opportunities to teach and exhort as much as to induce, and the voice that rang the loudest was the emperor's.[6]

If assemblies were central to the theory and practice of Christian order under the Carolingians, so too were there written products, capitularies.[7] Issued by Frankish rulers, they derive their name, *capitularium*, from the fact that they are subdivided into chapters or topics (*capitula*). They transmit the decisions of assemblies and synods, in so far as these met with royal or imperial approval, sometimes as directives to royal legates (*missi*). The period was far from uniform. Capitularies proliferated in the latter years of Charlemagne's life (that is, between 802 and 814); under his son, Louis the Pious, imperial direction soon gave way to episcopal initiative.[8] By the mid-ninth century, with empire under strain, conciliar activity continued, but the number of records began to wane.

Capitularies have undergone considerable reappraisal since Ullmann read their statements on welfare so literally, as evidence of a programme of social change, conceived and enacted by churchmen.[9] Capitularies are no longer understood as straightforward records of legislation, as decrees that were formulated and then

---

C. Wickham, 'Consensus and Assemblies', in V. Epp and C. H. F. Meyer, eds, *Recht und Konsens im frühen Mittelalter* (Ostfildern, 2017), where pp. 401–15 address Francia and Italy. Halfond, *Frankish Church Councils*, sketches continuities between Merovingian and Carolingian practice.

[4] CCSL 148A, pp. 331–6; McKitterick, *Frankish Church*, 13–14; Halfond, *Frankish Church Councils*, 87–8.

[5] J. L. Nelson, 'The Intellectual in Politics', in L. Smith and B. Ward, eds, *Intellectual Life* (London, 1992); R. McKitterick, 'Charlemagne's *missi*', in S. Baxter et al., eds, *Early Medieval Studies* (Farnham, 2009), 257–9.

[6] J. L. Nelson, 'Charlemagne and the Bishops', in *Relig. Franks*.

[7] Mordek, 'Karolingische Kapitularien', esp. 49: 'Die Kapitularien: sie bedeuten ja den sehr ernst zu nehmenden Versuch der fränkischen Herrscher, ein heterogenes Großreich regierbar zu machen, es verwaltungsmäßig zu durchdringen, die Mächtigen und Großen zurückzubinden an die zentrale Gewalt, das Volk zu formen zu einer an den sittlichen Maßstäben des Christentums ausgerichteten Gemeinschaft.' On their Carolingian character, Ganshof, *Recherches sur les capitulaires*, 2–7, 74–89, 103–5.

[8] Nelson, 'The Voice of Charlemagne', 77–9; Nelson, 'The Last Years of Louis the Pious', in *Ch. Heir*. The turning-point has been placed in 813, with bishops seizing the initiative from the palace in the creation of legislation, but also in 829 as the climax, and end, of government driven by a 'unified and comprehensive reform' (McKitterick, *Frankish Church*, 12; G. Schmitz, 'The Capitulary Legislation of Louis the Pious', in *Ch. Heir*, 436).

[9] Ullmann, 'Public Welfare'. For critiques of his positivist approach, F. J. Felten, 'Konzilsakten als Quellen für die Gesellschaftsgeschichte', in *Proc. of the Ninth Int'l Congress of Medieval Canon Law* (Vatican City, 1997), 346–7; Nelson, 'Legislation and Consensus'.

obeyed.[10] They are highly varied in form and intent, shaped as much by the scribes and compilers who fashioned or recomposed collections, as by the agendas of the assemblies themselves.[11] Some were less the record of an assembly than material to aid communication between the palace and local agents, or to propose new initiatives. Recent work has tended to stress their discursive and rhetorical qualities: that capitula were not simply the product of deliberations but the articulation, orally and in writing, of a shared conviction in the emperor's voice.[12] Capitula could be dispositive (resolving an individual dispute) as well as normative (to create standards), yet they should be read as exhortations or administrative or moral lessons as often as legal in character.[13] This multiplicity of form has left its mark on the statements regarding xenodochia, yet what stands out across this diversity is a stubborn consistency in the scope and aim of these statements.

The capitula on xenodochia are distinctive, even as a product of these bigger Carolingian agendas. So many perennial topics of law relating to the church saw intensified regulation under the Carolingians, from bishops to churches, clerical hospitality and tithes to monks and nuns. Even the most innovative of these statements rested on canonical authority. This authority had a fluid quality: with no official compendium of law at this time, canonists sought out biblical, conciliar, and patristic sources to recover models that were believed to have been lost.[14] So when councils spoke of priests or monasteries they acted within—indeed, sought to identify and promulgate—a canonical inheritance. This was not the case for xenodochia, for which there was no patristic or conciliar tradition. There were no inherited ways of thinking canonically about welfare houses, and no clerical frameworks.

As a topic in law, xenodochia were brought in and then snatched away on the tide of Carolingian activity, arriving—without language or an explicit definition—

---

[10] McKitterick, 'Charlemagne's *missi*', offers an introduction and bibliography. See, too, P. Wormald, *The Making of English Law*, I (Oxford, 1999), 49–70; F. L. Ganshof, *Recherches sur les capitulaires* (1958).

[11] C. Pössel, 'Authors and Recipients of Carolingian Capitularies', in R. Corradini et al., eds, *Texts and Identities* (Vienna, 2006), 253–9; S. Patzold, 'Capitularies in the Ottonian Realm', *EME* 27:1 (2019); Mordek, 'Karolingische Kapitularien', and Mordek, 'Fränkische Kapitularien'; De Jong, 'Charlemagne's Church', 107–11; Nelson, 'Intellectual in Politics'.

[12] M. Costambeys et al., *The Carolingian World* (Cambridge, 2011), 182–92. Kramer, *Rethinking Authority*, 43–9, goes so far as to argue for a 'discourse community', drawing on W. Pohl, 'Social Language, Identities and the Control of Discourse', in E. Chrysos and I. Wood, eds, *East and West* (Leiden, 1999), 138–41. Wormald, 'Lex Scripta', 3–7, 27–37, explores the ideological and performative quality of writing.

[13] Paraphrasing Mordek, 'Karolingische Kapitularien', 27; A. Rio, *Legal Practice and the Written Word* (Cambridge, 2009), 206–10; S. MacLean, 'Legislation and Politics', *EME* 18 (2010), illustrates how and why simplistic categories fail for this material. The 'messiness' of law and heterogeneous quality of capitulary material is laid out in M. Innes, 'Charlemagne, Justice and Written Law', in Rio, ed., *Law, Custom, and Justice*, 192–3.

[14] This was no conservative impulse, but the means by which innovation was imagined and carried out. R. McKitterick, 'Knowledge of Canon Law before 789', *JEH* 36 (1985), 99; Moore, 'Ancient Fathers'.

on the shore in *c*.780 and disappearing from view after *c*.860. Yet the intervening activity did introduce hospitals into the Western legal tradition, and eventually into church law. Chapter 6 will look at the work of specific councils and, via their manuscripts, at the development of key initiatives. Here, we focus on the more discursive properties of capitularies, across the variety of Italian convocations, and at the long process of *cognitio*: that is, of finding language, or finding a practice that could give language to a problem in law.[15] We begin with how Italian assemblies first staked out a claim to speak.

New Horizons, New Subjects

In turning to hospitals, we must take care not to look for a legal concept that did not then exist.[16] We cannot read backwards, nor can we read forwards, for the Lombard assemblies and synods seem to have no antecedents. As the previous chapter observed, earlier church councils in the West had not devised law for hospitals.

Nor were welfare facilities among the objects of Carolingian reform. Monasteries and churches, which had been a priority for Merovingian councils, were addressed with renewed vigour under the Carolingians. To rectify decades of neglect in Francia, Carloman's great council of 742/3, the *Concilium Germanicum*, had launched a programme under the missionary Boniface 'to restore the church canons and ecclesiastical law and amend Christian religion' (c. 1). It targeted priests (cc. 3–6) and monastic life (cc. 6–7), requiring that monks and nuns now adopt the rule of St Benedict.[17] Under Charlemagne and Louis the Pious, this vision was taken to new heights with the *Admonitio generalis* (789) and the

---

[15] On *inventio* and *cognitio* in Roman legal theory, C. Humphress, 'Telling Stories about (Roman) Law', in P. Dresch and J. Scheele, eds, *Legalism: Rules and Categories* (Oxford, 2015), 100, 103. In a sense, we will be reading outwards from the texts to uncover their social logic: here by the 'production of meaning' wrought both by the inscription of the fruits of a council's deliberation and by the accumulation of statements. On the social logic of the text, G. M. Spiegel, *The Past as Text* (Baltimore, MD, 1999), 24–8.

[16] A caution effectively levelled by Siems, '*Piae causae*', 83, who asks how far Justinian's legislation for *piae causae* was adopted, and even developed, for *xenodochia* in the early medieval, and largely Merovingian West.

[17] (c. 1) 'Statuimus per annos singulos synodum congregare, ut nobis presentibus canonum decreta et aecclesiae iura restaurentur, et religio Christiana emendetur.' MGH *Conc.* II.i, 2–4. The council issued seven directives in total. In the preface, Carloman declared: 'ut mihi consilium dedissent, quomodo lex Dei et aecclesiatica relegio recuperetur, que in diebus preteritorum principum dissipata corruit'. That ruinous state is laid out in a letter of St Boniface to Pope Zachary, in anticipation of the council: 'Franci enim, ut seniores dicunt, plus quam per tempus octuginta annorum synodum non fecerunt nec archiepiscopum habuerunt nec aecclesiae canonica iura alicubi fundabant vel renovabant.' *Die Briefe des heiligen Bonifatius und Lullus*, ed. M. Tangl (Berlin, 1916), 82. On Boniface's reforming synods, see Mordek, 'Fränkische Kapitularien', 11–12; J. M. Wallace-Hadrill, *The Frankish Church* (Oxford, 1983), 150–5; A. Diem, 'The Carolingians and the *Regula Benedicti*', in *Relig. Franks*. I. Wood, 'Reform and the Merovingian Church', in *Relig. Franks*, offers a Merovingian prehistory of reform.

Aachen reforms of 816–19. None of these initiatives addressed hospitals.[18] In fact, xenodochia were not a target of Frankish efforts to restore church canons and amend religion (they would not appear in Frankish councils until 845/6). Nor do we find a concerted programme in Lombardy. What the capitularies reveal, instead, are a series of deliberations that took place on the periphery of the Carolingian drive for Christian order. And they are all the more interesting for that.

The Call for *Restauratio*

Recent work has invited more careful thought regarding the languages of change. Whereas once 'reform' served as a catch-all term for initiatives to improve the practice of Christian religion, we now recognize a more varied vocabulary.[19] Carolingian councils did not use the word 'reform' (*reformare*), but set out rather to amend (*emendare*) and correct (*corrigere*) the quality of religious life.[20] Carolingian *ordines*, which laid out the procedure for church councils, reveal *emendatio* and *correctio* to have been obligations of leadership, at the heart of a prelate's pastoral duty.[21] The terms evoked specific ideals. *Correctio* inspired a renaissance in learning. It sought to raise the standard of religious life through knowledge, by educating monks, nuns, and priests in what they should be doing and why; it also underpinned a programme of pastoral instruction that reached deep into the dioceses.[22] It went hand in hand, under Louis the Pious, with an

[18]   It is likely that xenodochia were implied in c. 73 of the former, among 'those diverse places to which guests, pilgrims, and paupers should be received in accordance with the rule and the canons' ('ut hospites, peregrini et pauperes susceptiones regulares et canonicas per loca diversa habeant'), a passage inspired by the Benedictine rule, whose point was that monks and clergy be hospitable. (*Die Admonitio generalis Karls des Großen*, ed. H. Mordek et al., MGH *Fontes iuris* XVI (Hanover, 2012), 226–8; Hartmann, *Synoden*, 107). For monastic reform across the period, M. de Jong, 'Carolingian Monasticism', in R. McKitterick, ed., *New Cambridge Medieval History*, II. *c.700–c.900* (Cambridge, 1995). On Aachen (816) and the rule for canons, see pp. 72–8.

[19]   Barrow, 'Ideas and Applications', 350, 353–7; T. Reuter, '"Kirchenreform" und "Kirchenpolitik" im Zeitalter Karl Martells', in J. Jarnut et al., eds, *Karl Martell in seiner Zeit* (Sigmaringen, 1994).

[20]   P. Brown, *The Rise of Western Christendom* (Malden, MA, 1997), 439–41; J. M. H. Smith, '"Emending Evil Ways"', in K. Mills and A. Grafton, eds, *Conversion in Late Antiquity and the Early Middle Ages* (Rochester, 2003), 189–92, 214–15 nn. 15 and 16.

[21]   E.g. the prayer on a council's final day extolled *correctio* as a task that ensured the prelates' salvation, exhorting them to amend (*emendare*) their clergy and revive (*renovare*) those things agreed by the synod. R. Kramer, 'Understanding Councils and Performing Ordines', *EME* 25:1 (2017), 61; *Die Konzilsordines*, ed. H. Schneider (Hanover, 1996), 312.

[22]   R. McKitterick, *Charlemagne: The Formation of a European Identity* (Cambridge, 2008), 299–320; R. Kramer, 'Teaching Emperors', in E. Hovden et al., eds, *Meanings of Community* (Leiden, 2006), 309–10. On *correctio* of *leges*, Innes, 'Charlemagne, Justice and Written Law', 160–2; and priestly *correctio*, with a priest's handbook as a '*correctio*-dossier', C. van Rhijn, 'Carolingian local *correctio*', in *Relig. Franks*, 169–70.

emerging ideal of ministry (*ministerium*), a responsibility of leaders both lay and ecclesiastical to foster the salvation of the people.[23]

Initiatives for change are not perennial or even cyclical, but distinctively historical. They are rooted in cultural programmes of their moment, which in turn give shape to the logic, goals, and means of that change. This is significant when turning to xenodochia, because it challenges us not to think of a drive for improvement in generic terms, for example, as a cyclical attempt to counter the same entropy that stalked these houses in other eras and so keep hospitals on one correct path. Instead, it asks us first to consider not what is acted upon (xeno-dochia), or even the actors (councils), but the activity itself, that is, what councils thought they were doing. It quickly becomes apparent that the terms associated with the Carolingian transformation of religious life—*correctio, emendatio,* even *ministerium*—were not used in relation to xenodochia. To understand the appearance of hospitals in capitularies, we must identify another discourse of renewal, one that looked back to an antique past.

The ideal of restoration (*restauratio, restaurare*) saturates Carolingian capitularies.[24] It appears in the 743 councils of Boniface and Carloman, which aimed to 'restore' the laws of the church and, by imposing the Benedictine rule on monks and nuns, a standard of religious life.[25] This early use was an outlier and a synonym for *emendare*, before the latter term had gained common currency. It was under Charlemagne that *restauratio* began to be used often and to underpin a new sense of mission: injunctions to Italian *missi* began with concern for 'the state of ecclesiastical affairs and the *restauratio* of the churches of God'; those issued at Salzburg 803×4 order first 'that the churches of God be well built and *restaurata*'.[26]

There is also evidence beyond the capitularies that *restauratio* was an objective of Carolingian reform.[27] In his oft-cited letter to the emperor, confirming that he

---

[23] De Jong, 'Charlemagne's Church', 107–8; G. Koziol, 'Christianizing Political Discourses', in Arnold, ed., *Oxford Handbook of Medieval Christianity*, 482–6.

[24] This is not a term that has attracted notice, except in a list of terms for rebuilding: E. Thomas and C. Witschel, 'Constructing Reconstruction: Roman Rebuilding Inscriptions', *Papers of the British School at Rome* 60 (1992), 169. In comparison, *renovatio* has attracted attention as a spiritual and religious *Renovatio Imperii* after 800 (F. L. Ganshof, 'Charlemagne's Programme of Imperial Government', in his *The Carolingians and Frankish Monarchy*, tr. J. Sondheimer (London, 1971)) and as a political imperial ideology under the Ottonians, *Renovatio imperii Romanorum* (P. E. Schramm, *Kaiser, Rom und Renovatio* (Berlin, 1929); K. Görich, *Otto III: Romanus Saxonicus et Italicus* (Sigmaringen, 1993); L. Roach, 'Emperor Otto III and the End of Time', *TRHS* 23 (2013)).

[25] (c. 1) 'Abbates et monachi receperunt sancti patris Benedicti [regulam] ad restaurandam normam regularis vitae', MGH *Cap.* I. 28.

[26] (c. 1) 'De ordinacione ecclesiastica at restauracione ecclesiarum Dei, omnes generaliter bonam habeant providenciam.' (c. 1) 'Ut ecclesiae Dei bene constructae et restauratae fiant, et episcopi unusquisque infra suam parrochiam exinde bonam habeat providentiam, tam de officio et luminaria quamque et de reliqua restauratione.' MGH *Cap.* I. 206, 119. Also, *Cap.* II. 168, 220 (c. 13).

[27] Einhard's *Life of Charlemagne* notes the 'many projects he began for the ornament and benefit of his kingdom' ('opera...plurima ad regni decorem et commoditatem...inchoavit'): the great church at Aachen, the bridge over the Rhine at Mainz, palaces at Ingelheim and Nijmegen. 'More important still, and throughout his whole kingdom, wherever he discovered sacred buildings that had fallen into ruin from age, he commanded that they be restored (*ut restaurarentur, imperavit*) by the bishops and

had fulfilled Charlemagne's instruction to rejuvenate the province of Lyons, Archbishop Leidrad reported on how he had revived religious life and restored church buildings, what Mayke de Jong characterized as the 'two distinct but intricately connected domains...the cult of God and its material infrastructure'.[28] It was the latter that was the target of *restauratio*. Leidrad organized his report into categories of *restauratio*: 'Of the restoration of the churches [monasteries], insofar as I could ... Apart from the restorations of monasteries, I have also restored one episcopal house...In the same city I have restored other churches...'[29] This was no antiquarian mission: *restauratio* required that buildings be repaired so that religious life could be rejuvenated and even improved, by the introduction of a larger community of nuns or monks, for example, or the buildings necessary for a common life in order to live under a rule.[30]

In capitularies *restaurare* and its cognate *restauratio* have a clear if varied meaning. They were used most often in relation to the church, referring not to The Church and its spiritual mission but to the material forms that sustained that mission. It thus spoke often of churches (in the plural) and occasionally of the domestic buildings of a monastery, and it required that the physical buildings be repaired, particularly their walls and roofs.[31] The broader mission of *restauratio ecclesiarum* referred to a responsibility to repair the material fabric of Christian life, a category that extended beyond buildings. Individual injunctions focused on the duty of repair as well as the customary obligation to pay for these repairs, especially by those who held the benefices.[32] *Restauratio* was therefore bound up

churchmen who were responsible; ensuring through commissioners that his orders were carried out.' Einhard, *Vita Karoli Magni* II, c. 17 (ed. O. Holder-Egger, MGH *SS rer. Germ.* XXV (Hanover, 1911), 20-1).

[28] De Jong, 'Charlemagne's Church', 103. For the emperor's charge to Leidrad, MGH *Epp.* IV. 542. And see the example of Walcaud in A. Dierkens, 'La Christianisation des campagnes', in *Ch. Heir*, 319-23.

[29] 'De restauratione quoque ecclesiarum, in quantum valui, non cessavi...Praeter monasteriorum restaurationes domus quoque episcopales unam restauravi...In eadem civitate alias restauravi ecclesias.' MGH *Epp.* IV. 543.

[30] MGH *Epp.* IV. 543-4: 'Monasterium quoque puellarum in honorem sancti Patri dedicatum...ego a fundamentis tam ecclesiam quam domum restauravi...ita restauravi, ut tecta de novo fierent et aliqua ex maceriis a fundamentis erigerentur, ubi nunc monachi secundum regularem disciplinam numero nonaginta habitare videntur.'

[31] Frankfurt (794) specified that the roof, timber, stone, and roof-tiles be repaired: (c. 26) 'Ut domus ecclesiarum et tegumenta ab eis fiant emendata vel restaurata, qui beneficia exinde habent. Et ubi repertum fuerit per veraces homines, quod lignamen et petras sive tegulas, qui in domus ecclesiarum fuerint et modo in domo sua habeat, omnia in ecclesia fiant restaurate, unde abstracte fuerunt.' (MGH *Conc.* II.i, 169).

[32] The simplest statement was (c. 1) 'De ecclesiis nondum bene restauratis' (MGH *Cap.* I. 150, 152). The obligation to pay tended to fall on benefice holders, although more general arrangements, such as 'ancient custom', might be cited: MGH *Cap.* II. 84 (c. 1); and see MGH *Cap.* I. 175 (c. 24), 210 (c. 6), 287 (c. 5). The laity were to aid bishops and priests to whom the duty to repair a local church fell: (c. 36) 'Ut plebs ad ecclesias suas restaurandas episcopis et presbiteris diligenter adiuvent.' 'Capitulare generale Caroli Magni (a. 813)', ed. H. Mordek and G. Schmitz in their 'Neue Kapitularien und Kapitulariensammlungen', *Deutsches Archiv für Erforschung des Mittelalters* 43 (1987), 422, repr.

with a sense of custom and the customary: the income pertaining to a church, its property as well as its rent ('ninths and tenths'), was to be restored to its proper use, especially to repair of buildings.[33] Occasionally, church lights and ornaments, and even alms to Jerusalem, were swept up in the ideal of *restauratio*.[34]

Reinstating customary income and repairing church buildings was the bedrock of a wider mission to rejuvenate Christian life. Nevertheless, *restauratio* did extend beyond the ecclesiastical. It was also a call to restore bridges and streets, with their customary systems of maintenance, and even ancient palaces and courts 'where pleas should be'.[35] It encompassed the ancient public infrastructure, as well as that of Christian life. Under Carolingian rule, and especially in Italy, the two were often intertwined, drawn together by ideals of the public good and the governmental.[36]

The origins of this duty were civic, rather than religious. Early church councils had avoided this and other words that suggested change, even when they were working to transform religious norms and practices.[37] In contrast, the ideal can be found readily in the late antique period to praise rulers who restored civic

Mordek, *Studien*, at p. 142 (c. 36). More generally, MGH *Cap*. I. 65 (c. 2), 104 (c. 56), 142 (c. 3), 191 (c. 1), 196 (c. 3), 304 (c. 5), 307 (c. 24); *Cap*. II. 12 (c. 3), 33 (c. 11), 64 (c. 9), 79, 82 (c. 6), 126, 220 (c. 13), 268 (c. 3), 420 (c. 78), 433, 513 (c. 28).

[33] 'Praecepimus ut singulae plebes secundum antiquam consuetudinem fiant restauratae; quod si filii eiusdem ecclesiae eas restaurare noluerint, a ministris rei publicae distringantur, ut volentes nolentesque nostram observant praeceptionem.' MGH *Cap*. I. 327 (c. 8), whose public interest and governmental commitment to *restauratio* is developed in a capitulum of 832 (MGH *Cap*. II. 64 (c. 9)). MGH *Cap*. II. 13–14 (c. 9), offers a particularly detailed exhortation to *restauratio*. For benefice holders and their rents, MGH *Cap*. I. 100 (c. 10), 136 (c. 4), 153 (c. 14), 449 (c. 31); *Cap*. II. 394 (c. 62), 413 (c. 62); Constable, 'Nona et decima', esp. 228–9; Wood, *Prop. Ch.*, 199, 216, 459–72. *Plebes* refers to parish churches: Wood, *Prop. Ch.*, 69, 86ff.; A. Lunven, 'From Plebs to Parochia', in M. Cohen and F. Madeline, eds, *Space in the Medieval West* (Farnham, 2014).
[34] Among other concerns, royal *missi* were to enquire of monastic houses: (c. 3) 'quomodo aut qualiter in domibus aecclesiarum et ornamentis aecclesiae emendatae vel restauratae esse videntur' (MGH *Cap*. I. 131). In one case it extended so far as to incorporate 'luminaria seu officia etiam et missas necnon et sacri tecta [*sic*, texta?]', MGH *Cap*. I. 189 (c. 4). For alms sent to Jerusalem, to restore its churches: MGH *Cap*. I. 154 (c. 18), 447 (c. 31).
[35] (c. 25) 'Ut loca ubi placita esse debent bene restaurata fiant', MGH *Cap*. I. 151. Also, MGH *Cap*. I. 192 (c. 4), 306–7 (c. 22), 437 (c. 11); *Cap*. II. 64 (c. 7), 87 (c. 6–8), 277 (c. 4). Bridge building was a public duty to which exemptions did not apply, C. West, *Reframing the Feudal Revolution* (Cambridge, 2013), 22–3. On public works, M. Innes, *State and Society* (Cambridge, 2000), 159–64; B. Ward-Perkins, *From Classical Antiquity to the Middle Ages* (Oxford, 1984), esp. chs 7–9. On *placita*, Wood, 'Disputes', 7–14; Wickham, 'Consensus and Assemblies', 403–4, 413.
[36] E.g. Pippin's 782×86 capitulum: (c. 4) 'Ut de restauratione ecclesiarum vel pontes faciendum aut stratas restaurandum omnino generaliter faciant, sicut antiqua fuit consuetudo, et non anteponatur emunitas nec pro hac re ulla occasio proveniat.' MGH *Cap*. I. 192; and for immunity see, K. F. Drew, 'The Immunity in Carolingian Italy', *Speculum* 37:2 (1964), 185. '[Q]ui debeant palatia restaurare, qui pontes' were among the objects for the inquiry by the *missi* of Louis II in 865 on the state of public matters (*De statu rei publicae inquirendum*), MGH, *Cap*. II. 93–4 (c. 4). On the language of *publica utilitas* and *res publica*, M. de Jong, *Epitaph for an Era* (Cambridge, 2019), 178–90; Y. Sassier, 'La res publica aux IXe et Xe siècles', *Médiévales* 15 (1988), 9, noting its first appearance in Lombardy after the Carolingian conquest.
[37] C. Sotinel, 'The Church in the Roman Empire', in C. M. Bellitto and L. I. Hamilton, eds, *Reforming the Church* (Farnham, 2005), 156–9.

infrastructure, often explicitly the *res publica* of Rome.[38] King Theoderic was celebrated as 'a lover of buildings and restorer of cities [who] restored the aqueduct of Ravenna which Trajan had constructed'.[39] It was a use picked up in Fredegard's *Chronicle* and the *Annales regni Francorum*, for the rebuilding of castles and city walls.[40] Its use in the latter source to describe Charlemagne's rebuilding of the lighthouse at Boulogne was singled out by Karl Leyser for its 'unmistakable imperial overtones'.[41] From the end of the seventh century, the lives of the popes in the *Liber pontificalis* deployed the term routinely, if sparingly: after celebrating a pope's character, a life recorded his works of *restauratio*, *renovatio*, and building or foundation.[42] In this sense, it may have retained vestiges of *euergesia*, the classical virtue of gifts for the civic and public good, now directed to a more overtly Christian ideal of government.

A change occurred under pope Hadrian (772–95), who inaugurated an unprecedented campaign of building and rebuilding that intensified further in the 780s.[43] Thomas Noble has dated this escalation from the time of Charlemagne's visit to Rome in 781, after which he also detected new political symbols on papal coinage and in papal diplomatic.[44] Under Hadrian, *restauratio* became a papal mission in Rome: his *vita* is thick with these acts of building and with the term and the ideal of *restauratio*.[45] By the late 770s, he had drawn in Charlemagne and his

---

[38] The fifth-century Theodosian Code required that 'the ornaments of public works be preserved' (C.Th. 16.10.15) and, of temples, that 'their buildings remain unimpaired' (C.Th. 16.10.18): C. J. Goodson, *The Rome of Pope Paschal I* (Cambridge, 2010), 48.

[39] His biographer first used the term upon Theoderic's entry into Rome in a triumphal procession, when the king gave annual loads of grain to the *populus Romanus et pauperes* and money 'ad restaurationem palatii seu ad recuperationem moeniae civitatis'. Returning to Ravenna the king 'erat enim amator fabricarum et restaurator civitatum. Hic aquae ductum Ravennae restauravit, quem princeps Traianus fecerat'. He also fined the *populus Romanus* in order to rebuild (*restaurare*) the synagogues of Ravenna, burned down by Christian mobs; *Excerpta Valesiana*, ed. J. Moreau and V. Velkov (Leipzig, 1968), 19–20, 23. And see the examples in Thomas and Witschel, 'Constructing Reconstruction', 166 n., 167 n.

[40] Fredegard, *Chronica* (2.57; cont., 43), ed. B. Krusch, MGH SS rer. Merov. II (Hanover, 1888), 82, 187–8; *Ann. reg. Franc.* (a. 766, 776), 24, 47.

[41] *Ann. reg. Franc.* (a. 811), 135; K. Leyser, *Communications and Power in Medieval Europe*, ed. T. Reuter (London, 1994), 151 n. 34. For a literary reuse of the imperial past: M. Innes, 'The Classical Tradition in the Carolingian Renaissance', *International Journal of the Classical Tradition* 3:3 (1997).

[42] *Liber Pont.* I. 305, 346, 348, 363, 366, 385, 388, 419, 432, 440–1. Its sparse use suggests that *restauratio* was a duty but not yet a programme. Nevertheless, the term was used routinely and even with a sense of the imperial past or the *res publica*: 'sed et provincia Africa subiugata est Romano imperio atque restaurata' (John VII); 'Huius temporibus plurima pars murorum huius civitatis Romane restaurata est' (Gregory III), *Liber Pont.* I. 366, 420.

[43] T. F. X. Noble, 'The Making of a Papal Rome', in M. de Jong and F. Theuws, eds, *Topographies of Power* (Leiden, 2001), 49–56, who calls it 'a building upsurge that still staggers the imagination' (55). Goodson, *Rome of Paschal I*, 66–7, dates the surge in building work in Rome slightly earlier, from *c*.775.

[44] Among other markers, his coins switched to Frankish weights and his deeds abandoned Byzantine imperial dates, adopting the figure of Christ and pontifical then (by 798) Carolingian regnal dates; Noble, 'Papal Rome', 73–83. Hadrian's friendship with Charlemagne is treated in T. F. X. Noble, *The Republic of St Peter* (Philadelphia, PA, 1984), 138–83. J. Nelson, 'Charlemagne and Ravenna', in J. Herrin and J. Nelson, eds, *Ravenna* (London, 2016), offers a different perspective.

[45] *Liber Pont.* I. 500–14. The term occurs often on each page, nine or ten times on pp. 508 and 509, and includes the restoration of the walls and towers of Rome (p. 501). N. Christie, 'Charlemagne and

queen, who assisted substantially with the material burdens of building.[46] It may be that the vision had already captured Charlemagne's imagination during his visit to Rome in 774, the year he seized Pavia and was crowned king of the Lombards. In that year he began using the title *patricius Romanorum* (Patrician of the Romans), and Hadrian encouraged Charlemagne to think of himself as Constantine to his Sylvester.[47] The mantle of the Roman imperial past was already passing to the Frankish king.

Charlemagne's own programme of *restauratio* was inspired by Hadrian and fostered by his conquest of Lombardy. It preceded the distinctively religious *renovatio imperii romani* that followed his coronation as emperor in 800 under Hadrian's successor, Leo III.[48] It focused upon the material inheritance of Francia and Italy and it may have found a particularly ready reception in Lombardy, with its keener sense of the traditions of Roman law and government. It sought to repair buildings and infrastructure, and to reinstate customary systems for their maintenance; these were both a precondition to and a stage for the rejuvenation of religion, government, and public life. Although often centred on ecclesiastical sites, *restauratio*, as we have seen, extended beyond the clerical to include palaces, fortifications, streets and bridges, and ancient monuments; it therefore embraced a wider (and more material) scope of government than *correctio*, more explicitly Roman in its resonance. Its use from the 780s suggests a sense of trusteeship for the built infrastructure that served the public good, and so of the material inheritance of government and faith. It looked particularly to the landscape, with its standing reminders of antique and Christian enterprise, as well as of public obligation, incorporating a sense of ancient custom (*antiqua consuetudo*) and the *res publica*.

Finding a Place for *Xenodochia*

The call to *restauratio* saw councils look anew at their material inheritance and, in so doing, in Lombardy, they noticed xenodochia. The topic was broached in the

the Renewal of Rome', in Story, ed., *Charlemagne*, gives a sense of the wealth and art behind Charlemagne's 'renaissance' in Italy, and especially in Rome and Ravenna.

[46] In letters of 779/80 and 781×86, Hadrian asked the king to fulfil his promise to provide timbers *ad restaurationem* of St Peter's and to ensure that 'quantas ecclesias Dei ex ipsas trabes restauratas fuerint... restaurantur', as a lasting memorial of Charlemagne, his queen, and their progeny, MGH *Epp*. III. 592, 609–10.

[47] R. Kramer and C. Gantner, 'Building an Idea of Rome', *Viator* 47:3 (2016), 2 and n., 23–4, and 18 for the 'pomp and circumstance' of Charlemagne's Easter visit. Charlemagne's identification with Constantine fuelled a bold building programme in Francia, including his Aachen palace, modelled in ideal on Constantine's Lateran palace, R. Krautheimer, *Studies in Early Christian, Medieval and Renaissance Art* (New York, 1969), 230–7.

[48] On which see, Ganshof, 'Charlemagne's Programme'. For the changing shape of empire, M. de Jong, 'The Empire that was Always Decaying', *Medieval Worlds* 2 (2015).

earliest capitularies under the Franks. Xenodochia first appear in the capitulary for a royal council at Mantua (?781), in a capitulum that simply states that 'As to *xenodochia*, we wish and order that they be restored'.[49] Another early council under Pippin (782×86) was only slightly less brief: that brethren of xenodochia be fed (maintained) according to the ability of the house. The capitulum that followed (c. 4) required the restoration of churches, building of bridges, and repair of streets, 'according to ancient custom'.[50] To a scribe arranging the capitulary, xenodochia seemed to fit more naturally beside monasteries, so he attached the statement to the end of c. 3, that monasteries of men and women live under a rule. Yet its content (in contrast to that of monasteries) links it to discussions on material restoration and so to the group of public works that follow. Asked to look to *restauratio*, and to the built features of the landscape, Lombard councils noticed xenodochia.

Yet when they spoke, they said little. An initial glance at their statements on xenodochia reveal why Ullmann commented on their number, not their content. Pronouncements were short and repetitive, and they lack the administrative information (and drama) of the canon at Orléans (549)'s 'murderers of the poor'. It is easy to see why this Carolingian work has been dismissed as thin, and the councils as weak.[51] Yet this thinness was no accident. Like the Lateran decrees 300 years later, these were also crafted responses whose consistent restraint marks out a shape in law.

So how did councils categorize 'xenodochia'? Their placement in capitularies provides an initial clue.[52] Here they are not related to injunctions to be hospitable or care for the poor, a cohort of capitula that has so often been used by historians to define early hospitals. Councils issued many such exhortations, but these were not associated with xenodochia by the councils themselves.[53] Capitularies place hospitality as a virtue alongside other Christian traits, or as an obligation enjoined especially upon bishops, priests, and monasteries.[54] Such injunctions rarely occur even in the same capitularies as xenodochia, suggesting that the promotion of Christian virtues and the actual welfare facilities were the products of different

[49] (c. 12) 'De sinodochiis volumus adque precipimus ut restaurata fiant.' MGH *Cap.* I. 191.

[50] MGH *Cap.* I. 192 (cc. 3–4), following the arrangement in Vatican, Chig. F.IV.75, fol. 84v.

[51] *HDC* 10; Brodman, *CRME* 50; De Spiegeler, *Liège*, 36–7. Ullmann's comments are in his, 'Public Welfare', 9–11.

[52] On the ways in which 'thematic clusters' may reflect discussion at an assembly or a subsequent arrangement by the compiler, Pössel, 'Authors and Recipients', 257–8.

[53] The exception is Pippin's directive that bishops and abbots must continue to offer hospitality, where it anciently has been, in their own xenodochia and monasteries, MGH *Cap.* I. 210 (c. 9).

[54] E.g. at Frankfurt (794) where (c. 35) 'De hospitalitate sectanda' follows (c. 34) 'De avaricia et cupiditate calcanda' (MGH *Conc.* II.i, 169). Louis the Pious's Paris council of 829 provided a particularly long exposition of the obligation as it pertained to priests, MGH *Conc.* II.ii, 621 (c. 14). See also, MGH *Cap.* I. 60 (c. 75) and 231 (c. 6); *Conc.* II.ii, 707 (c. 3); and 'Capitulare ecclesiasticum Caroli Magni (a. 805–13)', c. 15, ed. Mordek and Schmitz, 'Neue Kapitularien', 125. For the grandeur and cost of hospitality, particularly towards royalty, nobility, and churchmen, Wood, *Prop. Ch.*, 271–9.

conciliar agendas. In a similar fashion, obligations to the poor, widows, orphans, and pilgrims—so often repeated[55]—are not grouped in, or near, decrees for xenodochia.[56] The organization of normative statements and rhetorics of law must not be confused with the motives that propelled people to act; the same call to love the poor that inspired these injunctions also inspired the creation of xenodochia.[57] Nevertheless, capitularies kept xenodochia separate from such calls, nor did they associate xenodochia with *diakoniae* or *matriculae*, which do not occur in councils of this late date. Instead, where possible, a statement on xenodochia was usually placed after those for monasteries or, less often, baptismal churches.[58] In capitularies xenodochia were classified not as an extension of charitable activity or virtue, but as a type of Christian foundation, a built feature of the landscape.

Yet xenodochia were usually the subject of their own capitula, and were not confused or conflated with churches or monasteries.[59] Even when mentioned alongside monasteries, they were distinguished from them.[60] The few decrees that mention both monasteries and xenodochia tend not to address the places

---

[55] This ethos penetrated the wider claim and practice of government. In Charlemagne's directions to *missi* in 802 e.g. c. 5 saw the emperor act as their defender, forbidding harm to come to them in God's holy churches; c. 14 directed bishops, abbots, abbesses, and counts to console and protect paupers, widows, orphans, and pilgrims; and c. 27 forbade anyone to deny hospitality (defined as a roof, fire, and water) to the wealthy, the poor, or pilgrims, whether vagabonds or those on a particular journey. MGH *Cap.* I. 93, 94, 96.

[56] The exception was Pavia (787), where xenodochia were included in the familiar exhortation that justice be done to all, including the poor, widows, and orphans; yet, even here, the term was paired with churches: 'ut omnes iustitiae pleniter factae esse debeant infra regnum nostrum absque ulla dilatatione, tam de aecclesiis quamque de senodochiis seu pauperibus et viduis et orfanis atque de reliquis hominibus secundum iussionem Karoli regis.' An earlier variant (?781) had mentioned only churches, widows, orphans, and the less powerful (MGH, *Cap.* I. 190 (c. 1)). The 787 decree was incorporated into the *Liber papiensis* (MGH *Leges* IV. 517 (c. 11), also, MGH *Cap.* I. 198 (c. 1)). Schmitz, 'Capitulary Legislation', 432–3, examines *pauperes* in the capitularies, as a group lacking *potens* in Carolingian society.

[57] On the call, Brown, '*Patriae Amator*'.

[58] E.g. Mantua II (813), which addressed royal churches (c. 1), monasteries (c. 2), *senodochia* (c. 3), baptismal churches (c. 4), bishops (cc. 5–6), etc., MGH *Cap.* I. 195. The duties and income of *ecclesiae baptismales* suggest that they were, in essence, parochial; Dierkens, 'Christianisation des campagnes', 317–19.

[59] A decree that might appear to do this occurs in antiquarian publications, attributed to Carloman's *Concilium Germanicum* in 742/3: 'Decrevimus . . . ut monachi, et ancillae Dei monasteriales, iuxta regulam sancti Benedicti, coenobia vel xenodochia sua ordinare, gubernare, vivere studeant. Et vitam propriam degere secundum praedicti patris ordinationem non negligant.' (Mansi XII, col. 367). However, the actual decree read simply: (c. 7) 'Decrevimus . . . ut monachi et ancille Dei monasteriales iuxta regulam sancti Benedicti ordinare et vivere, vitam propriam gubernare studeat.' (MGH *Conc.* II.i, 4). The corrupt version has caused confusion, partly due to its poor Latin: e.g. Merzbacher, 'Kanonischen Recht', 80, read it as a directive that monks and nuns establish and run *xenodochia*. I have not been able to identify the source of the corrupt version.

[60] E.g. in 845×50, Louis II laid out a series of issues for his bishops to consider, including those 'de restauratione aeclesiarum; de ordinatione plebium et xenodochiorum; de monasteriis virorum seu feminarum, quae secundum regulam sancti Benedicti vel ea, quae secundum canonicam auctoritatem disposita esse debent', MGH *Cap.* II. 79–80.

themselves, but the responsibility of a patron or bishop to appoint appropriately to its headship or benefice.[61] Most significantly, injunctions for xenodochia were not a by-product of discussions regarding monasteries. Abbots, abbesses, monks, nuns, and the quality of their religious life and supervision, remained a central preoccupation of councils, but hospitals were not included in these discussions, or the many and lengthy decrees that emerged.[62] The exception, the Aachen rules for canons and canonesses, prove the rule, treating hospitals not as a target for reform, or a community needing regulation, but as part of the built infrastructure necessary for the canons' or canonesses' common life.[63] Xenodochia came to the attention of councils less frequently than monasteries, but when they did it was as their own object of concern. In their first recorded appearance, in Pippin's Mantua (?781) council, they occur at the end of the capitulary, after a run of governmental business on tolls, mints, thieves, and Lombard vassals (cc. 8–11) and before the final decree (c. 13), on royal vassals.[64] Here, xenodochia are gathered up with a range of secular concerns linked to royal dominion. A few years later, the king responded to new problems, the first of them (c. 1) being custodians of xenodochia who refused to administer their facility's charity as of old.[65] The issue was its own item of business.

'Xenodochia' constituted a different kind of problem from that of monasteries and comprised their own category in legislation. Nevertheless, the tendency to place statements regarding xenodochia beside those for monasteries—and also for historians to associate them, as institutions—provides an opportunity for study.[66] Comparing the two offers a means to investigate xenodochia as a legal or institutional form and to explore what was distinctive about them.

Regulating Xenodochia

By the late eighth century, collections of canons included substantial material on monasteries, much of it from ecumenical and regional councils. There was also a well-established Carolingian practice of issuing injunctions regarding monasteries.

---

[61] Notably, the exercise of (royal) patronage or (episcopal) appointment, MGH *Cap.* I. 189 (c. 5), 201 (c. 6), 316 (c. 1).

[62] See the many questions about monastic life that Charlemagne directed to his bishops: Nelson, 'Voice of Charlemagne', 85–8.

[63] See my Chapter 3.   [64] MGH *Cap.* I. 190–1.

[65] MGH *Cap.* I. 200: 'Incipit capitulare qualiter praecepit domnus rex de quibusdam causis. Primo capitulo de senedochia: iussit ut...' It is the first of seventeen decrees covering a wide variety of business, the next one (c. 2) is on baptismal churches.

[66] 'Die Abgrenzung zwischen Kloster und Xenodochium ist eine offene Frage der Geschichte der Fürsorgeeinrichtungen', Sternberg, *Orientalium more secutus*, 158–61, with quotation at p. 158. In practice, lines between *xenodochium* and *monasterium* could blur (Stasolla, 'Proposito', 20, 23, 27, offers several potential examples in Italy, although surprisingly few given the wider picture; Le Maho, 'Hospices...de Rouen', 49–61).

Italian assemblies did not draw on this material when they turned to xenodochia. Their pronouncements reveal a defined type of facility, one distinctive from monasteries in law.

What were *Xenodochia*?

As an example, I shall take the second council of Mantua in 813, when discussion had reached a level of maturity.[67] Here, *restauratio* was decidedly on the agenda.[68] In the name of the young king of Italy, Bernard, the assembly and synod issued two capitularies, one directed to bishops and abbots, the other to the kingdom's *missi*, counts, and judges.[69] The former addressed monasteries and xenodochia side by side, and under a similar remit, to ensure their proper arrangement. The two chapters decreed that:

> (c. 2) Monasteries both of men and of girls that have been under a rule for a long time now, and which are situated within our domain of government, must be set in order and then live according to the rule. And if abbots or abbesses be found living without a rule or without discipline, and these men or women, once chastised, prove unwilling to change their ways, they should be ejected and an abbot or abbess elected from the same congregation, if worthy candidates should be found, or otherwise from elsewhere. And similarly, for royal monasteries.

> (c. 3) On the subject of the *senodochia* that belong to us: those that have been arranged well must continue in the same way; but those that have been brought to ruin, as is the nature of the times, we desire to be guided to their former state in order that the Lord's poor should be refreshed. And they should be arranged by the type of people who will direct them according to God and subtract nothing from the alms of the poor.[70]

---

[67] Boretius's date of 787 was revised to 813 by F. Patetta, *Sull' introduzione in Italia della Collezione d'Ansegiso* (Turin, 1890), 10–11; P. Wormald, 'In Search of King Offa's "Law-Code"' in I. Wood and N. Lund, eds, *People and Places* (Woodbridge, 1991), 34 n.

[68] MGH *Cap.* I. 196. The general capitulary was concerned with tithes (c. 8), customary bridge and other works (c. 7), and 'that baptismal churches be repaired (*restaurentur*) by those responsible for this, and the amount allotted to each one to be repaired (*restaurandi*) according to his ability' (c. 3).

[69] Labelled by Boretius 'purely ecclesiastical' and 'general', although both include ecclesiastical matters.

[70] (c. 2) 'Monasteria que iam pridem regularia fuerunt, tam virorum quamque et puellarum seu que sub nostro regimine dominio site sunt, volumus ut secundum regulam disponantur et vivant. Et si abbates vel abbatisse sine regula vivere seu inordinate inventi vel invente fuerint, si correpti vel correpte emendare noluerint, abiciantur, et de ipsa congregatione, si digni inventi fuerint, abbas vel abbatissas eligantur; sin autem, aliunde: et de monasteriis regalibus similiter.' (c. 3) 'De senodochiis vero nobis pertinentibus, que bene ordinata sunt in ipso permaneant; que vero destructa sunt secundum qualitatem temporum ad priore cultum perducere cupimus, ut ibi pauperes Domini reficiantur: et per tales personas fiant ordinata qui ea iuxta Deum regant et de helemosynas pauperum nihil subtrahant.' MGH *Cap.* I. 195.

The difference begins with the basis and remit of the actions. They differ in jurisdiction, or reach of action: c. 2 encompasses all regular monastic houses in lands under royal dominion, including royal monasteries;[71] c. 3 pertains only to hospitals that belong to the king. They also see different problems: one requires monks and nuns to follow their rule (*regula*) and provides for the correction or replacement of defiant heads; in the other there is no rule, or even a basic concern for the manner of life and its amendment. The hospital capitulum does not notice a community; instead, it speaks of how the facilities have been arranged (*ordinata sunt*) and the preservation of this arrangement, in order that the poor may continue to be refreshed there. Its concern is the administration of resources, not the quality of life that a community leads. If c. 2 worries about the government of people, the issue for c. 3 is the administration of goods. Its stewards were to keep God in mind when directing the facility and to ensure that the alms go wholly to the poor.

Carolingian capitula regarding monastic life were frequent, varied, and invasive. Individual councils might issue several injunctions, with (sometimes detailed) interventions into the manner of life led by the community. Councils in Italy as well as Francia addressed obedience, enclosure, clothing, drunkenness, discord, conducting secular business, and interactions with the opposite sex. Charlemagne's general assembly of 802 promulgated multiple directives regarding the life and chastity (*de vita et castitate*) of monks and nuns (cc. 15–20), as well as expectations for their leaders (cc. 11–14).[72] The more ecclesiastical the synod, the more extensive its activity regarding monks, nuns, canons, and heads of houses. Late in the day, the papal council of Rome (853) required that hospitals (and monasteries) should be returned through the intervention of the bishop to the purposes for which they had been built (c. 23). None of its other decrees mentioned hospitals, but several addressed the appointment of abbots (c. 27), how monks and abbots should live (c. 28), and women who received a religious habit (c. 29).[73]

Most fundamentally, councils reiterated that monks and nuns must adopt a rule and adhere to it. Such activity was a fundamental part of Carolingian *correctio* of religious life, which aimed to bring communities of monks and canons under one rule and one custom.[74] The desire to instil rigour and uniformity in monastic

---

[71] On the benefice of royal monasteries and *xenodochia*, see Pippin's capitulary of c.790: (c. 6) 'De monasteria et senedochia qui per diversos comites esse videntur et regales sunt; et quicumque eas habere voluerint, per beneficium domno nostro regis habeant.' (MGH *Cap.* I. 201, rev. *ut regales sint* to *et regales sunt*, as Wood, *Prop. Ch.*, 238 n. 29; an alternative reading is Schönfeld, 'Xenod.', 46). On royal monasteries, M. Innes, 'Kings, Monks and Patrons', in R. Le Jan, ed., *La royauté et les élites* (Lille, 1998), 308–10.

[72] MGH *Cap.* I. 93–5. See also Frankfurt (794), *Conc.* II.i, 168 (cc. 11–24).

[73] MGH *Conc.* III. 345, whose hospital canon adapts Rome (826), c. 23, by adding monasteries. Also, Rome (826), c. 7; Quierzy (858), cc. 8–9; in MGH, *Conc.* II.ii, 557; III. 417–18.

[74] *una regula et una consuetudo*, De Jong, 'Carolingian Monasticism', 629–33.

life, whose roots went back to the reform of 743, prompted many programmes of *correctio*, with the Benedictine rule at its heart.[75] The efforts were no mere rhetoric. The Aachen synod of 802 not only decreed that abbots and monks should adhere 'steadfastly and vigorously' to the rule, but also gathered the abbots and monks in attendance to hear the rule read aloud and explicated by wise men.[76] Visitors were then dispatched to discover whether monasteries were following the rule and to ensure the quality of their life and dwellings.[77] This did not mean that monasteries proved eager to reform—as late as the 820s the great royal abbey of Saint-Denis in Paris was not under a rule[78]—but it did constitute a programme embraced by councils and followed up through agents. In 789/90, for example, Pippin dispatched royal *missi* (one monk, one cleric) to inquire throughout the kingdom as to the quality of dwellings, life, and conduct, as well as the adequacy of their income, for the 'monasteries of men and of girls, who must live under a holy rule'.[79]

In contrast, injunctions regarding xenodochia were few, terse, and limited in scope. They made no mention of a rule. When a council did act, it usually issued only a single, thin statement, and there is little distinction even between those emanating from royal, episcopal, or papal gatherings. Monastic capitula usually spoke of monks (*monachi*) or nuns (*monachae* or *sanctimoniales*); if they referred to 'monasteries' they added 'living under a rule' or 'of men and girls', formulae that recognized the community of the house.[80] In contrast, those on xenodochia left the term unadorned.[81] Indeed, it is hard to detect any phrasing that might

---

[75] Chief among them the 816–19 Aachen council's programme for monasteries: 'Legislatio Aquisgranensis', ed. J. Semmler, in K. Hallinger, ed., *Corpus Consuetudinum Monasticarum*, I (Sieburg, 1963), 433–81, 501–36; Diem, '*Regula Benedicti*', 243–61; S. Meeder, 'Monte Cassino and Carolingian Politics', in *Relig. Franks*; T. F. X. Noble, 'The Monastic Ideal', *Revue Benedictine* 86 (1976), 242, 249–50.

[76] MGH *Cap*. I. 94 (c. 17), 103 (cc. 32–5). As recorded in the Lorsch annals in 802: 'Similiter in ipso synodo congregavit universos abbates et monachos qui ibi aderant, et ipsi inter se conventum faciebant, et legerunt regulam sancti patris Benedicti, et eum tradiderunt sapientes in conspectu abbatum et monachorum'; *Annales Laureschamenses*, ed. G. H. Pertz, MGH *SS* I (Hanover, 1826), 39; Diem, '*Regula Benedicti*', 247. On the events at Aachen, Innes, 'Charlemagne, Justice and Written Law'.

[77] For similar inquiries, MGH *Cap*. I. 131 (c. 3), 321–2 (cc. 1–2), 410 (c. 116); II. 64 (c. 10). In a list of questions from after 803, abbots were to be asked, 'si regulam scitis vel intellegitis, et qui sub regimine vestro sunt secundum regulam beatissimi Benedicti vivant an non, vel quanti illorum regulam sciant aut intellegant' (MGH *Cap*. I. 234 (c. 10)).

[78] M. Lapidge, *Hilduin of Saint-Denis* (Leiden, 2017), 39–40.

[79] (c. 11) 'Stetit nobis, ut missos nostros, unum monachum et alium capellanum, direximus infra regnum nostrum previdendum et inquirendum per monasteria virorum et puellarum que sub sancta regula vivere debent, quomodo est eorum habitatio vel qualis est vita aut conversatio eorum, et quomodo unumquemque monasterium de res habere videtur, unde vivere possit.' MGH *Cap*. I. 199; MGH *Leges* IV. 518–19 (c. 20).

[80] Compare the simple statement on hospitals (c. 6) with the multiple questions on monastic life and its correction (cc. 8–13) in the bishops' responses to palace questions, MGH *Cap*. I. 369, a text that seems to be Italian, from *c*.823 (see pp. 180–3). The synod of Milan in 863 did issue a second decree, for xenodochia 'in remote places', apparently a reference to the hospitals on the Alpine passes; MGH *Conc*. IV. 161 (cc. 4–5).

[81] The difference is apparent even when the two are mentioned together: 'monasteriorum sub regula degentium seu sinodochiorum…'; 'monasteria videlicet virorum ac puellarum et senodochia . .'.

suggest a legal rhetoric, or even a common way of writing about hospitals in law. They borrowed none of the formulae familiar from monastic injunctions. As bishops began to play a larger role in council agendas, especially after *c.*820, the divide between statements on monasteries and xenodochia grew more pronounced as councils offered more extensive regulation of monastic life.[82] Directives for hospitals grew longer, but they tended to elaborate on the same basic concerns regarding resources and administration; any community or personnel beyond a notional steward remained largely invisible.

With hospitals, restoration remained the main theme. We should not interpret this literally, as others have done, as evidence of a movement in decline, its houses fallen to ruin.[83] Xenodochia were vulnerable facilities, and many were old by *c.*780, so the challenge of failing houses was real.[84] Yet the drive to salvage older facilities was also part of a wider effort to cultivate hospitals, for there is evidence of sustained enthusiasm for welfare houses until the final quarter of the ninth century, and many new facilities were erected.[85] When the first council of Mantua directed that hospitals should be restored, it was aiming to reinstate disrupted royal facilities. But its initiative had a more significant meaning, as part of a wider ideological and governmental call to *restauratio*. In this light, the Mantua decree becomes a declaration that hospitals have a place in Carolingian renewal and, more specifically, in discussions of the public good and social order

(MGH *Cap.* I. 192 (c. 3), 211; *Cap.* II. 80; *Leges* IV. 222 (c. 4)). In such cases, there were usually additional capitula on monastic life.

[82] Although *monasterium* was an expansive term that embraced communities of monks or clerics, it was always treated separately from xenodochia in capitularies. What is absent in statements on *xenodochia* is any sense of a *vita communis*, the very element that blurred the boundaries between clerics and monks, who were both 'living in a state of ritual purity...[and so as] effective mediators between God and mankind' (De Jong, 'Carolingian Monasticism', 629).

[83] Imbert, 'Les conciles', 44; Schönfeld, 'Xenod.', 13, 15–16; Boshof, 'Armenfürsorge', 160–3.

[84] Lombardy had experienced a sustained wave of foundation since the early eighth century (Boshof, 'Armenfürsorge', 159–60, 162). Mantua II (813) addressed both the flourishing facilities and those 'brought to ruin, as is the nature of the times' ('destructa sunt secundum qualitatem temporum'). (MGH *Cap.* I. 195 (c. 3)).

[85] For regional pictures of foundation into the ninth century, Stasolla, 'Propositio', 14–20; Boshof, 'Armenfürsorge', 159–60, 162; Le Maho, 'Hospices...de Rouen', 49–61. Celebrated foundations include those of Adalhard, abbot of Corbie (d. 827) and Aldric, bishop of Le Mans (d. 856) (Paschasius Radbertus, *Vita sancti Adalhardi*, MGH *SS* II. 530; *Gesta Aldrici*, 148–9, and my Chapter 5 n. 86). Aldric established two hospitals, one for paupers, the other for nobles; similar pairings can be found at monasteries at Rebais, Jumièges Fleury-sur-Loire, Fulda, and Lobbes (E. Lesne, *Histoire de la propriété ecclésiastique*, 6 vols (Lille, 1910–43), 123–4 and, more generally, 142–51). Surviving evidence skews the picture towards episcopal and monastic foundations, yet even this provides glimpses of a wider public appeal and response. When Athanasius, bishop of Naples (850–72), made a *xenodochium* for pilgrims by the steps of his ecclesiastical court, he endowed it from his own estates and encouraged the faithful to make similar offerings ('illoque exortante plures fidelium simili contulere devotione', *Gesta episcoporum Neapolitanorum*, ed. G. Waitz, MGH *SS rer. Lang.* I (Hanover, 1878), 444, 434).

in Lombardy.[86] For xenodochia, the exhortation 'restore!' justified the right of assemblies to address hospitals.

It also provided a framework for their intervention. *Restauratio* was a claim to order (and that something might be ordered). If something needed repairing or reinstating, how and to what end depended on the nature of that thing: for bridges and streets, it was the customary duty of everyone that needed reinforcing; for churches, it was the income of the benefice and the responsibility of the benefice holder to pay; for monasteries, it was the buildings, so that communities might better be able to follow a rule. The goals of *restauratio* for xenodochia were not so clearly defined; in fact, initially they were barely defined at all. Assemblies embraced a deceptively simple task: to restore and, later, to guard what was already there. It followed less the model for monasteries, with their rule, than that for bridges and streets: to reflect and reinforce existing custom. So what was being restored, and what was it being restored to?

At first glance, pronouncements on hospitals have little in common with one another. A sample of different statements will demonstrate a range of approaches:[87]

1. . . . ut quicumque senedochia habent, si ita pauperes pascere voluerint et con-silio facere quomodo abantea fuit, habeant ipsa senedochia et regant ordinabiliter.

that whoever have xenodochia, if they are willing thus to feed (maintain) paupers and on advice to proceed as it was in the past, they should have these xenodochia and rule them properly.

Pippin (*c*.790), c. 1 (royal)

2. . . . ut secundum possibilitatem vel temporis fertilitatem testamentorum scripta sequantur.

that they follow the prescriptions of wills according to the ability and fertility of the age.

Lothar I (825), c. 4 (imperial)

3. . . . ad easdem utilitates, quibus constituta sunt, ordinentur, ut debiti panes atque cure pertinentibus revertantur.

they must be directed towards those uses for which they were established, in order that the due food and charges be restored to those to whom they belong.

Rome (826), c. 23 (papal)

---

[86] The council was largely concerned with justice, social order, and royal government. A near-contemporary council under Pippin in 782×6 proclaimed *restauratio* at the outset: (c. 1) 'Ut ecclesias baptismales seu oraculas qui eas a longo tempore restauraverunt mox iterum restaurare debeant' (MGH *Cap.* I. 191).

[87] In order, MGH *Cap.* I. 200; MGH *Cap.* I. 328; MGH *Conc.* II.ii, 576–7; MGH *Cap.* II. 121 and *Conc.* III. 226; MGH *Cap.* II. 94.

4.... secundum dispositionem eorum, qui ea instituerunt, gubernentur.

they must be managed according to the arrangements of those who instituted them.

Pavia (850), c. 15 (synodal)

5.... ubi sunt neglecta, ad pristinum statum revocent.

where they have been neglected, the missi *must restitute their original state.*

Louis II (865), c. 5 (directives to his *missi*)

In each case, the directives are brief and the tasks unelaborated. Curiously the language is not repeated: there is only a slight echo between *ordinabiliter* (1) and *ordinentur* (2). The verbal directions reveal the variety: to rule (*regare*), to follow what is written (*sequor*), to direct towards its charity (*ordinare*), to manage (*gubernare*), and to restitute (*revocare*) a former state. Even the object and the terms of action are different. One reinforces the duties of custodians; the next, obedience to testators; another, the uses to which the facility is directed; the fourth, that its management follow the founder's arrangements; the last, the restoration of neglected houses. It appears as if each injunction is doing something different.

Yet all of them share a fundamental consistency. They embrace preservation as an ideal. They stress management and require that, where this had failed, the facility should be returned its own original condition. For monasteries, *restauratio* sought a qualitative improvement of the community and its way of life through a common rule. For xenodochia, *restauratio* looked not forwards but backwards, and to the particular rather than the universal. The acts of correction target resources (the facility's assets) and their proper administration.[88] This encompassed both the use of those assets (its appointed charity) and the arrangements for their administration (its system of management). If monastic *restauratio* ultimately sought to harmonize arrangements for living under the rule, the injunctions for xenodochia aimed to preserve or reinstate the directives that were specific to each facility, laying out its particular use and administration. Each council used different language for what these directives were, but the idea was consistent: they were the arrangements put in place at the facility's inauguration, as enjoined by those who built (*construere*), made (*facere*), or founded (*instituere*) the hospital.

Behind these attempts at correction we can distinguish an institutional form. A xenodochium was defined by the administration of resources, and its objective was to preserve its assets and administer them to their assigned charitable use. The

---

[88] For a legal perspective on the significance to early churchmen of its property or assets (*Vermögen, Stiftungsvermögen*), see Siems, '*Piae causae*', 78–9.

basis for this, as well as the means for achieving it, was its original foundation and funding. These afforded the buildings and income to provide shelter, fuel, food, and the person or staff who carried this out. We glimpse, too, the mechanism by which this was brought about. A founder (*institutor*) established the hospital, providing its principal assets as well as the *dispositio*, the arrangement or directive, and so the framework, by which they must be administered. These were the charitable ends ('food and charges') to which the assets must be directed. Yet the charity itself was not the xenodochium's constitutive element—what defined it as a xenodochium and so what was looked to in order to define its constitution.[89] That is, a welfare house was not divided into institutional types: a xenodochium was not held 'to feed the poor' and a hospital 'to shelter pilgrims'; there was no expectation of a particular kind of charity. Instead, the question was about the institutor's act of giving. In the process of discovery and restitution, the issue was the equation between assets and their assigned uses; that is, what had been provided and what it was to be used for. It was this equation that defined the charity, both the activities to be performed and the facility itself.

This allows us to lay out the legal process by which a xenodochium was made and shed light on its constitution. A benefactor provided buildings and an original bequest, whose income would sustain charitable activity. This gift came with a directive (*dispositio*) as to how it must be used and according to whose terms it was to be administered. The original bequest thus did more than simply endow the xenodochium: it was its constitutive element. The donor's directive was inscribed on their material gift. In concept, the xenodochium was merely the vehicle through which the gift was held and administered. It is possible, too, that a subsequent bequest might add new assets and an enhanced directive to the original arrangement (*institutio*), as the vague 'prescriptions of wills' that *xenodochia* (pl.) must follow, in example (2), may suggest.[90] This original arrangement, or arrangements, constituted the facility's 'pristine' or original state. It served as the design by which the place was governed and to which it must be held.

If a monastery was a community, observing a common way of life, a xenodochium was a compilation of assets, to be administered to specific charitable uses. These assets were, in concept, a gift that remained marked in perpetuity by its giver. The donor's directive provided the template (*dispositio*) by which and to which the facility be ruled.

---

[89] As e.g. the constitutive element of a monastery was the community who had left the world to dedicate themselves to God and to a life of prayer, as laid down at the council of Chalcedon (451).

[90] E.g. in a 790 Luccan will, Jacopo Diacono, enhanced a *xenodochium* on his land in order that it might support an additional seven paupers, bringing the total to twelve: *Memorie e documenti per servire all'istoria del Ducato di Lucca*, ed. D. Barsocchini, V/2 (Lucca, 1837), no. 231.

Reinstating its 'Pristine State'

The model of a fixed original condition was simple in theory, but not in practice. It bequeathed to councils their main challenge: how to align a dynamic present with that fixed past. It was simple enough to exhort 'that xenodochia must be restored', it was another thing to provide mechanisms or even models for that restoration. We have seen how councils worked to find ways to articulate the problem that must be resolved, as one of stewards, arrangements, neglect, or changing fortunes. And they agreed, too, that the original design be maintained. But how was this to be effected? The issue of jurisdiction is addressed in Chapter 6. What follows explores the conceptual models for remedy. In general, these are noteworthy for the basic quality of their character. Most councils did little more than agree, proclaim, and enjoin that hospitals be preserved in or restored to their original state.

An assembly held in Olona under Lothar I in 825 was an exception, for it attempted to formulate a methodical programme to intervene in and remedy xenodochia. It survives in a capitulary that contains four capitula, all directed to the bishops of Lombardy.[91] The absence of monasteries in this capitulary, an unusual omission given the run of business, suggests that it was partner to another capitulary, on the regulation and correction of monastic houses; and what was presumably a third capitulary of the group concerned secular law.[92] Taken together, these constituted a three-pronged effort, to address secular business, monastic correction, and (in our capitulary) the secular pastoral duties of bishops. Among this business, the hospital resolution stands out. It was an agreement with the bishops to lay out a system by which hospitals could be corrected, and it offered a framework for diagnosis as well as remedies for different problems. It reads:

> (c. 3) That [i] in xenodochia that have been reasonably laid out (*disposita*) and still endure in their original/unspoiled state, the charters of testators should be entirely preserved. However, [ii] in those that were deprived from the beginning of the arrangement (*dispositio*) provided by a legitimate plan (*iusta ratio*), we wish that a fifth of its income be given to the poor. Similarly, [iii] in those that

---

[91] It addresses consecration by bishops (c. 1), priests cohabiting with women (c. 2), xenodochia (c. 3), and baptismal churches (c. 4). The capitulary is preserved in three manuscripts, alongside material produced during Lothar's Italian mission, 823–5: MS Blankenburg, fol. 115r–v; 'Gotha, Forschungsbibliothek, Memb. I 84', fols 406v–407r; 'Vercelli, Biblioteca Capitolare Eusebiana, CLXXIV', fols 82r–83v, the latter two consulted via *Capitularia* (acc. 17 July 2019). Boretius edits the capitulary as *Capitula de rebus ecclesiasticis*, offering a tentative date of ?825: MGH *Cap.* I. 331–2 (no. 166). The Olona councils are addressed in my Chapter 6.

[92] MGH *Cap.* I. 329–31 (no. 165). The monastic capitulary is ed. as no. 160, MGH *Cap.* I. 321–2; it survives only in MS Blankenburg, at fol. 106v.

CAROLINGIAN LOMBARDY   101

had a reasonable arrangement (*dispositio*) and nevertheless through some form of negligence are deprived of the order (*ordinatio*) of their original state, we wish that the aforesaid stipulation (*conditio*) [of the fifth] be observed until through the providing of good regulations and the abundance of the times they might graduate to their prior arrangement (*dispositio*).[93]

The provision distinguished three categories of hospitals: (i) those that possessed their original *dispositio* and continued, unspoiled, in that state; (ii) those that lacked this directive and so a 'legitimate plan'; and (iii) those that possessed a *dispositio* but could no longer fulfil it in practice. In these categories, the council has recognized the two essential elements of a hospital: its original design (*dispositio*) and the material ability to fulfil it. Each of the three categories required a different response. The first, with its two elements in place, must simply continue to follow its *dispositio*. The second required a substitute directive. The third needed a remedial directive by which it might recover its resources and eventually reinstate its *dispositio*, and so its assigned charity. For those that lacked a *dispositio*, the council provided a common substitute directive: to distribute a fifth of income to the poor.[94] This was also the remedial measure to return impoverished houses to their proper state.

The Olona resolution affords a unique window into the ways in which hospitals were understood, at least by this well-informed congress. It not only laid out the two necessary elements, it also prioritized them. The possibility that two different elements might fail should produce four categories: if neither fail, if one fails (×2), if both fail. The decree provides for two categories separately, where the original *dispositio* survived and the material state was (i) adequate or (ii) inadequate to follow it and required a remedial measure. The other two categories had been united, defined by one overwhelming failure: their lost directive (iii). In these

---

[93] (c. 3) 'Ut [i] in senodechiis rationabiliter dispositis et adhuc *in pristino statu manentibus testatoris omnino conscripta serventur. [ii] In his vero quae ab initio iustae rationis dispositione caruerunt, volumus ut quinta pars fructuum pauperibus detur. Similiter [iii] in illis quae rationabilem dispositionem habuerunt et tamen qualibet neglegentia pristini status ordinatione carent, volumus ut conditio suprascripta servetur, quousque per bonorum ordinatorum providentiam et temporum habundantiam ad priorem valeant ascendere dispositionem.' MGH *Cap.* I. 332. MS Blankenburg, fol. 115r–v, gives *in primo testamento testatoris omnino conscripta servetur *voluntas*; 'Vercelli, Biblioteca Capitolare Eusebiana, CLXXIV', fol. 82v, *in primo statu manentibus.

[94] The 'fifth' seems to be an innovation at Olona. It was not inspired by the quadripartite division of income (between bishop, clergy, church fabric, and poor), the so-called Gelasian formula, that had been enjoined on bishops since the mid-fifth century, but which predated Pope Gelasius in a letter of Pope Simplicius in 475 (*Epistolae Romanorum pontificum . . . a S. Hilaro usque ad Pelagium II*, ed. A. Thiel, I (Brunsberg, 1868), 176; for the Gelasian formula, Boshof, 'Armenfürsorge', 155–6; Caron, '*pia fundatio*', 139–40). I can find only one example of fifths and charitable distribution: when the East Roman emperor Julian the Apostate (361–3) ordered that hostels be established in the cities of Galatia, he provided corn and wine, ordering that one-fifth be allocated to the poor who served the priests, with the rest distributed to travellers and beggars (*The Works of the Emperor Julian*, ed. and tr. W. C. Wright, 3 vols (London, 1923), III. 69–71). This was not a model for Lothar's council, not least because the allocations are reversed.

cases, whether or not the resources were substantial was immaterial. This is because, however great they were, they could never fulfil a directive. That the remedial measure for (ii) was provided as a permanent substitute directive for these last suggests that hospitals that lacked their *dispositio* were also, and permanently, eroded. Of the two essential elements for a hospital, then, one was paramount: its original *dispositio*. If lacking, it could not be recovered, and the facility's mission was lost. The resources to fulfil that mission were a secondary and potentially recoverable consideration. Finally, the remedial provision made clear that a return to a 'pristine state' was not an issue of quality of life, but the reconstitution and correct administration of its resources, according to its original arrangement.[95]

There were thus three constitutive acts in law that can be glimpsed in capitularies. First, inauguration, or endowment, where a bequest was provided by the donor or founder. Second, charge (*dispositio*), the legitimate arrangement (*iusta ratio*) laid down by that donor and the model by which the facility must be administered and corrected. Finally, administration, or the mechanisms by which its resources were to be preserved and deployed, which included the staffing and supervision of the facility. In a sense, all three were intertwined, laid down by the donor and encompassed in the term *institutio*. Yet in law the three represented different challenges. The first (inauguration), forward-looking, was an issue of securing the bequest and its terms; the second (charge), retrospective, one of constitution and its recovery; the third (administration), a matter of personnel and oversight.

Even the most unusual interventions conformed to this model. Perhaps the most extreme was a late council under the archbishop of Milan in 863. It was one of the only councils to issue two capitula regarding xenodochia, both unusually intrusive. The first (c. 4) noted that long ago (i.e. at Olona) it had been established that xenodochia that were unable to fulfil their testators' *institutio* should distribute a fifth of their income to paupers and guests. But 'since this, too, is often and by many disregarded', it ordered that a priest, a pious and faithful man, be appointed to ensure this was done. Meanwhile, hospitals that were able to fulfil their testators' charges, must continue to do so. The second capitulum (c. 5) noted that xenodochia in remote places were not carrying out their distributions as lawfully established due to their rectors' neglect. For those where there were great numbers of guests and pilgrims, as well as paupers, the council required that 'by the arrangement of the bishops, the crops and the income from such crops owed to such a place should be distributed there to guests and paupers through the

---

[95] For other examples, see MGH *Cap.* I. 195 (c. 3); II. 63 (c. 1), 94 (c. 5) 121 (c. 15); *Conc.* III. 226 (c. 15), 324 (c. 23), 479 (c. 14); IV. 161 (c. 4). Cf. Tours (813), in which the return of 'monasteries of monks' *ad pristinum statum* was a matter of observance of the Benedictine rule and, especially, of abbots keen to observe that rule; MGH *Cap.* II.i, 290 (c. 25).

diligence of a faithful attendant provided by the (diocesan) bishop'.[96] The latter capitulum, unique among conciliar material, reflected the political conditions of the age, notably a concern to maintain the mountain passes into France given that Louis II, emperor of Italy, had extended his territory that year north of the Alps.[97] The former addressed hospitals more widely, reinforcing the Olona provisions and designating an agent (a priest) to ensure that its remedial charity should be dispensed.

The Milan decrees are extraordinary in the degree to which they stake a claim for bishops to intercede in the running of hospitals, especially the facilities on the Alpine passes, and for the level of that intrusion, in appointing agents. The appointment of a priest reminds us that, while there may often have been priests administering xenodochia, they have not before been noticed in the capitularies.[98] Yet, as elsewhere, the concern of the bishops at Milan was not to reform any community, but to apply a hospital's resources to their appointed use. This was reinforced when, in response to the Milan council of 865, Louis II dispatched visitors to correct the monasteries and xenodochia of Northern Italy two years later. Whereas he required visitors to correct monastic communities according to the Benedictine rule, they were merely to return neglected xenodochia to their original (*pristinus*) state and restore hospitals 'fully and with great care'.[99]

Milan also reminds us that capitula tell us very little about the facilities themselves. In contrast to the rules for canons and the foundation at Lyons by

---

[96] (c. 4) 'Iam pridem constitutum est, ut de senodochiis, quae iuxta testatoris institutionem consistere nequeunt, quinta saltim pars hospitibus vel pauperibus erogetur. Sed quia hoc quoque a plerisque neglegitur, statuimus, ut fidelis et religiosus ex sacerdotibus constituatur, qui ipsam quintam partem recipiat et hospitibus pauperibusque convenienter dispenset; quae autem iuxta testatoris dispositionem permanere possunt, in ipsa dispositione permaneant.' (c. 5) 'Ea vero senodochia, quae in remotioribus locis posita sunt—et quia sub testimonio ipsa distributio statuta non peragitur, ab eorum rectoribus neglegitur—statuimus, ut episcoporum dispositione fruges vel reditus ipsorum tali loco debeantur, ubi frequentia hospitum et peregrinorum atque pauperum fuerit, ibique religiosi dispensatoris diligentia sub episcopi providentia hospitibus et pauperibus erogentur.' MGH *Conc.* IV. 161.

[97] In 863 he seized the southern provinces of the kingdom of Province, *Annals of Saint-Bertin*, ed. J. L. Nelson (Manchester, 1991), 104.

[98] An early decree of Pippin (782×786) mentions *fratres* in *senodochia cuiuslibet sint*. That some had chapels is suggested at Olona in 825, by a reference to the consecration or dedication of xenodochia, and by Louis II in 845×50, 'de ordinatione plebium et xenodochiorum' (MGH *Cap.* I. 192 (c. 3), 332 (c. 1); II. 79–80). At his hospital for elite guests such as bishops, earls, and abbots, Aldric, bishop of Le Mans, dedicated a church (*aecclesiam . . . sollempniter dedicavit*), *Gesta Aldrici*, 148–9.

[99] MGH *Cap.* II. 94 (c. 5): 'Upright abbots should visit monasteries of monks and women and xenodochia. They should inquire [of monasteries], from wherever they are administered, whether they perform their due services and live together in harmony; whatever irregularities they find, they must correct them according to the rule. But for xenodochia they should proceed thus: where they have been neglected they must recover their pristine state; and hospitals for the poor both in mountains and wherever they are known to have been, should be restored fully and with great care.' ('Directi abbates monasteria monachorum et puellarum ac senodochia circumeant; [monasteria] si, unde administran- tur, debita obsequia habeant et concorditer degant, inquirant; quicquid inordinatum reppererint, regulariter corrigant; senodochia autem sic, ubi sunt neglecta, ad pristinum statum revocent; hospitales vero pauperum tam in montanis, quam et ubicumque fuisse noscuntur, pleniter et diligenti cura restaurentur.')

Childebert and Ultrogotha, the capitularies do not worry about the people within, the types of charity to be administered, or the routines by which this should be done. Instead, they treat a xenodochium as a site to which income was attached, whose fruits must be distributed in accordance with its foundation (*institutio*). Their concern was the preservation and proper administration of this original state.[100]

Public Interest and Private Will

If the capitula for xenodochia had a consistent vision and purpose, why was its articulation so varied? The answer to this question reveals how a governmental conversation was developed over decades.[101] It was an Italian discussion, fuelled by Lombard concerns, and at its heart was the question of public interest in the private will.

Learning to Talk about Xenodochia

Restauratio was a charge to Lombard councils that allowed them to look at their landscape and demand its rebuilding. It heaved xenodochia into view, but it did not offer a way to talk about what was seen. The statements that survive suggest a slow process of learning.

In the first few decades, statements on xenodochia are intermittent and haphazard, suggesting that specific matters of business were being raised by participants. Carolingian assemblies often addressed an immediate problem, generalizing from a specific case to craft a public response.[102] The hospital statements are too thin to establish what the specific cases were, but they do suggest several

---

[100] Only one brief note mentions brothers in the hospital, and even then it was about the administration of incomes, upholding their own right to be fed from them: (c. 3) 'simul et senodochia, cuiuslibet sint, fratres in omnibus pascantur iuxta illorum possibilitatem.' MGH *Cap.* I. 192; *Leges* IV. 514.

[101] Questions of who was speaking are addressed in the following chapters; this section examines what was said. It takes a view that collective action, or at least collective recognition, lies behind these many statements on *xenodochia*. Here, we might see Timothy Reuter's 'political community', which 'through embodying itself as an assembly ... was empowered and enabled to practice politics ... It was a public which did not ... have a permanent existence: it came into being at assemblies, and dissolved again when they ended.' T. Reuter, 'Assembly Politics', in P. Linehan and J. L. Nelson, eds, *The Medieval World* (London, 2001), 442.

[102] Debate as to whether councils were addressing 'real-world' problems has been answered in the positive. Many items in capitularies were not esoteric questions of law or theology but 'remedies [that] are being prescribed for quite local and/or short-term problems'; Nelson, 'Legislation and Consensus', 205, 210–11, with quotation at p. 210; Nelson, 'Law and its Applications', 313–15; Felten, 'Konzilsakten als Quellen', 350–2; McKitterick, 'Charlemagne's *missi*', 261; Halfond, *Frankish Church Councils*, 99–130.

issues of concern. The earliest dealt with hospitals in royal custody, asserting a royal right to act, but also reminding a new (Frankish) ruler and his agents of their responsibility to these places and specifically to their *restauratio*.[103] Discussion soon moved beyond royal holdings. In the case that hospital brothers must be fed from the hospital's income, as far as this was possible, we seem to glimpse a dispositive ruling. Its singularity and specificity suggest local controversy even though the ruling encompassed all 'xenodochia, to whomever they belong'.[104] Another case focused on the responsibility and accountability of stewards. Here, a sense of urgency rings through: as the *primum capitulum*, in Pippin's *c.*790 capitulary, 'on *xenodochia*', offered the fullest treatment thus far of these facilities. It ruled that stewards must be willing to perform customary doles and follow advice as to how this had been done, or be ejected and replaced.[105] These cases suggest sporadic questions, prompted by local problems, which focused on administration. The number of them in the first decade suggests that these had been concerns of long local standing, laid before the new regime. Frankish councils provided an opportunity to air and even begin to address them.

In confronting a dispute, confusion, or scandal, councils faced concrete rather than abstract challenges. They needed to rule on how a place or person was working, not to define concepts of *xenodochia* in law. But to give such a ruling, they had to delineate principles of hospital government. It is surprising how circumscribed these responses were. Before Olona (825) capitularies avoided wide-ranging resolutions. Each focused on a single issue: that hospitals 'be restored', that the brothers be fed there, that bishops or abbots practise customary hospitality in their xenodochia, or that ruined sites in royal custody be returned to their prior state. As a result, the decrees appear disjointed, even random. Together, they amount to an assortment rather than a corpus.

In addressing hospitals, councils were responding to well-known features in the landscape, yet they lacked templates through which to speak. It was not until the mid-ninth century, sixty years in, that councils made use of written models, and then Frankish bishops turned to Orléans (549), Italian bishops to Olona (825), and the pope to Rome (826).[106] As we have noticed, early Lombard capitularies deployed no common frameworks or linguistic formulae, as they did in capitula

---

[103] MGH *Cap.* I. 191 (c. 12) and I. 189 (c. 5): 'De eclesiis et monasteria et senodochia que ad mundio palatii pertinet aut pertinere debent: ut unusquisque iustitiam dominorum nostrorum regum et eorum rectum consentiat.' On the meanings of *iustitia* and *rectum*, see M. Lupoi, *The Origins of the European Legal Order*, tr. A. Belton (Cambridge, 2000), 420–6. Royal prerogative and the assertion of royal justice was a consistent theme under Pippin, the first Frankish ruler of Lombardy, e.g. MGH *Cap.* I. 198 (c. 1), 201 (c. 6).

[104] See n. 100.

[105] MGH *Cap.* I. 200, wherein example 1 (p. 97 above) is followed by 'Et si hoc facere noluerint, ipsas dimittant; et per tales homines inantea sint gubernatae, qualiter Deo et nobis exinde placeat'.

[106] Explored in my Chapter 6.

for monasteries, churches, and even bridges. Even the themes of preservation and administration were laid down by each scribe or council in its own terms. As our five examples revealed, this was not merely an issue of word-choice: the very concepts of *what* should be stable in a hospital and *how* this might be upheld were different. This suggests that the facilities (and their problems) lacked written models for judgement and intervention.

Indeed, early efforts suggest that councils were struggling to give language to something that was familiar in practice but not yet in written law. Even in material where words could have multiple spellings, that of 'xenodochia' stands out in its variety: we find *xenedochia, senodochia, sinodochia, synodochia, senedochia, synodoclica, exenodochia, cenodoxia, exsinodocius, exinodotie.*[107] We can almost see the scribe sounding out the term to write it down. It is a microcosm of the wider challenge, commonly faced by scribes, of transposing spoken directives into text— a challenge exaggerated for hospitals, which lacked a body of law or even basic formulae through which to conduct legal discussion. The assortment of concepts and the banality of early rulings suggests that councils were struggling to frame and articulate their statements.

A shift is reflected in the five examples across the period *c.*790–*c.*865, from clunky specificity to a more elegant abstraction, suggesting that law-makers were rising to the task. We can detect development in the terms in which they confronted the problem. The earliest focus simply on feeding the poor, language familiar from eighth-century deeds, which most often spoke simply of maintenance or feeding (*pascere*).[108] Other early concepts were that alms might fluctuate with income;[109] that government rested on the quality of the administrator;[110] and that the facility should be run as it had once been.[111] Some assemblies did more than others to advance the terms of legal discussion. Pippin's assembly of *c.*790 was the first to bring these concepts together in its *primum capitulum de senodochia*, permitting the replacement of inadequate stewards. Mantua II (813), cited above, included a directive regarding royal facilities, which offered the earliest statement of the model by which xenodochia should be run. Finally, Olona (825)

---

[107] The spellings suggest awareness of the term's components (*xeno* + *dochia*), as sounds rather than morphemes. Other sources can be still more wayward; the *Chronica patriarcharum Gradensium* (c. 5) refers to *sinochagia* (ed. G. Waitz, MGH SS rer. Lang. (Hanover, 1878), 394). This diversity of spelling has obscured many references to hospitals.

[108] MGH *Cap.* I. 192 (c. 3), 198 (c. 1), 200 (c. 1). A 764 will from Lucca made arrangements for feeding paupers 'just as is observed in other senodochia' ('sicut et in alia senodochia pauperes ad mensa pascere uidetur'), *CDL* II, doc. 175 (pp. 138–41). Stasolla, 'Proposito', 36, notices the repetition of *pascere* in charters.

[109] MGH *Cap.* I. 192 (c. 3), 195 (c. 3), 328 (c. 4).

[110] MGH *Cap.* I. 200, 195: (c. 1) 'per tales homines inantea sint gubernatae [gubernandas cum consultii proprii episcopi], qualiter Deo et nobis exinde placeat' (*c.*790); (c. 3) 'per tales personas fiant ordinata qui ea iuxta Deum regant' (813). The former has been adapted slightly in a later copy, in Munich, BSB Clm 29555/1 fol. 1r (c. 6).

[111] MGH *Cap.* I. 200 (c. 1), 195 (c. 3).

put in place mechanisms for correction and laid out core concepts that would echo through successive Italian decrees, from directives of will-makers to the 'pristine state' to which hospitals should be returned.[112] Individually, capitula reveal scribes and councils working to translate practice into prose. As a group, they share a sense of the nature of the problem for xenodochia and of the scope of the legal response, one that was always cautious but that grew in confidence.

In both assemblies and synods, the Carolingian and Italian elite were forging ways to think about and act on xenodochia. The terms 'public' and 'private' are contentious ones,[113] but they can speak helpfully to the challenge of hospitals in law at this time. The effort to forge a collective discussion was a public activity, in that it was at once governmental and Christian. Behind each individual statement lay an attempt to recognize underlying principles regarding xenodochia and to create a language for them. Each capitulum was a statement of order as well as consensus, articulating—even forging—a principle to be held in common. If bringing the question into the domain of government was the first consequential public act, and assemblies taking it up to resolve it the second, then writing the decision into a capitulary was the third. However banal any statement might be, it was law-making and this, for *xenodochia*, was pioneering. For councils inherited no tradition of hospital law in which they could work, and through which they could claim the right to act in law. Their challenge was therefore to stake a claim to speak in public terms. This governmental challenge was exacerbated by the character of xenodochia, facilities that were the result of (and answerable to) the will of an individual, oddly *privatus*.

Dispositio: A Will and Testament

A recent turn in legal studies asks us to see law as 'about making rather than knowing'.[114] In this view, law is its own closed workshop and law-makers are less reflecting the world around them than, in each law, making a new rhetorical object. Each statement is its own 'verbal performance', and a distinct thing, even though any new law is created by a common process: 'a mode of knowledge that aims at self-observation'. Any creation is thus the product of self-conscious manufacture, as law-makers watch themselves—in their workshop—making 'law'. Because any new rhetorical object must be made from components that have meaning, each Lombard council was finding the parts from which to build

---

[112] MGH *Cap.* I. 316 (c. 1), 328–9 (cc. 4, 7/7a), 331–2 (cc. 1, 3).

[113] Nelson, 'Legislation and Consensus', 205, 221; P. Fouracre, 'Eternal Light and Earthly Needs', in *PPEMA* 55–6; M. Innes, 'Charlemagne's Government', in Story, ed., *Charlemagne*, 86.

[114] For the calls to such an ethnology of legal rhetoric, see A. Pottage, 'Law After Anthropology', *Theory, Culture and Society* 31 (2014), with quotations from pp. 152, 156, 162; and Humphress, 'Telling Stories about (Roman) Law'.

their law, by identifying language that could be used but also practices regarding xenodochia to which they could give language. For the former, we might think of *pascere* (feeding), for the latter the requirement to look back to establish the original (*pristinus*) state. It is the self-observation of these councils, in navigating xenodochia, that allows us to use their words to explore both what was made (law) and what it was made from. The oddities of language and the varieties of terms are significant.

Assemblies recognized the xenodochium as a distinctive institution. Whereas their concern for monasteries was focused on the community, the quality of religious life, and imposition of a common rule, for xenodochia it was the material resources, their correct administration, and the preservation of the *dispositio*, the arrangements laid down for the specific facility. These qualities have wider implications, for they suggest that the role of a founder of a xenodochium in law was different to that of a monastery, especially in the nature of their endowment.

We begin with the act of hospital creation. It has been usual to use the terms 'founder', 'foundation', or 'founded' when discussing early medieval xenodochia, a vocabulary (*fundatio, fundare*) that has also been readily, if not straightforwardly, associated with monastic houses as well as hospitals in the late middle ages.[115] It was also, in a sense, what was done in practice in the early middle ages, when a new facility was established and endowed.[116] Yet these were not the terms used by councils, which embraced a more suggestive range of expressions. Even Childebert and Ultrogotha were said to have 'formed' or 'fashioned' (*condiderunt*) their xenodochium, which was to be administered 'according to the arrangement (*institutio*) that has been fixed/imposed (*secundum inditam institutionem*)'. The language of the capitularies—*instituere, ordinare, ab initio iustae rationis dispositione, ad easdem utilitates quibus constituta sunt*—similarly focused upon arrangement and the act of instituting. It is a language of reasoned design and individual determination.

A handful of decrees identify those who have instituted hospitals as 'will-makers' (*testatores*). The terminology appears in a range of different kinds of assemblies, royal and synodal. Louis II's Pavia council (850) threatened imperial coercion of any heirs who concealed or ignored the *institutio* of the will-maker

---

[115] HDC 44; Caron, '*pia fundatio*', 142. On the late development of the concept of *fundatio* in different national contexts, see R. Feenstra, 'Foundations in Continental Law', in *Itin. Fid.*, esp. 317–26). The German term 'Stifter' has a more nuanced meaning.

[116] Indeed, the biography of Pope Stephen II (752–77) used both *fundare* and *facere*: 'Mox vero *restauravit* et quattuor in hac Romana urbe sita antiquitus xenodochia, quae a diuturnis et longinquis temporibus *destituta* manebant et *inordinata*... Pari modo a novo fundasse dinoscitur et xenodochium in Platana, centum *pauperum Christi, dispositum illic faciens*, cotidianum videlicet victum eorum decernens tribui. Nam et foris muros huius civitatis Romane secus basilicam beati Petri apostoli duo fecit xenodochia...' (*Liber Pont.* I. 440–1). Author's italics mark out terminology familiar from the capitularies.

(*testatoris institutionem*), while one of Lothar's capitularies from Olona (825) required that the custodians of a hospital 'follow the prescriptions of wills (*testamentorum scripta*) as far as the ability and fertility of the age'.[117] Other Lombard councils, among them the Milan synod under Archbishop Tado in 863, emphasized the *conscripta testatoris*, the charters of testators.[118] This was no marginal detail, but the substance of the issue. When a contemporary law collection distilled the capitula into brief summaries they became: 'Regarding the preservation of the *institutio* of a xenodochia and that its property not be divided between coheirs' (Pavia, c. 15) and 'Regarding the preservation of the wills (*testamenta*) of xenodochia' (Olona, c. 4).[119] The very term *dispositio* meant 'decision' and 'layout', but also 'a testamentary provision'.[120] The *institutio* of a xenodochium, and so the directives according to which it was run and to which it was held, were what had been laid out by a *testator*, when assigning the bequest.

The terminology of 'will-making' does not occur in decrees for monasteries, and Carolingian councils worried little about their origins. When they did address monastic foundation, it was to reinforce the necessity of episcopal consent, as laid down by the council of Chalcedon (451).[121] As we have seen, their focus was rather on a community's present and future: that it observe a rule, and that a monastery continue to be a monastery in perpetuity, as also laid down at Chalcedon.[122] Fifth- and sixth-century councils had been preoccupied with bequests to monasteries and churches, but their concern had been with heirs who failed to hand over gifts.[123] At issue was the fulfilment of the act of handing over. It was recognized that a dying or deceased donor faced (and presented for the monastery) a distinct challenge. Whereas a living benefactor could ensure their gift was delivered to a

---

[117] As above, MGH *Cap.* I. 328 (c. 4); *Conc.* III. 226 (c. 15). Siems, '*Piae causae*', 81, noticed that '[k]onkret soll das Testament entscheidend sein', although did not develop this observation.

[118] MGH *Cap.* I. 332 (c. 3); *Conc.* IV. 161 (c. 4). Also, MGH *Cap.* I. 369 (c. 6); *Conc.* II.ii, 591 (c. 6). Pavia (850) also used 'institutors', clearly also meaning testators: 'sed iuxta institutorum decreta per heredes vel pertinentes ... Quodsi heredes, sive clerici sive seculares, adeo inportune contra maiorum suorum decreta ire temptaverint, ut testatoris institutionem subprimere vel obscurare nitantur'. MGH *Conc.* III. 226 (c. 15).

[119] MS Blankenburg, fols 71r, 71v: 'De institutione senedochiorum custodienda et de rebus eorum non dividendis inter coheredes / De senodochiorum testamentis custodiendis.' The first line of this manuscript's copy of Olona's *Capitula de rebus ecclesiasticis*, c. 3 is 'That in xenodochia that have been rationally arranged and where the written will is still wholly preserved in the first testament of the testator' (fol. 115r–v), see n. 93 to this chapter. The distilled titles can be illuminating: the targets of Pavia on magic, for example. are put more directly as 'De maleficio feminarum et magica arte earum' (fol. 71r; referring to MGH *Conc.* I. 229, c. 23).

[120] J. F. Niermeyer, *Mediae Latinitatis lexicon minus* (Leiden, 1976), 341.

[121] It was reinforced in the sixth century, but more rarely under the Carolingians, although note Aachen (802). CCSL 148, p. 205 (c. 27); CCSL 148A, p. 26 (c. 10); MGH *Cap.* I. 111 (c. 17).

[122] This was reinforced at Orleans (511) and Arles (554) and frequently by Carolingian councils (CCSL 148A, pp. 10 (c. 19), 171 (c. 3); MGH *Cap.* I. 102 (c. 15), 111 (c. 17), 183 (c. 11), 400 (c. 31) as well as the *Admonitio generalis*, MGH *Fontes iuris* XVI. 198–9 (c. 31).

[123] My Chapter 3. For the suggestion that early councils were creating law to counter the right of heirs in Roman law to inherit their full patrimony, see Magnou-Nortier, 'Enemies of the Peace', 61–2. In the East, heirs were required to carry out the wishes of monastic founders, even at their own expense (R. Morris, 'The Problems of Property', in Noble and Smith, eds, *Early Medieval Christianities*, 340).

monastery, the dead or dying relied on others to deliver the gift, and not to retract anything already given, to execute their 'will' in both senses of the term: as testament and personal resolution. In law, the resolve of a monastic benefactor was to hand over a gift, an action to be completed.[124] Post-mortem, this resolve relied on heirs and executors; it was to its fulfilment that councils stepped in.

When it comes to the *dispositio* of a hospital by a will-maker, councils stake out a subtly distinct set of legal concerns. The first council to notice hospitals, Childebert's council at Orléans (549), worked with the well-established legal tradition regarding gifts to churches. It injected the term *xenodochia* into an older, oft-repeated canon that defended bequests against heirs who failed to hand over gifts. When, 250 years later, Italian councils turned to hospitals, they did not use this tradition. Their decrees were not addressing the release by heirs of post-mortem or deathbed gifts. Curiously, they were not concerned with the challenges of donation itself, and did not even distinguish between bequests *inter vivos* and *post mortem*. At issue was not the act of giving, but the long afterlife of the bequest. Fixed arrangement was the priority, so that xenodochia were administered to 'the uses for which they were established' and 'governed according to the arrangement of those who instituted them'.[125] Whereas church councils had sought to secure the actual gift to monasteries, Italian councils now sought to secure the *dispositio* itself for xenodochia: the decree and rational design laid out by the founder/testator. Law-makers did not mention other methods of creating hospitals. 'Writings of testators' were the only *scripta* they mentioned.

In contrast to monastic benefactors, whether living or dead hospital founders faced the same legal challenge: how to keep alive the memory of their arrangements after their death. The challenge wrestled with the notion of 'will' not as 'act to be executed' but as 'ongoing resolution'. This resolution provided the fixed purpose of the bequest and so how it must continue to be administered. The legal challenge was not to complete an action; on the contrary, it was to hold a directive continuously in place. The donor's will was a living determination (*dispositio*) that was to persist after death. The founders of xenodochia might also face uncooperative heirs, but the charge they had laid before their heirs was not simply to hand over a gift: it was to ensure that the testator's directives should live, and be followed, long after the mind that conceived them was no more.

---

[124] This is viewing monastic benefaction through the eyes of clerical law-makers. Benefactors and their heirs might see the act differently, often exerting claims over property that had been given, even to the point of possession of the monastery or church itself (Wood, *Prop. Ch.*, 42–7, and her chap. 5–7). In practice, a gift was not simply handed over: it inaugurated a series of reciprocal actions and relationships, 'bonding' donors to monastic communities: B. H. Rosenwein, *To be the Neighbor of Saint Peter* (Ithaca, NY, 1989), 4; Innes, *State and Society*; J. Nightingale, *Monasteries and Patrons in the Gorze Reform* (Oxford, 2001), 39–58; S. D. White, *Custom, Kinship, and Gifts to the Saints* (Chapel Hill, NC, 1988), 130–76; Bijsterveld, 'The Medieval Gift as Agent'.

[125] (c. 23) 'ad easdem utilitates, quibus constituta sunt, ordinentur'; (c. 15) 'secundum dispositionem eorum, qui ea instituerunt, gubernentur.' MGH *Conc.* II.ii, 577; *Conc.* III. 226.

This resolution of an individual was not merely to endure, it was given institutional form. The material bequest that produced a xenodochium was not handed over, but inscribed with the requirements of the donor, what in later centuries would become known as 'the will of the founder'.[126] The hospital was both the container of that will and its servant. As Harald Siems has argued, for the period until the seventh century, there was no law of trusts or trustees, and so, on the face of it, no explicit legal mechanism to secure charities in perpetuity.[127] But the pronouncements of synods and councils, as well as the practice of making and preserving hospitals, reveal a shared model of the xenodochium, one held to the arrangements (*dispositio*) laid down by the original donor, and perhaps to an enhanced *dispositio* of a second donor. The challenge was to secure those arrangements indefinitely. This was the dilemma faced by Childebert and Ultrogotha in 549, who used the great council of Orléans as a public instrument, soliciting the council's collective resolve—and confirmation—to buttress 'this our arrangement' against the dangers of the coming years, especially the predation of elites, especially the bishop, and the incompetence or corruption of administrators.[128]

What must be preserved for xenodochia was therefore distinctive. Decrees for monasteries aimed to preserve the house in perpetuity, as a monastery, and its property against diminution or alienation; beyond that, they sought a better quality of religious observance by its community. It was to maintain something far more particular that councils acted for hospitals: a testamentary bequest, whose directives must remain fixed and be obeyed. This, its original, 'pristine' state, was—as Olona made clear—primarily the arrangements laid out by the testator and, secondarily, the material ability to fulfil it. This made a living will in two senses: as the directives of an individual (*ratio, dispositio*) whose resolution must endure after the individual was gone; and as the written statement of that will: the *testamentoris scriptum* which served as the facility's charter.

It was not only the act of the gift that was different, but also its reception as property. David Ganz and Michael Paulin Blecker have explored how sixth-century churchmen reconceived the very notion of property and ownership, in defining what was given to monastic communities.[129] A gift to a monastery (in concept) was an act of renunciation. An oblate surrendered possession as part of a

---

[126] Watson, 'Origins', 83–7, 94. The Carolingian material gives new weight to Imbert's discussion of the late middle ages: HDC 102–10.

[127] Siems, '*Piae causae*', 57–83. I agree with Siems's main contention that assets were at the core of a hospital, but the Carolingian material allows us to go further, to perceive a legal model rooted in perpetual will. While assets were important, the terms of the bequest were paramount.

[128] The phrase refers to the bishops' own act (and charter) at the council, but this confirmed the royal directives.

[129] Ganz, 'Ideology of Sharing', considers how monastic communities reconceptualized property, in accordance with apostolic ideals. Blecker examines the influence of Roman law on the early *Rule of the Master*, especially as it related to ownership and use of property, M. P. Blecker, 'Roman Law and "Consilium"', *Speculum* 47 (1972). I am indebted to Judy Frost for discussion on the question of endowment.

wider renunciation of self-will; a benefactor, giving 'to God through the monastery', relinquished the human notion of wealth.[130] This picked up on Augustine's distinction between human and divine property, which contrasted the renunciation of wealth to God with human law, wherein an owner imprints his claim onto a possession: '[b]y human law a man says "this is my villa, this is my house, this is my slave"'.[131] An image offered by Arator, the sixth-century Roman deacon and poet, defined its reception by the community: for the gift was placed at the feet rather than into the hands of the apostles, a symbol that management of material wealth had been surrendered and that, once received, monastic property belonged 'to everyone and no-one'.[132] The monastic community held dominion over the property, allowing it or its representative to make decisions as to its retention, disposal, and use. This was an ownership defined in turn by an abrogation of will.

The property of a xenodochium constituted a different kind of endowment. It furnished a facility with ongoing income via a bequest that had been handed over, but not wholly renounced. Its beneficiaries—the poor, pilgrims, or the sick—had no dominion, but neither did the administrators of a xenodochium, who were charged with fulfilling the terms of the bequest. Theirs was not to renounce human wealth, but the opposite: they were appointed for their managerial competence, and their charge was to cultivate its profits and deploy them to uses laid down by the donor, the hospital's *institutor*. The originating bequest retained the human will of this benefactor, in whose service the administrator was now held. The facility itself was defined by the command imprinted onto this original gift. To adapt Arator, the bequest was placed not at the administrators' feet, but firmly in their hands, although their hands were obeying the will of another. And to follow the Augustinian distinction, this endowment was held in human (secular) law.

In Carolingian councils, Lombard elites enacted principles and laws for the management of xenodochia. Through their eyes, across the Italian landscape, we glimpse a wide range of these facilities, great and small, in the hand of the palace and others, in the Alps and nearby, run by brothers and stewards. They offer a messy local contrast to the two great royal-imperial impositions of the previous chapter, in Francia. Yet Italian and Frankish xenodochia still share basic traits:

---

[130] '...donatio rerum suarum Deo per monasterium'. *La règle du maître*, ed. A. de Vogüé, 2 vols (Paris, 1964), II. 374; Blecker, 'Roman Law', 10. In practice, of course, a human notion of wealth was not so easy to abandon, Lesne, *Prop. Eccl.*, 118–23, 133–7. On child oblation and the handling of the inheritance of oblates, M. de Jong, *Child Oblation* (Leiden, 1996), 28–9, 71–5, 119–21, 217–18.

[131] Ganz, 'Ideology of Sharing', 18–19; M. Wilks, '*Thesaurus Ecclesiae*', in B. Sheils and D. Wood, eds, *The Church and Wealth* (1987), 42–3. The distinction is Roman, between what was in and what outside private ownership, and can be found in the second-century *Institutes* of Gaius; G. Kantor, 'Property in Land in Roman Provinces', in G. Kantor et al., eds, *Legalism: Property and Ownership* (Oxford, 2017), 57.

[132] Ganz, 'Ideology of Sharing', 21; 'res monasterii omnium est et nullius est', *La règle du maître*, I. 362; Blecker, 'Roman Law', 7.

they were held to a specific design (*institutio/dispositio*) laid down in writing by the founder or testator;[133] the central concern of councils was that this charge be upheld and the resources administered accordingly; external authorities— governmental, conciliar, and church dignitaries—were called on to protect the facility against maladministration and predation. The Lombard capitularies reveal that xenodochia were a particular kind of foundation. They were Christian institutions but not part of the Chalcedonian charge (in its Carolingian form, the work of *correctio* and *emendatio*). Instead, they appear as material forms, revealed through *restauratio*, the call to restore the built inheritance, religious and civic, of the *res publica*. As foundations, xenodochia were not held to a common rule, nor to any shared undertaking. The concern of councils was to preserve the original bequests to their assigned uses, and to return any that had strayed to their appointed form. Their challenge was to craft a governmental conversation about private will; in upholding the *dispositio*, councils reinforced an institutor's right to design and fix a charity post-mortem.

To speak about xenodochia, councils sought out familiar terms and gave language to recognized practices. In finding components from which to build their laws, however brief, they reveal what xenodochia were or should be in contemporary eyes. And, standing back, we notice that their pronouncements show no awareness of Justinianic institutions or Justinianic legislation. There are no *piae causae* here, or *venerabiles loci*, and no statements that a hospital is accountable to the bishop, even when law-makers did begin to look to bishops to step in. It is time now to explore the origins of these well-established facilities in the West and at their underlying legal form. What were these components from which the Lombard councils were building their laws? The question begins with Roman law.

---

[133] In the case of the Aachen rule, the rule itself provides the *dispositio*, since its goal was to create a communal (not an individual) charge.

5

Roman Law and the Western Tradition

As we have seen, the Lombard capitularies reveal that there was a well-known model for 'xenodochia', familiar from practice but not from written law, when assemblies turned their attention to these facilities in *c*.780. Armed now with a picture of this model, we look for its earlier history: it is time to turn to Roman law.

The new question demands a new stage, on a vast scale; for it moves us from the gathered assemblies of Carolingian Lombardy to the sweeping geography of the late Roman empire. It takes place against the backdrop of a Christianizing Roman empire which, having moved its capital from Rome to Constantinople/Byzantium in the 320s, began in fits and starts to separate into (Greek) East and (Latin) West. By *c*.400, the earliest welfare facilities had arrived in Rome from the Eastern Roman empire, and over the next four centuries *xenodochia* and *ptochia* dotted the West.[1] These were Eastern creations and they brought with them their Greek names. It has been assumed, therefore, that Justinian's law followed suit, emigrating from Byzantium to supply legal definition to the facilities of the West, just as they had to those of the Eastern empire. The relationships—political, religious, and legal—between East and West are at the heart of the question of Christian welfare's early history.

To explore these relationships, it is not possible to talk simply of 'Roman law'. The evolving law of the empire can be mapped onto the changing grid of power across these centuries. 'Roman' law was thus manifest in different forms around the Mediterranean over the millennium that followed Constantine's move East, to what would become Byzantium. To limit confusion, the legislation promulgated under his successor Justinian (527–65) will be referred to here as 'Byzantine' law, to distinguish it from the native ('vulgar' or 'provincial') traditions in the West.[2]

This chapter rethinks the legal origins of hospitals, and the relationship between East and West. It begins by interrogating the only evidence that Justinian's laws were observed in the Carolingian West: two chapters of

---

[1] For welfare institutions in the East, Constantelos, *Byzantine Philanthropy*, 149–65 (*nosocomeia*); 185–93, 207–13 (*xenones*); 222–9 (*gerocomeia*); 241–3, 248–9 (*orphanotrophia, brephotropheia*); 257–64 (*ptocheia*); and map on p. 17. The arrival in the West is treated below.

[2] There is some debate as to whether we can speak of 'Byzantine law' and, if so, from what moment. A case can be made for the year 534, when Justinian's *Code* was completed, after which Western and Eastern traditions diverged. Justinian's subsequent legislation, his *Novellae constitutiones* (Novels), were written in Greek, B. H. Stolte, 'The Law of New Rome', in *CCRL* 355–6, 369–70.

On Hospitals: Welfare, Law, and Christianity in Western Europe, 400–1320. Sethina Watson, Oxford University Press (2020). © Sethina Watson.
DOI: 10.1093/oso/9780198847533.001.0001

Byzantine law, copied by Ansegis, abbot of Saint-Wandrille, into his collection of capitularies in 826/7. The chapter then moves back to the earliest traditions, first in Byzantine law and then in Roman provincial law in the West, where it argues for a separation between East and West and for a distinctively Western and deeply embedded legal tradition. A final section, 'A New Story', presents a new account of the development of welfare houses, and of the law of charities, in the West.

Abbot Ansegis and Julian's *Epitome* (826/7)

Ansegis completed his *Collectio capitularium* in the month before 28 January 827.[3] It would be the largest and most significant collection of royal capitularies of the Carolingian era, and was swiftly and widely disseminated. Over sixty manuscripts survive, leading its modern editor, Gerhard Schmitz, to believe that it found its way into almost every major library in Francia.[4]

Its compiler had forged a long and distinguished career in royal service. As a young monk Ansegis had been introduced at Charlemagne's court in the 790s by his abbot (and relative), Gervold.[5] There he found rapid promotion as an administrator and monastic reformer, turning around the fortunes of a series of abbeys and serving as master of royal works (*exactor operum regalium*) at the palace under Einhard. As a trusted agent of both Charlemagne and Louis the Pious, Ansegis was often dispatched as legate (*missus*) in Francia, as well as to Italy and Spain. In 823, Louis made him abbot of Fontenelle, also known as Saint-Wandrille, a house on the Seine to the west of Rouen, where Ansegis had first become a monk. Here, Ansegis embarked on a programme of building and reform, reinstating the Benedictine rule and growing the size of the community.[6] It was here that he produced his *Collectio*.

The compiler's career is important for the light it sheds on his compendium. A long-running debate as to whether this was a personal or official work, and thus a private or public collection, tended to stress its personal and monastic origins.[7] Recent work has rejected such simple binaries. Carolingian political culture did not make such ready distinctions between empire and monastery, as exemplified

---

[3] In his prologue, Ansegis gives a date of 827 in the 13th year of Louis' rule, which ended on 27 January 827. Frankish years began on Christmas Day (Story, *Carolingian Connections*, 104).

[4] G. Schmitz, 'Einleitung', in his ed., *Collectio Capitularium Ansegisi*, MGH Cap. NS I (Hanover, 1996), 2. Also, *CCEMA* 92–9.

[5] The biography is drawn from Schmitz, 'Einleitung', 4–10, 12, 14.

[6] He is remembered, too, for his alms and gifts of books and treasures, *Chronique des abbés de Fontenelle*, ed. F. P. Pradié (Paris, 1999), 150, 152–70, 176–90, on which text see I. Wood, 'Saint Wandrille and its Historiography', in I. Wood and G. A. Loud, eds, *Church and Chronicle* (London, 1991).

[7] For the debate: S. Airlie, '"For it is Written in the Law"': Ansegis and the Writing of Carolingian Royal Authority', in Baxter et al., eds, *Early Medieval Studies*, 221–2, 231; Mordek, 'Fränkische Kapitularien', 34; Schmitz, 'Einleitung', 10–40, 56–70; Wormald, *Making of English Law*, 52–3.

by Ansegis's own career, in which his roles of reformer and royal agent were indissolubly linked. To Stuart Airlie, the collection was a personal, pious act and also 'part of the overarching public *ministerium*', whose very product 'made all its material royal'.[8] Ansegis was the creative force behind the collection, and his efforts were closely tied to the court and royal agendas. Its genesis was bookended by Louis the Pious's great legislative acts. The final chapter of Louis's *Admonitio ad omnes ordines* from 823×25 directed archbishops and their counts to gather copies of royal capitularies;[9] this text opens Ansegis's book 2, just as Charlemagne's *Admonitio generalis* opened his book 1. And his collection's sudden, wide dissemination has been linked to Louis's capitulary of Worms in 829, which cited Ansegis's text nine times. Copies of the Worms capitulary are so often bound together with the *Collectio* that they have been termed the 'Worms-Ansegis corpus'.[10] So central was its role in the dispersal of royal law that it has even been credited with transforming the very practice of law. Because of the *Collectio*, the argument goes, royal law became present and accessible in a whole new way, reducing the need for *missi* and for new capitularies after 829, whose council at Paris is now seen as the climax of an intensifying phase of royal law-making under Louis the Pious.[11] Ansegis may have been an abbot, but this had been no monastic labour. The *Collectio* was a product of his royal service; his own abbey celebrated Ansegis as abbot, including his many gifts of books, but it made no mention of his *Collectio*.[12] The collection was of Ansegis's making, yet decidedly (and immediately) royal.

The *Collectio* was composed of royal legislation ascribed to Charlemagne, Louis the Pious, and Lothar. In its preface Ansegis states that he composed it from affection for these emperors and to preserve their capitularies, which were at risk of being lost or forgotten, because they were 'scattered on various little parchment leaves' (*in diversis sparsim scripta membranulis*). The capitularies were to serve as

---

[8] 'No matter where he was, Ansegis could never be away from the court; he worked within a potent discourse of Carolingian authority... [a] discourse that spoke through him, that uttered his own text.' Airlie, 'Written in the Law', 222. De Jong, *Epitaph*, 52–6, explores the theme for two other abbots and royal servants.

[9] MGH *Cap.* I. 307 (c. 26); Ganshof, *Recherches sur les capitulaires*, 63–4. The chancellor was to record who had what, and to ensure that none neglect this duty. On Louis's *Admonitio*, Schmitz, 'Einleitung', 1, 14; De Jong, *Penitential State*, 37, 131–3; S. Patzold, *Episcopus: Wissen über Bischöfe im Frankenreich* (Ostfildern, 2008), 140–3.

[10] Schmitz, 'Einleitung', 1–2, 24. It is not clear which manuscript tradition was used at Worms, G. Schmitz, 'Intelligente Schreiber', in H. Mordek, ed., *Papsttum, Kirche und Recht* (Tübingen, 1991), 91–2.

[11] G. Schmitz, '...*pro utile firmiter tenenda sunt lege*', in D. R. Bauer et al., eds, *Mönchtum—Kirche—Herrschaft* (Sigmaringen, 1998), 226–8; De Jong, *Penitential State*, 53. On its influence: Mordek, 'Karolingische Kapitularien', 40, 48; P. Depreux, '*Hincmar et la loi* Revisited', in R. Stone and C. West, eds, *Hincmar of Rheims* (Manchester, 2015). On the significance of 829, Patzold, *Episcopus*, 149–62.

[12] It was not even among the list of manuscripts that Ansegis gave to the abbey, Schmitz, '...*pro utile lege*', 213; *Chron. Fontenelle*, 164–6, 172–6. The abbey had particularly close ties to the crown, Wood, *Prop. Ch.*, 212–13, 221.

'a useful law to be firmly held' (*pro utile firmiter tenenda sunt lege*) for the benefit of the church and Christian religion.[13] The *Collectio* is not a systematic collection, for it does not break material into legal subjects, nor select definitive statements in law. Yet it does have a basic structure. Four books separate ecclesiastical from secular business, and the capitularies of Charlemagne (books 1, 3) from those attributed to Louis and Lothar (together in books 2, 4). Ansegis moved confusing or duplicate material from Charlemagne's capitularies into appendices. Individual capitularies were thus 'torn apart and distributed across various books and appendices', according to this basic (but by no means consistent) structure.[14] Schmitz saw Ansegis as an archivist rather than a jurist, seeking to preserve any capitulary he could find, but not to make sense of the laws themselves. The result is a collection that included antiquated, moribund, and contradictory capitula, and made use of only twenty-six of the one hundred known capitularies between 768 and 826.[15] While the overarching arrangement seems simple, the collection included texts that were not strictly capitularies, nor even royal; these were inadvertent errors, Schmitz believed, from working with small parchment leaves (*membranula*) that lacked headings or dates.[16] Nevertheless, the texts can be linked to the court: for example, as responses to *missi*, or programmes of religious correction encouraged by the palace.

Curiously, these problems are concentrated in book 2, the messiest of the collection. This book (*libellus*) aimed to gather the ecclesiastical laws of Louis the Pious and Lothar;[17] but it included much that was either not ecclesiastical or not from Louis. In the first half, the secular chapters of Louis's *Admonitio* were retained, suggesting a preference to keep that text whole (cc. 1–24); and, compounding the issue, that text was followed by a series of directives as to where and how *missi* were to hold their legations (cc. 25–8). Schmitz characterized the book's second half (cc. 29–46) as particularly 'problematic', since much of the material was from Charlemagne's reign. This was an error of ascription, he suggested, that was left uncorrected because the palace was concerned with the body of laws, not their authorship.[18] The explanation seems at odds with a collection whose basic organizing principle was to distinguish Louis's acts from those of Charlemagne, and secular from ecclesiastical business. It is odd, too, to think that Ansegis the royal agent and reformer should be most confused by the

---

[13] MGH *Cap.* NS I. 431–3; Schmitz, 'Einleitung', 12–14.
[14] 'Ansegis mußte einzelne Kapitularien auseinanderreißen und über verschiedene Bücher bzw. Appendices verteilen.' Schmitz, 'Einleitung', 18. This is not the case for book 2. On the collection, and the tendency to dististinguish ecclesiastical from secular business at this time, Ganshof, *Recherches sur les capitulaires*, 13, 69–70.
[15] Schmitz, 'Einleitung', 4, 15–16, with its structure and (opaque) editorial criteria on 17–22; Mordek, 'Karolingische Kapitularien', 37.
[16] As 'Nicht als Kapitularien anzusehende Stücke', in Schmitz, 'Einleitung', 26–34, and 32–3 for the *membranula*.
[17] The book's preface offers little more than this statement in explanation, MGH *Cap.* NS I. 517.
[18] Schmitz, 'Capitulary Legislation', 425–6; Schmitz, '... *pro utile lege*', 216–19.

ecclesiastical material of the court he served. Perhaps the problem of understanding lies not with Ansegis but with us, and it is we who have yet to get to grips with the corpus that constitutes book 2, the one most immediately allied to Ansegis's own mission: to gather a *lex* for the church.[19] His selection may be less random, or mistaken, than some have believed, a question to which we shall return.

For now, it is enough to note that, even among this problematic material, two chapters stand apart. They do not fit into any definition of Frankish legislation and, to Schmitz, should be 'delete[d] ... from the list of Louis's capitularies', for they are two chapters (cc. 29–30) of Byzantine legislation.[20] These two chapters are important here, because they are the only examples of Byzantine law relating to xenodochia in the West; they have attracted considerable interest among historians of law because they stand out in Carolingian capitularies as the only copies of *any* Byzantine law to appear across the range of these texts.[21] The closer one looks, the more exceptional these chapters become.

Ansegis included his extracts in his second book, copying them verbatim, without comment or accreditation. They are, in fact, not direct copies of legislation, but summaries from Julian's *Epitome,* a digest of 124 of Justinian's 168 novels.[22] The Greek texts of these laws, promulgated between 535 and 545, were not available in the West, except via a Latin teaching aid created in 556/7 by the Byzantine legal scholar, Julian *antecessor.* It was Julian's chapters 32 and 33, along with their titles, that Ansegis copied.[23] They addressed the first two chapters of Justinian's novel 7, a new law of 535 that extended an earlier law of Leo I (457–74) to protect property belonging to churches. Novel 7 expanded the latter's reach geographically, beyond Constantinople to the whole empire, and institutionally, to include welfare houses with churches and monasteries, translating a local into a general law with clearly defined terms.[24] The original novel was long, regulating

---

[19] MGH *Cap.* NS I. 432–3. At the very least, book 2 challenges Schmitz's strict definition of capitulary, as royal legislation. Pössel's broader definition, of material emanating from or through the auspices of the palace, would recast the conclusions somewhat, although it would still not account for the *Epitome* chapters (Pössel, 'Authors and Recipients', 267–8). On thinking in terms of *lex*, Ganshof, *Recherches sur les capitulaires*, 74–6; T. Tsuda, 'Was hat Ansegis gesammelt?', *Concilium aevi medii* 16 (2013).

[20] Schmitz, 'Capitulary Legislation', 425–6. There is a third extract from the *Epitome*, 'Si servus clericus fiat'. This seems to have been added later, after Ansegis. It occurs in only four manuscripts, where it is inserted immediately after the prologue, MGH *Cap.* NS I. 444, esp. n. 21.

[21] J. Gaudemet, 'Survivances Romaines', *Tijdschrift voor Rechtsgeschiedenis* 23 (1955), 205; F. L. Ganshof, 'Le droit romain dans les capitulaires et dans la collection d'Ansegise', *Ius Romanum Medii Aevi*, pt 1, 2b, *cc* alphabeta (Milan, 1969); S. Esders and S. Patzold, 'From Justinian to Louis the Pious: Inalienability of Church Property', in *Relig. Franks*, 400–6.

[22] On the novels, T. G. Kearley, 'The Creation and Transmission of Justinian's Novels', *Law Library Journal* 102:3 (2010–11); on Justinian's corpus of law in the West, *CICMA* 36–65; and W. Kaiser, *Die Epitome Iuliani* (Frankfurt am Main, 2004), on the manuscript traditions of the *Epitome*.

[23] Const. 7, kp. 32–3, *Iuliani epitome Latina Novellarum Iustiniani*, ed. G. F. Hänel (Leipzig, 1873; repr. Osnabrück, 1965), 32.

[24] Cod. 1.2.14.

long-term leases (§3) and short-term uses (§4), laying out penalties for abuse by parties (§§5–8) and authorities (§§9–10), protecting the sites of monasteries and churches (§11), and prohibiting the acquisition of sterile properties (§12). All twelve chapters were summarized by Julian (kp. 32–43), but Ansegis incorporated only the first two into his collection.

The first, 'That properties pertaining to a venerable place must not be alienated',[25] set out the terms of the prohibition. It defined (i) the institutions to which it applied (any church established under Roman authority, or any *xenodochium, ptochotrophium, nosocomium, orphanotrophium, gerontocomium, brephotrophium*, or monastery of monks or nuns with an abbot or abbess); what constituted (ii) immovable property, such as a house, field, garden, and rural slaves; and (iii) alienation (a sale, gift, exchange, or perpetual lease). It then (iv) addressed possible transgressors and provided status-specific penalties, to priests and stewards of a house, to their successors, and to public officials who certified a wrongful grant, such as the notary and magistrate.[26] At the end (v) Julian added an explanatory section, defining six terms, each as 'a venerable place':

Xenodochium, that is, a venerable place in which pilgrims are received;
Ptochotrophium ... in which poor and sick men are maintained;
Nosocomium ... in which diseased men are tended to;
Orphanotrophium ... in which children deprived of parents are maintained;

---

[25] DE REBUS AD VENERABILIA LOCA PERTINENTIBUS NON ALIENANDIS (Const. 7, kp. 32), although the places are rendered by Ansegis in the singular *ad venerabilem locum* (2.29).

[26] MGH *Cap.* NS I. 549–52 (2.29): '(i) Nulla sub romana ditione constituta ecclesia vel *ex*enodochium vel ptochotrophium vel noso*ch*omium vel orphanotrophium vel geron*th*ochomium vel brephotrophium vel monasterium tam monachorum quam sanctimonialium, archimandritam habens vel archimandritissam, *ergo his omnibus non* ¹*liceat* [licentium habeat] alienare (ii) rem immobilem, sive domum sive agrum sive [h]ortum sive rusticum mancipium vel panes civiles, neque creditoribus specialis hypothecae titulo obligare. (iii) Alienationis autem verbum contine*at* venditionem, donationem, permutationem et emphi[y]teuseos perpetuum contractum. (iv) Sed omnes omnino sacerdotes huiusmodi alienatione abstineant poenas timentes, quas Leoniana constitutio minatur¹, id est, ut is quidem, qui comparav*er*it rem, loco venerabili reddat [eam ei], cuius et antea fuerat, scilicet cum fructibus aliisque emolumentis, quae in medio tempore facta sunt; *hyc*onomum [oeconomum] autem ecclesiae praestare [oportet] omne lucrum, quod ex huiusmodi prohibita alienatione senserit vel ecclesiam damno *eff*ecerit, ita ut in posterum *hyc*onomus [oeconomus] non sit. Non solum autem ipse, sed etiam successores eius teneantur, sive ipse *archyc*onomus [oeconomus] alienaverit, sive respiciens alienantem episopum non prohibuerit, [et] multo magis si consenserit. Tabellionem autem, qui talia interdicta [in]strumenta conscripts[er]it, perpetuo ex[s]ilio tradi oportet. Magistratus autem, qui eadem [in]strumenta admiserunt, et *ad* officiales, qui operam dederunt, et monumentis intimentur donationes vel ceterae alienationes actis intervenientibus confirmentur, non solum magistratus, sed etiam dignitate et facultatibus suis c*e*dant. Remittit autem constitutio ea, quae in praeterito tempore acta sunt; excepit autem quosdam contractos, quos in sequentibus exponit capitulis, per quos *et* ecclesiarum immobiles res alienari possunt.' Here and below major variances are marked between Ansegis' text and Julian's *Epitome*, as ed. by Hänel (*Iuliani epitome*, p. 32), using italics for letters only in Ansegis and square brackets for those only in the *Epitome*. Esders and Patzold, 'Inalienability', 390–1, offer an English translation of the chapters from Ansegis (2.29–30), offering 'economist' for steward and *prochotrophium* for ptochotrophium.

Gerontocomium... in which poor men, infirm only due to old age are tended to;
Brephotropium... in which infants are nourished.[27]

When historians claim that Western law-makers established a typology of charitable institutions in law, adopted from Eastern law, they are referring to this list,
from Julian's *Epitome*.

Julian's list was no statement of law, however. It runs, in order, through the
institutions listed at the head of the chapter. It omits 'church' and 'monastery',
because Julian could use known Latin terms (*ecclesia, monasterium*), translations
for the Greek *ekklēsia* and *monastērion*. But Julian lacked Latin terms for the six
welfare institutions or, at least, terms recognizable to his Latin audience. So he
retained the Greek in the chapter and appended a list of definitions at the end, in
the order they had appeared, transcribing the names into Latinized Greek: thus
nosokomeion is rendered '*nosochomium*... where diseased men are tended'. It is a
didactic endnote for his students, and Ansegis dutifully copied each definition into
his *Collectio*. Manuscripts of the *Collectio* recognized their role as a glossary,
setting the words apart with large spaces and using capitals (or large script),
perhaps attempting to break the word into parts:

> ecclesiaru[m] immobilesres alienaripossunt. Exe Nodo
> cHIUM   Idestlocusvenerabilis inquoperegrinisus
> cipiuntur   PTocho TRO Phium   Idestlocus
> venerabilis inquo pauperes&infirmihominespascuntur
> NOSO CHOMIUM   Idestlocusvenerabilis inquo
> aegrotihominescurantur   ARPHANO TROPHIUM
> Id est locusvenerabilis inquoparentibus orbatipueripascuntur...[28]

The definitions were not meant as, nor were they mistaken for law. They served
a similar purpose for Ansegis's readers as they had for Julian's, since the array of
institutions were as alien in ninth-century Francia as they had been to sixth-
century Latins. Indeed, much more of the chapter would have been alien to
Frankish readers, including terms for leases, as well as church and civic offices.
In contrast, the next chapter (c. 30) was brief and clear. Here, under the title,
'Concerning this [topic], how the emperor is permitted to transfer the property of

---

[27] '(v) *Exenodochium*, id est locus venerabilis, in quo peregrini suscipiuntur. *Ptochotrophium*, id est
locus venerabilis, in quo pauperes et infirmi homines pascuntur. *Nosochomium*, id est locus venerabilis, in quo aegroti homines curantur. *Orphanotrophium*, id est locus venerabilis, in quo parentibus
orbati pueri pascuntur. *Gerontho*[co]*mium*, id est locus venerabilis, in quo pauperes et propter
senectutem solam infirmi homines curantur. *Brephotrophium*, id est locus venerabilis, in quo infantes
aluntur.' MGH *Cap.* NS I. 552–3.

[28] Munich MS Bayerische Staatsbibliothek, Clm 29555/1, fol. 4v, to illustrate a wider tradition. BnF
lat. 4568, fol. 29v, offers a more confident rendition of the Greek terms.

a holy place', Ansegis copied Julian's full chapter (kp. 33), which gave the prince the right to exchange property with that held by a holy place.[29]

Today, these Byzantine chapters are the best-known in Ansegis's collection, yet little light has been shed on how they came to be in the collection, or how they relate to his Frankish world. It is their out-of-place character that has attracted attention. The assumption by their first editor, Alfred Boretius, that they were capitularies promulgated by Louis the Pious has been roundly dismissed, as has Imbert's vision of Ansegis as a confector of law, forging an imperial weapon against clerics who plundered church property.[30] Schmitz found an abbot with no interest in the content of the laws he collected, suggesting that Ansegis had copied in error what he had found on a loose membrane. In so doing, he brings the explanation full circle: the *Epitome* chapters were not from capitularies, but Ansegis thought they were. Curiously, while debate has focused on how the chapters came to be promulgated as law, their status as law in Francia has not been questioned. Their appearance in Ansegis's collection has been taken as evidence that such law was not foreign in Francia, but would seem to contemporaries as closely reflecting matters pertaining to the church (i.e. welfare houses).[31] A recent study by Stefan Esders and Steffen Patzold goes further, finding an active quest to adopt Justinianic law at the royal court and, with it, his concepts of imperial rule, especially notions of inalienability (Ansegis 2.29) and imperial sovereignty (2.30).[32] The idea that the Frankish court enacted Justinianic law, broadly or selectively, if systematically, continues to endure, a bullish take that rests on these two chapters in Ansegis's *Collectio*. How these came to be part of a legal collection of the 820s is therefore central to bigger questions, of court culture and legal heritage. The evidence is contextual, yet adequate to offer a series of interpretations or scenarios.

As we have seen, the presence of these chapters among such Frankish material was unique. Justinian's legislation was largely unknown in the West. The collections of law had emerged in Byzantium too late to find purchase in Italy, where the outposts of Eastern empire were on the military defensive. It would not even be

---

[29] (2.30) 'DE HOC, QUOMODO LICEAT AD IMPERATOREM RES SANCTI LOCI TRANSFERRI [TRANSFERRE]. Si princeps voluerit rem immobilem sancto loco praestare et accipere ab eo aliam immobilem rem et eo modo permutationem contrahere, liceat hoc facere ei divina pragmatica sanctione ab eo promulgata.' MGH *Cap.* NS I. 553; *Iuliani epitome* (Const. 7, kp. 33).

[30] Schmitz, 'Einleitung', 26–7. The vision of Ansegis as a proto-Benedict Levita rests largely on the fact that Benedict later made use of the *Epitome*, Imbert, 'Droit Romain', 65–7; Ganshof, 'Le droit romain', 28–9. On Benedict's use of the *Epitome*, Kaiser, *Epit. Iul.*, 464–5.

[31] Schmitz, 'Einleitung', 34; Airlie, 'Written in the Law', 230–1.

[32] Esders and Patzold, 'Inalienability', trace the concept of inalienability in Byzantine legislation to the West, resting its adoption on Ansegis (pp. 389–402). Their subject was less the law itself than the political meaning of its appropriation in the 820s. What follows owes a debt to their work, although I take a different position on the law itself and so suggest a different shape to activity under Louis the Pious.

adopted in the Italian regions where Byzantine rule had for a time persisted.[33] Manuscripts in Western collections are few and contain little evidence of scholarly interest or legal understanding; there are no glosses, for example, that make associations between ideas or chapters.[34] Only Julian's *Epitome* was known or copied in the West. A handful of manuscripts demonstrate a renewed if slight interest centred in Rome in the decades around 800, but even here—where Greek popes had predominated into the mid-eighth century—Greek remained a foreign language, associated with Byzantium, and increasingly tinged with the suggestion of error.[35] The pattern continued into the ninth century, when several manuscripts can be linked to Frankish ecclesiastical centres, and one, Paris BN lat. 4418, to the Frankish court; but this is a thin haul given the vigorous book production under the Carolingians and, significantly, it evinces little evidence of reading or use of the corpus.[36]

In the second half of the ninth century, evidence of contact with the material emerges, and brief quotes appear in ecclesiastical letters or treatises. They have long been seen as 'mined' for ammunition in arguments rather than drawn from knowledge, in a 'Carolingian Europe [that] was largely indifferent to Roman law'.[37] Such a bleak picture is now coming under challenge, as manuscript evidence suggests a wider interest in and use of Roman legal texts.[38] Several new collections of Roman law were compiled in North Italy, notably *Lex Romana canonice compta* (not before 829×837), *Collectio Anselmo dedicata* (882×896), and the *Excerpta Bobiensia*.[39] Yet references to Roman law in Frankish law codes

---

[33] Law schools in Rome did teach the Institutes, Digest, Code, and Novels from the 540s, but this was short-lived and limited (the imperial centre for such teaching had moved to Beirut). Several teaching aids did emerge, based largely on the Novels (D. Liebs, 'Roman Law', in Cameron et al., eds, *Cambridge Ancient History* XIV (Cambridge, 2000), 253, 256–7). The odd acquaintance with a Justinian novel has been detected at the council of Tours (567), S. Esders, *Römische Rechtstradition und merowingisches Königtum* (Göttingen, 1997), 180–1 n.

[34] *CICMA* 36–65. References to Roman law in Carolingian law books seem rhetorical rather than learned, R. McKitterick 'Some Carolingian Law Books', in B. Tierney and P. Linehan, eds, *Authority and Power* (Cambridge, 1980).

[35] T. F. X. Noble, 'The Declining Knowledge of Greek', *Byzantinische Zeitschrift* 78 (1985). This came to a head in 825 when, responding to a letter from the Byzantine emperor to Louis the Pious, Frankish bishops refuted the Greek position on images: T. F. X. Noble, 'The Settlement of Doctrinal Disputes', in Baxter, ed., *Early Medieval Studies*, 247ff.; for its associations with Greek and the Greeks, MGH *Conc.* II.ii, 497 (c. 53), 501–2 (c. 62), 534–5 (c. 64).

[36] *CICMA* 49; Kaiser, *Epit. Iul.* 30–3; T. Faulkner, *Law and Authority* (Cambridge, 2016), 224–5, who sees the *Epitome* as 'the dead end of a tradition', one sought out in North Italy but not used in Francia.

[37] *CICMA* 52–5, with quotation on p. 52; Gaudemet, 'Survivances Romaines', 205; Ganshof, 'Le droit romain'.

[38] Especially the work of Stefan Esders and Steffan Pazold. Also, T. Faulkener, *Law and Authority*, 222–44; D. Trump, 'Die Überlieferung des römischen Rechts', *Concilium medii aevi* 19 (2016).

[39] On the collections, *CICMA* 55–61. The complexity of the Roman law tradition is revealed in Kaiser, *Epit. Iul.*, where pp. 493–521 and 526–87 discuss the *Lex romana canonica compta*. The latter survives in one manuscript, ed. C. G. Mor, *Lex romana canonice compta* (Pavia, 1927). It copied many chapters of the *Epitome*, including the whole of Const. 7 (at cc. 96–106, 166). These include chapters mentioning *xenodochia* and *ptochia*, which appear interspersed within sections on administrators,

did tend to be generic ('sicut lex Romana praecipit') or to cite early Western compilations of Roman law, such as the *Lex Romana Visigothorum*. F. L. Ganshof's point still stands that 'one never finds an entire Roman law text inserted into a capitulary'.[40] And, in the 820s, the new Roman law collections were still a generation away. Ansegis' Roman chapters (2.29–30) remain unique.

It seems unlikely that Ansegis extracted the chapters from the *Epitome* himself. His method as a compiler argues against this. Ansegis was an unusually conservative editor, who did not intervene in the texts he copied and took little interest in the meaning of his material, a characteristic that extends to his *Epitome* chapters.[41] With the exception of the title of the second chapter (2.30), the texts appear untouched.[42] The end of the first chapter announced that exceptions are 'expounded in the following chapters', a word left in the plural.[43] Ansegis shows little interest in legal ideas; it is unlikely that he had read such a rare text as the *Epitome*, and likely that someone else had extracted the two chapters.

So how could these membranes have come to Ansegis? One option might be via a monastic library, perhaps Ansegis's own at Saint-Wandrille, but this seems unlikely. The few *Epitome* manuscripts of this early date are linked to cathedral and papal libraries, and their later use bears out a connection to episcopal argument rather than religious study. This may be why several manuscripts are linked to Lyons, Agobard's archiepiscopal see, and how one arrived from North Italy at Corbie Abbey, where the Pseudo-Isidorian forgers were soon to be at work.[44] A monastic interest did emerge in the definitions of the Greek terms for welfare houses, as given by Julian and transmitted by Ansegis. The definitions were copied as curiosities by lexicographers alongside other Greek words and

---

bequests in last wills, and management of property (cc. 19, 47, 84, 96–7, 108, 122, 128–9), but not in the section on monks, nuns, and monasteries (cc. 141–68). The arrangement suggests an awareness of welfare houses but no concern to address them as a topic; it also classes them among administrative not monastic business. On the collection, its inexpert compiler and its context: *CICMA* 55–62.

[40] Ganshof, 'Le droit romain', 3–43, with quotation on p. 41.

[41] Schmitz, 'Einleitung', 4, 15–16, and 'Intelligente Schreiber', 91–2. Ansegis's manuscripts share common variants for kp. 32, 33 that cannot be related to a particular manuscript tradition, although Kaiser found echoes in his Groups A and C (Kaiser, *Epit. Iul.* 92–5, 469–70, esp. p. 469 n.).

[42] Minor variants in the long first chapter can be found in other manuscripts linked to the region: i.e. 'Nulla . . . ergo his omnibus non liceat alienare' (*Iuliani epitome*: 'Nulla . . . licentiam habeat alienare') and the use of *hyconomium* and *praestare ~~oportet~~*, can also be found in BnF lat. 4568, fol. 29r, a manuscript at Corbie by the eleventh century (Kaiser, *Epit. Iul.* 23–7).

[43] ' . . . in sequentibus exponit capitulis'. MGH *Cap.* NS I. 552.

[44] For Agobard, see below, p. 129–30. On the libraries, Kaiser, *Epit. Iul.* 92–5; *CICMA* 49. The Corbie manuscript, BnF lat. 4568, was not the source of the *Collectio* extracts: its kp. 32–3 (fols 28v–30r) include many variants from Ansegis: *hostum* (for *ortum*), *speciales* (*specialis*), *emphyituseos* (*emphiteuseos*), *permutuum conspectum* (*perpetuum contractum*); *ut his* (*ut is*). Neither was the *Summa de ordine ecclesiastico*, which survives in one manuscript (Benedict Levita's source) that omits kp. 33 and contains a massively abbreviated kp. 32 (at c. 22, 'De sanctis eclesiis'), omitting any reference to welfare houses—and much else—except the word *xenodochium* at the beginning. *Die 'Summa de ordine ecclesiastico': Eine römisch-rechtliche Quelle Benedicts*, ed. G. Schmitz and M. Weber (2004), 17–18, available at <http://www.benedictus.mgh.de/quellen/summa.pdf>.

letters or into Greek–Latin dictionaries.[45] It is unlikely that Ansegis came upon his text in this way, however. The date is too early (the fashion for Greek was in its infancy in 826)[46] and Ansegis's copy is too long, preserving the whole of Justinian's two chapters, not just the list of definitions. Since the practice of copying the definitions is first known from the mid-ninth century at the monastery of St Gall, it seems more likely that Ansegis was the lexicographers' source, not the other way around.[47] The earliest instance of their lexical copying can be identified with Grimald, abbot of St Gall (841–72), who seems to have brought the tradition to St Gall.[48] The highly educated Grimald became abbot during a long career as an imperial chaplain, and has been detected in this position as early as 824.[49] He links the circulation of these definitions as much to the royal palace, therefore, as to St Gall.

Despite its apparent incoherence, Ansegis's book 2 is created from only four texts. To the *Admonitio* of Louis the Pious (cc. 1–24) and directives for *missi* (cc. 25–8) were appended the *Epitome* chapters (cc. 29–30) and a messy series of synodal rulings (cc. 31–46). The latter were copied from the Munich *rotulus*, Munich, BSB MS Clm 29555/2, a rough membrane, hastily compiled with a series of chapters from three of the five reform synods of 813.[50] They date to Charlemagne's reign and were ecclesiastical synods, one petitioning the emperor. A conceptual disorder and even repetition of canons (as well as subjects) reveals that the *rotulus* was neither a capitulary nor the draft of one. It seems to be a series

---

[45] B. M. Kaczynski, 'Some St. Gall Glosses on Greek Philanthropic Nomenclature', *Speculum* 58 (1983); H. Omont, 'Glossarium Andegavense, MS 477 (461) de la bibliothèque d'Angers', *Bibliothèque de l'école des chartes* 59 (1898), 688; A. C. Dionisotti, 'Greek Grammars and Dictionaries in Carolingian Europe', in M. W. Herren, ed., *The Sacred Nectar of the Greeks* (1988). The wider collection of glossaries, poor in quality, are considered in B. M. Kaczynski, *Greek in the Carolingian Age* (Cambridge, MA, 1988), 57–74. Also, M. L. W. Laistner, 'Notes on Greek', *Bulletin of the John Rylands Library* 7 (1923), whose later examples copy only the definition of *xenodochium* (p. 445).

[46] The study of Greek would take flight twenty years later (c.845–880) under Johannes Scottus Eriugena (W. Berschin, *Greek Letters and the Latin Middle Ages*, tr. J. C. Frakes (Washington, DC, 1988), 107–55, 384–7). An early Greek grammar, perhaps produced to assist Hilduin of St Denis in 827, did not include the terms for welfare houses: BnF lat. 523, fols 134v–135r; M. Lapidge, *Hilduin of Saint-Denis* (Leiden, 2017), 32–5, 69–80.

[47] Kaczynski, 'St. Gall Glosses', 1013, where they are found in glossaries or educational collections alongside poems and songs: St Gall, Stiftsbibliothek MSS Cod. Sang. 196 (front flyleaf), 299 (p. 292), and 397 (p. 38), and Munich, BSB MS Clm 19413, fol. 118r, a tenth-century manuscript with links to a St Gall manuscript (Rio, *Legal Practice*, 249–51).

[48] It is included in his *vade mecum* (personal handbook): St Gall, Stiftsbibliothek MS Cod. Sang. 397, p. 38; noticed, too, in Enders and Patzold, 'Inalienability', 397. Kaczynski, 'St. Gall Glosses', lays out the variant readings (pp. 1010–11) and later tradition (pp. 1015–16).

[49] On Grimald, M. M. Hildebrandt, *The External School in Carolingian Society* (Leiden, 1992), 108–12; B. Bischoff, 'Bücher am Hofe Ludwigs des Deutschen', in his *Mittelalterliche Studien*, III (Stuttgart, 1981), 192–3, and 201ff. Grimald was interested in Greek words: the welfare houses appear alongside other Greek terms in his *vade mecum*, while Ermenric's didactic letter, which Grimald preserved, contains a lengthy discussion of Greek terms, MGH *Epp.* V. 543–5, 549, and A. L. Taylor, *Epic Lives and Monasticism* (Cambridge, 2013), 118, on the letter.

[50] Schmitz, 'Einleitung', 21, 27–8, and 'Capitulary Legislation', 426–7; Mordek, 'Karolingische Kapitularien', 33–5. On the councils of 813, Kramer, *Rethinking Authority*, 61–9.

of notes, gathered hurriedly by a scribe.[51] The script suggests a scribe from Mondsee Abbey and a date near 813, raising questions as to how a text from Bavaria might be linked to Ansegis in northern France.[52] A solution was presented by Schmitz, in the person of Hildebald, archbishop of Cologne and arch-chaplain of the royal palace (787–819), who was also abbot of Mondsee from 802.[53] It was common for abbots to introduce talented monks into palace service, as Ansegis's own career bears witness. The *rotulus* may thus have been compiled by a palace chaplain for palace use. We may perceive its influence, or at least echoes of its concerns, in later legislation. The impoverishment of heirs through donations to the church was addressed by Louis in 818/9, while a council of bishops held in 818/9×29 treated lay instruction (c. 3), punishment of parricides and homicides (c. 6), and concern by officials for the poor (cc. 7, 8).[54] The *rotulus* was in active use—or at least relevant—during the early years of Louis's reign, when Ansegis was a senior figure at the palace. The *rotulus* offers a possible explanation for how another *membranulum*, with its two *Epitome* chapters, was scooped up by the abbot. It is possible that both parchments were working material at the palace, deployed in the fashioning of new policy.

The links between the *rotulus* and palace encourage a return to the problem of Ansegis's book 2, which defies its compiler's own organizing principles. Book 2 does not include Louis's most important ecclesiastical council, of 818/9, which Ansegis placed in book 1, and so notionally under Charlemagne's acts.[55] Book 2 is odd in other ways. It opens with Louis's *Admonitio* of 823×25, a capitulary that we know of almost solely because of Ansegis's collection; there is little evidence to indicate independent circulation.[56] This also appears in Ansegis's 'ecclesiastical' book 2, including all of the *Admonitio*'s secular material. Book 2 is much smaller than the others, with forty-six chapters to book 1's 162, 3's ninety, and 4's seventy-four. Book 2 was also barely noticed at the council of Worms in 829, which otherwise made ready use of Ansegis's collection.[57] Given that Ansegis's stated

---

[51] Two decrees of the council of Mainz (2.34, 35) are repeated at Arles (2.44, 45), Schmitz, 'Einleitung', 21. In addition to ancient churches (cc. 4, 15) and education of children (cc. 5, 14) topics of interest to the scribe include orphans and the poor (cc. 1, 2), penalties for those who are unchaste or murder or refuse to pay tithes (cc. 7, 11), instruction of the laity (cc. 8, 9, 13), and reception of the eucharist (cc. 8, 13). MGH *Cap.* NS I. 553–63.

[52] Schmitz, 'Einleitung', 27.   [53] Schmitz, 'Capitulary Legislation', 427 n.

[54] MGH *Cap.* I. 277, c. 7; *Conc.* II.ii, 594–5, which echo Ansegis 2.38–9, 41, 32. The chapter on the mass (c. 3) includes the same quotations as Ansegis 2.38.

[55] Schmitz, 'Einleitung', 19–20. For the council's reforms in context, Wood, *Prop. Ch.* 792.

[56] Beyond the *Collectio*, it survives in only one (Italian) manuscript, MS Blankenburg, fols 73r–79r, discussed in Chapter 6, and two small fragments in a northern French manuscript. In contrast, Charlemagne's *Admonitio generalis* and Louis's *Capitulare ecclesiasticum* (818/9), both in Ansegis's book 1, survive in over forty and twenty other manuscripts, respectively: 'Admonitio generalis' and 'Capitulare ecclesiasticum', in <https://capitularia.uni-koeln.de/capit/pre814/bk-nr-022> and <.../capit/ldf/bk-nr-138> (accessed Aug. 2019). For the fragments, 'Valenciennes, Bibliothèque municipale, 162', in *Capitularia*, <https://capitularia.uni-koeln.de/mss/valenciennes-bm-162>.

[57] The council only cited 2.21, *De nonis et decimis*, from Louis's *Admonitio*; in contrast, the council cited Louis's secular laws six times, from 4.13, 25, 30, 36, 38, 55. It noticed Charlemagne's legislation

goal for the collection was to gather law to conserve holy church (*ut ad sanctae ecclesiae statum longevis conservandum temporibus*), book 2 is at best a rudimentary (and at worst a failed) centrepiece to his collection.

This crude amalgamation of texts in book 2 makes more sense if we think of this book not as a finished compilation, but as part of a mission to gather law that had not yet been brought to fruition. For book 2 seems less a collection of laws than a preliminary gathering of texts from the palace with a view to fashioning a new *lex* for the church.[58] The council of Paris (829) is widely held to be a high-water mark of Carolingian law-making, with its vision of a Christian *ministerium* embraced by emperor, clerics, and nobility. The case has been made for a long preparation among the bishops;[59] is it possible that the texts of Ansegis's book 2 were material that was accumulated by the royal palace in preparation for just such a comprehensive endeavour?[60] If so, it had little impact on the capitulary that emerged from the June meeting in Paris. Laid out by Jonas, bishop of Orléans and imperial cleric, this drew upon other traditions for its composition.[61] Rather, it was the August meeting of a council at Worms that made use of Ansegis's collection. While Worms made no reference to the *Epitome* chapters, it did address one of their concerns. The instructions to *missi* (c. 5) upheld 'reasonable and useful' alterations (*commutationes*) to church property that had been made under Charlemagne and Louis, allowed the dissolution of 'unprofitable, troublesome or unreasonable' transactions, and required that the emperor be notified when mortmain was involved.[62] It does not use language from the second *Epitome* chapter (2.30), but both statements concern exchanges of church property and the prince's overarching authority.

So, what purpose did the *Epitome* chapters serve? Contemporary law-makers focused on the second of the two. It was not the statement on inalienability (2.29) that was gathered into Frankish law, but its exemption (2.30), reserving authority

---

less often, from 1.157; 3.26, 40: MGH *Cap.* II. 13–14 (cc. 5, 9), 14–16 (cc. 1, 5, 8), 18–20 (cc. 1, 5, 8). The Worms council's preference for Ansegis's secular material stands out at what was remembered as a great ecclesiastical council (Depreux, 'Hincmar et la loi Revisited', 160–1).

[58] The so-called *Capitula Ecclesiastica* (810×813?) in book 1 (cc. 140–58; MGH *Cap.* I. 178–9) also has a provisional quality, prompting Schmitz to characterize it as 'vielleicht eine Art Memorandum, partiell jedenfalls ein Tractandenkatalog von zu regelnden Problemen, also allenfalls die Vorstufe eines Kapitulars' (Schmitz, '... *pro utile lege*', 219).

[59] Patzold, *Episcopus*, 147–53.

[60] The language of the general prologue for book 2 differs slightly from the other books: it is the only one to prefer *edere* (bring forth/raise up) to *facere* (compose, produce), and transcribed (*descripsi*) to assembled (*adunavi*) in books 1 and 3, and gathered (*congessi*) in book 4. MGH *Cap.* NS I. 433.

[61] Patzold, *Episcopus*, 153ff.; J. Scharf, 'Studien zu Smaragdus und Jonas', *Deutsches Archiv für Erforschung des Mittelalters* 17 (1961), 348ff. Jonas was concerned to prevent secular uses of ecclesiastical property, including by the emperor (Wood, *Prop. Ch.* 794), a vision that flies in the face of the *Epitome* chapters.

[62] '... rationabiles atque utiles ... inutiles et incommodae atque inrationabiles', MGH *Cap.* II. 15. Schmitz, '... *pro utile lege*', 226–8; Esders and Patzold, 'Inalienability', 398–9.

to the emperor to permit exchanges of church property. Inalienability was well-established in church law and reiterated by Frankish councils. Most recently, reform synods of Mainz and Arles in 813 had forbidden that possessions of ancient churches should be alienated (*priventur*), a decree copied twice by Ansegis (2.34, 45) from the Munich *rotulus*.[63] Conceivably, the first of the *Epitome* chapters proffered further details on this protection, forbidding sale, gift, exchange, or mortgage. Yet neither the terms nor the concepts in this chapter left a mark on Frankish law, which continued to rest on Gallic and Merovingian precedents, embracing Julianus Pomerius's definition of church property, and a developing rhetoric against plunderers, robbers, and murderers of the poor.[64] If the inalienability of church property and its protection against ecclesiastical and secular officials was well-established in the West, it was the second chapter (2.30) that provided a new element in an exclusion and a privilege that might be afforded by the prince. This was the statement in law that mattered at the time. These were also the statements excerpted by a later collector, Regino of Prüm, when he copied this material into his collection (891–913). Regino included the whole of the second chapter, but only the central provision from the first (the basic prohibition of alienation from which the second chapter provides an exemption).[65] The few adjustments in Ansegis's *Collectio* were concentrated on the title to this second chapter, and they worked to extend a princely right to act into a right to grant exemption.[66]

The exemption had an immediate political context. A new form of royal privilege that licensed and confirmed the exchange of church property had emerged under Louis the Pious, who issued two such confirmations in 815/6 and another three between 823 and 825.[67] Originally prestigious protections, issued to the most powerful abbots and bishops, over time they also allowed the

---

[63] (2.45) 'DE ECCLESIIS ANTIQUITUS CONSTITUTIS. Ut ecclesiae antiquitus constitutae nec decimis nec alia ulla possessione priventur.' MGH *Cap.* NS I. 556, 563; *Conc.* II.i, 252 (c. 20), 271 (c. 41).

[64] Pomerius's definition was deployed at the Paris council of 829 and copied by Grimald, later abbot of St Gall, into his *vade mecum*, St Gall, Stiftsbibliothek MS Cod. Sang. 397, p. 27. For the longer tradition, Wood, *Prop. Ch.* 428–9, 794, and above, p. 68 n.41.

[65] Regino's excerpt is marked ⁱ xxx ⁱ (above, n. 26), and titled UT NULLUS REM ECCLESIAE IMMOBILEM ALIENARE PRAESUMAT, *Das Sendhandbuch des Regino von Prüm*, ed. F. W. H. Wasserschleben and W. Hartmann (Darmstadt, 2004), 190 (1.372–3). For Regino's use of the collection more widely, G. Schmitz, 'Ansegis und Regino', *ZRG* 150 *Kan. Abt.* 74 (1988).

[66] Ansegis or his exemplum added 'De hoc', linking the chapter to the preceding one. It also rendered the active verb passive, transforming permission that the prince may transfer land into a claim that transfers were under his authority. Although many manuscripts of Ansegis's text retain the active verb (*transferre*), the oldest and cleanest prefer the passive (*transferri*): MGH *Cap.* NS I. 553 n.; on the manuscripts, Schmitz, 'Einleitung', 197–205.

[67] A few early confirmations can be identified under Charlemagne, but the privilege gained substance in law under his successors and, in practice, came to replace the charters that effected the exchange (P. Depreux, 'The Development of Charters Confirming Exchange', in K. Heidecker, ed., *Charters and the Use of the Written Word* (Turnhout, 2000), 46–9). Louis confirmed exchanges made by Benedict of Ariane (in 815); Atto, bishop of Freising (816); Adalhard, abbot of Corbie (823); Noto, archbishop of Arles (825); and Hildebald, bishop of Mâcon (825): Depreux, 'Charters', 49, 51, 54–5, 57–8. It is likely they were linked to privileges of immunity-defence, also first associated with Benedict

crown to manage benefices and estates. At the same time, there were efforts in royal capitularies to protect churches and monasteries, as well as benefices in the royal fisc, from detrimental exchanges, even permitting ecclesiastical officers to annul bad deals made by their predecessors.[68] The earliest royal statements can be found in 818, revealing that the directive to *missi* (c. 5) at Worms was not the first of its kind. The *Epitome* chapters belong in the midst of these initiatives about property exchanges and royal prerogatives, but the question is how. The early formulation of the privilege took place in the decade before Ansegis began his *Collectio*, in royal charters and capitularies that drew their terms not from the *Epitome* but from examples of Charlemagne's charters.[69] Yet the underlying legal argument of princely prerogative, which emerged in this moment, made use of the *Epitome*'s exemption: that is, the brief second chapter. So, some time in the first decade of Louis's rule, the exemption was discovered in the *Epitome* and the two chapters copied on to a parchment for use by palace clerics. The second chapter's title was gently altered and the long first chapter was retained because it provided necessary context, clarifying inalienability as the issue and establishing the force of its injunction, and so, in turn, the force of princely exception. A decade later, Ansegis copied this parchment and the *rotulus* into his *Collectio*.[70]

It seems to have mattered that the exemption reflected Roman practice, for it was remembered in this way.[71] The reasons why are lost, although one possibility is offered by a capitulary, preserved in BnF lat. 4613, an Italian collection of the laws of Lombard and Carolingian kings. Inserted below a capitulary for Charlemagne's *missi* is an imperial decree under the title 'Concerning the property of churches'.[72] It permitted a gift of property to be retrieved using the testimony of

---

of Ariane in 814, under which 'church property would be treated like fisc, [but] not turned into fisc', Wood, *Prop. Ch.* 252, 257, with 260–3 on its royal exercise.

[68]   Early legislation includes the *Capitulare missorum* of 819, MGH *Cap.* I. 289, c. 7, which found a home in Ansegis (4.48), Depreux, 'Charters', 48–50, esp. 48 n. 34.

[69]   Compare *permutatio, alienare,* and *loco venerabili* of the *Epitome* with *commutatio, ecclesiae rebus,* and a language of benefit or usefulness in Charlemagne's charters. Depreux, 'Charters', 47–50, 59–61, explores the early formulation of the privilege and the use of formularies and dates the requirement for royal consent to later in the ninth century. The language of advantageous exchange remained fundamental, Wood, *Prop. Ch.* 770–1.

[70]   Ansegis's copy may have shaped the formulation of a later *capitulum,* inserted at the end of Hincmar of Reims's copy of Ansegis's *Collectio,* BnF lat. 10758, p. 180 (c. 162). The *capitulum* uses Frankish terms throughout but may have been inspired by Ansegis (2.29) when speaking of 'praeter mobilem possessionem...praedia vero, terras, villas, ecclesias, census, quia inde magni redditus possunt exire in commune bonum'. The undated *capitulum* is ed. MGM. *Cap.* I. 334, c. 5.

[71]   Charles the Bald confirmed the right as cited in the capitularies of his father and grandfather and *sicut lex romana praecipit,* Depreux, 'Charters', 50; Esders and Patzold, 'Inalienability', 400.

[72]   It appears after the 789 'Duplex legationis edictum' (MGH *Cap.* I. 62–4) and before an imperial capitulary of 802 (MGH *Cap.* I. 91–9), perhaps a royal instruction that was appended to the previous capitulary by a *missus* (Ganshof, 'Le droit romain', 6–8). It may have been an amendment to Charlemagne's ruling of 801, which addressed Lombard custom in Italy and required that post-mortem bequests *pro salute animae suae* be given 'absolutely', with only the right to reserve usufruct

witnesses, since '[a gift] cannot be made steadfast through a last will made by Romans unless it is confirmed through five or seven'.[73] The first *Epitome* chapter offered a means to counter the permanency of ecclesiastical tenure by refuting its basis in Roman law; the chapter's opening words draw attention to Roman rite (*Nulla sub romana ditione constituta ecclesia...*). If this were at issue, the overtly alien qualities of the *Epitome* chapter would become an asset, a way to uphold the inviolability of church property in the most Roman of terms.

A recourse to Roman law texts is unusual but not without precedent, at least in the mid-820s. At Lyons a learned cleric, Florus the Deacon, mined the Roman legal manuscripts of his cathedral library to support Archbishop Agobard's polemical tract against the Jews (823).[74] Agobard's efforts were part of a wider dispute with the palace on imperial policy, which saw him produce another tract in the following year, demanding the return of church property in lay hands.[75] Pope Eugenius II (824–7) also made use of Roman law once, in a letter of reply to Bernard, bishop of Vienne (an ally of Agobard's), who was seeking support in his

---

(MGH *Cap.* I. 204–5, c. 1). Wood, *Prop. Ch.* 737, notices a ruling under Lothar in 825 that permitted donors to make changes to their bequest (MGH *Cap.* I. 326, c. 3).

[73] (c. 4) 'ITEM DE REBUS ECCLESIARUM. Volumus ut qui aliqui per testes exinde quale[m]cumque rem tollere voluerit, per quinque vel septe[m] testimonia dicant suum testimonium, et sic tollantur qualecumque rem; quia testamento quod romani faciunt firmum non posset nisi per quinque aut per septem confirmatur.' BnF lat. 4613, fol. 83r–v (ed. MGH *Cap.* I. 216, as 'Capitula Italica'). It is a Frankish response to native Roman law on the validity of last testaments e.g. *Lex Romana Visigoth.* 4.4.1 (= C.Th. 4.4.1) (Ganshof, 'Le droit romain', 8–9; Wood, 'Disputes', 19), one noticed by Hincmar (S. Corcoran, 'Hincmar and his Roman Legal Sources', in Stone and West, eds, *Hincmar of Rheims*, 130).

[74] In this case he used the Sirmondian constitutions, a collection of imperial decrees (333–425) compiled in Gaul by *c.*585, which often circulated as an appendix to the Theodosian code, M. Vessey, 'The Origins of the Collectio Sirmondiana', in J. Harries and I. Wood, eds, *The Theodosian Code* (London, 1993), 178–99; S. Esders and H. Reimitz, 'After Gundovald, Before Pseudo-Isidore', *EME* 27:1 (2019). A longer version of the Sirmondians survives in only one manuscript, Berlin MS Phillipps 1745, a Lyons manuscript in which Florus made notes (Corcoran, 'Hincmar', 133–4, 137; K. Zechiel-Eckes, 'Sur la tradition manuscrite des Capitula', *Revue Bénédictine* 107 (1997); Florus's *Capitula ex lege et canone collecta* is edited in *PL* 119, cols 419–22). In the early ninth century, Lyons held an exceptional repository of Roman law manuscripts, with several dating back to *c.*500, when law may have been taught there (Liebs, 'Roman Law', 255); others were gathered later, Vessey, 'Origins', 181–4, 194. Three of the four Frankish copies of Julian's *Epitome* have been identified in Lyons, although among the tradition with particular links to Lyons, 'Group B', no witnesses of kp. 32, 33 survive (Kaiser, *Epit. Iul.* 92–3, 469). On Agobard, E. Boshof, *Erzbischof Agobard von Lyon* (Vienna, 1969), esp. ch. 4.

[75] 'On the Stewardship of Church Property', a case he first put to the synod at Attigny in 822 (P. Depreux, 'The Penance of Attigny', in *Relig. Franks*, 383; De Jong, *Epitaph*, 195; C. de Clercq, *La législation religieuse franque*, 2 vols (1936, 1958), II. 36–8; *De dispensatione ecclesiasticarum rerum*, ed. L. van Acker, *Angobardi Lugdunensis opera omnia*, CCCM 52 (Turnhout, 1981). The tract did not refer to Roman law, but does show evidence of research in the library at Lyons. Its arguments were framed in terms both familiar (*pericula de rebus ecclesiasticis, quas contra uetitum et contra canones tractant, et in usus proprios expendunt homines laici*, at c. 4), and soon to be familiar: *ad hanc roborandam* (c. 7); *Si uero his, qui propria uota non reddit, infidelis esse conuincitur iuxta Ecclesiasten... qui ea, quae alii uouerunt ac reddiderunt, usurpat, inuadit, diripit et diripienda concedit* (c. 12). The latter anticipate the Pseudo-Isidorian case (in Chapter 6), as does its echoes of the council of Tours (567), c. 25, CCSL 148A, 192–3.

efforts to restore church property.[76] Having investigated the papal archives, he claimed, Eugenius cited the *Epitome* (kp. 511) as grounds to allow churches a longer period of time in which to contest and so regain lost or missing property.[77] How it was that someone came to look in the *Epitome* and then find and copy the two chapters remains unclear. But in the mid-820s, a growing debate about the lay use of church property was directed against the palace, which was increasingly relying on lay abbacies and benefices.[78] It was marshalled from Lyons, where scholars were turning to the treasures of its cathedral library, and especially to extracts from Roman law manuscripts, to forge forceful political arguments.

In his undigested book 2, Ansegis captured a parchment that had been used by the royal palace to underpin a new form of royal privilege, to claim an imperial right to approve exchanges of church lands. What has been preserved is a remnant of the wider argument behind this privilege, one that would have been lost if not for Ansegis's archival copying. The parchment was thus neither capitulary nor preparation for a capitulary, except in the broadest administrative sense. Here, as elsewhere, the recourse to Roman law was an act of politics rather than legal inquiry, one centred on the second (non-hospital) chapter.[79] Yet its chance survival in the *Collectio* provides a glimpse into the making of law on two levels. Canonically, via Ansegis, we see material being gathered together to formulate church law and, perhaps, in preparation for a new conciliar vision of church law. Behind that, administratively in the palace, we see a membrane copy of two small sections of Roman law, incorporated into a dossier of material relating to the church, and used to inform arguments for imperial rights. The rights themselves, articulated in Frankish terms, obscure any underlying use of Roman law. Were it not for Ansegis, this activity would have been lost.

When I embarked on a study of the *Epitome* chapters, it was with the expectation of uncovering an initiative about hospitals; yet the deeper I looked, the more irrelevant hospitals became to this case. They have emerged not as subjects of law, nor even categories of peripheral interest. They are merely incidental references in a section copied for its contextual definition. So, beyond Ansegis, where does that leave us?

It is clear that Byzantine law did not shape hospitals or hospital law in the West. The *Epitome*'s list of definitions, so eagerly copied by Greek lexicographers, was never a legal or institutional template: its typology of Greek charities did not

---

[76] *CICMA* 53, which suggests this was merely a useful quotation, not evidence of deeper understanding of the law.

[77] *PL* 105, col. 643. 'et quidquid post auctoritatem Romanam, in Justiniana etiam lege comperimus, tuae sanctitati per nostros apices intimamus.' It extended the statute of limitations to forty years.

[78] Context is provided in the growing use of church lands for secular purposes, as *precaria* for military followers or lay abbacies for members of the royal family, Wood, *Prop. Ch.* 798; P. Fouracre, 'Carolingian Justice: The Rhetoric of Improvement', in *La giustizia nell'alto medioevo (secoli v–viii)*, II (Spoleto, 1995), 77.

[79] Cf. *CICMA* 60.

reflect conditions 'on the ground' in the West.[80] Several could be found between the fifth and eighth centuries in Rome, but no typology of institutions took root.[81] Instead the term *xenodochium* (and occasionally *ptochium*) became a more generic label for charities. Individually, such establishments might appear under a shifting range of (Latin) terms.[82] Western foundations also supported a slightly different range of charitable objects than their Eastern counterparts, focusing on widows, orphans, the poor, and pilgrims or travellers.[83] Of these, widows were often set apart: Abbot Adalhard of Corbie (d. 827) paid individual stipends to destitute widows, while the Aachen rule for women (816) distinguished the *hospitalis* outside the gate for paupers and travellers from the *receptaculum* within the enclosure for widows and poor girls.[84]

In general, however, and in contrast to the East, charitable objects are not reflected in categories of institutional form. Adalhard's xenodochium housed orphans, the weak, and travellers; Abbot Ansbert of Saint-Wandrille's late seventh-century xenodochium housed twelve feeble and aged paupers; while Pippin's *Capitulare Papiense* (787) referred to '*sinodochia*, whether for paupers, widows or orphans'.[85] Ansegis's near-contemporary Aldric, bishop of Le Mans, founded two *hospitalia*: one by the river for elite visitors; the other near the church and for the destitute, blind, and lame.[86] Regardless of the specific arrangements for

---

[80] Schönfeld, 'Xenod.', 19; Boshof, 'Armenfürsorge', 153–4; Stasolla, 'Propositio', 27. It is misleading to read Julian's list as a formal typology of charities, even in Eastern law, where an institutional typology is not as clear as assumed, E. Patlagean, 'La pauvreté Byzantine au VIe siècle au temps de Justinien', in *EHP* 70–5, 77; P. W. Duff, *Personality in Roman Private Law* (Cambridge, 1938), 179; cf. A. Philipsborn, 'Der Fortschritt in der Entwicklung des byzantinischen Krankenhauswesens', *Byzantinische Zeitschrift* 54:2 (1961). And n. 107 of this chapter.

[81] Rome acquired an *orphanotrophium* (for children), *nosocomium* (for the sick), and Gregory II (715–31)'s *gerocomium* (for the aged): Hubert, 'Hôpitaux et espace urbain', 116–19; Dey, '*Diaconiae*'. Several others were inspired by Byzantine models: Ravenna, a city like Rome with strong Greek connections, also gained an *orphanotrophium* and *gerocomium*, the latter near-contemporary with Gregory's foundation in Rome; in distant Clermont, Praejectus's *nosocomium*, built 'in the Eastern manner', stands apart. Gregory II had close Greek affiliations and had visited Byzantium, A. J. Ekonomou, *Byzantine Rome and the Greek Popes* (Lanham, MD, 2007), 244–6, 299. For Ravenna, Ward-Perkins, *From Classical Antiquity*, 242, 244. On Praejectus, Chapter 3 n. 17.

[82] The *Liber Pont.* I. 296, 309, 397, 440–1, noted Gregory's *gerocomium* but otherwise used *xenodochium* and *ptochium* for a range of welfare houses. Stasolla, 'Propositio', for the variety of names and duties in early medieval Italy. And see the discussion below, esp. pp. 153–7.

[83] For early medieval refrains regarding the poor, orphans, and widows, Moore, *Sacred Kingdom*, 262–3, 283. The categories, at least rhetorically, were remarkably enduring: e.g. in the late twelfth century, 'Nam preter pauperum et infirmorum, languidorum et leprosorum, uiduarum et orphanorum xenodochia que stabiliuit et gubernauit', *The Book of St Gilbert*, ed. R. Foreville and G. Keir (Oxford, 1987), 54.

[84] Paschasius Radbertus, *Vita Adalhardi*, PL 120, cols 1538–9; MGH *Conc.* II.i, 455–6, c. 28.

[85] 'Orphanorum quoque et debilium, necnon et hospitum in iisdem locis opportunius velut xeno-dochium constituerat', Paschasius Radbertus, *Vita Adalhardi*, PL 120, col. 1539; 'etiam exenodochium inbecillium ac decrepitorum pauperum, ad instar duodeni apostolici numeri constituit, deputatis eisdem rebus, qui sufficienter praeberent alimoniam', *Vita Ansberti episcopi Rotomagensis*, ed. W. Levison, MGH *SS rer. Merov.* V (Hanover, 1910), at p. 628; 'quam de sinodochiis seu pauperes et viduas vel orfanos', MGH *Cap.* I. 198, c. 1.

[86] *Gesta Aldrici*, 148–9: 'Unum itaque iuxta praefatam Ca[e]no[man]nicam urbem supra fluvium Sartae a radice pontis sanctae Mariae propter habundantiam aquarum et pascuarum construere certavit

a facility, the places themselves were known generically as *hospitalia* or *xenodochia*. This was summed up in a St Gall manuscript from the mid-ninth century where, above a list of Greek words, Julian's definitions have been copied. At the end of them, the scribe provided a label for his readers: *vi gen[era] hospitalorum* ('six kinds of hospitals').[87] In the West, *hospitalia* or *xenodochia* became the terms for a welfare institution, whatever its charge (*institutio* or *dispositio*).[88]

The *Epitome* chapter did not shape Carolingian law for welfare houses. As we have seen, by 827 there was an established tradition of legislating on hospitals under the Carolingian court in Italy that spoke in very different terms, of administration according to the founder's testament. Ansegis's *Collectio* was widely distributed in the wake of the council of Worms (829); many of his chapters were extracted and reused over the decades, but not the *Epitome* chapter on welfare houses (2.29). Later canonists used its section defining alienation but omitted any mention of welfare houses.[89] Late councils, anxious to safeguard xenodochia by extending the protections of church property to welfare houses, did not make use of its forceful statements on inalienability. Instead, synods such as Meaux-Paris (845/6), Pavia (850), and Quierzy (858) reached back (in Francia) to Merovingian precedents or (in Italy) reinforced existing protections, to return facilities to their original purposes.[90] We find an echo only once, at Pope Leo IV's council of Rome in 853, whose canon on hospitals appended the five other Greek words to *xenodochia* in its title.[91] But the canon itself made no use of the *Epitome*, or any Byzantine concepts, and merely reiterated a papal decree of 826, firmly in the Lombard tradition. The Greek terms were window-dressing: by the 850s Greek was firmly in fashion.[92] The *Epitome* text on hospitals was, and remained, alien in the West, in practice and law. It found contemporary relevance only to language students, keen to incorporate its Greek definitions into their dictionaries.

Carolingian legislation for xenodochia neither looked to, nor built upon the legislation of Justinian. So what did underpin the Western tradition? The answer

---

ad receptionem videlicet episcoporum et comitum atque abbatum sive cunctorum advantantium; in quo et aecclesiam construxit…sollempniter dedicavit…Alterum ergo hospitale iuxta matrem et senioris civitatis scilicet aecclesiam infra urbem construxit, in quo pauperes et debiles, ceci ac claudi sive aliarum debilitatum subnixi et indigentes multi reciperentur, in quo constituit, ut duodecim pauperes condigne reciperentur, quibus alimenta et lectorum stramenta sufficienter et discrete ministrarentur.'

[87] St Gall, Stiftsbibliothek MS Cod. Sang. 196 (flyleaf). Kaczynski, 'Some St. Gall Glosses', 1011, misreads this as 'Vigeni hospitalorum'. And see the Old English glosses to the term *xenodochium* in C. Morini, '*Xenodochium* nelle glosse anglosassoni ai "*Bella Parisiacae Urbis*"', *Aevum* 69 (1995).

[88] Italian sources used *xenodochia*; in the ninth century, Frankish sources begin to prefer the Latin-based *hospitales*, alongside *xenodochia* and *receptacula*.

[89] Kaiser, *Epit. Iul.* 464; *Sendhandbuch des Regino von Prüm*, 190 (1.372–3); Bonizo of Sutri, *Liber de vita christiana*, ed. E. Perels (Berlin, 1930), 216 (5.22).

[90] MGH *Conc.* III. 94 (c. 17), 226 (c. 15), 418–19 (c. 10); IV. 161 (c. 5). Discussed in Chapter 6.

[91] MGH *Conc.* III, 324 (c. 23).   [92] See n. 46.

brings us back to Roman law, but an earlier Roman law that was to underpin native tradition.

East and West: Divergent Paths

By the early sixth century, East and West had largely parted ways, and Byzantine reforms under Justinian failed to penetrate Western Europe.[93] Justinian's corpus of legislation would not be reconstituted and fully interrogated until the twelfth century, when the schools embraced the *Corpus iuris civilis*. So important did its Roman law then become that it has been easy to assume it had always served Western institutions.

As a consequence, the early legal history of hospitals is told through Justinianic law. To historians of pre-modern institutions the concern is largely that hospitals were given legal form as independent ecclesiastical institutions, allowing the Code, Digest, Institutes, and Novels to be used as historical sources according to which the institutions might be described or defined.[94] The question is more challenging for legal historians, who have been concerned with how hospitals were made into legal entities. This is a more technical problem of legal personality, which rests on where (that is, in what aspect of the facility) ownership, the right to act, and thus the means of action, was vested. The answers are multiple, the picture confused, in part because lawyers have sought the origin of a concept or device of today's law, such as a trust or foundation.[95] The cautious counsel against these dangers, warning that modern legal concepts were not fully formed or theorized in the sixth century;[96] yet concepts have still been explored and articulated using familiar legal terms. This means that the toolkits used to hypothesize historical ideas have been modern ones; they have also been—as

---

[93] Stolte, 'Law of New Rome', 356. For the local complexity behind this statement see S. Corcoran, 'Roman Law in Ravenna', in Herrin and Nelson, eds, *Ravenna*. On its resurgence in the second half of the eleventh century, W. P. Müller, 'The Recovery of Justinian's Digest', in *BMCL* 20 (1990); M. Ascheri, *The Laws of Late Medieval Italy* (Leiden, 2013), 20ff.

[94] Among the many: *HDC* 25; Merzbacher, 'Kanonischen Recht', 74–5, 77–8; Caron, '*pia fundatio*', 140–2; Rocca, *Il diritto osped.* 35–41; Patlagean, 'Pauvreté Byzantine', 72–5; Frank, 'Hospitalreformen', 6, 10–11; cf. J. P. Thomas, *Private Religious Foundations in the Byzantine Empire* (Washington, DC, 1988), 37–58, where philanthropic foundations are considered with monasteries.

[95] The most illuminating investigations are Duff, *Personality*, 173ff; Siems, 'Piae causae', 60–9. The problem has a long legal history, which treats *piae causae* as a class of institution, 'a species of Church property . . . subjected to the control of the Church': R. Sohm, *The Institutes: A Textbook*, tr. J. C. Ledlie (Oxford, 1907), 198; W. W. Buckland, *A Text-Book of Roman Law* (Cambridge, 1963), 178–81; E. F. Bruck, *Über Römisches Recht im Rahmen der Kulturgeschichte* (Berlin, 1954), 70ff.

[96] Siems, 'Piae causae', 58–9, 83, offers bibliographies on this problem in Germany, where scholarship has been concentrated.M. Borgolte, 'Die Stiftungen des Mittelalters', *ZRG* 150 *Kan. Abt.* 74:1 (1988), repr. in his *Stiftung und Memoria*, offers an effective critique of such teleological approaches to 'foundations' in Germany and their failure to identify legal personality. On terminology, M. Borgolte, *Enzyklopädie des Stiftungswesens*, I (Berlin, 2014), 23–31, 57–67; Chitwood, 'Endowment Studies', where pp. 6–7 address the problem of defining a 'foundation' for historical purposes.

in the nature of legal systems—national.[97] So German law thinks most instinct-
ively of *Stiftung*—a foundation defined by its purpose and resting on the
independent status of its endowment; like monasteries, hospitals were endowed
pro salute animae. Italian law thinks in terms of *associazione* (an association of
persons), and English law of fiduciary arrangements (the trustee and the mechanisms of accountability).[98] The question of a legal trust can thread through any
of these approaches, but the national building blocks of analysis have led, in
turn, to different preoccupations.[99] Such building blocks have been adopted,
because core concepts remain elusive in Justinian's legislation, even the basic
issue of personality. Historians agree that welfare institutions had legal personality, for they existed in law and made contracts, but not where that personality
resided or even what that personality was. The challenge now is to identify the
place of hospitals in law in the West without recourse to Justinian's legislation.

What follows is a historical not a legal analysis. It aims to move beyond a case
that hospitals had a legal form to offer some insight into the nature of that form.
This will not be an exploration of legal personality; there is not the body of law for
such an examination, and even if there were, this is not the study (and I am not the
person) to excavate the juridical nature of the hospital. Instead, what follows
explores the pattern of laws and legal ideas that underpinned institutional constructions of welfare. It is an analysis that looks to the activity of law, as well as the
shifting forms of legal discussion. Legal scholars will (justly) find my terminology
untechnical, and therefore unspecific on fundamental modern concerns, such as
ownership; but the intention here is to digest and reflect the ideas in the historical
material. The focus, here as elsewhere, is on the normative concepts in law; as
always, practice was far murkier and muddier.

The early medieval West was not an age of jurists or legal scholarship. We have
looked at the statements in capitularies regarding xenodochia, which were brief

---

[97] The studies in *Itin. Fid.* give a sense of the dazzling variety of devices across time and place. For
beyond the West, Hennigan, *Birth of a Legal Institution*, 52–70.
[98] Examples that demonstrate the potential of each approach are: M. Borgolte, 'Die Stiftungen', and
Borgolte, 'Foundations'; Feenstra, 'Foundations', 305–26; Rigon, 'Schole, confraternite e ospedali'; Duff,
Personality.
[99] So e.g. the retention by a founder (or owner) of a proprietary interest in a foundation/its
endowment is at the basis of the German concept of *Stiftung*. Endowment status thus determines the
legal nature of an institution in a way that it does not for English and Italian scholars, and has prompted
the many German studies that so rigorously examine the nature of endowment, especially the binary
between proprietary (*Eigenkirche*) and endowed churches. In contrast, English studies are less concerned about the status of 'ownership'. They see the institution as a defined type and the ever-changing
claims of laity as part of a continuum of experience that is historically and culturally bounded. Italian
studies take a people-centred approach, looking to the role of confraternities in the innovation and
endurance of charity (M. Gazzini, ed., *Studi confraternali: orientamenti, problemi, testimonianze*
(Florence, 2009), esp. essays by Natalini, Frank, and Terpstra). For a thoughtful examination of
approaches to endowment, from within the German school, see Z. Chitwood, 'The Proprietary
Church and Monastery in Byzantium', *Viator* 47:3 (2016); also, C. Moddelmog, 'Stiftung oder
Eigenkirche?', in F. Rexroth and W. Huschner (eds), *Gestiftete Zukunft im mittelalterlichen Europa*
(Berlin, 2008), 220–2.

and practical. Lombard councils struggled to find ways to articulate the problem in law, but they agreed on its basic legal components: that assets must be preserved and administered, according to the terms laid down by an original donor/will-maker. If in very different language, these were also the principles that underlay the confirmation at Orléans (549) of the royal xenodochium at Lyons. In both contexts, xenodochia are revealed as familiar in practice. The challenge now is to look before these councils, and even before Justinian, in order to identify the xenodochium's legal contours.

The Inheritance of the East (*c.475–c.535*)

Xenodochia arose in the mid-fourth century, spreading across the empire in the following decades. As with other early Christian forms, their creation preceded any recognition in law. Since Constantine (d. 337), imperial legislation had begun to encompass Christian forms and Christian priorities.[100] In parallel, prelates of the church had begun to meet in ecumenical councils, beginning with the council of Nicaea I (325), to bring order to faith, resolve theological questions, and define heresy and orthodoxy. Their meeting at Chalcedon in 451, as we have seen, secured monasteries and churches under the bishop, but ignored welfare houses (*ptochia*). It would define ecclesiastical jurisdictions, and so the responsibilities of prelates, for both the Greek East and Latin West. For both, its failure to claim *ptochia* was to have defining consequences for hospitals in law, bequeathing to them a legal history that was extraordinary, in both its vernacular ('exceptional') and ecclesiastical ('beyond the reach of the bishop') senses.[101] Yet this shared inheritance would have different consequences as the empire divided into East and West. In the East, *ptochia* continued to be noticed in imperial decrees and were gathered into Justinian's corpus of law, which united church and secular law under a mighty Christian emperor.[102] In the West, deprived of Byzantine law and imperial law-making, welfare faced a different fate. It is to both of these very different worlds that we must turn to look for Western hospitals in law.

The place to start, perhaps counterintuitively, is Justinian's body of laws. The legislation of the Code, Digest, Institutes, as well as Justinian's own Novels have

---

[100] Duff, *Personality*, 171–3. The emergence of churches, especially in the fourth century, is considered in C. Sotinel, 'Places of Christian Worship and their Sacralization', in Sotinel, *Church and Society in Late Antique Italy*, no. 12 (Farnham, 2010).

[101] Many modern ecclesiastical accounts rest on the so-called Arabic canons of Nicaea (325), which will not be treated here. These *Pseudo-Nicaean* canons are spurious: H. Kaufhold, 'Sources of Canon Law', in W. Hartmann and K. Pennington, eds, *The History of Byzantine and Eastern Canon Law* (Washington, DC, 2012), 299. A recent iteration of that ecclesiastical model is, C. Keyvanian, *Hospitals and Urbanism in Rome, 1200–1500* (Leiden, 2015), 33–6.

[102] On imperial law and the church: Chitwood, 'Proprietary Church', 29–46; Thomas, *Private Religious Foundations*; B. Stolte, 'Law for Founders,' in M. Mullett, ed., *Founders and Refounders of Byzantine Monasteries* (Belfast, 2007).

been read by historians comprehensively, as a body of law that defined hospitals, and developmentally, as an accrual of legal protections that secured these institutions for the following millennium. The intention now is to read the law backwards, for Justinian's jurists were not only devising but consolidating. The *Corpus iuris civilis* rested on a longer legal process, with its roots sunk in earlier traditions.[103] What follows offers a kind of legal archaeology to identify these roots and glimpse the legal structures into which hospitals had been inserted.

It has often been noted that the *Corpus iuris civilis* extended to philanthropic (that is, welfare) houses a number of protections that were already enjoyed by churches; the question is how. These protections included freedoms of personnel from secular exaction (Cod. 1.3.32), legal rights to claim gifts (Cod. 1.2.15, 17, 19, 22, 23; Cod. 1.3.45, 48) or manage property (Nov. 54.2), and protections of property against alienation (Cod. 1.2.17; Nov. 7) and abusive administrators (Cod. 1.3.41; Nov. 131.10). This legislation may seem piecemeal, and it includes acts that date back to the mid-fifth century, but it was concentrated under Justinian's reign, when efforts were made between 528 and 545 to consolidate philanthropic institutions in law. Justinian's reforms placed them in the category of 'divine property' (*res divinae*) rather than 'human property' (*res humanae*) (Cod. 1.2.22), a matter not of private but of 'divine and public law' (*divinum publicumque ius*, Cod. 1.2.23), that is, of things beyond private ownership.[104] They were inserted into the *Code* under book 1, titles 2 and 3, titles that addressed ecclesiastical property and people.[105] To do so, Justinian's jurists crafted new categories. Where once the adjective 'venerable' had honoured ecclesiastical sites and activities generally, from synods to churches, it now gained a more particular use. From 530 edicts distinguished churches, as *sacrosanctes* (holy), from foundations (*domus*), as *venerabiles*;[106] the latter category included monasteries and hermitages (Cod. 1.3.46), as well as a growing assortment of philanthropic houses, known collectively as *ptochia* (e.g. Cod. 1.3.41.11; Nov. 7.5, 6, epilogue).[107] This

---

[103] E. Levy, *West Roman Vulgar Law* (Philadelphia, PA, 1951), esp. 12–14; W. Kaiser, 'Justinian and the *Corpus Iuris Civilis*', in *CCRL*.

[104] The categories of divine and human extended back to classical Roman law, and were laid out by Gaius, P. du Plessis, 'Property', in *CCRL* 177–8; Kantor, 'Property in Land', 57. Justinian's wider programme of reform was extraordinarily ambitious: it aimed to curtail aristocratic power, assert imperial authority, and regulate clerical and lay life, P. Sarris, *Economy and Society in the Age of Justinian* (Cambridge, 2006), 206–12.

[105] Title 2, 'On holy churches, their property and privileges' ('De sacrosanctis ecclesiis et de rebus et privilegiis earum'). Title 3, 'On bishops, clerics, orphanages and foundling hospitals, and *xenodochia*, hermits, and monks and their privileges . . .' ('De episcopis et clericis et orphanotrophis et brephotrophis et xenodochis et asceteriis et monachis et privilegio earum . . .').

[106] Cod. 1.2.23; Cod. 1.3.41.3, 11; Cod. 1.3.43, 45, 48; Nov. 120.6.1; Nov. 131. Prior to this such terms were not consistent. But see Nov. 54.2 which introduces *venerandae* (worshipful).

[107] There appears not to have been any formal typology of these philanthropic institutions, but rather a profusion of types over time. Only one, the *orphanotrophium*, was distinguished in law when its director was afforded rights in 472 to act for his charges (Cod. 1.3.31, 34; Nov. 131.15). Two laws provided five types as examples (Cod. 1.2.22; Cod. 1.3.41.11, with *gerontocomia* and *nosocomia* alternatively). Six types appear together only twice: in a 530 list of officials (below n. 109) and once

framework of 'divine and public' law justified the inclusion of *ptochia* with ecclesiastical facilities under key imperial protections. But the framework also had its limits.

Imperial law maintained clear boundaries between monasteries and philanthropic institutions, confusing neither the places nor their superintendents with monks. Many laws acted only on the religious (monks, holy virgins, and hermits).[108] In contrast, the superintendents (*administratores*) of philanthropic institutions were assumed to be managers, a particular kind of steward (*oeconomi*).[109] Justinian's laws upheld major church councils, including Chalcedon (Cod. 1.3.23), which secured the special status of oratories and monasteries, which could only be built on a site consecrated by the bishop (Nov. 131.7; Nov. 5). No consecration (and no bishop) was required to build *ptochia*.[110] Justinian also recognized the different challenges confronting founders. A law of 530 provided three years for heirs and executors to establish a chapel (this was extended to five years in 545), but only one year to establish a *ptochium*. The time-frame recognized the complexity of the former process, which required both bishop and civil magistrate, and stressed the simplicity of the latter, in the hands of heirs or executors alone. A hospital could easily be made in one year, it explained, for the 'time is sufficient to implement the will of the deceased, because they can even hire a house and put the sick into it while the hospital building is completed'.[111]

A *ptochium* required simply a site where its charity could be administered, and this could be easily moved, in contrast to a monastery. The novel that prohibited alienation of hospital property (Nov. 7) included a chapter (11) specifically for

---

in Nov. 7.1 (535), whose other references use three, four, or five of the terms. Other acts do not give full lists. *Ptochotrophium/ptochium* was the basic term, the latter as *ptochia* sometimes used to refer to philanthropic houses generally (Nov. 7.5, 6; Cod. 1.3.41.3); *xenon/xenodochium* was its frequent pair. After these, it was most common to add *nosocomium* (Nov. 54.2), then *orphanotrophium* (Nov. 120.1, 6.2, 7) and *gerontocomium* (Nov. 131.13; Cod. 1.2.22, 23; Cod. 1.3.45.1b, 3a), but there was no systematic logic to this. (The Code's Title 3 itself referred simply to 'orphanages, foundling hospitals, xenodochia' ('orphanotrophis et brephotrophis et xenodochis'), along with bishops, clerics, monks, etc.). Taken together, the lists offered illustrative examples of a genus of house; they were not attempts to establish an official cohort of institutions but to accommodate a growing profusion of charities (Cod. 1.3.41.3).

[108] Cod. 1.3.20, 22, 38, 39, 43, 46; Nov. 5.
[109] Cod. 1.3.45.3 (530) lists the heads of the six welfare institutions (*xenodochos ptochotrophos nosocomos brephotophos orphanotrophos gerontocomos*) alongside *paramonarios* [servants at a monastery], *oeconomos* [stewards] *vel denique piarum causarum administratores* [superintendents of pious causes]'. The group is of officials charged with the management of wealth or income. See, also, the early Cod. 1.3.32.7, the first to mention such houses, which inserted 'orthodox *xenodochii* and *ptochii*' (terms for those who were running the xenodochia and ptochia) alongside 'priests and clerics of whatever grade, and monks'.
[110] A *ptochium* might also have an oratory and *adorantes clericorum* (Nov. 120.6.1), which would require consecration.
[111] '...sin xenonem, infra unum annum eum facere cogantur, cum hoc tempus ad defunctorum voluntatem implendam sufficiat: possunt enim et domum conduci ibique aegroti deponi possunt, dum xenonis extructio perficiatur.' Cod. 1.3.45, updated in 545 as Nov. 131.10.

monasteries (*venerabilia monasteria*), which it then defined as places 'in which an altar has been established and holy services are held (*sacrum exhibitum minister- ium*), of the kind customarily celebrated in the holiest churches, with holy scriptures read and the holy and ineffable sacrament administered, and the monks' dwelling made there'.[112] In line with Chalcedon, it 'entirely forbade' that these should be converted from a holy state, pleasing to God, to private uses, making offenders accountable to the diocesan church. The monastery was *vener- abile*, but its activities were *sacrosancta*. The same novel guarded what had been given to a philanthropic house, but not the site itself, which could be changed. A privilege of 529 had distinguished two categories of place that warranted protection for reasons of piety: one ecclesiastical, the second 'other houses that have been deputed to pious consortia'.[113] Justinian's reforms worked to extend the imperial embrace beyond the strictly ecclesiastical (*sacrosancta*), enveloping *pto- chia* as a type of Christian institution that was not *sacrosancta*, but worthy of protection in property, administration, tax, and lawsuits.

The grounds on which this inclusion rested are revealing. The new category was set out in an early decree of Justinian, in 528 (Cod. 1.3.41). It dealt with the appointment of bishops (§§1–2), safeguarded church property against a bishop's private interests (§§3–10), and forbade simony (§§19–23). Here (§§11–18) law- makers also 'held it necessary to lay down regulations regarding those who have undertaken or will undertake care of venerable *xenones, nosocomia, ptoch[otro- phia], orphanotrophia*, and *brephotrophia*', a group presented as examples of *ptochia*.[114] Their superintendents may retain and bequeath private property, defined as what they had held prior to appointment or received subsequently from family (§11). All other property belonged to the venerable house (§12), including gifts to the superintendent (§13), which must not be used for his benefit (§14), but expended on the poor (§15). Any surplus must be invested (§16), the property augmented (§17), and full account rendered to his successor upon leaving (§18). So the regulations laid out a superintendent's duties as to income and expenditure. His accountability, however, was to a greater contract. The edict rested on a more general Christian obligation to safeguard the gifts of the faithful, who give 'on account of the hope that they place in God and that they might make safe their souls', in order that such gifts 'might be expended upon beggars and the

---

[112] '…in quibus et altare collocatum est et sacrum exhibitum ministerium, quale moris est in sanctissimis ecclesiis celebrari, sacris quippe lectis scripturis et sacrosancta et ineffabili tradita com- munione, et monachica illic facta habitatione'. Nov. 7.11.

[113] 'lege scilicet…in parte autem ecclesiastica vel aliarum domuum, quae piis consortiis deputatae sunt, suum vigorem pietatis intuitu mitigante.' Cod. 1.2.22.

[114] 'Etiam de iis aliquid definiendum esse credidimus, qui curam venerabilium xenonum nosoco- miorum ptochiorum orphanotrophiorum brephotrophiorum susceperunt vel suscipient.' Cod. 1.3.41.11. The first reference uses *ptochium*, thereafter *ptochotrophus*, the leaders given as examples of a wider category, 'those placed in charge of *ptochia*' ('quive ptochio praeficiendus'; 'ptochio praepositum', §§ 20, 23).

poor and other pious uses'.[115] Their faith in this divine order, one that enabled salvation and fulfilled acts of Christian good, must be upheld.

Just as it was *absurdum* for bishops to betray their trust regarding holy churches (§3), so it was for superintendents of *ptochia*. But theirs was a distinctive kind of trust:

> (§13) For it is manifest that whoever bequeaths or donates anything to a facility for strangers, for the sick, for the poor, or for orphans, whether that person does so in writing or not, gives so that it may be dutifully (*pie*) expended by [the superintendent] as one who has many opportunities for kindness (*pietas*) on account of those who are under his care.[116]

At issue was not the act of giving, but the faith that donors had in the meaning of that act, a faith demonstrated by the very fact that they had given to such a facility. The resonance of *pietas* (piety, duty, kindness, devotion) is lost in translation, but the links are important. *Pietas* here is filled with emotion, will, and human connection. *Pietas* induced the gift and manifested the charity; it also directed the superintendent, who carried out the kindness on behalf of the donor. It tied all three (the expenditure, its good, and the agent) together in one action, performed in service to the donor's wishes and imbued with his or her *pia* intent. This obligation was reinforced to superintendents, who were exhorted as trustees to augment 'that which has been designated for pious uses' so that 'anyone *who wants to do something* for the salvation of their soul will give more readily, confident that *what is given* will be dutifully (*pie*) administered'.[117] The faith that prompted a donor to give must be upheld. Charities were not merely vehicles of redistribution, they were trustees of the piety that had brought the gifts into being. Such faith was the very basis of the redemptive economy in a Christian society.[118] It was thus not the places that

---

[115] 'Nam cum quidam propter spem quam in deo habent et ut animae eorum salvae fiant ad sacrosanctas ecclesias accedant iisque ipsis facultates suas offerant et relinquant, ut in ptochos et pauperes aliosque pios usus expendantur, absurdum est episcopos haec in proprium lucrum vertere vel in liberos suos cognatosque expendere.' Cod. 1.3.41.3.

[116] 'Manifestum enim est eum, qui xenodocho vel nosocomo vel ptochotropho vel orphanotropho quid relinquit vel donat sive in scriptis sive sine scriptura, ideo dare, ut per eum pie erogetur, quippe qui multas pietatis occasiones habeat per eos qui sub ipsius cura sunt.' Cod. 1.3.41.13. A similar notion is rather movingly articulated in 531 (Cod. 1.3.48.3): 'for who is poorer than men who are oppressed with want, set aside in a *xenon* and, afflicted with bodily infirmities, unable to obtain for themselves the food necessary to survive?' ('qui et inopia tenti sunt et in xenonem repositi et suis corporibus laborantes necessarium victum sibi non possunt adferre').

[117] 'Ubique enim id enitimur, ut quae ad pios usus destinata sunt incrementum vel augmentum capiant: ita enim *quisquis pro animae suae salute aliquid facere vult*, promptius donabit, quando confisus fuerit *ea quae offeruntur pie administratum*.' Cod. 1.3.41.17 (author's italics).

[118] *Pius* acts were part of a long Roman tradition of loyalty and civic *euergesia*; here, though, the term takes on a new Christian meaning, one infused with ideas of social care—the 'cry of the poor' (Matt. 25: 31–46) and salvation, Brown, *Poverty and Leadership*, 87–91. For earlier acts of (non-Christian) munificence, D. Johnston, 'Munificence and Municipia: Bequests to Towns in Classical

were pious, but the motives that prompted (and thus imbued) donors' gifts. The *pietas* performed at *ptochia* was that of the donors, embodied by the superintendent.[119] The gift was material, but it mattered because it was imbued with the Christian kindness, devotion, and connection of the giver to the needy person; it was the vehicle for, as well as the manifestation of, the faith and *caritas* in Christian social and salvific order.

The donors' motive was the basis for imperial action. The first laws under Justinian acted to protect the gifts of the faithful because they were motivated by devotion, rendered in the conviction of heavenly reward, and intended for Christian purposes. We find its legal origins much earlier, in Zeno's ruling of 474×491 (Cod. 1.2.15). This defined the principle of the pious promise (*pia promissa*), wherein a donation to build a chapel was perfected in law not through material transfer of that gift (i.e. handing over the wealth), but by the promise itself. From that moment, 'both the donor and his heirs were held to that pious promise' (*ut et ipse et heredes eius teneantur pie promissis*). This had four consequences, laid out in Zeno's law. The first was enforcement: bishops and stewards of the great church were empowered to bring suit in court to enforce what had been piously promised (*quae pie pollicita sunt*) (§2). The second was surrender: upon the promise, the gift no longer belonged to the donor; the heirs and even the donor himself were now servants to that promise. The third was obligation: the gift was committed to the object (e.g. the chapel) whether or not that object existed. And when it did exist, upon receipt of the gift, the recipient remained a servant of that promise, for 'the property must be managed according to the donors' wish and following their stipulations, in order to fulfil what has been brought into being by the donors' pious promise'.[120] A pious promise did not transfer property from one party to another; rather, it attached the property to that promise. Finally, as the law recognized (§1), this had immediate implications for philanthropic houses 'that anyone has promised he would build *as a gift*', and

Roman Law', *Journal of Roman Studies* 75 (1985); Bruck, *Über Römisches Recht*, 70–82; Borgolte, 'Die Stiftungen', 71–4; G. le Bras, 'Les fondations privées du haut empire', in *Studi in onore di Salvatore Riccobono* (Palermo, 1936), III. 23–67; and the long tradition, in Italy, Ward-Perkins, *From Classical Antiquity*.

[119] A companion law of 528 elaborated on an older principle, 'ut donationes super piis causis factae' were valid up to 50 *solidi* even if unwritten, in order to secure gifts to holy churches, philanthropic houses, the poor, and cities (Cod. 1.2.19).

[120] 'Sub hac tamen definitione, ut impletis iis quae hac lege placuerunt et *pia donatorum promissione ad effectum adducta* administratio rerum donatarum ex sententia donatorum et secundum condiciones iis impositas procedat.' Cod. 1.2.15.3 (author's italics). Compare to legacies *sub modo*, an underdeveloped classical mechanism for charitable bequests: D. Johnston, 'Trust and Trust-Like Devices in Roman Law', in *Itin. Fid.* 45–56, and for an early history, Johnston, 'Munificence'; Bruck, *Über Römisches Recht*, 72–84; J. Hillner, 'Families, Patronage, and the Titular Churches of Rome, c.300–c.600', in K. Cooper and J. Hillner, eds, *Religion, Dynasty, and Patronage in Early Christian Rome* (Cambridge, 2007).

so the law was to apply 'to *xenodochia*, which are also called both *nosocomia* and *ptochia*'.[121] It was the earliest law to name charities as places.[122]

It was via the notion of 'pious promise' that charities were manifest in law and also, in its creation, the moment they were guaranteed in Byzantine law. Although the contrivance of pious promise secured gifts to churches and monasteries, monastic service itself was not defined by a donor's promise, as the definition of monasteries above made clear (Nov. 7.11). *Ptochia*, on the other hand, were agents of their donors' pious gifts, their superintendents held to fulfil donors' pious intent. It was Zeno's 'pious promise' that underwrote this obligation and, beyond that, secured the institution in law, as a gift held to a pious promise. With a promise to build a *ptochium* 'as a gift', the charity could be upheld against donors, heirs, and other potential malefactors. Neither the house nor the people—superintendent, staff, or beneficiaries of charity—were at the heart of the law of *ptochia*, but the gift. The issue at law was not who owned the property, but the right of the gift to exist and to preserve within it the donor's promise. It then obliged others to uphold this.

Pious motive was the legal innovation, but not the underlying constituent of charity law. Before there was a right to fix the gift in law, there was a mechanism to make that gift. Legislation was little concerned with activities of a living donor, who could ensure completion of their gift.[123] Rather, it was concerned with the gift in the absence of the donor (Cod. 1.3.41) or knowledge of their will (Cod. 1.2.15). Most legislation was concerned with testamentary bequests, and it is here that the first legal mechanisms were developed. The earliest, in 455, ensured that '[w]hat is left to the poor in a last will or a codicil [to a will] shall not lose effect *if left to uncertain persons*, but remain wholly valid and enduring'.[124] Thirteen years later, Leo warranted the bequest of a pious testator (*dispositio pii testatoris*) for the ransom of captives, another work of Christian mercy (Cod. 1.3.28). In both, the issue was not transfer of assets, but the maintenance of a resolution after the resolver's death. Leo's edict required heirs, beneficiaries, and executors to defend that resolution. It established accountability for the fund to the testator's named agent, if there was one, or if not to the bishop (§1), who was given one year to declare his arrangements (§2). It clarified episcopal authority regarding testators who were foreigners (§3) or rural residents (§4), and exhorted informers to report malfeasance to the provincial governor or bishop. The two edicts have been

---

[121] 'Eadem omnimodo valeant in xenodochiis quae dicuntur vel nosocomiis vel ptochiis, quae quis *donandi animo* ad modum supra dictum aedificaturum se pollicitus est.' Cod. 1.2.15.1 (author's italics).

[122] A 472 law of Leo I included their staff alongside priests and monks in its new protections from secular exactions (Cod. 1.3.32.7–8); another in 468 regulated bequests to ransom captives (Cod. 1.3.28).

[123] Cf. Cod. 1.2.19.

[124] 'Id, quod pauperibus *testamento vel codicillis relinquitur*, non *ut incertis personis* relictum evanescat, sed modis omnibus ratum firmumque consistat.' Cod. 1.3.24 (author's italics).

noticed as the first steps in allowing charitable beneficiaries to inherit and hold property, the central thrust in discussions of legal personality.[125] The point here is a different one: that testamentary law was the clay being moulded in both; in the first, to make valid (i.e. give a form in law to) a will as an ongoing resolution; in the second, to lay down mechanisms to enforce that resolution. The bequests of Christian will-makers were the seeds from which the 'pious promise' was grown.

The rights of testators underpin Justinian's own charity law and the central role that it gave to the bishop. The legislation that lays out obligations of administrators (Cod. 1.3.48), rights to recover bequests (Cod. 1.2.23), make contracts (Nov. 120.6.1), or bequeath to uncertain recipients (Cod. 1.3.48)—all acts to protect will-makers. The major edicts of 545 (Nov. 131) and its prototype of 530 (Cod. 1.3.45), which both deal with the establishment, endowment, management, and supervision of *ptochia*, announce in their opening lines that they address testaments and acts of the dying. The latter distinguish the law for churches, chapels, and monasteries on the one hand from pious gifts for *ptochia* on the other.[126] They lay out terms for construction, the former group requiring the bishop, whether the founder is alive (Nov. 131.7) or dead (Nov. 131.10). For the latter, *ptochia*, the law was concerned only with the heirs or executors, who have sole responsibility for fulfilling a testator's bequest. Only if they fail in their task do they cede that responsibility and lose their right 'to exclude the most religious bishops from that administration' (Cod. 1.3.45.1). The right of a bishop in a *ptochium* rested on a duty to ensure that a testator's directives were carried out: against heirs or executors who failed to act (§§1, 4); to oversee superintendents (§2); and to uphold ongoing provisions such as annuities (§§9–13), even those that arise after the death of the heir (§8). Based in testamentary law, these arrangements were intertwined with provisions for the ransom of captives, i.e. as a fund entrusted to a charitable use. In both cases, the bishop was charged to intervene if heirs failed:

> Because we want holy bishops to ensure that everything proceeds according to the will of the deceased in all such pious wills, even if testators or donors have especially forbidden that [bishops] have any part in these things.[127]
>
> (Nov. 131.11.2)

---

[125] Patlagean, 'La pauvreté Byzantine', 73–5. An evocative example, which focuses on the status of the poor, is C. Humfress, 'Poverty and Roman Law', in M. Atkins and R. Osborne, eds, *Poverty in the Roman World* (Cambridge, 2006), 194–7.

[126] And see Nov. 131.6, which allows forty years to recover property 'for holy churches and all other venerable places' ('sacrosactis ecclesiis et aliis universis venerabilibus locis'), extending the provision 'to the collection of legacies and inheritance which have been bequeathed for pious purposes' ('in exactione legatorum et hereditatum quae ad pias causas relictae sunt').

[127] 'In omnibus enim talibus piis voluntatibus sanctissimos locorum episcopos volumus providere, ut secundum defuncti voluntatem universa procedant, licet praecipue a testatoribus aut donatoribus interdictum sit eis habere ad haec aliquod participium.'

The issue is one of enforcement, rather than jurisdiction. Should the bishop fail, it fell to the metropolitan of the province, or to any citizen (*civis*) who might wish to prosecute, 'for since the matter of piety belongs to all, so the desire that it be realized must belong to all'.[128] Should heirs fail to respond to a bishop's reprimand, the provincial governor must punish them. The bishop was the first and natural agent to police the public interest in upholding pious promises. Out of this charge emerged a wider responsibility that bishops should appoint and oversee the superintendents of hospitals.[129] In practice, by 544, Byzantine bishops had a jurisdictional claim over the management of hospitals; in law, their claim stemmed from a public duty to ensure that a testator's pious promise was not abandoned or subverted.

In Byzantine law, *ptochia* were testamentary institutions, developed through testamentary legislation. Imperial edicts developed a series of legal mechanisms that would give structure—legal form—to testators' provisions. The most significant was the 'pious promise', which attached a bequest to the promise itself, charging the bequest with purpose and requiring heirs, executors, and superintendents (even donors themselves) to serve that promise and, eventually, governors, citizens, and, above all, bishops to act as guardians of that intent. Beyond the reach of church councils and established without the licence of a bishop, *ptochia* were not ecclesiastical foundations under church law, and not *sacrosancta*, but in the East imperial law reached out to envelop them in its protective custody. Jurists claimed them as Christian institutions on the basis of the donor's Christian motive, which prompted the gift and gave it redemptive and social meaning. It was in service to this motive that jurists under Justinian acted, placing *ptochia* alongside monasteries as 'venerable places', under divine and public law.

Pious promise and pious motive offered a new legal infrastructure, built in Byzantine imperial law; but it was an edifice that rested on an older bedrock (will-making). In so doing, Justinian's reforms reinforced 150 years of testamentary practice. Such practice had and would continue to bring *ptochia* into being in the East, if now with public systems of accountability. It was a pattern of practice that had been established, too, in the West, but one that would develop without Justinian and on its own terms.

---

[128] '...cum enim pietatis ratio communis sit, commune etiam studium esse debet, ut ea impleantur.' Cod. 1.3.45.6. Also, Nov. 131.11.4.

[129] A late (544) edict to guard church property established measures to check abusive administrators in monasteries, churches, and *ptochia*. To do so, it distinguished *ptochia* with an oratory, whose contracts were made with the consent of its clergy and the steward, from those without, whose managers drew up the contract and must take an oath before the bishop who put them in charge (Nov. 120.6.1). Other categories included holy churches and religious houses under the bishop (Nov. 120.6.1) and monasteries (Nov. 120.6.2). We should be cautious in assuming that what Justinian claimed in law would then prevail, even in the East. On the backlash against his assertion of *imperium*, Sarris, *Age of Justinian*, 219–24.

Roman Law in the West (*c.400–c.800*)

Justinian's reforms did not penetrate the West, but earlier Roman law had been well established under the empire, in Italy and Gaul, and Spain. The forerunner to Justinian's more comprehensive programme, the Theodosian Code, had penetrated the West. Comprising sixteen books, this Code had also been compiled in Constantinople by an imperial commission, charged by Theodosius II in 429 to create a definitive collection of law from the edicts of the Christian emperors (and so for the hundred years since Constantine). The Theodosian Code was promulgated in the East in February 438, and in the West by the Roman senate in December of that year.[130] It found a ready reception in the West where, a century before Justinian, Italy was still an integral, if increasingly besieged, part of an empire that spanned the Mediterranean. It remained the basis of law for those who identified as Roman in the West, and its sixteenth book, on matters pertaining to the church, served as 'an ecclesiastical Magna Carta'.[131] When westerners spoke of 'Roman law' in the early middle ages, they were referring to the Theodosian Code or to its offshoot, the *Lex Romana Visigothorum* (or *Breviary of Alaric*), a compilation promulgated in 506 by the Visigothic king, Alaric, for his Roman subjects.[132] Its law was that of the first century of Christian Rome.

The Theodosian Code made no mention of welfare houses, pious motive, or pious promise (it predated Zeno's development of 'pious promise' by fifty years); however, like much of Roman law, it paid great attention to inheritance and the right to make wills.[133] It therefore captures an earlier history of Christian testament. From the earliest laws of Christian Rome, the ability to make a last will was a basic right of citizens, and its defence was a priority of government. In 321, Constantine decreed that:

> Every person shall have the liberty to leave at his death any property that he wishes to the most holy and venerable council of the Catholic [church]. Authoritative decisions (*iudicia*) shall not become void. There is nothing that is more due to men than that the expression of their last will (*supremae voluntatis*),

---

[130] J. Harries, 'The Background of the Code', in Harries and Wood, eds, *Theodosian* Code; T. Honoré, *Law in the Crisis of Empire* (Oxford, 1998); Liebs, 'Roman Law', 245–7.

[131] For its use in the third quarter of the ninth century, and for the phrase, see J. L. Nelson, '"Not Bishops' Bailiffs but Lords of the Earth"', in D. Wood, ed., *The Church and Sovereignty* (Oxford, 1991), 23.

[132] *CICMA* 45–6, modifying I. Wood, 'The Code in Merovingian Gaul', in Harries and Wood, eds, *Theodosian Code*. The Breviary opened with the sixteen books of C.Th., then added novels of fifth-century Roman emperors and several earlier Roman collections of law: *Lex Romana Visigothorum*, ed. G. Haenel (Leipzig, 1849). The Visigothic kingdoms extended across what is now Spain and south-western France.

[133] Justinian's *Digest*, for example, dedicated ten whole books to questions of wills, *Digesta*, ed. T. Mommsen and P. Krueger, 16th ed. (Berlin, 1954), books 28–37.

after which they can no longer will anything, be free and that the power of choice (which does not return again) be unhampered.   (C.Th. 16.2.4)[134]

As this law anticipates, the ability to make a will had been quickly bound up with faith. In 381 the right to make a will was revoked for those of suspect or heretical religion. Manichaeans were 'deprive[d] of all right to make a will and to live under the Roman law', although the right of any untainted children to inherit was upheld; the rights of Eunomians, an extreme Arian sect, were also revoked, and regranted and revoked, over the next thirty years.[135]

The intertwining of Christianity and testament is best revealed in the title 'On apostates'. This opens with a straightforward law of 381 that:

> Those who have left Christinity to become pagans shall be deprived of the power and right to make testaments and the testament of every such deceased person, if that person made one, shall be rescinded as annulled in its very foundation (*submota conditione*).   (C.Th. 16.7.1)[136]

All seven laws in this title centre on will-making. The property of apostates could pass along the line of family succession to parents, siblings, children, grandchildren (C.Th. 16.7.6), but apostates were denied the right to exercise their own will and so to make their own choices. 'Blinded in mind' (*mente caecati*, C.Th. 16.7.5) they could not bequeath their goods to others (literally, 'outsiders', *ut testandi in alienos*, C.Th. 16.7.6). As the fourth century gave way to the fifth, there was a growing sense that a will, and the mind behind it, was not either just or unjust, but either a Christian mind/will or mind/will that had been deceived.[137] Imperial law

---

[134] 'Habeat unusquisque licentiam sanctissimo catholicae venerabilique concilio decedens bonorum quod optavit relinquere. Non sint cassa iudicia. Nihil est, quod magis hominibus debetur, quam ut supremae voluntatis, post quam aliud iam velle non possunt, liber sit stilus et licens, quod iterum non redit, arbitrium.' Tr., with minor adaptations, follows C. Pharr et al., tr., *The Theodosian Code and Novels* (Princeton, 1952). Constantine also relaxed the formal requirements for laying out a will, permitting testators to write on any material and using their own words (Cod. 6.23.15), an act discussed in N. Everett, 'Lay Documents and Archives', in W. C. Brown et al., eds, *Documentary Culture and the Laity* (Cambridge, 2013), 68–9. Women could gift their property, although their right to do so *in extremis* was restricted, lest (it was feared) they fall prey to unscrupulous agents (C.Th. 16.2.27), Humfress, 'Poverty and Roman Law', 196.

[135] '...quoniam isdem sub perpetua inustae infamiae nota testandi ac vivendi iure Romano omnem protinus eripimus facultatem'. C.Th. 16.5.7, pr. and 2. On the Eunomians: C.Th. 16.5.17, 23, 25, 27, 36, 58.4.

[136] De apostatis: 'His, qui ex christianis pagani facti sunt, eripiatur facultas iusque testandi et omne defuncti, si quod est testamentum submota conditione rescindatur.' On the context and intention of the law, and the case that *submota conditione* means 'failure to complete the formalities', see L. Atzeri, 'Submota conditione: Una questione terminologica', in K. Muscheler, ed., *Römische Jurisprudenz: Dogmatik, Überlieferung, Rezeption* (Berlin, 2011), 20–32. Wider context is supplied by T. Jürgasch, 'Christians and the Invention of Paganism', in M. R. Salzman et al., eds, *Pagans and Christians in Late Antique Rome* (Cambridge, 2015), 128–9.

[137] Jewish citizens could make testaments but not disinherit a Christian heir (CTh. 16.8.28).

acted to fortify Christian wishes and dissolve what was degenerate. It was not the bequest that was just or degenerate, but the faith, and so the will, of the testator.

The opposite was also true: the validity of a will might be demonstrated by the Christian decisions of a testator. A novel of Marcian (N.Marc. 5; Cod. 1.2.13), an emperor of the Eastern empire (450–57), overturned a previous law that had prohibited widows and deaconesses from making bequests to clerics in their last will. At issue was the testament of one Hypatia, who had included Anatolius the priest as an heir. Her provision was upheld on the grounds that the rest of her will was 'so justly and prudently' arranged 'that the testator [had] neglected no person who deserved well of her', notably 'conferr[ing] much property upon the sacro-sanct churches, much upon the poor, much upon monks, out of her reverence for religion, and much for the redemption of captives, since she was deeply moved by their miserable lot'.[138] The rectitude of Hypatia's wishes proved that her testament was worthy and so to be upheld in all its parts. The case necessitated a change in law that women of various venerable estates might leave bequests to churches, shrines of martyrs, clerics, monks, or the poor, and that 'such testament shall stand ratified and valid in all respects', whatever the form of gift (N.Marc. 5.2).[139] The novel was promulgated in the West and found its way into the *Breviary of Alaric*. The suggestion here is not that Western jurists built a law for xenodochia from these legal remains—there is no explicit law for xenodochia (even the *Breviary* is silent on the subject)—but rather, that a legal context did exist into which xenodochia might fit. The rights of Christian citizens to make a will, and the public enforceability of that will, resting upon the Christian rectitude of the testator, offered a fertile soil for the practice of making welfare facilities. It offers one prehistory for the picture glimpsed in Lombardy before the arrival of the Carolingians.[140]

Given the absence of legislation on xenodochia from the Theodosian Code and the *Breviary of Alaric*, it is not surprising that other Western law codes were largely silent on the topic. This makes its chance appearance, in those of the Lombard kings Liutprand (712–44) and Aistulf (749–56) all the more remarkable. Xenodochia first occur at the end of an edict datable to 720/1 on legal age (*de*

---

[138] '...cum repertum fuisset alias quoque partes eiusdem voluntatis ita iuste ac prudenter institutas, ut nullum bene de se meritum neglexerit, multa sacrosanctis ecclesiis, multa pauperibus, multa monachis religionis intuitu, multa captivorum redemptioni commota miserabili eorum sorte contulerit'. N.Marc. 5.1. One of the edicts it modified was CTh. 16.2.27, for which see n. 134.

[139] '...id modis omnibus ratum firmumque consistat'.

[140] It is a picture upheld in the letters of Gregory the Great. Having spent a year in Constantinople (although he later claimed to know no Greek, *Greg. Epp.* 11.55), Gregory was familiar with Justinian's law. Such familiarity was strange in the West and did not reflect wider conditions (*CICMA* 40–1). He was aware of its laws on welfare institutions, although Gregory only applied one to xenodochia in the West: Cod. 1.3.45/Nov. 131.10, that directives in a will will be fulfilled and in a timely manner (*Greg. Epp.* 1.9, 4.9, 4.10, 9.35, 9.90, 13.26). One apparent exception—that *xenodochia* in Cagliari submit regular accounts to the bishop, under whose instruction they exist (*Greg. Epp.* 4.24)—cited local custom in Byzantine Sardinia and was not enjoining new practice.

aetate), which recognized 19 as the age of majority for a Lombard man and restricted the activities of an underage heir. This ended with an exception: an underage heir might make arrangements on his deathbed by assigning 'his own property as he wishes to holy places for pious reasons or to a xenodochium, and what he will have resolved for his soul must endure without change'.[141] The first appearance, in a Western law code, is thus in the context of testamentary bequests made *in extremis* and *pro anima*. Here, too, they are placed beside holy places but distinguished from them; the use of the singular 'to a *xenodochium*' perhaps hints at a more specific act, like the creation of a facility. Subsequent appearances follow a similar pattern: a clause of *c.*726 excepted from *launigild* (and so upheld as valid) anything given 'for [a donor's] own soul to a church, or to places of the saints, or to a xenodochium'; a law of 753 forbade heirs to challenge any agreement made with bishops, abbots, custodians of churches, or heads of xenodochia, if heirs had given consent in the presence of appropriate witnesses; and another (753/4) protected from double taxation any monasteries, basilicas, and xenodochia known to be under royal protection (*que in defensione sacri palatii esse noscuntur*).[142] Incidental as they are, these early edicts create a context for our Carolingian assemblies, whose first notices also concerned xenodochia under royal control and whose wider preoccupation was to uphold the arrangements of will-makers. It suggests that the capitulary decrees emerged from a longer, Lombard tradition of law-making for xenodochia. These early discussions were limited, but they upheld the Christian acts of donors, focused on will-making, and worked to fortify the wishes of testators post-mortem.

   Although the subject emerged in Lombard law, it did not codify Lombard custom. To understand its roots, we must look to the late empire and to post-imperial relationships between rulers and local populations. Late antique forms of administration, record-keeping, and law were adapted to provincial demands, establishing ways of working that persevered through the disruptions of the late fifth century, providing the fabric of local life and 'barbarian' government.[143] In this period, it was peoples (not kingdoms) that had their own *lex*, so native

---

[141] '... ut si cuicumque ante ipsos decem et octo annos euenerit egritudo, et se uiderit ad mortis periculum tendere, habeat licentiam de rebus suis pro animam suam in sanctis locis, causa pietatis, uel in senedochio iudicare, quod uoluerit; et quod iudicauerit pro animam suam, stabilem de[b]eat permanere.' Liut. no. 19. This reworks an earlier decree of 713—Liutprand's first revision of Rotheri's code—casting it specifically for minors and *pro anima* gifts: *Leges Langobardorum, 643–866*, ed. F. Beyerle, 2nd edn (Witzenhausen, 1962), 101 (no. 6), 110. On the role of *iudices* at the palace and local judicial assemblies, Wickham, 'Consensus', 401–4.

[142] '... in ecclesiam aut in loca sanctorum aut in exeneodochio pro anima sua'. Liut. no. 73, Ahist. nos. 7–8 (*Leges Langobardorum*, 133–4, 201–2). As Liutprand's *c.*726 edict explains 'quia in loga sanctorum aut in exeneodochio nec thinx nec launigild inpedire deuit, eo quod pro anima factum est' (*Leges Langobardorum*, 134).

[143] Everett, 'Lay Documents'. For the complex relationships between custom and law during the late Roman period, and the significance of the former, C. Humfress, 'Law and Custom under Rome', in Rio, ed., *Law, Custom, and Justice*.

populations could follow Roman law, which meant, in essence, preserving Roman habits of law. On the ground, Roman ways of working endured. Increasingly local, adapted to changing social structures, absorbed and codified under Germanic kings, these habits rested on the practices of the late empire and the principles of late antique Roman law, especially the Theodosian Code.[144] This tenacious continuity has been known as 'vulgar' Roman law, although the term 'provincial' better fits its regional, customary forms.[145]

Evidence for its endurance across the former Roman world is scattered, but compelling. It was most developed in Ravenna, a Byzantine stronghold into the eighth century. Here Roman legal and administrative practices continued, in the production of documents, their registration in a central archive, and in the *tabelliones*, trained legal professionals who maintained Roman legal traditions into the eleventh century.[146] Here, written documents were at the centre of that tradition, and of a legal culture that 'privileged writing as a form of proof'.[147] Elsewhere there is evidence of administrative continuities. Into the seventh century, Roman forms of documents, systems of authentication and publication, and practices associated with registration in *gesta municipalia* (municipal archives), can be identified in Italy, Spain, and Merovingian Gaul.[148] If anything, these practices were reinforced in the seventh-century Visigothic Code, which was preoccupied with the use, authority, and proof of documents. Here the validity of acts in law depended upon systems of drafting, publicizing, preserving, and proving documents.[149] Document types were transmitted via formularies, collections whose models might be reproduced by scribes.[150] In the Rhine valley,

---

[144] Roman law was quick to saturate so-called Germanic law-codes, and we should be cautious of drawing too clear a line between the two: N. Everett, 'Literacy and the Law in Lombard Government', *EME* 9 (2000), 106–7; P. Wormald, 'The Leges Barbarorum', in H.-W. Goetz et al. eds, *Regna and Gentes* (Leiden, 2003). For critical discussions of the field, D. Liebs, 'Roman Vulgar Law', in B. Sirks, ed., *Aspects of Law in Late Antiquity* (Oxford, 2008); Rio, 'Introduction', in her *Law, Custom, and Justice.*

[145] On the term, and continuities of Roman law and 'Romans' in the new kingdoms, Wormald, '*Leges Barbarorum*', p. 29; Gaudemet's 'tradition savante', in his 'Survivances Romaines', 158ff. The term 'Roman vulgar law' has been attached to and cultivated many pejorative interpretations, perhaps most influentially Levy's sweeping model of a 'vulgar' law born in the early fourth century of 'long pent-up energies [that] now broke forth immediately through the disintegrating dams' (Levy, *Vulgar Law*, with quotation on p. 7). Challenges to the condescension inherent in this framework include J. B. Sirks, 'Shifting Frontiers in the Law', in R. Mathisen and H. Sivan, eds, *Shifting Frontiers in Late Antiquity* (Aldershot, 1996); and K. Fischer Drew, 'Another Look at the Origins of the Middle Ages', *Speculum* 62:4 (1987).

[146] Everett, 'Lay Documents', 70–82; Corcoran, 'Ravenna', 184–95. For early administrative structures, E. McCormick Schoolman, 'Local Networks and Witness Subscriptions', *Viator* 44 (2013), 32, 41. On Ravenna's place between Byzantium and Rome, V. Ortenberg West-Harling, 'The Church of Ravenna', in Herrin and Nelson, eds, *Ravenna.*

[147] Everett, 'Lay Documents', 63, 66ff.

[148] Wood, 'Disputes', 12–14; Corcoran, 'Ravenna', 184–5. An 'echo' of *gesta municipalia* persisted in a series of public practices, W. C. Brown, 'The Gesta Municipalia in Frankish Europe', in Brown et al., eds, *Documentary Culture*; Rio, *Legal Practice*, 179–82.

[149] E.g. VC 2.5.12–18. See also, Everett, 'Lay Documents', 82–93.

[150] Wood, 'Disputes', 9, 12–13, and A. Rio, 'Charters, Law Codes and Formulae', in P. Fouracre and D. Ganz, eds, *Frankland* (Manchester, 2008), which stresses how *formulae* do not follow any simple (or Roman) frameworks.

formularies and trained scribes ('the guardians of legal tradition') ensured continuity of practice and, from the seventh century, informed a revival of legal culture where licit action was public and visible, deploying written documents, inspired by Roman forms.[151] These traditions were strongest in North Italy.[152] Here, Lombard invaders embraced Roman legal ideals more quickly even than Catholicism. The earliest written collection of Lombard laws, Rothari's Edict of 643—'an attempt to write the Lombards into the still lively legal culture of post-Roman Italy'[153]—had little to say on Christian practice. Donations to the church only appear in 714 under Liutprand, when Roman influence also intensified.[154] Liutprand's edicts addressed both Roman and Lombard subjects, as the latter adopted local practices, including Christian will-making. Under the Carolingians, Frankish law-making would take on a new hue.[155] But Roman provincial law was a law of convention, not edicts and jurists, and it was sustained by long-embedded practices of document drafting, use, preservation, and authentication.[156]

At the centre of this documentary culture were testamentary arrangements. Wills remained fundamental, although now part of a wider category of deeds that included provisions in anticipation of death or the afterlife.[157] In concept, last testaments exemplified both the ability and the value of law. In a lawless society acts are secured by force, and so ultimately by the agent (or his emissary). For an act to be carried out in the absence of its agent—to ensure that a disembodied will is enacted regardless of loyalty—law is needed. In their creation, wills could be the most personal of acts, arranging the material accumulations of a life to honour the people, ideals, and obligations that mattered most to a testator, as well as making provision for their soul. Their essential, plebeian qualities had been reinforced in Constantine's law that wills might be written on any material and expressed in any words, however ungrammatical.[158] It is not surprising, ten, that will-making emerges as a practice that was both common and of intense concern, and that

---

[151] Innes, *State and Society*, 111–18, with phrase at 118.

[152] C. Wickham, *Early Medieval Italy* (Ann Arbor, MI, 1989), esp. 124–8.

[153] Wormald, '*Leges Barbarorum*', 35; Everett, 'Literacy'; Wickham, *Early Medieval Italy*, 122–8.

[154] Wormald, '*Leges Barbarorum*', 22, 38–9. C. Wickham, 'Land Disputes and their Social Framework', in W. Davies and P. Fouracre, eds, *The Settlement of Disputes* (Cambridge, 1986), 113. For Lombard relations with the church, T. S. Brown, 'Lombard Religious Policy', in G. Ausendda et al., eds, *The Langobards before the Frankish Conquest* (Woodbridge, 2009). On Liutprand, Wickham, *Early Medieval Italy*, 43; cf. Everett, 'Literacy', 103–4.

[155] A long-standing view that the Carolingians did not consult Roman law books is now being overturned, especially for Italy: Wickham, 'Land Disputes', 112, 122–3; Trump, 'Überlieferung des römischen Rechts'.

[156] McKitterick, *Written Word*, 23–31 and the references above.

[157] The Roman form of testament continued in Gaul until the eighth century, when, Kasten argues, inheritance became more personal and commemorative (B. Kasten, 'Erbrechtliche Verfügungen des 8. und 9. Jahrhunderts', *ZRG* 107 *Kan. Abt.* 76 (1990), esp. 237–8). If so, such a development may have reinforced the use of wills to lay down directives for *xenodochia*, as several of Kasten's own examples suggest (pp. 253, 256–7).

[158] 'it makes no difference whatever what grammatical forms of the verbs indicate in his will, or what way of speaking pours out' (Cod. 6.23.15), tr. Everett, 'Lay Documents', 68–9.

wills are among the oldest deeds to have been preserved.[159] Donors went to great lengths to ensure that their intentions were followed. In the Visigothic Code, a compilation concerned with the authority and use of documents, some of the most elaborate edicts are those regarding the making, proving, and contending of wills.[160] The code also laid out mechanisms by which bequests to a church might be upheld. In one edict, the wills of benefactors were to be read to an incoming priest that he might know 'the rights to which [his church] is justly entitled' (VC 5.1.6). The example is relevant here both as a comparison to the picture of Lombard hospitals (in giving the founder's will a perpetual afterlife) and as a contrast, since it looks outward, to the church's rights against others, rather than inward, at duties imposed on the facility. These wills of benefactors were more traditionally a list of bequests, not a command to be obeyed. The edict also echoes Cod. 1.3.45.5, in permitting a founder's heirs, the governor, or any citizen to bring suit against a bishop who despoils a church, but it provided different grounds: because a bishop who misused church property was guilty of sacrilege and of 'break[ing] the vows of donors'. The Visigothic Code made no mention of xenodochia, but it did reinforce two threads laid out in late antique law: the legal force of a will and, especially, its use by Christians to make provisions for their souls. Here, too, we can see the ways in which a bequest might become a testament.

So where do welfare facilities fit in this picture? It is easy to identify them in the practice of document-making: their study today rests on the many scattered deeds that established or confirmed the creation of a hospital. Our wider picture of the pattern of hospital foundation in the early medieval West, which sees Frankish initiative wane in the seventh century and Lombard activity surge from the early eighth, rests on the ebb and flow in the survival of these references, and especially the many testamentary arrangements that survive among the Lombard char-ters.[161] The motley content of these has dictated the approach of many previous studies. As we have seen, the extensive information about Childebert and Ultrogotha's sixth-century foundation in Lyons stands out, accounting for its

---

[159] The earliest deed to survive from the middle Rhine was Adalgisel-Grimo's 634 (Romanized) will (Innes, *State and Society*, 112). See, too, the wills from 474–552 in the municipal registers, among the earliest acts in the Ravenna papyri, McCormick Schoolman, 'Local Networks', 26ff. On will-making, McKitterick, *Written Word*, 61–7; Everett, 'Lay Documents', 87–8.

[160] In the VC, when it came to making a will, concern focused on those being drafted by the dying (*morientium extrema voluntas*), so as to ensure that what was written conveyed their genuine intentions (VC 2.5.12). It lays out four ways of drafting wills, the roles of witnesses, publication via an ecclesiastic, investigation by a judge, and mechanisms to verify their authenticity. The latter included 'a search to be made by both parties, among household papers for instruments in writing, so that it may be compared with the subscriptions and signs of other documents' ('querenda ab utrisque partibus in scriniis domesticis instrumenta cartarum, ut contropatis aliarum scripturarum suscriptionibus adque signis possit agnosci, utrum habeatur idonea, an reprobetur indigna.') (VC 2.5.12–18, at 17).

[161] Notably the *Codice diplomatico longobardo*, deployed effectively in Schönfeld, 'Xenod.', esp. 14–16. Also, HDC 36–54; Mollat, 'Premiers hôpitaux'; Stasolla, 'Proposito'; Sternberg, *Orientalium more secutus*, chs 4–5.

definitional status in many accounts of early medieval hospitals. Most *cartulae*, whether a confirmation deed or a will with many provisions, include only a brief statement on the xenodochium, specifying the charitable activities or listing incomes from small properties, such as an orchard. Such statements defy easy schemes of arrangement, but they tantalize with their human detail: to distribute tithes to the poor, to welcome pilgrims and the indigent, to feed four pilgrims each week or twenty-four paupers daily, or to provide beds for three days to pilgrims.[162]

Indeed, it is the very variety of detail that has drawn scholarly attention. Each site was assigned its own package of responsibilities, some merely to feed, others to distribute alms, still others to accommodate the poor or pilgrims, for one or more nights. In their variety, it is possible to perceive basic kinds of charity, but nothing more formal than that, and no types of facilities. Rather, the statements make clear the distinctiveness of each arrangement. So, in a Pistoian will of 748, Ratpertus *in infirmitate* confirmed a church he had built for a monastery and, among other provisions, gave his daughter, should she wish to join the monastery, the power to rule a *senodochium* he had also established and entrusted to the abbot. The xenodochium, he specified, was to receive the indigent and paupers, bestow alms, and accommodate paupers and pilgrims for up to one week.[163] A Luccan will of 790 entrusted to the monastery of San Vitale a xenodochium on property with a bath, where twelve paupers must be received and fed, on one day of every week, and in Easter week a bath heated so that paupers might wash there throughout that week.[164] Each example is mesmerizing for its own quaint detail, a quality that has encouraged a descriptive approach to the evidence: by reciting the charters' directives, studies illustrate the profusion of facilities and the kinds of welfare available. The approach reinforces a messy, rather folksy picture of xenodochia. It also brings out the immediate quality of each founder's vision.

The contrast between these humble directives and the assurance with which they were advanced has not been lost on the earlier generations of historians who studied them. Donors formulated their charity and prescribed its performance with a confidence that made clear that they, at least, believed they had a right to dictate the facility's charity, and that these directions would be upheld. The question those historians then posed was how these actions fitted with law; believing that law to be the *Corpus iuris civilis*, their answer was 'they don't, but

---

[162] *CDL* I, nos. 24, 32, 48, 82, 96, 114; II, nos. 127, 140, 163, 175, 194, 203, 218, 224, 231; Stasolla, 'Proposito'; Kasten, 'Erbrechtliche Verfügungen', 253, 256–7.

[163] *CDL* I, no. 96: 'in sua habeat potestate regendum, in senodochio egenos uel pauperes recipiendum et elemosina tribuendum et guuernandum per ebdomata una pauperes uel peregrinas animas et una cum Dominico abbate rectore'. Costambeys et al., *Carolingian World*, 112, offers context.

[164] '... ut sint insimul pauperes duodecim, qui una die per singula ebdomadas in ipso Sinodocchio S. Vitalis suscipere, et a mensa pascere deveant ... ut semper in ebdomada una Pasca, presbit[er] de ipso Senodochio ipsum Balneum calere facias, ut tota ipsa ebdomada ipsi pauperes laventur.' *Memorie e documenti ... di Lucca*, ed. Barsocchini, no. 231. The gift is by Jacopo Diacono, to take effect after his death.

somehow they must'. Stasolla suggested that the whole scope of hospital activity could be classed as Justinianic if viewed under the general type of *piae causae*.[165] Imbert separated discussion of the activity of foundation (in charters), 'le système de la déclaration de volonté unilatérale', from the *structure juridique*, which he ascribed to Justinian.[166] Schönfeld meditated on the disconnect between Justinian's law and Western practice, seeing it as the result of a clash of legal systems, as the Germanic right of founders hijacked the institutions of Roman law (a Teutonic insurgency brought to North Italy by the Lombards).[167]

But what if we regard the conviction of founders—replicated time and again, in regions across the former Roman empire, and through different documentary forms—as a continuity rather than a corruption? What if the confident assertions of founders are not the problem to be explained away, but the answer? Historians' observations are a response to the *agency* of founders, witnessed time and again in the deeds; the 'will (*voluntas*) of the founder', a later expression, provided a convenient short-hand for this activity. Imbert and Schönfeld adopted it to mean the 'demands' or 'dominion' of founders, who refused to surrender their claim to property. In a more conceptual survey of *Stiftungen* (foundation/endowment), Michael Borgolte also pinpointed the *Stifterwille* (donor's intention) as the fundamental component of legal personality. He saw this as an embodied will without a physical body, offering the founder as an 'ongoing legal entity' (*fortdauernder Rechtssubjekt*), a legal person who continued even after death. Until the law of foundations developed in the nineteenth century, this legal person constituted the foundation's legal personality and *Stifterwille* a way to read this personality.[168] What matters here is not the various answers proposed by each historian, but the issue with which they all wrestled: the documentary record makes clear that xenodochia were set up by and thereafter held to the directives laid down by their founder.

Practice and theory align if we place this documentary activity into the context of provincial Roman law and, specifically, into the legacy of late antique will-making. A founder's agency, their *voluntas*, is a concept rooted in testamentary law. This partly explains the frequent use of last testaments to lay down or finalize directives.[169] But we should not take 'will' too literally here. The legal foundation on which a hospital rested was not the document itself, but the right in law of the

---

[165] Stasolla, 'Proposito', 39–41, an answer framed in the most general of terms.

[166] *HDC* 41–2, 44. Imbert seems to argue that this practice arose from an 'easy confusion' of the poor and sick in a hospital for a community, but the case is made very generally (pp. 26–7).

[167] Schönfeld, 'Xenod.', 40–4; Sternberg, *Orientalium more secutus*, 155–7.

[168] Borgolte, 'Die Stiftungen', 84–93.

[169] That so many provisions were laid out *in* wills has often been noted, Siems, '*Piae causae*', 63, 69; *HDC* 39, 41 n., 52 n.; Rosenwein, *Neighbor of Saint Peter*, 87. Complex politics—familial, seigneurial, and diocesan—might underlie apparently straightforward statements of donation: R. Balzaretti, 'The Politics of Property in Ninth-Century Milan', *Mélanges de l'Ecole française de Rome—Moyen Age* 111:2 (1999), 754–7, 761–3, a study centred on a xenodochium.

faithful to allocate possessions for a Christian purpose in hope of redemption. The mechanism—and so the document—by which this action was expressed might vary considerably. Regional power-structures and cultures of record shaped what was created, and the vicissitudes of survival what is available today.[170] For Italy we have a preponderance of wills. Further north, where Roman legal practices had not been so well-embedded, founders relied more heavily on ecclesiastical frameworks: donation charters that echo monastic deeds and appeals to ecclesiastical authority for security.

Post-mortem provision was not simply realized through written record, it was also transformed by it. As Matthew Innes notes, 'written documents were useful precisely because they could be read aloud and brandished aloft before the inhabitants of a locality'.[171] Written instructions, whether in the form of a will, bequest, or episcopal confirmation, ensured that a donor's directives could echo from beyond the grave. It is possible that some, following antique practice, carved their statements in stone. The 1080 foundation deed of Santa Maria Nuova in Viterbo (Figure 5.1), whose canons were to maintain pilgrims and ailing paupers in an attached hospital, was inscribed onto a marble slab, a permanent reminder of the founder's arrangements.[172] The more powerful the donor, the greater the options for articulating and protecting their arrangements. Childebert and Ultrogotha made use of the council of Orléans (549) to secure their xenodochium, and the collective authority of its bishops to reiterate and reinforce the founders' arrangements. The council's voice blended law with the sacred; an approach that may have been favoured more often in Francia than in North Italy, with its stronger legal tradition and professions.[173]

---

[170] A reliance on ecclesiastical archives skews material, and few lay wills survive, J. L. Nelson, 'Literacy in Carolingian Government', in R. McKitterick, ed., *The Uses of Literacy* (Cambridge, 1990), 13.

[171] Innes, *State and Society*, 111. For their increasing weight in Lombard courts, Wickham, 'Land Disputes', 114, 117. The words were informed by others, and by diplomatic convention, yet they would have resounded to later audiences as the donor's direct instruction.

[172] On the date of the inscription, M. Bottazzi, 'Tra Papato e Impero', *Studi medievali*, 3rd ser. 47 (2006), 311–19. Thecharter is edited in I. Ciampi, *Cronache e statuti della città di Viterbo* (Florence, 1872), 282–4, and cites the whole of c. 141 of the *Institutio canonicorum* (see Chapter 3, n. 58). Examples of epigraphy can be seen in Ward-Perkins, *From Classical Antiquity*, 3, 73–6, 247–8.

[173] Marculf's formulary offers another Frankish example, in a charter 'for someone who wants to build an *exsinodocio* or monastery from a great property': part 2, no. 1, *Marculfi Formularum: Libri Duo*, ed. A. Uddholm (Uppsala, 1962), 162–74. Its location in book 2, on local matters, and the fact that the deed refers to a 'xenodochium' and not a 'monastery', suggests that it was written for the former, although too careful a contrast is unwise here and for such a major enterprise, 'from a great property', with a *oratorium* (a reference to *ipsis sanctis Dei pauperibus* also blurs any easy boundary, but cf. *Marculfi Formularum*, part 1, nos. 1, 2, 19, 24, 35). The deed is in the donor's voice and provides his directives: '*elegi* ad prefato oraturio vel cellola iuxta apostulorum numero duodecim ad presens pauperum pro remissione peccatorum meorum…Ubi etiam per presentem epistolam donacionis mei dono ad presente die—quod in luminaribus ipsius oratorii vel alimonia ac substanciale victu, vestitu quoque, substancatione ipsorum pauperum vel clericorum ibidem serviencium, Deo gubernante et opitulante proficiat' (p. 166). It ends by requiring that the *presens epistola* remain *firma, incorrupta, intemerata inviolataque*, committing the protection of 'this my will' (*huic voluntate mea*) to the bishop, who might punish via anathema and fines. This was an ecclesiastical deed and a template for episcopal action, putting two options before the donor, who handed the land titles (*instrumenta*) to the bishop, of

Figure 5.1. Marble inscription at the church of Santa Maria Nuova in Viterbo, *c*.1084. It marks the foundation by brothers Biterbo the priest and Leo in memory of their brother John, mother Sassa, and Leo's wife Carabona. It was established 'beside the hospital above their marketplace' and to serve its pilgrims. The inscription summarizes parts of their 1080 charter, and includes the election of priors (front), the life of the canons (near side), and works of remembrance (far side). This example is for a church with canons, a high-status affair; but as an inscription, it suggests another possibility for how a founder's *institutio* might have been preserved and proclaimed.

A Testamentary Institution

We now have a clearer sense of welfare institutions in law. Fixed to the directives laid down by their institutors, xenodochia were testamentary institutions. Their right to endure was, in principle, a donor's right to assign property for charitable uses. Legally, this was based on a citizen's ability to bequeath their possessions as they saw fit, i.e. to make a will. It was an ability retooled under Christian emperors

---

greater or lesser episcopal custody (p. 172). It also defended the house and its property against the episcopal predation. On the formulary and its context, A. Rio, *The Formularies of Angers and Marculf* (Liverpool, 2008), esp. 10–18, 178–9.

in support of Christian ends, allowing property not simply to be transferred to designated heirs (lay, clerical, and monastic), but to be held indefinitely to a charitable use prescribed by the donor. Their bequest was an act of faith, given in the hope of redemption and in support of the ideals of Christian society. It was thus the Christian duty of rulers, bishops, and citizens to uphold that act of faith and to defend not just the property that was assigned, but the terms on which and to which it was assigned. In the East, Byzantine jurists, especially under Justinian, developed law to safeguard the pious intentions of donors and to defend the facilities as Christian institutions, as a matter of public/divine law. In the West, where Roman law rested on an earlier legal tradition, xenodochia were simply held to the directives of their donors. It was a right readily accommodated and perpetuated in the documentary culture of provincial Roman law, although the weaker that documentary tradition the more a donor turned to ecclesiastical structures and models to articulate and preserve their project.

It might be tempting to characterize the Byzantine tradition as sophisticated, and to contrast it with a Western model that was immature, a model abandoned and left to flounder until Justinian's corpus of law was discovered by the schools in the twelfth century. This would be wrong. As we shall see in Part III, the *Corpus iuris civilis* would not shape the Western model of hospitals: the West developed its own tradition. And the legal story of xenodochia starts before Justinian. Xenodochia developed out of a call to Christians to allocate their goods for charitable ends and a duty of leaders, and law, to ensure that that gift did not dissolve at the death of its giver. The West consolidated its own legal model, rooted in testamentary law and forged through the documentary culture of provincial Roman law. The practice of making, preserving, and following written directives was the vehicle by which charitable bequests were realized, codified, and enforced.

Individual xenodochia were constituted through this testamentary practice, and the form itself was also developed within it. An example is the will of Urso, son of the late, noble Petronus and priest-brother of the mother church of Cremona in 768;[174] in it Urso instructed that on the day of his death (*a die obitus mei*) his dwelling on the street to *Buxito*, and his properties should be used to found an oratory (*oraculum*) of God the Creator and the archangel Michael. He enjoined his brothers at the mother church to ensure that the following be carried out:

---

[174] The will is among the Cremona forgeries, but is included here because its first part typifies eighth-century arrangements for xenodochia. The role of a *mensa* may be lifted from a genuine deed; if not, the forger went to great effort to ensure that it reflected one, demonstrating in turn an awareness of how such texts were used to make xenodochia. There are oddities: *xenodochia peregrinorum*, better Latin than usual, and what seems to be a spurious second part, tying the facility to Cremona's mother church. The first part is similar to an authentic Pavian will of 769, which also exemplifies the points drawn above (*CDL* II, no. 231); since this, in turn, echoes a 764 will from Lucca (*CDL* II, no. 175), there may have been a model text or formulary on which the Cremona deed was based.

And that there [at my dwelling] an *exenodochium* for pilgrims should be built, so that from the fruits of my inheritance all the pilgrims who might be there throughout the year should be fed in that place at a common table and have a bed to sleep in for three days and three nights and no more for each person, if they be in good health. And at times when pilgrims are not there, thirteen of Christ's paupers should be fed until they are full on every feast day at the same table. And when from my property pilgrims and paupers receive a dish and drink, and give thanks to God the father, they might be able to attain peace for my soul and [those of] my parents, Petronus and Bertrana...[175]

Urso's will illustrates the degree to which a donor might dictate a charity's set-up, including its accommodation, duties, regulations, and government. The documentary tradition allowed a donor to lay out directives on his or her own terms. It highlights the unusual nature of such a bequest, which was not a gift handed over to a church—and so an action completed—but a directive that was to endure—to hold—in perpetuity.[176] The property remained inscribed with the donor's directives and so beholden to that donor's will.[177] And because the document lived on after a donor had died, it became a vehicle through which he or she could continue to speak. Through its writing others could reattach a donor's directives to a bequest. It also allowed founders to lay out details. An individual's *voluntas* might be composed of multiple provisions, particular to the bequest and to the donor. The bequest could be provided to perform a series of specific tasks, for specific types of needy, at specific times and for specific durations.[178] The types of charities were inspired by the enthusiasms of the moment and shaped by precedent, yet the package was distinctive to a bequest. What was willed by the donor had also been imagined by him or her (or, at least, credited to that person's

---

[175] *CDL* II, no. 224: 'et inibi construatur exenodochium perecrinorum, quatinus de fructibus facultatis mee perecrini omnes, qui per omne anno ibi fuerint, ibi ad mensa comuni reficiantur, et lectulum pro dormitu habeant tribus diebus et tribus noctebus et non plus si sani fuerent pro singuli, et quando perecrini ibi non fuessent, trexdecim Christi pauperes per omne diem festo ad ipsa mensa ref [i]ciantur ad satietatem; ut, cum ex rebus meis perecrini ut pauperes escam et potu acceperent et Deo auctori gratias retulerent, pertigere possent ad pacem anime mee et parentes mei Petroni et Bertane statuo etiam et hordino, ut ab ipso die obitus mei omne anno in perpetuum...'

[176] Compare the 'handing over' (*trado, transfundo*) of property to churches and monasteries in a very different will, J. L. Nelson, 'The Wary Widow', in *PPEMA* 97, 99.

[177] *CDL* II, no. 231: 'de rebus meis propriis...de fructibus suprascriptarum rerum nostrarum.'

[178] A late example is provided by the will of Anspertus, archbishop of Milan (868–81). This converted his own enclosure in Milan, where he had already built a basilica, into a *xenodochium*. He entrusted these to the monastery of St Ambrose with instructions that they ensure that eight monks perform offices at the basilica each day and that at the xenodochium, different rations of bread, wine, bacon or cheese, and pulses be fed daily to 100 paupers and to the twenty poor men and women who made up the *scola sancti Ambrosii*. Daily in Lent 100 paupers were to be fed with bread, fish, and wine, and then offer praises to God for the souls of king Arnulf and of Anspertus and his family. On Anspertus's anniversary, twenty-four priests were to be fed in an appropriate manner and given wax, offerings, and 6d. to benefit the souls of the archbishop and his family. *Codice diplomatico sant'Ambrosiano*, ed. A. Fumagalli (Milan, 1805), 456–64 (esp. 458–9).

imagination) and enshrined in the donor's own legal statement, the xenodo-chium's constitutional text.

The messiness of wills and charters reinforces this picture. They focus on the directives attached by the donor to the property, often with imaginative details. Rather than a straightforward facility for pilgrims, or for paupers, these deeds prescribe a more distinctive arrangement, for example, that it should feed six paupers a day and house three pilgrims for three nights. The idiosyncrasy suggests that donors particularly valued—and certainly embraced—the ability to person-alize their charity. Indeed, the arrangements can be so distracting that we fail to notice that the charter neglects to give a name to the facility itself. The charity may be classified as a xenodochium only because a stray clause uses the term: for example, that the place should exist 'just as other *senodochia*'.[179] Some use informal or descriptive names for the charity, such as *mensa pauperum, mensa communis*, or *aula miseris auxilii pueris*; many are easily overlooked as xenodo-chia because they seem to be simply a bequest for the performance of specific charities.[180] It was not the place or its name that mattred, but the charitable acts to be performed. In the early medieval West, there was little interest in institutional types or even the notion of an institution. What mattered, and what legal custom protected, was the act of making charity. Donors took pleasure in elaborating their own directives, even when a charity was strikingly humble, for example feeding four paupers once a week or running a bath in Holy Week.

The legal culture that upheld both a secular right to dispose of property and a Christian ability to provide for the soul was the crucible within which welfare was forged in the West. It was a place founded on late antique Roman law, but realized in practice over the coming centuries. Bequest became a constitutional act: *institutio*. The practice was not continuous, universal, or necessarily devel-opmental. The scattered documentary record that survives suggests regional cultures of record, and the ebb and flow of activity. In Northern Italy, the will was king and so, when Carolingian councils (in Lombardy) came to articulate the practice as law, they looked to that native tradition. What they laid out suggests a rather muddled sense of the term *xenodochium*, but a clear sense of the practice of making, administering, and upholding a charity. It was natural, then, that they laid this out in terms of a language of testators and the writings of will-makers.

---

[179] In a Luccan will of 764, Anspaldo required that twelve paupers and pilgrims be fed each week for three days at table (*ad mensa*) in the house he established beside his church, 'sicut et in alia senodochia pauperes ad mensa pascere uidetur.' *CDL* II, no. 175, and see no. 231, which echoes its provisions, including using *mensa pauperum* instead of *xenodochia*.

[180] *CDL* II, nos. 140, 218; V. Forcella, ed., *Iscrizioni delle chiese e degli altri edifici* (Milan, 1889), no. 105. The charter in Marculf's formulary also lays out the donation and its uses; we only know the result is a *xenodochium* from a clause that identifies the bishop because *in cuius opidum exsinodocius ipsi ponetur, Marculfi Formularum*, 168.

East and West: A New Story

It is time to give a new account of the hospital in the West, and of the relationship between East and West, Roman and church law. Xenodochia were Christian institutions. They were the product of a pious bequest, given in the hope of redemption, and a material expression of Christian social ideals. To found, provide for, or administer one was an act of devotion, as well as kindness. But xenodochia were a particular category of foundation and distinct from monasteries, one being intended to serve the needy of the world, the other a retreat from the world into a life of fasting and prayer. The latter definition was laid down by the council of Chalcedon (451), which focused upon the religious, who had left the world, and the service at the altar, thereby defining monasteries and altars as ecclesiastical (*sacra*) sites. The council noticed *xenodochia* or *ptochia*, but declined to claim these facilities as an ecclesiastical form.[181] As a result, their creation did not require episcopal consent (they could be made by anyone), nor were they secured under episcopal authority and so church law. This was recognized by Isidore of Seville, who did not include *xenodochium* and *nosocomium* in his chapter *De aedificiis sacris* ('On sacred buildings', 15.4), which contained 'oratory', 'monastery', 'convent', 'temple', 'basilica', 'martyrium', 'altar', and 'pulpit'. Instead, he put them in his previous chapter, *De habitaculis* ('On dwelling places', 15.3) alongside 'house', 'palace', 'chamber', 'inn', 'lodging-house', and 'solarium'.[182] Welfare facilities were not sacred places. Of course, an ample foundation might acquire a church or oratory, and a larger one still might be served by a body of clerics, who might then be answerable to the bishop. Yet in its most basic form, charity was material. As a material object, *ptochia* were left to the (secular) testamentary law that had fostered their formation.

It was in this law that welfare in both the East and West shared the same legal foundations. The first Christian emperors made no mention of xenodochia in their laws, but they consolidated the right of Christians to make wills and, with them, to dispose of property for the sake of their soul. The activity of making charities—and, more significantly, the duty to ensure that what another did was enacted—was secured through testamentary legislation. This had a classical pre-history, of legacies *sub modo*, a culture of making bequests for the common good; but under Constantine the relationship between Christian motives to bequeath property and the ends that gift was to serve became part of a religious and salvic order, one in law, with the emperor at the centre. The appearance in the East and then the West of *xenodochia* and *ptochia*, charities with a Christian purpose and a

---

[181] Chalcedon referred to *ptochia aut xenodochia* in passing, among the possible business of a major church (*COGD* I. 143, c. 10). At c. 8 it included clerics who oversaw *ptochia* among other clerics answerable to the bishop, but this canon was not to be associated in the West with welfare facilities.

[182] *Isidori Hispalensis Episcopi Etymologiarum*, ed. W. M. Lindsay (Oxford, 1911). Isidore gives *nosocomium* only in Greek.

Christian name, inaugurated a new dialogue between practice and Roman law. As testamentary institutions, they were given form by, and beholden to, the bequest of their donor. As empire split and East and West parted company, however, Roman law diverged and, with it, the legal course of welfare.

In the East, powerful emperors buttressed and extended Christian matters through imperial legislation. They gathered up *ptochia* and other welfare institutions, carving out a place for them as matters divine/public. This was developed out of testamentary law and, especially, a duty to defend the Christian arrangements made by a testator. The first mechanism was the idea of a 'pious promise'. The arrangements laid down by a testator—what they gave and what they required of it—were now given an enduring status in public law. Executors and agents were obliged to enact a testator's directives, and officers of state and church, as well as concerned citizens, were required to act when they failed. Justinian's jurists named and formalized the growing number of philanthropic institutions, by regulating their creation, administration, and oversight. Such institutions continued to be distinguished from churches and monasteries, but a duty to ensure that testators' directives were followed by heirs, executors, and superintendents, was increasingly laid at the feet of bishops.

During the same period, the political structures of the West were fragmenting, and the ability to refine and promulgate law disintegrated. Roman law became local and practical, sustained through custom and, especially, documentary practices. It proved a fertile seed-bed for charity. Never explicitly mentioned in Roman law, welfare facilities remained testamentary products, fashioned through the principles and practices that indemnified Christian wills. The right to make provision for one's soul was cultivated across a range of written deeds, appointing or confirming a bequest and conveying the benefactor's instructions for its uses. This became the directive to which a charity was accountable. By giving voice to a donor's personal instructions, documents became active agents in constructing charities. This basic custom was maintained in Italy, Francia, and Spain, although practices varied across time and place. Branded (when they had to be) *xenodochia*, the results could be more akin to charitable endowments than institutions, any name fading in significance behind an ability to devise acts of Christian aid. Western charities could be humble, messy, and idiosyncratic because they were the product of personal initiative and beholden to a donor's own directives. This was not a consequence of their form, it was their fundamental character. For what Western *institutors* had, and what they valued most, was the ability to imagine and fix their own design.

These charitable endowments developed in practice, without explicit law. Only in the wake of the Carolingian conquest of Lombardy in 774 was local concern for charities given voice via the call to reinstate (*restaurare*) the built and customary inheritance of church, empire, and *res publica*. The Carolingian council, wherein the governmental unity of church and empire was most clearly embodied, now made possible a pastoral conversation about a phenomenon rooted in secular, rather than church law.[183] When it came to xenodochia, these councils worked within a native tradition of testamentary arrangements, Initially, comments focused on minor matters and were directed at royal administration, but deliberations about the material reconstitution of xenodochia developed into questions of the use of resources, accountability of administrators and, eventually, oversight. The breakthrough moments came at the councils of Mantua II (813) and Olona (825). Under their guiding hand, xenodochia became a matter of the *res publica* and, from there, of churchmen.

Divergence in law between East and West resulted in a divergence in the very nature of charitable creations. In the East, charities became institutions fixed in legislation and defined institutional types: a hostel for visitors (*xenodochium*), poor-house (*ptochodochium*), medical facility (*nosocomium*), foundling hospital (*brephotrophium*), orphanage (*orphanotrophium*), or old-age home (*gerontocomium*). In the West, the donor's will remained pre-eminent. Charity focused on the donor's act, the *institutio*. Donors embraced their right to compose and selected from an ever-expanding buffet of choices to construct their own charitable platter. With it, came changing terms for the facilities themselves.

Our picture of welfare institutions in the West has long been based on a list of six Greek terms, which historians must then translate and explain. Our sense of their foreignness underpins the historical story that has long been told, of a self-consciously Byzantine form, held to foreign typologies and foreign law. But we have missed something basic. The Greek terms were alien to Julian's sixth-century Latin students, just as they were to Carolingian readers, which is why they found their home in Greek dictionaries. They remained foreign and were not taken up in the West. We see the issue as one of Greek origin, but this is not what makes the story of welfare remarkable. The nouns of the Christian church *are* Greek: Christ (Khristos, *Christus*), eucharist (eukharistia, *eucharistia*), church (ekklēsia, *ecclesia*), cathedral (kathedra, *cathedrale*), monastery (monastērion, *monasterium*), cemetery (koimētērion, *coemeterium*), bishop (episkopos, *episcopus*), cleric (klērikos, *clericus*), priest (presbuteros, *presbyter*). We tend to forget their Eastern origins because these Greek words became Western words, first in Latin, then in the vernacular. The first welfare houses in the West, as in the East, were given Greek names; but unlike those in the East, neither the facilities nor their Greek names were claimed and fixed by the church, or in law: the terms were not pegged to a concept.

The problem of what to call *xenodochia/hospitales* is bound up with this omission. Semiotics helps to explain its peculiar experience. For *monasteria*, the referent (object) could transform—a *monasterium* in eighth-century Pavia was

---

[183] The Lombard kingdom had kept secular and church law separate, Wickham, *Early Medieval Italy*, 55.

different to that in fourteenth-century Pavia, or twelfth-century Yorkshire—but not the signifier (the word *monasterium*). To a degree, what was signified (the manifestation of *monasterium*) was subject to changing fashions and expectations; but it was pegged fundamentally to an enduring definition, guarded by church leaders and beholden to canonical tradition. Every foundation was a manifestation of beliefs, culture, technologies, and laws of its age, but it was never divorced from—and was often wilfully brought into line with—an enduring language and growing canon law that defined *monasteria*. This was not the case for welfare houses. Had the church claimed *ptochia* as an ecclesiastical form, we would be talking now of 'tocha'. The term would be in the title of this book, its topic familiar to modern audiences, and the institution readily translatable across English, Italian, German, and French legal traditions, its manifestations readily identified in documents as 'tocha'. But since church and Western Roman law remained silent, neither the terms (signifiers) nor the objects (referents) were fixed to a definition under the church. Unpegged, both the referents and signifiers floated free in the world: charities took on diverse forms across the centuries, meta-morphosing most when passions to create ran highest. What did endure at the very heart of *ptochia* was right to create. This is why Carolingian law-makers, the council of Vienne (1311/2), and historians today have struggled to define 'tocha' (welfare houses) and even to give it a name. And just as those Carolingian law-makers and the councils of the Lateran and Vienne, we have neither term nor definition in law, yet we know 'tocha' when we see them: charities, assigned indefinitely to uses that were laid down by the founder. To grasp the form of a facility, or even give it a name, we must first identify the founder's will, what it was founded for.

The phenomenon arrived in the West from the East, but was not articulated in law. The social and redemptive ideals of Christianity made a basic idea possible: of a Christian act that could establish a place and income to provide for those who needed care. Nurtured in the West by the documentary culture of provincial Roman law, this idea took flight, as donors embraced the ability to establish places to tend (specified) needs of (specified) needy in (specified) ways through (speci-fied) actors. It was an idea exalted by the church, but handed over, fundamentally, to the whole of the faithful. Over centuries the faithful—laypeople, clerics, and religious—enacted new visions and provided them with new names. Churchmen and law-makers shaped this language and these forms, but they never owned them. Welfare houses were known by a shifting Latin vernacular because the very idea of these charities lived not in canon law but out in the world, among the Christian population at large. It was a vernacular form.

6

Carolingian Claims and Innovations

With a clearer understanding of their legal status and form, it is time to put xenodochia back into their world. What follows identifies the development of law and policy for welfare foundations, in the late eighth and ninth centuries. The first section asks a more contextual question, about supervisory jurisdictions: in whose hands did they lie and what means existed to protect these places and to correct failures? The question matters not just for the ninth century, and our understanding of the work of its councils, but also for the long story of hospitals. For late medievalists the confusion of hospitals—the gap between theory and practice— rests on the notion that xenodochia were originally an ecclesiastical form but that the church lost control, either temporarily or permanently in the twelfth century. For early medievalists the conceit that xenodochia were subject to the bishop has rested on two legal pillars: Byzantine law that was then reinforced in the sixth-century councils via a legal device of 'murderers of the poor'; we have seen that these pillars no longer stand. This first section rests heavily on North Italian material, for the insight that it affords into local practice and because it was this North Italian model, as we shall see, that fed forward into subsequent law. Our focus remains on the concepts rather than the practice of law but, for jurisdiction, theory cannot help but meet practice, and any distinction is messy at best.

The last two sections identify key initiatives in Lombardy and Rome, and in Western Francia, which saw councils and even individuals fashion new statements in law. Their work can only be understood in terms of the wider jurisdictional context. For any effort to act in the public interest—by crown, papacy, episcopacy, or royal assembly—was defined by a fundamental challenge: an absence of any overarching jurisdiction. It was the need to navigate this situation that provides the key to understanding any innovation. Because xenodochia did not fall under any general jurisdiction, any statement in law was also a new claim for the right to act. Seen in this light, the environment emerges as more complex, activity more dynamic, and regulation more challenging than has been appreciated.

Potestates: Custody and Supervision

We begin with the question of jurisdiction. For these local facilities, this was an issue not of *ius* (right), but of custody; and we begin with the custodians.

On Hospitals: Welfare, Law, and Christianity in Western Europe, 400–1320. Sethina Watson,
Oxford University Press (2020). © Sethina Watson.
DOI: 10.1093/oso/9780198847533.001.0001

The Circumscribed Claims of Palace and Bishop

There is one immediately distinguishable category of hospital: those of the king. It was the responsibilities inherent in this authority, over facilities in the royal hand, that first introduced xenodochia into capitularies, at Mantua (?781) among a raft of royal business.[1] Successive capitularies issued statements regarding xenodochia 'that pertain to us', sometimes grouped together with royal monasteries and churches in the administration of the palace.[2] As with monasteries, this category included facilities of royal foundation and those given or transferred into royal custody. Each was an individual action, placing a specific house under the king.[3] For monasteries there was a third category: of houses made royal via a grant of royal protection. Such grants, extended to politically important monasteries, provided immunity from episcopal jurisdiction.[4] The exercise of such a privilege is significant when thinking about wider jurisdiction. Since at least the synod of Ver (755), Carolingian monasteries were acknowledged to be accountable either to king or bishop.[5] The two jurisdictions can be seen in capitularies, which either address royal monasteries as a single group or appear united into one, when the palace and bishops acted together to reform all the monasteries of the realm. The binary jurisdiction of palace/bishop was clearer in theory than practice, but the theory was clear.[6] Bishops had an authority over monasteries; Carolingian law then permitted the palace to exempt individual houses from this overarching claim.

No language of such a binary jurisdiction can be observed for xenodochia. The contrast can be seen in another early *capitulum* from Mantua (782×786), which stated that 'Monasteries of men and of women, both those known to be under the *mundium* of the palace or in the episcopal *mundium*, as well as [those] found to be

---

[1] MGH *Cap.* I. 190–1 (c. 12).

[2] (c. 3) 'De senodochiis vero nobis pertinentibus', MGH *Cap.* I. 195, also, 201 (c. 6), 328 (c. 4). In c.780×90, Lombard bishops consented to a continuation of royal custom (and so control) over churches, monasteries, and xenodochia pertaining to the royal palace: (c. 5) 'De eclesiis et monasteria et senodochia que ad mundio palatii pertine[n]t aut pertinere debent: ut unusquisque iustitiam dominorum nostrorum regum et eorum rectum consentiat.' (MGH *Cap.* I. 189). As early as 753 'monasteria, basilica vel exenodochia que ad palatii defensione esse videntur' were exempted from double taxation (MGH *Leges* IV. 202, c. 17).

[3] See the late plea by bishops regarding the emperor's responsibilities to 'those who have placed monasteries and *sinodochia sub defensione sacri palatii*', MGH *Conc.* III. 226 (c. 16), at the council of Pavia (850).

[4] These grants were used as royal policy, to extend royal authority and erode a bishop's power in their locality: De Jong, 'Carolingian Monasticism', 624–7. Kasten, 'Erbrechtliche Verfügungen', 248, offers one such example.

[5] De Jong, 'Carolingian Monasticism', 626. The synod was upholding a decree of a previous (now lost) synod, 'ut illa monasteria, ubi regulariter monachi vel monachas vixerunt ... ut exinde, si regales erant, ad domnum regem fecissent rationes abba vel abbatissa; et si episcopales, ad illum episcopum.' MGH *Cap.* I. 36 (c. 20).

[6] For the complexity of practice, and the leading role played by nobles, De Jong, 'Charlemagne's Church', 120; Innes, *State and Society*, 180–222. Monasteries could be commended to bishops and kings between the mid-eighth and late ninth centuries, Wood, *Prop. Ch.*, 339–45.

under other men, every single one (in whosesoever *mundium* they are) must be compelled to live regularly; and xenodochia, whomever they belong to, must maintain their brothers in everything according to their capability'.[7] When it came to monasteries, the injunction relied upon two different types of jurisdiction. The first, *mundium*, was a Lombard legal status of protection, a kind of responsibility of guardianship. While this could be held by many persons, the injunction called on two wide-ranging (and thus, to a degree, public) *mundia* to act: that under the palace (singular) and under bishops (plural). The second type of jurisdiction was implicit in the council's right to compel monks and nuns to live regularly, regardless of the *mundium* in which they sat. This was a right that superseded *mundium* for monasteries: the long-standing claim of ecclesiastical jurisdiction over religious. When it came to xenodochia, the capitulum could stake no such claims. There was no statement of greater *mundia*, only a more messy system of possession, 'whomever they belong to'. Nor does this capitulum offer a vision of correction, and so a claim to be able to correct. In terms now familiar, the council agreed simply that a facility must juggle a basic responsibility to maintain their brothers with the resources that were available. In this ruling on a specific controversy, the council articulated its shared sense of a facility's existing responsibilities under the law.

Carolingian bishops did have facilities in their care and under their protection,[8] perhaps many more than the palace, but no general diocesan jurisdiction over xenodochia. Such a claim over monasteries rested on Chalcedon (451), as the bishops at Olona made explicit in 825, when asked by whom and how a negligent abbot should be corrected: this had been 'manifestly set forth', they said, 'by canon 8 of Chalcedon', which gave the bishop the power to excommunicate him.[9] Chalcedon's rulings that a monastery could only be made with episcopal consent (c. 4), that monks were subject to their bishop (c. 4), and that a consecrated monastery could never return to secular uses (c. 24) had been repeated in Gallic and Merovingian councils, the *Dionysio-Hadriana*, and Charlemagne's *Admonitio generalis*.[10] The principles were so familiar that they were usually articulated in

---

[7] MGH *Cap.* I. 192 (c. 3): 'Monasteria virorum et puellarum, tam que in mundio palatii esse noscuntur vel etiam in mundio episcopales seu et de reliquis hominibus esse inveniuntur, distringat unusquisque in cuius mundio sunt, ut regulariter vivant; simul et senodochia, cuiuslibet sint, fratres in omnibus pascantur iuxta illorum possibilitatem.'

[8] MGH *Cap.* I. 316 (c. 1).

[9] MGH *Cap.* I. 369, c. 11 (corrected here using MS Blankenburg, fol. 105r): 'A quo et quomodo corrigi abbas neglegenter agens debeat, canon Calcidonensis titul. VIII evidenter exponit, cum ab episcopo loci dissilienter communione privare non ambigit.' The capitulum also adapted language from Chalcedon's canon ('nec per contumeliam ab episcopo suo dissiliant; Qui vero audent evertere huiusmodi formam... communione priventur.' *COGD* I. 141–2). On Olona, see below, and pp. 180–3 for the *relatio*.

[10] CCSL 148, p. 205 (c. 27); CCSL 148A, pp. 10 (c. 19), 26 (c. 10), 171 (c. 2); MGH *Fontes iuris* XVI. 198 (c. 31), MGH *Cap.* I. 102 (c. 15), 111 (c. 17), 183 (c. 11), 400 (c. 31). Episcopal jurisdiction over monasteries in fifth-century Gaul was treated in H. R. Bittermann, 'The Council of Chalcedon and

wholly Carolingian terms by both synods and councils, who spoke of monasteries, basilicas, baptismal churches, and *plebes* (parish churches), but not of xenodochia.[11] Capitularies also reinforced a general episcopal authority over churches, including a right to consent to the appointment and dismissal of priests,[12] but this authority was never explicitly related to xenodochia. Chalcedon's less-circulated canon 8 had included 'clerics who presided over *ptochia*' alongside those in monasteries and *martyria* as answerable to the bishop.[13] It was never associated with xenodochia, even by the bishops at Olona in 825, who answered in very different terms when asked about xenodochia.[14] No statement, at Mantua or elsewhere, spoke in Chalcedonian terms of xenodochia, nor even of a *mundium episcopales* over xenodochium. When the palace took a monastery into the *mundium palatii*, it extracted the house from an overarching episcopal jurisdiction; in contrast, it simply gathered a xenodochium under its protection.

Frankish church councils largely ignored xenodochia, continuing the pattern of Gallic and Merovingian forebears. Hospitals do not appear among the ordinary (or extraordinary) business of Carolingian prelates; even the great council in Paris (829), the high-water mark of sacral kingship and the Frankish ideal of episcopal government, ignored hospitals.[15] 'Among what especially pertains to bishops', its many and lengthy statutes addressed faith and baptism, priestly behaviour,

Episcopal Jurisdiction', *Speculum* 13:2 (1938), whose wider argument on Roman law rests problematically on Justinianic law.

[11] It was reinforced, too, by the Benedictine rule (c. 64). Charlemagne to his *missi* in 802: (c. 15) 'And we will and command that abbots and monks in all ways be subject to their bishops in all humility and obedience, as the canonical ruling requires. And that every church and basilica remain under ecclesiastical protection and authority (*potestas*). And none may dare to divide or parcel out the property of a basilica...And monks must be corrected by their diocesan bishop; and if they do not mend their ways the archbishop must summon them to synod and if still they do not reform themselves they must come before us with their bishop' ('Abbates autem omnis modis volumus et precipimus, ut episcopis suis omni humilitate et hobhedientia sint subiecti, sicut canonica constitutione mandat. Et omnis eclesiae adque basilicae in eclesiastica defensione et potestatem permaneat. Et de rebus ipse basilicae nemo ausus sit in divisione aut in sorte mittere...Et monachi ab episcopo provinciae ipsius corripiantur; quod si se non emendent, tunc archiepiscopus eos ad sinodum convocet; et si neque sic se correxerint, tunc ad nostra praesentiam simul cum episcopo suo veniant.') (MGH *Cap*. I. 94). Of course, practice was messier than theory: Wood, *Prop. Ch.*, 86–7, 92–3, 96, 191–210.
[12] G. Schmitz, 'The Capitulary Legislation of Louis the Pious', in *Ch. Heir*, 429–31; Wood, *Prop. Ch.*, 519–23. Diocesan authority was proclaimed, too, over churches founded and retained by secular lords, Wood, *Prop. Ch.*, 789–94.
[13] *COGD* I. 141 (c. 8), regarding 'Clerici qui praeficiuntur ptochiis vel qui ordinantur monasteriis et basilicis martyrum, sub episcoporum qui in unaquaque civitate sunt...' Canon 8 was among the twenty-seven capitula in Pope Zacharias's letter of 747 to Pippin, among material on the clergy and priestly discipline (MGH *Epp*. III. 483). On the letter, D. Jasper, 'Papal Letters of the Merovingian and Carolingian Periods', in *PLEMA* 105. Cf. Schönfeld, 'Xenod.', 38, who misread the original decree.
[14] For the bishops at Olona, see later in this chapter. 'Thociis' was used in place of Chalcedon's 'ptochiis' in the *Collectio Vetus Gallica*, from Lyons in c.600, suggesting that even at this early date the Greek term was foreign to a Frankish audience: H. Mordek, *Kirchenrecht und Reform im Frankenreich: Die Collectio Vetus Gallica* (Berlin, 1975), 402 (at 13.7); *CCEMA* 50–3.
[15] On the council, Patzold, *Episcopus*, 149–68; Schmitz, 'Capitulary Legislation', 436; M. de Jong, *The Penitential State* (Cambridge, 2009), 170–84; Patzold, *Episcopus*, 149–68.

basilicas, and religious life, including monks and nuns.[16] The council was particularly exercised by church property and an episcopal duty to administer this
correctly and to those in need, a topic on which it wheeled out a weighty
bibliography of holy councils and church fathers.[17] This might have been a perfect
moment to introduce xenodochia; but the council did not. Similarly, *capitula
episcoporum*, the many sets of statutes issued for dioceses across the ninth century,
fail to mention xenodochia.[18] And when a Frankish synod did finally address
hospitals, at Meaux-Paris (845/6), it was in a petition to the king to act on his
responsibilities. This pattern of silence suggests that xenodochia were not considered a matter of church business. And, as we have seen, they were not objects of
correctio and *emendatio*, to reinvigorate religious practice, but *restauratio*, a
rebuilding of the material (if often Christian) landscape.

Yet when xenodochia did finally appear, among a list of royal duties in
Lombard royal assemblies, they were not worldly objects. They were often placed
with ecclesiastical topics, finding a home as institutions beside pronouncements
on monasteries and basilicas; yet here, too, they were treated at a cautious remove.
The *mere ecclesiasticum* of Mantua II (813) encompassed monasteries, baptismal
churches, basilicas, and clerical or religious men in general, but only xenodochia
that were in royal hands ('senodochiis vero nobis pertinentibus').[19] The point here
is not that bishops failed to take an interest in xenodochia, nor even that bishops
exercised the same type of authority as any other patron. Indeed, as we shall see,
there was a sense that bishops were the natural protectors of these Christian forms
and, as such, they were at the centre of intensifying efforts to address these
facilities after 825. The point here is that bishops neither inherited nor claimed
any general jurisdictional right as diocesan. And this lack of a recognized right was
the challenge they faced in those intensifying efforts.

Nevertheless, there were rights by which bishops could act on individual
xenodochia. We detect them in late decrees, which turned increasingly to bishops.

---

[16] (c. 6) 'QUOD INTER CETERA AD CURAM EPISCOPORUM SPECIALITER PERTINEAT...', esp. priestly
hospitality (c. 14), monks and nuns (cc. 28, 37, 39, 43–4, 46), reinforcing that monks be subject to their
bishop (c. 28), MGH *Conc.* II.ii, 614–68. See, too, Jonas of Orléans, *Relatio episcoporum* (report) on the
four councils of that year, MGH *Cap.* II. 27–51.

[17] MGH *Conc.* II.ii, 622–5 (cc. 15–18). Its c. 15 quoted Gelasius, Pomerius, and Jerome (twice); there
are later quotations from the canons of Chalcedon (c. 26) and Antioch in 330 (c. 25), the latter stating
that, 'Episcopus ecclesiasticarum rerum habeat potestatem, ad dispensandum erga omnes qui indigent,
cum summa reverentia et timore Dei' (*PL* 67, col. 164). While Pomerius and Jerome have a long history
in Frankish legislation, the Paris council was the first to use Gelasius (Hartmann, *Synoden*, 183).
A fondness for Pomerius has been linked to Wala, D. Ganz, 'The *Epitaphium Arsenii* and Opposition to
Louis the Pious', in *Ch. Heir*, 545.

[18] They span *c.*800–*c.*950 and focus on priestly behaviour and responsibilities, including hospitality
(MGH *Cap. episc.* I. 122 (c. 25), 241 (c. 11); II. 85 (c. 4); III. 29 (c. 5), 98 (c. 8), 127 (cc. 14, 16)), but they
also address monks, monasteries, and basilicas (I. 30 (c. 13); II. 129 (cc. 6–7): III. 41 (c. 3), 55 (cc. 10,
12), 276 (c. 30), 362 (cc. 13–15)). On the material, C. van Rhijn, *Shepherds of the Lord* (Turnhout,
2007).

[19] This royal council was acting as much to preserve the people and places of the church from abuse
by bishops as to reinforce discipline under bishops, MGH *Cap.* I. 195 (c. 3).

In 850, the bishops of Lombardy met in Pavia under the archbishop of Milan, the patriarch of Aquileia, and the royal arch-chaplain to consider the state of the realm. They presented twenty-four decrees to Louis II in the form of a synodal letter. Most were directed at the bishops themselves, addressing pastoral duties, marriage, baptismal churches, and a duty to restore monasteries brought to ruin by poor custodians or by the laity. The synod then turned to xenodochia in two decrees, the second (c. 16) pleading that the new emperor fulfil his responsibilities regarding those in his possession. The first addressed the bishops themselves:

> (c. 15) Similarly also, concerning xenodochia we establish that [i] those in the *potestas* of bishops be governed according to the arrangement (*dispositio*) of those who instituted them. Moreover, [ii] those that are in fact under the protection of a church but must be ruled according to their institutors' decrees by heirs or by those to whom they pertain who shall have lived a religious life: the bishop should ensure that they not be neglected by these [heirs or assigns] who, if found guilty of bad management in anything, should be subject to ecclesiastical discipline. But [iii] if heirs, whether cleric or secular, should have been tempted to go against the resolutions of their ancestors (*maiorum*) to such a degree that they try to suppress or conceal the testator's instructions and divide the resources of the xenodochium between themselves, it should be reported to the most holy emperor, so that by his authority the wickedness of such transgressors might be repressed.[20]

Here we can distinguish a series of ways by which a bishop might acquire a right in or over a xenodochium, and the differences in the reach of those rights. The synod recognized two forms of episcopal jurisdiction. The first [i] was straightforward: 'in potestate episcoporum' referred to facilities in a bishop's hand and directly managed under him. These included those founded by a previous bishop and retained to the episcopal estate, and those founded by others and entrusted to the bishop or perhaps seized by the bishop with the passage of time.[21] Even in these cases, a bishop was obliged to observe the founder's arrangements (*dispositio*), revealing that this was not an ordinary jurisdiction, but a form of managerial

---

[20] 'Similiter et de senedochiis statuimus ut [i] quecumque in episcoporum sunt potestate secundum dispositionem eorum, qui ea instituerunt gubernentur. [ii] Que autem sub defensione quidem sunt ecclesie, sed iuxta institutorum decreta per heredes vel pertinentes qui religiosam vitam duxerint regi debent, procuret episcopus ut ab eis non neglegantur, et si in aliquo male tractationis obnoxii reperiuntur, ecclesiastice subiaceant discipline. [iii] Quod si heredes sive clerici sive seculares adeo importune contra maiorum suorum decreta ire temptaverint, ut testatoris institutionem subprimere vel obscurare nitantur et inter se senedochii substantiam dividere nuntietur sacratissimo imperatori, ut eius auctoritate huiusmodi transgressorum nequitia coherceatur', ed. here following MS Blankenburg, fol. 110v. It is also ed. MGH *Conc.* III. 226, where p. 217 discusses the letter.

[21] It was to prevent the latter that Frankish founders, in particular, were anxious to add clauses to charters, including Childebert and Ulthrogotha at the council of Orléans (549). Also, Wood, *Prop. Ch.*, 52–3, 173.

supervision, a trusteeship for the testator/founder. It would include the right to appoint (or supervise the appointment of) its steward.

A second episcopal jurisdiction, [ii] 'sub defensione ecclesiae', encompassed hospitals in the hands of others but under church protection. The synod suggests two routes by which this might be extended. One was as xenodochia under the control of a monastery or house of canons; these would include facilities established by the community itself and those founded by others and entrusted to the community to oversee.[22] In such cases the bishop's right of action was through diocesan jurisdiction over the monastery, a duty to inquire into and correct the community; he could not oversee the facility itself but he could threaten its guardians with ecclesiastical sanction if they failed in their duties. A second group was secured under church protection by specific agreement with the founder. A wide range of charters survives in which founders entrusted their facilities to heirs or to clerical assigns and also arranged for ecclesiastical protection, to guard the facility and its *dispositio*.[23] These were not handed over into a standard custody. Instead, founders agreed terms with the bishop, specifying the extent of a bishop's authority. Some dictated that their facility never be subject to the bishop, others that he would supervise the priest but not appoint him, or that he oversee the facility's government.[24] We see its legal authority in a lawsuit of 762 in which Alpert challenged his brother's widow, Rottruda. Alpert had seized his late brother Auripert's property as his natural heir, even though Auripert had made a will directing that the property be used to make a xenodochium. At the heart of the case was 'what your brother himself established (*instituit*) in the charter of his arrangement for the xenodochium, in food and aid for the poor'.[25] The judges read a copy of the will, ruling that it should stand and that the xenodochium be 'just as he had ordered'. They found in favour of Rottruda, to whom Auripert had entrusted his project. The will included provisions for its custody, for 'he established that its guidance and government be conducted by the bishop of Pisa without neglect, but should he neglect this then its guidance will be conducted by Rottruda'. The founder had hoped that the bishop might offer secure guardianship, a form of executorship over his will; but should this fail it

[22] Because much of our documentary evidence survives in monastic archives, these two groups constitute our most numerous examples of actual foundations. They are noticed in Stasolla, 'Propositio', 15–20; Kasten, 'Erbrechtliche Verfügungen', 253; Schönfeld, 'Xenod.', 24–7, 30–1. These were discrete facilities, their 'assets autonomous from the parent institution', Schönfeld, 'Xenod.', 27.

[23] E.g. Schönfeld, 'Xenod.', 36, 39; Stasolla, 'Propositio', esp. 24, 29–32.

[24] Marculf's sample charter sets out two categories between which the founder might choose (*Marculfi Formularum*, 162–74; Ch. 5 n. 173 in this volume). Also, Schönfeld 'Xenod.', 39.

[25] '... eo quod ipse germanus tuus per cartulam sue ordinationis instituit exenodochio in alimoniis et subsidiis pauperum, et statuit ut per pontificem civitatis Pisane rectum et guvernatum fieri deberit absque neglegentiam, et si ipse neglegeret rectum fierit per ipsa Rottruda', *Chartae Latinae Antiquiores*, ed. G. Cavallo and G. Nicolaj, LVIII (Zurich, 2001), no. 15. The word *rectum* seems to be an abstract noun made out of *regere*.

would be returned to his wife. The right of supervision was a matter of Auripert's gift.

Over such facilities, the rights of a church or bishop were contractual. Founders took advantage of an ability to lay down precise directives in writing and make custody contingent upon their fulfilment. This could produce complicated and competitive arrangements. One enterprising founder in Salerno entrusted his xenodochium to his heirs, but established a series of safeguards. Should the heirs fail to fulfil their responsibilities or should they remove anything from that place, the facility was to be placed in the power (*potestas*) of the abbot of St Benedict. Should he fail, it should be handed to the abbot of St Vincent. And should he fail, the property would revert (*in proprietate*) back to the heirs, who would control it as their own property but never diminish its possessions and ensure its lodging and alms were provided.[26]

The term used across a range of material, and in relation to the range of custodians, is *potestas*. It is used technically in the Lombard material and carried specific meanings, extending back to classical Roman law. *Potestas* was the term used to demarcate the power of a father over his children and a master over his slaves; it was a kind of private power, but not dominion.[27] In the cases of xenodochia it emerges as a right that was attached to the property not the person, and could be transferred to another if the person failed to uphold the terms of their *potestas*. Such rights were diverse, contingent, and assigned with the property, even for the bishop. This delimited permission meant that a bishop's scope of action was inherent in and specific to a facility, it was not a *ius* over facilities. On one extreme, were those in his *potestas*, whose management he directed; on the other, those in *potestates* over which he had no direct authority. Many, perhaps most xenodochia probably sat between these two poles.

A Multiplicity of *Potestates*

The defining characteristic of xenodochia was the multiplicity of *potestates* in which they sat, often beyond the reach of palace or bishops. The Pavian council recognized church protection as a claim extended to individual houses, through specific channels. It also recognized a third group: [iii] xenodochia over which no ecclesiastical jurisdiction had been established. These facilities were in the hands

---

[26] *Codex diplomaticus cavensis*, ed. M. Schiani et al., 12 vols (Naples, 1873–2015), I. 79–84 (no. 64). Despite poor Latin, the meaning emerges through the length and repetition of the charter. It uses neither *xenodochium* nor *hospitale*, although such is clearly intended given its focus on the site and arrangements to ensure that 'reception and alms' always be performed there ('ut fiat inde ospitium et elemosinam').

[27] A. Lewis, 'Slavery, Family, and Status', in *CCRL*; Pottage, 'Law After Anthropology', 154, drawing on Y. Thomas, 'La langue du droit romain', *Archives de la philosophie du droit* 19 (1974), 105.

of a founder's heirs or assigns, who might be laity or clerics and who were not subject to the bishop. One such example was established by the archdeacon Pacificus and his sister Ansa in Quinzano in 844, whose house was to be converted into a xenodochium, supervised by their niece Anselinda and nephews Rodibert and Placibert, a deacon. It was to feed sixty paupers each month, and more on the Saturdays in Lent, and to host a feast of bread, beans, cheese, meat, and wine for 140 paupers and twelve clerics on the anniversaries of Pacificus's and Ansa's deaths.[28]

For historians these are the most invisible facilities since, beyond the reach of monastery, bishop, or king, their deeds have usually been lost. Nor were they a target of councils, whose exhortations for xenodochia were directed mainly at the king and bishops. Nevertheless, several royal capitularies notice them in statements regarding xenodochia 'whoever has them' or 'anyone to whom they belong'.[29] Exceptional circumstances, like the suit against Rottruda, might bring an individual facility into public view. A few can be glimpsed as earlier foundations, beside a church to whose cleric they were subsequently entrusted.[30] This was the group of xenodochia that had perplexed Schönfeld, who noticed their private character and their subjection to 'the founder [who in charter after charter] assigned the *potestas* to himself, because this *potestas* is nothing but the *proprietas*'.[31] Schönfeld's explanation, of a German 'legal earthquake' that overcame (Justinianic) law, must now be set aside, but not his hard-won observations from so many documents. For the founder did assign control over the xenodochium, a *potestas* that was attached to the *proprietas*, a form of trusteeship that could be lost if the trustee failed to uphold its terms. This *potestas* was grounded in testamentary law, in an ability to assign property to specified uses and to appoint executors (trustees).[32] The result was a multiplicity of arrangements, as founders devised their own custodial arrangements.

---

[28] After their heirs' deaths, the charities were to be entrusted to a school of canons and their priors. *Codice diplomatico veronese*, ed. V. Fainelli, I (Venice, 1940), no. 176; Kasten, 'Erbrechtliche Verfügungen', 256–7. See, too, *CDL* I, no. 48.

[29] (c. 3) 'et senodochia, cuiuslibet sint' (782×86); (c. 1) 'ut quicumque senedochia habent' (c.790); (c. 7/7a) 'De senodochiis precipimus, ut quicumque illas habet / ... ad palatium vel ad quorumcumque iura pertinentibus' (825). MGH *Cap.* I. 192, 200, 328–9. There is some ambiguity in the second, which may refer to temporary (managerial) custody rather than an ongoing *potestas* that would pass to successors. The former was the meaning of *habere* in a subsequent capitulum on monasteries and xenodochia that 'quicumque eas habere voluerint, per beneficium domno nostro regis habeant'. (MGH *Cap.* I. 201, c. 6).

[30] Stasolla, 'Propositio', 15–16, 24–5, 30.

[31] 'Dies alles ist nur möglich, weil der Gründer sich die potestas zuschreibt; denn diese potestas ist nichts anderes als die proprietas, das Eigentum': Schönfeld, 'Xenod.', 39.

[32] In the early middle ages, any such ability was expressed via local institutions and systems of record, which shaped its expression and scope. Records that survive for Francia present a more ecclesiastical picture, in part because Roman law practices had been less deeply rooted here, in part because its *gesta municipalia* (public archives) have not survived, depriving us of the more secular picture. The pictures are not mutually exclusive, since the ecclesiastical archives may have subsumed some of the function of *gesta municipalia*, Rio, *Legal Practice*, 179–82.

We see this multiplicity most clearly when later synods tried to intervene in order to rescue failing houses. This was the ambition behind the late Pavian decree, which exhorted bishops to manage their own hospitals correctly and punish neglect of those subject to church protection. For facilities beyond episcopal reach [iii] it threatened (unspecified) imperial penalties when heirs and assigns proved 'wicked'. This novel penalty was also a new claim to punish, and thus a new claim of jurisdiction. The limits of its reach suggest its basis in law. In contrast to facilities under royal and episcopal control, or subject to church protection, private heirs and assigns were not punished for routine neglect or failure to follow a testator's directives; instead, they were reported *in extremis*, when a xenodochium was dissolved and its property seized for private gain, and to the emperor. In so doing, it reminds us of the canon of Orléans (549) against 'murderers of the poor', which protected bequests to xenodochia from appropriation by heirs. The canon's anathema clause was rediscovered and widely reused in Francia in the 840s to guard monasteries and hospitals against dispossession;[33] similarly at Pavia we see calls for protection, should a xenodochium be pillaged by its own guardians. In Italy it was a response entrusted to the palace.

But we must beware. Categorizing hospitals as royal, episcopal, or private oversimplifies the means by which an executor might hold a hospital or by which another authority might intervene to protect it. It also obscures the more fundamental issue, of the legal framework under which and to which a xenodochium was administered. For this was not an ecclesiastical institution forged under the bishop and held to a common model of government, such as the Benedictine rule. Each was its own unit of resources administered to an assigned use. In working to bolster and intrude rights of oversight, the Pavian synod underscored what was vital to the government of hospitals, a defining condition to which every facility was subject: that it be directed by and in accordance with the instructions of its founder. This was the case regardless of governing authority. The Pavian synod (c. 15) directed that a bishop must ensure that xenodochia in his hand were 'governed according to the directive of those who instituted them'; those under church protection 'ruled according to the decrees of their institutors by heirs' or assigns, who could be clerics, monks or nuns. Heirs beyond episcopal reach must not 'be tempted to go against the resolutions of their ancestors'. Each hospital was held on its own terms, as laid out by its founder. This was even the case for those in the emperor's hand. The synod's following capitulum urged the emperor to uphold the trust of those who had entrusted their facilities to the palace, 'the highest power of protection', and not assign them 'against the decrees of founders', lest he incur the condemnation of God.[34] Whoever the supervisorial

---

[33] See below, on Meaux-Paris (845/6). The Orléans canon is treated in Chapter 3.

[34] It was couched as a general warning to emperors: (c. 16) 'The most blessed emperors should be advised that they who have entrusted monasteries and xenodochia to the protection of the royal palace,

authority, it could have no will of its own, even (as was the case for monasteries) a reforming will. It acted in service to another's directives by ensuring that the agent charged to carry out (embody) that will carried this out, be they an on-site manager, custodian, or heir.

Chapter 4 established that a xenodochium was fundamentally a gift (assets), attached to a directive (*dispositio*), and held to its specific charitable charges. This, its basic constitutional equation, was laid down by the original donor, who directed by whom and to what ends the resources be administered. As chapter 5 uncovered, it was a framework rooted in testamentary law, and in the duty of a Christian to recognise and tend to the needs of others. This cultivated a right to imagine, and fix, in one's own terms. The Pavian synod, among others, reveals that the *institutor* also established custodial arrangements: the internal staffing, its external custody (in whose *potestas* it sat), and whether it was subject to a superior protecting authority. The efforts to provide protections for failing houses bear witness that xenodochia were Christian facilities but not fundamentally ecclesiastical: they did not require episcopal consent to be built and were not forbidden to return to worldly uses.[35] Welfare foundations were created in fulfilment of Christian ideals, but under a Roman right to make testamentary provision for one's soul. As a result, in law, they did not pass into ecclesiastical jurisdiction unless an agent did so. In practice, lines would not have been so careful, especially in Francia. There the concern to protect a foundation from future bishops suggests both the ability of bishops to intrude into individual houses and the heavier reliance on the church in lieu of secular law.

The multiplicity of arrangements was not an issue of types of xenodochia. To call a facility royal, episcopal, monastic, aristocratic, clerical, or lay, may capture a characteristic of that hospital, but it did not define a type of hospital nor even of jurisdiction. (The xenodochium of Bishop Bertrand, bishop of Le Mans, for example, was founded by a bishop, yet entrusted to a monastery.[36]) Nor can it be simply said that some xenodochia were 'private', in remaining in the hands of heirs. All facilities, even those beyond the reach of bishop or palace, had an ongoing charge, whose continuation was a matter of Christian service and public

[and] been proven to have done so, trusted them to be defended by none better than the highest powers. And so, if [emperors] have given such places to unlawful persons, in contravention of their founders' decrees, then the very persons who had been charged to defend [such places] must be condemned as their assailants. And rulers should especially beware that they who face judgement now on this matter by no one be not more harshly judged in a future ruling by omnipotent God, because according to the apostle "it is a fearful thing to fall into the hands of the living God" [Heb. 10: 31]. Indeed, we who are under an obligation to faithfully make known do humbly advise on that account what we dare not keep silent about.' Tr. from MGH *Cap.* II. 121; *Conc.* III. 226–7. Although the capitulum refers to both monasteries and *xenodochia*, its main target is the latter, as its position in the capitulary makes clear.

[35] Some do appear to have been consecrated or dedicated and may have been seen as *spiritualia*: MGH *Cap.* I. 332, c. 1.

[36] *Das Testament des Bischofs Berthramn*, 26. See, too, *Cod. dip. sant'Ambrosiano*, 458–9.

concern. And all facilities were governed by the directives of a founder. This meant that even governmental authorities, acting in the public interest, were acting to support the will of a private person; even the terms of their action were subordinate to that will.

Innovations and Interventions

Xenodochia were Christian foundations but not as a category secured under the bishop, as ecclesiastical or consecrated sites. It is worth stressing that the most profound (and the simplest) innovation was not attempted: a claim to such a diocesan jurisdiction from a council, by extending Chalcedon. Indeed, it was the absence of such a right that proved the main obstacle to any synod or assembly who wished to address xenodochia. Here we return to the capitularies, to look at familiar material through a new lens, to observe how mechanisms to act were built.

Lack of jurisdiction did not mean lack of concern, but it did define a council's task and its response. It laid a basic challenge at law-makers' feet, one that shaped conciliar material in two ways. It defined their scope of action, which was not to intrude into the house but to police it externally, by confronting those in whose *potestas* it rested; and it meant that a growing sense of obligation to act was met by a lack of a general right (and so ability) to act. Conciliar activity was therefore directed less towards creating actions than crafting a means of action. Capitula should be read as attempts to devise protections for facilities that lacked a structure of oversight. This was not a question of enforcement since councils were not reinforcing an existing state (this is one reason why their decrees lacked repetition or legal rhetoric). Rather, they sought to bolster and even manufacture means by which to extend an umbrella of protection. Their statements were assertions, at once ingenious interventions and blunt instruments, and still restricted in their reach.

We have seen how xenodochia emerged, if fitfully, as a matter of business in Italian royal assemblies of the 780s. These assemblies laid out a model for restoring xenodochia, based on the administration of resources in accordance with its institutor's directive. Relatively quickly and without templates from previous councils or canonical collections, assemblies resolved what to act on, and in what terms. It took much longer to determine how to act or to enforce compliance with these models. The challenge was how to create systems of oversight that might reach xenodochia and rebuke custodians. The lack of a general jurisdiction prompted different activities in Lombardy and Francia. It may account for the total silence of Frankish councils, until the more radical episcopal activity in the 840s and 850s, considered below. In Lombardy, Frankish arrivals found a more centralized system of government, with the royal palace at the heart of law-making and the administration of justice.[37] The introduction of the Carolingian assembly expanded the government's legal remit. Here, in this interplay between Carolingian ideology and local structures, the hospital emerged as a topic of public deliberation.

Initially, the assembly itself was the mechanism for action. For those xenodochia in the royal power and so under a basic supervisorial jurisdiction, there existed a right of action. Royal assemblies now offered a forum in which to act or, more exactly, by which to prompt the palace to observe basic principles regarding those facilities in the royal hand. This is why early activity focused on royal xenodochia. The first injunctions hinged on the palace's obligation to appoint fitting custodians and to require them to fulfil their duties.[38] Their focus, on the act of appointment, offered limited remedy. Their force was less in the specifics of any pronouncement, such as they were, than its collective statement by the assembly. This collective voice affirmed the value of xenodochia and exhorted Frankish rulers (and their local agents) to observe a basic duty of care.

The tougher problem was how to create mechanisms to guard other facilities. Two early snapshots shed light on this absence of means and the response of assemblies. The earliest reference to xenodochia as a category ('whomever they belong to') appears under Pippin and declares, without elaboration, that the brothers of a hospital be fed or maintained as the facility's resources allow.[39] The significance of this simple statement lies not in the matter but in the fact of its declaration. With the consent of 'every bishop, abbot, and count and faithful man with the king, both Frank and Lombard', and the king himself, xenodochia became a subject of law-making by the governing elite. It opened a door through which assemblies would walk with more conviction a few years later, in c.790 when, in the king's voice, the assembly determined:

(c. 1) That whoever have xenodochia, if they are willing to provide for paupers there and seek advice on how it had been in the past, then they should hold these xenodochia and rule them properly. And if they are unwilling to do this, they must be relieved of the same [places], which should henceforth be governed by such men as are pleasing to God and thus to us.[40]

The statement went beyond mere principle to articulate a model towards which hospitals should be run and basic mechanisms to ensure this was done. It was

---

[37] By the early eighth century, Lombard kings sat atop a judicial process with Pavia at its centre (C. Wickham, 'Aristocratic Power in Lombard Italy', in A. C. Murray, ed., *After Rome's Fall* (Toronto, 1998)). The Lombard role in the reorientation of Ravenna is treated in D. H. Miller, 'The Roman Revolution', *Mediaeval Studies* 36 (1974).

[38] MGH *Cap.* I. 195 (c. 3).   [39] MGH *Cap.* I. 192 (c. 3).

[40] '...ut quicumque senedochia habent, si ita pauperes pascere voluerint et consilio facere quomodo abantea fuit, habeant ipsa senedochia et regant ordinabiliter. Et si hoc facere noluerint, ipsas dimittant; et per tales homines inantea sint gubernatae, qualiter Deo et nobis exinde placeat.' MGH *Cap.* I. 200.

directed at its steward or administrator, who should be willing to perform his duty, and included a right (if not yet a mechanism) to enforce this. An unwilling steward may be relieved of the house, although the capitulum does not say by whom. It does give the authority by which this might be done: the king's pleasure provides the authority to do what is agreeable to God, the assembly's consent gives it form.

These directives, as those from Olona (825) and Pavia (850), remind us that the power to act lay fundamentally with the king. Royal assemblies provided the forum for action, royal authority underpinned any directives, in service to a broader vision of Christian *imperium*. This was not a matter of secular versus temporal rule. The important point is that oversight for hospitals was not crafted by defining new rights of jurisdiction: it was crafted by making use of organizational structures of government, including shared ideals of *ministerium*.

Curiously, such use stopped short of royal legates (*missi*). This lack is grounded in the relationship between governmental and diocesan authority. Under Charlemagne *missi* were essential to government, ensuring communication between centre and locality and carrying out a council's directives. From *c*.800, the palace turned increasingly to local land-holders to act as *missi*, preferring archbishops and other senior churchmen for their institutional authority, high rank, good judgement, and wisdom.[41] Some initiatives rested upon cooperation between *missus* and diocesan.[42] We have already noted how *missi* were charged with the correction of monasteries or houses of canons, often dispatched in pairs consisting of a monastic and a clerical *missus*.[43] In such cases, the palace was using (and bolstering) diocesan structures in pursuit of a wider vision of Christian order. There is no such example for xenodochia in Francia, an absence that probably reflects the lack of an ecclesiastical jurisdiction onto which royal initiatives might be grafted.[44] There are only two examples of such use of *missi*, both Italian and relatively late. In 832, Lothar directed his *missi* to 'inquire of each monastery or xenodochium how they were arranged by those who established them, as well as their present state and by which persons they are held'.[45] Its terms suggest

[41] McKitterick, 'Charlemagne's *missi*'; Wormald, *English Law*, 50–1; Fouracre, 'Carolingian Justice', 780–3, 787; Costambeys et al., *Carolingian World*, 179–81; K. F. Werner, '*Missus, marchio, comes*: Entre l'administration centrale et l'administration locale', in W. Paravinicini and K. F. Werner, eds, *Histoire comparée de l'administration* (Zurich, 1980), 196–205; MGH *SS* I. 38–9.

[42] E.g. in *c*.790 the bishop and *missus dominicus* were to work together to reallocate a bequest of alms when a recipient had died before receipt, MGH *Cap*. I. 201 (c. 8); *Leges* IV. 520 (c. 31).

[43] Chapter 4, p. 94–5; MGH *Cap*. I. 199 (c. 11); *Leges* IV. 518–19 (c. 20). For similar inquiries, MGH *Cap*. I. 131 (c. 3), 321–2 (c. 2), 410 (c. 116); II. 64 (c. 10); De Jong, *Penitential State*, 131.

[44] As noticed above, for Lombardy, xenodochia in the custody of monasteries might have been corrected by the bishop or *missi* on the basis of ordinary jurisdiction, but there is no Frankish statement to this effect.

[45] It is the first of thirteen directives to his *missi* (c. 1): 'Ut inquirant de singulis monasteriis vel senodochiis, qualiter a conditoribus ordinata sunt vel quomodo nunc permaneant et a quibus personis detineantur.' Subsequent capitula address baptismal churches (c. 9) and the state of cathedral churches, including 'qualiter canonicorum vita et conversatio ordinata sit' and whether the bishop ordains his

xenodochia were in fact the object. The task was devised by piggy-backing these facilities onto a practice of monastic oversight. Yet it did not adopt the terms of monastic visitation, to inquire as to rule and quality of life, forging instead a new directive with its own language of enquiry.[46] We have evidence of only one other inquiry. In 865, Louis II of Italy issued a brief set of charges, substantially ecclesiastical, to *missi*. Among them was one directing 'upright abbots' to visit monasteries, xenodochia, and hospitals, restoring the latter to their pristine state.[47] It is one of the last references to hospitals before the records go silent.

The more of the picture that is painted, the further the bishop seems to fade. This is largely due to the elements that compose the picture: on the one hand, the records themselves, of capitularies and so the agency of Carolingian *imperium*; on the other, the absence of a general diocesan jurisdiction over xenodochia that might serve as a tool for those royal assemblies, as it did for monasteries. The first makes up the action of the picture, the second limits that action's reach. Where royal authority reached *out* to the bishop for monastic supervision and invigorated his role as diocesan, public deliberations regarding xenodochia (even those articulated by churchmen) turned back to the centre, bidding the palace to act. For this reason, bishops are unfairly obscured in our material, and wholly absent before 825, the most active period of conciliar activity.

Yet bishops were always there. They were fundamental to Carolingian government. In assemblies their voices would have joined calls to address hospitals, and as local agents they were integral to many of the actions agreed. This was not only because bishops administered their own and supervised other xenodochia; they were also at the centre of a moral discourse that bubbled below the surface of capitularies. The ideal of *amator pauperum* continued to characterize good pastoral leadership, including that of the king. Churchmen spoke out collectively in embodiment of this ideal, and perhaps most readily when gathered together. Their collective moral calls are most clearly discerned in late ecclesiastical councils at Meaux-Paris (845/6), Pavia (850), and Milan (863), but they played a part in earlier assemblies, too. As individuals, bishops and abbots were also a main target as assemblies moved to counter abuses, from granting facilities as sinecures to despoiling houses in their charge. Several of the most detailed directives for xenodochia survive among ecclesiastical business, suggesting that bishops were their intended recipients. While bishops had no general right of action over xenodochia, they seem to have seen themselves (and been seen) as having a duty to act, and increasingly from the 825. It was a view fostered at papal councils

---

churches (c. 10), MGH *Cap.* II. 63–4. For context, see J. L. Nelson, 'The Last Years of Louis the Pious', in *Ch. Heir*, esp. 151.

[46] It is based on policy laid down under Wala at Olona (825) and Rome (826). Wala was present in 832.

[47] 'Directi abbates', MGH *Cap.* II. 94 (c. 5).

at Rome in 826 and 853, which exhorted bishops to have 'a watchful concern' that the charities of xenodochia not fail.[48]

As the challenge of protecting hospitals grew more acute, bishops were at the head of efforts to defend them. Xenodochia were vulnerable facilities with a tendency towards decay, as memories of their directives were lost or administration failed, a problem compounded as secular power fragmented. Family conflict in the 820s gave way to open warfare and the division of empire in 843. Churches suffered, too, when plundered of property and leadership.[49] Churchmen increased their cries for restitution, while late councils, like that of Savonnières (859) bewailed 'the discord and destruction of disaster' of the times.[50] The partnership between *regnum* and *sacerdotem* shifted its emphasis from the former to the latter as bishops seized the initiative. Patzold finds a new concept of episcopacy arising in northern France in the 820s, as bishops claimed a self-conscious role in the government of the realm, one based on early Christian precedents and cogently articulated at the Paris council of 829.[51] As we shall see, the claim grew in force and ambition over coming decades.

Lombardy and Rome

The changing political climate of the mid-ninth century—a period when bishops became a stronger voice in government and royal power came under greater challenge[52]—shaped the public conversation about xenodochia, and in starkly different ways in Italy and West Francia. In each region a group of law-makers worked to reframe the terms on which hospitals were addressed. One, in Italy, at the cusp of this period of change, the other in West Francia as episcopal claims became more radical. The first sheds light on the underlying local role of bishops, the second on their capacity to stake new claims.

The Olona Programme (825)

The most serious attempt to devise policy for hospitals took place at Olona where in 823 and 825 assemblies were convened under Lothar I, king of Italy (822–55)

---

[48] 'per sollicitudinem episcoporum', MGH *Conc.* III. 324 (c. 23), considered below.

[49] Nelson, 'Last Years of Louis the Pious', 155–6.

[50] 'Nota et—pro dolor!—nimis est nota discordia atque calamitatis pernicies', MGH *Conc.* III. 438 (c. 1). Of Bishop Aldric's hospitals in Le Mans it was said: 'Sed haec et reliqua bona innumerabilia a praedictis tyrannis, sive hospitalia VII quae ad pauperes et hospites recipiendos et recreandos fecerat, funditus vastata et diruta sunt.' *Gesta Aldrici*, 173; Goffart, *Le Mans Forgeries*, 30–5.

[51] 'den Wandel im Denken über Bischöfe', Patzold, *Episcopus*, 105–84, with quotation at p. 146; Moore, *Sacred Kingdom*, 328–67.

[52] For the complexity of the (heavily moral) political culture in this period, with church and crown closely aligned: De Jong, *Penitential State*, esp. ch. 3; C. M. Booker, *The Penance of Louis the Pious* (Philadelphia, PA, 2009); Meens et al., eds, *Relig. Franks*.

and co-emperor with his father Louis the Pious. For half a century, Italian assemblies had issued brief, descriptive statements to address specific controversies. Olona ended that tradition. Here, xenodochia featured conspicuously alongside monasteries, churches, and oratories in protections against episcopal greed.[53] They were also the particular object of three capitula that, individually, were unlike anything that had come before and which, together, amount to a programme of regulation unlike anything to be seen again. Their aim for xenodochia—to restore their possessions and charitable services—was uncontroversial; what is remarkable was the ambition with which this was done. They devised overarching policies, formulating frameworks for evaluation and intervention, and principles on which these were based. Theirs was the most significant body of material to be promulgated on welfare houses, as well as the most innovative.

These observations may come as a surprise, because the Olona assemblies have attracted such little attention.[54] Only one of their acts has been noticed, the so-called 'Edict of Olona', which required that schools be established in cathedral cities across North Italy.[55] This has inspired study of Carolingian, and especially Italian education, but not the law-makers who produced it. Olona's hospital programme puts the law-makers front and centre: not only was the agenda theirs, but their policies would have a defining impact over the coming generations.[56] In this new context, the 'Edict' becomes part of a longer story, that moves from Francia, to Olona, to Rome.[57]

The place of Olona in Carolingian law deserves wider study than can be offered here, for its significance extended beyond xenodochia and schools. Its legislation was incorporated into Italian and Frankish collections, including later manuscripts of Ansegis's *Collectio*, and the Roman law compilations, *Lex Romana canonica compta* and the *Collectio Anselmo dedicata*.[58] When other texts are attributed only to an emperor, these insertions were sometimes labelled as 'from Olona', suggesting that Olona had a reputation among compilers

---

[53] In capitula that nullified exploitative leases and banned fees for consecration, MGH *Cap*. I. 316 (c. 1), 332 (c. 1). The former, the 823 *Cap. Olonnense*, opens with 'senodochia aut monasteria vel baptismales ecclesias' that belong to a bishop's church.

[54] See the brief notes in Mordek, 'Fränkische Kapitularien', 22; Ganshof, *Recherches*, 16. For a digest of the legislation, de Clercq, *Législation religieuse*, II. 43–8.

[55] MGH *Cap*. I. 327 (c. 6); R. G. Witt, *The Two Latin Cultures* (Cambridge, 2011), 35–6, 39–41; Hildebrandt, *External School*, 67.

[56] For its impact: MGH *Cap*. II. 82 (c. 7), 121 (cc. 15–16); *Conc*. II.ii, 576–7 (c. 23); III. 213 (c. 7), 226 (cc. 15–16); IV. 161 (c. 5).

[57] For the question of schools in Francia and Rome, MGH *Cap*. I. 369 (cc. 6, 13); *Conc*. II.ii, 581 (c. 34).

[58] MGH, *Cap*. NS I. 478–9 (1.79–80), 494–5 (1.105–7), 533 (2.16–19), 661 (4.72), 664 (4.76), 767, with the manuscripts at pp. 80–1, 93, 102, 114, 168, 171, 175, 199. Italian legislation, esp. that of Olona, make up a good number of the later insertions into Ansegis's collection. On the Roman law collections, *CICMA* 57–9.

of law.[59] Undoubtedly, its capitularies were widely copied. Eight Olona capitularies are scattered across nineteen manuscripts (and two fragments), although there are particular concentrations in three: two manuscripts of c.1000 from central and southern Italy gather the same six capitularies from Olona, while Wolfenbüttel, Herzog August Bibliothek, MS Blankenburg 130 (herein MS Blankenburg), from North Italy, c.855, is the only manuscript to collect all eight.[60] Compiled by someone with a knowledgeable interest in law and access to a considerable collection of legal material from Francia and Italy, MS Blankenburg constitutes one of the most substantial Carolingian collections of law.[61]

The story of Olona begins in Francia, when Louis sent his son Lothar to North Italy, after the council of Attigny in August 822. At his side Louis placed two leading counsellors, one of them the newly rehabilitated Wala, a cousin of Charlemagne who had become a monk at Corbie when exiled by Louis in 814.[62] 'With their advice', the Astronomer wrote, '[Lothar] was to put in order, promote and watch over Italy's public and private affairs'.[63] The years between the group's arrival in Italy that autumn and their return to Francia in the summer of 825 were busy ones, during which Lothar issued many capitularies, went back and forth to Francia, and was crowned emperor (again) in Rome at Easter 823; he also sent Wala to the consecration of Eugenius II in June 824 and to negotiate the *Constitutio Romana* (Nov. 824), an agreement that secured the latter as pope.[64] But the group's main charge was to 'dispense justice' and make law. This was the task laid down by Louis the Pious when he dispatched his son, and on which Lothar reported in 823. Apparently unimpressed, Louis then bolstered the royal party by sending the count of the palace and Mauring, count of Brescia, to help complete the task.[65] Lothar's mission was bookended by residence at Corte Olona, a royal palace outside Pavia,[66] and by two bursts of legislative activity there. The

---

[59] For comparison, MS Blankenburg, fols 70v–71v, 106r–117v; Vatican City, Chig. F.IV.75, fols 93r, 94v; 'Gotha, Forschungsbibliothek, Memb. I 84' (fol. 406r–v), at *Capitularia* (acc. 07/22/2019); MGH *Cap*. I. 326.

[60] Vatican City, Chig. F.IV.75, fols 90r–94v, and Cava de' Tirreni, Biblioteca della Badia, 4, fols 238v–245v, omit the otherwise common *Cap. Olonnense* (MGH, *Cap*. I, no. 157). The monastic capitula (MGH, *Cap*. I, no. 160) only survive in MS Blankenburg, fol. 106v.

[61] B. Mischke, 'Manuscript of the Month January 2016: Wolfenbüttel Cod. Guelf. 130 Blank', in *Capitularia* <blog/handschrift-des-monats-blankenb-130> (acc. July 2019).

[62] *Ann. Reg. Franc*. (a. 822), 159; D. Ganz, *Corbie in the Carolingian Renaissance* (Sigmaringen, 1990), 25, 28–30.

[63] Astronomus, *Vita Hludowici imperatoris*, c. 35; ed. E. Tremp, *Astronomus, Das Leben Kaiser Ludwigs*, MGH SS rer. Germ. LXIV (Hanover, 1995), 410; tr. T. F. X. Noble, *Charlemagne and Louis the Pious* (University Park, PA, 2009), 263.

[64] MGH *Cap*. I. 316–32. On Lothar's Italian mission, *Ann. reg. Franc*. (a. 822–3, 825), 157–64, 167–8; De Jong, *Penitential State*, 32–3; Noble, *Republic of St Peter*, 308–22; L. Weinrich, *Wala: Graf, Mönch und Rebell* (Lübeck-Hamburg, 1963), 48–50.

[65] *Ann. reg. Franc*. (a. 823), 160–1: 'Qui cum imperatori de iustitiis in Italia a se partim factis partim inchoatis fecisset indicium, missus est in Italiam Adalhardus comes palatii, iussumque est, ut Mauringum Brixiae comitem secum adsumeret et inchoatas iustitias perficere curaret.'

[66] In the Frankish manner, Lothar preferred royal estates to cities, Wickham, *Early Medieval Italy*, 50. For the place of palaces in the performance of Carolingian government and power, J. L. Nelson,

first, in early 823, saw two capitularies promulgated, one each for bishops and counts.[67] The second burst, concentrated in May 825, produced a messier series of texts for counts, bishops, *missi*, and monastic visitors.[68] It is here, in late spring of 825, that we find the hospital programme.

Hospitals were on Lothar's mind. Several months earlier, in February 825, he had issued a charter for the hospital of Mont-Cenis, which was located on the main Alpine pass between France and Italy. This was being established for pilgrims at his father's order, to fulfil a vow Louis had made as he crossed the pass. To ensure property 'sufficient to sustain the daily assembly of Christ's poor', Louis wished to endow the hospital with nearby properties, but these belonged to the abbey of Novalesa, a Benedictine abbey on the downward slopes of the pass.[69] Lothar's charter realized Louis's plans, and was likely the culmination of negotiations that dated from the party's arrival in Italy. It recounted the creation of the hospital and confirmed the charitable use to which its property was assigned; it also granted a smaller abbey (at Pagno) to Novelesa in recompense, placing both abbeys under Novelesa's abbot.[70] Three months later, Lothar's court was at Olona, debating policy for hospitals. Nevertheless, it is unlikely that the acts in Lothar's name at Olona were of Lothar's devising. The young emperor was a man with little interest in government or the *res publica*.[71]

Insight into the genesis of the hospital programme is offered by another text, one yet to be affiliated with Italian councils: a 'report (*relatio*) of the bishops to the emperor on ecclesiastical matters', published by Boretius as no. 179 among the capitularies of Louis the Pious. This text dates after February 821 and has most recently been included by Philippe Depreux in a group of texts as 'working documents' from Louis the Pious's council of Attigny (822) in Francia.[72] The texts survive together in one manuscript (from North Italy), which is also noteworthy for preserving the only copy of Louis the Pious's *Admonitio* that exists

---

'Aachen as a Place of Power', in M. de Jong et al., eds, *Topographies of Power* (Leiden, 2001); Costambeys et al., *Carolingian World*, 173–8.

[67] Edited as *Cap. Olonnense* (MGH *Cap.* I, no. 157) and *Mem. Olonnae comitibus* (no. 158).

[68] *Cap. Olon. eccl. primum* (*De episcoporum causis*) (MGH *Cap.* I, no. 163); *Cap. Olon. eccl. alterum* (no. 164); *Cap. Olon. mundanum* (no. 165); *Cap. de rebus eccl.* (no. 166). A fifth, *Cap. de inspiciendis monasteriis* (no. 160), would seem to constitute the monastic piece of this set.

[69] *Die Urkunden Lothars I und Lothars II*, ed. T. Schieffer (Berlin, 1966), 61, no. 4 (825): 'dum ad domni et genitoris nostri Hludouuici serenissimi atque religiossimi augusti sacrosanctum votum in monte Ciniso quoddam hospitale... fieret constructum, voluit tanta illud rerum propriarum substantia locupletare, per quam sufficeret diurnus pauperum Christi concursus tolerari.'

[70] *Urkunden Lothars I und II*, 62: 'considerantes, ut sub unius abbatis regimine utraque monasteria regulariter deo militarent'.

[71] According to Nithard, the bishops would denounce Lothar as deficient in both 'knowledge of how to govern the commonwealth' and 'good will in his government', J. L. Nelson, 'Kingship and Empire', in R. McKitterick, ed., *Carolingian Culture* (Cambridge, 1994), 67; Leyser, *Communications and Power*, 19–25.

[72] It postdates the death of Benedict Abbas 'beatae recordationis', MGH *Cap.* I. 368–9. Depreux, 'Penance', 382; and cf. Patzold, *Episcopus*, 147–8. Its title was assigned by Boretius.

outside Ansegis's collection.[73] Depreux suggests that the texts were copied into the personal notebook of a royal cleric, then brought to Italy, possibly in 834, by Wala or Agobard, when they went into exile with Lothar that year.[74] While several of the texts clearly relate to Attigny—including a set of five episcopal capitula, which follow the *relatio* in the Italian manuscript—there is little evidence to link the *relatio* itself to the council, as Depreux admitted.[75]

However, there are reasons to tie it to Olona. The *relatio* records a series of episcopal responses to questions about the *ordines* (orderly arrangements) according to which ecclesiastics and religious should live, taking in the wide picture from bishops, priests, and clerics, to abbots, nuns, canons, and monks. The answers are qualitatively different to those offered in the bishops' capitula from Attigny, for the former present sharper, more distilled answers offering a fuller testimony as to the state of Christian life. Several mutate into petitions to the emperor, to harmonize reform and correct religious life. Significantly, the Italian manuscript is the same one that gathers the full component of Olona capitularies: MS Blankenburg, where the *relatio* and the Attigny capitula immediately precede the first Olona capitulary (823) for the bishops, recorded as 'Olonna constituit'.[76] Among the questions asked of the bishops was 'how the orderly arrangement (*ordo*) of xenodochia must be observed', to which the bishops responded:

> they must show the testaments issued by those who instituted them (the xeno-dochia). If, shrouded in errors arising from superficiality or perhaps want of detail the wills are not in a reasonable state, they should await the decision of a *provisor catholicus*.[77]

It is unlikely that this question was posed in Francia for, as we have seen, Frankish councils had taken no interest in xenodochia (and would fail to notice them for another twenty years). More certainly, the bishops were offering an Italian answer, regarding will-makers. Its focus on the detail of wills anticipates Olona's arrangements for the restoration of or substitution for a *pristinus* (original)

---

[73] MS Blankenburg, fols 73r–79r. There is a fragment in Valenciennes, Bibliothèque municipale, 162, fols 87r–88r: *Capitularia* <en/capit/ldf/bk-nr-150> (acc. July 2019).

[74] Depreux, 'Penance', 382, 385.

[75] Depreux, 'Penance', 374, 382–4. On the presentation of material at Attigny, MGH *Cap.* I. 357–8, Patzold, *Episcopus*, 147.

[76] MS Blankenburg, where the *relatio* is fols 104r–105v, under the title *Item alia capitularia domini Hludowici imperatoris*; the capitula, fols 105v–106r. A second copy of the latter appears at the back of the *Collectio Quesnelliana*, a late eighth-/early ninth-century manuscript of ecclesiastical law, produced in north-eastern France and kept by the Frankish royal court, Einsiedeln, Stiftsbibliothek MS Codex 191, fol. 232r–v.

[77] (c. 6) 'Qualiter senodochiorum ordo servetur, promulgata ab auctoribus eorum testamenta fatentur; nam si levitatis aut fortasse simplicitatis erroribus obvoluta rationabili statu caruerint, catholici provisoris arbitrium prestolentur.' MS Blankenburg, fol. 104v (where it is marked as c. 7), ed. MGH *Cap.* I. 369.

state, provided by a legitimate arrangement (*iusta ratio*).[78] The answer ties the *relatio* to preparations for Olona's May 825 assemblies. This moment would account, too, for the *relatio*'s chapter 13, where the bishops asked for clearer details as to how schools were to nurture ecclesiastical discipline, and for its monastic demands, both to be answered at Olona.

The *relatio* was prepared for the royal party. It is structured by a series of questions as to the proper arrangement for the *ordo*/*ordines* of bishops (cc. 1–4), episcopal property (c. 5), xenodochia (c. 6), canons (c. 7), monks and abbots (cc. 8–11, 15), and nuns (cc. 12–13). It was a survey of the church—information-gathering in preparation for law-making. Its inspiration, and the language of *ordo*/*ordines*, seems to have been inspired by Louis's *Capitulare ecclesiasticum* (818/9), whose 'Capitula pertaining particularly to bishops and to each category (*ordines*) of ecclesiastical persons' immediately precedes the *relatio* in MS Blankenburg.[79] What the *relatio* preserves, then, is an intriguing give and take between a Frankish royal agenda and the Italian bishops and abbots, testifying to local practice. So readily dispatched by the bishops, xenodochia seem to have been a concern of the royal palace; the bishops' query regarding schools, in contrast, suggests a more complicated response to the bland terms of an instruction in the *Admonitio*, that schools be established for the preparation and education of the ministers of the church.[80]

The *relatio* is significant here for three reasons. First, it connects MS Blankenburg even more closely to Olona, and to the Frankish law-makers of 823 and 825. The manuscript seems to incorporate a formal archive from Olona, and so perhaps from the palace: not merely the full collection of capitularies produced, but those brought from Francia and those developed in preparation for its synods and councils. Second, it ties the Olona programme closely to Frankish agendas, shedding light on the careful—and highly documentary—work that underpinned Louis's directive to Lothar to dispense justice and make law in Italy. Perhaps unsurprisingly, it connects their Italian mission closely to contemporary agendas of the Frankish palace. More intriguingly, it links the *Admonitio* to the Olona mission and—by its moment (825), through the *Admonitio* itself, and by the many Olona capitula entered into Ansegis's *Collectio*—suggests a wider context that situates Ansegis's project among contemporary palace initiatives. Finally, the *relatio* offers to us Wala as the likely royal agent who brought the

---

[78] MGH *Cap.* I. 332, c. 3, whose language might echo the *relatio* ('In his vero quae ab initio iustae rationis dispositione caruerunt, volumus') and whose substitute directive supplies the answer to the problem laid out in the *relatio*'s c. 6. Other references, to *Romane legis statuta rite conservata* (c. 5) and the *reipublice* (c. 14), are also suggestive of an Italian synod, if not definitively.

[79] 'Haec capitula proprie ad episcopos vel ad ordines quosque ecclesiasticos pertinentia', MS Blankenburg, fols 101r–104r, where it preserves the full title, as ed. MGH *Conc.* I. 275–80 (no. 138).

[80] Its placement, immediately following the topic of episcopal property, also suggests Frankish categorization. Schools had been discussed at Attigny: Depreux, 'Penance', 374 n. The *Admonitio* postdates the royal party's arrival in Italy, but not necessarily its reinforcement in 823.

Frankish texts to Italy and instigated the testimony in the *relatio*, in preparation for the Olona decisions.

Cousin to Charlemagne and adviser in Lombardy to Lothar, Wala's interest in hospitals was personal as well as governmental. His was a family concern and seems to have been influenced by a previous visit to Italy when, in 812, he joined his brother Adalhard, abbot of Corbie.[81] Since July 810, Adalhard had been regent of Italy for the child-king, Bernard, a position he also assumed thirty years earlier, in 781, as guardian and regent for Bernard's father Pippin.[82] The timing means that Adalhard had presided over the first councils of Pippin, when xenodochia were first noticed, as well as Mantua II (813), which presented the first mature statement on xenodochia, with Wala likely in attendance. The brothers also worked together at Corbie, where Adalhard instituted a series of charities, establishing stipends to support destitute widows and single men, and a xenodochium for orphans, the weak, and visitors.[83] In 822, under Adalhard, written customs were provided for the abbey's hospital, a facility under a monastic *hospitalarius* that distributed clothing and footwear, fed paupers and pilgrims, provided nightly accommodation, and ministered to the sick.[84] The *hospitalarius* in these years was none other than Wala. Wala had entered Corbie abbey when exiled by the new emperor in 814 and he earned there a reputation for his service to the poor and for his labour among the dirt, smells, and sufferings of the wretched.[85] As Paschasius Radbertus, his companion and biographer, would vividly later recall:

> Have you not seen him when he was in charge of our hospitality? What a wonderful person, how great, humble, devoted! Have you even seen any of our notables longing for such vile tasks, enduring such harsh matters, and assiduously handling such repulsive, stinking things? I am not referring to dirty shoes of guests, but to sores of the poor and their stinking clothes. He always washed them as though he were carrying spices. All such matters he endured tirelessly, never growing weary.[86]

---

[81] Weinrich, *Wala*, where his first visit to Italy is pp. 26–8; De Jong, *Epitaph*, 25–34.

[82] For Adalhard in Italy, *Vita Adalhardi* (*PL* 120, col. 1517; tr. A. Cabaniss, *Charlemagne's Cousins* (Syracuse, NY, 1967), 36, 43; McKitterick, *Charlemagne*, 152–5; Nelson, 'Aachen', 226–32; De Jong, *Epitaph*, 24. On Adalhard, Ganz, *Corbie*, 22–9. D. A. Bullough, '"Baiuli" in the Carolingian "regnum Langobardorum" and the Career of Abbot Waldo (d. 813)', *EHR* 305 (1962), 627–8 sheds light on Pavia as centre of law and justice.

[83] Paschasius Radbertus, *Vita Adalhardi*, *PL* 120, cols 1538–9, the arrangement echoes Pippin's capitulum of 787, 'sinodochiis seu pauperes et viduas vel orfanos' (MGH *Cap.* I. 198, c. 1).

[84] 'Consuetudines Corbeienses', ed. J. Semmler, in Hallinger, ed., *Corpus Consuetudinum Monasticarum*, 372–74.

[85] For his time as a monk, Weinrich, *Wala*, 33–40. De Jong, *Epitaph*, 29–30, suggests he may merely have received a clerical tonsure at this time.

[86] *Vita Walae*, ed. G. H. Pertz, MGH *SS* II (Hanover, 1829), 533–69, with quotation at p. 536; tr. Cabaniss, *Charlemagne's Cousins*, 111–12.

Wala's commitment to hospitals lasted throughout his monastic life, even to its end, as abbot of Bobbio, near Pavia, in 836.[87]

Together, Adalhard and Wala had a hand in the most significant attempts to regulate hospitals of the early middle ages: from Mantua II (813) to Olona (825), to the papal council at Rome (826), as well as in the regulations for the hospital at Corbie in 822. It was Wala who emerges as the driving force behind the hospital reforms between 822 and 826, as chief adviser to the emperor and, soon, to the pope. To carry this through, he relied on Italian expertise and, probably, on Italian servants of the royal court. One such example was Leo, whose long career as *iudicatus* and adviser saw him serve with Adalhard in 812–14 and with Wala in Rome (823) and at judicial sessions at Reggio (824); he was also with Lothar (and Wala) during their Italian exile in the 830s.[88] No doubt the governmentally minded Wala would have relied heavily on such local expertise.

Olona answered a Frankish question with Italian solutions and, under Wala's guiding hand, theirs was no conservative response. We have met one capitulum already, in Chapter 4. Edited from an undated capitulary by Boretius (as 'Capitula de rebus ecclesiasticis', c. 3), this was the only attempt by a synod or assembly to lay out a schema for restoring xenodochia, defining both a 'pristine state' and a programme for its preservation or substitution.[89] A second short capitulary, dated May 825, edited by Boretius as 'ecclesiasticum alterum', contains two further capitula for hospitals. The first (c. 4) is a brief statement 'that xenodochia follow the written directives of their will-makers, as far as they are able and the abundance of the times allow'.[90] The other appears in two forms, each in two manuscripts.[91] One (c. 7) demanded the restoration of all xenodochia, 'whosoever should have them', and the return of any possessions wrongfully withheld from the poor since King Pippin's death in 810. It threatened to suspend the *potestas* of any who refused to do so, 'until he should come before us with the *missi*, and the *missi* with the bishop systematically list (*imbrevient*) in our presence those things [that have been neglected]'.[92] The briefer version (c. 7a) 'reserved to imperial

---

[87] In 834, Wala retired to Italy as abbot of Bobbio, Ganz, *Corbie*, 30. The first mention of a xenodochium in Bobbio, at Casale Lupani, occurs in Wala's *Breve memorationis*, 'Consuetudines Corbeienses', 421; M. Gazzini, 'Le rete ospedaliera di Bobbio', in E. Destefanis and P. Guglielmotti, *La diocesi di Bobbio* (Florence, 2015), 485.

[88] D. A. Bullough, 'Leo, qui apud Hlotharium magni loci habebatur', *Le Moyen Age* 67 (1961), 224, 228–9, 233–4.

[89] MGH *Cap.* I. 332, no. 166 (c. 3). And see chapter 4, pp. 101–2.

[90] (c. 4) 'De senodochiis visum est nobis ut secundum possibilitatem vel temporis fertilitatem testamentorum scripta sequantur', MS Blankenburg, fol. 112r. The capitula are ed. MGH *Cap.* I. 328–9, no. 164 (cc. 4, 7/7a).

[91] What follows uses MS Blankenburg, fol. 112r, for c. 7a; Vatican City, Chig. F.IV.75, fol. 94v, for c. 7. But see, too, 'Cava de' Tirreni, Biblioteca della Badia, 4', fol. 244r (c. 7), and 'Ivrea, Biblioteca Capitolare, XXXIV', fol. 54r (c. 7a), in *Capitularia* <mss/cava-dei-tirreni-bdb-4>, and <mss/ivrea-bc-xxxiv> (acc. July 2019).

[92] (c. 7) 'De senochiis precipimus, ut quicumque illas habet, omnia secundum Deum et secundum canones inde faciat; et quicquid inde non fuit datum pauperibus post hobitum domni Pippini in

justice anyone who defies the admonition of bishops regarding monasteries or xenodochia that are disordered or ruined, whether they pertain to the palace or to whomever'.[93] The relationship between these four capitula ('de rebus' 3, and 'alterum' 4, 7, and 7a) is worth unpicking, to shed light on the council's workings as well as the systems it put in place to police xenodochia.

The imperial reference to Pippin's death reveals a more immediate aim: to reconstitute facilities after the disruptions of Bernard's rule. To do this, the council established a procedure, appointing a prosecuting agent (the local *missi*) and providing a mechanism for enforcement (royal power). Its reference to local bishops speaks to the integral partnership between the two authorities, royal and episcopal, both judicial and moral. This was no ongoing system of accountability; the act was justified by a temporary claim to repair the damage of the interregnum. To do so, it had to confront the jurisdictional challenge of xenodochia: to construct a supervisory authority to hold those with *potestas* to their obligations, and a procedure by which to do this. In keeping with previous efforts, that authority was royal, and the procedure's aim was to restore xenodochia to their former state. But it was reconceived at Olona as political theatre. Under imperial authority, *potestas* could be suspended. To reclaim possession, a negligent heir or assign must attend court and stand before the emperor and their bishop while royal *missi* act as prosecutors, to hold him to account. They were to *inbreviare*, a term used when *missi* reported faults in writing to the king, that 'most effective sign, as well as instrument, of royal power', in the words of Janet Nelson.[94] In so doing, a xenodochium's design (its *dispositio*) would need to be given, in order to catalogue its failures, and both would be performed by *missi* before the court. In undoing the damage of the interregnum, this was a particular kind of theatre, less of hospital regulation than imperial restoration. That it uses xenodochia in such a political fashion, linking local neglect to governmental power, underscores the significance of xenodochia, as a visible sign of Christian order and correct rule, and the particular reliance in Italy on imperial power for its enforcement.

The second capitulary ('alterum') provides clues about the negotiations from which the arrangements emerged. It also presents the most obvious problem, in the two formats of c. 7/7a, which return to a topic addressed in c. 4. This made their nineteenth-century editor suspicious; at best, he wondered if they had been

---

omnibus fiat restauratum. Quod si aliquis hoc facere noluerit, de ipsos senodochios non habeat potestatem, usque dum veniat cum ipsis missis in nostra presentia; et missi cum ipso episcopo illa imbrevient in nostra presentia.'

[93] (c. 7a) 'De monasteriis et senodochiis inordinatis et destructis ad palatium vel ad quorumcumque iura pertinentibus, qui admonitionem episcoporum contemnunt, placuit nostre imperialis providentie iudicio reservari.'

[94] Nelson, 'Literacy', 14–19, with quotation at p. 19. MGH *Cap.* II. 267, 298. On the use of Aachen as a 'theatre of power', Nelson, 'Aachen', 226–32.

added later from another capitulary.[95] But why would two scribes, in two different places, select such a similar capitulum to append to the same capitulary, especially one whose existing statement on xenodochia is so bland, for example, in comparison to that in 'de rebus' with its 'pristine state'? The answer to the problem of 7/7a lies in the structure of the capitulary itself, which is in fact composed of two parts. The first part, preserved in all four manuscripts, comprises capitula 1–6, which address baptismal churches (c. 1) and their priests (c. 2), bishops and the business of the *res publica* (c. 3), xenodochia (c. 4), and women cohabiting with priests (c. 5). Finally, it refers (c. 6) any bishop who failed to act on 'a declaration or reproof of these kinds [of errors]' within forty days of 'this synodal council' to the judgement of his metropolitan. Part one is the record of a synod. Each chapter is directed at bishops and in the collective voice of synod.

Appended to this is either (c. 7) or (c. 7a), whose two versions are so different that, at first glance, they suggest two different capitula. Yet closer inspection reveals a fundamental similarity, since both address xenodochia that have been reduced by recent events, reserving imperial judgement to those who either (c. 7) refuse to make restoration, or (c. 7a) disdain the admonition of bishops. These are two sides of the same recalcitrant coin. In addition, both versions are explicitly in the voice of the emperor: they speak of *in nostra presentia* and *nostrae imperialis providentiae* and are directed to royal *missi*.[96] This was no longer the bishops' voice, and so a synod, although the imperial statement seems to be responding to the synodal business. It was not uncommon that bishops and abbots might hold a synod, and laity their own separate meeting, in addition to the joint assembly, when all had gathered for a royal council.[97] Here, it seems, we find business from the synod then brought before the emperor.[98] While the business took one route, from synod to general council, the text at this moment diverges. It suggests two scribes, with identical copies of the synodalia, who produced their own version of what was said at council in the emperor's name. The difference between their efforts is evidence both of the imagination needed to distil wide-ranging oral discussions into a written ruling, and of a capitulum's role as aide-memoire to that more complex deliberation.[99] Both scribes looked to models to formulate their written statement: one (c. 7a) to monastic decrees, whose structure and language he adapted to address a house, its disorder, and the prelate as admonisher; the

---

[95] MGH *Cap.* I. 328.

[96] Pössel, 'Authors and Recipients', 259–70, on the significance of audience.

[97] Hartmann, *Synoden*, 98; Ganshof, *Recherches*, 24–9.

[98] Under the archbishop of Milan, patriarch of Aquileia, and royal arch-chaplain, the synod at Pavia (850) produced a series of requests to lay before the emperor, MGH *Conc.* III. 220.

[99] For relationships between orality and literacy in the formulation of law, text, and memory, Mordek, 'Karolingische Kapitularien', 32–5; Ganshof, *Recherches*, 18–21; and esp. Nelson, 'Literacy', 9–10, 24, who observes that 'things written down often lacked formal precision or completeness precisely because they assumed the complement of things spoken and remembered'. One author's role in crafting capitularies is uncovered in Nelson, 'Intellectual in Politics'.

other (c. 7) drew his phrasing and structure, if not his content, from the early decree by Pippin cited above.[100] The three capitula (cc. 4, 7, 7a) in one capitulary represent efforts at recording the same piece of business, as it progressed through stages at the council.

If so, this permits a reading that reconstitutes the deliberations and, behind them, an agenda. The business was first brought to synod, where a generic call that hospitals follow their will-makers' directives was laid before the bishops. Its similarity to the answer in the *relatio* suggests that the business was placed by the royal party from Francia before the synod which seemed unable to act. The full synodal text captures several concerns of their meeting. One was the relationship between governmental and ecclesiastical authority, since it urged (c. 2) priests of baptismal churches to show customary obedience to the *res publica* and honour to the bishop,[101] and noted (c. 3) what bishops should do when unable personally to fulfil a governmental duty. The bishops were also concerned to specify how any resolution might be enforced or forgiven, whether by bishops on priests or by the synod on bishops. Only the xenodochia decree lacked an agent or accountability. It seems that this synod (or its palace handler) was not content with a customary statement of the principle of restoration and, reconvening in full council, placed the question of enforcement at the emperor's feet.

The first capitulary ('de rebus'), with its long chapter on how to diagnose and respond to failure of a xenodochium, develops this picture. The capitulary itself is so closely related to the synodal text ('alterum') that it follows the latter's resolutions: c. 2 and c. 4 of 'de rebus' duplicate the synod's cc. 5–6 and cc. 2–3, respectively, and largely word for word. They correct the odd detail and append to one (c. 2) a statement on clerical conduct and to the other (c. 4) that those reported by *missi* for oppressing a church be punished by a canonical invective, promulgated by the emperor.[102] Besides their (brief) opening chapters, which both address baptismal churches, the main difference is between the synod's short statement (c. 4) that xenodochia follow their testators' writing, and the lengthy unpacking of this in no. 164 (c. 3).[103] Placing the two side by side, 'de rebus'

---

[100] The *c*.790 decree is: (c. 1) '*ut quicumque senedochia habent*, si ita pauperes pascere voluerint et consilio facere quomodo abantea fuit, habeant ipsa senedochia et regant ordinabiliter. Et *si hoc facere noluerint*, ipsas dimittant; et per tales homines inantea sint gubernatae [*cum* consilio proprii *episcopi*], qualiter Deo et nobis exinde placeat.' MGH *Cap.* I. 200, with language in Olona (c. 7) marked by italics. The square brackets insert a phrase that was interpolated into Pippin's decree in the *Liber papiensis* (c. 24), whose echoes suggest a wider conversation between these texts (MGH *Leges* IV. 519). The monastic template for (c. 7a) accounts for the phrase 'secundum canones', one often used for monastic regulation but not for xenodochia.

[101] *Res publica* seems here to refer to the performance of obligations to the state, given voice through the palace, Nelson, 'Kingship and Empire', 64–8.

[102] MGH *Cap.* I. 332. Of the three manuscripts with 'de rebus', only one includes 'alterum': MS Blankenburg, at fol. 112r. Its corrections reverse the numbers to improve 'a septem usque ad tres idoneis testibus', and it gives bishops fifty days after the synod to act.

[103] The synod (c. 1) ordered that baptismal churches have one priest as rector; 'de rebus' (c. 1) prohibits bishops from taking payment to consecrate or dedicate baptismal churches, xenodochia, or oratories, MGH *Cap.* I. 328, 332.

emerges as a more digested and explicitly imperial version of the bishops' deliberations in synod ('alterum'). It is this palace version that takes the close interest in
xenodochia. And in its policy for xenodochia (c. 3), we might even glimpse the
template it used. For its three groups of hospitals (those run according to their
directive, those unable to fulfil their directive, those without a directive) were a
development of Mantua II's (813) two types of xenodochia, the well-ordered and
those brought to ruin and to be restored 'ad priore cultum'.[104] Here, again, we may
see the hand of Wala.

And what of the diocesan's role, glimpsed but not revealed in the addendum?
Royal muscle underwrote the Olona policy: *missi* seized xenodochia from
intransigent heirs, assessed the losses, and prosecuted heirs before the emperor.
The power to prosecute and punish belonged to the emperor, but the *missi* were to
carry out the final reckoning *cum ipso episcopo*. This small phrase does not do
justice to the wider importance of the diocesan, at every stage of the Olona
business. When Wala sought an *ordo* for xenodochia, he turned to the Lombard
bishops, first in a fact-finding inquiry that produced the *relatio*, and then at the
synod of 825. In both cases, they responded with a basic statement of principle,
that facilities follow their will-makers' instructions. The use of bishops marks a
change in Lombard practice, where deliberations about xenodochia had previously been directed at royal possessions, when directed at any authority. This had
been the case, too, at Mantua II (813), when it addressed 'xenodochia that
belonged to us [the palace]'.[105] It is hard not to detect, once again, a Frankish
approach, for these northern regions relied more heavily on religious authority to
defend xenodochia. The issue was laid at the bishops' feet as a question of
Christian order, one reinforced by referring wills without a directive to a *catholicus provisor* (an odd term which suggests the contortions of the group to frame
a form of Christian authority that was not 'the bishop').[106] Yet the bishops
themselves were unable to punish offenders. Their synod threatened no ecclesiastical judgement, as it had when prohibiting women and priests from cohabiting,
for example. For enforcement, they looked to the emperor.

The capitularies from Olona capture a governmental conversation between
Frankish royal agendas and Italian ways of working. They were also, and fundamentally, shaped by the problem that dogged xenodochia as a public concern: that
contemporaries turned to bishops to act, yet bishops had no right of action. To
this problem, Olona offered two answers. First, it charged the diocesan to act by

---

[104] Mantua II survives in three manuscripts, two of which include the synodal text (no. 164, cc. 1–7):
Vatican City, Chig. F.IV.75 and Cava de'Tirreni, Biblioteca della Badia, 4 (MGH *Cap.* I. 194).

[105] MGH *Cap.* I. 195 (c. 3).

[106] I can find no other use of the term *catholicus provisor*. It seems not to refer specifically to bishops,
who are *episcopi* in the text. It seems to suggest a more general category, of a trusted churchman,
perhaps a royal *missus* or, more likely, a diocesan agent backed by royal authority.

confronting heirs and assigns who failed to uphold the institutor's arrangements: he was to admonish (c. 7a) and demand restitution (c. 7). Second, should his local, moral voice fail, royal government provided the sword. The final royal capitulary in 'de rebus', once again, laid out the principles (i.e. what should be corrected) but not the agents (i.e. who should correct), never charging bishops explicitly. Yet, taken together with the policy of imperial enforcement in the addendum to the synod (cc. 7, 7a), it suggests that the initiative, and the front-line moral authority, was entrusted to the bishop. The schema for policing hospitals seems to have been developed by royal agents under Wala, with the advice of the Italian synod, and with the participation—and force—of the general assembly.

Olona law-makers aimed to go beyond the principle that 'hospitals be restored' to forge mechanisms by which they might be restored. This was innovation, although not *emendatio*. It did not seek to transform hospitals, even for their improvement, as did the imposition of a rule for monasteries and canons. It crafted means by which xenodochia might be policed or, more accurately, by which the wills of hospital institutors might be upheld. It relied on bishops as the principal agents but rested on imperial authority. The latter continued in Lombardy. So, when Lothar initiated an inquiry into the state of xenodochia in 832, he directed this to his *missi*, and at the synod of Pavia (850) disrespectful heirs were threatened with imperial punishment.[107]

The Council of Rome (826)

In November 826, xenodochia crossed from royal into canon law. A Roman council under Eugenius II was the first papal council in the West to address xenodochia, for among its decrees was the brief (c. 23), 'On xenodochia and other pious places'.[108] This stated that: 'Through the watchful concern of the bishops in whose dioceses they sit, they should be arranged to the same uses for which they had been established, so that customary bread and duties be resumed for those to whom it is owed.' Behind this apparently unremarkable statement lay a series of initiatives, and at its basis lay Wala.

Eugenius II had been consecrated pope in June 824, although his position was not secured against a rival candidate until November of that year, through the *Constitutio Romana*, an agreement with Louis the Pious in Lothar's name. Wala, a friend of Eugenius II, had been present at his consecration and instrumental in

---

[107] MGH *Cap.* II. 63 (c. 1); *Conc.* III. 226 (c. 15).

[108] (c. 23) 'DE XENODOCHIIS ET ALIIS PIIS LOCIS. Per sollicitudinem episcoporum, quorum dioceseos existunt, ad easdem utilitates, quibus constituta sunt, ordinentur, ut debiti panes atque cure pertinentibus revertantur.' MGH *Conc.* II.ii, 576–7. Two manuscripts give *similibus* rather than *piis* (p. 576 n.).

negotiating the *Constitutio Romana*.[109] Indeed, the *Constitutio Romana* survives in only three manuscripts, the same three that preserve the large caches of Olona capitularies.[110] Eugenius's council was implementing the reform programme of northern Francia, although Frankish prelates were not in attendance: the sixty-eight bishops who attended were all from Lombard regions and the Roman province.[111] The council cannot therefore be considered universal, but it can be closely tied to Wala and, in the case of xenodochia, to his Italian reforms. Not only was the subject likely introduced by Wala, coming fresh from his Olona pro-gramme, but its definition of hospitals was clearly based on Lombard capitularies: that a xenodochium be arranged to the uses for which it had been established.

Yet Rome was no simple reiteration of Olona; it added a new element, some-thing only implicit at Olona: episcopal agency. It was carefully worded, being the only canon among the thirty-eight of the council to speak of 'the watchful concern of bishops'; others instructed that bishops 'must do', using language of licence, subjection, or obedience.[112] And their duty was carefully circumscribed, not to arrange or oversee a facility, but simply to restore its customary bread or duties. The right in hospitals was simply a commission to reinstate alms. But behind the decree we can detect a more ambitious initiative.

The key is *pia loca* ('pious places'), a term introduced at this council that was the fruit of historical inquiry at the papal curia. It echoes Justinian's *piae causae* but it is not Justinianic: Byzantine legislation attached the adjective 'pious' to a donor (Cod. 1.3.28) or to the donor's intention (Cod. 1.2.15), act (Nov. 7.2), or to the purpose (Cod. 1.2.19; Cod. 1.3.41; Nov. 131.11, 12) for a gift. The Code and Novels preferred *venerabilia loca* for the places themselves, the term also used in Ansegis's *Epitome* chapter. The source was neither Justinian nor Ansegis: it was the letters of Gregory the Great. Three centuries earlier, Gregory, familiar with Justinian's corpus, had cited select laws and terminology, including *venerabilia loci* and *piae voluntatis* in relation to xenodochia.[113] He also used *pia loca*, apparently his own term, in letters regarding the foundations of Queen Brunhild and her grandson,

---

[109] MGH *Cap.* I. 316–32. On Wala and Eugenius, Noble, *Republic of St Peter*, 310–11; Weinrich, *Wala*, 48–50.

[110] Vatican City, Chig. F.IV.75, fols 97r–98r; Cava de'Tirreni, Biblioteca della Badia, 4, fol. 240v, and MS Blankenburg 130, fol. 117r–v, where it is in the middle of the Olona material.

[111] De Jong, *Penitential State*, 38; Wood, *Prop. Ch.*, 793; Hartmann, *Synoden*, 174. For a breakdown of the canons, T. F. X. Noble, 'The Place in Papal History of the Roman Synod of 826', *Church History* 45:4 (1976), 450–4, whose interpretation of the council is different from that presented here.

[112] E.g. cc. 3, 4, 7 (ms *VI*), 18, 21. The latter required that priests in monasteries or oratories on private estates be appointed through episcopal consent 'ut ad placita et iustam reverentiam ipsius episcopi oboedienter sacerdos recurrat' (MGH *Conc.* II.ii, 576). On such language, Patzold, *Episcopus*, 129–34.

[113] *Greg. Epp.* 4.9, 4.10, 4.24, 9.35, 9.90. Modern surveys of hospitals in law can give substantial weight to Gregory's letters; however, this pope seems to have left little mark on Western law for xenodochia, beyond this term adopted by Eugenius. When it came to welfare facilities, Gregory's main preoccupation was to ensure that the requirements of a will be fulfilled and in a timely manner (Chapter 5 n. 140).

Theoderic; these included one for their xenodochium in Autun, Gregory's only letter of protection for a xenodochium.[114] Resourceful clerics at the curia found a second letter, Gregory's other substantial treatment of a xenodochium. This concerned facilities wilting from grave neglect, for which Gregory appointed agents 'to strive to arrange these xenodochia carefully and to good purpose'.[115] Eugenius found inspiration in Gregory's language, but not in his actual directives. Rather than the more open charge suggested by Gregory's letter, Rome embraced the North Italian model of a specific, fixed arrangement—but it seized on the term *pia loca* as a way to talk about *xenodochia*.

The term was then adopted and developed for the Roman council. It was used in five decrees, four of them in a run beginning with *De xenodochiis* (cc. 23–6). One (c. 25) demanded that churches 'and any *pia loca*' be restored (*restaurentur*), if necessary by local subscription; two others forbade bishops (c. 16) from taking property from their flock 'or from other pious places' or (c. 26) from demanding gifts from clerics and 'pious places'. In these cases, the term was inserted into familiar decrees that protected the property of priests and churches from abuse by bishops and called for the restoration of church buildings. Adding *pia loca* was no mere embellishment: it added a category of places to these protections. Most ingenious was a longer decree that immediately followed *De xenodochiis*: (c. 24) 'On pious places that are without (their) priests', which bemoaned that 'certain pious places' that ought to have priests 'are now turned abjectly to the benefit of laymen'.[116] It enjoined bishops to remedy the situation and recognized two theatres of action: in a place subjected 'proprio iure' to a church (i.e., in its own right or hereditary entitlement), the bishop must establish priests with adequate means of support; however, for those that had been established in the jurisdiction of laity (*saecularium hominum sunt iurae constituta*), the local bishop should admonish that layperson (taking care not to slight the prince's authority) and if they fail to act after three months should advise (*suggerat*) how the matter should be remedied. The canon was forging a way for the bishop to protect places that were not in church hands, by affording him the right to admonish laity in whose *potestates* they might sit. It is easy to assume that this decree did not concern xenodochia, because the new term *pia loca* was left undefined. Only the previous chapter (c. 23) mentioned welfare facilities and only its title, *De xenodochiis et aliis piis locis*, made the link. *De piis locis* (c. 24) had quietly subsumed xenodochia among this wider new category of 'pious places'.

---

[114] *Greg. Epp.* 13.11; JE 1875 (1492), *Quando ad ea*: 'ne hac occasione ea quae a fidelibus piis locis offeruntur aut iam oblata sunt consumantur.'

[115] *Greg. Epp.* 14.2; JE 1915 (1534), *Experientia tua indicante*: 'ut eadem xenodochia ipsi in periculo suo sollicite ac utiliter studeant ordinare.'

[116] 'DE PIIS LOCIS, QUE SINE PRESBYTERIS EXISTUNT. Sunt quaedam pia loca...nunc autem ut aliae domus utilitate saecularium hominum sordide inveniuntur.' MGH *Conc.* II.ii, 577.

Behind the term *pia loca* was a wider vision, cautiously advanced by the council. Ullmann saw in Eugenius's council an effort to delineate clerical from lay spheres.[117] *Pia loca* did extend episcopal reach into a new sphere, but the initiative was not the pope's: the two chapters on xenodochia echo policies crafted at Olona the previous year and suggest that Lothar's court worked closely with the new pope. But Eugenius did not parrot Olona's agenda, his approach was carefully thought through in its own terms. It was shaped by archival investigation, if with little reward, and an awareness that its claims were both novel and contentious. The canons were therefore crafted cautiously. The council provided a new term of indeterminate meaning (*pia loca*), at once making a claim for episcopal action (*pia*), but without explicitly defining *loca*. By then adding the term to other, more familiar canons, it enfolded their sites and assets into wider protections against abuse and decay. Rome did not claim *pia loca* as ecclesiastical forms, nor did it place them under the bishop; indeed, it explicitly recognized that many existed under secular right, and that those that did belong to a church had arrived there through specific arrangement. At Olona, the right to admonish had been underpinned by imperial authority and directed at the administration of goods; to craft an equivalent right in ecclesiastical law, Eugenius had to establish a *cura* (responsibility) and priests were the mechanism. This subtle approach provided a package of ecclesiastical rulings on xenodochia for those who sought it, without contravening practice more widely.

Were it less subtle, Rome (826) might have provided a mechanism by which hospitals found a place under episcopal jurisdiction and among the canons that laid out ecclesiastical rights—what would soon become canon law. But the claim was so faintly made that the effort passed unnoticed. Any association of xenodochia with *pia loca* was swiftly lost, even in copies of the council's decrees.[118] Only *De xenodochiis* (c. 23) would be associated with hospitals, although copied without its title, it lost any connection to *pia loca*.[119] When Leo IV reissued Eugenius's canons at Rome in 853, he stumbled at the 23rd decree. He altered its title, replacing 'xenodochiis' with the Greek list of welfare institutions and 'aliis piis locis' with 'monasteries of monks and nuns'.[120] He also added a long clause at the

---

[117] W. Ullmann, *The Growth of Papal Government in the Middle Ages* (London, 1962), 128.

[118] The abbreviated version of c. 24 excises any mention of *pia loca*. It reads: 'Episcopi in propriis suis aeclesiis presbyteros ordinent; quodsi quislibet alius homo in sua infra trium mensium spacium ab episcopo admonitus presbyterum non miserit, episcopus principi suggerat, ut hoc emendetur.' (MGH *Conc.* II.ii, 577.)

[119] E.g. Munich, BSB Clm 29555/1, fol. 1r, where (c. 8) is on 'Exsenodochia et reliqua monasteria' in a collection of ecclesiastical decrees, whose c. 6 is Pippin's chapter on xenodochia (MGH *Cap.* I. 200, c. 1). Some early manuscripts even changed the title to 'De xenodochiis et aliis similibus' (MGH *Cap.* II. ii, 576 n.).

[120] (c. 23) 'DE XENODOCHIIS ET PTOCHOTROFIIS, NOSOCOMIIS ET ORFANOTROPHIIS ET GERENTOCOMIIS, BREFOTROPHIIS ET MONASTERIIS TAM MONACHORUM QUAM SANCTIMONIALIUM.' MGH *Conc.* III. 324. The list was probably copied from Ansegis's *Collectio*. At the pope's request, Lothar had dispatched four Frankish envoys to the council, chief among them Joseph of Ivrea, who

end of the decree, an attempt to clarify how restoration of bread and duties was necessary to feed those who pursue a religious life.[121] Only one generation later, *pia loca* had made no sense to the papal curia, who refashioned the decree for monastic life (another indication that the 826 demand was not papal but Frankish, from Wala).

The term *pia loca* would be rediscovered in the twelfth century, in part because Gratian incorporated Eugenius's prohibitions on episcopal demands into the *Decretum*;[122] it took a further century before it would be associated with welfare institutions.[123] Eugenius's efforts were quickly forgotten, but they were extraordinary. Due to Wala's influence, Rome (826) was the only papal council in the West to address hospitals before 1311. And, as the only ruling 'On xenodochia', it would be resurrected four hundred years later, by a canonist desperate for law on hospitals.

It is therefore to Wala that we owe an effort to formulate policy for—and public jurisdictions over—xenodochia. The issue moved from the imperial councils at Olona to the papal court at Rome, which, aware of its novelty, pushed boundaries to create rights by which governmental authorities, and especially bishops, might act; it never lost sight however of the basic legal equation that made up a xenodochium, of a bequest given for specified charitable purposes by a donor or testator. That its resources continued to be used according to these original terms, was the purpose of any intervention. Wala's commitment to xenodochia endured, as *hospitalarius* at Corbie, adviser to Lothar and Eugenius II, abbot of Corbie in 826, then abbot of Bobbio in 834. It may even have reached beyond his death, to Meaux-Paris (845/6). There a new hospital decree can be linked to forgers, working at Corbie under Paschasius Radbertus, Wala's erstwhile companion and, by then, abbot. If there was an echo of Wala in their act, it was of his passion to protect hospitals, not of his Italian solutions. The Frankish forgers would propose a very different model.

---

served as interim abbot after Ansegis at Saint-Wandrille (M. Schäpers, *Lothar I. (795–855) und das Frankenreich*, Rheinisches Archiv 159 (Cologne, 2018), 566–8; *Chronique des abbés de Fontenelle*, 194).

[121] (c. 23) 'that customary bread and duties be resumed for those to whom it pertains, so that those who have dedicated themselves to God might never be consumed by scarcity and needs, but with all cares expunged might more faultlessly be able to abide in their hearts in the service of God' ('ut debiti panes atque cure pertinentibus revertantur, qualiter deo vacantes inopia vel necessitatibus nullatenus occupentur, sed omni expulsa cura purius in dei servitio valeant mentibus permanere') MGH *Conc.* III. 324.

[122] C.12 q.1 c.27 (Rome, c. 16); C.16 q.1 c.62 (Rome, c. 26).

[123] The term reappeared in the twelfth century, when it was used to refer generically to a range of eleemosynary, religious, and quasi-religious sites, e.g. by Innocent II (*PL* 179, cols 92, 325, 356). It became widespread in the thirteenth century, deployed in standard clauses in papal privileges ('per quem ecclesiis et monasteriis sive aliis piis locis honor et commodum proveniret') and local testaments, such as a 1251 Toulouse will leaving money 'ecclesiis et hospitalibus et pontibus et aliis piis locis et miserabilis' (J. H. Mundy, *Studies in the Ecclesiastical and Social History of Toulouse* (Aldershot, 2006), 46 n.). The term's popularity is due to its reappearance in the *Liber Extra*.

Western Francia

A different picture emerges in Western Francia, when a council of bishops broke three centuries of silence to address xenodochia. Theirs was a period of conflict: civil war after the death of Louis the Pious (d. 840) had seen the empire divided in 843 between his sons into three kingdoms; thereafter, dynastic conflict became more common, while Viking raids intensified, along the coasts and rivers. Institutions continued to thrive, among them palace, church, and intellectual life, but there were new political fissures, especially between churchmen and the emperor.[124] An assembly at Yütz in 844, the last to gather all three kings together, warned the royal brothers 'not without deep sorrow and in fear of divine vengeance' of the punishment that awaited them for allowing the church, in particular, to suffer such destruction.[125] In councils, churchmen still spoke of *ministerium*, but more often now, too, of the vengeance of God.

Meaux-Paris (845/6) and Pseudo-Isidore

In 845, a church council was convened under archbishops Wenilo of Sens, Hincmar of Reims, and Radulf of Bourges. They met in Meaux in June but, forced to disperse, reconvened in Paris the following February. The Meaux-Paris council promulgated decrees from previous Frankish councils, at Coulaines (cc. 1–6) and Laurière (cc. 13–16) in 843, Yütz in 844 (cc. 7–12) and Beauvais in 845 (cc. 17–24); they also issued another fifty-seven decrees.[126] Among the latter was one on hospitals (c. 40), composed of two halves. The first half laid out the problem: in a thunderous clerical voice it admonished the royal majesty concerning 'hospitals, which had been set in order (*ordinata*) and carefully tended in the age of his predecessors and now have been reduced to nothing'. Even the hospitals of the Irish, 'built by holy men of that nation and augmented because of their sanctity, have been utterly estranged from their office of hospitality', with travellers finding no reception there and religious staff cast into mendicancy.[127] The longer second

---

[124] For the political culture of this period, Nelson, 'Intellectual in Politics'; Costambeys et al., *Carolingian World*, ch. 8; A. Rio, 'Waltharius at Fontenoy?', *Viator* 46:2 (2015). From the 820s, the episcopacy played an increasingly forceful role in crafting councils and their written products, a change chronicled in Patzold, *Episcopus*, chs 3–5.

[125] (c. 4) '...quod non sine gravi dolore et metu ultionis divinae dicimus, in vestri regiminis tempore in destructionem, non in aedificationem, sicut Paulus docuerat, accidisse conspicimus.' MGH *Conc.* III. 32–3.

[126] For Meaux-Paris and Épernay, the royal assembly that followed it in 846: Hartmann, *Synoden*, 208–17; de Clercq, *Législation religieuse*, II. 111–23. The preceding councils are discussed in Nelson, 'Intellectual in Politics'; Moore, *Sacred Kingdom*, 353–62.

[127] MGH *Conc.* III. 103–4, which opens: 'Admonenda est regia magnitudo de hospitalibus, que tempore praedecessorum suorum et ordinata et exculta fuerunt et modo ad nihilum sunt redacta. Sed et hospitalia Scothorum, que sancti homines gentis illius in hoc regno construxerunt et rebus pro

half provided canonical quotations to make clear the cost of inaction. It rained down 'canonical judgement' to threaten anathema to such a wrongdoer 'as a murderer of the poor' and betrayer of Christ, in the manner of Judas. Finally, it appended the anathema clause from the Orléans council's confirmation of the Lyons xenodochium, its first reappearance since 549.

This was a clerical broadside, in which Frankish churchmen admonished the king in terms of divine order and damnation. It spoke not of xenodochia but, like Aachen (816), of *hospitalia* and focused on the *hospitalia Scottorum*, of the Irish, an early religious order of hospitallers, the destruction of whose religious life it vividly painted ('those who have fought for the Lord dedicated to a religious way of life from their infancy in these places have been cast out from them and forced to beg from door to door'). It is strikingly different from the Italian capitula, which were articulated in terms of custom, law, and imperial authority; and different, too, from the papal canons of Rome (826) in the Lombard image. Meaux-Paris was not working within the Italian framework to reinforce guardianship but forging a canonical case for royal action. To do so, it was using the religious hospitals of the Irish to make a wider case for hospitals, to defend xenodochia, a connection made explicit in the Orléans anathema clause. In one way, the call did echo a familiar pattern: it was not framed within the church's theatre of action— that is, bishops were not enjoining bishops or even hospital custodians to act— rather, it was the first of the small cohort of decrees directed to the king on matters under royal control or influence.[128] The council's was a moral voice, an exhortation to action. As had the Lombard councils, it recognized that any authority to act lay with the king.

The council of Meaux-Paris was a radical assembly. Much of its work was rejected when the king and nobles assembled at Épernay later that year and, barring the bishops from attending, upheld only nineteen of their eighty-three canons.[129] Since the hospital decree was among the nineteen that was not dismissed, it is tempting to read it as an uncontroversial, even conservative act, and this is what modern commentators have done.[130] It will be argued here that this

---

sanctitate sua adquisitis ampliaverunt, ab eodem hospitalitatis officio funditus sunt alienata. Et non solum supervenientes in eadem hospitalia non recipiuntur, verum etiam ipsi, qui ab infantia in eisdem locis sub religione domino militaverunt, et exinde eiciuntur et ostiatim mendicare coguntur.'

[128] Hartmann, *Synoden*, 211; MGH *Conc.* III. 103–4, cc. 40–2, which begin 'Admonenda est regia magnitudo de hospitalibus...'; 'Providendum est regie maiestati, ut monasteria...'; 'Monenda est sollertia regia, ut strenuos et fideles missos per regnum sibi commissum dirigat'. The latter address monasteries in lay hands and commission *missi* to inventorize (*inbrevient*) church property.

[129] MGH *Cap.* II. 261–2; Hartmann, *Synoden*, 216.

[130] Imbert, 'Les conciles', 40, 42, 44–6; Moore, *Sacred Kingdom*, 365, which saw its citations as 'a conservative—one might even say a scholarly—reference to pre-Carolingian canon law, reflecting the influence of Hincmar'. Hartmann saw in council of Épernay's dismissals not hostility to the reform programme but concern that laws be adequately rooted in old law, finding a preference for those that cited earlier laws (W. Hartmann, 'Vetera et nova', *Annuarium Historiae Conciliorum* 15 (1983), 87–8).

was, in fact, a bullish broadside, with links to the Pseudo-Isidorian project. 'Pseudo-Isidore' is the name given to an unknown forger or, more likely, team of forgers working in the province of Reims in the mid-ninth century.[131] They have been identified at work in the library of Corbie abbey, near Amiens, and connected to the deposed archbishop of Reims, Ebo (816–35, 840–1).[132] Pseudo-Isidore produced a large dossier of canon law, in multiple parts. Its main elements are the *Collectio Hispana Gallica Augustodunensis*, the 'False Capitularies' of Benedict Levita, and the 'False Decretals' of Isidore Mercator (from which Pseudo-Isidore has been named).[133]

The latter two are our focus here, and their integral connections mean that one cannot be read without the other. Both were huge productions, a confection of genuine biblical, patristic, and legal sources, tampered decrees, and outright forgeries. The scale, craft, and swift dissemination of the work is widely recognized, as is its central concern to reinforce the position of bishops and forge protections against their trial and deposition. But there were other themes, too, from defending suffragan bishops against their metropolitans to using papal authority to strengthen episcopal power. They shared the wider ideals propounded at the council of Paris (829) and embraced by churchmen of the region, a reform agenda characterized by Steffen Patzold as a Paris-Aachen episcopal model, from the two councils.[134] At their heart was the church's claim to steer the government of the realm and its defence of church property in the face of growing political instability. These concerns place the forgeries in the world of the 830s or 840s, although their precise date remains uncertain. The earliest undisputed use of Pseudo-Isidorian material was at the council of Quierzy in February 857, sometime after the forgeries had been completed, although Hincmar of Reims and Thietgaud of Trier may have cited material in 852.[135] Recently, Eric Knibbs has made a new case for an old date, moving the forgers' work from the 830s into the conflicts of 845–51.[136] He has even detected 'faint traces' of the False Decretals in a Maundy reference at the council of Meaux-Paris and, if so, an

---

This may explain why the hospital decree, one of the most extensively 'proven' through quotations, was among those upheld.

[131] An extensive bibliography and exposition of the main interpretive issues can be found in E. Knibbs, 'Ebo of Reims, Pseudo-Isidore, and the Date of the False Decretals', *Speculum* 92:1 (2017).
[132] The identification with Corbie was made by K. Zechiel-Eckes, for which see H. Fuhrmann, 'The Pseudo-Isidorian Forgeries', in *PLEMA* 145, 171–2, and for Ebo, 171, 175; Patzold, *Episcopus*, 224–6; M. de Jong, 'Paschasius Radbertus and Pseudo-Isidore', in V. L. Garver and O. M. Phelan, eds, *Rome and Religion* (Farnham, 2014), 154–6. Knibbs, 'Ebo', 177–81, revisits the connection to the archbishop.
[133] The material, and the components of the False Decretals in particular, is laid out in Fuhrmann, 'Pseudo-Isidorian Forgeries', 135–95; *CCEMA* 69–70, 100–22.
[134] Patzold, *Episcopus*, 222–6; Hartmann, *Synoden*, 153–7; Knibbs, 'Ebo'; De Jong, 'Paschasius'; Fuhrmann, 'Pseudo-Isidorian Forgeries', 142–3.
[135] Fuhrmann, 'Pseudo-Isidorian Forgeries', 173–6; De Jong, 'Paschasius', 154–8.
[136] Knibbs, 'Ebo', 173–81; and now, E. Knibbs, 'Pseudo-Isidore's Ennodius', *Deutsches Archiv für Erforschung des Mittelalters* 74 (2018), 35–41.

early date for their influence.[137] The hospital canon takes on new life when examined within this context.

The canonical condemnations that constitute the canon's second half warrants close examination. It states that:

> For which canonical condemnation must be feared, and especially what has been laid out in a decretal of pope Symmachus, [i] because he who is known to be the progenitor and perpetrator of this crime/sin (*scelus*) *should be struck with anathema* now and in perpetuity, as *a murderer of the poor* and as *Judas* himself, the betrayer of Christ. [ii] *Those*, says Pope Symmachus, *who seek from kings the property of* or whatever belongs to *a church, and* incited by a corrupting piety *plunder the resources of the needy; what they possess shall be made void and they shall be excluded from the community of the church whose inheritance they desire to steal.* Also in a canon of Orléans: [iii] *But if anyone at any time should attempt to act against this our regulation or remove anything from the customary rights or endowment of* a xenodochium *so that the xenodochium (God forbid!) might cease to be, he should be struck with an irrevocable curse as a murderer of the poor.*[138]

Although it refers to a decretal of Pope Symmachus, the passage is in fact stitched together using three Gallic councils. They were used one after another, their borrowed language marked above in italics. Only one of them, Orléans (549) [iii], is acknowledged, although it has been altered in small ways that convert a protection for a specific xenodochium into a general statement of the inviolability of any xenodochium's property. The more substantial effort is focused on the preceding part, where canon 5 of the 535 council of Clermont is quoted largely in full [ii],[139] after a statement [i] confected from ideas in canon 25 of the council of Tours (567). Together, they are used to supply language for a decretal of Symmachus, [i] by association and [ii] directly, by putting language from Clermont into the pope's mouth. The goal at Meaux-Paris was to construct a canonical condemnation, complete with the threat of anathema to any who

---

[137] Knibbs, 'Ebo', 179; Hartmann, *Synoden*, 210, 212–13.

[138] (c. 40) 'Unde pertimescenda est canonica sententia et maxime decretalis Symmachi pape definitio, [i] quia ut *necator pauperum* et Christi traditor *Iudas* isdem, qui huius sceleris auctor et perpetrator esse dinoscitur, praesenti et perpetuo est *anathemate feriendus.* [ii] *Qui reiculam*, inquit Symmachus papa, vel quicquid fuerit *ecclesie, petunt a regibus* et corrumpende pietatis instinctu *egentium substantiam rapiunt, irrita habeantur, que obtinent, et a communione ecclesie, cuius facultatem auferre cupiunt, excludantur.* Item in canone Aurelianensi: [iii] *Si quis quolibet tempore [cuiuslibet potestatis aut ordinis persona] contra hanc constitutionem nostram venire temptaverit aut aliquid de consuetudine vel facultate senodochii [ipsius] abstulerit, ut senodochium, quod avertat deus, esse desinat, ut necator pauperum inrevocabili anathemate feriatur.*' MGH *Conc.* III. 103–4. Author's italics mark language from [i] Tours (567), c. 25; [ii] Clermont (535), c. 5; [iii] Orléans (549), c. 15 (CCSL 148A, pp. 106, 153, 192–3). The language in the other square brackets has been excised from [iii].

[139] Meaux-Paris's c. 40 substitutes 'corrumpendae pietatis instinctu' for 'horrendae cupiditatis impulsu'.

despoiled xenodochia and deprived the needy of their alms. Its significance lies in the means by which this was done.

The choice of the sixth-century Symmachus (498–514) is significant. Elected pope on the same day as a rival, Symmachus hweathered factionalism and criminal accusations. He and his allies responded in firm tones, in several synods and via a collection of forged documents known as the Symmachan forgeries that were to find wide circulation from the sixth century for their claims of papal immunity.[140] His (genuine) synods of 499, 501, and 502 were gathered into the *Dionysio-Hadriana*, through which they were widely available in Francia, as were his letters to Caesarius of Arles. The synod of 6 November 501, in particular, contained uncompromising statements on the inalienability and proper administration of church property. It was rediscovered in the 820s by the Frankish bishops and cited, as 'decretals' of Pope Symmachus, in defence of these principles at the councils of Paris (829) and Aachen (836).[141] Its most forceful statement was quoted at the council of Aachen (836): 'For it is unjust and a kind of sacrilege that what each person gave [in life] or bequeathed with assurance [upon death] to a venerable church, because of its poor [clergy or religious] there and for the salvation and repose of their own souls, should be transferred to another use by those who have agreed above all to protect them'.[142] Symmachus's was a voice that had begun to ring loudly against infringements by secular powers in Francia at this moment.

The hospital canon rested upon this growing reputation. Yet, the canon did something odd. It claimed the pope's name and authority, even his voice, but not his words. Gone are his own measured tones, replaced by thunderous threats against plunderers of property and murderers of the poor. It is a meaningful change.

Given his contemporary currency, it is not surprising that the figure of Symmachus was to be adopted (and developed) by the forgers. As Knibbs has shown, his 502 Synod Palmaris was at the heart of Benedict Levita's fabricated case for *excepto spolii*, a set of protections for bishops facing trial; it was also at the centre of Ebo's forged privilege of Gregory IV of *c*.845, a text with Pseudo-

[140] E. Wirbelauer, *Zwei Päpste in Rom: Der Konflikt zwischen Laurentius und Symmachus* (Munich, 1993). For the councils, W. T. Townsend, 'Councils Held under Pope Symmachus', *Church History* 6:3 (1937); Hillner, 'Titular Churches'. For the *Dionysio-Hadriana*, CCEMA 13–20. For the forgeries, concerned with papal immunity, and their circulation, D. Jasper, 'Papal Letters and Decretals', in *PLEMA* 69 n.; and Knibbs, 'Ennodius', 3–9, on the Symmachan corpus in the ninth century.

[141] Paris (829), c. 17, 'QUOD NULLI EPISCOPORUM LICEAT RES ECCLESIAE EXTRA CONSTITUTA CANONUM PASSIM IN ALTERIUS IURA TRANSFERRE'; Aachen (836), c. 48, 'DE CONSERVANDIS REBUS QUAE A FIDELIBUS CONFERUNTUR'; and c. 95, untitled (MGH *Conc.* II.ii, 624, 718–19, 766). The 501 synod is ed. by T. Mommsen in *Cassiodori senatoris variae*, MGH *Auct. Ant.* XII (Berlin, 1894), 438–55.

[142] MGH *Auct. Ant.* XII. 446–7: 'iniquum est enim et sacrilegii instar, ut quae vel pro salute vel requie animarum suarum unusquisque venerabili ecclesiae pauperum causa contulerit aut certe reliquerit, ab his, quos hoc maxime servare convenerat, in alterum transferantur,' in Aachen (836), c. 95.

Isidorian echoes.[143] Pseudo-Isidore continued in this tradition. He/they gathered Symmachus's letters and councils into book 3 of the False Decretals and fabricated new synods in the pope's name. One of these, the so-called Sixth Synod, was set in Rome in 504 and consisted of a series of exchanges between the 'holy synod' and Symmachus, in long expositions purporting to be speech ('dixit . . ,').[144] (To limit confusion, in what follows, I shall refer to the genuine synods by their date and the false synod as the 'Sixth Synod'.) Here, Pseudo-Isidore addressed only one subject: transgressions against the property of (and thus gifts to) churches. He was particularly keen to stress, repeatedly, that violators must be condemned and anathematized. Pseudo-Isidore's Sixth Synod was an argument for the heinousness of these crimes and for their just punishment by anathema, as the penalty prescribed by holy canons.[145] One striking passage—often cited to epitomize the synod's tone and rulings[146]—laid down the rationale behind such judgement: that any who seize or unjustly possess church property and refuse to return it should be judged a murderer of the poor and 'eradicated' from the body of the church.[147] The statement, of course, was not produced by Symmachus but by Pseudo-Isidore. It was interpolated from the council of Paris (556×73), an extended version of canon 26 of the council of Tours (567). Both Pseudo-Isidore and Meaux-Paris retool these sixth-century Gallic statements and move them to Rome, placing them in the mouth of Pope Symmachus to threaten invaders of church property.

A campaign to defend ecclesiastical property (*res Dei*) intensified in the troubled years of the 840s. The division of empire in 843 saw new levels of warfare and, with it, the use by kings of ecclesiastical estates for military supporters. Bishops, abbots, and synods responded with a greater quantity of fulminating

---

[143] Knibbs, 'Ebo', 158–64, 175–6.

[144] The best published edition remains *Decretales Pseudo-Isidorianae et Capitula Angilramni*, ed. P. Hinschius (Leipzig, 1863), 679–84, for whose flaws see Fuhrmann, 'Pseudo-Isidorian Forgeries', 154–9. A new critical edition by Eric Knibbs is under way and I cite here from his working text of the Sixth Synod. I am grateful to Prof. Knibbs for this text, and for generous advice on several points in this discussion.

[145] As one of his opening statements makes clear: 'Et facto silentio Symmachus episcopus dixit: Communis dolor et generalis est gemitus, quod intra ecclesiam nostris et retroactis temporibus *de invasione rerum ecclesiasticarum* et vexatione sacerdotem cognovimus, quae res non nos solos, sed omnes Domini tangit sacerdotes. Et, licet *haec a praecessoribus nostris iam prohibita sunt, et tales praesumptores damnati et a sanctis canonibus anathematizati*, ne tamen denuo praesumantur, est enim super eis promenda sententia, ut qui eorum casum non timent, timeant saltem perpetuam eorum damnationem, et quod saepe praesumitur, saepius, ut inhibeatur, necesse est. (Author's italics, to the central arguments).

[146] The tradition goes back at least to C. J. Hefele, *A History of the Councils*, tr. W. R. Clark, IV (Edinburgh, 1895), 72–3.

[147] '*Indigne enim ad altare Domini properare permittitur, qui res ecclesiasticas audet* invadere, aut *injuste*, id est sine licentia episcopi, *possidere* aut *iniqua* vel iniusta *defensione* in eis *perdurat. Necatores enim pauperum iudicandi sunt* praefixo tenore, et si non emendaverint vitium, exstirpandi.' (Author's italics mark language taken from Paris (556×73), c. 1, ed. CCSL 148A, pp. 205–6). The Sixth Synod continues to cite, largely verbatim, much of the Parisian canon.

prohibitions against the practice.[148] They also responded, it seems, by sharpening the terms of those prohibitions. Their case shifted from the principle that church property was inviolable, to the judgement that any violator must face. With the king among the chief offenders, they needed a new court of justice, one that rested now on God's wrath. Since this was an argument based on divine order and divine judgement, it had to rest on the holy antiquity of its claims. The quest for canonical authorities intensified. This change in tactic, from principle to judgement, can be identified in a series of related texts, each one a pioneer in articulating the case. Table 6.1 lays out components and characteristics of these arguments. It was a case built through orthodox and spurious means, and the lines between the two could blur.

Forerunners can be glimpsed at earlier councils, which crafted protections for ecclesiastical property and laid out basic authorities. Paris (829) deployed Symmachus's 501 synod to forbid alienation of ecclesiastical property. Aachen (836) took this further, to move from the principle that land was protected to the right to inflict punishment, a case it argued through an assertion of scholarly authority that, in writing, was more bluster than scholarship. Two of Aachen's decrees (cc. 93–4) claimed that the writings of many holy fathers, in both Latin and Greek, might be produced in support of punishment but that, to save time, only two were selected.[149] These were presented in the next decree (c. 95), with little additional comment beyond their identification as chapters 7 and 8 of the council of Gangra (c.340) and as a decree ('in decretis') of Pope Symmachus, from his 501 synod (as above). Neither would have been new to the churchmen assembled at Aachen. Symmachus was already familiar, although a sharper citation was chosen here because it labelled the activity as 'unjust and a kind of sacrilege'. The council of Gangra was widely known. Circulating in the *Dionysio-Hadriana*, its canons had been regularly cited ever since Charlemagne's *Admonitio generalis*, usually to promote religious discipline.[150] Here it is deployed for a new target. The Aachen council was pushing to develop a weapon to agitate for the restitution and protection of church property, but it went no further than to state, within the Grangra canons, that violators 'should be anathema.'

Behind the scenes, more radical work was taking place. A dossier of excerpts from patristic and canonical sources survives, if incompletely, that were copied

---

[148] On the escalating problem of royal use of church property and lay abbacy, De Jong, *Penitential State*, 142–4, 166–9; De Jong, *Epitaph for an Era*, 193–9; Patzold, *Episcopus*, 211–18. The canon that followed the hospital canon at Meaux-Paris reprimanded the king regarding monasteries handed over to lay tenants, MGH *Conc.* III. 104 (c. 41).

[149] MGH *Conc.* II.ii, 766: (c. 93) 'Multa siquidem sanctorem patrum, qui non solum Latinae, verum etiam Grece scripserunt, documenta proferri poterant, quae ob prolixitatem vitandam omittuntur, qui res Deo dicatas atque sacratas nullatenus impune auferri posse testantur.'; (c. 94) '...de multis brevitatis gratia duo huic subnectere opusculo'.

[150] MGH *Fontes iuris* XVI (cc. 47–8), *Cap.* I. 227 (c. 9); *Conc.* II.i, 209 (c. 4), 269 (c. 35), 365–6 (cc. 65–9). Gangra's c. 8, threatening anathema to those who divert offerings for the poor to other purposes, had been cited at Aachen (816), c. 66.

Table 6.1. Techniques deployed in arguments to punish violators of church property

	Dossier for ?Aachen†	Aachen (836), cc. 48, 95	Ben. Levita (False Capit.)	Meaux/Par. (845/6), c. 40	Corbie privilege (846/7)	Ps. Isid. Synod VI
GALLIC COUNCILS:						
for anathema:						
AUVERGNE (535)	x		x			
CLERMONT (535)			*c. 14*	*c. 5*		
+ *necatores pauperum*:			*c. 5*	*x*		
ORLEANS (549)	c. 13		*c. 13*	*c. 15*		
TOURS (567)			*c. 26+25*	*c. 25*	(cc. 25, 26)	
PARIS (556×73)						*c. 1*
Case for anathema	x		x	x		x
GANGRA (324)	cc. 7, 8	cc. 7, 8	cc. 7, 8		x	*cc. 7, 8*
Symmachus	501 (sacrilege)	501 (sacrilege)	*502*		c. 8	x
'*necatores pauperum*'			x	x		x
violators/crime			x	x	x	x
prose argument					x	x
Misuse of authorities			x	x		x
Specific to universal			x	x		

'x' signals that a technique or decree was used; if a particular element was used, it is specified.

Italics signals that the technique or decree has been spuriously adapted or altered.

† BnF, MS nouv. acq. lat. 1632, fol. 97r–99r.

into a manuscript at Orléans, around 850 or shortly thereafter. It seems to represent preparatory work (*Vorarbeiten*) for Aachen or another council in the 830s, assembled perhaps at Orléans, possibly by Jonas of Orléans.[151] The final chapter ('cap[itulum] xx') consists of a group of conciliar canons or extracts from canons: Gangra cc. 7 and 8; two quotations from Symmachus's 501 synod (one of them 'Iniquum est...transferre');[152] and six passages from five canons, from councils of Orléans (511, 535, 549) and Toledo (655).[153] All of them concern the property (*res*) or inheritance (*facultates*) of churches and threaten excommunication or anathema. Immediately preceding them, marked 'cap[itulum] xix', the group is introduced by a statement that is also found at Aachen, here given the title 'That many documents of the holy Greek and Latin fathers are neglected which bear witness that property dedicated and consecrated to God cannot be taken away with impunity.'[154] The canons of the council of Aachen thus included 'chapter xix' and the first three of the ten extracts from the final chapter.

The council's selection obscures the agenda of the dossier's composer, who concludes his extracts with a clear statement of his purpose:

We have transcribed these from the principal canons enacted in the cities of Gaul, that we should expose to view how much the bishops of churches in that time were laying claim to the church resources that were committed to them, and under how great authority and anathema they bound those who attempted to take possession of these things unjustly, because by the definitions of the canons it is fitting to punish anyone who after such prohibitions regarding church properties should presume to be able extract anything with impunity.[155]

---

[151] BnF nouv. acq. lat. 1632, where the collection is fols 78v–99v. It has been partially edited in, C. Erdmann and G. Laehrs, 'Ein karolingischer Konzilsbrief', *Neues Archiv* 50 (1935), 120–34; and A. Wilmart, 'L'Admonition de Jonas au Roi Pépin', *Revue Bénédictine* 45 (1933), 221–32, for which see G. Schmitz, 'Die Synode von Aachen 836 und Pseudoisidor', in P. Depreux and S. Esders, eds, *La productivité d'une crise* (Ostfildern, 2018), 329–42; S. Heinen, 'Pseudoisidor auf dem Konzil von Aachen', in K. Ubl and D. Ziemann, eds, *Fälschung als Mittel der Politik?* (Wiesbaden, 2015), 97–126; Patzold, *Episcopus*, 202–4. I am indebted to Prof. Knibbs for his introduction to this manuscript.

[152] The second is 'modis omnibus synodali...commissa docetur'. The two excerpts are titled, 'De rebus ecclesiae conservandis, Symachi capitulo secundo', and 'eiusdem III', misleading headings that refer to their source, the *Dionysio-Hadriana*, tit. Decretorum papae Symmachi IIII, at 'II. Exempla scriptura' and the section that followed: *Collectio Dionysio-Hadriana*, ed. J. W. Cochlaeus (Mainz, 1525), fol. 161r–v.

[153] BnF nouv. acq. lat. 1632, fols 97r–99r. There are two extracts from Orléans (511), c. 15; the others are Orléans (535), c. 5; Orléans (538), c. 25; Orléans (549), c. 13; Toledo (655), c. 1.

[154] 'QUOD MULTA SANCTORUM PATRUM LATINORUM ATQUE GRECORUM DOCUMENTA PRAETERMITTANTUR, QUI RES DEO DICATAS ATQUE SACRATAS IMPUNE AUFERRI NON POSSE TESTANTUR Multa siquidem sanctorum...posse testantur' (as Aachen, 836, c. 95), BnF nouv. acq. lat. 1632, fol. 97r–v. Curiously, and unlike the other chapters, this one does not provide a source for the statement.

[155] BnF nouv. acq. lat. 1632, fol. 99r. 'Haec de praecipuis canonibus galliarum civitatibus actis transcripsimus, ut hostenderemus quanta auctoritate praesules ecclesiarum illo tempore facultates ecclesiae sibi commissas defendendo vindicarent, et sub quanta auctoritate et anathemate constringerent eos, qui illas indebitae possidere conarentur, quia canonum constitutionibus dignus est puniri

The dossier pushed the case further than the council was able or willing to go. Its Gallic excerpts were chosen for their threats of excommunication, and as a model for how a council might offer formidable visions of punishment. This was not taken up at Aachen (836), which offered a more conservative case against the rash (*temeraria*) practice of seizing church property, making a case for punishment only indirectly, via familiar canons and a promise (threat?) of many more. It seems that the council's discussions went far further than its canons suggest and that someone among the party, at least, made a more forceful case for the council to threaten anathema in its own voice and in Gallic terms. This, the Aachen council declined. Nothing in the dossier suggests an interest in xenodochia. Yet here is evidence not only of the agendas that were bubbling behind Aachen's more cautious statements, but also of the rediscovery of the Gallic councils, among them Orléans (549). It is likely that something like this dossier underpinned the hospital canon at Meaux-Paris.[156]

The fruits of wider library research emerge as something of a 'big bang' in the next stage of argument. A new and remarkably mature case can be identified in a group of texts dating to within a few years after 845 that changed both the techniques and direction of argument. All of them use material from the Gallic councils, drawing from a shared cohort of decrees (and perhaps a shared dossier of material) selected for their language of violation, accusation, and curse. This was the moment when the phrase 'murderers of the poor' (*necatores pauperum*) was rediscovered, from the sixth-century Merovingian councils.[157] It was also the moment when focus shifted from the inviolability of church land to the violators and their crimes.

The techniques appear for the first time in two sources. The largest group can be found in the False Capitularies. Benedict Levita had discovered the phrase 'murderers of the poor', which he presented via canons from Orléans (549, c. 13) and Tours (567, c. 26). He deployed them in defence of church property, along with Gangra (cc. 7–8), Auvergne (535, c. 14), and Clermont (535, c. 5).[158] Most, including the Orléans and Gangra canons, were incorporated without changes,

---

quisquis post tot prohibitiones de rebus ecclesiasticis putaverit aliquid inpune posse tractare. Contumeliae enim studio sit, sicut ait beatus papa innocentius ad marcianum quicquid interdictum totiens usurpatur.' Two more contemporary canons on ecclesiastical property then follow, both unattributed, from the councils of Antioch (c. 24) and Aachen 816 (c. 116). The former was used at Aachen 836 (c. 48), where it was given its other name, Nicea. (MGH *Conc.* II.ii, 718–19; II.i, 398). This, and the fact that cap. xix makes no mention of Aachen, suggests that the dossier was used at the Aachen council.

[156] The dossier argues against the possibility that the Gallic canons were innocently assigned to Symmachus at Meaux-Paris. It and the Aachen council suggest that larger aim of the dossier's researchers, to introduce Gallic claims into Carolingian practice, was controversial; the material was recognized as different.

[157] On the phrase, see Chapter 3.

[158] He uses several of them twice, including Orléans (at 2.136; 3.419). The others are 2.134, 428; 3.7, 8, 265, 409. The *False Capitularies* of Benedict Levita are edited in MGH *Leges* II.ii, 17–158, but, where

but given titles that offered a specific interpretation, for example, 'Concerning those who seize or withhold property assigned to the church'. The titles emphasized the malefactors, that is, the transgressors—not the property or the principle of its inviolability.[159] To make the case, Benedict focused his energies on chapter 26 of the council of Tours (567), which he quoted in full, with additions and alterations. He gave it the rather confusing title 'Concerning those who not only give something to a church from their own property but also unjustly possess what has been given by others'.[160] The original Tours canon had castigated those who refused to hand over a gift that they or a predecessor had promised to a church in writing. It justified punishment by excommunication as a 'murderer of the poor' and outlined a procedure by which this must be done: the transgression must be proved, the violator admonished by the bishop, and excommunicated if the admonition was ignored; the punishment was not to be lifted until the property had been restored. Benedict did not change the substance of the canon, but he made two interpolations: some small changes in its justification for excommunication, to draw attention to the transgressors of the crime;[161] and a statement at the end, purporting to be a continuation of the original but in fact using phrases from a previous Tours decree (c. 25).[162] This vowed to punish any who infringed on 'this our sanction' and not merely through excommunication but anathema. Here, as in his selection generally, Benedict revealed his goals: to use the violators to construct a crime and a case for punishment; to establish anathema as that lawful punishment; and to exemplify his case, and particularly the crime, in forceful terms. In pursuit of the latter, Benedict preferred the phrase 'murderers

possible, I have preferred the ongoing edition by Gerhard Schmitz for the MGH, at <http://www.benedictus.mgh.de/edition/edition.htm> (Aug. 2019).

[159] This is not always done, but there is a clear tendency. To take the main run of decrees in book 2: (134) 'DE REBUS ECCLESIAE ABLATIS AUT FRAUDATIS VEL RETENTIS' (Auv., 535, c. 14); (135) 'UT NEMO RES ECCLESIAE, NISI CUI IURE DEBENTUR, IN QUIBUSLIBET REGIONIBUS CONIACENTES COMPETERE AUDEAT VEL TENERE' (Orl. 549, c. 14); (136) 'DE HIS, QUI FACULTATES ECCLESIAE DELEGATAS AUFERUNT VEL RETENTANT' (Orl. 549, c. 13). Those whose titles do not begin 'De his' tend to have canons that open with 'Si quis', notably Gangra (cc. 7–8), Clermont (535, c. 5) and, as above, Auvergne (535, c. 14).

[160] (2.428) 'DE HIS, QUI NON SOLUM DE REBUS SUIS ALIQUID ECCLESIAE CONFERUNT, SED ETIAM AB ALIIS CONLATAS INIUSTE POSSIDENT.'

[161] 'For it is intolerable to allow one to approach the altar of the lord who has even dared to seize church property or unjustly take it as his own. Indeed whoever hold out in injurious defence of this, all must be judged as murderers of the poor because they have deprived them in such a manner of their food.' ('Indigne enim ad altare domini properare permittitur, qui res ecclesiasticas aut audet rapere aut iniuste possidere. Qui vero in hac iniqua defensione perdurant, ut necatores pauperum omnes iudicandi sunt, quod eorum taliter alimenta subtraxerint.') The language from Tours (567), c. 26, is marked in italics.

[162] 'Qui vero his nostris sanctionibus contraierit et, quae neglexit, legibus emendare tardaverit vel deinceps in praedicta nequitia perdurare voluerit, omnes honores, quos habere videbatur, perdat et a nobis seculariter et legaliter strictim fortiterque puniatur et a sacerdotibus caelesti gladio feriatur. Et si se non correxerit, non solum excommunis, sed etiam anathematizatus moriatur.' With Tours (567), c. 25, marked in italics.

of the poor'. His aim was not to reinforce the principle that church lands were inviolable, but to forge a system to prosecute, judge, and punish malefactors. Benedict was sharpening old law into a judicial weapon for the times.

The same techniques were deployed in the Meaux-Paris hospital decree. Its canonical case also focused on violators ('because he... Those... who seek... But if anyone').[163] Its three conciliar extracts were chosen because they required a penalty of anathema and because they constructed the crime or criminal, and in dramatic terms: 'murderer of the poor' (twice), 'Judas, the betrayer of Christ', and 'plunder the resources of the needy'. The author used essentially the same Gallic councils as Benedict to make his case, although their selection and use was tailored to xenodochia. So, the hospital canon preferred canon 25 of Tours for its reference to Judas, and Benedict canon 26 for its procedure for punishment. Benedict used Clermont (535, c. 5) to castigate those who sought church property from kings, and Meaux-Paris selected its phrase 'resources of the needy' (*egentium substantia*) as fitting for hospitals.[164] Finally, Meaux-Paris preferred the anathema clause for the Lyons xenodochium (Orléans, c. 15) to that council's general statement on church property (c. 13); Benedict used the latter twice, but never the former. There is thus no textual relationship between the hospital canon and the False Capitularies: one was not a source for the other, since two of the canons used for Meaux-Paris were not included in Benedict's collection. Nor is it possible to say which was first to deploy this corpus of early material, to embrace 'murderers of the poor', or to use the latter to argue that anathema was the just penalty for malefactors. What can be said is that they were working from the same clay. The two texts were discrete performances of a shared knowledge and approach, in pursuit of a shared goal, one enacted first in these two theatres. The connection was not textual but authorial: the authors may not have been the same person, but they were part of the same pursuit.

The privilege of Corbie develops this picture further. Issued the following winter of 846/7 at another council of Paris, it confirmed Corbie abbey's right to elect its abbot and administer its own property.[165] It was written under the guidance of Paschasius Radbertus, a scholar in his own right, as well as Wala's biographer and now successor as abbot. It has also been suggested that Paschasius was the directing mind behind the Pseudo-Isidorian project, largely on the grounds of the forgers' connection to Corbie's library.[166] The privilege includes

---

[163] See n. 138.

[164] The change in Meaux-Paris of its *horrendae cupiditatis impulsu* to *corrumpendae pietatis instinctu* could be read in this light, although its specific reference is now lost. It may refer to the goods of xenodochia being diverted to other religious uses, e.g. by monastic custodians.

[165] MGH *Conc.* III. 144–7, with the manuscripts and the council, 140–3; Hartmann, *Synoden*, 217–18; Ganz, *Corbie*, 30–2; De Jong, *Epitaph*, 57–64.

[166] A proposal advanced by Zechiel-Ecke, but now challenged: De Jong, *Epitaph*, 199–205; Knibbs, 'Ebo', 151, 181.

a long denunciation of those who despoil monastic property.[167] This differed from the moral tones of recent councils, such as the council of Ver (844), which presented a zealous case against lay abbots and those who withdrew resources from monasteries.[168] Ver's long plea bemoaned the deprivations wrought on the servants of God, on the poor, guests, and captives, as well as Christians who had pledged gifts to God, imbuing its case with Old and New Testament references, the longest of them (Ps. 82: 13–15) reiterated in the privilege. The privilege's case has a more contemporary feel: against any 'invader or wolf' (*pervasor, immo lupus*) who might seize the abbacy, it justified the penalty of anathema, on the authority of the current Paris council and 'all the holy fathers who issued the holy canons' that required this. It is a largely rhetorical case, bolstered by biblical references. It then turned to plunderers of church property, in a statement inspired by Tours (567, cc. 25–6). As Meaux-Paris, it used the first to curse as a murderer of the poor, and as Judas, whoever invaded or confiscated the wealth or living 'of the servants and poor of Christ'.[169] But whereas Meaux-Paris used its ideas to confect a decretal of Symmachus, the privilege extracted other elements, to compose a ringing condemnation in the voice of the Paris council. It then laid out a procedure for admonishing malefactors ('once, twice, and a third time or more') before cursing as anathema any who refused to reform, citing Gangra's c. 8 in full.

The privilege's approach echoes that of Meaux-Paris, but its argument is more closely aligned with a third text. The spurious Sixth Synod of Symmachus takes a similar line and laid out an argument whose underlying structure was taken from the council of Paris (556×73, c. 1). This laboured to establish a procedure by which violators 'must be judged murderers of the poor in the manner laid out above and, if they do not correct their fault, be cut out'.[170] It laid out this penalty by citing the council of Gangra (cc. 7–8), as part of a longer interpolation from the council of Aachen (836).[171] The privilege contains a highlights-tour of Pseudo-Isidore's longer case, following the structure of the latter's arguments and resting on a shared corpus of sources.[172] It was aware not only of the final product of the Sixth

---

[167] It occurs after the section that defines the privilege and the process of election. It begins 'Quodsi aliquando contigerit, ut aliquis pervasor', at the bottom of p. 145 of the MGH edition, continuing through the next page.

[168] MGH *Conc.* III. 42–4 (c. 12). The hand of Lupus of Ferrières has been detected in the capitulary, especially in the 'elegant Latin and aggressive tone' of this decree: Nelson, 'Intellectual in Politics', 11; Hartmann, *Synoden*, 204–5.

[169] 'Et quia *cupiditate* ductus etiam pecuniam ac substantiam servorum et pauperum Christi invadere et asportare voluit, una cum *Iuda* sacre pecuniae dilapidatore et proditore domini nostri Iesu Christi, *maledictiones illas, quae* in eum prolate sunt, excipiat, utpote invasor gregis Christi et *necator pauperum*.' MGH *Conc.* III. 146, with language from Tours marked in italics.

[170] 'Necatores enim pauperum judicandi sunt praefixo tenore et, si non emendaverint vitium, exstirpandi.' The case begins at 'Scimus spiritu domini . . ,' at the top of p. 680 in Hinschius's edition.

[171] Using Aachen's c. 95 (MGH *Conc.* II.ii, 766). The Sixth Synod continues (p. 682) by drawing on Paris (556×73, c. 2).

[172] The common exchange of Tours for Paris suggests a shared, if tightly controlled, bank of underlying sources, and so perhaps a dossier similar to that in BnF nouv. acq. lat. 1632. The two

Synod, but of the elements behind its making.[173] The denunciation deepens the links between Paschasius Radbertus, Corbie, and the forgers, taking them beyond the abbey's library. It suggests that the Parisian council of 846/7 made use of the spurious synod, perhaps via its creators rather than the text itself.

The privilege is one of a family of texts that advanced a distinctive argument to punish violators of church property. The family included, too, the Meaux-Paris hospital canon, and the False Capitularies and False Decretals, whose authors shared a body of research, agenda, and core argument. Among them only the privilege faithfully represents its authorities and so offers an orthodox version of this argument. In so doing, it highlights the goals and techniques of the forgers. First, the development of an argument that invaders (*pervasores*) or violators of church property face anathema as murderers of the poor, a case based around the similar texts of Tours (567, cc. 25–6) or Paris (556×73). This defined the crime and its culprits, then laid out a procedure to establish guilt, to admonish, and then to anathematize. It was a case falsely given voice through Pope Symmachus, the penalty confirmed via the council of Gangra (cc. 7–8). Their goal was to codify a crime and establish anathema as its penalty, as prescribed by divine judgement and the ancient canons.[174] They aimed to lay out a judicial process whereby bishops could prosecute and punish, and so to find justice.[175]

It also sheds light on the evolving techniques of the forgers in the years 845–7. Unlike the privilege, Meaux-Paris abused authorities to argue for anathema. Like Benedict's False Capitularies, it made its case through a bundle of denunciations from Gallic councils, both genuine and confected. In modifying the Orléans anathema clause for the Lyons xenodochium, it displays one of Benedict's favourite techniques, of reframing the specific as universal.[176] That it shared a source-base with the False Capitularies suggests the latter's research was fresh, perhaps still active in the summer of 845, when the Meaux-Paris canons were

councils were natural alternatives, since Tours c. 26 made up the first half of Paris c. 1. With its reference to Judas Tours (c. 25) was preferable for maledictions; Paris, whose second half bewailed abuse under the banner of royal liberality and outlined a procedure to punish a malefactor who was in a different diocese than his victim, better for discussions of enforcement.

[173] For Symmachan forgeries at Corbie: R. H. Rouse and M. A. Rouse, 'Ennodius in the Middle Ages', in J. R. Sweeney and S. Chodorow, eds, *Popes, Teachers and Canon Law* (Ithaca, NY, 1989), 97–101; Knibbs, 'Enodius'.

[174] An early instance might be glimpsed in Agobard's *De dispensatione ecclesiarum rerum*, ed. van Acker, for which see my chapter 5, n. 74.

[175] The extreme efforts to craft a judicial framework, based on the threat of divine wrath, throws a different light on Hartmann's observation, 'Das Privileg für Corbie ... kann als Beleg für die starke Stellung der Bischöfe im Reich Karls des Kahlen gelten: Nicht der königliche Schutz, sondern die Drohung mit dem Anathem durch die Bischöfe erscheint dem Kloster die wirksamste Stütze gegen die Einwirkung von außen, die vor allem vom regionalen Adel drohen mochte.' (Hartmann, *Synoden*, 218). On the weakening power of royal protection in the mid-ninth century, Wood, *Prop. Ch.*, 345.

[176] On the technique, Knibbs, 'Ebo', 161.

crafted.[177] But in packaging two of its extracts as a decretal, the hospital decree anticipates the more 'digested' work of the False Decretals, crafting a new case that it ventriloquized through a confected decretal of Symmachus.[178] A year later in the winter of 846/7 the longer, more elegantly reasoned case in the privilege suggests that Pseudo-Isidore's Sixth Synod of Symmachus had already been drafted. The hospital canon offers itself as a transitional moment between the corpus of canons gathered in the False Capitularies and the production of at least one major forgery of the False Decretals. As such, it supports Knibbs's argument to return the forgeries to the 840s and, specifically, the period 847–52.[179]

The hospital canon revitalizes the question of the links between the forgers and the Meaux-Paris canons. Traces of Pseudo-Isidorian influence had been suggested by their editor, Wilfried Hartmann, who noticed a preference for citing papal letters and a requirement that holy chrism be consecrated on Maundy Thursday, a day only otherwise found in the False Decretals.[180] Hartmann drew attention to chapters 60–2 on church property, where he found traces that seemed to reflect the False Capitularies: use of the term *sacrilegium* (theft of consecrated property) and the penalty of anathema, as well as echoes of what the council proclaimed to be 'the ancient dictum, that he who neglects his taxes should lose his field'.[181] In the latter Hartmann saw his strongest tie to the forgeries, 'a literal correspondence with a passage in Benedict Levita', although the axiom may have been in wider use.[182] These traces prompted Hartmann to wonder, 'Can one conclude that the

---

[177] The decrees were formulated at Meaux in June 845 and confirmed at Paris in 846, Hartmann, *Synoden*, 208.

[178] The term is that of Knibbs, who contrasts the forger's evolution from 'Benedict [who] transmits the raw product of our forgers' imagination' to the False Decretals, 'which provide much of the same material in more digested form, bent towards more specific ends' (Knibbs, 'Ebo', 164). Paris (829), c. 17, and Aachen (836), c. 95, both refer to 'decretals' of Symmachus; Meaux-Paris, c. 40, to 'decretalis Symmachi pape definitio', MGH *Conc.* II.ii, 624, 766; MGH *Conc.* III. 103.

[179] Knibbs proposes a return to an earlier scheme that dated our version of the False Capitularies to after Feb. 847 and the False Decretals at or slightly later (847–52). This does not exclude the possibility that both were under way by 846. On dating, see Knibbs, 'Ebo', 180; and, now Knibbs, 'Ennodius', 35–41.

[180] Hartmann, *Synoden*, 210, 212, discussed in Knibbs, 'Ebo', 179 n. Although previous Carolingian councils had required priests to journey to their diocesan seat to collect the chrism on *coena Domini* (the Last Supper, or Maundy Thursday), e.g. in 769 (c. 8) and 818/9 (c. 18), MGH *Cap.* I. 45, 278, 407 (c. 93).

[181] '…antiquum dictum qui neglegit censum, perdat agrum.' MGH *Conc.* III. 114; Hartmann, *Synoden*, 213. The word *sacrilegium* is taken from the passage in Symmachus's 501 synod, as cited at Aachen (836, c. 95; MGH *Conc.* II.ii, 766). It echoes Jerome's letter to Nepotian, also cited by the 442 council of Vaison-la-Romaine: 'Amico quippiam rapere furtum est, ecclesiam fraudare sacrilegium est', Jerome, *Ad Nepotianum* (ep. 52), at c. 16 (2, 3).

[182] Compare Meaux-Paris's *'iuxta legale et antiquum dictum qui neglegit censum, perdat agrum'* (c. 62) with the more diffuse language in Benedict Levita (1.13), 'et illos *census* vel illas decimas ac nonas ibidem dare pleniter debeant sicut eis ad Vernum ordinavimus. *Et qui hoc non fecerit, ipsas res perdat.'* (Author's italics to highlight the versions of this language.) Both draw from a longer tradition and were inspired by different capitularies. Benedict's phrase comes from Hirstal (779), whose c. 9 threatened tenants who failed to hand over brigands, 'et qui hoc non fuerit, beneficium et honorem perdat', and whose c. 13 permitted those who now paid tax (*census*) from church lands to pay 'decima et nona' with those taxes (MGH *Cap.* I. 48, 50). Meaux-Paris affirmed Louis's 818/9 decree, which ends, 'Et hoc qui

Pseudo-Isidorian forgers also participated in the formulation of many canons at the council of Meaux-Paris?'[183] But he went no further than to wonder.[184] The hospital canon suggests not simply that Pseudo-Isidorian texts were familiar to its drafter, but that a Pseudo-Isidorian drafted this decree. The hospital canon offers a possible glimpse of Pseudo-Isidore at work, and its bigger argument—that the extraction of church property is a crime against God, punishable through anathema—unites the councils of Aachen (836), Meaux-Paris (845/6), and Paris (846/7), researchers at Corbie and perhaps Lyons, and the producers of the Pseudo-Isidorian corpus in a wider mission to develop a court of divine justice, with Symmachus's voice booming with increasing volume, to protect church possessions against lay intrusion, especially by the king.

Here is not the place to follow the trail into the Meaux-Paris canons, although a few points might be flagged. Threats of anathema from the council of Orléans (549) against 'murderers of the poor' were appended at Meaux-Paris not only to the hospital canon but to a confirmation (c. 17) of a decree from Beauvais (845) that required heirs to hand over post-mortem bequests.[185] The former used the confirmation of the Lyons xenodochium from Orléans (c. 15), the latter that council's general protection of church property (c. 13), preferred also by Benedict Levita. The Meaux-Paris canons on church property (cc. 60–2) reveal other similarities to Benedict in their focus on malefactors, in setting up crimes in excoriating language, and making a case for anathema as the just penalty.[186]

---

nonas et decimas dare neglexerit...ne saepius iterando beneficium amittat'. The threat, in similar language, echoes through French and Italian capitularies and the axiom is repeated, perhaps from Meaux-Paris, in a Le Mans forgery that purports to be by Louis the Pious in 832: 'Et praevideat unusquisque, ne illam ibi audiat sententiam, *qui negligit censum, perdat agrum*, et per hanc auctoritatem, sive pro eorum negligentia vel contemptu, ipsa perdant beneficia.' *Geschichte des Bistums Le Mans*, ed. Weidemann, II. 294, who notes the language in Louis's *Formulae imperiales*, c. 21 (ed. K. Zeumer, MGH *Formulae* I (Hanover, 1886), 301–2). Also, Goffart, *Le Mans Forgeries*, 26, 289.

[183] 'Darf man daraus schließen, daß die pseudoisidorischen Fälscher auch an der Formulierung mancher Kanones auf dem Konzil von Meaux-Paris beteiligt waren?' Hartmann, *Synoden*, 213.

[184] An earlier and more cautious statement, Hartmann, 'Vetera et nova', 85–7, explored the techniques at Meaux-Paris within a wider context of 'canonical distortion' among West Francian reformers who, keen to advance their goals, turned away from tradition. After the failure of Meaux-Paris, they learned to package their initiatives in terms of old law, a practice that encouraged the Pseudo-Isidorian forgers. The technique was perfected by Hincmar of Reims, whose 'artifice', but not forgery, saw him 'surround[ing] his own novel legal constructions with the aura of tradition'. ('Mit diesem Kunstgriff vermochte Hinkmar—ohne regelrecht eine Fälschung zu begehen—eigene, neuartige Rechtskonstruktionen mit der Aura der Tradition zu umgeben.') Hartmann, 'Vetera et nova', with quotation at p. 92. This article noted two other moments of potential correspondence between Meaux-Paris and the forgers: concern about *corepiscopi* (c. 44) and a sentence on the right to burial in church (c. 72) that mirrored Additio 4.146 of Benedict Levita: Hartmann, 'Vetera et nova', 86–7.

[185] MGH *Conc.* III. 54–5 (c. 3) and 94. Beauvais had also railed against the attackers and oppressors of church property, but without the excoriating touches of Pseudo-Isidore, or the Orléans anathema. On the separate copy of Beauvais's canons, possibly reflecting Hincmar's editorship, see Hartmann, *Synoden*, 205–7.

[186] (c. 60) 'Ut hi, qui...infringunt et...abstrahunt et...non solum dehonorant, verum et...affligunt; velut sacrilegi canonice sententia...subigantur'; (c. 61) 'Ut pervasores rerum ecclesiasticarum, qui...non solum retinere, verum et crudeliter depopulari noscuntur...inmisericorditer

Here, too, the canons work to establish a system of ecclesiastical judgement when the secular arm failed to act. Canon 61 says this explicitly: 'And if [the malefactors] refuse to do this and have not been exhorted or forced by royal power, let the terrible apostolic sentence be pronounced against them, as is said [by previous councils]'.[187] Chief among their authorities is Pope Symmachus, who declared (in his genuine Roman synod of 501, c. 7) that the removal of church property 'is unjust and a kind of sacrilege'.[188]

Late Frankish Councils

If the drafting of the hospital canon was Pseudo-Isidorian, the desire to address hospitals came from the council itself. The Pseudo-Isidorian forgers had no interest in hospitals: their huge dossier failed to address them.[189] The council was however the first to address hospitals in West Francia for centuries, suggesting a new agenda whose backstory is now lost. Since the topic appears at Meaux-Paris, the temptation is to see the influence of Hincmar of Reims, and this may not be wrong.[190]

Only one other council of northern Frankish churchmen would address hospitals: Quierzy in 858, a synod of the bishops of Reims and Rouen provinces. Hincmar presided over this council and wrote its canons.[191] References in his

---

expoliant, devastant et opprimunt, ut rapaces, qui secundum apostolum a regno dei excluduntur, ex criminali et publico peccato publica penitentia satisfaciant...ab omni ecclesiastica communione ut sacrilegus debet arceri'; (c. 62) 'Hi vero, qui ex rebus ecclesiasticis...non solum neglegunt, verum et per contemptum dimittunt atque...obprimunt...ab ecclesiastica communione separentur', MGH *Conc.* III. 112–14.

[187] (c. 61) 'Quodsi hoc agere noluerint et potestate regia ad hoc exortati vel coacti non fuerint, proferatur contra eos apostolica terribilis sententia, qua dicitur'.

[188] See n. 142.

[189] 'Sinodochiae/synochia' occur only once and then incidentally, in a version of Const. 7, kp. 32, from Julian's *Epitome*, forbidding rectors of churches, *xenodochia*, and monasteries to alienate property. It is the same decree that Ansegis copied into his collection, but Benedict's version came from *De ordine ecclesiastico* (c. 22), a collection of abbreviated chapters from Julian's *Epitome*. Benedict copied the text and title (*De sanctis ecclesiis*) into his Additio 3 (c. 56) as the last of a run of decrees on the duties of clerics. Benedict used the collection frequently and as the spine of Additio 3, whose cc. 28, 31, 34, 37, 40, 43, 46–7, 50, 53, 56, 59, 62, 69, 72, 75, 78, 81, 84, 87, 90 sequentially follow *De ordine ecclesiastico* 8, 11, 14–18, 20–2, 34–5, 39–41, 43–4, 48–9, and 51. Unlike so many of these other cases, Benedict made no changes to c. 22 beyond amending the Latin for sense. *De ordine ecclesiastico* is edited, alongside Benedict's texts, in Kaiser, *Epit. Iul.* 476–92.

[190] MGH *Conc.* III, 61–4; and for context, Stone, 'Introduction', in Stone and West, eds, *Hincmar of Rheims*, 6–9.

[191] Hincmar took a strong stand in favour of ecclesiastical rights and against violators of church property, promulgating a treatise, 'Collectio de raptoribus', at Quierzy in 857, which quoted the False Decretals. Nevertheless, Hincmar's style of authorship was very different to that observed by the Pseudo-Isidorians; he, too, preferred accusing language ('Audiant rapaces et praedatores...!'), but built a more biblical and theological case. He preferred Ansegis as a source and Augustine (Depreux, 'Hincmar's Use of Capitularies'; Nelson, 'Intellectual in Politics', 12–14; MGH *Conc.* III. 392–6).

other writings suggest that he noticed xenodochia and may have taken a wider interest in them.[192] Quirezy's hospital canon reflected that of Meaux-Paris, even echoing the latter's opening sentence. In keeping with wider practice, it also addressed the king, ordering him to maintain those 'hospitals for pilgrims', and particularly those of the Scots, established in the time of his royal ancestors. As a text, however, it was woven from very different threads:

> Maintain hospitals for pilgrims, such as *those of the Scots* and *those which in the time of your* royal *ancestors had been* built and arranged, so that they are held to the purpose for which they were appointed and are regulated and guarded by rectors who fear God, lest the hospitals be squandered. And order the rectors of monasteries and xenodochia, that is hospitals, that—just as canonical authority teaches and the capitula of your grandfather and father command—they be subject to their own bishop and that they rule the monasteries and hospitals committed to them with the counsel of the same [bishops], since bishops will strive to apply fatherly concern to them as is their office.[193]

Gone are the Pseudo-Isidorian signs: the language of damnation, the case for punishment by anathema via Symmachus and Gallic councils, and even casting hospitals as communities of religious whose life has been lost. Instead, we find three elements. A return to the language of the established (Italian) tradition: of construction and arrangement, of facilities held 'to the purpose for which they were assigned', and ensuring that rectors preserve and not dissipate its charity. Here, too, are echoes of the council of Rome (853), especially in its call for the *sollicitudo* (concern) of bishops. But Quierzy's final clause is boundary-breaking, for it adapts a canon that abbots and monks be subject to their bishop to require the king to order rectors of xenodochia as well as monasteries to be subject to their diocesan and administer their charges through his counsel. The extension of the canon was perhaps inspired by the addition of 'monasteries' to the title of the hospital canon at Rome (853). Quierzy's was the only Carolingian decree, in

---

[192] He included xenodochia alongside episcopal palaces and monasteries, as manifestations of the gifts of the faithful for which bishops owed honour through fervent prayer to kings and to others in authority over the *res publica*: 'Nam et episcopi de oblationibus fidelium, de quibus episcopia et monasteria ac senodochia constant, regibus et his, qui in sublimitate rei publice sunt, honorem cum orationis instantia non sine traditione ecclesiastica exhibemus, ut quietam et tranquillam vitam cum pietate agamus.' Hinkmar von Reims, *Collectio de ecclesiis et capellis*, ed. M. Stratmann, MGH *Fontes iuris* XIV (Hanover, 1990), 108.

[193] (c. 10) '*Hospitalia peregrinorum, sicut sunt Scottorum et quae tempore antecessorum vestrorum* regum constructa et constituta *fuerunt*, ut ad hoc, ad quod deputata sunt, teneantur et a rectoribus deum timentibus ordinentur, custodiantur, ne dissipentur, obtinete. Sed et rectoribus monasteriorum et xenodochiorum, id est hospitalium, praecipite, ut sicut canonica docet auctoritas et capitula avi et patris vestri praecipiunt, episcopis propriis sint subiecti et monasteria atque hospitalia sibi commissa ipsorum regant consilio, quoniam, episcopi paternam sollicitudinem eis secundum ministerium illorum studebunt impendere.' MGH *Conc.* III. 418. Language from Meaux-Paris (c. 40) is marked by italics, that from Rome 826 (c. 23) with underlining.

Francia or Italy, including the papal canons, to stake such a clear claim for episcopal jurisdiction over xenodochia. It found no imitators and it was repeated neither by other councils nor in canonical collections.

Further afield, one other French injunction was issued, at Langres (859), a council of the provinces of Lyons and Vienne in Burgundy, a region under the young Charles of Provence, Lothar's son. It adapted its subject from Quierzy ('Ut hospitalia peregrinorum...'), enjoining the king to exercise fitting patronage and concern (*sollicitudo*) to more traditional ends: that pilgrim hospitals and hostels for other needy persons, once equipped by pious emperors for the health of their souls, be restored 'to those uses to which they were appointed through his predecessors' piety'. It reminded the king that 'those who cheat the poor of love, pilgrims of sustenance, and the dead of alms are called their murderers among the holy fathers'.[194] Rather fittingly, this final Frankish act reads like a compilation of 'greatest hits' from the great Carolingian proclamations on hospitals: *restaurare* (Italy, c.780 onwards), 'for those tasks for which they had been established' (Italy, c.790–850), *receptacula* (Aachen, 816/7), *sollicitudo* (Rome, 826), 'hospitals of pilgrims' (Quierzy, 858), and that he who defrauds the poor of their sustenance is a 'murderer of the poor' (Meaux-Paris 845/6). It reveals the variety of languages that have been developed to talk about hospitals, often in very different conversations. Yet, fundamentally, it reinforces how little had changed. The bishops were concerned but unable to act, except via the king. They offered a moral rebuke to the king whose *potestas* rested on his status as heir. They entreated him to ensure that the facilities be maintained as directed according to the instructions of the royal donors who had set them up. Law had learned to talk about welfare facilities, but it did not reshape them.

The picture of welfare that emerges across the early middle ages is most notable for its variety. This is because xenodochia belonged to the traditions of Christianity, but not to those of church law. Left out from the Chalcedonian charges, there was no diocesan claim through which synods might act and onto which Carolingian *correctio* and *emendatio* might have been grafted. Indeed, there was no established arena to address xenodochia. There was also no written inheritance: no canon or legal rhetoric that might provide a model or authority

---

[194]   (c. 14) 'Ut hospitalia peregrinorum videlicet et aliorum pro remedio animarum receptacula a piis imperatoribus, patrum scilicet vestrorum, in timore et amore dei preparata, ab omni usu et libitu humane temeritatis absoluta, in eos usus, quibus sunt constituta, pietatem praedecessorum vestrorum sequentes, sub patrocinio vestro dignum est vestro tempore et vestra sollicitudine restaurentur. Qui enim agapem pauperum et sustenationem peregrinorum et elemosinam defunctorum defraudant, apud sanctos patres eorum necatores vocantur.' MGH *Conc.* III. 479. The decrees of Langres have been preserved among those of the joint synod of Savonnières in June 859, which included forty bishops from provinces including Reims, Sens, Bourges, Lyons, and Vienne. Hartmann, *Synoden*, 257–9; P. R. McKeon, 'The Carolingian Councils of Savonnières (859) and Tusey (860)', *Revue Bénédictine*, 84 (1974).

for action or a language by which to act. Xenodochia had to be intruded onto a council's agenda and responses fashioned by participants.

It is important to remember that law in the ninth century was not a system. For our purposes, it might be more helpful to think of it as a metal workshop, which had its patterns of business and ways of working, as well as its patrons, master craftsmen, tools, and materials of choice.[195] Intruding welfare houses into this space was like bringing a wounded animal into the workshop: the sense of responsibility and desire to help was clear; yet, while the expertise could be adapted, the power to act was limited and the tools not suited to the task. The responses of councils were therefore ad hoc, heterogeneous, and local. In Italy Olona (825) used Mantua II (813) to develop means to address failing custodians, combining the moral voice of bishops with a diagnostic programme that was reinforced through the palace's judicial might; later Italian councils followed in its path. Rome (826) looked to a papal model, in Gregory the Great, to develop language of 'pious places' and so appeal to the *sollicitudo* of bishops. The bishops of Meaux-Paris (845/6) reworked the thunderous threats of Gallic councils, to exhort the emperor into action. In the different workshops, activity produced small acts that were unusual, even radical in their own way. Their very distinctiveness is evidence of widespread concern and of concerted attempts to protect vulnerable facilities.

And they share other common themes. If the act was immediate, the statement that was crafted looked backwards and forwards in time. It made an argument for how things should be, and so for the justice of the act, in terms that reached beyond one time and place. Each strove to extend or contrive means to restore hospitals to their original uses, by policing those who kept them. Over time, small questions grew larger and governmental conversations nurtured a culture of responsibility. Any enforcement rested fundamentally on the palace, although from the mid-820s councils turned increasingly to bishops, to act as local agents (Olona, 825) and have a duty of concern (Rome, 826). From *c*.845 this growing episcopal charge underpinned a new demand that kings act, by synods in West Francia, Burgundy, and Northern Italy, underpinning a series of bullish initiatives in the mid-ninth century.

Most remarkably, all embraced a consistent model of xenodochia. In practice many xenodochia may have been easily confused with monasteries or houses of canons, but not in law. Monasteries were a Chalcedonian charge, a community whose quality of life was the central issue: they were the object of *correctio* and *emendatio* and, during the ninth century, of campaigns that they submit to a rule. Xenodochium was a catch-all term for a place whose resources had been dedicated to tending humans in bodily need. Some were institutions, many were facilities,

---

[195] See the discussion on p. 107–8, and Pottage, 'Law After Anthropology'.

others were simply charitable charges placed on a property. Without a conceptual language in law, law-makers agreed on what xenodochia were: each was a gift by the faithful, which had been assigned for specific acts of human care. In a sense, a xenodochium was a pure product of law, for it was property attached to the directive of a dead person. But that is not how contemporaries saw it. When early medieval prelates and law-makers looked at these places they saw not the place itself, but its creator. Welfare houses did not merely perform charitable tasks, they embodied an act of human *caritas*, a moment when someone of means had surrendered their wealth to tend 'the least' of Matthew's gospel. In performing its charges, the xenodochium, in embodying its donor's act, was seeing those who were too often invisible, and tending to them. What mattered was not the identity of the donor, but the Christian determination in their act: their *dispositio*. A xenodochium's testamentary charge was also the ongoing witness to a Christian act and, in it, a testimonial of Christian community and salvation.

Even in their small statements, the councils enhance our picture of welfare in the early middle ages. The documents that survive from this period paint two very different pictures. The ecclesiastical archives of Francia, together with the councils of Orléans (549) and Aachen (816), offer a picture of few but substantial founda-tions in Francia, strongly ecclesiastical and perhaps easily confused with small monasteries. The civic and Roman law traditions of Italy preserve a more messy collection of charters, which has suggested, in turn, a more messy picture of many and minor, less enduring charities. The differences were no illusion: the power structures, authorities, and documentary practices of a region shaped welfare itself. Yet the councils pull us away from the landscape, and offer a wider lens through which to view Christian welfare. Their statements bear witness to the easy profusion of its charges, as well as its forms—the religious *hospitalia Scottorum*, consecrated houses, those with brothers or communities of priests, or attached to a monastery, facilities under a priest or a steward or the founder's heirs. If measured by their institutional arrangements, welfare seems chaotic. Yet, in the eyes of councils they were united as acts of welfare, as wealth given to be used for those without. Councils knew what these houses were, not from law but from what was enacted in their world, as relics of an act of human compassion and the ongoing agents in service of that *caritas*. To endure across regions and centuries, and the seismic disruptions of the period 'after Rome', it must have been funda-mental to the very expression of Christianity.

Even in the last decades when prelates reached to monastic models to protect Christian sites under threat, xenodochia retained their form. Quierzy (858) may have grouped xenodochia with monasteries in its exhortation that bishops attend to their preservation, but it followed a canon that monasteries (and only monas-teries) be run according to their religious rule.[196] Milan (863) authorized bishops

---

[196] MGH *Conc.* III. 418 (c. 9).

to intervene, not to uphold a Christian community or church, but to preserve a bequest, ensuring its suitable management and distribution 'according to the arrangement of its testator'.[197] Late decrees uphold the legal model for hospitals but soon turn away from law and towards the threat of divine punishment to craft protections in desperate times. A final decree saw King Wido of Italy (889–94) and a council of bishops in Pavia forbidding anyone to subject bishoprics, abbeys, xenodochia, nor any place dedicated to God, to violence or injury.[198] Councils fell away as Carolingian power waned, only to revive under the reform papacy in 1049. The seventy years to Lateran I (1123) have been described as 'the most active period of synods in the history of the papacy';[199] yet legislation on xenodochia did not revive with these church councils. It would be 1312 before another council would explicitly address welfare houses.

As the tide of Carolingian activity retreated, it left two objects on the beach: the Greek definitions of welfare institutions in Ansegis's *Collectio* and the canon of Eugenius II's council of Rome (826). This driftwood would be gathered up by canonists in the coming centuries and used to make whole new statements on welfare houses in law. We return now to the twelfth century, and to the start of the Charitable Revolution to look behind the councils of that era. For the early medieval picture provides an institutional and legal model, and a sense of messy endeavour behind the scenes, that offers a key to reading canon law in the later middle ages. There, too, yet in wholly different terms, we find that interest swirled around welfare houses and their status in the church.

---

[197] MGH *Conc.* IV. 161 (cc. 4–5), which follow (c. 3) that 'quae semel monasteria dedicata sunt, perpetuo maneant monasteria'.

[198] MGH *Cap.* II. 105 (c. 3). An end to the creation of capitularies draws a close to legislation on xenodochia, although it did not mean the end of assemblies, or the use of capitularies themselves (Nelson, 'Legislation and Consensus', 214; Patzold, 'Capitularies in the Ottonian Realm', 120–32). On this period of documentary silence, see C. Cubitt, 'Bishops and Councils in Late Saxon England: The Intersection of Secular and Ecclesiastical Law', in W. Hartmann, ed., *Recht und Gericht in Kirche und Welt um 900* (Munich, 2007).

[199] U.-R. Blumenthal, 'Conciliar Canons and Manuscripts', in P. Landau and J. Mueller, ed., *Proc. of the Ninth Int'l Congress on Medieval Canon Law* (Vatican City, 1997), 358, citing Paul Hinschius.

PART III
STALKING THE BORDERLANDS
(1100–1320)

7

Canonists and Commentators at the Edges of Canon Law (1100–1260)

When we left hospitals in the twelfth century, in Chapter 2, they were as places, not communities in law and the Lateran councils had responded carefully, not addressing them directly but talking around them to wider communities over which they had a conventional claim: self-proclaimed nuns (Lateran II) and the Christian faithful, especially clerics (Laterans III and IV). We return now to the high middle ages with a new backstory and, with it, a new toolkit. Gone are frameworks based on Justinian's Code and Novels, or even an episcopal claim via the formula 'murderers of the poor', replaced now by a vast array of small, diverse acts outside the canon. These odd remnants looked disappointing to a canonist of the twelfth century, just as they would to modern historians; yet, as the only relics in law, several found an afterlife in the new collections and commentaries. We have, too, a different definition of the hospital in law, as a Christian creation that had not been claimed as ecclesistical. As testamentary creations, the right of a welfare house to exist was underpinned by the right of the faithful to make a disposition (*dispositio*) of their property to Christian ends for their soul. Over time this had yielded a wide variety *ptochia*, *xenodochia*, *hospitales*, *receptacula*, and *mensae*, versatile yet vulnerable creations that had, by 1100, populated the cities, streets, and mountain passes of Western Europe for 700 years. In the West, welfare was a Christian practice, promoted by bishops, kings, and monasticism, but it was in the hands, too, of the people. A new era brought new experiments and challenges.

In the long twelfth century, three revolutions would interact to reimagine welfare: the quest for a *vita apostolica*, which cultivated new forms of religious life from *c.*1100; the intensification of the study and collection of canon law from the early twelfth century; and the so-called charitable revolution, which intensified at the end of the twelfth century to produce a profusion of foundations. We know a great deal of the charitable revolution and of its intersection with the *vita apostolica*, which in the twelfth century spawned the military and other, local hospitaller orders, the congregations of *regulares*. The focus of this chapter is on the comparatively unmapped interaction between local welfare and classical canon law: on 'xenodochia', the term in law for the descendants of testamentary foundations; what the scholarly priory of Northampton had defined in 1200 as a form that, in its very definition, was neither a church nor college of monks,

On Hospitals: Welfare, Law, and Christianity in Western Europe, 400–1320. Sethina Watson,
Oxford University Press (2020). © Sethina Watson.
DOI: 10.1093/oso/9780198847533.001.0001

canons, templars, hospitallers, or nuns.[1] Part III places the Northampton definition in its scholarly context, by looking behind the Lateran councils to a wider,
messier conversation about Christian life.

This chapter tackles the canonists and the discursive (and, eventually administrative) edifice they built during the classical period of canon law. At the centre
of the development of law, in theory and practice, was the papal curia, although
the activity itself was defined more by locality and the variety of its demands and
initiatives.[2] Out of this activity emerged a wide and relatively cohesive body of
canon law in authoritative collections, even if the path of creation was neither
straightforward nor direct. Consolidated efforts began in the later eleventh century, as canonists gathered biblical, patristic, conciliar, and papal rulings into
collections that aimed to define basic principles of church law, an endeavour that
culminated in Gratian's *Decretum*, or *Concordance of Discordant Canons* (*c.*1145).
As the twelfth century progressed, decretals (papal letters) played an increasingly
significant role. Papal letters had always been used to define law, but from the
pontificate of Paschal II (1099–1118) onwards, as the flurry of business steadily
grew, the papal curia relied more heavily upon these letters to formulate and
communicate legal decisions.[3] They were being circulated and, soon, extracted
and gathered into systematic collections, an endeavour which, in turn, culminated
in Gregory IX's *Decretales* (1234), also known as the *Liber extra*. Commentaries
that interpreted canonical and decretal collections circulated with the collections
as glosses, or separately as *summae*; a gloss that was recognized as authoritative
was known as the *glossa ordinaria*. Underpinning this activity was not only the
expanding reach of the papacy and local demand for legal clarity, but the rise of
the schools, especially the universities at Bologna, then Paris and Oxford. They
brought scholastic approaches to the formulation of canon law, which was
stimulated in turn by study of Justinian's Code, Institutes, Digest, and Novels
(now known collectively as the *Corpus Iuris Civilis*).[4] This was a period marked by
legal curiosity and a desire to clarify and define.

---

[1] See Chapter 1, p. 25.

[2] For introductions, Clarke, *Interdict*, 4–12; J. T. Gilchrist, *Canon Law in the Age of Reform*
(Farnham, 1993); K. G. Cushing, *Reform and the Papacy in the Eleventh Century* (Manchester,
2005); and, more widely, L. Melve, 'Ecclesiastical Reform', *History Compass* 135 (2015).

[3] U.-R. Blumenthal, 'Conciliar Canons and Manuscripts', in *Proc. of the Ninth Int'l Congress of
Medieval Canon Law* (Vatican City, 1997), 373–9. The False Decretals of Benedict Levita had been
deployed with new zeal in the late eleventh century, F. Delivré, 'The Foundations of Primatial Claims',
JEC 59 (2008). Jasper and Fuhrmann, *PLEMA*, explore earlier practice.

[4] On the schools, J. A. Brundage, 'Teaching Canon Law', in J. Van Engen, ed., *Learning
Institutionalized* (Notre Dame, IN, 2000); P. Landau, 'The Origins of Legal Science', in M. Brett and
K. G. Cushing, eds, *Readers, Texts and Compilers* (Farnham, 2009). On the emergence of Roman law:
S. Kuttner, 'The Revival of Jurisprudence', in R. L. Benson, G. Constable, and C. D. Lanham, eds,
Renaissance and Renewal (Toronto, 1991), 299–323; K. Pennington, 'Roman Law at the Papal Curia', in
U.-R. Blumenthal et al., eds, *Canon Law, Religion and Politics* (Washington, DC, 2012); and the essays
in *HMCL*. On its rediscovery: *CICMA*; U.-R. Blumenthal, 'The *Collectio Canonum Caesaraugustana*',
in Blumenthal et al., eds, *Canon Law, Religion and Politics*.

The body of law grew exponentially from c.1150, and so did its subjects; yet even here, xenodochia comprised an odd class of their own. They were a non-topic, without a title (*De xenodochia*, 'on the subject of hospitals') or place for discussion until the thirteenth century. Early commentators said little on the subject; later commentators repeated the same contradictory refrains that confused rather than clarified the place of welfare foundations in the church. Its disappointing harvest prompted Brian Tierney to skip the subject, lamenting that 'commentaries [on hospitals] are not so interesting for the student of poor law principles as might have been expected'.[5] Yet, reading around the edges, in this world of manuscript and scholarly exchange, we find a largely underground conversation about hospitals. Among its fragmented and contradictory comments this chapter identifies, for the first time, the legal efforts of canonists to make a place for hospitals, and the legal origins of the two contradictory principles: that anyone could make a hospital, without the bishop; and that hospitals were religious houses, subject to the bishop. It also sketches the development of legal protections and jurisdictional ideals, which would begin to reshape welfare from 1186.

Before and After Gratian

If the early medieval story of hospitals has looked to Francia, the high medieval definition has tended to begin (or end) with Gratian. His name has been taken in vain (by Imbert), his *Decretum* and its commentators said to have consolidated the hospital form according to Justinianic law and, more recently, to have ignored hospitals entirely, as uncontroversially ecclesiastical.[6] The Justinianic model for hospitals in the West can no longer stand, yet Justinianic law cannot be simply dismissed in this period. For Gratian was writing at Bologna, where scholars had been discovering Justinian's *Corpus Iuris Civilis*; indeed Anders Winroth has revealed that the *Decretum* itself was composed in two recensions, Gratian I (c.1140) and Gratian II (c.1145), the latter largely to accommodate the new findings from Roman law.[7] Roman law is once again at the centre of the study of

---

[5] Tierney treated hospitals only briefly, via the commentary of Lapo da Castiglionchio (d. 1381), in Tierney, *Medieval Poor Law*, 85–7, with quotation at p. 87). B. Tierney, 'The Decretists and the "Deserving Poor"', *Comparative Studies in Society and History* 1:4 (1959), 362–70, examined the grounds on which an almsgiver should discriminate between recipients. Focused on D.42 c.1–3, especially its line *In hospitalitate autem non est habendus delectus personarum*, the canonical discussion addressed individual not institutional charity.

[6] HDC 55; Caron, '*Pia fundatio*', 137–59; Merzbacher, 'Das Spital', 84–5; Drossbach, 'Das Hospital', 513. Any simplistic notions that Gratian marked a watershed in the development of canon law are laid to rest by the essays in Rolker, ed., *New Discourses*, especially those of Wei, Dusil, and Summerlin.

[7] A. Winroth, *The Making of Gratian's Decretum* (Cambridge, 2000), 140, 142, 175–96; A. A. Larson, 'Early Stages of Gratian's *Decretum*', BMCL 27 (2007). Its study had been growing since the late eleventh century, Pennington, 'Roman Law at the Papal Curia'.

Gratian, posing a new question for understanding hospitals in this text, in its reception, and in the Western canonical tradition.

The *Decretum* and Early Collections (*c*.1000–*c*.1150)

Only seven chapters in the *Decretum* contain references to *xenodochia, ptochia,* or other (Greek) charities.[8] All are early references, two of them Byzantine, the other five from the early church: two each from the council of Chalcedon (451) and the letters of Gregory the Great (d. 604), one from a letter of Jerome to Pope Damasus (d. 384). Each one is an incidental reference to welfare houses, in a chapter and argument that pursues other matters, such as alms from profits of simony, clerics granting tithes, or heads of religious houses taking up a post elsewhere. The most elaborate references are in the two Byzantine texts. One, on simony, quotes Patriarch Tarasius (787) that whoever used money to procure their position as manager or head of a monastery, churches, religious house, or *ierocomiorum, seniorum,* or *orphantrophiorum,* should be removed from that post.[9] The *causa* (case) addressed recanting heretics, and this *questio,* whether a former heretic might be made a bishop; the welfare houses are fortuitous mentions. Indeed, their names have been muddled, from *gerontocomia* and *xenones,* probably because they were unrecognised by a Western scribe. These were debris, washed in among more relevant examples. The same is true of the final excerpt, this one from Justinian's Code, and an insertion in Gratian's second recension.[10] It cited Cod. 1.2.22 that gifts of property 'to venerable churches or *xenones,* monasteries, or *ptochotrophia,* or *brephotrophia,* or *orphanotrophia,* or *gerontocomia*' were not to be taxed (C.23 q.8 c.23).[11] This was from Justinian's privilege of 529 that had distinguished between ecclesiastical sites and 'other houses that have been deputed to pious consortia', as two categories of foundation that warranted protection. It might have been a useful selection to establish, at least, that the possessions of welfare houses should be protected, but it was never used that way by later

---

[8] The decrees are C.1 q.1 c.27, C.1 q.7 c.2, C.16 q.1 c.39, C.16 q.1 c.68, C.18 q.2 c.10, C.21 q.2 c.3, C.23 q.8 c.23. T. Reuter and G. Silagi, eds, *Wortkonkordanz zum Decretum Gratiani,* 5 vols (Munich, 1990), 463, 3234, 3868, 4959.

[9] C.1 q.7 c.2 §5: 'Quicumque per pecuniam, dispensationem uel curam sortiti sunt monasteriorum uel ecclesiarum, uel religiosarum domorum, ierocomiorum, seniorum, orphanotrophiorum, cum depositione expellantur a dispensatione illa et cura.'

[10] The later additions are C.16 q.1 c.39, C.18 q.2 c.10, C.23 q.8 c.23. Winroth, *Gratian's Decretum,* 1–18, 204–27. Caron, '*Pia fundatio*', 142–7, made use of C.18 q.2 c.10 and C.16 q.1 c.68.

[11] 'Inperator Iustinianus: §2 Sanccimus res ad uenerabiles ecclesias, uel xenones, monasteria, uel ptochotrophia, uel brephotrophia, uel orphanotrophia, uel gerontocomia, uel si quid tale aliud consortium descendentes ex qualicumque curiali liberalitate, siue inter uiuos, siue mortis causa, siue in ultimis uoluntatibus habita, lucratiuorum inscriptionibus liberas esse et immunes; lege scilicet, que super huius modi inscriptionibus posita est, in aliis quidem personis suum robur obtinente, in parte autem ecclesiastica, uel aliarum domuum, que his piis consortiis deputatae sunt, suum uigorem pietatis intuitu mitigante.'

canonists, perhaps in part because it did not include *xenodochia*, the recognized Latin term. Nor did they attract Gratian's attention. He included the extract in his well-known *causa* on the principle of just war.[12] The list was part of a longer comment, itself on the question as to whether a bishop or any cleric might raise arms. The *Decretum* provides no evidence that Gratian or the scholars around him were thinking about welfare houses, even when they turned to the *Corpus Iuris Civilis*. Indeed, the confusion of terms suggests they may not have recognized much of what they found.

The *Decretum* accorded welfare houses neither a place in law nor recognition as contemporary institutions. They were not the subject of any *causa*, question, or chapter. In contrast, monasteries were the subject of *Causae* 16–20. While the list of references to monks and monasteries in the *Wortkonkordanz* runs to sixteen pages, there are none to *hospitales* or *domus leprosorum*.[13] Nor, as we shall see, did decretists see welfare institutions as a matter raised by the *Decretum*. When glossators mentioned hospitals, which they did sporadically, their notes found no natural (or consistent) home in Gratian's collection, although the five Greek terms in the 'just war' chapter presented an obvious initial attraction.

Gratian's lack of interest in xenodochia was no break from the past. The previous century had seen 'a vast undergrowth of canonical interest' in ecclesiastical law, which produced many, varied, and local canonical collections.[14] In these collections, too, xenodochia had failed to attract notice. Most, like the *Collection in 74 Titles* (*c*.1076) and that of Bonizo of Sutri (d. *c*.1095) contained no extracts that mentioned xenodochia. It was not because such facilities were unknown to these authors. Bishop Bonizo's prologue to book 8 included 'building xenodochia' among several Christian acts to which merchants were neither permitted nor forbidden to apply their profits.[15] The facilities existed, and their Christian activity was encouraged, but the law remained silent.

---

[12] The *causa* and the topic has a long history of study: R. W. Cox, 'Gratian', in D. R. Brunstetter and C. O'Driscoll, eds, *Just War Thinkers* (Abingdon, 2018).

[13] *Wortkonkordanz*, 2836–51, 2143, 2553–4.

[14] Martin Brett characterized this local demand for jurisprudence, 'diverse and untidy', as the driving engine for the growth of ecclesiastical law: M. Brett, 'Canon Law and Litigation', in M. J. Franklin and C. Harper-Bill, eds, *Medieval Ecclesiastical Studies* (Woodbridge, 1995), with quotations at 33, 39–40; G. Austin, 'Bishops and Religious Law', in J. S. Ott and A. Trumbore Jones, eds, *The Bishop Reformed* (Aldershot, 2007). For the individual and highly selective nature of canonical collections pre-Gratian, see Blumenthal, 'Conciliar Canons'; and for the array of material, C. Rolker, *Canon Law and the Letters of Ivo of Chartres* (Cambridge, 2010), 50–88.

[15] '...elemosinas exinde facere et scenodochia edificare et ecclesias fabricare et sarta tecta reficere', Bonizo, *Liber de Vita*, 252. *Diuersorum patrum sententie siue Collectio in LXXIV titulos digesta*, ed. J. T. Gilchrist (Vatican City, 1973). We glimpse welfare houses much earlier, when Abbot Regio of Prüm (d. 915) used an extract from the council of Chalcedon, that priests in charge of *ptochiorum* or officiating in monasteries and basilicas obey the bishop. In titling his chapter (1.255) DE CLERICIS QUI PRAEFICIUNTUR PTOCHIIS, the abbot took phrasing from Chalcedon to make a decree that prioritized the *ptochia*, or houses for the poor (Regino of Prüm, *Libri duo de synodalibus causis et disciplinis ecclesiasticis*, ed. F. G. A. Wasserschleben (Leipzig, 1840; repr. Graz, 1964), 122). Regio's example was not followed by later canonists. Polycarpus included the same canon without the title, transforming it

Only Anselm of Lucca's *Collectio canonica* (*c.*1086) stands apart, offering a glimpse of a path not taken. His book 5, on the ordination and law of churches, presented three chapters whose content or titles mentioned xenodochia. Together they constitute an early attempt to recognize welfare houses in law.[16] One (c. 53) recasts the final clause from the confirmation by the council of Orléans in 549 of the royal xenodochium at Lyons. Anselm used only its ending, the threat of anathema, which he edited to create a more general decree. A compiler, close to the Pseudo-Isidorians, had done a similar thing at Meaux-Paris (845/6). Anselm selected the same clause and for the same reason, that it was for a xenodochium, but his edits were different. Anselm's clause now threatened with excommunication as a murderer of the poor any who took the customary dues or inheritance of *xenodochia* (*pl.*) *or churches.*[17] In contrast to the original, which had defended a specific house and against its bishop, Anselm was asserting ecclesiastical protection over hospitals and churches generally and so, ironically, diocesan responsibility over such places. A second chapter (c. 58) used a report of an edict of Justinian, as provided in Anastasius Bibliothecarius's ninth-century *Chronographia tripartita*, which Anselm now deployed to speak to the concerns of contemporary reformers. He gave it the title, 'that bishops or *oeconomi* or the heads of orphanages or xenodochia should have nothing by inheritance unless they acquired it *before their ordination*', transforming a ruling about property managers into a distinction of the priestly office.[18] The third (c. 28) cited Gregory the Great's letter against simoniacs, selecting its sentences on alms and omitting the pope's more pointed condemnations of simoniacal

---

into a decree about episcopal authority: *Polycarpus* (4.35.17), cited from *Die Sammlung 'Policarpus'*, ed. C. Erdmann, U. Horst, and H. Fuhrmann, MGH, accessed Aug. 2019, <http://www.mgh.de/datenbanken/leges/kanonessammlung-polycarp/>.

[16] They are titled: (c. 28) QUOD MONASTERIA VEL XENODOCHIA, QUAE EX PECUNIA PRO SACRIS ORDINIBUS DATA CONSTRUUNTUR, MERCEDI NON PROFICIUNT SED NOCENT; (c. 53) SI QUIS ECCLESIARUM [VEL] XENODOCHIORUM FACULTATES ABSTULERIT, UT NECATOR PAUPERUM EXCOMMUNICETUR; (c. 58) UT EPISCOPI VEL OECONOMI VEL ORPHANOTROPHI VEL XENODOCHI NICHIL HEREDITARIE POSSIDEANT NISI QUOD ANTE ORDINATIONIS HORAM POSSEDERUNT, cited here from *Anselmi episcopi Lucensis Collectio canonum*, ed. F. Thaner (Innsbruck, 1906–15; repr. 1965), 242, 252, 256. The major study of Anselm's work is K. G. Cushing, *Papacy and Law in the Gregorian Revolution* (Oxford, 1998). I am grateful to Dr Cushing for checking these transcriptions against key manuscripts.

[17] '[Quod] si quis quolibet tempore, cuiuslibet potestatis aut ordinis persona, [contra hanc constitutionem nostram venire timptaverit aut] aliquid de consuetudine vel facultate [e]xenodochi[i]*orum vel ecclesiarum* [ipsius] abstulerit, [ut exenodotium,] quod avertat Deus, [esse desinat,] ut necator pauperum i[n]revocabili anathemate feriatur.' Author's italics mark Anselm's additions, square brackets language that he removed from the original (MGH *Conc.* I. 105, c. 15).

[18] Author's italics, to indicate Anselm's redirection of the extract, which spoke of *promovere*, meaning promotion to the position of steward, and made no mention of priestly office. The officers were those responsible for managing goods. Anastasius' source was the chronicle of Theophanes (d. 817/8), both ed. in Theophanes, *Chronographia*, ed. C. de Boor, 2 vols (Leipzig, 1885), II. 133. Justinian's edict distinguished private property, which may be bequeathed, from goods acquired after appointment, which must be used for the church or other pious causes (Nov. 131.13; Cod. 1.3.41.11).

heresy.[19] Anselm provided a title, from the text, that made monasteries and xenodochia the subject, underscoring that those built from money given for holy orders might not merit reward for the giver. Anselm's creative use of authorities has long been recognized.[20] It is difficult not to see, in his deliberate manipulations of these texts, a thoughtful attempt to insert hospitals into ecclesiastical law.

Anselm's chapters constitute the only early gathering of canonical extracts to engage with xenodochia. Much of his work passed directly into Gratian's *Decretum*, but not these chapters. Gratian did employ Gregory's letter, but not for Anselm's purposes and not from Anselm, since Gratian's edition used fewer clauses on alms and more on the sin of simony (the letter's more common use). Under the title 'Alms cannot be performed from money acquired symoniacly', the hospitals were once more incidental.[21] In contrast, Anselm had made the places (not the simony) explicit. Here was a canonist who wrestled with the problem of hospitals and may even have offered an embryonic answer. His *Collectio*, at least, made xenodochia visible; it may also have taken cautious steps to recognize xenodochia alongside churches and monasteries. If so, the effort did not bear fruit.

Like Gratian's *Decretum*, other early collections contain only incidental references to xenodochia, a number from Gregory the Great. The simony letter was employed in Cardinal Gregory of San Grisogono's *Polycarpus* (*c.*1109×13), to stress Gregory's original proposition that wealth acquired simoniacally could not redeem a culprit if given in alms. This letter is also the only reference to welfare houses in Alger of Liège's (d. 1131/2) *Liber de misericordia et iustitia*, where it appears at 3.44, 'That even alms cannot be made from the wages of simony'.[22] The *Polycarpus* and Cardinal Deusdedit's *Collectio Canonum* (1087) extract from a long letter of Gregory VII who cites his namesake in defence of his own actions. If his predecessor 'has laid down that kings who broke his decree over a single hospital were not only deposed but also excommunicated...who may take us to task for having deposed and excommunicated Henry'?[23] The 'single hospital' is a reference taken from Gregory the Great and used here to signal

---

[19] *Greg. Epp.* 9.219 (JE 1747 (1263)).

[20] His has been characterized as sloppy, his use of Roman law 'casual, with little real understanding': *CICMA* 105. The material for xenodochia suggests a more deliberate approach, supporting Cushing's argument that 'with his rubrics, his omissions and his excerpts, [Anselm] could also most effectively distort and transform those sacred authorities', Cushing, *Papacy and Law*, 102.

[21] C.1 q.1 c.27: 'NON POTEST FIERI ELEMOSINA EX PECUNIA SYMONIACE ADQUISITA... §1. *Unde etiam certum est, quia etsi monasteria uel xenodochia, uel quid aliud ex pecunia, que pro sacris ordinibus datur, construantur, non proficit mercedi.*'

[22] 'QUOD NON POSSIT ETIAM ELEEMOSYNA FIERI EX PRETIO SIMONIAE'. Alger of Liège, *Liber de misericordia*, PL 180, col. 952. *Polycarpus* (2.1.28) cites Gregory's letter more fully.

[23] 'Quodsi beatus Gregorius, doctor utique mitissimus, reges, qui statuta sua super unum xenodochium violarent, non modo deponi, sed etiam excommunicari...quis nos H.... deposuisse et excommunicasse reprehendat, nisi forte similis eius?' 8.21, from *Das Register Gregors VII*, ed. E. Caspar, 2 vols (Berlin, 1920–3); *Polycarpus* 1.20.11; Deusdedit 4.184, from *Die Kanonessammlung des Kardinals Deusdedit*, ed. V. W. von Glanvell (Paderborn, 1905). For Deusdedit's activity, and distinctive

meagreness, for it represented to Gregory VII the tiniest of prompts for papal punishment of a king. For Gregory VII, defending his most controversial action, the question of hospitals could not have been further from his mind.

Deusdedit and *Polycarpus* also preserve incidental references in Justinian's legislation, from a law that extended the statute of limitation for legal actions to defend church property. At one point (3.176), Deusdedit made a small adjustment, replacing the Greek list of charities with the phrase *et aliis piis locis* after 'venerable churches and monasteries and xenodochia'.[24] It marks a notable departure from the Julian phrase, *venerabiles loci*, which was widely employed through the late eleventh and twelfth centuries. Instead, Deusdedit adopted the term from Eugenius II's Roman council (826), whose decrees he had consulted for his *Collectio*.[25] Curiously, these new, if fleeting, references to Justinian's legislation did not develop as the twelfth century progressed. Even as the schools embraced Roman law with mounting enthusiasm, discussions of xenodochia ignored relevent laws in the Code and Novels. In fact, it was Deusdedit's editorial intervention, using Eugenius's council, that presaged the efforts, a century later, finally to address hospitals in canon law.

Another early experiment was not to survive the eleventh century. The *Decretum* of Burchard of Worms (1012×1022) included a chapter under the title 'On the administration of xenodochia and tithes'. The excerpt was copied from an early medieval penitential and placed in Burchard's book 19, *On penance*; it required three years of penance and full repayment by any who had taken the income of xenodochia of the poor or the tithes of the people for his own gain.[26] The excerpt targeted the sin (of mismanagement) and appeared in Burchard's collection between two other sins: of men who bathe with women and women who attend church while menstruating. Ivo of Chartres copied Burchard's penitential decree, among the same material, into book 15 (on penance) of his

---

ecclesiology: D. B. Zema, 'Economic Reorganization of the Roman See', *Studi Gregoriani* 1 (1947), 145–6; W. L. North, 'The Curious Case of Bruno of Segni', *Haskins Society Journal* 10 (2001), 116–17.

[24] Nov. 111.1 reads 'nunc venerabilibus ecclesiis et monasteriis et xenonibus nec non orphanotrophiis ac brephotrophiis et ptochiis quadraginta annorum protelatio conferatur'. Other citations list the types of welfare houses: Deusdedit 3.173, 4.285; *Polycarpus* 3.12.37.

[25] Deusdedit used seven decrees from Rome (826), including two that refer to *pii loci* (cc. 16, 26), although not c. 23 on *xenodochia*: 1.148, 151; 2.63; 3.19, 51–2, 179.

[26] (19.139) 'DE ADMINISTRATIONE XENODOCHIAE, ET DECIMAE. Si quis xenodochias pauperum administrat, vel decimas populi susceperit, et si quis exinde vel suis saecularibus lucris sectandum aliquid subtraxerit, quasi rerum alienarum invasor: reus damnum restituat, et sub canonico judicio reformetur, et agat poenitentiam tribus annis. Scriptum est enim: Talem dispensatorem Dominus quaerit, qui sibi de suis nihil usurpet.' Burchard of Worms, *Decretum Libri XX, PL* 140, col. 1010. It is the last of five prescriptions from the *Paenitentiale Hubertense* and occurs, too, in the 'Liber Poenitentialis' of Theodore of Canterbury: H. Hoffmann and R. Pokorny, *Das Dekret des Bischofs Burchard von Worms* (Munich, 1991), 238; *Ancient Laws and Institutes*, ed. B. Thorpe, I (London, 1840), 316.

Decretum (after 1095).[27] Thereafter, this penitential tradition disappeared. It is noteworthy here for the early glimpse it offers of xenodochia, among sins of the faithful, and partnered with the stewardship of tithes, as income to be applied to its (Christian) use.

There was one practice in these early collections that would endure; indeed, it would become the only way to mention hospitals for much of the twelfth century. Ivo's *Decretum* included two other references to welfare houses, both of them excerpts from Julian's chapter, (II. 29) in Ansegis's *Collectio* of 827. In book 3, on churches and ecclesiastical things, Ivo copied the chapter's first half, an injunction not to alienate goods that had been given to a church, a monastery, or the six charities. Its final three-quarters, prohibiting priests or stewards from alienating a house's goods, constitutes the very last chapter of Ivo's final book (17), on the *speculativa* of the holy fathers on faith, charity, and hope.[28] This second excerpt includes Julian's definitions of the six Greek charities, an odd inclusion since the terms occur not in the second excerpt but in the first part of Julian's chapter, fourteen books earlier in Ivo's *Decretum*. The excerpt hangs oddly at the end of his *Decretum*, as though Ivo intended something more but failed to follow through.

There are signs of a changing world in Ivo's writing, spurred by the early signs of the new wave of charitable foundation that would define the coming centuries. The canonist's silence did not stem from ignorance of the topic, for Ivo was an active promoter of hospitals. As bishop of Chartres, he created a rule for the leper-house of Grand Beaulieu at Chartres, which claimed him as founder.[29] He also issued a charter of protection for the leper-house of nearby Châteaudun, which suggests he was thinking about the status of such places in the church. The charter affirmed the Christian impulses behind endowment and the responsibility of churchmen to maintain such houses, laying down an argued case that:

> Since what was wont to be given to *xenodochiis, ptocotrophiis* and *other religious houses* by the devotion of the faithful, for the redemption of their souls and for the maintenance of those who dwell there, must no longer be reckoned as the things of man, because they belong to God; it is fitting that rectors of churches receive [these gifts] as divine patrimony for the protection of the church and, with the sword of the spirit thrust forth, not shrink from striking their usurpers and dissipators with canonical severity as despisors of God. [The bishop and the

---

[27] Ivo of Chartres, *Decretum* 15.149, cited from Martin Brett's edition at <https://ivo-of-chartres.github.io/decretum.html> (Sept. 2015).

[28] Ivo of Chartres, *Decretum* 3.183; 17.137. On Burchard, Ivo, and the reformers, see Rolker, *Ivo of Chartres*, 60–88, 107–12; G. Austin, *Shaping Church Law around the Year 1000* (Farnham, 2009); and Austin, 'Authority and the Canons in Burchard's *Decretum* and Ivo's *Decretum*', in Brett and Cushing, eds, *Readers, Texts and Compilers*.

[29] S. C. Mesmin, 'Waleran, Count of Meulan and the Leper Hospital', *Annales de Normandie* 32:1 (1982), 8–10; F.-O. Touati, 'Les groupes de laïcs dans les hôpitaux et les léproseries', in *Les Mouvances laïques* (Saint-Étienne, 1996), 142 n; Touati, *Maladie et société*, 258–9, 660–1; and see now his *Yves de Chartres (1040–1115)* (Paris, 2017), 22, 57–68.

church of Chartres then take the *ptocotrophium* in Châteaudun] into their guardianship, denouncing their usurpers and dissipators, to be dreadfully condemned before the heavenly tribunal as Judas.[30]

In one sense, Ivo's statement is familiar, since it draws from a long tradition to defend church property. Readily apparent is the excoriating language of sixth- and ninth-century Frankish councils, embraced especially by the Pseudo-Isidorians, of usurpers (*pervasores*) and dissipators (*distractores*), in the model of Judas, which Ivo also used to justify anathema, that 'heavenly sword wielded by priests'.[31] But Ivo added something of his own. He distinguished the spiritual from the temporal: refashioning 'patrimony of the poor' so that what was once 'property of mankind' (*in humanis rebus*) is now 'divine patrimony', defended by a spiritual sword. The terms echo Justinian's classification of charities as divine (*res divinas*) rather than human property (*res humanas*) (Cod. 1.2.22), although Ivo inserts them into a more classically Western framework: Julianus Pomerius's definition of church property as 'the offerings of the faithful, the penitential payments of sinners, and the patrimony of the poor'.[32] Ivo's charter claims welfare houses among this divine order, notably as houses not communities, putting them alongside 'other religious houses' with the exhortation that rectors of churches defend them as divine inheritance. Ivo was also self-consciously importing Greek terminology from his law books, deploying *xenodochia* and *ptochodochia* to suggest a formal classification of such houses as belonging to the church (his appropriation of the latter to refer to leper-houses was to be more widely embraced).[33] In Ivo's charter, it was not simply this house at Châteaudun that belonged to God, but any welfare house.

---

[30] 'Cum ea quae xenodochiis, ptocotrophiis vel aliis religiosis domibus devotio fidelium pro redemptione animarum suarum dare consuevit, ad sustentationem eorum qui ibi commorantur, non jam in humanis rebus computanda sunt, quia Dei sunt, oportet rectores Ecclesiarum ut ea tanquam divina patrimonia in defensionem Ecclesiae suscipiant, et exerto gladio spiritus pervasores eorum et distractores tanquam Dei contemptores canonica severitate ferire non differant...in tuitionem sanctae Carnotensis ecclesiae et nostram paterne suscipimus, et pervasores eorum atque distractores ante tribunal aeterni Judicis terribiliter condemnandos esse denuntiamus'. Ivo of Chartres, *Epistula* 282, *PL* 162, col. 282. See, too, letters 192 and 283 to monastic communities, *PL* 162, cols 200, 283.

[31] '...a sacerdotibus *caelesti gladio feriatur*' deployed by Tours (567), c. 25, and refashioned by Benedict Levita (2.428), who added 'by priests': MGH *Conc.* I. 134; CCSL 148A. 192–3.

[32] Julianus Pomerius, *De vita contemplativa* 2.9 (*PL* 59, col. 454), see my Chapter 3, n. 41. Later iterations, conserving the gifts of the faithful against those who would tear them asunder (*distrahere*) can be found at Paris (829) and Aachen (836), MGH *Conc.* II.ii, 624 (c. 17), 718–19 (c. 48). Ivo took an early interest in Roman law, Rolker, *Ivo of Chartres*, 108, 178.

[33] The pairing of *xenodochia* and *ptochotrophia* seems to have been used by Ivo to mean hospitals for pilgrims and leper-houses (indeed, the charter calls the leper-house at Châteaudun *ptocotrophium*). This may have been a misunderstanding of *ptochotrophia*, which was used in Byzantium for paupers, or perhaps Ivo was appropriating the idea of *pauperes* for those with leprosy. The paired terms were used by others, e.g. in referring to Lanfranc's twin foundations at Canterbury ('Xenodochia vel prothrophia duo extra civitatem aedificavit', Robert de Torigni, *Chronique*, ed. L. Delisle, 2 vols (Rouen, 1872), I. 73; *Chron. Maj.* II. 29, where they are 'xenodochia vel ptochotrophia'; in both cases a neuter plural has become a feminine singular). It was common to call early twelfth-century leper houses *domus pauperum*.

There was a contrast between bishop and canonist. As bishop, Ivo promoted local hospitals and developed mechanisms to defend and regulate them. The opening statement of his charter suggests that the bishop was thinking in more universal terms, for it articulates a broader conviction that welfare houses should belong to the church and to prelates as their rectors, a conviction that fuelled Ivo's own work. And in this charter the bishop was laying out such a claim, playing with several legal traditions to craft a contemporary argument. Yet this effort was not given voice in his legal works.[34] Ivo the canonist staked no explicit claim for welfare houses in his collections and drew no decree from earlier councils. Only Julian's antiquated list, inserted into the book in the *Decretum* on churches and ecclesiastial things, and appended awkwardly at the end of its final book, hints at Ivo's interest. The latter acknowledged such houses, and the responsibility of priests to guard their goods, but did so obliquely, by linking the Greek definitions at its base to Ivo's title, 'On property pertaining to a venerable place, that it not be alienated'.[35] Julian's chapter was skilfully abridged but it could not say what Ivo wanted it to, and what his Châteaudun charter had argued. Here, in the canonical tradition, Julian's didactic typology seems to act as a legal place-holder. It marked a spot for facilities without law and without a place in law: as places not communities, whose goods like 'other religious houses' must be properly managed as God's own (states the bishop, if not the canonist).[36]

The Decretists, *c*.1150–*c*.1200

A similar canonistic caution can be observed in the early glosses to Gratian. In the mid-twelfth century, as numbers of actual hospitals and leper-houses rose, decretists remained oddly silent on the subject. Rolandus made no reference in his *Summa* (1150s–1160s), while Stephen of Tournai (*c*.1166) mentioned xenodochia only once, in passing, among a list of immobile ecclesiastical possessions that, if

---

[34] For Ivo's body of work, see Rolker, *Ivo of Chartres*, whose ch. 7 casts particular doubt on Ivo's authorship of the *Panormia*. Ivo's silence as to hospitals contrasts with his careful reflection on ideals of *caritas*, L.-A. Dannenberg, 'Charity and Law: The Juristic Implementation of a Core Monastic Principle', in G. Melville, ed., *Aspects of Charity* (Berlin, 2011), 18–20.

[35] 'DE REBUS AD VENERABILEM LOCUM PERTINENTIBUS NON ALIENANDIS.' Ivo of Chartres, *Decretum* 17.137. By starting mid-way through Julian's chapter (Const. VII, kp. 32 from 'omnes omnino sacerdotes . . '), Ivo's version removed the churches, monasteries, and nuns in the opening portion. It also stressed priestly responsibility for *rem loci venerabilis*, the latter now defined only via the Greek definitions.

[36] Innocent II may have used Ivo's chapter in a protection for a hospital at Tournai. In a change from his previous protections, which had been addressed to a bishop or abbot who held the facility, this was 'Gerardo administratori hospitalis domus' and his successor, 'statuentes ut quascunque possessiones, quaecunque bona idem venerabilis locus inpraesentiarum legitime possidet . . . firma tibi tuisque successoribus et illibata permaneant.' PL 179, col. 442.

consecrated, must not be directed by the laity.[37] Those who did notice hospitals limited their comments to the list of Julian's Greek definitions, initially inserted at C.23 q.8 c.23, v. *xenones*. Paucapalea (*c.*1146×50) copied the list, omitting *nosocomium* and *brephotrophium* and defining inhabitants as *xenones*.[38] Rufinus (in *c.*1164) followed suit, but included *brephotrophium*, and prefaced them with a helpful introduction:

> It is known that any 'venerable place' except a church or a monastery is called by the general term '*ptochium*'; this, however, comprises many forms within it. Thus another kind of *ptochium* is a *xenodochium*, another a *ptochotrophium*, another an *orphanotrophium*, another a *geruntocomium*, another a *brephotrophium*. [Then begin versions of the Julian definitions:] *Xenodochium* is a *locus venerabilis* where paupers are received, the inhabitants of which place are called *xenones*. Ptochotrophium is a *locus venerabilis* in which infants are nourished...[39]

To Caron this was the defining statement in Western law, which now gave hospitals their own legal personality; however, it is difficult to interpret the preface in this way.[40] Rufinus's comment sought to explain Justinian's term *locus venerabilis* (C.23 q.8 c.23 §2), and the extract's foreign terms more generally, including *xenones*. His response largely extemporized from the *Epitome* chapter, although an awareness that *ptochium* was a 'general term' suggests familiarity with its use in Justinian's Code. Yet it is hard to find any definitional interest in the houses themselves, since Rufinus confuses the definitions of *brephotrophium* and *ptochotrophium*. His comment was not copied or adapted, nor did it become part of the canonical conversation.[41] Rufinus was using the Justinianic concept of 'venerable

---

[37] At C.16 q.3. Stephan von Doornick (Étienne de Tournai), *Die summa*, ed. J. F. von Schulte (Giessen, 1891; repr. 1965), 226.

[38] At C.23 q.8 c.21–3, v. *xenones*: 'Xenodochium est locus venerabilis, in quo peregrini suscipiuntur; a quo loco habitatores illius loci xenones vocantur. Vel *phochotrophium...orphanotrophia... Geronthomachomia...*' Paucapalea, *Summa*, ed. J. F. von Schulte (Giessen, 1890), 103.

[39] At C.23 q.8 c.23: 'Sciendum quod omnis locus uenerabilis preter ecclesiam et monasterium generali uocabulo ptochium nuncupatur; hoc autem multas sub se continet species. Ptochium enim aliud est xenodochium, aliud ptochotrophium, aliud orphanotrophium, aliud geruntocomium, aliud brephotrophium. Xenodochium est locus uenerabilis, ubi pauperes suscipiuntur: a quo loco habitatores xenones uocantur. Ptochotrophium est locus uenerabilis, in quo infantes aluntur; orphanotrophium erat locus...Gerontocomium erat locus uenerabilis...brephotrophium erat locus uenerabilis, in quo pauperes infirmi homines pascebantur.' Rufinus von Bologna, *Summa Decretorum*, ed. H. Singer (Paderborn, 1902; repr. 1963), 413. His statement is repeated in John Faventius's *Summa* (*c.*1171), at C.23 q.8 c.23, v. *zenones*: BL Add. MS 18460, fol. 107v; Royal 9 E VII, fol. 126v.

[40] Caron, '*pia fundatio*', 148–50.

[41] The definition may have been noticed by the anonymous author of *Summa Parisiensis* (*c.*1169) who, eschewing the full slate of Greek charities, noted only that *ptochiis* meant 'venerable houses', at C.21 q.2 c.3, v. *sive ptochiis*: 'videlicet domibus venerabilibus'. *The Summa Parisiensis*, ed. T. P. McLaughlin (Toronto, 1952), 199.

place' to make (confused) sense of the Greek terms; it was not the concept, or term, that was to take root in canon law.

The recitation of Greek terms has been noticed by others and interpreted as proof that canonists took no interest in hospitals. To Imbert it revealed them as lost in ancient books and ignorant of the world beyond their window: Tierney, who did not recognize Julian's *Epitome* as the source, saw the terms in the *glossa ordinaria* as Johannes Teutonicus 'merely showing off his erudition by explaining what all these quaint old-fashioned terms meant'.[42] However, the use of these terms across the long twelfth century was too systematic and too exclusive to be dismissed so casually. The Latin definitions of Julian's *Epitome* thread through the glosses and commentaries to the *Decretum*. The canonists were not interested in their source, or the heritage it might have represented, and do not refer to the novel or to Julian's chapter.[43] Instead, the definitions were familiar as curiosities. They were copied from gloss to gloss, bouncing between commentators in various stages of corruption or decay. Their location in the text was scattered; they initially appeared beside the alien terms in the *Decretum*, especially v. *xenones* (C.23 q.8 c.23), v. *ptochiis* (C.21 q.2 c.3) but over time they began to detach from Gratian's seven references. What remained consistent was that, until the end of the twelfth century, the *Epitome* definitions remained the only means by which decretists could speak of welfare institutions.[44]

There are signs that their use was neither reflexive nor uncrafted. We have already noted how an apparently casual insertion or edited definition suggests deeper intellectual labour. Stephen of Tournai's addition of *xenodochia* to a list of ecclesiastical possessions might seem to anticipate X 3.36.4, below, but his rationale was quite different because it stemmed from Roman law, of which he was an early assimilator.[45] In his list of definitions Rufinus made a small change to its verb tenses, leaving the present tense (*est*) for *xenodochia* and *ptochotrophia*, but providing the past (*erat*) for the others. This served to distinguish the forms that existed in the West, in line with the redefinition of *ptochotrophia* as leper-houses, suggesting that here, at least, Rufinus was recognizing the activity outside his window. Ivo of Chartres had been eager to address contemporary houses, in practice and in theory, able to act as a bishop but not as a canonist, where he lacked the tools though which to talk. For Ivo's successor canonists the Julian definitions were also the only authoritative means by which welfare houses could be discussed. Until new legal statements were offered, the Greek definitions

---

[42] *HDC* 115n.; Tierney, *Medieval Poor Law*, 142 n. 8.

[43] For the *Epitome* and its Greek terms, see Chapter 5.

[44] The *Summa* of Simon of Bisignano was the first to move away from the definitions, as discussed below.

[45] On his use of Roman law, G. Conklin, 'Stephen of Tournai', in Chodorow, ed., *Proc. Eighth Congress*.

remained an antiquated place-holder for charities in canon law. The strain behind their use suggests that decretists had far more that they wanted to say.

The definitions were therefore the only clay from which observations might be moulded. Attempts to classify welfare houses used these definitions. It was how Rufinus defined them as 'venerable places', distinct from churches and monasteries. His contemporary, Johannes Beleth, was even more methodical. He opened his *Summa de ecclesiasticis officiis* (c.1162) by defining *loci venerabiles*, whose many forms he divided into two categories, those 'consecrated to prayer' and those 'assigned for human needs'. The first comprised three forms, drawing on Roman law: sacred (*sacra*) places, ritually dedicated through the bishop and sanctified to God, such as churches, temples, oratories, monasteries, basilicas, and chapels; holy (*sancta*) places, with immunity, as that around a monastery or the cloister of secular religious; and religious (*religiosus*) places, where any human body or head was buried. The second category was of Beleth's own devising. It consisted of *xenodochia, nosocomia, gerontochomia, orphanotrophia, ptocotrophium,* and *brephotrophium,* anciently instituted by the holy fathers and religious emperors to receive pilgrims, orphans, the aged, worn out, sick, feeble, and wounded.[46] Without new law this was as much as a canonist could say: that hospitals were in a different category from monasteries and churches; that they were not sacred (*sacra*), holy (*sancta*), or religious (*religiosus*), but 'assigned for human needs'; and that they were of ancient Christian pedigree and for many kinds of human needs.

Only at the turn of the century did a new legal statement arise, on contemporary hospitals, as 'hospitales'. It was the late fruit of a slow-growing weed.

Ad Petitionem and Early Decretal Collections

Our first clue that there was something new appears in Johannes Teutonicus's *glossa ordinaria* to Gratian's *Decretum* of 1216/7. Here we find the statement that a hospital might be built without the bishop: it is the earliest and most authoritative mention in commentary of this first of the two legal principles that would be

---

[46] (c. 2) 'DE LOCIS UENERABILIBUS ET EORUM DIUERSITATE. Locorum ergo uenerabilium alia sunt orationi dicata, alia humane necessitati deputata. Loco humane necessitati statuta sunt hec: Xenodochium, nosocomium, gerontochomium, orphanotrophium, prototrophium [*sic*], brephotrophium. Sancti enim patres et religiosi imperatores quedam instituerunt loca, ubi peregrini, orphani, senes, emeriti, infirmi, inbecilles et saucii reciperentur. Locorum autem, que orationi sunt dicata, alia sunt sacra, alia sancta, alia religiosa. Sacra loca sunt, que per manus pontificum sunt rite dicata et Deo santificata, que diuersis uocantur nominibus, istis scilicet: *Ecclesia, sacrarium, sacellum, templum, oratorium, Dei tabernaculum, monasterium, cenobium, kyrica, dominicalis, domus orationis, basilica, capella.*' Iohannis Beleth, *Summa de ecclesiasticis officiis*, ed. H. Douteil, CCCM 41A (Turnhout, 1976), 4–5. Beleth's section was incorporated by Sicard of Cremona (c.1200) where he offered 'ut hospitale est compassio mentis', *Sicardi Cremonensis episcopi Mitralis de officiis*, ed. G. Sarbak and L. Weinrich, CCCM 228 (Turnhout, 2008), 23.

repeated by later canonists. Johannes's words appear among a series of notes on oratories, where he writes:

> neither an oratory nor a hospital can be built without episcopal licence, as *extra I* (*de religiosis domibus*, 'Ad haec'); but if there is no oratory in the hospital then a simple hospital can be built without the bishop's licence, as *extra II*. (*de ecclesiis edificandis*, 'Si hospitale').[47]

His first reference is 1 Comp. 3.31.4 (X 3.36.4), a decretal to be discussed in the final section of this chapter. Here, it is Johannes's second statement, of a *hospitale simplex*, that catches the eye, for he is citing a decretal. His reference leads us to title 26 ('On the building of churches') of the recently compiled collection by John of Wales, the *Compilatio secunda* (1210–15), and to a statement beginning *Si hospitale* (2 Comp. 3.26.1 = –X):

> [*Si hospitale*] If you (pl.) establish a hospital in any place without an oratory, you are free to build that house without the knowledge of the bishop in whose parish it should be. But if you wish to establish an oratory there, you may not do so without the bishop's permission, preserving his jurisdiction in all things.[48]

Compilatio secunda attributes the statement to Alexander III. John's main source was a collection dated to 1203, compiled by Gilbertus Anglicus, an English jurist at Bologna. And it was from Gilbertus's *Collectio* that John took *Si hospitale* and the title under which it was nestled (Gb. 3.26.1).[49] What is this statement and where did it come from?

The answers lie in the forest of early decretal collections that arose in the decades after 1170.[50] These gathered papal letters and pronouncements, as

---

[47] C.18 q.2 c.10, v *aut oratoria*: 'non solum oratorium sed nec etiam hospitale potest sine licentia episcopi construi ut extra i *de religi. dom. c. ultra* sed si oratorium non est in hospitali tunc simplex hospitale potest construi sine licencia episcopi ut extra ii *de eccl. edifi. si hospitale*.' For Johannes Teutonicus's comments the following have been consulted: Troyes, Bibl. mun. MS 192, fol. 117r; BnF lat. 3904, fol. 155v and lat. 14317, fol. 165v. This statement does not appear in his first recension, Vatican City, Vat. lat. 1367, fol. 170v.

[48] 'DE ECCLESIIS EDIFICANDIS, c. 1: Alexander III. pars c. Ad petitionem. Si hospitale in aliquo loco absque oratorio feceritis, liberum erit uobis absque conscientia episcopi, in cuius parochia fuerit, ipsam domum construere. Quod si oratorium ibidem facere uolueritis id absque licentia episcopi non faciatis, iustitia in omnibus seruata.' (JL 14190 (9257))

[49] R. von Heckel, 'Die Dekretalensammlungen des Gilbertus und Alanus', *ZRG Kan. Abt.* 29 (1940), 204. It occurs at the end of book 3, without a title and in the same form as that in n. 48, in BL Harley 3834, fol. 181r. On Gilbertus: K. Pennington, 'Decretal Collections', in *HMCL* 304–5.

[50] On the collections, C. Duggan, *Twelfth Century Decretal Collections* (London, 1963); C. Duggan, *Decretals and the Creation of 'New Law'* (Aldershot, 1998); Kuttner and Rathbone, 'Anglo-Norman Canonists'; Holtzmann and Kemp, *Papal Decretals rel. Lincoln*, pp. xi–xvi; J. J. H. M. Hanenburg, 'Decretals and Decretal Collections', *Tijdschrift voor Rechtsgeschiedenis* 34:4 (1966); C. Duggan, 'Decretal Collections', in *HMCL*; Pennington, 'Decretal Collections', and his online database, *Bio-Bibliographical Guide to Medieval and Early Modern Jurists*, <http://amesfoundation.law.harvard.

extravagantes, new statements of law. Many were products of Alexander III's chancery, *decretales epistolae* dispatched in response to a case before a judge delegate or to episcopal questions on obscure points of law (we have met them already, in Chapter 2, when the bishops of the province of Canterbury relayed a series of potential rulings to Alexander for confirmation, one of them on leprosy). Centres of law, several attached to an active bishop and jurist as were those at Exeter, Worcester, and Canterbury, began to gather and share these rulings.[51] The practice of compiling collections originated in England, spreading to France by the 1180s then Bologna. The early products were constantly in motion, because a manuscript was not simply copied but often refashioned, its material edited and developed. Manuscripts therefore survive in evolving families of texts. Soon, more systematic methods to organize material would develop, extracting passages from a case-specific response, to codify wider law.[52] Gilbertus's extract, *Si hospitale*, was a late product of this process: a sentence removed from a longer text and deployed by this Bolognese jurist under a new title. Here, Gilbertus's attribution, '*Alex III pars c. Ad petitionem*', suggests a longer decretal. Threading back through these collections, it has been possible to reconstruct this lost decretal, as it was circulating in the late 1170s. An edition is presented in Appendix A, where the textual evidence that underpins what follows can be found. Extracts of this decretal became known as *Ad petitionem* (§1), *Uxoratus* (§3), *Si hospitale* (§5), and *Si cum aliquo* (§6), marked among the sections (§) in the edition.

Alexander III and the Cruciferi (*c*.1170)

The main fragment of the decretal, *Ad petitionem* (JL 13972), appears in Jaffé, who wrongly attributed it to the Hospitallers of St John and so by implication to Gerard their first prior (d. 1120).[53] In fact, the decretal was a rule, provided by Alexander III to 'prior Girard and the brothers living according to the teaching of Cletus of

---

edu/BioBibCanonists/MainEntry_biobib2.php>, whose dates have been consulted throughout this chapter.

[51] C. Duggan, 'Papal Judges Delegate and the Making of the "New Law"', in T. N. Bisson, ed., *Cultures of Power* (Philadelphia, PA, 1995); C. Duggan, 'Decretals of Alexander III to England', in F. Liotta, ed., *Miscellanea Rolando Bandinelli, Papa Alessandro III* (Siena, 1986); C. Duggan, 'The Reception of Canon Law in England', in S. Kuttner and J. J. Ryan, eds, *Proc. of the Second Int'l Congress of Medieval Canon Law* (Vatican City, 1965), repr. in Duggan, *Canon Law in Medieval England* (London, 1982), no. 11. This was as much about the practice as the theory of law, with bishops eager to clarify their authority and systematize their jurisdictions, Duggan, '*De consultationibus*', 193–5. A. Morey and C. N. L. Brooke, *Gilbert Foliot and his Letters* (Cambridge, 1965), 230–44.

[52] For Alexander's legal team, codification by scholars beyond the papal curia, and these 'drastically abbreviated extract[s]', see A. Duggan, 'Master of the Decretals', 377–8, 382–7, and its bibliography.

[53] Bernard of Pavia may have been the source of Jaffé's confusion, since he ascribed the decree to 'G. Priori et fratribus S. Ioannis' (1 Comp. 3.28.8 = X 3.32.8). Bernard's error seems to have followed *Brugensis*, which labelled the extract that followed *Ad petitionem* (19.2) as *idem eisdem*, although the

good memory'. Girard's was a Venetian community, soon to be known as the Cruciferi, which ran hospitals for the poor and for pilgrims en route to the Holy Land. They first appear in charters of 1162/3, with hospitals as widely dispersed as Ancona and Como, and a deed of 1163 records brother Girard and a companion 'receiving on behalf of Saint Cletus a grant of land to build a hospital in Rimini'.[54] The order is little known and has attracted notice primarily for its ties to the papacy.[55] These ties date back to Alexander, who worked so closely with the order that he became known as its founder. The brothers had come to his attention by 1167, when he directed the bishop of Vicenza to provide the *Cruciari* with an oratory and cemetery at their site in Vicenza, a request that had been blocked by a local convent of nuns.[56] At about the same time, in *c*.1170, Alexander provided the burgeoning community with a rule. Shortly thereafter he laid the foundation stone for a house in Bologna, which in 1179 he would confirm as head of the order.[57] An earlier effort in Verona in 1173 may have been a first attempt at this reorganization, when Alexander confirmed to *magistro* Ventura and the whole *congregatio* that he had rebuilt its hospital there from his own funds and provided resources to add a church, which was to be answerable only to the papacy.[58]

The Cruciferi rule survives in a seventeenth-century copy; it is in Alexander's name, and contains much of his early rule, but it is clearly a later version, whose interpolations reflect the order's subsequent reorganization into a congregation under a *magister*.[59] Clunky changes in register between the original rule and its additions, together with the reconstituted decretal, make it possible to distinguish the shape and structure of Alexander's rule. A careful reading of this early rule shifts our attention away from papal power and onto the streets of Italy. The rule is relatively brief and focused on the challenges presented by a new kind of religious life centred on hospitals. Its main concern was how vows of obedience, poverty, and chastity might play out in such an informal community. It stressed the overarching authority of a superior prior (*maior prior*) over the scattered houses as well as over the brothers themselves. Property was to be held in

latter was a papal privilege to the Hospitallers (JL 13963), similar to that of 1137 or 1154: *CS*, p. 150; *PL* 179, col. 313; Anastasius IV, *Epistolae et privilegia*, *PL* 188, col. 1079.

[54] 'recipientibus vice sancti Cleti ad hospitale ibi edificandum ut ibi Deo pauperibus honor exhibeatur': G. P. Pacini, 'Fra poveri e viandanti ai margini della città', in *Religiones novae* (1995), 62. On the early order, G. P. Pacini, 'I Crociferi e le comunità ospedaliere', in A. Rigon, ed., *I percorsi della fede* (Padua, 2002).

[55] K. Baaken, 'Papsturkunden für die Crociferi', in K. Herbers et al., eds, *Ex ipsis rerum documentis* (Sigmaringen, 1991), and the articles by Pacini in n. 54. For Alexander, more generally: M. Pacaut, *Alexandre III: Etude sur la conception du pouvoir pontifical* (Paris, 1956).

[56] Alexander's deed is preserved in BL Add. MS 8602, fol. 255r, and mentions the *fratres Cruciari* 'et familia sua, et pauperes quos in hospitio recipiunt'. Also, Pacini, 'I Crociferi', 165.

[57] Pacini, 'Fra poveri', 65, 81 n.; Baaken, 'Papsturkunden', 336, 339.

[58] 'Papsturkunden in Venetien', ed. P. Kehr, *Nachrichten von der Königl.* (Göttingen, 1899), 231.

[59] 'Papst. in Venetien', 227–30. On the differences in terminology, and the change in register, see Appendix A, esp. n. 3.

common; if a brother was found with unexplained money at his death, he was 'not to be buried in a church or hospital but deposited outside the city in the fields'.[60] Scandal was a particular concern, in ways that suggest the lower social status of its converts. Probation for a novice lasted for half a year if the candidate was well known (*cognitus*), a year if unknown (*incognitus*). To be received into the order, a serf required his lord's consent and had to be returned if received (in ignorance of his status) without it, unless he had subsequently been promoted to priestly orders. A married man might join if his wife agreed; if of irreproachable reputation, she was to then live chastely with family but, if not, she was to take a vow of chastity and remove herself to a religious house. No women might be received into or live with the community.

A highly abridged version of the rule was circulating as a decretal by the late 1170s. It began at *Ad petitionem* and included an abbreviated address; it was apparently composed of §§1–6, as presented in Appendix A. The decretal was first used by the Bolognese jurist Simon of Bisignano, who cited §§1, 3, 5, and 6; a few years later, the whole decretal found its way into several early English collections and, from there to Reims, where it was copied into the *Collectio Brugensis* (1187/8), which preserves our fullest copy.[61] It seems initially to have circulated as a loose text, and had probably been abridged and circulated first at Bologna. The redactor seems to have had little interest in hospitals themselves. He kept the two main statements concerning hospitals but these, which had been in longer sections of the rule, were now beside different neighbours. In the decretal, *Si hospitale* is placed before a statement that a brother found at death with unexplained money must not receive Christian burial, and after a series of terse statements that none may build a hospital without the prior's licence, nor may he have his own possessions, but must hand anything he acquired to his *rector*. They therefore appear among a series of injunctions directed towards individual brothers, which appear to forestall disputes over property and authority. In the decretal, a hospital appears as something a (wealthy) new entrant might want to build from private resources, when the rule demanded that such resources be held in common, their use commonly determined under the prior and, if to create an oratory, under the bishop, too. Such a reading is the product of the redactor's work. Reinserting the missing text transforms the reading of Alexander's rule.

The rule set out to structure an order not of conventual priories (*ecclesiae*) but of hospitals. Where the former required a full convent, the latter had a more informal staff. Alexander laid this out with care. Brothers served in hospitals, each run by a *rector* but together subject to the (superior) prior. Individual communities

---

[60] This clause (§6) is missing from the seventeenth-century copy of the rule, but was clearly part of the original decretal. Burial for such brothers *quasi excommunicatus* also appears in the first Hospitaller rule (1125×53) at c. 13 and in Lateran III (c. 10): *Cartulaire général de l'ordre des Hospitaliers de S. Jean de Jérusalem*, ed. J. Delaville Le Roulx, 4 vols (Paris, 1894–1906), I. 62–8; COGD II. 135–6.

[61] Appendix A considers the relationships of these copies.

might be small: only seven brothers (clerical or lay) had to be present at divine service. Significantly, while the rector had local charge over a hospital, and the brothers there, it was not as a religious superior. He presented any new brother to the prior to receive the mark of the order (a cross). A brother was also freer to move between facilities, seeking the rector's advice (*consilium*), not his permission, before moving to another location. If a brother felt unduly burdened by the rector or had another kind of quarrel, he took his complaint to the prior, an event that involved a journey. Hospitals were therefore at the centre of the rule: administering multiple facilities across a region was the object of this religious order, who were dispersed across these facilities; the hospital was the unit in which they lived, although it was not the unit of religious belonging and discipline. That none could build a hospital without the superior prior's licence was a control not on personal property but on the growth of the order. A new hospital, and with it a new community to staff it, needed supervision and resourcing.

Alexander, it emerges, took a particular interest in welfare houses. We have already noticed how, in the late 1160s and resettled in Italy after his exile, this pope turned with concern to the suffering of those with leprosy, crafting new ways to help support leper-houses and exhorting Christians to compassion in New Testament language.[62] There are wider hints, too, that he worked to promote the status of episcopal hospitals when confirming a new bishop. Earlier papal confirmations had focused upon a bishop's churches, noting a hospital as a minor possession, usually in terms of the mechanism by which it had become a possession.[63] This changed from 1168/9, when Alexander began to extol the importance of their charge, in elevated language. He began to entrust them to the new diocesans through apostolic authority, not as possessions but as a category of *cura* (responsibility).[64] His cultivation of the Cruciferi at this moment was therefore part of a wider vision. And in the wake of the Vicenza dispute, when a new Cruciferi community had been blocked by the local convent, *Si hospitale* takes on a new hue. It becomes in the rule a statement of communal right, clarifying that Cruciferi might build a new hospital, and thus establish a new group of brothers, without treading on parochial rights. In the face of local opposition, brothers might establish a facility and serve the poor without an oratory. Alexander's statement was part of a religious *ordo*, yet it was based in law. It rested on the

---

[62] Chapter 2; Bolton, 'The Absentee Lord?', 176–9.

[63] See e.g. the *hospitale domus* 'ex dono bonae memoriae Sanctii, quondam illustris Hispaniarum regis' in the confirmation to the bishop of Burgos in Castile in 1163, *PL* 200, cols 251–3. Also, *PL* 179, cols 442, 489–90; Lucius II, *Epistolae et privilegia*, *PL* 179, col. 847; *PL* 200, cols 305–6, 314–15, 320–1.

[64] '. . . tibi et successoribus tuis nihilominus auctoritate apostolica communimus', *PL* 200, cols 578, in an 1169 charter to the bishop of Ferrara. Also, the 1167/8 confirmation to John, bishop of Maguelone: 'auctoritate apostolica statuimus ut ecclesia cum hospitali, auctoritate tua noviter in silva Galteri constructa, ita pure et absolute in tua dispositione consistat, quod nemini liceat eamdem ecclesiam cum hospitali a jurisdictione tua subtrahere, aut jus tuum diminuere, vel in alterius ordinationem transferre'. *PL* 200, col. 522.

council of Chalcedon's chapter 4 (C.18 q.2 c.10), whose language it knowingly echoed, to confirm that an oratory required episcopal licence, and therefore agreement with the rectors of a parish; but this was not the case for a basic hospital. Alexander worked on multiple fronts to promote welfare facilities. In each case, he recognized the limits of law.

Early Decretal Collections and *Si Hospitale* (*c.*1175–*c.*1190)

Initially, canonists took no interest in the decretal's statements on hospitals. In abridging the rule for circulation, its redactor had stripped out any organizational material, including its design for a hospital network under a religious congregation. He had focused on its comments on religious vows, especially those regarding property and chastity. This was how the decretal was picked up by early decretalists, who deployed its sections in legal questions concerning monastic conversion and obedience. First, in Bologna, Simon of Bisignano extracted many of its statements in his *Summa* on the *Decretum* (1177×79) to clarify aspects of monastic life.[65] In English decretal collections the first manuscripts, in the early *Wigorniensis* group, transcribed the decretal largely in full for its comments on religious life.[66] Soon, the fuller text gave way to extracts in the *Appendix concilii Lateranensis* (*c.*1184×85), 'the fountainhead of the main decretal tradition'. It used the main portion in a title on rules for religious (27.5) and *Uxoratus* on a married person wanting to enter a monastery (5.9).[67] When the *Appendix* made its way to Rouen, then Tours and Bologna, it brought this division of topics: *Ad petitionem* (§§1, 4–6) on 'religious rules' and *Uxoratus* (§3) on conversion of spouses made its way through the (Tours) Bamberg group, in *Bambergensis* (15.1, 49.9) and *Casselana* (25.1, 57.10), and its descendant, the north-eastern Italian *Lipsiensis* (15.1, 58.9).[68] This passed into Bernard of Pavia's *Breviarium extravagantium*,

---

[65] *Summa in Decretum Simonis Bisinianensis*, ed. P. V. Aimone (Fribourg, 2007), 338, 341–2, 354, 419–20 (online at <https://www3.unifr.ch/cdc/de/dok.html>), citing §6 for burial of monks (C.18 q.1 c.1 v. *statuendum*), §5 for monks needing licence to build a church (C.18 q.2 c.12 v. *De monachis*); §1, for virgins moving to a stricter rule (C.20 q.4 c.1 v. *virgines*); and §3 for a promise of chastity when a spouse converts (C.27 q.2 c.22 v. *Si quis* and c.25 v. *agatho*).

[66] It opens part II of *Collectio Wigorniensis*, under the title: Incipiunt decretales epistolae a [lex.] papae III de statu religiosorum et de eorundem priuilegio quorum prima destinatu est Gerardo priori et fratribus, BL Royal 10 A.ii, fol. 14r.

[67] Where part 5 is entitled, De coniugatis et sponsis monasterium ingressis, vel ingredi volentibus (Mansi XXII. 285, 374). For the *Appendix*, Kuttner and Rathbone, 'Anglo-Norman Canonists', 283); C. Duggan, 'English Canonists and the Appendix concilii Lateranensis', *Traditio* 18 (1962); P. Landau, 'Die Entstehung der systematischen Dekretalensammlungen', *ZRG* 96 Kan. Abt. 65 (1979),128–32; C. Duggan, *Twelfth-Century Decretal Collections*, 51–7, 135–9.

[68] Under titles (15) De ordine et specialitate quorundam regularium and (49) De sponsis coniugatis monasterium ingressis vel ingredi volentibus, in *Bambergensis* (*CS*, pp. 98, 110; *QCA*, 193, 205). On the group, C. Duggan, 'New Case Law', 280–2. On continental contacts: A. Duggan, 'Master of the Decretals', 374–6; C. Duggan, 'New Case Law', 249, 272–5.

the first authoritative collection of *extravagantes* (decretals), as *Ad petitionem* (§1 only, as 1 Comp. 3.27.1) and *Uxoratus* (§3, as 1 Comp. 3.28.8).[69] Only the latter would make it into the *Liber extra*, as X 3.32.8. This main legal strain paid little heed to hospitals and gradually dropped the section *Si hospitale* (§5) from *Ad petitionem*, as irrelevant to monastic vows.

Yet beneath this main strain a new interest was fermenting. It can be seen in the decretal's first use, when Simon of Bisignano offered an early aside in his *Summa*. At C.18 q.2 c.12, Chalcedon's requirement that none might found a monastery without episcopal permission, Simon noted that religious men or women may build a hospital house without episcopal licence, but not a church or an oratory.[70] The more significant change happened at Reims in *Brugensis* (1187/8).[71] Its compiler copied the full text of the original decretal (§§1–6), likely from an ancestor of the *Wigorniensis* group.[72] By this time, compilations had changed, gathering excerpts from decretals under topic headings and so, at first glance, the full copy in *Brugensis* seems like an odd throwback to the earlier methods of compilation. In fact, *Brugensis* was breaking new legal ground, for it was forging a new title: (19) 'On the privileges of religious, the penalty for their abuse, and from what they must abstain'.[73] Here *Brugensis* offered eighteen chapters on rights and restrictions accorded to groups of religious and, especially, to the Hospitallers of St John and the Cistercians. Among the chapters was *Ad petitionem* (19.2) and, at (19.13), a decretal of Urban III (1185–7) that addressed episcopal confirmation of hospitals (discussed below). For the first time, *Ad petitionem*'s statements on hospitals were placed into a wider context, if a rather woolly one. This compiler had noticed welfare houses; he just did not yet know what to do with them.[74]

Si hospitale was no game-changer. Alexander's sentence had offered no new rulings regarding hospitals: it merely reflected wider practice, using Chalcedonian language to render explicit what that early council had left implicit. It set no new precedent in canon law. In fact, it had reinforced the vernacular quality of xenodochia, and their status beyond ecclesiastical control, to create a loop-hole for the Cruciferi. This loop-hole ensured that an order of low-status converts— one whose limited social capital left them easily blocked by great churches and ignored by bishops—could grow, serving the marginalized, beneath the high politics of church and city. Xenodochia as a category were not the subject of

---

[69] Under DE REGULARIBUS TRANSEUNTIBUS AD RELIGIONEM and DE CONVERSIONE CONIUGATORUM (1 Comp. 3.27 and 3.28).

[70] *Summa*, ed. Aimone, 341.   [71] On which, C. Duggan, 'New Case Law', 285–6.

[72] Master Ralph of Sarre (in Kent), a member of Becket's network of clerics and a colleague of John of Salisbury, was dean of Reims at the time, C. Duggan, 'New Case Law', 285.

[73] 'DE PRIVILEGIIS RELIGIOSORUM ET PENA ABUTENTIUM EIS ET A QUIBUS DEBEAT ABSTINERE', CS, p. 150. On new law, Landau, 'der systematischen Dekretalensammlungen', and note 75 below.

[74] *Brugensis* was uniquely aware of welfare houses. Other compilers had used Lateran III's *Cum dicat Apostolus* for benefices; *Brugensis* (22.1) recognized it as a spiritual indulgence for lepers (CS, p. 152; cf. Avril, 'Le III[e] concile du Latran', 36).

Alexander's rule and they attracted little interest among the early decretalists. But the next generation of canonists, hungry for legal rulings on hospitals, would turn to his words. The very existence of the statement *Si hospitale* intruded 'hospitals' into the legal conversation. It allowed canonists to move beyond the Greek definitions and notice contemporary charities.

Bernard of Pavia and his Legacy

At the same time, in Bologna, there was a parallel initiative that would finally make hospitals a topic in canon law. The agent was Bernard of Pavia, a legal scholar and canonist who went on to serve the papal curia in Rome. Bernard was one of the great architects of scholastic canon law, on whose work rested the thirteenth-century collections, including the *Liber extra*. It is therefore a surprise to find in this man the great radical of hospital law.

Bernard Stakes a Bold Claim (*c.*1177–*c.*1200)

Bernard's efforts began in his first decretal collection, *Collectio Parisiensis II*, which was compiled in 1177×79, at roughly the same moment that Simon de Bisignano was composing his *Summa* on the *Decretum*.[75] But where Simon was thinking within the monastic tradition, Bernard was stretching its legal boundaries. He did this by creating a new title (60), 'That religious houses be subject to their bishop'.[76] This he illustrated with two texts: an excerpt from a letter of Gregory the Great, that a monastic house attached to an abbey in another diocese was still answerable to the local bishop; and the xenodochia decree from the council of Rome (826), familiar to us but unknown to Bernard's contemporaries.

There are reasons to detect in his act a new agenda. His title was a new creation, devised by Bernard to create a new subject of law: not the monks themselves but the houses or places of religious. *Parisiensis II*'s other titles were lifted from Gratian's *Decretum*.[77] Titles 56 to 64 followed *Causa* 16, which explored the relationships between monks and parish churches; only his title 60 on 'religious

---

[75] Named for its manuscript, BnF lat. 1566, *Parisiensis II* is seen as the moment when 'old law [was replaced] by new' in decretal collections (Hanenburg, 'Decretals', 599). To reflect its importance, Pennington suggests a new name, *Collection in 95 Titles*, in his 'Decretal Collections', 296, whose 294–300 discuss Bernard's collections more widely. On Bernard, Pennington, 'The Decretalists 1190 to 1234', in *HMCL* 211–15; P. Landau, 'Bernardus Papiensis', in M. Stolleis, ed., *Juristen* (Munich, 2001), 81–2. For this pivotal period in Bologna, S. Kuttner, 'Bernardus Compostellanus Antiquus', *Traditio* 1 (1943).

[76] 'UT RELIGIOSAE DOMUS SUOS EPISCOPOS SINT SUBIECTAE', cited herein from *CS*, p. 42.

[77] Hanenburg, 'Decretals', 594–5.

houses' had no precursor.[78] Bernard populated his new title with two obscure texts. Gregory's letter (JE 1846 (1422)) appeared only here and in *Lipsiensis* (34.1), a slightly later collection that follows *Parisiensis II* so closely that Bernard has been thought to be its author.[79] He also dredged up the Roman decree, which had languished unnoticed since the ninth century, and attributed it simply to 'pope Eugenius', creating an easy confusion with the more recent Eugenius III (1146–53), which continues to mislead.[80] He made small changes to its text, integrating its original title into the decree and removing the final phrase, so that the decree now read:

> [*De xenodochiis*] Concerning xenodochia and other similar places, these should be arranged through the watchful concern of the bishops in whose dioceses they sit, to the same uses for which they had been established [*and so removing*: so that the customary bread and duties be resumed for those to whom it is owed].[81]

Eliminating the final clause expanded the reach of the decree. Whereas the original permitted a bishop to intervene when a house's management had failed in order to restore specific alms, the revised version suggested a more general responsibility for a bishop to intervene and a right to arrange the house more comprehensively, in accordance with its foundation. Bernard's new title had a purpose. It offered an embryonic legal corpus which aimed to establish episcopal jurisdiction over daughter houses of religious congregations and over local hospitals, two types of houses that had spread rapidly during the twelfth century. It distinguished places from communities.

As Bernard developed his argument in subsequent work, its target emerges. His second collection, *Breviarium extravagantium* of *c.*1190, proved a defining moment for hospitals in law. Here, Bernard modified his new section into title

---

[78] We can detect the building blocks out of which Bernard fashioned his chapter in this *Causa*. At its base was C.16 q.1 c.12, from Chalcedon ('MONACHI, QUI SUNT IN CIUITATIBUS, EPISCOPO DEBENT ESSE SUBIECTI'). To expand the category beyond monks to the sites themselves, Bernard relied on the authority of C.16 q.7 c.10 ('OMNES BASILICAE AD EUM PERTINENT EPISCOPUM, IN CUIUS TERRITORIO POSITAE SUNT') and the terminology of C.16 q.4. c.2 ('QUADRAGINTA ANNORUM PRESCRIPTIO RELIGIOSIS DOMIBUS CONCEDITUR').

[79] *CS*, p. 123. On Bernard's unlikely authorship of *Lipsiensis* see n. 92 of this chapter.

[80] E.g. Frank, 'Hospitalreformen', 11. When Bernard used material from early councils, he tended to cite the council with the exception of those held in Rome, which he ascribed to its pope. For Bernard's sources, *QCA*, pp. vii–xxiii.

[81] 'EX DECRETIS EUGENII PAPAE. De xenodochiis et aliis similibus locis per sollicitudinem episcoporum, *in* quorum dioecesi exsistunt, ad easdem utilitates, quibus constituta sunt, ordinentur [ut debiti panes atque cure pertinentibus revertantur].' *Parisiensis II* 60.2 (*CS*, pp. 123/42) (1 Comp. 3.31.2 = X 3.36.3). The Roman council is examined in my Chapter 6. It was not unusual for compilers to make editorial interventions: K. Pennington, 'The Making of a Decretal Collection', *Proc. of the Fifth Int'l Congress of Medieval Canon Law* (Vatican City, 1980), 83–9; S. Kuttner, 'Raymond of Peñafort as Editor', *BMCL* 12 (1982); and H. Singer, *Die Dekretalensammlung des Bernardus Compostellanus antiquus* (Vienna, 1914), 27–8.

(3.31) 'On religious houses, that they be subject to the bishop'.[82] It contained the chapters from *Parisiensis II*, including *De xenodochiis* (at 3.31.2),[83] and added two more. The first (3.31.1) was a statement by Gregory VI (1045–6), another obscure authority excavated by Bernard. It clarified that, should it be unclear in which diocese a territory lay, then a basilica in that territory would be consecrated by the bishop who had last exercised jurisdiction there (JL 4127).[84] The second (3.31.4) was the decretal of Urban III, seen in *Brugensis*, in which an episcopal confirmation secured a hospital to its charitable task in perpetuity. Of the four chapters, two specifically address hospitals. The other two establish diocesan jurisdiction over sites that were contested or claimed by others; in so doing, they address two ecclesiastical aspects of hospital foundation: oratories, licensed by the bishop but often not then supervised by him; and hospitals that were entrusted to a hospital order or to another custodian, such as a monastic house. Bernard's main concern in this chapter was the status of hospitals; his ambition, to fashion canon law for hospitals.

The argument was reinforced in Bernard's *Summa* on his *Breviarium*. His discussion of this title was concerned not with the nature of episcopal power, but with the status of religious houses. In particular it worked to classify hospitals, first with monasteries and churches, and then as falling under episcopal jurisdiction. In so doing, Bernard was arguing against custom and law, as it had been recognized by Alexander III and the decretists before him, including Rufinus and Johannes Beleth. Bernard trod carefully, but with determination, writing:

> We have spoken of monks and other religious; now we shall look at religious houses. We should consider by whose authority they might be made and to whom they ought to be subject. §1. It is well established that churches and monasteries must not be made without the authority of the diocesan bishop, as C.16 q.1 c.44; D.1 de cons. c.40; C.18 q.2 c.12; I say the same of hospitals, in *Nov. 131.10; 1 Comp. 3.31.4*. §2. They should be subject to the diocesan bishop, as *1 Comp. 3.31.2;* C.9 q.3. c.1; C.18 q.2 c.17; D.61 c.16; *Cod. 1.3.28*. §3. That in summation it must be noted that a religious house cannot be commuted into secular habitation: *1 Comp. 3.31.4* §4. Likewise that the setting up and decommissioning in a religious house pertains to the bishop: *Nov. 131.10; C.1 q.7 c.2*.[85]

---

[82] 'DE RELIGIOSIS DOMIBUS UT EPISCOPO SINT SUBIECTAE.'

[83] 1 Comp. 3.31.2 and 4 (X 3.36.3 and 4).

[84] For an example of such a controversy, see Rufinus, *Summa*, C.16 q.3 c.6 v. *Inter memoratos*.

[85] 'Diximus de monachis et aliis religiosis; nunc de religiosis domibus videamus. Consideremus igitur, cuius auctoritate sint faciendae, et cui debeant esse subiectae. §1. Constat autem, quod ecclesiae et monasteria fieri non debent absque dioecesani episcopi auctoritate, ut...; idem dico de hospitalibus... §2. Subiectae autem debent esse episcopo dioecesano, ut... §3. Illud in summa notandum, quod religiosa domus non potest in seculare habitaculum commutari, ut infra... §4. Item illud notandum, quod institutio et destitutio pertinent ad episcopum in domo religiosa, ut...' Bernard of Pavia, *Summa decretalium*, ed. E. A. T. Laspeyres (Regensburg, 1860; repr. Graz, 1956), 116. Author's italics mark citations used for hospitals.

Bernard opened with a statement of his new subject: no longer monks (people) but houses (places). The contrast between what had long been established (*constat*) for monasteries and what Bernard now argued (*dico*—'I say') for hospitals underscores the novelty and the target of his effort. That monasteries were subject to the bishop and made with his licence (§1, §2) was supported by a wealth of law, cited easily from Gratian's *Decretum*. That law was so well established, and its statement of general jurisdiction so clear, that Bernard dropped monasteries after the first two sections, to focus on the problem of hospitals.

And a problem they were, as his authorities make clear. Neither of those cited underpins the first proposition (§1), that hospitals require episcopal licence. The first, a Novel of Justinian (Nov. 131.10), allowed heirs or executors five years to establish an oratory and one year to establish a welfare house (on either a permanent or temporary site).[86] An oratory required them to consult civil and episcopal authorities; a welfare house none, unless a testator had specified a system of government for the facility, in which case the bishop was to ensure the arrangement was carried through. No consent was required; rather, the bishop was acting in service to a will-maker's directive. The second was Urban III's decretal that, as shall be seen, preserved a hospital in perpetuity if it had received episcopal confirmation. No confirmation was required to establish the hospital.

Urban's decretal also served as Bernard's authority for his third claim (§3), that a hospital might not be converted into a secular dwelling. Here he was on stronger ground, although the decretal applied by definition to foundations that had received episcopal confirmation, a subset of hospitals, as other canonists would recognize. For his second claim (§2) that hospitals were subject to the bishop, Bernard used his own reworked decree from Rome (826) and a chapter of Justinian's Code (Cod. 1.3.28). The latter required that executors fulfil any bequests that were made for the redemption of captives and, should a testator fail to name an executor, directed the testator's hometown bishop to ensure it was fulfilled. This chapter was also cited in support of claim four (§4), that the setting up or decommissioning of a hospital pertained to a bishop, to which was added C.1 q.7 c.2. The latter concerned ecclesiastics who had abjured heretical behaviour: the quotation of Patriarch Tarasius that listed three Greek charities (*ierocomia, xenia, orphantrophia*) among the places whose superintendants should be deposed if appointed simoniacly. The citations make clear the seriousness of Bernard's attempt, as well as the novelty (and weakness) of his case. His precedents were inadequate for his claims and not only because he had to reach beyond Western canon law. No authority directly, or even implicitly, supported his general claim that hospitals belonged to the bishop. The closest was Eugenius's decree from 826, after Bernard had edited it.

---

[86] See, too, Cod. 1.3.45.1 and the discussion in Chapter 5.

Bernard was trying to forge a legal rationale to establish hospitals as a category of ecclesiastical house. Given how far his *Breviarium* was inspired by Justinian's Code, it is curious that Bernard did not draw from its extensive legislation on welfare houses.[87] Bernard did not even use the edict of Emperor Leo II from 470, which extended protections for the goods of churches 'to other venerable places and all colleges that a pious act has established'.[88] This edict had been incorporated into Gratian's *Decretum* and Bernard would use it in his *Summa de electione* to define a church as a religious house. But he did not use it for hospitals, even though its term 'venerable places' could be tied to welfare houses through the Greek definitions, and had been so defined by Rufinus and Beleth. His contemporary, Huguccio, had made such a link, offering just such a Roman law definition of 'pious act' and listing the Greek charities with 'all churches'.[89] But Bernard did not use the term 'venerable places', nor any Roman law term or legal argument. This is because Leo's edict had distinguished welfare houses as 'venerable places' from 'holy and religious' churches, as had Rufinus and Beleth. Bernard was working to define them both in one category, as religious houses.

Bernard made this argument implicitly in his collections and explicitly in his *Summa*. It was one he had made, too, in his *Summa de electione* (*c.*1191×98), where he stated that, 'In name, religious houses are understood to be churches, monasteries, and hospitals, because they are built out of love of religion and contemplation of the divine'.[90] His grounds were different from those in Roman law, which distinguished the acts of foundation. Bernard sought to unify hospitals, monasteries, and churches as places in service of religion. Here, all were created because a founder turned away from worldly motivations to face God. Those who

---

[87] Bernard adopted many titles from the Code and Digest, to the point that Pennington characterized the *Breviarium*'s structure as 'underlin[ing] the interdependence of Roman and canon law in the late twelfth century', Pennington, 'Decretal Collections', 296–9, with quotation at p. 298. Contemporary debate as to the relationship between canon and Roman law gave the former authority, with Roman law in its service: C. Munier, 'Droit canonique et droit romain', in G. Le Bras, ed., *Etudes d'histoire du droit canonique* (Paris, 1965); A. J. Duggan, 'Justinian's Laws, Not the Lord's', in I. Fonnesberg-Schmidt and A. Jotischky, eds, *Pope Eugenius III* (Amsterdam, 2018). On the interplay between Roman and canon law, Kuttner, 'Secular Law and Institutions', 351–62; C. Gallagher, *Church Law and Church Order* (Aldershot, 2002), 114–52.

[88] C.10 q.2 c.2: '*Inp. Leo.* Ea enim, que ad beatissimae ecclesiae iura pertinent, tamquam ipsam sacrosanctam et religiosam ecclesiam intacta uenerabiliter conuenit custodiri. CONSTITUTIO NOUA. Hoc ius porrectum est ad omnem locum uenerabilem, omneque collegium, quod actio pia constituit.' (Cod. 1.2.14.2; and see Nov. 7.1).

[89] C.10 q.2 c.2, v. '*Actio pia*, id est actus ex pietate proueniens, hoc dicit ut excludantur collegia laicorum siue licita siue illicita et comprehendit generaliter omnes ecclesias et xenodochia et b[r]-ephotrophia et orphanotrophia et gerontocomia et nosocomia et huiusmodi' (BnF lat. 3892, fol. 181r, and see the brief definitions, fols 125v–126r, 250r, 256r). Huguccio took little interest in hospitals and had little impact on the legal tradition for this topic, which preferred the Western tradition (and term) of 'pious places'. Cf. Caron, '*pia fundatio*', 152–5, esp. 152.

[90] (§1) 'Nomine autem religiosae domus ecclesiae, monasteria et hospitalia intelliguntur, quia religionis amore ac divino intuitu construuntur; ecclesiae, ut [C.10 q.2 c.2]; monasteria, ut [C.16 q.4 c.3]; hospitalia, ut C.1 q.7, v. *Ipsum.*' 'Summa de electione', in Laspeyres, ed., *Summa*, 307. This last authority had defeated his editors: it is in fact C.1 q.7 c.2, the same authority that Bernard had used in his *Summa*.

served within also shared an orientation towards the divine. In his *Summa* on the *Breviarium,* a discussion on clerical property offered three forms of conversion: professed (*conversus professus*), simple (*conversus simpliciter*), and vowed (*devotus*). Only the first had to renounce property and could not marry, vows that required a solemn ceremony of profession, 'unless a profession is tacitly understood, as with those who render themselves in conversion to a monastery or as a canon regular or to a hospital'.[91] The place itself was dedicated to service of God, regardless of its rule.

Bernard was working to establish hospitals within the church, using the language and law of the Western church. He sought to give them ecclesiastical status, under the bishop, on the grounds that devotional impulses drove both their creators and those who served within. It was an argument inspired by Roman law, in so far as it was based on an idea of motive, but it was not built from Roman law. Bernard rejected the latter's terminology of 'pious uses' or its wider category of 'venerable houses', working instead to incorporate hospitals into canon law for monasteries and using language familiar from charters (*religionis amore ac divino intuitu*). He ignored Justinian's edicts on welfare institutions, selecting instead those that protected testators, by ensuring their material bequest be fulfilled according to their intentions. Bernard recognized hospitals as testamentary institutions and worked to institutionalize them as religious houses. Across two collections—*Parisiensis II* (1177×79) and *Breviarium* (*c.*1190)[92]—and two *Summae*—on election (1191×98) and on his *Breviarium* (*c.*1200)—Bernard laid the groundwork for a monastic model of the local hospital, one based not on the nature of its service (as in a church) or its community (as in a monastery) but on the Christian intentions that brought them into being and sustained them (its testators). By focusing on hospitals as places, not communities, Bernard encompassed all welfare houses, not only those under religious congregations. His case for episcopal supervision was based on a bishop's duty (in Roman law) to ensure that executors fulfilled the bequests laid out in a will. The implication was that bishops had authority over the gifts of the faithful, when given for Christian purposes.

---

[91] 'In conversis professis ipsa professionis sollemnitas usque adeo necessaria videtur, ut sine ipsa non credatur professus... nisi professus tacite intelligatur, ut qui se reddit monasterio vel canonicae regulari vel hospitali in conversum.' Bernard, *Summa,* 94.

[92] A third collection, *Lipsiensis* (*c.*1185), has been attributed to Bernard (C. Duggan, 'New Case Law', 281; Landau, 'der systematischen Dekretalensammlungen', 135–6; L. Kéry, 'Die Systematisierungsbemühungen des Bernhard von Pavia (†1213),' in W. P. Müller and M. E. Sommar, eds, *Medieval Church Law* (Washington, DC, 2006), 235–6), although the attribution is now questioned (Hanenburg, 'Decretals'; Pennington, 'Decretal Collections', p. 296 n.). The welfare material supports the latter position. *Lipsiensis* drew the title and texts from *Parisiensis II* but expanded the title (34. UT DOMUS RELIGIOSAE EPISCOPO SINT SUBIECTAE ET DE DIVISIONIBUS PARROCHIARUM, ed. *QCA,* 198) and added three chapters on diocesan authority over churches, especially those owing the papal *census*. Bernard was the only canonist to direct the title towards hospitals; others used it to explore wider questions of diocesan authority, as did *Lipsiensis*.

Bernard's was the most sustained and ambitious attempt in the West to claim hospitals for the church and in canon law. It would not be picked up by other canonists. His argument disappeared so comprehensively as to suggest it was rejected out of hand.

Si hospitale and the *Liber extra* (1200–1234)

In the early thirteenth century, canonists took notice of hospitals, and not in Bernardian terms. At about the same time another canonist, Gilbertus Anglicus, was taking an interest in hospitals. By 1203, as we have seen, he had extracted §5 of *Ad petitionem* to make a new statement in law: *Si hospitale*, that anyone could make a hospital, but not an oratory, without involving the bishop (3.26.1).[93] At the very end of book 3 he created a new title for his statement, 'On the building of churches',[94] and *Si hospitale* was its only content. This was the arrangement that passed into the *Compilatio secunda* (1210–12). But it was not the end of Gilbert's interest. His augmented collection of 1203/4, *Bruxellensis*, bears witness to a new development, inspired by Bernard. For here Gilbertus added the new title, 'On hospitals' (3.27, *De xenodochiis*), to his collection.[95] He adopted the title from Bernard's *Breviarium*, but not its content, for instead of Eugenius' decree Gilbert substituted *Ad petitionem* (3.27.1).[96] These early efforts reveal the success and failure, in equal measure, of Bernard's effort: his subject, *De xenodochium*, found ready reception but not his legal argument regarding the place of hospitals under the church. To put this another way: he had made hospitals a topic in canon law but did not define that law. Instead *Si hospitale* reinforced the autonomy of local hospitals, contradicting Bernard's claim that hospitals belonged to the bishop and should be identified with monastic houses.

---

[93] Gilbertus also inserted *Ad petitionem*'s §6, *Si cum aliquo*, in the title DE STATU REGULARIUM (3.22.1), although he did not note that this came from *Ad petitionem* (BL Harley 3834, fols 179v, 181r; Heckel, 'Dekretalensammlungen', 203). The two sections §§5–6 were also adopted by the *Compilatio secunda*: 2 Comp. 3.26.1 (= –X); 2 Comp. 3.22.1 (= –X).

[94] The source of his title is unclear. It was not Justinian's *Digest*, which was the source for Gilbert's preceding title 25, DE CENSIBUS (Dig. 50.15). One possible source was the *Summa circa ius naturale*, which had a title 35, DE ECCLESIIS DE NOUO EDIFICANDIS. The *Summa* was probably composed at Paris in *c*.1186 by Richard de Mores, an Englishman who within ten years had moved to Bologna, Kuttner and Rathbone, 'Anglo-Norman Canonists', 334–9, 355.

[95] On this longer recension, see P. D. Clarke, 'The Collection of Gilbertus', *ZRG Kan. Abt.* 117 (Berlin, 2000), 139–42, 172.

[96] It was followed in *Bruxellensis* by a letter of Innocent III regarding sanctuary (Potthast 1141; *PL* 214, cols 875–6), whose connection to hospitals cannot be discerned. There may be none. The letter was appended to the original recension, perhaps placed here because its comment that a *servus* be returned to his lord echoed a sentiment in *Ad petitionem*, or perhaps a redactor simply placed it at the end of book 3. Innocent's decretal was popular among contemporary canonists, who included it in their version of this book, but not to address hospitals (Clarke, 'Collection of Gilbertus', 172).

Si hospitale was soon cited in Johannes Teutonicus's *Glossa ordinaria* (1216/7) to the *Decretum*. Johannes did not place it beside the list of Byzantine charities that had inspired decretists to recite the Julian definitions (at C.23 q.8 c.23), and where Johannes himself offered an erroneously abbreviated version of these definitions.[97] Nor was it placed beside any other Byzantine reference to *xenones, xenodochia*, or *ptochia*. Instead it was related to the phrase 'aut oratorii', from the council of Chalcedon (C.18 q.2 c.10), that none may build a monastery or oratory against the will of the bishop. Here, Johannes noted that even a hospital cannot be built without episcopal licence, unless it was a simple hospital with no oratory.[98] For the latter statement he cited *Si hospitale* (via *Compilatio secunda*); for the former, Urban III's decretal (*Ad haec*) in Bernard's *Breviarium*, for which Johannes adopted Bernard's assertive interpretation. It is here that Johannes introduced the term *simplex hospitale*. As so often with *simplex* in such commentaries, the term was to distinguish the basic, unadorned form of a concept (here, *hospitale*). *Simplex* differentiated the charitable element of the hospital from the ecclesiastical interest in an oratory. Canon law did not define two types of hospital; instead it acknowledged competing rubrics, none of which directly confronted the problem of hospitals: a definition of 'venerable places' (Roman law), episcopal licence to establish an oratory (Chalcedon), and new papal statements to confirm the independent status of hospitals (Alexander III's *Si hospitale*) and extend the reach of episcopal confirmation (Urban III's *Ad haec*). Johannes's *glossa ordinaria* wrestled uncomfortably with the last three of these and could not clarify how they worked together. His own statement (at *aut oratorii*) is significant less for its muddled answer than for its clear rejection of Bernard's claim that hospitals were ecclesiastical.

In fact, any explicit argument in law ended with Bernard of Pavia. It was Bernard's title and two chapters that appeared in the *Liber extra* (1234) and was therefore Bernard—and not the latter's compiler, Raymond of Peñaforte, or its disseminator, Gregory IX—who assembled the small corpus of canon law on hospitals that predated *Quia contingit*. Its reuse in the *Liber extra* was mechanical rather than creative, for the title, 'On religious houses, that they be subject to the

---

[97] C.23 q.8 c.23 v. *xenones*: 'Xenodochium est locus uenerabilis ubi pauperes peregrini recipiuntur, Ptochium est locus ubi pauperes [*here a line is missing*: pascuntur, Gerontocomium est locus uener-abilis, in quo pauperes] et propter senectutem solam infirmi homines curantur. Orphanotrophium est locus uenerabilis in quo pueri parentibus orbati pascuntur. Brephotrophium locus est in quo infantes aluntur.' Troyes, Bibl. mun. MS 192 fol. 129v. Bartholomew of Brescia's later gloss included *Gerontocomium* with slightly altered language: 'est locus ubi senes et valetudinarii et propter senectutem…', *Corpus juris canonici*, 3 parts (Rome, 1582), I, col. 1819.

[98] Above, n. 47. Bartholomew of Brescia copied Johannes Teutonicus's gloss with only a minor linguistic change: 'sed si oratorium non est *sine licentia episcopi construendum*, tamen simplex hospitale potest construi sine licentia episcopi', *Corp. jur. can.* I, col. 1593 (author's italics). Johanne's source was neither Laurentius Hispanus nor Huguccio (Munich, BSB MS Clm 28174, fol. 145v; BnF lat. 3892, fol. 250r). For his frequent reliance on these predecessors, R. Weigand, 'The Development of the *Glossa ordinaria*', in *HMCL* 82–6.

bishop' was directed to more traditional ends. Bernard may have made the title for hospitals but subsequent canonists then used it to explore the scope of episcopal jurisdiction, often in the diocese as a territory. It began in the glosses to the *Breviarium* itself, whose only comment on *De xenodochia* was to clarify that jurisdiction over a church or religious place belonged to the particular bishop in whose own diocese it sat, a reaction to the plural forms in the Roman council's phrase 'of the bishops in whose dioceses they are'.[99] Canonists used the title to gather material on episcopal jurisdiction, not hospitals, as did Bernard of Compostella in his *Compilatio Romana* of 1208.[100] *Compilationes tercia* (1209) and *quarta* (1215) added five decretals of Innocent III, all concerned with episcopal authority over monasteries and regular life.[101]

Bernard's claim might have been dismissed, and his initiative abandoned, but it made a lasting mark in canon law. Its materials remained in his *Breviarium*, which was to supply the scaffolding for the decretal collections that followed. Soon to be known as *Compilatio prima antiqua*, its structure was adopted by successor *compilationes* and passed, with much of its material, into the *Liber extra*. In its two chapters, hospitals now had a place in law (if only a cubbyhole); the opening words of *De xenodochiis* ('On hospitals') offered them as potential subjects for those who wrote glosses or *summae* on the *Liber extra*. And Bernard's title ensured that places could now be distinguished from religious communities in law. Geoffrey de Trani (d. 1245) noticed this small revolution when he introduced the title by noting that 'the above treatment addresses the conversion and condition of religious [men and women]; here below is the treatment of the houses of the same'.[102]

At first glance, the *Liber extra* appears to retreat even from the efforts of compilers who followed Bernard. Raymond included neither *Si hospitale* nor the other sections of *Ad petitionem* that mention hospitals.[103] By definition, xenodochia

---

[99] E.g. the *glossa ordinaria* of Tancred of Bologne: *De xenodochiis*, v. *diocesi*: 'eo ipso quod ecclesie uel alia loca religiosa sunt in diocesi alicuius episcopi ad eius iurisdictionem debent pertinere, ut hic C.16 q.2 c.8; C.18 q.2 c.26; C.16 q.2 c.10': Vatican City, Vat. lat. 1377, fol. 56r; BnF lat. 15996, fol. 39r.

[100] H. Singer, *Dekretalensammlung des Bernardus Compostellanus*, p. 83; BL Harley 3834, fols 302r–303r. See, too, *Lipsiensis*, above n. 92.

[101] 3 Comp. 3.28.1–2 (X 3.36.5–6); 4 Comp. 3.13.1–3 (X 3.36.7–9). The last of these was Lateran IV, c. 13, forbidding new religious rules (*COGD* II. 175).

[102] At X 3.36, DE RELIGIOSIS DOMIBUS: 'Tractatum est supra de conversione et sta[t]u religiosorum; hic subiicitur tractatus de domibus eorundem, et ideo ponitur hic rubrica de religiosis domibus ut episcopis sint subiecte.' Goffredus Tranensis, *Summa* (Lyons, 1519; repr. Aalen, 1992), fol. 155v. See, too, *Glo. ord.* to X 3.36: 'Supra visum est de statu religiosorum, et quibus subiiciantur, nunc de eorum domibus et ecclesiis, et quibus sunt subiecte, est videndum, ideo, etc.' *Corp. jur. can.* II, col. 1302.

[103] Gilbert's title under which *Si hospitale* was lodged had become DE ECCLESIIS AEDIFICANDIS UEL REPARANDIS (X 3.48), where Lateran III's *Cum dicat Apostulus* found a home (X 3.48.2) as 'Lepers must be permitted, without prejudice to ancient parishes, to have their own church and priest and are not required to pay tithes on their gardens or animal produce.' ('LEPROSI PERMITTI DEBENT, SINE PRAEIUDICIO ANTIQUARUM PAROCHIARUM, HABERE ECCLESIAM PROPRIAM ET PRESBYTERUM, NEC TENENTUR SOLUERE DECIMAS DE HORTIS UEL NUTRIMENTIS ANIMALIUM.')

were not included in the titles on monastic houses or the regular life.[104] And they begin to fade, too, from Bernard's title on religious houses. Here, Raymond merely corralled the material from *Compilationes prima, tercia*, and *quarta*, reducing hospitals to a minor notice, in only two of nine chapters.[105] *Compilatio quinta* (1226) had included two letters of Honorius III concerning hospitals, but neither were incorporated into the *Liber extra*. One, on changing petitioners during a lawsuit (5 Comp. 2.3.1 = X-), addressed an issue of legal process not of hospitals, but the other (5 Comp. 1.19.1 = X-), from 1224, pressed the bishop of Arras to support the sisters of the hospital at Douai in their desire to assume the rule of St Victor. Elsewhere, Raymond did use two decretals of Innocent III from *Compilatio tercia*: one, under the title 'On judgements', clarified the role of consent, and the ultimate power of a supervisory patron, in choosing a hospital rector (3 Comp. 1.25.4 = X 1.43.7); but the other, under the title 'On donations', upheld a hospital's right to give itself to a religious order (3 Comp 3.18.5 = X 3.24.8).[106] Along with Honorius's intervention at Douai, the latter suggests that the early thirteenth-century papacy was more active in addressing hospitals than the thin corpus of canon law material suggests. It was cultivating routes by which a xenodochium might become a community of *regulares*. They did not find a home alongside 'On hospitals'.

In fact, the conservative scope of the corpus in the *Liber extra* belies efforts of care and creativity. Raymond incorporated Eugenius' decree of 826 in its edited, Bernardian form and gave it an even more forceful summary, that 'All pious places are under the bishop and through his watchful concern arranged to their assigned use'.[107] It is this summary that historians cite to argue that the church maintained or asserted a general jurisdiction over hospitals between 1100 and 1300, the claim that Bernard had attempted (and failed) to fashion.[108] Raymond's action was subtler than has been appreciated. His copying was not without reflection, and some research.

His reintroduction of the phrase 'pious places' reveals that Raymond had examined the original decrees from 826. There, Eugenius had linked xenodochia with 'other pious places', a term he had adopted from Gregory the Great to forge a wider (if tentative) claim to act for hospitals. The decree that followed his 'On hospitals and other pious places' (*c.*23) at the Roman council had reinforced

---

[104] E.g. DE STATU MONACHORUM ET CANONICORUM REGULARIUM (X 3.35) and DE REGULARIBUS ET TRANSEUNTIBUS AD RELIGIONEM (X 3.31) refer to Hospitallers and Templars (X 3.31.18) but made no mention of welfare houses.

[105] X 3.36.3–4.

[106] Pottast 3482, 3672. Hospitals were mentioned incidentally in other chapters, such as X 2.13.12; 2.28.48; 3.35.6; and *Cum dicat Apostolus* occurs at X 3.48.2.

[107] X 3.36.3: 'EPISCOPO SUBSUNT OMNIA LOCA PIA, ET AD EIUS SOLLICITUDINEM DEBENT ORDINARI AD USUM DESTINATUM.'

[108] Drossbach, 'Das Hospital', 512–15, and Frank, who also notes 'Das vorangestellte *Summarium* spitzt den Inhalt noch zu', in his 'Hospitalreformen', 11 n. 28.

episcopal authority over 'pious places', a category that included chapels under secular jurisdiction. It required a bishop to appoint its priests, if his jurisdiction allowed, and enjoined him to intervene in places under secular jurisdiction when lay authorities proved remiss.[109] If the first requirement was uncontroversial in the thirteenth century, the second (for hospitals) lay beyond diocesan claim. For this reason, neither Bernard nor Raymond could append the statement to De xeno-dochiis and claim a right to intrude into facilities established in secular law. Instead, Raymond's summary advanced episcopal claims by retaining a useful ambiguity as to what constituted a locus pius. His reintroduction of the term marked a change in canonistic language from Justinian's (and Julian's) venerabiles loci.[110] Like Deusdedit a century earlier, Raymond reached back to the Western tradition to point a way forward. Henceforth, the language of 'pious places' would replace that of 'venerable places'. But where all hospitals had been venerable places in Roman law, not all were 'pious places'. The power of the term was not in any claim but in its ambiguity.

The temptation is to read the Liber extra's chapter 'On hospitals', or its summary, as a reflection of an ecclesiastical right—either a right that had been established or was now being claimed in law.[111] This would be an error. As we have seen and shall see, canonists and popes shied away from such a claim. Rather, De xenodochiis, and Raymond's reintroduction of 'pious places', was part of a longer story: two of a series of fragmented, cautious responses to welfare since the 1170s, the most influential of which were Alexander's Cum dicat Apostolus and the development of Si hospitale. Together they amount to a quiet but dynamic legal framework that responded to and reinforced calls to expand episcopal intervention. Between 1179 and 1317, this activity chipped away at the limits of jurisdiction, as concerned churchmen pushed inwards to reach hospitals. Its sharpest chisel may have been not the instruments of law themselves but the slow cultural change cultivated by Raymond's 'pious places' and the association of hospitals with the term 'religious'. Over time, it worked to reimagine many hospitals as 'pious places' and to embolden episcopal claims.

Urban III (1185–7) and Ad haec (X 3.36.4)

Raymond was able to take this leap, to name a new category, because the world was already changing. The change was powered by a new instrument in law, a

---

[109] See Chapter 6.

[110] The previous rarity of the term 'pious place' is apparent in the Wortkonkordanz to the Decretum, 2630–2, 2636–41, where locus had many modifiers, including venerabilis, but pius occurs only twice: C.12 q.1 c.27, citing Rome (826), and C.16 q.1 c.62. As discussed earlier in this chapter, during the twelfth century, Roman law (via the glossators' Greek definitions) provided the scholarly definition of charities as venerable places.

[111] Cf. Drossbach, 'Das Hospital', 514; Frank, 'Hospitalreformen', 11.

quiet conceptual workhorse that was crafted specifically for xenodochia. It had been transforming hospitals across Europe for fifty years when Raymond reintroduced the term 'pious places'. The new instrument was preserved as the second of the two hospital chapters in the *Liber extra* (1 Comp. 3.31.4 = X 3.36.4). It has been overlooked in modern scholarship because it seemed trivial, even inane, when hospitals were defined as monastic forms; however, with hospitals stripped of this status, the decretal takes on new meaning.

The decretal, *Ad haec* (JL 15723 (9866)), was a papal intervention from 1186, clarifying a status for hospitals as ecclesiastical sites. It was prompted when Rufino, bishop of Rimini (1185–91), sought the advice of Pope Urban III about decommissioning a hospital. Urban's response was to prove the defining statement of hospitals in canon law, and was quickly and widely disseminated, appearing by 1188 at Reims in the *Collectio Brugensis*.[112] Urban stated:

> on that [clarification] which has been sought from us—whether a hospital house can be wholly changed back to a worldly state—to your inquiry we answer the following: that if this place should have been fixed by episcopal authority for the use, as is the custom, of hospitality and provisioning of the poor [then] since it should thus be religious it must not be consigned to worldly uses, just as ancient custom respects without doubt (and the sanctions of the venerable fathers teach) concerning vestments, wooden vessels, and other utensils allotted by the bishop to religious practice.[113]

Although the question was posed regarding a 'hospital house', the answer spoke generically of place (*locus*): once again, it was not a community at issue, but the site and its use.[114] The form is now familiar to us. But here Urban was making new

---

[112] The text, as it survives, is undated. It was the second of two queries, sent together, the first concerning marriages involving those of servile status (X 4.9.3). The first year of Urban's pontificate seems likely. A papal confirmation of October 1186 to the chapter of Pistoia concerning their hospital articulates similar themes, if with small differences, notably the protection of the chapter's rights ('ut nullus in preiudicium iuris vestri circa statum hospitalitatis ipsius temere quicquam audeat immutare vel ipsum ad alium locum transferre'). *Acta Pontificum*, ed. J. V. Pflugk–Harttung, 3 vols (Tübingen, 1880–6), III, no. 388; JL 15681, 15723. It marks a dramatic change in terminology from the usual papal charters for hospitals, which tended to undertake the guardianship (*tutelam*) of the hospital or protect its possessions: e.g. JL 10320, 15772, 15960. Imbert noticed the Rimini letter, seeing in it an expression of *affectation perpetuelle*, an enduring principle fixed by the church since at least 826, HDC 79–81.

[113] X 3.36.4: 'LOCUS, AUCTORITATE EPISCOPI AD USUM HOSPTIALITATIS DEPUTATUS, EST RELIGIOSUS, ET AD MUNDANOS USUS REDIRE NON DEBET. Ad haec *super eo, quod quaesitum est a nobis, utrum hospitalis domus possit in saecularem habitum commutari*, inquisitioni tuae taliter respondemus, quod, si locus *ille* ad hospitalitatis usum et pauperum prouisionem fuerit, sicut moris est, auctoritate pontificis destinatus, quum sit religiosus, non debet mundanis usibus deputari, sicut de uestibus et ligneis uasis, et aliis utensilibus ad cultum religionis per pontificem deputatis, antiqua consuetudo indubitanter obseruat, et venerabilium Patrum edocent sanctiones.'

[114] Hospitals were its recognized subject: *Glo. ord.*, at C.19 q.3 c.4 [QUE SEMEL SUNT DEDICATA MONASTERIA SEMPER PERSEUERENT], v. *Maneant*: 'similiter nec hospitale potest conuerti ad alium usum, ut [1 Comp. 3.31.4 = X 3.36.4] sed nec permutari possunt mancipia ecclesiae [1 Comp. 3.16.3 = X 3.19.3] dari tamen possunt priuato, ut [C.12 q.2. c.67]'. *Corp. jur. can.* I, col. 1610.

law, creating a new category of hospitals: those confirmed to their use by a bishop. Here he was crafting a new means of protection by the church: when fixed through episcopal authority, hospitals must be held in perpetuity to their charitable purposes; that is, to what they had been established to do. To put it another way a hospital's *institutio*—the founder's directive (*dispositio*)—could now be guarded in perpetuity under canon law through episcopal confirmation.

It is the legal basis that is most fascinating. Urban's case did not rest on Roman law, protecting welfare houses as fixed to a pious promise, their goods dedicated to God and subject to divine law; nor did it rest on the early medieval arguments of church property, as the patrimony of the poor.[115] Urban did not claim hospitals as ecclesiastical institutions or as church property. Instead, he redefined the act of episcopal confirmation. To do so, he relied on Gratian's *Decretum*, part III, 'on consecration'. Urban did not turn to its sections on churches and monasteries (cc. 1–24), defined therein as *loci sacrati* (sacred places): the only places where mass might be celebrated and the eucharist performed; perpetual, under the bishop's jurisdiction, and consecrated by him to God.[116] Nor did he turn to its chapters on altars and oratories (cc. 25–36). Instead, Urban rested his case on the material culture of worship (cc. 38–46): the church timbers, episcopal chairs, the candles, altar cloths, holy vessels or vestments, and priest's clothing. As objects consecrated to religious uses, these were not to be handed over to the laity and the most holy of them (those pertaining to the sacristy) were to be burned when worn out, their ashes entombed in the church's baptistry, walls, or flagstones.[117] Urban secured hospitals just as (*sicut*) vestments, wooden vessels, and other utensils allocated *ad cultum religionis*, and so as a material tool dedicated to a religious use. Urban takes his language from the opening of Gratian's 'On consecration', which summarizes God's commandment that Moses equip the tabernacle with candles, vases, utensils, and holy vestments that 'perform divine worship'.[118] If confirmed by the bishop to a use, the very material form of the hospital would now be a protected vessel.

This act made hospitals 'religious' and Urban took care to distinguish what this meant. He wrote not of *vasis* (as Exodus) or *sacra vasa* (as Gratian) but of wooden

[115] On the former, Nov. 7; Étienne de Tournai, *Summa*, 226; and Chapter 5. On the latter, Julian Pomerius, p. 76–7.

[116] D.1 de cons. Much of Gratian's material came via Burchard of Worms and Ivo of Chartres. For the definition of *loci sacri*: 'SACRIFICARE ET MISSAS CELEBRARE NON LICET, NISI IN LOCIS SACRATIS ... quoniam in aliis locis sacrificari et missas celebrari non licet, nisi in his, in quibus episcopus iusserit, aut ab episcopo regulariter ordinato, tenente uidelicet ciuitatem, consecrati fuerint.' D.1 de cons. c.14 (Ivo of Chartres, *Decretum* 3.62).

[117] D.1 de cons. c.39: 'non licet ea, que in sacrario fuerint, male tractari, sed incendio uniuersa tradantur.'

[118] 'Tabernaculum enim Moysen Domino precipiente fecisse et sacrasse, cum mensa et altari eius, et [c]ereis *uasis* et *utensilibus ad diuinum cultum* explendum legimus ... Dominoque cum *uestibus* sanctis sacrati.... quam in Domino sacratis *ab episcopis*' (author's italics). D.1 de cons. c.2 (Ivo of Chartres, *Decretum* 3.60–1), referring to Exodus 25: 9, 30: 26–7.

vases (*ligneis vasis*). His reference was to an early debate, settled by the ninth century, that wooden vessels not be used for the mass: a chalice or patten must be made of gold, silver, or pewter.[119] It was a ruling upheld in the twelfth and thirteenth centuries, even among the Cistercians.[120] The reference roots Urban's ruling in Western tradition. It also makes a clear statement, one that would have been explicit to contemporaries, of the kind of material tool with which he was equating hospitals: vessels that did not hold the body and blood of Christ. A confirmed hospital was a place (*locus*), not a sacred place (*locus sacratus*); as were wooden vessels, they were part of a wider material culture of Christian service, which did not pertain to the sacristy. Such a distinction was also made in the act of confirmation. For whereas a *locus sacratus* was made (and made perpetual) through consecration, a hospital was simply built, without the bishop, but made perpetual if fixed (*destinatus*) through episcopal authority to an assigned use. Thereafter, a *locus sacratus* could not be transformed (*fieri*) into secular dwellings;[121] in contrast, a hospital could not be reassigned (*deputari*) to worldly uses. The former was a holy place, its site rooted into the soil and transformed by consecration; the latter sat above the soil, located but not placed, as resources assigned to a use.

From the first, Urban's statement *Ad haec* was paired with *Si hospitale*; indeed, the two seem to have given rise to one another. *Ad haec* was itself a response to the place of simple hospitals, which could exist beyond the reach and protection of the church. Urban's new protection introduced canon law for hospitals and this, in turn, required a statement of that wider circumstance, of the other side of the coin. In response, canonists found a sentence buried in Alexander's decretal *Ad petitionem*. *Ad haec* first appeared in *Brugensis* (1187/8) at Reims: it was preceded in the same chapter by our fullest surviving copy of *Ad petitionem*, with all of the latter's statements on hospitals. The relationship was temporarily severed when Bernard of Pavia stretched the limits of *Ad haec*, in his argument that all hospitals were religious places, under episcopal jurisdiction. In response, *Si hospitale* appeared, extracted now from *Ad petitionem* and with an identity of its own.[122]

[119] A decree of the council of Tribur (895), IN LIGNEIS UASCULIS DOMINICI CORPORIS ET SANGUINIS SACRAMENTA NON SUNT CELEBRANDA, was cited by Gratian: D.1 de cons. c. 44; see, too, c. 45.

[120] D. J. Reilly, 'Art', in M. B. Bruun, ed., *The Cambridge Companion to the Cistercian Order* (Cambridge, 2013), 129. The material tools of the mass are explored in E. P. Maclachlan, 'Liturgical Vessels and Implements', in T. J. Heffernan and E. A. Matter, eds, *The Liturgy of the Medieval Church* (Kalamazoo, MI, 2001).

[121] C.19 q.3 c.4 (Ivo of Chartres, *Decretum* 3.17): 'QUE SEMEL SUNT DEDICATA, MONASTERIA SEMPER PERSEUERENT. Que semel sunt dedicata monasteria consilio episcoporum, maneant perpetuo monasteria, et res, que ad ea pertinent, monasteriis reseruari oportet, nec posse ea ultra fieri secularia habitacula. Qui uero permiserint hec fieri, subiaceant his condempnationibus, que per canones constitutae sunt.'

[122] We might see here a parallel with a 'paradox' observed in the rise of privileges, that 'particular privileges contributed to the establishment in medieval societies of the idea and practice of a generally applicable law.' (A. Boureau, 'Privilege in Medieval Societies', in Linehan and Nelson, eds, *The Medieval World*, 622.)

It appeared in 1203 and 1203/4 in Gilbertus Anglicus's collections and then in *Compilatio secunda* (1210–15), under the title *On the building of churches* (2 Comp. 3.26.1). Glossators reinserted the statement, and so the balance of religious and private into Bernard's own *Breviarium*, or *Compilatio prima*. Attached to *Ad haec*, their comments confirmed 'that a private person cannot make a consecrated place' and that 'it is permitted to build a hospital without the licence of a bishop', citing *Si hospitale*.[123]

Aftermath: The Problem of *Religiosus* (1234–70)

Urban's decretal introduced canon law on hospitals. It was a new law, rooted in the traditions of the Western church; but it was also an act very much of its moment. Urban had consolidated a new protection and with it a new power of episcopal confirmation, to fix in perpetuity a hospital (and so its property) to its charitable use. It was fixed as a material object, not as a *locus sacratus*, and regardless of the existence of an oratory. The mechanism that made this perpetual was not consecration (this was not a site made sacred) nor religious profession (this was not a community made religious). It was a legal act, one that was expressed via charter. It made use of the increasing administrative and legal reach of bishops at this moment and the growing significance of documents. And there was one other element that was of its moment: its (subtle) flirtation with Roman law in the term 'religious'. This would cause problems for canonists. For nearby, Bernard of Pavia was also trying to define hospitals as 'religious', but his use of this term was at odds with Urban's.

Urban III and Bernard of Pavia were applying themselves to the same problem: how could the church protect a material object (the hospital)? By 1187, Bernard had staked out the core of his argument that a hospital was a religious house. He inserted Urban's decretal into *Parisiensis II* and the *Breviarium* beside his edited decree from Eugenius' council of 826, welcoming its prohibition against a hospital, once confirmed, returning to worldly uses. But Urban's decretal sat uncomfortably with Bernard's argument in other aspects, including the second statement for which it was cited in Bernard's *Summa*: that hospitals 'must not be made without the authority of the diocesan bishop'. Nevertheless, the two solutions were similar enough to sow confusion. Both rested on notions of *locus* (place) and *religiosus* (as a mark of ecclesiastical status), but defined each differently. As places, Bernard equated hospitals with monasteries, making them 'houses', a

---

[123] 'Ad hec super, *pontificali*: §quam priuatus locum non fac[it] sacrum § ... sine licentia/consensu episcopi licet hospitale construere ... *Si hospitale*'. In between are statements on burial and consecration (*sacrum locum*). The Latin in the glosses varies considerably (e.g. *quam priuatus locus quo ad hospitaliaros non facit sacrum*), but the clarity of *Si hospitale* rings through: Vatican City, Vat. lat. 2509, fol. 53v and Vat. lat. 1377, fol. 56r; BnF lat. 15996, fol. 39r).

term that spoke of people as much as place; Urban placed them among the accoutrements of Christian worship, with linen clothing and wooden bowls, as mundane items that could be applied to Christian service. Bernard's concept of *religiosus* was explicitly adapted from monastic life, where religious men and women had made a profession to God; Urban gave *religiosus* a modern twist, (silently) taking a definition from Roman law, which distinguished *religiosus* from *sacer* (consecrated).

By 1203, Bernard's argument had been dismissed in favour of *Si hospitale*, but the *Liber extra* brought the two models once more into collision. By importing Bernard's rubrics and his material, it left Urban's decretal under Bernard's title 'On religious houses, that they be subject to the bishop'. Raymond was the first to confront the resulting problem: how could a hospital be a 'religious place' in this way? His appropriation of the term 'pious places' was a way to address this, creating a distinctive category for certain hospitals (by implication, those that had been confirmed by a bishop to their specific charitable tasks). His title to Urban's decretal (X 3.36.4) trod carefully, offering a link between Eugenius's decree (now X 3.36.3, *De xenodochiis*), where such pious places 'are arranged through the watchful concern of bishops to their established uses', and Urban's constrained definition of *religiosus*: 'a place allotted to the use of hospitality by episcopal authority', it declared, 'is religious and must not be redirected to mundane uses'.

With the chapter *De xenodochiis* in the *Liber extra*, hospitals became a topic in canon law, even if they did not have a legal form provided by canon law. The chapter drew little attention from canonists, who preferred the wider topic of religious houses from the title. Geoffrey de Trani defined religious houses as 'monasteries, temples, hospitals, and other such places assigned to pious and religious uses', yet dedicated discussion only to oratories, churches, and, in particular, monasteries.[124] Innocent IV (*c*.1245) made a brief comment that recognized a conflict between the two hospital chapters and other authorities, which he left uncited but which were clearly chapters from the *Decretum*.[125] In the former, a private person needed episcopal consent to make a religious place; in the latter any lay person might have an oratory and hospital on their own property, so long as it did not take the form of a church or have the mass celebrated there without episcopal licence. He did not interrogate the discrepancy, noting only that: 'This however is certain that [anyone] can assign a house for the reception of

---

[124] At X 3.36, c. *de religiosis domibus*: 'Religiose domus dicuntur monasteria, templa, hospitalia et alia loca similia ad pios et religiosos usus deputata quocumque nomine censeantur ut [X 3.36.3] et [Cod. 1.3].' He defined an oratory as 'the same as a church or chapel' and even those in a private house, if established with episcopal authority, as religious places. He noted that *domus religiosae* were created via episcopal authority and could not be returned to secular uses. Goffredus Tranensis, *Summa* (fols 155v–156v).

[125] D.1 de cons. cc. 33–4.

the poor'.[126] Among the decretalists, hospitals remained an uncertain topic. As those that had gone before, Bernard of Parma (d.1263) focused discussion of the title on the diocesan and his reach. His only notice of *De xenodochiis* was a brief note of the Byzantine forms and those accommodated in each.[127]

One thirteenth-century scholar did take an interest in hospitals: Henry of Susa, or Hostiensis, one of the most original canonists of his age. His interest in hospitals may be due to serendipity as much as intellectual curiosity, for his early career as papal legate had taken him to England between *c*.1236/7 and 1244. During this time he acted as a royal agent and as such, for a short time, held the mastership of St Cross hospital, Winchester, one of the oldest hospitals in the country.[128] While it is unlikely that he spent much, if any, time at the hospital, it is tempting to wonder whether this tenure lay behind his attempt to interrogate hospitals in law. Certainly, the Winchester hospital made a lasting impression on him, for thirty years later he remembered it in his will, leaving to it three of his books.[129] His years as master correspond with the early phase of his first great work, his *Summa copiosa* on the *Liber extra*, which he wrote *c*.1239×53. He followed this with his *Lectura* on the *Liber extra*, first drafted between 1254 and 1265 and then fully revised before his death in 1271. It is the earlier works, the *Summa* and first draft of the *Lectura*, that contain his pioneering work on hospitals.

In his *Summa*, unlike previous canonists, Hostiensis wanted to clarify how it was that hospitals could be categorized with monasteries and churches as 'religious places' given that hospitals could be created by anyone and without episcopal authority. It forms Hostiensis's first question of the title, 'What should be called a religious place?' Monks, who cannot live without a cloister 'as a fish cannot live without water', must live in religious places, and a place where a body is buried is also religious, but the category includes unconsecrated places, such as

---

[126] At X 3.36.4, v. *Ad hoc auctoritate*: 'Ad hoc auctoritate pontifici quia priuatus sine auctoritate episcopi locum religiosum facere non potest...Alii tamen dicunt quod cuicunque laico licitum est habere oratorium et hospitale in domo propria, dummodo non habeat formam ecclesie, etiam sine auctoritate episcopi...sed ibi celebrari non poterit absque auctoritate episcopi, ut in predictis capitulis [X 3.36.3]. Hoc autem certum est, quod domum deputare potest ad pauperes recipiendos.' Innocent IV, *Apparatus super quinque libros decretalium* (Venice, 1491), fol. 163r–v, noticed also in *HDC* 68 n.

[127] At X 3.36.3, v. *De xenodochiis*: 'Ponitur in bepho. geron. orpho. pochoque [*sic*] xenon. Infirmus uetulus puer orphanus et peregrinus [C.23 q.8 c.23].' Cf. X 3.36.3, v. *Diocesi*: 'hic manifeste patet quod monasteria et alia loca religiosa pertinent ad episcopum loci de iure communi [C.16 q.5. c.8, C.16 q.7 c.10, C.18 q.2 c.17] nisi ostendant exemptionem [C.18 q.2 c.18]', *Compilatio nova decretalium domini Gregorii pape noni* (Speyer, 1486), fol. 206r.

[128] *CPR 1232–47*, 249, 252; *Chron. Maj.* IV. 352–3. A successor had been instituted by Nov. 1250 (*CPR 1247–58*, 79). For Hostiensis, see K. Pennington, 'Henricus de Segusio (Hostiensis)', in his *Popes, Canonists and Texts*, no. 16, pp. 2–3; N. Didier, 'Henri de Suse en Angleterre (1236?–1244)', in *Studi in Onore di Vincenzo Arangio-Rviz*, 4 vols (Naples, 1953), II. 339, 341; C. Gallagher, *Canon Law and the Christian Community* (Rome, 1978).

[129] N. Ramsay and J. M. W. Willoughby, eds, *Corpus of British Medieval Library Catalogues XIV* (Oxford, 2009), 432–3.

'*xenodochia*, that is hospitals'.[130] He then gave the Julian definitions, but not as a place-marker. Now the definitions offered another piece of the puzzle, as Hostiensis tried to make sense of contemporary hospitals in law. He noted that all these Byzantine forms were types (*species*) of approved religious ways of life, but also that many types of hospitals and similar places could be created by anyone, on private authority.[131] A new vocabulary was to point the way forward. As had Johannes Beleth before him, Hostiensis used Roman law to distinguish religious (*religiosus*) from sacred (*sacer*), relating the former to the latter as genus to species.[132] Sacred places were temples, churches, and houses dedicated to the service of God. Such were also *religiosus*, but this second category also included places not 'ceremonially dedicated to God, i.e. in the form of a church and by a bishop'.[133] Hostiensis concluded that 'A sacred place is religious, but not the reverse'. He distinguished charities from churches, made sacred through consecration.[134] But he failed to clarify what made a place *religious*: whether episcopal authority was necessary or how this might relate to private foundation.

The early version of his *Lectura* resolved this. Here, at 'On hospitals', he noted that *xenodochia* was a term generally taken to mean all hospitals, but he used Julian's definitions to show that the term had also referred specifically to pilgrim hostels.[135] A range of authorities made 'manifestly clear that monasteries and

---

[130] At X 3.36. 'DE RELIGIOSIS DOMIBUS RUBRICA: Quoniam monachi sine claustro vivere non intelligunter posse, sicut nec piscis sine aqua [C.16 q.1 c.5] et degere debent in locis religiosis & vacare orationibus... *Quis dicatur locus religiosus*: dictum est [Summa, *de sepulturis* quid sit sepultura]; sed sciendum quod hic ponitur domus religiosa pro sacra, unde exponendum est de religiosis id est sacris uel ideo dixit religiosis ut includat loca religiosa et non consecrata sicut xenodochia id est hospitalia et [X 3.36.3]' Cited here from Henricus de Segusia, *Summa super titulis decretaliu[m]* (Venice, 1480); Munich, Staatsbibl. MS Clm 14006, fol. 121r.

[131] '...hac autem omnes species religionis approbatae uidentur...Et sunt haec diuerse species hospitalium et talia loca uidentur, quod quilibet possit facere propria auctoritate...'

[132] A place was made religious through burial, even if unconsecrated (Dig. 11.7, esp. 2.5 and 44; also, Dig. 1.8.6 and 9). The tasks before Beleth and Hostiensis were very different. Beleth had distinguished charitable houses, dedicated to human needs, from other venerable places (religious, holy, and sacred), which were dedicated to prayer (Iohannis Beleth, *Summa de Ecclesiasticus Officiis*, c. 2). Hostiensis was confronted with a situation where charitable houses had already been defined as *religiosus* by the *Liber Extra* title (X 3.36) and *Ad haec* (X 3.36.4).

[133] 'Et nota quod locus religiosus et sacer habent se tanquam genus et species, transit enim in nomine speciali et dicitur sacer remanet in generali quod dicitur religiosus sic ad optio transit in nomine speciali et dicitur arrogatio remanet in generali et dicitur adoptio... ergo locus sacer religiosus est sed non conuertitur ideo dixit de religiosis et non de sacris ut sub genere speciem comprehendere posset. Dicitur autem locus sacer ille que rite id est iuxta ecclesie formam et per pontifices deo dedicatus est. Et aedes sacre id est ecclesie et domi que rite ad ministerium dei dedicata sunt sacra dicuntur ut calices uestimenta sacerdotalia et similia.'

[134] His more domestic use of 'religious' can be seen, too, in his statement that 'Someone who lives in a holy and religious way in his own house, although not professed, is also called religious in a broad sense not because that sort of person is bound to any precise rule but rather because he leads a stricter and holier life than other secular people', tr. Makowski, '*A Pernicious Sort of Woman*', p. xxvii.

[135] 'generaliter supponit pro omnibus hospitalibus proprie tamen dicitur xenodochium locus in quo peregrini suscipiuntur.' His early draft survives in only one manuscript, used here: Oxford, New College MS 205, fol. 157v. On the manuscript, K. Pennington, 'An Earlier Recension of Hostiensis's *Lectura*', *BMCL* 17 (1987).

other religious and pious places belong to the diocesan from the *ius commune*', the interplay of canon and Roman law that now underpinned church law.[136] In the following chapter, on Urban III's decretal, he drew a new distinction: only the bishop could make a place sacred, but any private person could make it religious. Anything, once dedicated to God, could not be returned to worldly uses, but this clearly meant sacred not religious places, since a place made religious through burial ceased to be religious upon disinterment.[137] Hostiensis expanded this section before his death, but his thinking on hospitals had all been laid out in the early draft. His final version meditated further on episcopal authority over churches, noting in passing its different nature depending upon the type of institution.[138] It also noted that, on the question as to whether something consecrated to God might return to worldly uses, some authorities had distinguished between temporalities (which are alienable) and spiritualities. Finally, he quoted Innocent IV, and by simply changing *religiosus* to *sacer* made a declaration out of what had been a conundrum: none can make a place *sacred* without the bishop, and some say laity can make a hospital or an oratory in their own house, so long as it has neither the form of a church nor celebration of mass, while it is certain that anyone can assign their house to receive the poor.[139]

Hostiensis had resolved an intellectual problem that had been created when two contradictory arguments were placed side by side in the *Liber extra*. On the face of it, his achievement seems to matter little: his ideas of genus and species did not underpin subsequent statements of law, for example. It would be easy to dismiss his efforts, as those of his fellow canonists, as indulgent scholasticism, but that would be to miss the bigger point. Canon law was a scholastic pursuit—it was articulated, curated, and interpreted by canonists in texts that took specialist training to command—and it was one where definitions mattered. By the thirteenth century, to redefine the expectations of a priest under canon law, for example, was to redefine what a priest should be. The challenge for hospitals

---

[136] 'Hic manifeste patet quod monasteria et alia loca religiosa et pia ad diocesanum pertinent de iure communi, de quo petens uel agens fundat intentionem suam, ut hic patet et [C.16 q.5 c.8; C.16 q.3 c.2; C.16 q.7 c.10; C.18 q.2 c.17; C.18 q.2. c.10].'

[137] '*Ad haec*, et infra auctoritate pontificis [X 3.36.4] Hoc ideo dicit quia priuatus locum non facit sacrum... Quamuis religiosum faciat sepeliendo etiam in alieno loco, dummodo hoc fiat de domini uoluntate... Sic econuerso per extumulationem desinit religiosus esse.'

[138] At X 3.36.3, 'quod omnes ecclesiae, omnia monasteria, hospitalia, et alia pia loca sub dispositione episcoporum subsistant: *ut uidelicet istud intelligatur uerum esse quantum ad hoc, ut seruent ea ad quam sunt ordinata.*' Henricus de Segusia, *Lectura sive Apparatus domini Hostiensis super quinq[ue] libris decretaliu[m]*, 2 vols (Strasbourg, 1512), II, fol. 145v (author's italics).

[139] At X 3.36.4. 'Quamuis autem nemo *possit sine authoritate episcopi locum sacrum facere*... tamen secundum quosdam cuicumque etiam *laico licitum est habere oratorium et hospitale in domo propria, etiam sine authoritate episcopi, dummodo non habeat formam ecclesiae, sed* sine *authoritate episcopi non est ibi celebra*ndum [D.1 de cons. cc. 33–4]. *Hoc autem certum est, quod ad recipiendos pauperes potest domum* suam quilibet *deputare.*' Henricus de Segusia, *Lectura* II, fol. 145v (the language quoted from Innocent is marked with italics).

was very different. For xenodochia, in their diverse forms, were not beholden to canon law; as a result, popes and canonists were not the arbiters of either the signifier (the words used) or its referent (the facilities themselves). What might appear to be an indulgent debate about language was therefore the consequence of a far more meaningful struggle: how to wrestle with the complexity of Christian welfare. In a field where definitions mattered, this was also a question of how to apply the language of church and canon law to a phenomenon that could not itself be defined in that law.

It was also an effort to engage with that phenomenon. Devising canon law without canons—in the absence, that is, of a recognized right to act or a body of material through which to act—produces a bitty and confusing picture. It hides careful thinking behind small statements that did not fully reveal their objects. In this context, and rather unexpectedly, it is Urban III and Bernard of Pavia who emerge as the great radicals of hospital law, a title they might claim merely for directly addressing hospitals. Yet it was also through their actions that the framework of canon law changed for welfare, and with it changed welfare.

Bernard's attempt to define all hospitals as ecclesiastical was an immediate failure, but it had two consequences. The first was its legacy in the *Liber extra*, whose chapter 'On hospitals' made hospitals a topic of canon law and whose title (X 3.36) defined hospitals as 'religious places which should be subject to the bishop', a statement that was to ring through schoolrooms and then into dioceses over the next century. The second was the response it prompted, in the discovery/creation of *Si hospitale*. Its repetition in glosses and commentaries may too easily obscure its significance as witness to the most important development in canon law regarding welfare: that it was concertedly agreed that anyone could make a hospital and without the knowledge of the bishop.

The quiet revolutionary agent was Urban III's *Ad haec* of 1186. This was the only major piece of legislation to redefine hospitals and to create a new legal tool. In episcopal confirmation, it offered a mechanism to fix a facility, in perpetuity, to its assigned use. This was a Western 'pious promise', a way to secure the endowment to its *dispositio*: the purpose laid out by the founder could now be guarded by the bishop. If there was a change between the early medieval xenodochium, a manifestation of a private bequest, and the later medieval hospital, an institution publicly accountable for its mission, it can be found in this small act.

The challenge in canon law during the classical period was to understand how a non-ecclesiastical form was also religious and to develop, where possible, support for what were acts of Christian faith. It was not to claim hospitals, which remained a phenomena that would exist in the world and of the world. The answers of Alexander III, Urban III, Raymond of Peñaforte, and Hostiensis did not provide classifications for hospitals. They left unclear, for example, the status of a hospital with a chapel, or with a group of priests who maintain the canonical hours, or with a devotional community that had not been constituted as an *ecclesia* or as conventual. What they did was preserve ambiguity while extending a new vocabulary. This new vocabulary (*pius locus, religious, sacer*) underpinned an expanding ability (and claim) of bishops to intervene, when needed, in welfare houses, to oversee priests, the moral and religious life of their communities, and, especially, that they were fulfilling the tasks for which they were founded. The consequence was not to bring hospitals under the church, but to provide public mechanisms to enforce arrangements laid down at foundation. The legal surety that anyone could make a hospital and fix it in perpetuity to a charitable use emboldened the laity and brought new clarity, and so security, to the role of patrons and assigns, especially urban governments. It encouraged—and may even have made possible—the profusion of experiments in forms of welfare in the century following 1186. It also fostered the ideal of an episcopal concern that charities be held accountable to their foundation.

8

Robert de Courson and the
Northern Reformers

In 1213 the papal legate Robert de Courson convened a council at Paris and issued a decree that required leper-houses and hospitals to adopt a rule. The decree was reissued at a council at Rouen in 1214 and, it has often been suggested, perhaps at another three councils held by Courson in France. It has been to these councils and to this decree that historians have turned in order to answer the question, 'what did the medieval church do about hospitals?' The decree has long defined our understanding of church policy towards welfare institutions: it has been used to suggest that hospitals were held to a (monastic) model and to identify the means by which such a model was effected, to give shape to the chronology for change in hospitals between 1100 and 1500, and to indicate the expectations of local bishops. For over a century, the hospital reform under Robert de Courson has defined the place of hospitals in the eyes of the church. Given its significance, it is amazing that it has never been studied.

Modern scholars have turned to the Paris/Rouen decree because it seems to explain a very real phenomenon: the application of written statutes, rules, or regulations to individual hospitals and leper-houses, and in increasing number, during the thirteenth century.[1] A new wind was sweeping across Europe, and something in hospitals was changing. *Quia contingit* (1317) was too bland and too late to account for the change, but the Paris decree seems to fit perfectly. It became the central pillar of an enduring model of reform, first laid out by Léon Le Grand in the 1890s.[2] Le Grand's model was composed of three pieces of evidence. First, a wave of statutes that he discovered, issued to French hospitals in the half century after *c.*1210. They constituted a loose corpus, varied in content, although there is evidence of cross-pollination between texts. Most significantly, they share a general ambition to regulate behaviour and devotional routines within hospitals, and even to require vows. Le Grand identified one early text, for the *hôtel-dieu* at Montdidier in 1207, which found its way over time into seven nearby *hôtels-dieu*.[3]

---

[1] The picture is laid out in the Introduction. For reflections on aspects of the problem, Saunier, 'Trame hospitalière'; Montaubin, 'Hôpitaux cathédraux', 23–39; Watson, 'Origins'.

[2] *Statuts*, 'Introduction'; Le Grand, 'Régime intérieur'; Le Grand, 'Leurs statuts'.

[3] It was used at Noyosn (1216×17), Amiens (1233), St Riquier (1233), Abbeville (1243), Beauvais (1246), Rethel (1247), and Montreuil-sur-mer (1250). Le Grand believed that it also inspired a second family of statutes given at Paris (1217×21), then Cambrai (in 1220 and 1227) (*Statuts*, pp. xiii–xiv, xvi,

On Hospitals: Welfare, Law, and Christianity in Western Europe, 400–1320. Sethina Watson, Oxford University Press (2020). © Sethina Watson.
DOI: 10.1093/oso/9780198847533.001.0001

Second, a contemporary passage in Jacques de Vitry's *Historia Occidentalis* (*c.*1219–21) praised well-ordered hospitals in the West and the East that now followed the Augustinian rule.[4] Le Grand opened his edition with this passage, which seemed to give a language and character to the French reform. Third was Courson's Parisian decree itself, which seemed to explain the whole movement. To Le Grand, the Paris-Rouen councils were the official drivers of regulation across France.

Le Grand's own research into the Paris council went no further than to quote the decree, as published by Labbe and Mansi. The Paris-Rouen model has continued to rest on his statements, although it has been developed over time by imagination. It has been a top-down model, with bishops centre stage. Le Grand imagined French bishops gathering at the Paris council and, inspired by the Montdidier rule, taking a stance against disorder in hospitals. He even character-ized the decree as a brief *résumé* of the Montdidier rule.[5] Soon, Imbert would give the drama a lead actor in Richard de Gerberoy, bishop of Amiens; and Mollat then imagined Gerberoy thrusting the rule before his fellow bishops, to provide the model for a new initiative.[6] While we have no list of who attended the Paris council, we can be sure Gerberoy was not among them, since the aged bishop had died three years earlier.[7] And it is unlikely that his successor, Évrard de Fouilloy, attended, since the council covered the province of Sens and Amiens was in that of Reims. The links between the Montdidier rule and Courson's council have yet to be uncovered. A second fanciful story was stripped away in Chapter 2: that the

---

with the Noyon date corrected slightly by Montaubin, 'Hôpitaux cathédraux', 29 n.). A.-M. Bonenfant-Feytmans, 'Les organisations hospitalières vues par Jacques de Vitry', *ASBHH* 18 (1980), 28–32, challenged Montdidier's early date, pointing to problems in its attached confirmation charter of Innocent III. In the latter she was correct; the genuine papal letter merely confirmed the hospital's *dispositio* and a grant by Urban III of an oratory (V. de Beauvillé, *Histoire de la ville de Montdidier*, 4 vols (Paris, 1857), III, pièces just. nos. 105, 111). Nevertheless, the rule requires more careful study before its own internal date of 1207 can be dismissed, and there is some suggestion that the Montdidier version preceded that at Amiens (M.-T. Lacroix, *L'Hôpital Saint-Nicholas à Tournai* (Louvain, 1977), 142–6). P. Montaubin, 'Le déménagement de l'Hôtel d'Amiens', in *HMMA* 51–85, teases out the history of the Amiens hospital.

[4] *The Historia occidentalis of Jacques de Vitry*, ed. J. F. Hinnebusch (Fribourg, 1972), 146–51; tr. J. Bird, 'Texts on Hospitals', in Biller and Ziegler, eds, *Religion and Medicine*, 109–13. The early thirteenth century is a period when historians shift from using first names to surnames. To be consistent and to avoid confusion, not least of Roberts, I use surnames ('Grosseteste') or abbreviated toponyms ('Courson'). The exception is Marie d'Oignies, because her holy reputation made her 'Marie'.

[5] Le Grand, 'Régime', 113.

[6] Mollat, 'Hospitalité', 40; *HDC* 268. Later, Mollat credited 'Richard, bishop of Soissons' (Mollat, 'Floraison', 56; followed by Brodman, *CRME* 78). This seems to be a slip of the pen, for Gerberoy. Montdidier was located in Amiens diocese, not neighbouring Soissons, whose bishop in 1213 was Aymard de Provins.

[7] His successor was in place in 1211. Gerberoy's advanced age had sparked a papal commission at his election in 1204 to establish whether infirmity prevented him from fulfilling his duties (Durand, 'Richard de Gerberoy', *Bibl. de l'école des chartes* 99 (1938), 269–70, 272).

Parisian hospital reform was promulgated at Lateran IV, which declined to issue a decree regarding hospitals. For any wider context for hospital reform we are now left with Jacques de Vitry's celebration of hospitals that were under the Augustinian rule, a comment that is still read in light of Le Grand, as confirmation that a European-wide movement was launched at Paris and Rouen.[8]

It remains unclear, then, where the Paris reform came from, why it appeared at the Paris council, and whether, and if so how, the initiative reached beyond the legate's regional councils. As chapter 2 observed, the decree itself cannot be found beyond the councils of Paris and Rouen: there is no sign of it in any other council or manuscript, nor was it noticed by canonists (it is not mentioned in any collection, gloss, or commentary). In fact, Paris-Rouen has endured as the model for church policy for one reason: it is the only known medieval decree to require hospitals to receive a religious rule. What disqualifies it as a general model thus makes it tantalizing as an initiative. It is unique. And it is all the more interesting for that.

While hospital historians have focused on the French bishops, in a parallel field Courson has taken centre stage. Courson was a teacher at Paris and a member of Peter the Chanter's circle, reform-minded scholars who brought moral theology to bear on the problems of their world, from warfare to tax, usury to justice. The group included Stephen Langton, archbishop of Canterbury (1207–28), and the future Innocent III, but it is Courson who has become Peter's avatar, his *Summa* characterized by John Baldwin as 'a perfected version of the *questiones* of Peter'.[9] This scholarly cohort is now recognized as the driving-force behind Innocent's Lateran IV reforms and in this, too, Courson's legation played a decisive role. His council at Paris is now seen as the moment when scholars produced a programme of reform, which Courson then carried to Rome.[10] The initiatives themselves have largely been studied through Innocent III and Lateran IV: in its major study, Baldwin drew on Courson's *Summa* to identify the scholastic origins of an impressive range of Innocent's ideas, in a study that took 'Paris' as the schools, not the council.[11] The moralists' ideas regarding usury and, to a lesser extent, inquest have also been brilliantly teased out, via Courson's *Summa*, through the

---

[8] Mollat, 'Floraison', 47–9; Brodman, 'Religion and Discipline', 125; Montaubin, 'Hôpitaux cathédraux', 28. A thoughtful exposition of Augustinian influence, in light of the order of canons and the diversity of texts in northern France, is given in M. Mollat, 'Complexité et ambiguité', in G. Politi et al., eds, *Timore e carità i poveri* (Cremona, 1982). Bonenfant-Feytmans, 'Organisations hospitalières', is a stimulating study, with some insight, although too loose with the material for its arguments to hold.

[9] *MPM* I. 19.

[10] *MPM* I. 20–1; Moore, *Innocent III*, 220–1, 225. The paradigm is based on Dickson, 'Courson'.

[11] J. W. Baldwin, 'Paris et Rome en 1215', *Journal des Savants* 1 (1997), covering preaching and education, profession of faith, marriage, clerical continence, clergy in lay chanceries, ordeals, punishing heretics, and the reformist power of ecclesiastical councils.

preaching campaigns of his Parisian cohorts, and into Lateran IV.[12] (Courson's anti-usury campaign during his legation proved a flash-point of controversy.)

Given their role in this picture, as the moment when theology became policy, it is surprising that the legatine councils themselves have received so little study.[13] Our view still rests on the 1934 article of Marcel and Christiane Dickson, an impressive treatment of Courson's 1213–15 legation, which focused on his itinerary and non-conciliar activities, especially his tense relations with Innocent III, the French and English Crowns, and the southern bishops.[14] The Dicksons saw the legislation promulgated at Paris as the model for successive councils, but they left the legislation itself largely unexplored; they suggested that it echoed Courson's *Summa* but did not elaborate as to how.[15] They have been taken at their word.[16] The celebrated decrees at Paris have received little dedicated attention and the hospital decree has been entirely overlooked.[17] One important study did point a way forward. Contextualizing two later sermons by Vitry for hospitals, Jessalynn Bird drew compelling connections between Vitry's writing and the concerns of Parisian moral reformers, among them almsgiving and an episcopal effort to regulate hospitals, an activity she noticed, too, in Flanders-Brabant.[18] Her recasting of reform drew the first link between Le Grand's rule-making and Baldwin's Parisian circle.

Geography matters. The two fields have offered two different models of reform, both of them rooted in the meaning ascribed to Paris, as the location of Courson's first council. Once Le Grand's capital city, where bishops launched a French

---

[12] For usury, *MPM* I. 296–311; J. Bird, 'Reform or Crusade? Anti-Usury and Crusade Preaching', in J. C. Moore, ed., *Pope Innocent III and his World* (Aldershot, 1999), 172, 184; R. Rist, 'The Power of the Purse', in B. Bolton and C. Meed, eds, *Aspects of Power and Authority* (Turnhout, 2007). The interest in Courson's anti-usury campaigns has deep roots: F. J. G. La Porte-du Theil, 'Notice et extraits', in *Notices et extraits*, VI (Paris, 1801). For inquest, J. Bird, 'The Wheat and the Tares', *Proc. of the Twelfth Int'l Congress of Medieval Canon Law* (Vatican City, 2008); J. Sabapathy, 'Some Difficulties in Forming Persecuting Societies', in G. Melville and J. Helmrath, eds, *The Fourth Lateran Council* (Affalterbach, 2017).

[13] The exception is the council of Montpellier, under Peter of Benevento, P. Montaubin, 'La légation du cardinal Pietro Beneventano en 1214–1215', in *Innocent III et le Midi*, Cahiers de Fanjeaux 50 (2015).

[14] Dickson, 'Courson', with pp. 100, 103, 106–7, 109, 126, for sketches of each council. Their focus on his non-conciliar activities set the scene for work that followed: *MPM* I. 20–3; II. 10–13; Moore, *Innocent III*, 221–6; J. M. Powell, *Anatomy of a Crusade* (Philadelphia, PA, 1986), 33–50.

[15] They offered only the pledge of faith by excommunicated barons (in the Bordeaux legislation) as an example. Their cursory treatment itemized decrees adopted at Lateran IV and noted basic differences between the legatine councils, all 'analogue à Paris et Rouen' and, as those, inspired by Courson's *Summa* (Dickson, 'Courson', 124–6).

[16] See n. 10.

[17] Even Baldwin left the legation and its legislation unexplored, resting on Dickson, 'Courson': *MPM* I. 20. The main topics of the decrees are given in O. Pontal, *Les Conciles de la France Capétienne* (Paris, 1995), 396–402; and R. Foreville, *Le pape Innocent III et la France* (Stuttgart, 1992), 321–4, which stresses the role of the French bishops. All omit the hospital decree.

[18] J. Bird, 'Jacques de Vitry's Sermons to Hospitallers', in Biller and Ziegler, eds, *Religion and Medicine*, 93–4, 98–100. And see De Spiegeler, *Liège*, 111–13, 147; Bonenfant, 'Hôpitaux', 27–9; Bonenfant-Feytmans, 'Organisations hospitalières'.

reform of hospitals, Paris has become Baldwin's university laboratory of moral reformers, whose ideas were digested by Courson the theologian, enacted through Courson the papal legate, and carried by him to Lateran IV. In order to understand the hospital reform, we must first recognize Le Grand's geography for what it was: a nineteenth-century national view of France. His search for a French initiative has locked the reform behind nineteenth-century borders, a false geography. What follows examines the origins, form, and consequences of Courson's decree. The story takes us into two very different medieval geographies: one, economic, on the edge of the empire; the other ecclesiastical, along the east of France. The picture is not what it has seemed.

Courson and the Hospital Decree

There was only a single decree, promulgated at Paris (1213) and then Rouen (1214). Appendix B presents a new edition, with translation. What was presented as one decree in the Paris manuscript (3.9 in Mansi's edition) appears divided into two in Rouen's (2.39–40).[19] With the exception of this division, the versions contain only minor scribal variations, confirming that Courson promulgated the decree, unchanged, at Rouen. The decree addressed leper-houses and hospitals for the sick or for pilgrims. It required first that those whose resources were adequate to support a common life should be provided with a rule, which was to contain three elements: renunciation of property, a vow of continence, and a promise of obedience to a prelate, or head. Residents were also to adopt a religious style of dress. The second part declared that it was unfitting to have more healthy than sick people or pilgrims in such houses, because the faithful had donated their gifts for the infirm not the healthy. It complained, too, that married people enter these houses, in some cases to escape secular authority, and then lead a life even more luxurious than before. These must now live religiously, in the habit of a religious, or be ejected, and care must be taken that they not abscond with goods that belong to the house and so profit from their fraud.

How far can we discern the legal framework for this decree? It has often been portrayed as the next step in the church's response to hospitals, building on Lateran III's canon for lepers, *Cum dicat Apostolus*.[20] In fact, it offers a better contrast to that canon. The language of *infirmi/sani* may be an echo of *Cum dicat Apostolus*, but its terms are strikingly different. Alexander had acted to remedy the deprivation of those denied spiritual care because of their disease, and he carefully avoided reference to any house or facility. Courson's decree announced its subject

---

[19] Mansi XXII. 835–6, 913. There has been some uncertainty as to how far the two were similar (e.g. Brodman, *CRME* 79–80 n.).
[20] Touati, *Maladie et société*, 403; Avril, 'Le IIIe concile du Latran', 65. For the canon, see Chapter 2.

in its opening line, 'On houses of lepers and hospitals of the sick and of pilgrims'. Its stated aim was to protect the places, not the residents, and its justification for action was to ensure that the house's wealth was deployed to its appointed use, 'for truly, the goods gathered there from the devotion of the faithful have not been assigned for the use of the healthy but rather for the infirm'. In acting to defend the bequests, the decree was protecting that wealth from its people. The residents were both the problem and the means of remedy, so the decree limited numbers of the healthy, imposed on them religious life and vows, and forced the recalcitrant to leave. Here, a common life was not a precondition to be supported, but the prescription, based the status of the house: 'if the wealth of the place should permit'.[21] Whereas Alexander had secured rights for groups who were denied spiritual care, Courson imposed a life of renunciation (of fleshly pursuits, leisure, luxury, and freedom from dominion).

In the Paris manuscript, the hospital decree occurs in a section labelled, 'For nuns' ('Ad moniales'). Its first eight chapters do address nuns, although its last thirteen concern male religious, largely abbots and priors. Between these groups falls the hospital decree. Mansi provided a title ('De iis qui manent...'), whose 'those' might appear to link the decree to those that precede it, on nuns. This would be a misreading. His 'those who dwell' is a descriptive phrase, needed because there is no noun in the decree, such as 'nuns', 'clerics', 'abbots', or 'religious'. It reflects a bigger absence, for there is no ecclesiastical status, or category for the people in the hospital decree. Comparison with Lateran II's 'false nuns' reveals the decree's oddness. One required nuns to remove themselves into a single-sex cloister, the other arranged a mixed community (the 'De domibus...' of its opening line signals a new subject, whose mixed congregation hangs oddly between the two halves of the section).[22] The objects were different (nuns vs. houses) and so, too, their justifications. Lateran II had ensured that those who claimed to be nuns follow a rule (i.e. that *regulares* have a *regula*); Paris preserved the faithful's gifts for their intended purposes. In the former, a woman's own resolution to take on a religious status, and assume a religious habit, invited the response of supervising authorities; in the latter, the people had not chosen a religious habit, or even a religious life. The resolution to be religious was not theirs; it was the council's. Wearing a religious habit was the council's solution to a problem not with disordered religious life, but disordered places.[23]

---

[21] Compare Lateran III's (c. 23) 'ut ubicumque tot simul sub communi vita fuerint congregati' to Courson's 'ut si facultates loci patiuntur quod ibidem manentes competenter possint vivere de communi'.

[22] In the Paris manuscript, sections have been labelled in the margin by another scribe, as: 'Ad clericos saeculares statuta concilii Parisi magistro Roberto de Curceon' (with 20 chapters); 'Ad viros regulares' (27); 'Ad moniales' (21); 'Ad archiepiscopum et episcopos' (21) (Paris, Bibl. de l'Arsenal MS 769, fols 115r–120r). The Rouen manuscript has no sections; neither has chapter titles.

[23] In early medieval prescriptive texts '[l]'acte de revêtir un habit religieux a donc une signification grave: il exprime la volonté de changer de vie'. Magnou-Nortier, 'Formes féminines', 199–200.

The hospital decree marks a break from earlier legislation in ways that suggest contemporary expertise. In 1213, Bernard's *Breviarium* was the legal text of the moment. It was closely bound up with the work of the Parisian reformers, conceptually (Courson's own *Summa* was structured using the *Breviarium*) and literally (the decrees of the Rouen council were bound beside the *Breviarium* in their only surviving manuscript, from Mont-St-Michel).[24] The decree itself was inspired by Bernard's new title, 'On religious houses' (3.31), going a step further to explore what it now meant for 'those who dwell within [such] a religious house'. Indeed, 'religious' and 'house' are the two live concepts that thread through the decree, which was particularly concerned with the relationship between them. The drafters seem unaware of, or unimpressed by Bernard's own definition of 'religion' in this title, which had been fundamentally Roman, a matter of categorization and jurisdiction, not religious discipline.[25] Instead, they focused on Urban's statement that places confirmed by episcopal authority to a charitable task 'should be religious' (1 Comp. 3.31.4 = X 3.36.4, *Ad haec*). The decree is like a legal riff on the problem posed by the *Breviariam*: what it means for a 'religious place' to be religious. Theirs was no legal interest, for the answers lacked legal precedent and contradicted basic concepts regarding the common life. Instead, they took 'religion' to be a moral question, of what was appropriate to do ('illud omnino indignum est'), and especially an issue of the manner of life: to 'live religiously in a religious habit'. Those who had 'removed themselves to such houses, under the canopy of religion' must live religiously, not secularly: in common, under vows, and in religious dress. The decree was looking to the world, not to the law.

Courson's decree took a genuine interest in welfare houses. It had a clear sense of the legal nature of hospitals, and it based its legal power to act on these grounds: that the faithful had assigned goods for a specific charitable use, and that this act must be upheld before all else. As had Carolingian legislation and *Ad haec* before, and as would *Quia contingit* a century later, it identified the *dispositio* of the gifts of the faithful as the defining element in law. What Courson added was a vision of a religious life in these places. It was not the religious life of *regulares*, because it was a mixed facility, with married people. The requirements that these men and women, together, profess to chastity, a life without personal possessions, and obedience to a prior, reveal the reformers playing with a new model of religious service. They were not trying to make hospitals monastic but to make hospitals 'religious'. At the core of the decree was a bold new agenda for hospitals. Where did the vision come from? The natural place to turn is to Courson's own *Summa*

---

[24] Avranches, Bibl. mun. MS 149, with the council at fols 3v–6r, the *Breviarium* fols 7r–78v.

[25] Bernard did so in Western terms, to argue that hospitals should belong to ecclesiastical not worldly law because, when they were created, their founders were facing towards God ('from a pious motive', as Justinian would have said).

de moralibus quaestionibus theologicis, as a distillation of the thinking of the moral theologians.[26]

The decree may owe a passing debt to theological ideas in Courson's *Summa*.[27] Written between 1208 and 1212, the 'Summa on the moral questions of theology' has been noticed for its innovative treatment of usury and alms; that is, of the moral gain and disbursement of wealth.[28] Given these preoccupations, it is odd that hospitals and leper-houses are largely absent, even from the section 'on alms' (16).[29] They do occur once in the section on usury (11), in a chapter that considers what a prelate should do if he learned that a church or other buildings had been constructed from offerings made by usurers.[30] Courson's answer, one of his more extreme positions, is largely concerned with churches 'built from sin [so] that those in them can scarcely eat except what comes from theft'.[31] If the church had already been consecrated (and so could not be returned to secular uses), then an abbot and chapter could 'redeem' it by repaying the full value of the gift, either to the usurer or as alms for the convent's souls; however, unconsecrated churches might be profitably destroyed. But usurers had also made bequests 'to provide windows, dormitories, hermitages, hospitals or leper-houses', what should then be done? Drawing upon sound counsel, the recipients should first determine the value of the gift, then make efforts at restitution.[32] Here hospitals and leper-houses are categorized, in now-familiar terms, not as communities (churches) but as objects or buildings. Financial compensation was adequate exchange for these material goods.

Hospitals and leper-houses are the subject of one chapter. It is the briefest of the nine that make up Courson's section 24, 'on the vows of the religious or of those

---

[26] A second proposal, that the papal curia provided the schema and French synodal statutes the content, can be rejected for the hospital decree, since no French synodal statutes had touched this subject. For the proposal: Foreville, *Innocent III*, 322–5.

[27] On the *Summa* see MPM I. 23–5; II. 14. V. L. Kennedy, 'The Content of Courson's *Summa*', *Mediaeval Studies* 9 (1947), publishes the chapter titles; the sections on usury have been edited by G. LeFèvre, *Le Traité* 'De usura' *de Robert de Courçon* (Lille, 1902). I cite here using BnF lat. 14524, but have also consulted BL Royal 9 E XIV and the primitive version, BnF lat. 3259.

[28] *MPM* I. 179–85, 302–11; Bird, 'Reform or Crusade', 172–3, 176–8. for the wider context of Parisian thinking on usury and alms, I. P. Wei, *Intellectual Culture* (Cambridge, 2012), 306–18; S. E. Young, *Scholarly Community* (Cambridge, 2014), 131–67.

[29] BnF lat. 14524, fols 69r–72r.

[30] (11.11) whose title is: 'QUID FACIENDUM PRELATO QUI HABET POTESTATEM DIRUENDI ECCLESIAS ET AEDIFICIA CONSTRUCTA SUB NOMINE ECCLESIAE A FENERATORIBUS CUM HOC EI CONSTITERIT'. Kennedy, 'Courson's *Summa*', 90.

[31] 'Quomodo ergo possunt ibi viventes habere mundam conscientiam scientes quod haec sunt tabernacula peccatorum et ex peccatis constructa, et quod in illis vix aliqua comedunt nisi ex rapina.' In *De usura*, ed. LeFèvre, the question is pp. 35–9.

[32] 'Item cum fœneratores passim offerant ecclesiis, construendo eas totas vel in parte de fœnore, ut vitreas vel dormitoria, vel eremitoria vel hospitalia aut domos leprosorum... In cathedralibus et domibus leprosorum et hospitalium, consilium esset sanum ut estimatione laboraretur ad restitutionem et satisfactionem faciendam spoliatis vel animabus ipsorum et per manus Ecclesiae aut per arbitrium in Ecclesia', ed. LeFèvre, *De usura*, 35.

becoming religious'.[33] The section addresses titles 27 (*De regularibus transeuntibus ad religionem*) and 28 (*De conversione coniugatorum*) of Bernard's *Breviarium*. Bernard's title 27 had opened with Alexander's *Ad petitionem*, but Courson ignored this decretal; in fact, he largely ignored the contents of title 27, reworking its heading but focusing on title 28, on the conversion of married people to religious life, whose chapters he more readily deploys. Courson's section explores the nature of vows, especially who can make a binding religious profession and under what circumstances. His chapters discuss youth (c. 1) and the movement between orders (cc. 8, 9), but most of them concern married people who wish to enter a cloister, take holy orders, or become bishops; that is, how someone might enter the church and leave a spouse behind (cc. 2–6). Bernard's material had also wrestled with the circumstances under which a spouse might leave a partner to become a nun, monk, priest, or bishop. In his collection of decretals, a total separation of the sexes—into different institutions, for example—was both presumed and enforced. Addressing married men, for example, *Ad petitionem* had decreed that 'none of you should dare to tonsure any woman or presume to receive her to live with you'.

Inserted between two discussions—on leaving a spouse for the church and on moving between religious orders—Courson's chapter 7 stands apart. It warrants quoting in full:

> Concerning men and their wives entering together into a house of lepers or a hospital in order to serve and remain there perpetually, we say that they must not cohabit or have carnal intercourse. On the contrary, as the aforesaid decretal of Alexander [III] says, they must rather dwell in separate dwellings.[34]

The terse statement is different from the eight other chapters: it is the only one in which married couples may enter the same house, and the only one that makes no mention of a vow or profession, the husband and wife simply 'entering together … to serve and remain there perpetually'. Finally, it is the only chapter not to rest on decretal authority. Courson, using the phrase 'dicimus quod' (we say that), does gesture vaguely towards a decretal of Alexander III, but he does not specify which decretal. The principle of separate dwellings might suggest *Uxoratus* (1 Comp. 3.28.8 = X 3.32.8), from *Ad petitionem*, which permitted a married man to join the order only with his wife's permission and then if she took a vow of

---

[33] DE VOTIS RELIGIOSORUM/SIVE AD RELIGIONEM TRANSSEUNTIUM, BnF lat. 14524, fol. 85r; BnF lat. 3259, fol. 105r, adds the latter portion.

[34] (24.7) 'DE VIRO ET UXORE INTRANTIBUS SIMUL DOMUM LEPROSORUM VEL HOSPITALE. De viro et uxore simul intrantibus domum hospitalem vel domum leprosorum ut ibi perpetuo serviant et contineant, dicimus quod non debent cohabitare vel *commisceri carnaliter*, immo ut dicit predicta decretalis alexandri debent potius in diversis domiciliis commorari.' BnF lat. 14524, fol. 86r, with title from BnF lat. 3259, fol. 106r; BL Royal 9 E XIV, fol. 27v. (Author's italics.)

perpetual continence and lived in her own house (*in domo propria*) with her children and family or, if of suspect reputation, entered a religious house. The language, however, draws from another decretal (1 Comp. 3.28.2 = X 3.32.2), which permitted the dissolution of a marriage when a spouse entered a monastery, so long as the pair had not had carnal intercourse (*carnalis commixtio*, the phrase reused by Courson); since they had not become one flesh (even saints have been called from marriage!), the remaining spouse might remarry.[35] Either decretal fails to underpin a requirement for chastity of established couples in the same hospital.

As with so many previous statements on welfare houses, Courson's contortions illuminate his agenda. Courson used Bernard's *Breviarium* but not its title 31, on religious houses, with its hospital decrees, and his approach ignores Bernard's own arguments for hospitals. In more traditional fashion, Courson made the people ('De viro et uxore') his subject, not the houses. He then worked to construct a new requirement: that married couples serving in hospitals remain chaste. It is premised upon the fact that spouses were together and not professed (there was no vow of chastity to fall back on). Courson's concern was to prevent sexual contact and, perhaps more than that, the suspicion of sex that would result from cohabiting (the section in the *Summa* that follows this one is *De scandalo*). It would be an error to overstate Courson's interest in hospitals, which was marginal at best. Welfare houses were not a Parisian topic, and his teacher, Peter the Chanter had made no mention of hospitals, *xenodochia*, or leper-houses in his own *Verbum abbreviatum*.[36] Courson's argument was a moral rather than a religious one.[37] His concern was the scandal of sexual activity rather than the houses themselves, even though the irregular status of these houses had created this particular problem, with couples entering together into a life of service, but not religious profession. The chapter was a product of his interest in vows, a concern that runs through his work.[38] Given that his *Summa* was preoccupied with the poor and alms, with the nature of gifts and the qualities of vows, it is the absence of welfare houses that stands out.

There are relationships between Courson's *Summa* and his conciliar decree. Both refer to 'hospitals and leper-houses', distinguished yet always paired. Both share a concern with married couples living together in these houses as they had in the world. Less assuredly, the decree's careful terminology of a 'vow' of chastity, a

---

[35] 1 Comp. 3.28.2 (X 3.32.2) 'Verum post [*illum*] consensum legitimum de praesenti licitum est alteri, altero etiam repugnante eligere monasterium, sicut *etiam* sancti quidam de nuptiis vocati fuerunt, dummodo carnalis commixtio non intervenerit inter eos, et alteri remanenti, si commonitus continentiam servare noluerit, licitum est ad secunda vota transire, quia, quum non fuissent una caro simul effecti, satis potest unus ad Deum transire, et alter in saeculo remanere.'

[36] Although he dedicated many discussions to the poor, to the corporal works of mercy, and especially to alms: Peter the Chanter, *Verbum adbreviatum*, ed. Boutry (Turnhout, 2004), 1.13, 46; 2.4, 13–19, 38–41.

[37] Courson's moral bent and his interest in scandal have been teased out by E. Corran, *Lying and Perjury in Medieval Practical Thought* (Oxford, 2018), 85–93; Sabapathy, 'Some Difficulties'.

[38] He dedicates four full sections (21–4) to vows and another (27) to oaths.

'renunciation' of property, and a 'promise' of obedience might reflect Courson's interest in vows.[39] Nevertheless, the contrasts are more significant. The decree is structured around Bernard's introduction of 'religious houses', the *Summa* ignores this. The decree built a more convoluted picture of scandal, where healthy men and women, and those 'joined by the fetters of wedlock', had relocated to hospitals as a fraud, continuing to revel in worldly living and fleshly pursuits.[40] Yet scandal was not its target, merely its argument to effect its main action, which was to subject adequately endowed houses to a rule, under a prelate, with vows and religious dress. This was a far more radical agenda than Courson's prohibition of sexual contact. Its legal rationale, to guard the gifts of the faithful to their assigned uses, might appear to echo Courson's discussion of usury, since the moral quality of the gift has consequences for the recipients. Yet in the *Summa*, a prelate was to intervene to protect religious life from contamination by tainted gifts; the decree introduced religious life to protect the gifts. We might thus detect Courson's influence in drafting the decree, but its agenda was not his.

The agenda, to subject hospitals and leper-houses to a common life with vows, cannot be found in the texts of the Parisian theologians, and it flew in the face of legal precedent. Of any written statements, it is best reflected in Jacques de Vitry's *Historia Occidentalis*, although not in his famous statement on hospitals. More relevant is a preceding passage in which Vitry argues that the many forms of cenobitic life share the same foundation, which consists of four requirements: to renounce the world, to have no private possessions, to render obedience to a superior, and to observe continence.[41] The ideas are not in themselves unusual, but their distillation and language is distinctive and they echo language of the decree. The passage occurs in the last of three chapters (cc. 11–13) to introduce a discussion of monastic, regular, and secular orders. Later in this discussion, between 'the religion and rule of the Humiliati' (c. 28) and 'secular canons' (c. 30), is Vitry's statement on reformed hospitals and leper-houses, living under a rule. The chapters that immediately precede his introduction to the religious life celebrate a band of famed preachers that grew up around Peter the Chanter that included Fulk de Neuilly, Stephen Langton, and Robert de Courson (cc. 6–10). The reference leads us back to the network of reformers and to the context in which the decree took shape.

[39] '…ut proprio renuntient, continentie uotum emittant, et suo prelato obedientiam fidelem et deuotam promittant.' Appendix B.

[40] '…quod quidam sani uiri et mulieres et matrimoniali uinculo copulati…qui tamen in domo religionis manentes, non minus, immo magis seculariter et delicate uiuunt, et operibus carnis uacant, quam antea uacare consueuerant.' Appendix B.

[41] 'Sunt autem cenobitarum diuersa genera, uariis institutionibus et diuersis uiuendi modis multi-pliciter distincta. Omnes tamen unum et idem habent principale fundamentum quasi lapidem quadratum. Oportet enim quod seculo renuncient, proprium non habeant, superiori suo obediant, et continentiam obseruent. Super hoc fundamentum tot sunt edificate mansiones quot sunt regularium uarietates.' *Hist. Occ.*, ed. Hinnebusch, 110. For its post-Lateran context, see J. Bird, 'The Religious's Role', in C. Muessig, ed., *Medieval Monastic Preaching* (Leiden, 1998), 212.

The Launch of Courson's Legation

In 1213, Courson was Innocent III's most zealous and influential agent in preparing for the pope's great council and new crusade.[42] His rise had been swift. The Derbyshire man had moved to Paris by the 1190s, where he became a leading scholar in the circle of Peter the Chanter, that great master from Reims who became cantor of Notre Dame in 1183, then dean of Reims in 1196, before his death in 1197.[43] During his time at Paris, Courson developed close ties with other students of the circle: the Lincolnshire man Stephen Langton, Jacques de Vitry from Reims, and the Italian Lotario dei Conti di Segni, the future Innocent III.[44] Courson first appears on the written record in 1200, when we glimpse him as *magister*. An active career as papal judge delegate began in January 1204, prompting a succession of appointments as canon of Noyon (1204–8/9), then Paris (1209–12).[45] It was during this period that he drafted and revised his *Summa* (1208–12). By June 1212 Innocent III had appointed him cardinal of Santa Stefano in Celio Monte.

Courson appears in Rome in February 1213 and is recorded there again on 18 April 1213.[46] The following day Innocent III issued his general summons to Lateran IV and letters dispatching legates to regions across Europe.[47] He commissioned Courson as legate to France, to preach the upcoming crusade to the Holy Land and prepare for the great council by identifying abuses. While the same charge was given to each legate, the latter was recognized as Courson's legacy, bound up with his Paris council and the moral theology of the schools. As a legate, Courson emerges as a controversial and difficult figure. He was castigated by contemporary chroniclers for his aggressive and illegitimate activities, although these have often been dismissed as partisan responses to the legate's political dealings, inflamed by his anti-usury measures.[48] So it is on Paris and his legatine councils that Courson's reputation rests. What follows does not contest the significance of the moralists' thinking, or its influence on policy of its day. It does question the shape and simplicity of our Paris-Rome conciliar model.

[42] For Courson's career: Dickson, 'Courson', 61–83; *MPM* I. 19–25; W. Maleczek, *Papst und Kardinalskolleg* (Vienna, 1984), 175–9. This summary follows Maleczek, except where noted.

[43] *MPM* I. 5–16; T. Gousset, ed., *Les actes de la province de Reims*, 4 vols (Reims, 1842–4), II. 326–7.

[44] Baldwin, 'Paris et Rome', 103.   [45] Dickson, 'Courson', 75–7, 81.

[46] Maleczek, *Papst und Kardinalskolleg*, 390.

[47] Powell, *Anatomy of a Crusade*, 22–7, explores who was commissioned and Innocent's sensitivity to regional politics.

[48] Moore, *Innocent III*, 226; Dickson, 'Courson', 126–7; *MPM* I. 22–3. Studies that focus on his conflicts with the king judge the legation most harshly, Powell, *Anatomy*, 34, 44–8.

The Council of Reims (1213)

The Dicksons have provided a schedule for the councils and an itinerary for Courson as he criss-crossed France.[49] It sees Courson announcing his arrival in France with a council in Paris in June 1213, and holding a second council in Rouen in February/March 1214. He then turned south to join the Albigensian crusaders in late spring, holding councils at Bordeaux (in English territory) on 25 June and Clermont-Dessous on 27 July. After King John's defeat at the battle of Bouvines, Courson spent the late summer of 1214 negotiating a truce between the English and French kings. At this point, his frenetic energy seems to flag. He moved slowly back from Picardy towards Tours. New councils were held at Montpellier on 8 January and Bourges in May 1215, although Courson did not attend the former: he issued its summons from Reims on 7 December 1214 but the council itself was convened under Peter of Benevento, a papal legate who had been in the region since April 1214, dispatched to help with the Albigensian crusade.[50] Instead, Courson turned west from Reims towards Le Mans, then Soissons.

In keeping up with all of Courson's frantic activity, it has been easy to forget that our knowledge of the councils can be uncertain. Ironically, we know most about Montpellier, the council that Courson did not hold.[51] Legislation survives in full only for Paris, Rouen, and Montpellier, the last a far briefer text. Bourges issued truncated decrees in the face of local rebellion, while those of Clermont and Bordeaux have been lost, although the latter (apparently a limited cohort of decrees) were reported in a letter from Courson to King John.[52] As to the dates, only those of Montpellier and Bordeaux are certain, while charters putting Courson in Clermont on 29 July 1214 and in Bourges in May 1215 suggest general dates for those councils.[53] It is the dates of the earliest councils that are least secure. A Rouen chronicle reported Courson's arrival under the year 1214 and,

---

[49] Dickson, 'Courson', 89–117, where full references can be found. For its influence, Maleczek, *Papst und Kardinalskolleg*, 176–7; *MPM* I. 20; Moore, *Innocent III*, 221–5; Powell, *Anatomy*, 36. Foreville, *Innocent III*, 321 gives a more general date of summer 1213 for the Paris council. S. Hanssens, 'De legatiereis van Robert van Courson', in *Miscellanea* (Louvain, 1946), I. 528–38, adds detail on his time in the Low Countries.

[50] Courson did not attend the council at Montpellier, as stated in Maleczek, *Papst und Kardinalskolleg*, 177. On Bonaventura, Montaubin, 'Pietro Beneventano', who dates Courson's summons to 1213, arguing that a month's warning was too short for a council (pp. 400, 404–5). Yet Courson was in Ooscamp in mid-December, and probably Arras before that (Hanssens, 'De legatiereis', 530–1; Dickson, 'Courson', 94–5). The summons is ed. S. Baluze, *Concilia Galliae Narbonensis* (Paris, 1668), 38–40. In what follows, for the itinerary, I cite Hanssens and M. and C. Dickson, except when new material can be brought to bear. Wherever possible, and in most cases, I have consulted the original material on which their statements were based.

[51] Montaubin, 'Pietro Beneventano', 407–11. The council itself is described by Peter of les Vaux-de-Cernay, *The History of the Albigensian Crusade*, tr. W. A. Sibly and M. D. Sibly (Woodbridge, 1998), 242–4. The council lasted for many days, and probably several weeks.

[52] Mansi XXII. 817–44 (Paris), 897–924 (Rouen); 931–4 (Bourges); Baluze, *Conc. Gall. Narbon.* 40–54 (Montpellier). For Bordeaux, see my n. 139.

[53] Dickson, 'Courson', 102, 112–14; *MPM* I. 22.

because charters place the legate in Brittany in January and, more particularly, in Hyenville on 13 April of that year, March seems a likely time for the Rouen council.[54]

The date of the Paris council is merely a best guess. Only one reference places Courson in the city during his legation when in August 1215 he promulgated statutes for the university at Paris, his final major act before turning south to Rome.[55] For the Paris council, the council's own legislation constitutes its main evidence: it survives in a thirteenth-century manuscript of the abbey of Saint-Victor, and its fuller collection of decrees, largely repeated at Rouen, points to the earlier period of the legation.[56] To the Dicksons it seemed 'perfectly natural' that Courson would proceed directly to Paris, because he carried letters from Innocent III to Philip Augustus, his son Louis, and Blanche of Champagne.[57] They had assumed that the king was resident in the royal capital; in fact, Philip and Louis were in Flanders in the late spring and summer of 1213, intent upon launching an invasion of England.[58] A more likely occasion for the Paris council might be late summer, when Courson was in the region south of Paris, around Melun and Sens in August and September 1213, before moving in October to Auxerre and Troyes.[59] There is no dated record of Courson's whereabouts between Rome on 19 April and Melun, in mid-August. His first four months remain unaccounted for.

Nevertheless, there is evidence that Courson was busy in these months, and that his legation did not begin in Paris. A statement by a contemporary Rouen chronicler recorded that 'Robert de Courson, papal legate, came to Rouen in the year of our Lord 1214, having celebrated a council first in Reims, then Paris'.[60]

---

[54] Dickson, 'Courson', 89, 96, 98. For the chronicle, see my n. 60.

[55] His march from Tours to Reims between 2 and 7 Dec. 1214 would have taken him (briefly) through regions near Paris, although too briefly for a council (Dickson, 'Courson', 89, 114). On the statutes, S. C. Ferruolo, 'The Paris Statutes of 1215', *History of Universities* 5 (1985).

[56] Paris, Bibl. de l'Arsenal MS 769, fols 115r–120r, where it is gathered with other material from the early decades of the thirteenth century (H. Martin, *Catalogue des manuscrits de la bibl. de l'Arsenal*, II (Paris, 1886), 90).

[57] Dickson, 'Courson', 89–90.

[58] J. W. Baldwin, *The Government of Philip Augustus* (Berkeley, CA, 1986), 209–12.

[59] Dickson, 'Courson', 91–2. In July and Aug., Courson was gathering evidence regarding the legitimacy of the heir of Henry, count of Champagne, charging the abbots of Montiéramey, Quincy, Vauluisant, and then Preuilly to gather testimony. Innocent III, *Register*, app. nos. 9–12 (*PL* 214, cols 979–82). His letters on behalf of Blanche date to Oct. of that year: *The Cartulary of Countess Blanche of Champagne*, ed. T. Evergates (Toronto, 2010), nos. 56 and 101.

[60] 'Anno Domini MCCXIV, Robertus de Corcione Legatus Apostolicus, celebrato Concilio, primum Remis, deinde Parisiis, Rotomagum venit: factoque sermone ad Clerum et populum super Crucis caractere in auxilium terre Jerosolymitane capiendo: cujus occasione legationis officio fungebatur, infinita multitudo Crucem cepit.' *Concilia Rotomagensis*, 110, from an old chronicle of Holy Trinity, Rouen, in a manuscript that I have not been able to trace but that was noticed, too, in Mansi XXII. 897; Dickson, 'Courson', 90 n. The description fits with other impressions of Courson's activity: at the castle of Limoges e.g. two abbots and thirty men and women were moved by his preaching to take the cross, including ten brothers from the chronicler's abbey (*The Chronicle of Bernard Itier*, ed. and tr. A. W. Lewis (Oxford, 2012), 96–7).

The Dicksons dismissed the note of Reims for lack of corroborating evidence;[61] but they acted too quickly. A second reference, among a series of additions to the Paris legislation, notices the penalties for a prelate or canon who might fall into a life of infamy 'after the council of Reims'.[62] And, third, there is a letter in Courson's name, as legate, enforcing what was established by a council at Reims.[63] This was not a reference to Innocent II's council of 1131, as Paul Bonenfant had assumed.[64] We know this because the ruling concerns the regulation of hospitals.

The letter survives in the cartulary of the priory of St Martin in Ypres and concerns the hospital in the town's marketplace. In it, Courson demands reform, castigating the hospital's brothers for failing to observe the statutes of the council of Reims.[65] They were living dissimilarly, yet from a common purse that was adequate for their support. Some were chaste, others had wives; some wore religious dress, others secular; and the number of healthy brothers and sisters almost exceeded that of the sick. This was because they lacked a prelate and a rule for living, as laid down by the Reims council. In remedy, Courson entrusted the spiritual care of the house to the prior of St Martin's, to whom the hospital's brothers would swear obedience. By his legatine authority, Courson required that the brothers and sisters be obedient to the prior, who must ensure that they live regularly and observe what was established at the council of Reims since (because the hospital was in the priory's parish) it fell to the prior to correct their behaviour

---

[61] Dickson, 'Courson', 90.

[62] 'Post Remense concilium inciderint', Mansi XXII. 849, who edits the additions from a manuscript of the abbey of Anchin. And see, too, la Porte-du Theil, 'Notice et Extraits', 218–22. I intend to work further on this manuscript.

[63] It was noticed by Hanssens, 'De legatiereis', 532, who, concerned with the legate's travels in Flanders and Hainaut, did not pursue the question of the council. Aware of Hanssens's essay, J. H. Lynch, *Simoniacal Entry into Religious Life* (Columbus, OH, 1976), 187 and Bonenfant-Feytmans, 'Organisations hospitalières', 30, list Reims as a seventh council, in 1214.

[64] Bonenfant, 'Hôpitaux', 26. Mansi XXI. 457–62, offers an edition of the 1131 decrees, although for the complex tradition of canons see M. Brett and R. Somerville, 'The Transmission of the Councils', in J. Doran and D. J. Smith, eds, *Pope Innocent II* (London, 2016), esp. 232–5.

[65] 'Significatum est nobis, quod fratres hospitalis infirmorum, quod situm est in foro Yprensi, licet *de communi vivant* et *competentes* ad hoc habeant *facultates*, dissimiliter tamen vivunt et Remensis concilii constituta non servant. Quidam enim ex eis uxores non habent et *contin*ent; alii uxores habent, et *non minus, quam* cum essent in seculo, *operibus carnis vacant.* Quidam *religioso habitu* et alii habitu *seculari utuntur.* Preterea tanta est ibi multitudo fratrum ac sororum *sanarum,* quod fere numerum *infirmorum exced*unt. Que omnia ex eo contingunt, quod prelatum non habent cui obediant, nec regulam secundum quam vivant. Cum igitur in Remensi concilio provida sit deliberatione statutum, ut tales domus *prelat*um habeant, cui fratres ipsarum *obedientiam fidelem et devotam promittant,* et *competens eis vivendi regula statuatur,* et alia que non sine periculo animarum a predicte domus fratribus omittuntur, sollicitudini tue curam ipsius domus in spiritualibus duximus commitendam, mandantes, ut fratres ipsos regulariter vivere, et Remensis statuta concilii diligenter ac reverenter facias observare, auctoritate legationis qua fungimur statuentes, ut tibi ac successoribus tuis imperpetuum fratres ac sorores ipsius hospitalis obediant, et vos potestatem habeatis corrigendi excessus eorum per competentis regule disciplinam, cum situm sit hospitale in parochia, cujus cura ad preposituram Yprensem noscitur pertinere.' *Cart. Ypres* II, no. 81. Author's italics mark language identical to the Paris/Rouen decree; on numerous other occasions the meaning follows Paris/Rouen but the wording differs (e.g. *multitudo* for *numero*).

according to the discipline of an appropriate rule. The letter might read as if a wayward hospital was being brought to heel, yet both the complaints and the remedies were borrowed from another text. The letter's structure and much of its language were lifted from the hospital decree: its qualification to act (that the brothers and sisters had adequate resources to live in common) as well as its requirements (of a rule, obedience to a prelate, continence, and a religious habit) all follow the decree, as do its criticisms that the healthy risk outnumbering the sick and that married members engage in carnal pursuits, as they had in the world. The brief letter invokes the council of Reims (*Remensis concilii*) three times. Ypres was in the diocese of Thérouanne, part of the province of Reims, so this was no copyist's error for Rouen (*Rotomagensi*) or Paris (*Parisiensis*). Both the legal framework of Courson's instruction and its authority derived from this forgotten council.

The circumstances of the letter shed light on Courson's hospital reform, and on its lawfulness. The letter was dispatched during Courson's legation, although it is unclear when, since the copy lacks a dating clause. Hanssens suggested that Courson was in Ypres in December 1213, en route from Arras to Oostkamp.[66] This is the likely period, although the connection seems to have been one of person rather than place. The letter's opening words suggest that Courson had not attended the hospital personally and was not necessarily in Ypres when he wrote the letter; indeed, its simple repackaging of the decree makes this an oddly bureaucratic response to the situation (rebuking prelates rarely passed up a chance to illustrate corrections with particular criticisms and local colour). The agent behind the act is suggested by the letter's only local detail, that 'the hospital is situated in a parish whose responsibility (*cura*) is known to belong to the prior of Ypres'. Indeed, the letter is addressed to Henry, prior of St Martin's, and herein lies the problem. For the hospital was a town foundation, under the supervision of the *scabini*, or civic officers. Their desire to secure a chapel and chaplain for the hospital had brought them into conflict with the priory, the great church of Ypres which held a monopoly of spiritual jurisdiction in the town.[67] For thirty years the controversy had raged. It had finally (and only just) been resolved, in an agreement confirmed by papal judges delegate in 1212, who stressed the many labours that had been undertaken by the *scabini* and burgesses.[68] The agreement allowed the priory to provide a priest from among their canons, who was to celebrate in

---

[66] Hanssens, 'De legatiereis', 530–1. He was in Brittany by 15 Jan. (Dickson, 'Courson', 96).

[67] *Cart. Ypres* I. 24. For the hospital, II, nos. 39–42, 64, 68, 78, 84, 90.

[68] The charter, ironically given Henry's actions in 1213, was copied into the cartulary as 'NOTA DE PACE SUPER CAPELLA HOSPITALIS IN FORO, ET SUPER OBLATIONIBUS ET VESTIMENTIS ET CONFIRMATIONE PACIS'. Three judges delegate declared that 'accedentes ad locum invenimus questionem que inter predictam ecclesiam et pauperes memoratos super capellano, quem idem pauperes petierunt, diutius fuerat agitata, de consensu scabinorum et burgensium loci, qui plurimum laboraverant, ut ipsi pauperes capellanum haberent, tali ad ultimum compositione sopitam.' *Cart. Ypres* II, no. 78. The initial settlement had been made in 1208, between the prior and *scabini* (II, no. 68).

the chapel and visit the sick yet live and dine at the priory; it was a contract for services that kept the canons away from the hospital government. Courson's letter was not the result of a new agreement, since it makes no mention of the *scabini*, who would have had to consent; instead, it is a directive made at Henry's petition, one that was enforced locally.[69] A second complaint by the priory over exactions taken by the town—apparently rights in churches and chapels—was also resolved in the priory's favour in May 1214, by judges delegate under Courson's legatine authority.[70] It is possible that these two petitions, one answered forcefully, another handed to adjudication, were laid before the legate at the same moment. If so, this would reinforce a date of early winter 1213/4.

The letter is evidence of an annexation by Henry. As head of a major church, he was almost certainly in attendance at the council at Reims. It may have been the priory's own delegation that spotted an opportunity to assert authority over the once contested (and now resented) hospital. His whole case rested on the decree. It employed the council's authority to target the brothers and sisters, requiring them to submit to a rule and wholly to the prior's authority. In complying, Courson reveals the jurisdictional claim that underlay his decree: a requirement that adequately endowed hospitals submit to a rule was fundamentally a statement that such places belonged under church supervision. In Henry's case, the plan failed. In 1217 Honorius III confirmed the 1212 agreement.[71] After 1215, there is no evidence of Courson's mandate nor of any right of the prior to regulate the hospital and correct its brothers and sisters.[72] The hospital's surviving ordinances, from 1268, were issued by the town, make no mention of the prior, and contain no religious vows.[73] Courson's intervention had been overturned (indeed, erased).

The Ypres letter suggests that the council of Reims predated that at Rouen, but by how long? The only compelling date for Courson in Reims, 7 December 1214, is too late for the council. An earlier journey in autumn 1213 from Troyes to Saint-Quentin offers one possibility, for this route may have taken him through Reims.[74]

---

[69] In another deed, dated 1215, the *scabini* have been forced to recognize an earlier mandate of 1187, which denied them any right to a chapel, altar, bells, or divine offices except by the will of the prior and chapter (*Cart. Ypres* II, no. 84). Henry had overturned the 1212 agreement.

[70] *Cart. Ypres* II, no. 82. The disputes likely involved the rights to offerings in the hospital and also of the lepers of St Mary Magdalene (II, nos. 53, 77, 89).

[71] *Cart. Ypres* II, no. 90 and, for the leper-house, no. 89.

[72] That said, the priory made good use of the letter. It was copied on the first folio of their *Registrum Rubrum* and may have inspired the arrangement of 1230 for the hospital of St Catherine, when lady Margaret, widow of Lambert Pedis, turned her own house into a hospital for the sick. Margaret entrusted its temporal oversight to the *scabini* and spiritual oversight to the priory, the latter arrangements deploying Courson's language (the episcopal letter was apparently drafted with a text of the Reims decree to hand), *Cart. Ypres* II, nos. 81, 114–15.

[73] '... cest li ordinance et li pourveance faite de commun conseil de le vile d'Ypre sour l'estat et sour le maniere dou vivre de chiaus qui serviront en lospital dYpre que on siut appeler freres et sereurs communement'. 'Réglement... de l'hôpital Notre-Dame á Ypres', *Annales... des Antiquités de la Flandre* 7 (1849), 247.

[74] Dickson, 'Courson', 140–2.

However, the words of the Rouen chronicle, 'first at Reims, then at Paris', urges us to look earlier and towards the launch of the legation.

The Preaching Tour of Early Summer, 1213

Across the channel and many years later in 1253, Robert Grosseteste, theologian and bishop of Lincoln, lay dying. At his deathbed was the St Albans monk and chronicler, Matthew Paris, who recorded the bishop's final pronouncements, a series of lecturing rebukes on the state of the church. Among them, a moment of the bishop's youth intrudes, when he recalls having seen and heard 'holy fathers and our teachers' driving usurers from regions of France with their preaching; he names Eustace, the Cistercian abbot of Flay; master Jacques de Vitry; the 'exiled' (*exulans*) archbishop, Stephen Langton; and master Robert de Courson.[75] Paris wrote about these preachers a second time, in his *Life* of Stephen Langton. Its only surviving folio gathers four episodes from Langton's time in exile, including one that has Langton returning from Rome towards England and preaching, first in Italy against heresy and then in north-eastern France against usury.[76] On the second leg, he was joined by Courson, 'cardinal of the Roman church, [and] together they prosecuted usurers to the point of eliminating usury'.[77] Paris then turns aside to note that copies of their sermons and parables, together with those of Jacques de Vitry, were preserved in a manuscript at St Albans abbey for anyone who wished to read them.[78]

These references have been noticed but never developed, because Paris's life presents a problem of chronology. The *Life* places Langton's preaching (§3) after his stay in Rome for Lateran IV, when he was upbraided by Innocent III (§2), and before his translation of Thomas Becket's body in 1220 (§4). This seems to date any preaching tour between 1216 and Langton's return to England in May 1218.[79]

---

[75] '…sancti patres et doctores nostri', *Chron. Maj.* V. 404.

[76] The folio survives, torn in two. On the manuscript and the events of this period: B. Bolton, 'Pastor Bonus', *Nederlands Archief voor Kerkgeschiedenis* 84:1 (2004).

[77] 'Rediens autem Stephanus archiepiscopus Cantuarie per partes Ytalie versus partes Anglicanas…In partibus autem Cisalpinis et in regno Francorum maxime apud Atrabatum et Sanctum Aodemarum et in partibus Flandrie, juvante eum quodam profundi pectoris magistro videlicet Roberto de Curcun, viro scientissimo, ecclesie Romane cardinali, adeo usuras eliminando usurarios persequebatur', Matthew Paris, 'Vita sancti Stephani archiepiscopi Cantuariensis', in *Ungedruckte Anglo-Normannische Geschichtsquellen*, ed. F. Liebermann (Strasbourg, 1879), 327–8. His source was Gervase de Melkley, a poet and pupil of Jean de Hanville (R. Glendinning, 'Eros, Agape, and Rhetoric', *Speculum* 67:4 (1992), 906). Gervase seems to have travelled with Langton, 1213–15.

[78] 'Cujus sermones, parabolas et virtutes, quas Dominus pro eodem archiepiscopo et magistro Roberto memorato, necnon et magistro Iacobo de Vitriolo, que speciales exigunt tractatus, [*qui*] legere desiderat, librum Additamentorum annalium, que apud Sanctum Albanum sunt, adeat inspecturus.' Paris, 'Vita', 328. This material no longer survives (322).

[79] *Acta Stephani Langton Cantuariensis episcopi*, ed. K. Major (Oxford, 1950), 165; Paris, 'Vita', 320–2.

Yet the archbishop and the legate could not have been together in those regions at that time.[80] The inability to pin down such a tour has lent it a legendary quality.[81] To square the circle, it has been suggested that the preachers toured separately.[82]

One date does work for a great preaching tour: late spring and early summer of 1213.[83] In this year, the exiled Langton left Rome after January 1213, travelling north; his whereabouts are unknown until mid-July, when he arrived in England, with fellow bishops in tow.[84] Matthew Paris gives an itinerary, moving Langton first to Cisalpine Italy and later into France then Flanders, where he was joined by Courson, the two of them preaching against usury near Arras and Saint-Omer and in the region of Flanders.[85] The route follows the *via Frankigena*, the main route from Rome to England, along eastern France, through Reims, and into Flanders, then Calais.[86] This is the direction that Courson also would have proceeded when he left Rome, in the days after 19 April, armed with letters for Blanche of Champagne, at Troyes, and Philip Augustus and his son Louis. By the end of May, Philip had left Gravelines where, his plans to invade England scuppered, he was now attacking the Flemish towns of the count of Flanders.[87] (Saint-Omer and Arras were west of the fighting, on the road to Gravelines from Reims.) There was cause to be in the area: Langton and Courson were at the centre of efforts to secure peace between the two kings, and this was the theatre of war.[88] A third key player, Jacques de Vitry, was also in the area in early summer. Three years earlier, he had moved there to be near Marie d'Oignies, now his spiritual adviser, a holy woman who had left the world to serve God in a leper-house, inspiring her husband and

---

[80] As papal witness lists reveal, Courson was resident in Rome after Lateran IV, until departing on Crusade in Aug. 1218; he died at Damietta in 1219 (Dickson, 'Courson', 127 n. and 130). Hanssens's suggestion of winter 1213/14 can also be discarded, since Langton was in England then (Hanssens, 'De legatiereis', 531; *MPM* II. 12–13). Bird considers the bishop of Arras's efforts to counteract heresy and usury 1203×1208, implying a possible link to (and thus earlier date for) the preaching tour (Bird, 'Wheat and the Tares', 771). An earlier date is not impossible, although it is unlikely, not least because Courson was only in France as cardinal during his legation of 1213–15.

[81] R. W. Southern, *Robert Grosseteste* (Oxford, 1984), relegates it to a footnote (66 n. 7), although does believe it happened at some point. The tour is not noticed in D. Baumann, *Stephen Langton* (Leiden, 2009).

[82] A. Forni, 'La "nouvelle prédication"', in *Faire croire* (1981), 23. This is also the implication of the conclusion reached by P. Roberts, *Stephanus de Lingua-Tonante* (Toronto, 1968), 18–19.

[83] *MPM* I. 20; II. 12; Paris, 'Vita', 322.

[84] On Langton's return to England, see *Chron. Maj.* II. 550; Robert of Auxerre, *Chronicon*, ed. O. Holder–Egger, MGH SS XXVI (Hanover, 1882), 279; *Acta Langton*, 164.

[85] Paris, 'Vita', 327–8, in note 77, above.

[86] See the routes laid out by Paris, in D. K. Connolly, 'Imagined Pilgrimage', *The Art Bulletin* 81:4 (1999), 609.

[87] Spiegel, *Romancing the Past*, 45–8; Baldwin, *Philip Augustus*, 209–12.

[88] On Courson's charges to negotiate peace and prepare for crusade, Powell, *Anatomy*, 33, 39–40. After years of interdict, King John submitted to papal terms on 13 May 1213 and on 6 July Innocent appointed special envoys to negotiate peace. One of these envoys was Courson; another was Nicholas, cardinal bishop of Tusculum, who was sent with letters by Innocent directly to Langton: *Selected Letters of Pope Innocent III*, ed. C. R. Cheney and W. H. Semple (London, 1953), nos 53–5, and esp. its footnotes.

others to follow.[89] In mid-June 1213, Marie lay dying at Oignies, twenty miles from Arras, and Vitry sat vigil at her deathbed.[90] Langton was not the only scholar remembered for a preaching tour against usury: Courson's preaching against usury was widely noted by chroniclers and caused such consternation that Philip Augustus complained to the pope in the spring of 1214.[91] Thereafter, the chroniclers turned against him, condemning the preacher for his attacks on clerical abuses and his 'indiscriminate' recruitment of crusaders, including 'children, old men, women, the lame, the blind, the deaf, and lepers'.[92] Only in early summer of 1213 do the people, the places, and the great anti-usury initiative align.

The picture is further developed by a long-standing network that was activated for the summer tour. The year before, Vitry and William, archdeacon of Paris, had been entrusted with preaching the Albigensian crusade in France and Germany. The chronicler of that crusade, Peter of les Vaux-de-Cernay, complained that Vitry and William were then called away by Courson, when the legate arrived, full of gusto, in France; Vitry did not return to preaching for the Albigensian crusade until December 1213.[93] Courson probably recruited William when the latter was in Rome as an envoy for the crusaders in March and April 1213. A central figure in Peter's story—the general on the front lines, building and rallying siege engines— William suddenly disappears from Peter's account at this moment. He reappears in April 1214, alongside Courson, suggesting that he stayed with the legate through the council of Rouen.[94] The famed preacher and Parisian scholar, Alberic of Laon, archbishop of Reims, would also join William in July 1214, along with the cantor of Reims.[95] These networks had deep roots: Courson,

---

[89]   On Marie, Simons, *Cities of Ladies*, 40, and below.

[90]   Marie died on Monday 23 June, 'The Life of Mary of Oignies by James of Vitry', tr. M. H. King, in A. B. Mulder-Bakker, ed., *Mary of Oignies* (Turnhout, 2006), §§96–7, 105–9. The Latin text of Marie's life is *Acta Sanctorum*, 5 June, pp. 542–72.

[91]   *PL* 217, cols 229–30. For Courson's anti-usury campaign, J. C. Moore, 'Pope Innocent III and Usury', in F. Andrews et al., eds, *Pope, Church and City* (Leiden, 2004), 72–3; *MPM* I. 296–311; Bird, 'Reform or Crusade?'

[92]   'Robertus de Corcon, apostolice sedis legatus, et multi cum eo et sub eo adhuc predicabant publice per universum regnum gallice et multos crucesignabant indifferenter, parvulos, senes, mulieres, claudos, cecos, surdos, leprosos; propter quod multi divites crucem tollere abhorrebant, quia hujus-modi confusion presumebatur potius impedire negotium crucis, quam posse succurrere Sancte Terre.' *Œuvres de Rigord et de Guillaume le Breton*, ed. H. F. Delaborde, 2 vols (Paris, 1882–5), I. 303.

[93]   Peter records that 'on this arrival in France the legate began to perform his allotted task with great energy . . . and advanced the cause of a Crusade to the Holy Land by every means available to him', which included co-opting 'the preachers working for the Crusade against the heretics' to preach alongside him. Peter did not name William and Jacques, but these seem to be who he meant, as those who had been made responsible for Crusade preaching in 1212. Peter was at pains to stress that only the bishop of Carcassonne continued to preach after spring 1213 (*Hist. Alb. Crus.* 142, 150, 199–200, 222, 229).

[94]   *Hist. Alb. Crus.* 151, 157–8 (Courson), 184, 200, 229–300 (William's absence). William had worked closely with the archbishop of Rouen, Robert de Poulain, when the latter participated in the crusade in 1212.

[95]   *Hist. Alb. Crus.* 159, 162, 164.

Langton, and William the archdeacon, fellow Parisian scholars, had worked closely together as papal judges delegate.[96] Also, Fulk, bishop of Toulouse, a friend of Vitry and Marie d'Oignies, may have been present at the preaching tour. He was in attendance as Marie lay dying and enacted anti-usury measures in Toulouse in 1215 that seem to have been influenced by Courson's campaign.[97]

The tour likely occurred between late May and early July. The memory of these great orators and visionaries of a new age inspired a generation of young churchmen. Forty years later, Grosseteste remembered it as a highpoint of moral action and a moment of great hope then lost.[98] Such a tour would fit the zeal behind Courson's mission, its twin motives of crusade and reform, and a pattern seen in the run-up to his other councils.[99] And it offers a new chronology and geography to the legate's first months, suggesting a likely date for the Reims council in July and the Paris council in August. In preparation, Courson and his closest allies preached in Artois and Flanders, although there is another way to define the territory they toured: the north of the province of Reims, whose twelve dioceses made up a long triangle, its short edge at the coast from Abbeville in the west to Antwerp in the north-east, its southern point the Perthois, to the east of Troyes.[100] The area encompassed north-east France, including Arras and Saint-Omer, and much of Flanders, including Ghent, Bruges, Ypres, and Brussels. Launching the legation here, and with a preaching tour, could serve pastoral, political, and practical ends: announcing the legate's arrival, broadcasting the new papal missions, engaging with local prelates, and biding time while calls for the early councils went out. It could also fulfil a key part of Courson's charge: to identify abuses in preparation for Innocent's great council. It moves his research from the schoolrooms of Paris to the cities of the northern province, its remedies unveiled at his first council, at the archiepiscopal seat in Reims. This creates a new frame in which interpret Courson's reform agenda and, specifically here, to search for the origins of his hospital reform.

---

[96] Dickson, 'Courson', pièces justificatives, nos. 2–7, 9. The network is best discovered through the work of Bird more generally.

[97] He blessed the altar beside her sick bed, 'Life of Mary of Oignies', 123–4; B. Bolton, 'Fulk of Toulouse', in D. Baker, ed., *Church, Society and Politics* (Oxford, 1975), 91–2.

[98] This may also have been the moment when Thomas de Cantimpré first encountered Jacques de Vitry, for he testifies that '[w]hen I was not yet fifteen years old and you were not a bishop, I heard you preaching in Lotharingia. I loved you with such veneration that I was happy just at the sound of your name. From then on a special love for you stayed with me. It is no wonder; the things we learn as children take firm root in us.' (Thomas of Cantimpré, 'Supplement', tr. H. Feiss, in Mulder-Bakker, ed., *Mary of Oignies*, 129–65. Thomas was born c.1200 and attended school at Cambrai or Liège until he entered the monastery of Cantimpré in 1217 (p. 132); Vitry was elected bishop of Acre at some point between 1214 and his consecration in 1216 (*Hist. Occ.*, ed. Hinnebusch, 6 n.).

[99] On these twin imperatives, Bird, 'Reform or Crusade?'; B. Bolton, 'Show with a Meaning', in Bolton, ed., *Innocent III* (Aldershot, 1995).

[100] The dioceses were Thérouanne, Tournai, Arras, Cambrai, Amiens, Beauvais, Senlis, Noyon, Laon, Soissons, Châlons-sur-Marne, and Reims itself.

A New Vision for Hospitals, from Brabant to Reims

In heading to this region in May 1213, Courson was returning to familiar territory. As a young man, in the 1190s, he had accompanied Fulk de Neuilly on his preaching tours of Picardy and Brabant, and he may have witnessed or even assisted in the campaign by the bishop of Arras against heresy and usury in the first decade of the new century.[101] Before becoming cardinal in 1212, he had been a canon of Noyon (1204–9), the mother church of a diocese of Reims. His activities as papal judge delegate were concentrated in the provinces of Reims and Sens and included disputed elections of the sees of Reims (1204), Amiens (1205), Troyes (1206), and Thérouanne (1209).[102] His responsibilities had been concentrated in the area between Troyes in the south, Reims in the east, and the diocese of Thérouanne in the north, an area that covered the province of Reims and the north-east of the province of Sens. In these cases, Courson had worked closely with local ecclesiastics and with fellow judges delegate who were often masters from Noyons and Paris and officials from the province of Sens.[103] He would have been well known and well connected among the leading ecclesiastics of the region.

The Spread of Hospital Rules (1170–1233)

It was a region where hospital reform was taking hold. It had not begun with the *hôtel-dieu* of Montdidier which, if it did have its rule by 1207, was an early product of a wave that was washing outwards from the trading towns of Flanders.[104] The earliest initiatives had been rules (*regula et ordo*) issued by town governments to their hospitals of St John at Bruges (1188) and Ghent (1196);[105] then, at Liège, master Jean de Nivelles was instrumental in providing rules to the abbey's hospital of St Christopher in 1199 and the cathedral's hospital of St Matthew in *c*.1200; at around this time, too, a rule was given by the chapter to the hospital at nearby Fosses-la-Ville.[106] In the next decade the *hôtel-dieu* at Laon received a rule in *c*.1209, as did the hospital of St John, Brussels in 1211, from the local cathedral chapter and bishop respectively.[107] New efforts were also afoot for leper-houses, especially in the diocese of Cambrai. The town gave constitutions to the leprosaria

---

[101] *MPM* I. 37; Bird, 'Wheat and the Tares', 771.

[102] Dickson, 'Courson', 77–82; *MPM* I. 20, 317–18.   [103] Dickson, 'Courson', 71–2, 75–7, 81.

[104] See n. 3. The sketch here is necessarily preliminary, for the manuscript and textual traditions of these rules await careful study.

[105] Maréchal, *Brugse hospitallwezen*, 94–8; Bonenfant, 'Hôpitaux', 27.

[106] De Spiegeler, *Liège*, 62, 67, 112–14; *Cartulaire de la commune de Fosses*, ed. J. Borgnet (Namur, 1867), 5–8.

[107] Saint-Denis, *Laon*, 76; *Cartulaire de l'hôpital Saint-Jean de Bruxelles*, ed. P. Bonenfant (Brussels, 1953), no. 10; Bonenfant, 'Hôpitaux', 27–8; Potthast 3155, 3157.

at Liège (1176), and the bishops to those at Berlaimont (1176×1177), east of Cambrai, Cambrai (1178×1179), and Mons (1202).[108] Further afield, the archbishop of Sens provided rules for leprosaria at Meaux (by 1193) and Châteaudun (1205).[109] When local prelates returned from Lateran IV, the focus on *hôtels-dieu*, and especially capitular *hôtels-dieu*, intensified. In the province of Reims, the Montdidier/Amiens rule was provided at Noyon (1216×17) and made its way through the dioceses of Amiens and Noyons in the coming decades, then into Beauvais (1246).[110] Cathedral chapters provided rules to the hospitals at St Julien, Cambrai (1220), and Notre Dame de Tournai (+1238), while bishops issued (sometimes identical) rules to those of St John, Cambrai (1227), and Tongres (1233), Ghent (1236), and Saint-Trond (1240).[111] A look further afield reveals how remarkable—and how concentrated—was this movement. For elsewhere we find only scattered instances before 1250: episcopal statutes for the hospital at Angers (1200×1202); a capitular rule at Paris (1217×21); an episcopal rule at Coëffort, near Le Mans (1231×1234) given to Ferté-Bernard; and capitular statutes to the hospital of Le Puy (1249).[112]

Le Grand's study of hospital statutes offered a powerful vision of reform in the nation of France, so much so that it became the template by which other regions have been measured. Some time ago, when first approaching hospitals, I set out to do for England what Le Grand had done for France but, looking for hospital statutes, came up short. Few rules or statutes appeared in England until well into the thirteenth century; instead, the texts that mattered, and that continued to matter, were charters, especially those that confirmed foundation arrangements.[113] Comparing this pattern to Le Grand's France, it seemed that England was unusual; but it was not, and nor was France. If we step out of national borders, we see a concerted movement to create rules for welfare houses in the decades around *c*.1200, one centred originally around Flanders and Brabant. It was this area that was unusual.

---

[108] *Régestes de la Cité de Liège*, ed. E. Fairon and J. Haust, 4 vols (Liège, 1933–40), I, no. 8; P. De Spiegeler, 'La Léproserie de Cornillon', *ASBHH* 18 (1980); De Spiegeler, *Liège*, 57–60, 107; *Actes et documents anciens intéressant la Belgique*, ed. C. Duvivier (Brussels, 1898), 304–5; de Keyzer, 'Évolution interne', 14–15. W. de Keyzer, 'Le léproserie Saint-Ladre de Mons', *ASBHH* 12 (1974).

[109] *Statuts*, 184–93. The Sens initiative may have built on an older tradition of rule-making for leprosaria by Ivo of Chartres, Mesmin, 'Waleran, Count of Meulan', 8–10; Touati, *Yves de Chartres*, 60–5.

[110] See n. 3; Montaubin, 'Hôpitaux cathedraux', 29; Lacroix, *Hôpital Tournai*, 113–30.

[111] *Statuts*, 53–60; Lacroix, *Hôpital Tournai*, 112–30; Maréchal, *Brugse hospitallwezen*, 101–2. Tongres and Saint-Trond received the rule from nearby Liège (De Spiegeler, *Liège*, 114). A concentration of activity in the province of Reims was noticed by Bonenfant-Feytmans, 'Organisations hospitalières', 31–2.

[112] *Statuts*, 21–33, 57–60, 96–100; J.-M Bienvienu, 'Pauvreté, misères et charité en Anjou', *Le Moyen Age* 73 (1967), 208–9. Montaubin, 'Hôpitaux cathedraux', 24–5, 29–30, suggests that Paris inspired rules in other capitular hospitals, including Reims and Châlons.

[113] Watson, 'Origins'. When statutes did emerge in different regions of England, they evinced little sign of any textual borrowing and there were no families of texts, such as the Amiens group.

The movement took hold in in the towns of the Low Countries and travelled through the trading networks that criss-crossed this area on the edge of the empire.[114] Early efforts were led by towns but by *c.*1200 there was a new ecclesiastical thrust. At its base was a vision of an ordered devotional life that accommodated both men and women, focused first on leper-houses then, increasingly, on hospitals for the pilgrims, poor, and the sick. The new ideas had already begun to spread west through ecclesiastical networks when Courson arrived on his preaching tour in 1213, but it was only thereafter that activity found new centres in north-eastern France. The vision behind this activity was not so obviously top-down, nor so clearly episcopal, as it has been seen. While individual bishops may have been supporters, the early agenda was not theirs: the efforts were too diffuse and moved too easily between civic, episcopal, and capitular drafters. Such fluidity suggests not a programme implemented, but efforts—at least in part—to manage a wider phenomenon.

Hospitals and the Early Beguine Movement

So where did the vision come from? Although several great churches in the region took an early interest, it was only after 1213 that cathedral chapters took centre stage, creating regulations for their own *hôtels-dieu.* This suggests that Courson's decree was a turning point for hospital reform in the region, amplifying an existing initiative but also repackaging it for a new audience. In its wake, the geography of reform shifted from the trading networks of the Low Countries to the ecclesiastical province of Reims where, over the coming decades, the practice spread. But it had not originated in these diocesan or provincial structures.

The initiative, given institutional thrust in Courson's decree, was cultivated by a group of allies who were working in the region, a network of Parisian scholars that threaded through these churches and cities. At the top, facilitating the reach of the legatine decree, were Alberic of Laon, archbishop of Reims (1207–18), Parisian scholar and crusader; and Robert de Poulain, archbishop of Rouen (1208–21), an ally in the fight against heretics and usury; and Peter of Corbeil, archbishop of Sens (1199–1222), another theologian and colleague of the Chanter.[115] And the Parisian roots went deeper and wider. Peter the Chanter himself began and ended his career at Reims, was a benefactor of the *hôtel-dieu* of Beauvais in 1183, and had been elected bishop of Tournai in 1193, only to be pipped to that post by his own advocate, Stephen (1193–1203), the former abbot of Saint-Geneviève in Paris.[116]

---

[114] Cologne may also have been an early centre: Bonenfant, 'Hôpitaux', 19–20.

[115] *MPM* I. 45–6; Bird, 'Reform or Crusade', 168. On the Parisian network's fight against heresy: Bird, 'Wheat and the Tares', 767–80. A tension between the advocates of Crusade and the French bishops is teased out in B. Bolton, 'Faithful to Whom?', *Revue Mabillon* 9 (1998).

[116] *MPM* I. 6–7, 9–10.

Since Fulk de Neuilly's efforts in the late 1190s, Parisian crusade preaching and anti-usury campaigns had swept the area, revivifying reform networks and drawing young students.[117] The diocese of Amiens also had close links to the schools, not least through Jean d'Abbeville, a regent of theology in Paris and canon then dean (1215–25) of Amiens.[118] He was among the many able administrators, fresh from the schools, who were populating diocesan administration at this time. It was a network sustained through close personal and ideological ties and, in many ways, it underpinned various efforts at hospital regulation.

Yet the agenda was not a scholastic one: Courson's own *Summa* is evidence that the hospital initiatives were not hatched in the schools. At the same time, it is evidence of something happening further afield: that new forms of religious life, based in hospitals and leper-house, were calling to these scholars. The *Summa's* only statement on welfare houses had addressed couples who served together in a leper-house, suggesting that Courson knew of couples like Marie d'Oignies and her husband, if not of Marie herself.[119] Jacques de Vitry had certainly heard of Marie in Paris. He was so inspired by these accounts that, in the words of his follower, 'he abandoned his theological studies in which he was immoderately interested and came to Oignies' to join her by 1210.[120] Vitry's source may have been Jean de Nivelles, who by 1199 was a canon at Liège and knew Marie well. Marie was from Nivelles and in the early 1190s had led her husband to the leper-house there, at Willambroux.[121] Jean de Nivelles had also worked closely with Fulk de Neuilly and had studied under Peter the Chanter alongside Vitry, with whom he would maintain a life-long correspondence.

For the longer ambition behind the hospital decree, we might look to three men: Jacques de Vitry, Jean de Nivelles, and Jean de Liroux. Nivelles and Liroux joined Langton, Courson, and Alberic of Laon, the archbishop of Reims, on Vitry's list of renowned preachers. Liroux worked closely with Nivelles; he was a canon of Liège and would die crossing the Alps with Vitry in 1216 to seek papal recognition of beguine life.[122] Nivelles was involved in the early rules for the hospitals at Liège c.1200, and in May 1212, when that city was sacked, he was with Marie in Oignies and, Vitry writes, 'grieved inconsolably for the holy virgins whom he had gained for the Lord by his preaching and example'.[123] These three men were the most important patrons of what has come to be seen as the early beguine movement. This was a more informal new form of religious life, characterised by a deeply

---

[117] The density of the network is illustrated by Bird, 'Wheat and the Tares', 767–76. On Fulk: Forni, 'La "nouvelle prédication"'; A. W. Jones, 'Fulk of Neuilly', *Comitatus* 41 (2010).

[118] Montaubin, 'Amiens', 63.

[119] Bird, 'Reform or Crusade', 174–7, draws in Marie as part of the reformers' anti-usury campaign and a 'quasi-regular ideal' for the laity.

[120] Cantimpré, 'Supplement', §1. For the question of dates, Simons, *Cities of Ladies*, 172 n. 20. On Vitry's network, Mollat, 'Floraison', 47–50, 55–6; Bolton, 'Faithful to Whom?'

[121] Simons, *Cities of Ladies*, 40: Vitry, 'Life of Marie d'Oignies', §§1, 13–14, 44.

[122] Simons, *Cities of Ladies*, 41–2, 48, 173–4.   [123] Vitry, 'Life of Marie d'Oignies', §57.

personal piety, whereby women (and some men) left the comforts of their lives to serve the poor, the sick, and the suffering. Marie d'Oignies has come to be recognized as the early exemplar of this new model of holy life (which was exactly what Vitry's *Life of Marie d'Oignies* set out to do).[124] In the decades after 1190 *mulieres sanctae* ('holy women') can be found across the Low Countries and into Champagne, but our early accounts centre on Huy, Liège, and Nivelles.[125] We know so much of these places because of the concentration of *vitae* written by local Cistercians and canons of Liège, as well as by Vitry and his follower, Thomas de Cantimpré: eleven lives known misleadingly as 'beguine *vitae*'.[126] It was the women who forged the new way of life; but here, near Liège, arose a concentration of (devoted and inspired) religious men who were keen to communicate and institutionalize that vision. It was not one vision of institutionalization; the Cistercian patrons, for example, fostered single-sex convents, if still with the stress on care for the sick.[127] And between *c.*1199 and *c.*1216 none worked harder than Vitry, Nivelles, and Liroux.

This new form of religious life was integrally associated with hospitals and leper-houses. It was to leper-houses that the first women, including Marie d'Oignies and Juetta de Huy, removed themselves; and it was through hospitals that later communities of women served. The summer of 1213 asks us to see hospital reform and this new life as two sides of the same coin, brought together in the person of Vitry. To modern historians, Jacques de Vitry has four identities, each extraordinary: a historian of the 'West' and the 'East'; a preacher, whose sermons survive in four collected cycles; the early patron and organizer of the beguine life; and the celebrator of a new kind of hospital, raised up from the world. June 1213 brought together the last three. It was at this moment that Marie died and Vitry shifted from disciple to apostle, and when he was surrounded by influential allies who were preaching (and seeking) a new moral order, with an eye towards Innocent's upcoming council. In these cross-currents, the hospital decree emerged. Placing the decree in this new context, we notice that it ignored

---

[124] J. Wogan-Browne and M.-E. Henneau, 'Liege, the Medieval "Woman Question"', in Dor et al., eds, *New Trends in Feminine Spirituality*, 3–5, 7.

[125] Walter Simons identifies the informal communities of the first phase, *c.*1190–*c.*1230, and the nearby centres at Huy, Nivelles, and Liège, Simons, *Cities of Ladies*, 36–48. See, too, Bolton's defining essay, 'Mulieres Sanctae'.

[126] For the *vitae*, Simons, *Cities of Ladies*, 37–40.

[127] See the work of Anne Lester, cited in n. 136. Famously, the Cistercian order began to clamp down on female convents, forbidding the incorporation of any new houses in 1228 (Lester, *Cistercian Nuns*, 93–6). The activity of the Cistercian order takes on a new hue when placed beside Courson's hospital decree. The Cistercian General Chapter had maintained almost total silence on the subject of nuns until, suddenly, in 1213 it issued a statute that prohibited them from stepping out of the house without licence from their abbess and required any new houses to observe 'full inclosure' (*penitus includendae*). This was repeated in 1219, 1220, and 1225, the latter requiring that new houses be fully built and endowed before being populated with nuns 'so that it is not necessary for them to beg' (*ita quod eas non oporteat mendicare*): *Statuta capitulorum generalium ordinis Cisterciensis*, ed. J.-M. Canivez, 8 vols (Louvain, 1933–41), I. 405 (c. 3), 502 (c. 84), 505 (c. 12), 517 (c. 4); II. 36 (c. 7).

bishops. It focused on reforming the houses themselves by organizing mixed communities into a more regular and less scandal-prone form of life, which included placing them under a *prelatus*, a male ecclesiastical authority to whom they should 'promise faithful and devoted obedience'. The decree was rooted in the bigger question of the *mulieres sanctae* and their reputation.

This casts Vitry's own well-known statement on hospitals in a new light. The *mulieres sanctae* were the object of widespread suspicion and slander, against which their biographers were keen to defend them.[128] One cannot help but see the reform of hospitals as part of this defence. Vitry's statement includes a long condemnation of the state of hospitals, acknowledging—polemically—the worst fears of critics, that 'houses of hospitality and piety are transformed into dens of robbers, prostitutes' brothels, and the synagogues of Jews'.[129] The picture was drawn to create a decisive contrast between welfare houses more generally and a new spirit of religious service that was bringing with it a new kind of hospital. To illustrate that the wider 'sort of pestilential corruption and abominable hypocrisy does not infect all hospitals', Vitry named a handful of new orders and individual hospitals. The first were exemplary religious congregations: Holy Spirit of Saxia in Rome, St Sampson's in Constantinople, St Anthony of Vienne, and St Mary of Roncevaux.[130] These were southern movements concentrated in France and Italy, although one, St Sampson's, had close ties to Flanders, and a new daughter house in Douai.[131] Another, in Rome, was Innocent III's great hospital, which he had begun creating in 1198, almost as soon as he became pope.[132] Vitry's second group consisted of houses with individual rules, at Paris, Noyon, Provins, Tournai, Liège, and Brussels. It is striking how closely the lists accords with our pattern of known rules before 1218, concentrated in Brabant and the provinces of Reims and Sens.[133] From his new perch as bishop of Acre, Vitry was celebrating the work

---

[128] Vitry, 'Life of Marie d'Oignies', §4 and n. 9.

[129] 'Texts on Hospitals', tr. J. Bird, 111; *Hist. Occ.*, ed. Hinnebusch, 149.

[130] On these houses, Chapter 1 n. 7. At least two of them had recently received a rule: Saxia in 1204 and the Antonines in 1217.

[131] St Sampson's was reorganized into a military hospitaller order after the Latins seized Constantinople in 1204, crowning Baldwin IX (count of Flanders and Hainaut) emperor of Constantinople. In June 1218, the archbishop of Thessalonica, a canon of St Amé in Douai, gave property in Douai to St Sampson's to be a daughter-house *ad receptionem pauperum*. D. Stathakopoulos, 'The Hospital of St. Sampson', *Viator* 37 (2006), 258.

[132] Drossbach, *Christliche Caritas*, 55–62.

[133] The earliest rule to survive for Tournai dates from +1238, although an undated oath for the canon-procurator does indicate some kind of a rule, with *conversi* and *conversa* who had to renounce property ('Item quemcumque vel quamcumque in conversum vel conversam recipiam omnifaciam renuntiare proprietatis'. The oath is based on episcopal constitutions of 1197, in the name of Stephen of Tournai, which did require the incoming canon-procurator to take an oath before taking up his stall: 'Documents... de l'hôpital capitulaire de Notre-Dame de Tournai', ed. J. Pycke, *ASBHH* 8 (1970), 26; Bonenfant-Feytmans, 'Organisations hospitalières', 34). Such an early rule for the hospital of Provins (in the diocese of Sens) is unknown, although one may predate the Paris statutes of 1217×20, which assigned its sisters the black headdress of 'the women of Provins'. A seventeenth-century copy of the 1263 'constitutions, statuts, et ordonnances', in French, survives as Dammarie-lès-Lys, Archives

accomplished in his home region, including in the immediate aftermath of Courson's decree. He was also promoting an ecclesiastical programme, one that distinguished the general picture of welfare houses from the new ideals, which brought a new order to hospitals. To Vitry the reform of hospitals was intertwined with the *mulieres sanctae*. Positively so, by seeking to reform hospital communities in imitation of the new religious service that the women inspired. And negatively, because the liminal character of hospitals, a general state of being, cast suspicion on the new devotional movement for which he had appointed himself chief advocate. It is hard not to see Vitry's as the agenda at work behind the Reims' hospital decree.

Once forged, the hospital decree took on a life of its own. It was no top–down reform. Instead, it was like a stone that skipped briefly from pool to pool, each time creating different, and smaller, ripples before disappearing into the deep waters of the papal curia.

It was born of a particular place and moment, when Courson returned to France to prepare for Lateran IV, in part by rooting out reforms to be taken up by the great council. His legation began with a preaching tour of Artois and western Flanders, which reunited Courson with the community of reformers from which both legate and pope were hatched, once-scholars who were now episcopal and spiritual leaders in the towns of north-eastern France and the Low Countries. At this moment, it must have seemed like they could change the world. The hospital decree was a product of the intensity and ambition of this group of allies, who were eager to put religion firmly at the heart of daily life. In this instance, at least, they looked to the streets, inspired by the *mulieres sanctae* and the vision of Vitry and his Liège cohorts. They attempted to give institutional voice, and bring institutional vision, to a movement that had taken root in local towns, and especially near hospitals and leper-houses.

The decree was first proclaimed at the council of Reims in July 1213, where it found a sympathetic audience. Prelates – the men in charge of dioceses, cathedral chapters, and urban religious houses – saw here an answer in terms they could recognise to what was substantially a lay, and female, movement. Regulation became an institutional project, as bishops and, especially, chapters, went on to create statutes for their *hôtels-dieu* across the province. In this new arena, the reform took on a new shape. In the stilted roll-out of hospital statutes over the coming decades, local arrangements took precedence in the regulations and local circumstances were probably behind their creation. We might see in the concentration of statutes for capitular *hôtels-dieu*, an echo of the Aachen (816) rule for canons, which cast a chapter's *hospitalis pauperum* as a public marker of the

départementales de Seine-et-Marne 11Hdt/A3 (I am grateful to Prof. Adam Davis for this reference). They are related to the rule for the hospital at Troyes (*Statuts*, 46, 101).

canonical community's own observance.[134] As did the Aachen rule, this new reform should redirect our view into the cities themselves. It might, in turn, pose questions about local beguine movements or about initiatives (or controversies) regarding women's religious life more generally in this region.

When the decree reached the council of Paris in August 1213, it prompted a more limited response. The province of Sens had already embraced rules for leper-houses, so the decree did not fall on stony ground.[135] Here, reform was cultivated through scholarly networks and, especially, within the region of Champagne, which had close ties to Reims and the trading networks of the Low Countries; there the Cistercian vision of reform proved particularly influential.[136] In contrast, the decree made barely a ripple in the province of Rouen, where it was issued at the council of March 1214. Thereafter the province evinces little evidence of hospital regulation.[137] The surviving copy of the decrees, in a contemporary manuscript from Mont-St-Michel, suggests here, at least, the decree was not wholly understood.[138]

After the council of Rouen, the decree disappears entirely even from Courson's legation. It was not among the decrees of the other legatine councils, even those of Montpellier (January 1215), which otherwise largely followed those of Paris and Rouen.[139] Beyond the security of his Parisian network, things turned sour for Courson. King Philip protested his strict regulations on usury, as did others, leading to a rebuke in March 1214 by Innocent for exceeding his legatine powers in his legal decisions; the following year, local bishops boycotted Courson's final council, at Bourges.[140] Its legatine history underscores the two local characters of

---

[134] The capitular context, in the wake of Aachen, is skilfully developed in Montaubin, 'Hôpitaux cathédraux'.

[135] For those in the province of Sens, see n. 109.

[136] Anne Lester has revealed the close connections between hospitals and new communities of Cistercian nuns in Champagne, especially in the decades after 1200. The house of Argensolles e.g. was established 1222×1224 by Blanche of Navarre, countess of Champagne, on the advice of Cistercians from Liège and by recruiting women from Liège: Lester, *Cistercian Nuns*, 28–33, 211–15; A. E. Lester, 'Cistercian Nuns and the Care of Lepers', in E. Jamroziak and J. Burton, eds, *Religious and Laity* (Turnhout, 2006), 219. Touati, *Maladie*, 659–78, explores work with leprosaria.

[137] M. Arnoux, *Des clercs au service de la réforme* (Turnhout, 2000), 21–2, 123–5; although see the encounters of Archbishop Eudes de Rigaud (1248–75) on his visitation (Davis, *Holy Bureaucrat*, 81–2). Arnoux, *Des clercs*, 75, 125n, notes the reform of communities into Augustinian canons at the leper-house of Val-au-Gris in 1188, and at the *hotels-dieu* at Neufchâtel-en-Bray, Caen, and Rouen under archbishop Robert de Poulain.

[138] The scribe misread *pauci sani* as *paucissimi*, changing the sentence from 'since a few healthy persons should be able to care very capably for many sick people' to 'since the very fewest (or very smallest) should be able to care.' The number of healthy in the hospital was a central concern in the original decree. In addition, the scribe has used this moment to start a second decree, potentially disassociating the *paucissimi* from hospitals.

[139] The canons for Bordeaux, in English territory, survive only in a digest, sent by Courson in a letter to King John (*Foedera*, ed. T. Rymer, I (London, 1745), 61). Those of Clermont do not survive but, given the broader pattern, were probably a restrained corpus. The council of Bourges only produced fourteen decrees for the cathedral chapter. For editions of the decrees, see n. 52.

[140] Moore, *Pope Innocent III*, 223–4; Foreville, *Innocent III*, 323–4; Pontal, *Capétienne* (Paris, 1995), 401.

the hospital decree: its roots in the new religious lives of the *mulieres sanctae* across the trading network of the Low Countries, then its episcopal and capitular uses in the province of Reims.

Afterlife: A Failure in Law

At Rome, Courson was swept aside. French chroniclers took delight in his disgrace at the Lateran council, when the pope undid so many of the excesses of this 'wicked man'.[141] Both Innocent and his successor, Honorius III, continued to overturn many of his legatine decisions. Courson's legatine legislation did not circulate in manuscript, even in the provinces where it had been promulgated. (It was the synodal statutes of Odo of Sully, bishop of Paris (1196–1208), that would shape synodal legislation across France as well as in England, Portugal, and Spain.[142]) And there are reasons to suspect that the hospital decree was specifically rejected at the curia. Courson's legislation had been carefully examined and elements adopted into the Lateran canons, drafted by Innocent himself.[143] No version of the hospital decree was incorporated into other conciliar legislation, synodal, provincial, or ecumenical, even by Stephen Langton.[144] The clear authority of *Si hospitale* from this moment, as the defining statement of a hospital, suggests that the decision may not have been quietly taken. Within months, it first appeared as a definition in commentary, in John Teutonicus's revised *glossa ordinaria* to the *Decretum*.

Two other decretals, noticed in Chapter 7, suggest why Courson's decree was set aside. In 1224 Honorius III would intervene on the side of the prioress and sisters of the hospital of St Nicholas, Douai, who wished to assume the Victorine rule (5 Comp. 1.19.1 = X-).[145] Their bishop was imposing a condition that they obtain episcopal consent to elect any abbess and to receive any sister, lay brother, or lay sister. In law the ruling is unexceptional: the curia required that, once *regulares*, they should have the freedoms accorded to other *regulares*. To us, it is interesting for the light it sheds on the reform of this area and the difference between a hospital under a local rule and a house of *regulares*, in an abbey or priory. For the hospital's prioress and sisters had clearly already been under some form of *regula* in which the bishop had invasive powers of oversight; once they

[141] '...vir improbus', Robert of Auxerre, *Chron.*, MGH SS XXVI. 280; Bird, 'Reform or Crusade', 172; *MPM* I. 22–3, 297.

[142] C. R. Cheney, *English Synodalia* (Oxford, 1941), 55–7, 82–4; P. Linehan, 'Councils and Synods in Castile and Aragon', in Cuming and Baker, eds, *Councils and Assemblies*, 104 nn. 1–2.

[143] *COGD* II. 154.

[144] Langton's diocesan statutes at Canterbury in 1213/14 did reproduce several of Courson's decrees, but made no mention of hospitals, *C&S* II. 23–36.

[145] Honorius III, *Opera Omnia*, ed. C. A. Horoy (Paris, 1879–82), IV, cols 622–3. Backed by the bishop's successor, the hospital would shortly became the abbey of Beaulieu-les-Sin-le-Noble.

joined the Victorine order, they would become *regulares* with the legal status this entailed. The law upheld the right of a community, through its own will, to submit to 'bind themselves more strictly in divine service' (*ut se arctius diuinis obsequiis obligarent*) and submit to a full religious rule. The second, more significant decretal would be incorporated into the *Liber extra* (3 Comp 3.18.5 = X 3.24.8). In it, Innocent III upheld the gift of a hospital in Piscia to the Hospitallers at Pisa, even though some of the Piscian brethren as well as the town itself objected. The pope upheld the gift because the fault lay on the part of the Piscian hospital, not the Hospitallers.[146] The gift had been effected properly, and the hospital's rector, patron, and representatives of the brothers had carefully deliberated and determined the course of action, in common, appointing three proctors.[147] The decretal made no mention of rules or vows; rather, it was concerned with the hospital as a material object. It was promulgated under the title 'On donations' (*De donationibus*), and the principle it upheld was that 'the people of a hospital, to their own prejudice, might subject themselves and grant their own house to another religious house'.[148] It even recounted the key moment of submission, when representatives from Pisa 'received the donation and assignment of the hospital' from the rector, the proctors, and other brothers in the chamber of the hospital's rector.[149] The question at law was who had the right to give the hospital as an endowed place to another religious house, and it was determined that the community and patron, acting together, could do so. Courson's decree violated the principles at the heart of both of these decretals. It imposed submission, to vows and to a prelate, regardless of the will of the interested parties. To make this concrete: the civic hospital at Ypres could not be placed under the priory unless it was handed over willingly, after proper deliberation, by the *scabini* and the rector and brothers and sisters of the hospital.

The reformers pushed beyond the limits of law. As had Bernard of Pavia before them, they attempted to claim hospitals for the church and as part of religious life. And, like Bernard, their efforts foundered at Chalcedon and its contemporary restatement, *Si hospitale*. But while they stalked the borderlands of the church's legal reach, and pushed too far, their efforts were not fruitless. Through their networks, their calls, and the models put into practice, the Northern reformers helped foster new approaches to the organization and regulation of hospitals.

---

[146] '... the law assists not the deceivers but the deceived' (*quia non deceptoribus, sed deceptis iura subveniunt*).

[147] '... quum G. quondam rector, et fratres ac patroni eiusdem hospitalis S. Allucii habito communi tractatu deliberassent hospitale ipsum hospitalariis supponere supra dictis'.

[148] 'POSSUNT HOSPITALARII IN PRAEIUDICIUM SUUM SE ET DOMUM SUAM ALTERI RELIGIOSAE DOMUI SUBIICERE ET DONARE.'

[149] 'Quum autem duos illuc de suis fratribus propter hoc transmisissent, ipsi in camera praedicti rectoris donationem et assignationem hospitalis praedicti tam a praefato magistro quam a supra dictis procuratoribus et aliis eiusdem domus fratribus receperunt.'

Once again, silence in law has disguised purposeful activity (and passion). The moment that produced the hospital decree reveals just how much welfare houses were at the centre of Christian life. Courson's decree offers one vision of reform that placed hospitals at its heart, but it was one of many at this moment. Around the edges of this tale we glimpse different ideals: the civic hospitals, as that at the marketplace at Ypres, a focus of civic charity and piety; the *mulieres sanctae* who forged new religious lives among the sick and the poor; the religious men who found inspiration in the way their devotion put the most difficult commandments of Christ into practice; Vitry and his allies, who believed therefore in the reform of welfare houses more generally; the local Cistercians who worked to create convents of women serving the poor and leprous; the cathedral chapters, whose *hôtels-dieu* could be monuments to their own good governance; Innocent III's grand foundation of the Holy Spirit in Saxia, welcoming visitors to St Peter's, Rome; and the military hospitaller order of St Sampson's in Constantinople, to name a few. To think in terms of one church reform of hospitals, a single vision for these places and activities, is thus to miss the point. Welfare houses were manifestations of Christian ideals so fundamental, so woven into medieval life, that they were expressions of its highest ideals across the spectrum, from piety and religion, to government and politics, from human compassion and the problems of affluence (and its absence), to self-sacrifice and pilgrimage. There was never one vision of a hospital.

The vision explored here owes its greatest debt to Jacques de Vitry, who saw hospitals and hospital service as the key to a religious transformation of lay society. In the summer of 1213, it seems to have captured the imagination of the band of preachers. Courson himself had a hand in drafting the hospital decree and the legate used (superseded) his judicial authority in imposing such reform in Ypres. Almost immediately, Fulk of Toulouse commissioned Vitry to write a life of Marie d'Oignies, as an example that might counteract the lure of heresy. The Victorines in Paris also seem to have been inspired, especially Robert of Flamborough, a member of the band of English scholars.[150] The abbey library preserved one of the two copies of Courson's Paris legislation, where it is bound beside a letter of the abbot to Jacques de Vitry.[151] It was noticed above, in Chapter 2, that the Third Lateran council's canon on lepers attracted only two statements about leper-houses; both of them were by Victorines, in 1215. Early in that year, and so before Lateran IV, Flamborough argued in his *Liber poenitentialis* that congregations of lepers and those who had rendered themselves to a *domus Dei* should be classed, with monks and canons, as *personas*

---

[150] Flamborough had served as papal judge delegate with Courson in 1205–7 and composed his *Liber poenitentialis* for Richard Poore, another English ally and reformer (*MPM* I. 32–4).

[151] Martin, *Catalogue des manuscrits*, 90.

religiosas.[152] Later that year, his colleague Peter of Poitiers wrote that the privilege credibly extends to *domus hospitales* for the poor and for lepers that adhere to an *ordo*, promising obedience to a prelate, leaving the world, and having no property.[153] Both comments reflect the initiative behind and the terms of the hospital decree.

In England, too, we see the influence of that summer's vision. One close associate of Langton and Courson did pursue hospital regulation: Richard Poore, bishop of Salisbury (1217–28) and Durham (1228–37).[154] Richard was the only English bishop to require that new hospitals obtain a 'rule or institution' from the bishop, in his Salisbury statutes (1217×1221). His statute ignored Courson's decree, adapting instead language from Lateran IV (c. 13).[155] It is a crafty (and slightly dishonest) statement in law. It did not address existing houses or communities, requiring only that new foundations receive a rule from the bishop. It does this by fudging its statement in two ways. First, Poore stripped out the references to religion or religious order (*religionem*) from his exemplar text. Second, he ignored the founder, who was free in law to create a hospital without a bishop's involvement. Instead he cast the community itself as the founder, aligning their will to found a *domum hospitalem* or *scenodochium* with acceptance of a rule by which they should live; he therefore elided foundation with consent. Poore's Salisbury statutes influenced a generation of conciliar and synodal statutes, yet none of its many adaptors used his hospital decree.[156] And one final participant did not forget his time in the region. In public, Robert Grosseteste, bishop of Lincoln, extolled begging in sermons to the Franciscans, but in private he confided to his friends 'that the Beguines are the most perfect and holy of religion because they live by their own labour, and do not burden the world with their requirements', a vision that goes back to the early years of the movement.[157] On his deathbed, it was the heady summer of 1213 that he remembered as the highlight of his youth, with its vision for a new moral order.

Frameworks for arranging hospitals were each of their moment. They were constructed locally and shaped by regional ways of working. Because they were

---

[152] 'Personas religiosas voco non solum monachos et canonicos, sed etiam templarios, hospitalarios, leprosos qui sunt de congregationibus (de vagis enim non loquor) et illos qui se domibus Dei dederunt et similes', in Longère, 'L'influence de Latran III', 92, 108.

[153] Longère, 'L'influence de Latran III', 109.

[154] On their friendship, *MPM* I. 19–31, esp. 20–1, 28.   [155] Chapter 2 n. 31.

[156] The statute was reproduced by Poore in Durham I (1228–36) and possibly by Langton for his Canterbury diocese after 1222. (*C&S* II. 201; J. Hardouin, *Acta conciliorum*, VII (Paris, 1714), col. 273; Cheney, *English Synodalia*, 65–7; this corrects Watson, 'Origins', 83, a regretted early error. Langton's provincial statutes rested substantially on Poore's Salisbury legislation, but omitted Poore's hospital statute (*C&S* II. 100–25).

[157] '…unde dixit quod Beginae sunt perfectissimae et sanctissimae religionis, quia vivunt propriis laboribus, et non onerant exactionibus mundum' (Thomas of Eccleston, 'Liber de adventu minorum in Angliam', in *Monumenta Franciscana*, ed. J. S. Brewer (London, 1958), 69; B. Bolton, 'Thirteenth Century Women Religious', in Dor et al., eds, *New Trends in Feminine Spirituality*, 132).

arranged locally, one personality, or a group, could instil a new vision of hospital life, as did Marie d'Oignies and, in her wake, Jean de Nivelles and Jacques de Vitry. What was exceptional was the opportunity of Courson's legation, and the zeal of its preaching tour of June 1213. To Vitry and the allies, the council of Reims, in preparation for Lateran IV, presented an opportunity to envision a new order. They needed law, and seized on Urban III's *Ad haec* with its statement that a hospital 'should be religious' to make an argument that the people within such a place should be religious (ignoring both the context of that phrase and the meaning of the decretal: that episcopal confirmation fixed a hospital, as a material object, to its use). It failed. Its significance is not that this effort failed, or even that ambitious visionaries tried to impose a new order: it is that all such efforts failed when made in law. In practice, as their registers reveal, Innocent III and Honorius III were cultivating new initiatives—their own great complex of the Holy Spirit in Saxia, new military and hospitaller orders—as well as confirming local initiatives for individual hospitals; at Lateran IV Innocent injected a sample letter, calling on Christians to give generously to those without, in hospitals; yet in law they remained silent. The church upheld *Si hospitale* as the basic definition of a hospital, as a Christian foundation that could be made by anyone, without a bishop, and in *Ad haec* it offered a way to fix a specific arrangement in the eyes of the church. These remained the basic tenets in canon law. We turn next, and finally, to the big picture in the eyes of the church, and to the one developed statement on hospitals: *Quia contingit*, or 'the magna carta of hospitals'.

9

The Council of Vienne (1311/2) and Late Medieval Hospitals

The council of Vienne (1311/2) was the only general council in the middle ages to design a policy for the reform of hospitals, and its *Quia contingit* (1317) was the only sustained legal treatment of hospitals and their government. The council and its canon are therefore unique. This has earned the latter its modern sobriquet 'the Magna Carta of hospitals', although its significance remains unclear. It appeared too late in the day to shape the creation of welfare houses and, for all its length, the canon's aims have continued to perplex historians. As law it seems disappointing, since it offers no detail on the running of these facilities, and arriving seemingly out of nowhere, and without any apparent legal context, even its intention is confusing. For these reasons it has usually been set aside, written out of the history of hospitals as institutions and, especially, in law. Read literally, it seems to be a catalogue of endemic abuses. In 1317, suddenly, law spoke; and its words seem to confirm the marginal, muddled, and neglected state of welfare houses.[1]

In this final chapter, we turn to *Quia contingit* and to its place in the wider picture of late medieval canon law. For the canon was both a statement of long-held views and the manifestation of tectonic change.

The Council and *Quia contingit* (1317)

A century after Lateran IV, the council of Vienne was a very different affair: if one had been Innocent III's show, the other was council by committee. Clement V was a Frenchman, with close links to the French king, Philip the Fair.[2] It was Philip who sought the end of the Knights Templar at this time; it was also Philip who solicited Clement to settle the papal curia in France and to celebrate a general council in his country.[3] On 12 August 1308, Clement V acquiesced to all three

---

[1] 'Face à la nécessité des réformes, les Pères conciliaires n'avaient pas mâché leurs mots; il s'agit d'incurie et d'abus, de ruines et d'usurpations, de négligences', Mollat, 'L'au-delà', 69–72 (with quotation at p. 72), who recognizes that the canon's approach to jurisdiction followed no simple template. For its character as a reform text, Frank, 'Hospitalreformen', 13–14.

[2] S. Menache, *Clement V* (Cambridge, 1998), 6–7, 11–13.

[3] J. Théry, 'A Heresy of State', *Journal of Medieval Religious Cultures* 39:2 (2013); *COGD* II. 362; cf P. Zutshi, 'The Avignon Papacy', in M. Jones, ed., *The New Cambridge Medieval History* (Cambridge, 2000), 653–4.

On Hospitals: Welfare, Law, and Christianity in Western Europe, 400–1320. Sethina Watson, Oxford University Press (2020). © Sethina Watson.
DOI: 10.1093/oso/9780198847533.001.0001

demands, issuing a summons for a council at Vienne.[4] The council that convened on 16 October 1311 was a slow and deliberate affair that ran for seven months. It established three committees, to address the Templars, a new crusade to the Holy Land, and the reform of the church. In preparation for the latter, local bishops and synods provided reports of concerns and abuses, known as *gravamina*, whose material was then sifted into six areas of complaint for examination by the committee.[5] The canons were drafted by the end of the council but then revised by a papal commission. They were finally promulgated by Clement's successor, John XXII as the *Constitutiones clementinae* (*Clementines*) on 25 October 1317. The council is best known today for its rulings against the Templars, the beguines, and the spiritual Franciscans, but its body of canons had significant impact as law. By *c.*1322 the great canonist, Johannes Andreae, had completed his commentary or apparatus on the *Clementines*.[6] This was quickly established as its standard gloss and distributed together with manuscript copies of the legislation.

Although easily lost among the weightier acts of this council, canon 17, *Quia contingit*, is substantial as a hospital decree. It finally gave canonists something to chew on and this they did over the following 150 years, an activity that Thomas Frank has teased out with such insight. *Quia contingit* was a reformist intervention yet, as Frank acknowledged, it had a serious deficit as a reform programme, because it failed to address basic issues, including conflicts that arose within hospital communities.[7] It will come as little surprise by now that historians have been polarized as to its meaning. The most enduring interpretation remains that of Claude Fleury, set out in the seventeenth-century, which saw this canon as the moment when the church finally relinquished its monopoly over hospitals. Because clergy had so often proven themselves incapable, the council now permitted lay administrators and, as a consequence, independent and even municipal houses would emerge.[8] In recent years, hospital historians have offered a very different view: that here, now, the church was claiming hospitals, perhaps even as monastic forms.[9] So was *Quia contingit* recognizing private (lay) control, or asserting ecclesiastical authority? Was the church finally claiming or releasing these houses? Here, we look not forwards but backwards, to understand *Quia contingit* as the culmination of a longer relationship between canon law and welfare institutions.

---

[4] This summary of the council rests on R. Saccenti, 'Concilium Viennense', in *COGD* II. 362–7; Menache, *Clement V*, 283–305. See, too, M. Mollat and P. Tombeur, *Le concile de Vienne* (Louvain-la-Neuve, 1978).

[5] *COGD* II. 365; E. Müller, *Das Konzil von Vienne* (Münster, 1934), 574–5.

[6] On Andreae, S. Kuttner, 'Joannes Andreae and his Novella', *Jurist* 24 (1964).

[7] Frank, 'Hospitalreformen', 13–14.

[8] J. Lecler, *Le concile de Vienne* (Paris, 1964), 158–9; Müller, *Vienne*, 575; Menache, *Clement V*, 300; Brodman, *Charity and Welfare*, 134.

[9] Drossbach, 'Das Hospital', 516, 521–2; Brodman, *Charity and Welfare*, 49.

The canon (reproduced below)[10] took care to distinguish the houses it addressed from those it did not. It was not to touch 'to the smallest degree' those *hospitales* that belonged to military orders or to other religious [5a], an exclusion stressed by Johannes Andreae.[11] Such houses already had a clear

---

[10] [1: *RECTORES*/MANAGERS] [a] Quia contingit interdum, quod xenodochiorum, leprosariarum, eleemosynariarum seu *hospitalium rectores*±, locorum ipsorum cura postposita, *bona*, res et iura ipsorum interdum ab *occupatorum* et *usurpatorum*± manibus excutere negligunt, [b] quin immo ea collabi et deperdi, domos et aedificia ruinis deformari permittunt [c] et, non attento, quod loca ipsa ad hoc fundata et fidelium erogationibus dotata fuerunt, ut pauperes infectique lepra reciperentur inibi et ex proventibus sustentarentur illorum, id renuunt inhumaniter facere, proventus eosdem in usus suos damnabiliter *convertentes*±, [d] cum tamen ea, quae ad certum usum largitione sunt destinata fidelium ad illum debeant non ad alium, salva quidem apostolicae sedis auctoritate converti,

[2] [*COLLATORES*/PATRONS] [a] nos, incuriam et abusum huiusmodi detestantes, hoc sacro concilio approbante sancimus, ut hi, ad quos id de iure vel statuto in ipsorum fundatione locorum apposito aut ex consuetudine praescripta legitime vel privilegio sedis apostolicae pertinet, loca ipsa studeant in praedictis omnibus salubriter reformare, [b] ac occupata, deperdita et alienata indebite in statum reduci debitum faciant, [c] et ad ipsarum *miserabilium personarum** receptionem et sustenta-tionem debitam iuxta facultates et proventus locorum ipsorum rectores praedictos compellere non omittant.

[3] [*ORDINARI*/BISHOPS] [a] In quo si forte commiserint negligentiam vel defectum, ordinariis locorum iniungimus ut, etiamsi pia loca praedicta exemptionis privilegio munita consistant, per se ipsos vel alios impleant omnia praemissa et singula, et rectores eosdem utique non exemptos propria, exemptos vero et alios privilegiatos apostolica ad id auctoritate compellant, [b] contradictores, cuius-cunque status aut conditionis exsistant, ac praebentes eisdem circa praemissa consilium, auxilium vel favorem, per censuram ecclesiasticam et aliis iuris remediis compescendo, [c] nullum tamen per hoc exemptionibus seu privilegiis ipsis quoad alia praeiudicium generando.

[4] [GOVERNMENT] [a] Ut autem praemissa promptius observentur, nullus ex locis ipsis saecu-laribus clericis saecularibus in beneficium conferatur, etiamsi de consuetudine, quam reprobamus penitus, hoc fuerit observatum, nisi in illorum fundatione secus constitutum fuerit, seu per electionem sit de rectore locis huiusmodi providendum. [b] Sed eorum gubernatio viris providis, idoneis et boni testimonii committatur, qui sciant, velint et valeant loca ipsa, bona eorum ac iura utiliter regere, et eorum proventus et reditus in *personarum* usum *miserabilium* fideliter dispensare, et quos in usus alios bona praedicta convertere praesumptio verisimilis non exsistat; [c] in quibus sub obtestatione divini iudicii illorum, ad quos dictorum locorum commissio pertinet, conscientias oneramus, [d] Illi etiam quibus dictorum locorum gubernatio seu administratio committetur, ad instar tutorum et curatorum iuramentum praestare, ac locorum ipsorum bonis inventaria conficere, et ordinariis seu aliis, quibus subsunt loca huiusmodi, *vel deputandis ab eis, annis singulis*+ de administratione sua teneantur *reddere rationem*+. [e] Quod si secus a quoquam fuerit attemptatum, collationem, provisionem seu ordinatio-nem ipsam carere decernimus omni robore firmitatis.

[5] [EXCLUSIONS] [a] Praemissa vero ad hospitalia militarium ordinum aut religiosorum etiam aliorum minime extendi volumus, [b] quorum tamen hospitalium rectoribus in sanctae oboedientiae virtute mandamus, ut in illis secundum suorum ordinum instituta et antiquas observantias providere pauperibus, et hospitalitatem debitam in illis tenere procurent, [c] ad quod per superiores eorum arcta districtione cogantur, statutis aut consuetudinibus quibuslibet non obstantibus in praemissis.

[6] [*SPIRITUALIA*] Ceterum nostrae intentionis exsistit quod, si qua sint hospitalia, altare vel altaria et coemeterium ab antiquo habentia, et presbyteros celebrantes et sacramenta ecclesiastica pauperibus ministrantes, seu si parochiales rectores consueverint in illis exercere praemissa, antiqua consuetudo servetur quoad exercenda et ministranda spiritualia supra dicta.

COGD II. 429–31; *DEC* 374–6, offers a Latin text and English translation. (Author's apparatus, to assist in reading and reference. With language marked from +Arles 1260; ± Ravenna 1311; and *William Durant, *Tractatus,* discussed later in this chapter.)

[11] 'Declarat constitutionem non extendi ad hospitalia religiosorum vel militarium ordinum.' Glo. ord. to Clem. 3.11.2, v. *Quia Contingit* §.3 under the title 'DE RELIGIOSIS DOMIBUS, UT EPISCOPO SINT SUBIECTAE'. For the Constitutiones Clementinae (Clem.), Friedberg, ed., *Corpus Iuris Canonici*, II (Leipzig, 1879; repr. Graz, 1959), cols 1133–1200, with Johannes Andreae's *Glossa Ordinara* from *Constitutiones mit der Glosse von Johannes Andreae* (Speyer, 1481).

framework to define expectations of administrators and they were to provide for the poor and observe customary hospitality, just as the institutes and ancient observances of their order directed [5b]. These places also had an existing system to remedy neglect or abuse, since through their own regular obedience the custodians were subject to religious superiors who should punish them for any failures, according to the discipline of their order [5c]. *Quia contingit* did not encompass these men and women, although the council, in clarifying their exemption, seized the opportunity to remind them of their obligations. Instead the canon addressed the mismanagement of '*xenodochia, leprosaria*, almshouses and hospitals', the many local welfare houses that were not in the hands of religious houses or religious orders.

The canon is composed of five sections. The first set out the problem: that due to the neglect of *rectores* it sometimes happened that the goods, property, or rights of these places had been alienated [1a] so that their endowment was lost and their sites were falling to ruin [1b]. The first three sections are arranged by person, although in the first two cases the terminology is intentionally imprecise. Nevertheless, it is clear from [2c] that *rectores* meant those charged with the day-to-day management of the houses.[12] The council fixed blame securely on these administrators, for failing to guard the possessions of the hospital, 'inhumanly' refusing to carry out its charities, and criminally taking its incomes for their own gain [1c]. In so doing it lay out the expectations for a correctly run house [1c–d], how management might fail, and its ruinous consequences. The next section turned from abuse to remedy, and so from those with administrative custody to those with permanent guardianship of the hospital, 'those to whom it pertains' by right, foundation, custom, or privilege [2a]. They had a duty to reform these places [2a]: to recover and return 'to its rightful state' what had been seized, lost, or alienated [2b]; and 'to compel the said rectors to receive the same pitiable people and maintain them, as they are bound, according to the resources and revenues of the places' [2c]. The canon was addressed not to the *rectores* but to this nameless group, and it is to them that the first command of the council was directed ('sacro concilio approbante sancimus, ut hi... studeant... reformare'). Andreae stressed this point, summarizing the canon as having 'established that hospitals be reformed by their *collatores*'.[13] He supplied this term for the

---

[12] For rectors as administrators, see Brodman, *Charity and Welfare*, 50–3.

[13] 'Ponens constitutionis causam statuit hospitalia reformari per collatores ipsorum et cogi rectores eorum ad conservationem locorum et suorum iurium et ad hospitalitatem tenendam statuens per locorum ordinarios suppleri defectum vel negligentiam collatorum etiam circa exempta.' Glo. ord. to Clem. 3.11.2, v. *Quia Contingit* §.1. See, too, the summary of the council of Angers (1366), c.21 that *Quia Contingit* acted on 'illi qui de consuetudine, de jure vel fundatione in nostra provincia eleemosynarias, leprosarias, xenodochia, vel domos Dei habent committere', *Les conciles de la province de Tours*, ed. J. Avril (Paris, 1987), 385–6. The term *collatores* was not used in *Quia contingit* but it has been employed in this chapter for the same reason that Andreae bequeathed it: because it is peculiarly difficult to discuss law without a word for the people it addressed.

(nameless) variety with responsibility, uniting the disparate group by a defining manifestation of that responsibility: the duty to appoint custodians. This was a publicly re-enacted mark of patronage, one recognized in canon and common law.[14] In one long sentence, these two sections laid out the situation that confronted the council. Problem and solution hinged on one basic mechanism: if *rectores* dissipated goods and neglected customary aid, *collatores* must regain the possessions and reinstate the charity. These opening sections reflect rather than redefine existing circumstances in hospitals. They call out to those who held hospitals to do what should be done.

The novelty of the canon comes in the next sections, which designed a framework to protect what should be done. Section 3 provided a remedy in cases when *collatores* failed to act, through neglect or defect. In such cases, it then enjoined the local ordinary—a bishop or another official with overall authority in an area[15]—to make up for this lack. He was now 'to carry out each and every one of the foregoing' in person or through an agent and to compel the rectors to fulfil their duties [3a]. To enable this, *Quia contingit* established rights to act: over houses without an explicit exemption via the bishop's own authority as ordinary and in this matter over exempt or otherwise privileged rectors by papal authority [3a], permitting ecclesiastical censure and remedies at law to be deployed against any who refused or who assisted in that refusal [3b]. Section 4 addressed the on-site government of hospitals, laying out basic measures for their better administration. Such places must not be used as benefices for secular clerics [4a];[16] instead, they must be entrusted to the government of prudent and suitable men, of good reputation. They must have the knowledge, desire, and ability to administer the house and its goods profitably, to distribute faithfully the revenues to the 'pitiful people', and not to divert income to other uses [4b]. The quality of person was not a legal requirement, but a moral plea to the consciences of *collatores* [4c]. Incoming rectors should take an oath 'in the manner of a protector (*tutor*) and guardian (*curator*)' and make an inventory of the goods, then submit an annual account of their administration to the ordinary or to whomever their house was

---

[14] See e.g. the twelfth-century assize of *darrein presentment* in English common law, which recognized the act of presentation, if undisputed, as evidence of its right.

[15] The term is used in the Clementines, as elsewhere, to recognize the variety of higher ecclesiastical jurisdictions. Canon 7 of the council e.g. considered the plight of exiled *episcopi*, who must navigate local *episcopi* and also local *ordinarii*.

[16] It is because of this provision that the decree has been interpreted as ending a clerical monopoly on running hospitals, by opening up a clerical order to now allow lay rectors. This is to misread the clause, which merely prohibited that a rectorship be conferred illegitimately as income for a secular cleric, who might then be working at the schools or a distant court (Hostiensis was one such example of a benefice-holder). Such was reinforced in Clem. 3.11.2: 'Per literas, a sede apostolica vel legatis ipsius super provisione quorumlibet clericorum directas, de xenodochiis, leprosariis, eleemosynariis seu hospitalibus, etiamsi ecclesias vel capellas, decimas, aut alia spiritalia iura noscantur habere, nulli posse decernimus provideri, nisi hoc in apostolicis literis caveatur expresse.' Glo. ord. v. *Per literas*: 'Literae super provisione clericorum non includunt hospitalia et loca similia et habentia iura spiritualia nisi id exprimatur.'

subject [4d]. The final sections defined protections. The first excluded hospitals of military and religious orders [5a–c]; the second guarded any existing arrangements regarding altars, cemeteries, or the ministry of their own or parish priests at any place and, indeed, required that these 'ancient customs' be fulfilled [6]. Of these sections, only section 3 created a new right or obligation in law. Other clauses provided legal protections to the houses and moral appeals as to the character of rectors. Its safeguard provisions for rectors—the oath, inventory, and accounting—might have had a regulatory force under willing bishops, but it is unlikely that they would have been adopted by *collatores* more generally.

Continuity and Change

Can we identify any legal origins for this canon? Hospitals do not appear among the compilations of *gravamina* that survive from the council, although that material is by no means complete.[17] What does survive reveals the huge research task engendered by the council: remnants of the reports, sent by regional churches, which the committees then sifted, extracting pertinent statements which they then corralled under titles of complaints. The lengthy hospital canon, clunky in its detail, likely went through this process. Indeed, we may be able to glimpse three different statements that reached the committee, if not always in the exact form in which they were received (they do not survive as *gravamina*).

Most significant was a decree from Ravenna in 1311, one of two councils held under archbishop Rainald of Concorezzo in preparation for Vienne.[18] Its 'On the rectors of hospitals' complained that hospitals' goods had been consumed and seized, even by lay persons, and their rents not applied to the paupers for whom they had been assigned.[19] In answer, Ravenna decreed that hospitals should only be entrusted to religious men without wives, who shall profess publicly to serve the poor there in perpetuity and who will keep a tonsure and be resident. Current

---

[17] Two stages of the sifting process are represented by the material edited in F. Ehrle, 'Ein Bruchstück der Acten des Concils von Vienne', *Archiv für Literatur- und Kirchengeschichte des Mittelalters* 4 (1888), 366–99; and E. Göller, 'Die Gravamina auf dem Konzil von Vienne', in *Festgabe, Heinrich Finke* (Münster, 1904). On the relationship between the two, L. E. Boyle, 'A Committee Stage at the Council of Vienne', in R. J. Castillo Lara, ed., *Studia in Honorem Stickler* (Rome, 1992).

[18] On Rainald, E. Bellomo, 'The Templar Order in North-Western Italy', in V. Mallia-Milanes, ed., *The Military Orders*, III (2008), 105–6.

[19] (c. 25) 'DE RECTORIBUS HOSPITALIUM. Item cum hospitalium bona consumantur, devastentur et occupentur, etiam per laicos, et saepe sine aliquo titulo usurpata detineantur, et eorum redditus in pauperes non convertantur, ad quod deputata sunt; statuimus, quod hospitalia alicui non concedantur, nec aliqui instituantur in eis, nec ea qui habent valeant detinere, nisi sint religiosi, et sine uxore, et tales, quod profiteantur perpetuo ibidem pauperibus deservire, et tonsuram et hospitalitatem teneant, et residentiam faciant in eisdem...' Mansi XXV. 463.

wardens had three months to comply, those who refused were to be sent away. The drafters at Vienne took the language of the target (*rectores*) and the problem from Ravenna, but nothing of Ravenna's answer. It took even less from Arles, where a decree of 1260, 'On the government of hospitals', complained that many had been entrusted through improper means to laity and secular clerics, who consumed their goods and administered nothing to the poor.[20] The problems are familiar, but not the solution, for the Arles' council then required that such officers be properly sought, wear a religious habit, live communally, and each year present an account to the founders, 'just as law provides'.[21] Only its requirement (and language) for an annual account was picked up by Vienne. Finally, William Durant's *Tractatus*, a call for a reform of the church at the Vienne council, included two chapters, on lepers (3.17) and hospitals (3.19).[22] The first noted of lepers 'and other pitiful persons' who were too infirm to support themselves that bishops had a duty to be generous, but it focused on the need to separate lepers as per Mosaic law because of the dangers they presented to the healthy. Durant suggested that they be fed from public alms, to remove any pretext for their 'intermeddling' in human society. The second, brandishing the definitions of Greek terms from the *Epitome*, called for failing hospitals to be reformed and new houses to be established where there were none. The council ignored both calls. Its only commonality with Durant was the term 'pitiful persons' (*persone miserabiles*).

The council saw and even used this material but ignored every one of the proposals. Its contrast to Durant is striking. Whereas Durant's 'pitiful persons' were a privileged category of the needy, the council rejected such judgements of ability to work, and their implicit blame.[23] Instead Durant's phrase became an image of charity: the 'paupers and those infected with leprosy' to whom welcome and maintenance were owed, and whose denial was an act of 'cruelty'. There is an echo here of Alexander III's *Cum dicat apostolus*, which also rejected Mosaic

---

[20] (c. 13) 'DE REGIMINE HOSPITALIUM. Item quia in civitatibus et oppidis provinciae nostrae, hospitalia pauperum multa sunt, quorum regimina ut frequentius laici et clerici saeculares, multiplici prece et pretio, aliquando etiam per litteras Papales et mandata principum et potentum, consueverant occupare; nec ibi pauperibus aliquid ministratur, sed omnia bona et eleemosynae talium hospitalium per hujusmodi rectores in usus proprios asportantur et devorantur: ordinamus et statuimus, prout in jure cavetur, ut de cetero per praelatos locorum, et alios ad quos id pertinere noscitur, proprie, congrue et ad id competenter perquirantur, qui habitu et signo aliquo religionis assumto, ibidem Domino famulantes, vitam agant communem: et annis singulis, ipsis institutoribus suis, vel deputatis ab eis, rationem de omnibus reddant: nihil sibi aut suis, praeter victum et vestitum, de omnibus eleemosynis hujusmodi hospitalium retinentes.' Hardouin, *Acta Conciliorum*, VII. 514–15.

[21] This may be a (distant) reference to Roman law (Cod. 1.3.41.11–18), although the use of *institutores sui* speaks more strongly of ninth-century capitularies.

[22] William Durant, *Tractatus de modo generalis concilii celebrandi* (Lyons, 1531), fol. 56r. On Durant, Müller, *Vienne*, 591–610; C. Fasolt, 'A New View of William Durant the Younger's "Tractatus"', *Traditio* 37 (1981); C. Fasolt, *Council and Hierarchy* (Cambridge, 1991), 290–3.

[23] The term *persone miserabiles* was used often in law in questions of legal jurisdiction and the special legal protection owed to the powerless, R. H. Helmholz, *The Spirit of Classical Canon Law* (London, 2010), 128–32. This was not its use here.

language to build a picture of human suffering and, in response, Christian charity. In the cases of Ravenna and Arles, Clement's council rejected any demand that rectors wear a religious habit, profess, or be tonsured. In fact, it protects 'secular places' from clerical abuse and leaves the status of person open, demanding only personal qualities of knowledge, will, and ability, as well as the integrity to dispense income correctly. Such a person was simply to take an oath 'as a protector or guardian' and to be held to account annually for their administration.

The council's own approach can be seen in its choice of language. Durant had trotted out the usual raft of Greek institutions to define his subjects; *Quia contingit* now provided contemporary names. As argued in Chapter 5, Western practice embraced not the product (an institution) in law but the right of founders to create; the result was a constellation of shifting forms and no fixed name or product. How to peg these places down in order to address them? The council selected four terms. The first, *xenodochia*, was the contemporary term in law, and secured the decree into that legal tradition; next came the two most common generic forms of foundation, *hospitalia* and *leprosaria*; the last, more unusual *elemosinaria* (alms or almonry) captured the broader activity of material Christian *caritas* that lay behind the different kinds of charities. The forms of the words are interesting, because we might expect to find the terms that were in more common use—*domus hospitalis, domus leprosorum,* or *domus elemosinarium*—but 'house' is entirely absent here. The list of *-aria* avoids *domus* and any difficult interpretive problems of 'religious house'. It also avoids the more descriptive (adjectival) terms for charities, offering instead nouns: a *leprosaria* instead of a 'house of lepers'. The nouns suggest institutions and, together, a cohort of facilities. The decision was semantic, but it suggests an inclination, perhaps even an intention, to create a Western vocabulary and dispense with the Greek list. There is other suggestive language. A phrase from the Arles's decree, 'reddere rationem', was a common phrase from the parable of a manager who had to render account when accused by a rich man of dissipating his possessions (Luke 16: 2). The council at Vienne had also looked over Roman law, finding inspiration in its focus on systems of charitable government (Cod. 1.3.41.11) and in two requirements for those who held wardship, in obliging rectors to take an oath 'in the manner of *tutores* and *curatores*' (Cod. 5.37.28.4) and to submit an inventory to whoever presides over the house (Cod. 5.37.24).[24] Yet the council did not otherwise adopt the concept of wardship in addressing hospitals, nor the models built in Roman law, of pious motive or venerable houses. Instead, they built a Western case.

---

[24] '...omnes tutores vel curatores non alias creari, nisi prius cum aliis sollemnibus verbis, quae pro gubernatione rerum...conscribuntur, et hoc specialiter expresserint, quod omnimodo sine ulla dilatione defensionem pro pupillis et adultis aliisque supra memoratis personis subire eos necesse est.' Cod. 5.37.28.4. 'Tutores vel curatores, mox quam fuerint ordinati, sub presentia publicarum personarum inventarium sollemniter rerum omnium et instrumentorum facere curabunt.' Cod. 5.37.24.

This is seen most readily in the council's struggle with terminology. The particular problem was what to call those who had responsibility for the houses. There was no term for the wide variety of arrangements or tenures. As had Carolingian councils, the canonists, cardinals, and bishops at Vienne struggled to find language for the multiplicity of jurisdictions. For those with on-site responsibility they adopted 'rectores', an open-ended term that captured a sense of correct government yet also referred to a range of custodial tenures, from administrative posts, to benefices, and the supervision of priests.[25] However, for those with perpetual dominion or charge—'to whom the commission of the said places pertains', Andreae's *collatores*—there was no ecclesiastical term. And the canon left them without title. Instead, it simply described them as 'those to whom this thing [id] pertains', elucidating the bases of such tenure: 'by legal right or by a statute applied at the foundation of the individual places, or according to legit-imate and written custom, or through a privilege of the apostolic see' [2a]. The broad catch-all of 'legal right' would include patronage and inheritance, as well as assignment, when the supervision over a place had been entrusted to a religious house or town government: a right of possession substantially adjudicated under secular (common) law. Terminology was also left open for the duties incumbent on these places where 'revenues were to be faithfully dispensed for the benefit of pitiable people'. Its open-ended terminology allowed the canon to reach widely, to encompass any welfare house.

Yet what we find in here is a familiar form, with deep roots. Confronted with contemporary problems, the council rejected contemporary proposals for reform, as well as Roman legal models. Instead they set out to articulate, then reinforce, a long-standing model. It is only when placed alongside Carolingian decrees that *Quia contingit* no longer seems obscure. At issue, in the fourteenth as well as the ninth century, was the decay caused by neglectful management by the wide array of administrators, priors, wardens, and priests, gathered here under the term *rectores*. The duty to correct lay with those to whom the place pertained, and so the heirs, patrons, officials, secular chapters, bishops, or urban governments who had responsibility for a place. Faced with accruing complaints, the council reminded rectors and *collatores* of their duties, then authorized the bishop to intervene to restore a house if those responsible failed. The procedure was familiar from late Carolingian councils, although the remit now was far wider, if only because of the reach of the Clementines, as law and policy of the Western church.

Ambitious in seeking widespread reform, *Quia contingit* offered limited pre-scriptions for *what* those reforms should be. It provided no shared model to which a place should be reformed. Instead, as had Carolingian councils, it upheld the arrangements that were specific to an individual place. These included the type of

---

[25] It is used in all three ways elsewhere by the council (*COGD* II. 408–9, 414–19, 435–6, 446–8, cc. 4, 10, 22, 30). The term had been used, too, by the council of Quierzy in 858, MGH *Conc.* III. 418 (c. 10).

aid and the other duties with which it was charged (i.e. the purpose of the house), its customs and practices (i.e. routines), varieties in administration and personnel (i.e. form, government, and community), and the range of tenure or superior authority (i.e. jurisdictions and oversight). The canon's respect for local arrangements even extended to agreements for the performance of divine service and administration of the sacraments, a point that Andreae stressed, going so far as to exclude expressly *hospitalia et loca similia* from the regulations regarding provision of prebends via papal or legatine letters.[26] *Quia contingit* fashioned a policy to correct when administration and oversight had both failed; it did not redefine the houses themselves, even to improve them. It consistently upheld arrangements that had been made at foundation even if—in the case of hospitals held as benefices, for example—these arrangements were contrary to the provisions of the canon itself.

This was very different to the work on monastic houses and religious orders. For these, the council issued many and lengthy decrees, which required, for example, that nunneries be visited and corrected annually by the bishop and directed, in detail, the forms of dress, instruction, discipline, and governance to which Benedictine monasteries must be held.[27] Clement also pledged to examine the rules of the Hospitaller order, which he promised to revise, to

> make decrees for its regulation and reform... [to] approve and confirm what is good, clarify doubtful points that we find in need of revision as to the order and its personnel, both head and members... [and so] restore the norm of truth, justice, and regular observance with the equilibrium of reason and equity, to the advantage and welfare of the order and for the help of the Holy Land.[28]

These efforts reflect the more universal jurisdiction of papal or ecclesiastical authorities to visit, correct, and regulate religious orders. They also underscore their priority, to uphold the quality of the community of these religious, by regulating their way of life.

In contrast, for hospitals, and in now-familiar fashion, *Quia contingit* acted to guard not the life of a community but the gifts of the faithful. In fact, even though many hospitals likely had some form of community or staffing, community is

---

[26] Glo. ord. to Clem. 3.11.2, v. *Quia contingit* §4: 'Conservat antiquas consuetudines talium locorum circa divina officia et sacramenta.' See also n. 16.

[27] *COGD* II. 422–7, cc. 14–15.

[28] (c. 7) 'Tertium circa praefatum ordinem per nos, ut praedicitur, ordinandum cedet ad regulationem et reformationem ipsius, videlicet quod ordinationes, statuta et statum et processum ipsius ordinis et personarum eiusdem videbimus et examinabimus diligenter et approbando ac confirmando bona declarandoque dubia illa, quae correctionis lima egentia tam in ordine quam personis ipsius in capite et membris inveniemus, ipsa ad veritatis et iustitiae morum et regularis observantiae normam cum rationis et aequitatis libratione, et prout utilitati et bono statui eiusdem ordinis expedierit, et terrae sanctae subsidio reducemus, ut sic ordo ipse et praeservetur a casu et in statu salubri et prospero conservetur.' *COGD* II. 402; following the translation in *DEC* 358, with minor adaptations.

absent from the canon. The canon was even careful to speak of them as *loca* (places) and not *domus* (house), with its implications of a residential household or convent. *Quia contingit* legislated for hospitals as a structure for the administration of donations: to guard the gifts of the faithful and apply their incomes to the charitable uses for which they were intended. As had Urban III's *Ad haec* (X 3.36.4), these facilities were protected as the site and agent of material service.

What *Quia contingit* was now doing, and what had not been done before in canon law, was to enjoin the *collatores*, the patrons and overseers, to fulfil their duty: to preserve these houses as they should be preserved. In chastising them, it first had to articulate what should be preserved, offering an overarching definition of a welfare house:

> [1c] And not paying attention [to the fact] that the same places have been founded for this [purpose] and endowed through the distributions of the faithful in order that the poor and those infected with leprosy should be received there and supported from the revenue of those [distributions] [some rectors] cruelly refuse to do this ... [1d] even though what has been assigned by the generosity of the faithful for a certain purpose (*usus*) must be applied to that purpose and not to any other, except by authority of the apostolic see.

Welfare houses were the administrators of a gift, entrusted by the faithful to a specified charitable use. From its revenues, the gift provided the material means by which those in need might be welcomed, housed, fed, clothed, warmed, and ministered to. It was the terms of their original gifts, their foundation, that defined the charitable obligations of the house and its fixed form. It is the same basic definition of a hospital as that offered by Robert de Courson in 1213, and the same basis on which the church claimed now to act: to uphold the faith of Christians in making these gifts, by protecting what had been entrusted, and for the uses for which it had been given.[29] *Collatores* must ensure that *rectores* upheld these arrangements and, should they fail, bishops were now to intervene.

To do this *Quia contingit* had to build a new instrument in law: a means by which bishops might now intervene. Indeed, *Quia contingit* marks the moment when bishops were given a defined authority to intrude into the affairs of an abused and neglected welfare house. The council neither assumed nor asserted that welfare houses fell under the bishop or papacy; indeed, it recognized that they existed under a range of custodial arrangements, beyond the definition (and terminology) of the church. Its new instrument was built through argument. It began with a selective assertion of Urban III's *Ad haec* (X 3.36.4) at [1d]: that what was assigned by the faithful for a purpose must be held to that purpose. But where

---

[29] Courson had used the phrase 'Bona enim ex deuotione fidelium ibidem collata'.

in *Ad haec* pontifical authority became a means by which a hospital might be fixed to a specific purpose under the church, *Quia contingit* turned that around, to claim for the apostolic see a right to release a house from its charge. Legally, *Quia contingit* was claiming to act on houses that had been secured under an episcopal confirmation (and thus under *Ad haec*); by a sleight of hand, it was staking a far wider claim. Its case for action was not based on a right over the places themselves, or the communities within, or even to protect the poor, but on a testamentary function: to guard the gifts of the faithful to their use and to ensure executors (rectors and *collatores*) were fulfilling their charge.

The ruling of *Quia contingit* on exemption is clever here. Exemption was a privilege afforded to specific churches and religious communities, releasing them from a general diocesan jurisdiction over such places and communities under canon law. By the later middle ages, it could apply, for example, to royal peculiars as well as to individual abbeys and whole orders, who were made directly answerable to a mother church or the pope.[30] Ecclesiastical status on the ground was a messy business. The essential point here is that churches and monasteries were presumed to fall under the diocesan, unless they had a specific and recognized exemption. In contrast, hospitals were dispersed under a variety of jurisdictions: there was no general episcopal authority from which they had to be exempt (even though certain houses, such as those of royal foundation, might be classed as exempt). *Quia contingit* was creating an authority to intrude, and it was doing so by deploying the concept of exemption [3a, c]. Its use was not about exemption itself, but about creating a general right by overriding the very notion of exemption. If even an 'exempt' house was no longer beyond the reach of episcopal correction, then the bishop now had a right to compel any *collator* of any house, even those that had never come under episcopal purview. It was creating a non-exempt status, even as it was denying exemption. The council's motive is revealed in the canon's own exemptions [5], for it did not apply to the hospitals of military orders, of religious, and 'of others' whose rectors could be compelled by their own superiors through disciplinary measures of their order. The goal of *Quia contingit* was not to stake a new jurisdictional claim, but to create a mechanism by which bishops might now act when rectors, heretofore beyond policing, proved abusive and their own *collatores* failed.

So, why this council, at this moment? It is unlikely that *Quia contingit* was connected with the same council's efforts to reform convents (c. 15) and prohibit beguines (c. 16). These preceding canons forcefully addressed women's religious lives, and were both, to an extent, a response to *Periculoso*, the 1298 papal bull

---

[30] On exemption, see the comparative discussions in C. West, ed., *Religious Exemption in Pre-Modern Eurasia* (2017).

requiring perpetual claustration of nuns.[31] These were built on entirely different foundations from *Quia contingit*, which was filed next to them only because the Clementines arranged its material according to the *Liber extra* titles, placing *xenodochia* under *De religiosis domibus*, where the beguine decree was also filed. It is more likely that the process of soliciting *gravamina* brought hospitals to the fore. The canon's own title 'Because it sometimes happens . . .' draws attention to a lived rather than a legal problem.

But the forces that brought *Quia contingit* into being were longer term and more structural. One of the themes of previous chapters has been the consistent undertow of concerns for welfare houses that could receive little answer in law. What had changed by the council of Vienne was law itself. In the background was a more universal shift, as the clash of political claims between crown and papacy in the century after *c*.1050, which had centred on jurisdiction, had given way across the long thirteenth century to the complex task of administering law. As demand for law had grown, so had expectations of law and the administrative burdens of meeting those expectations. By the fourteenth century, crown and localities were eager for local policing and the challenge was how to create a warrant for that policing. The partnership between crown and episcopacy was reinforced in 1414, when the English parliament finally addressed hospitals. A complaint had been brought that the gifts given by so many for 'maintaining there old men and women, leprous men and women, those who have lost their senses and memory, poor pregnant women, and men who have lost their goods and have fallen on hard times' had been dissipated and the facilities were falling to ruin.[32] In response, king and parliament instructed ordinaries to visit royal hospitals (and so to act as royal agents for those in the king's hand), and to follow through for other houses 'according to the laws of Holy Church' (i.e. *Quia contingit*).[33]

More specifically, for hospitals, small changes in the law had helped fuel a culture change in the expectations of bishops. In establishing that episcopal oversight could now fix a hospital, as an endowment, to its assigned uses in

---

[31] T. Stabler Miller, 'What's in a Name?', *JMH* 33:1 (2007), 61–2. E. Makowski, *Canon Law and Cloistered Women* (Washington, DC, 1997).

[32] 'Henry V: Parliament of April 1414', in C. Given-Wilson et al., ed., *The Parliament Rolls of Medieval England* (Leicester, 2005): 'ount founduz et faitz plusours hospitalx . . . as queux ount donez graundement de lour biens moebles pur les edifier, et graundement de lour terres et tenementz pur y sustenir veigles hommes et femmes, lazers hommes et femmes, hors de lour senne et memoir, poveres femmes enseintez, et pur hommes q'ount perduz lour biens et sont cheiez en graunde meschief, la murir, relever, et refresser ove ycelles. Et unquore est ensi, tresgracious seignur, qe la greindre partie des hospitalx deinz vostre dit roialme sont encheiez, et les biens et profitz d'icelles . . . retractz et expenduz en autri oeps, parount plusours hommes et femmes ount moruz en graunde meschief, pur defaute d'eide, vivre, et socour, al displesance de Dieu, et peril de lour almes q'ency gastent et exspendent les biens d'icelles poveres hommes ou femmes en autre oeps.'

[33] 'Et qant as autres hospitalx, qe sont d'autri fundacioun et patronage qe de roi, les ordinairs enquergent del manere de la fundacioun, estat, et governance d'icelx, et de toutz autres matiers et choses busoignables celle partie; et sur ceo facent ent correccioun et reformacioun solonc les leies de seinte esglise, come a eux appurtient.'

perpetuity, Urban III's *Ad haec* (1186) had not only created a mechanism by which founders could secure their *dispositio*, with episcopal backing, but expectations of episcopal enforcement. In addition, a legacy of Bernard of Pavia's initiative endured through the *Liber extra*, enhanced by Raymond of Peñaforte's 'pious places'. *Xenodochia* now belonged in canon law under the title 'Of religious houses, that they be subject to the bishop'. Generations of university students absorbed the *Liber extra* and went on to have careers as clerks, canonists, archdeacons, and bishops. It fostered episcopal activity in dioceses, from specific acts of correction to a more general sense of episcopal responsibility;[34] a few local synods even worried explicitly about hospitals.[35] When the call went out for *gravamina* in preparation for the councils, it is not surprising that queries and suggestions for hospitals were returned. In response, *Quia contingit* gave the matter explicit definition in law.

Yet what remains most striking about *Quia contingit* as legislation is its limits. It upheld existing arrangements for hospitals, both generally (in the many, including private jurisdictions in which they were created and operated) and specifically (that a facility was to be administered according to the terms of its foundation). It refused calls to make their rectors religious. Indeed, *Quia contingit* is noteworthy as the clearest articulation of a long tradition of law for welfare facilities. This tradition recognized: (1) that *xenodochia*/hospitals did not belong fundamentally to the church; (2) that they could exist under a variety of custodians and jurisdictions; (3) that they must be held to the arrangements of those who first established them, even when these arrangements contradicted ecclesiastical policy; (4) that the defining supervisorial issue was the preservation and allocation of its resources, the gifts of the faithful, to their assigned charitable purposes; and so (5) the quality of its administrators. Placed in this context, *Quia*

---

[34] More tantalizing wider claims to act rested on other rights. So, when Gregory IX charged the bishop of Langres in 1235 to visit and correct the hospitals in his diocese, this was 'certain hospitals', where men live with women, claiming a religious life that had been approved by no one and setting the worst example ('quaedam domus hospitales . . . in quibus viri cum mulieribus habitantes, sub quodam religionis velamine, licet nullam assumpserint de religionibus approbatis, vitam ducebant Deo et hominibus displicentem et pessimi exempli': *Les registres de Grégoire IX*, ed. L. Auvray (Paris, 1896), no. 2540; Montaubin, 'Hôpitaux cathedraux', 30). The right was over false religious, not hospitals themselves (an echo of Lateran II, c. 26). In France, Roman law seems to have underpinned a wider claim of episcopal supervision by the later thirteenth century. The customs of Philippe de Beaumanoir noted that 'according to common law the guardianship of leper-houses belongs to the bishop in the diocese where they are situated', although custom could clearly overrule such claim since 'we know of several leper-houses which are specially in the guardianship of secular lords . . . And the guardianship of each foundation should be maintained as it has been for a long time' (*The* Coutumes de Beauvaisis *of Philippe de Beaumanoir*, tr. F. R. P. Akehurst (Philadelphia, PA, 1992), 590). It is likely that it was just such a right, over unclaimed houses, that underpinned the statement of the regent of France, in a settlement of 1270, that 'domus leprosorum et domus pauperum Dei omnes sunt in protectione et custodia episcopi, et curam earum gerit tam in spiritualibus et temporalibus', *Cartulaire de l'église Nôtre-Dame du Paris*, ed. M. Guérard, 4 vols (Paris, 1850), I. 185–6; MacKay, *Hôpitaux à Paris*, 39.

[35] In addition to Salisbury (1217×22), considered in Chapter 8, we can find Coventry (1237) and Arles (1260) and (1275), *C&S* II. 92–3, 214, 965; Hardouin, *Acta Conciliorum*, VII. 514–15.

contingit reveals an extraordinary continuity in the manner by which ecclesiastical councils recognized local hospitals. It also reinforced a customary legal model that was entirely different from that which defined, in canon law, monasteries and houses of religious orders. It was a model based on the allocation of goods to a charitable purpose, rooted in testamentary provision. Urban III's *Ad haec*, which provided security for those material arrangements, and its eventual successor, *Quia contingit*, was as much as canon law could explicitly offer. *Quia contingit* became the church's defining statement on welfare houses. No future councils would act. The only other general congress to address hospitals was the council of Trent in 1563 and they simply confirmed 'the constitution of the council of Vienne which begins *Quia contingit*'.[36]

---

[36] Council of Trent (1563), Section 7, c. 15; Frank, 'Hospitalreformen', 8.

Conclusion

This has been a book about the church in the world, and about the limits of the reach of church law. It may be tempting, then, to see 'church' and 'world' as entities, pushing against one another. This would invite two basic responses to the failure of the church to claim welfare in law. First, if the law could not reach out, then how far did 'church' control 'world'? And, second, more imaginatively, why did the church let such a state of affairs exist, and leave welfare abandoned in this way?

Such a model would map neatly onto old, yet still oddly familiar paradigms. In religion, a question about the 'Christianization' of the laity once wondered how far the church could reach the beliefs ('superstitions') of the medieval population. In politics, modern notions of Church and State can, for students, easily still impose themselves on great contests in the middle ages, between emperor and papacy, for example. Among historians, simple binaries have, for the most part, been replaced by more complex approaches, but they could easily reassert themselves here, where law did not tread. It is these binaries that have seen the absence of canon law for hospitals as a mark of the lesser status of welfare in the church, and so in Christianity. But the broad picture of welfare in law asks us to look again at the relationship between 'the church' and Christian practice.

In many ways, the most curious finding of this book has been the consistency with which the church did not claim welfare in law. This is remarkable across a millennium, when we might have expected to find a few sweeping claims. There was the odd campaigner, who pushed things too far, like Bernard of Pavia or Robert de Courson, but their cases in law were swiftly dismissed. There were legal packages that set out to address specific problems, including the group of canons of the council of Orléans (549) or Eugenius II's idea of 'pious places', but their connection to hospitals was almost immediately lost, in part because of the subtlety with which the cases had been crafted. And there were moments—in the generations after 820, and in the thirteenth and fourteenth centuries—when more was asked of and demanded by bishops, who were armed in turn with new administrative tools, backed by imperial or papal authority.

Those who did build new mechanisms in law—Alexander III, Urban III, the council of Vienne, and, for a generation, Wala—navigated what could not be done or said in law, painstakingly. Eventually, it was the call of Eugenius II in 826 that bishops should have a 'watchful concern' over xenodochia that would do most to invigorate church claims. But this was not until the statement was rediscovered

On Hospitals: Welfare, Law, and Christianity in Western Europe, 400–1320. Sethina Watson, Oxford University Press (2020). © Sethina Watson.
DOI: 10.1093/oso/9780198847533.001.0001

almost four hundred years later, when it found an audience eager to heed the call. It would prompt *Quia Contingit* (1317), but even this did not claim hospitals for the church. It merely offered a key by which bishops, with a 'watchful concern', might open doors that had been locked, in order to set things back as they should be. The limits of this law were not dictated by ability or ambition, but by shifts in the place of law and the place of welfare, respectively, in Christianity.

The second finding is the wealth of material in which popes, councils, bishops, and canonists wrestled with the problem of welfare and the law. When law-makers wanted to address welfare in law, they met a blank page. Without a canonical tradition, and with no corpus of law to guide them, they had to invent their case. Each statement is wholly individual: a creation of its moment and unique to its author. Some have long been known, but in their very oddity they have caused confusion including *necatores pauperum*, Ansegis's *Epitome* chapters, and even *Quia contingit* itself. But behind them, around them, and between them, there was a constant endeavour in support of welfare. This is most readily observed in larger collections of material produced when law-makers were charting law in new venues, and so new kinds of text, notably in the Carolingian capitularies and the work of the decretalists. But it has appeared, too, behind what was not said in Laterans II, III, and IV; in preparation for the Olona council (825) and on the streets of Flanders, *c*.1200; and even in the small adaptations of the Greek definitions of welfare institutions. It may be that the present study, therefore, has barely scratched the surface of a discourse about the Christian order, at the edge of law.

What is most significant about this material is its overarching coherence. Over a millennium, and across different regions, welfare foundations took wildly different forms. Yet law-makers could see through these outer shells to a core definition of what made a xenodochium: property assigned by a (Christian) donor to tend the needy, according to the terms specified by him or her. Even without a language in law, they understood what it was they were looking at. They knew that hospitals were beyond the claim of church law, yet they shared a sense of what they could act on: to guard the gifts of the faithful to their assigned uses; that is, to ensure that the testamentary provision was being fulfilled.

The efforts in law show no signs of a power struggle between Church and laity, nor any attempt to control welfare, as if it was something unwieldy or out of control. On the contrary, law-makers sought to cultivate welfare, and the diverse activities of the faithful, through their efforts. They acted to guard existing houses and salvage failing ones, by exhorting guardians, clerical and lay, to fulfil their obligations, and emperors, kings, and bishops to police those who were recalcitrant. They worked to reinforce existing houses, through privileges and calls to alms. Most significantly, they did not try to organize welfare by standardizing templates for foundations; on the contrary, law-makers worked to bolster a founder's *dispositio*: the terms laid down for the use of their gift, from its charitable charges, routines, and staffing, to its systems of government and oversight. This was most often done through policies of exhorting or policing custodians, but it also reinforced the wills themselves (Olona, 825), or created mechanisms to fix the arrangements under the church (*Ad haec*, 1186). In so doing, councils, bishops, and canonists were reinforcing the right of a Christian to dispose. The variety of welfare, and its constantly changing forms, were possible because individual Christians kept creating welfare and because others, including churchmen, honoured this and worked to maintain it.

The place of welfare in Christianity that this study has pursued was so consistently held that it must have been deeply familiar. It was fundamental to an understanding not only of Christianity but of the church; that is, of the duties incumbent upon and the practices forged within the community of the faithful. At its core was salvation, and the image in Matthew of the sheep and the goats. But it was also, fundamentally, a social vision. It was best captured by Jerome, when he celebrated Fabiola, 'the first person to found a *nosocomium*' in the West, recounting her many acts of care to the unfortunate, tending to their sores, their diseased flesh, and infection. The significance of this care, he stressed, was that it recognized the shared humanity of even the most miserable and despised person, and stirred pity in those who would rather look away.[1] In similar ways, councils and popes so often added language that made apparent the human need at the heart of any act of welfare: the requirement to see the person that is easy to ignore, to feel for them, and to tend to them. Welfare was at the heart of Christian salvation, but its performance was fundamentally human and fundamentally social. It required the donor to see the person in need and to respond directly. It is this act of seeing and doing that lay behind the *dispositio*. It was a pursuit that belonged not to law nor to bishops, monks, or nuns—although these must embrace and encourage it— but to every Christian. Here was Christianity beyond church law. And here, at the edge of law, were xenodochia. In the eyes of the church, it was the very particularly of a founder's response to those who were without that gave the charitable foundation its identity and also its meaning. Each charity was a living testament to an act of *caritas*, an act of seeing and responding to want.

The picture of law that emerges from these pages asks us to think of medieval Christendom not as Church and World, but as three layered components, each of both church and world.[2] The most fundamental was the body of the faithful, the mass of humanity that made up the community of Christians, and so both

---

[1] 'The poor wretch whom we despise, whom we cannot so much as look at, and the very sight of whom turns our stomachs, is human like ourselves, is made of the same clay as we are, is formed out of the same elements. All that he suffers we too may suffer. Let us then regard his wounds as though they were our own, and then all our insensibility to another's suffering will give way before our pity for ourselves.' Jerome, *Letter* 77.6: tr. H. Wace, *Jerome: Letters and Select Works*, VI (New York, 1893).

[2] This is the what might be termed the View from Medieval Christianity. It is not a view to which all would have subscribed, from sceptics to non-believers.

'church' and 'world' in their widest senses. This body included sheep and shepherd, saint and sinner, nobility and peasant. The second component acted on the
first. It was the people of the institutional church: the monks, canons, nuns,
priests, and clerics, who were under the authority of church law, and so the bishop
or pope.[3] In theory at least, they embodied the principles and the mission of the
church in the world: we might think of them as the muscles, nerves, and sinews,
running through the body of the faithful and animating it. The third acted on the
second. It was the basic canonical framework of the church, the laws and canons
that might be thought of as a canonical *regula* for the people of the church, and
especially its bishops, clerics, monks and nuns—a term (*regula*) used here in its
Latin sense of a thing that straightens, balances, and corrects. Here were also
defined concepts and manifestations of what was most sacred in the world,
especially consecration of the host, altars, and churches. These provided a certain
and enduring framework, the skeleton, to which the animating fibres adhered.

Welfare threaded through all three layers. In the account of the Last Judgement,
it was the activity of feeding the hungry, clothing the naked, and visiting the sick—
of having served Christ by tending 'the least of my brothers'—that would separate
the sheep from the goats. This was one of the basic tenets of Christianity. It was
the anticipation of this moment, when Christ the king would come to judge, with
which the faithful were confronted when they stepped into a church: in the image
of Christ enthroned on the apse or over the central western doorway or in images
of the Last Judgement, with the vividly contrasting fates of the saved and the
damned. Welfare was also part of the charge laid upon the people of the institutional church. Priests were to be hospitable; bishops to protect the poor, widows,
and orphans; monks to welcome strangers, and wash their feet, and to give alms to
the poor. Such service could be a religious calling, and hospital orders—from the
hospitalia Scottorum of the early middle ages, to the hospitaller and pilgrim orders
of the twelfth century—arose alongside other forms of religious service during
periods of monastic revival. As a Christian calling, welfare was never solely 'of the
world', so it is not surprising that xenodochia and hospitals could also find a place
outside the orders of *regulares* but still as places of religious service, to which men
and (to the inspiration of many and the discomfort of others) women might
dedicate themselves. Welfare in these two layers has not been the focus of this
study, but it has appeared in every chapter.

Welfare houses stood apart from monasteries of religious, however, in their
place among the faithful, the wider body of Christians. When the council of
Chalcedon defined churches and monasteries as sacred and so ecclesiastical
forms under the bishop, it left welfare houses in the hands of the faithful. In the
West, they found a place in testamentary law, as a way for Christians to perform

---

[3] I am setting aside exemption here, so as not to get weighed down by technicality, although even the
exempt were under the authority of church law.

the corporal works of mercy in answer to Christ's call in Matthew. Even on their deathbed—maybe especially on their deathbed—a Christian might choose the path of a sheep, rather than a goat. When law-makers looked at a xenodochium and the many forms of welfare, what they saw was not the institutions or their chaotic variety, but the Christian determination that had produced each one: a provision by a donor to tend the 'least'. This determination was embodied by the *dispositio*: the arrangements laid out by the donor for the gift. It was therefore a particular kind of gift, one not handed over to the ownership of another but attached in perpetuity to that *dispositio*; it belonged in perpetuity to the will of the founder. The challenge for the testators/founders, and for those who came after, was how to enforce that *dispositio*. In the early middle ages, Lombard and then Frankish councils extended a protective umbrella, one that looked to the moral voice of bishops and the judicial authority of the palace to ensure those responsible did as they should. In the later middle ages, the church responded with small and carefully targeted legal mechanisms, the most significant being Urban III's *Ad haec* (1186). Such skeletal provisions needed bolstering in practice by local custom or initiative: we have glimpsed already how Roman law infused the frameworks of North Italy, bishops and monastic templates those of Northern France, and the *mulieres sanctae* those in the Low Countries. Wider comparative study of regional shapes and their languages for order awaits.

Welfare houses were one of the three great built foundations of medieval Christianity, but they were also extraordinary. Unlike monasteries and churches, they were not an ecclesiastical form; they belonged to the faithful, the body of Christians in the world. At the core of medieval Christianity was the exhortation to medieval Christians to see and address human suffering and human want. In law, this became a testamentary provision, to assign wealth for specific uses. In practice, it was the ability of any Christian to envision care and to create an enduring response. Here was a Christian form that was in the hands of the faithful and could be reimagined by any founder, and especially the laity. The consequence was one of the most familiar, enduring, and fertile forms in the church. The chaotic variety of its manifestations was not a sign of its liminality but, rather, a consequence of its very significance in Christian religion and Christian society. Welfare was at the edge of canon law in the middle ages, but at the heart of Christian community and salvation itself.

Ad Petitionem: A Lost Decretal of Alexander III

Fragments of this decretal have been known as JL 13972 (§§1, 3), 14190 (§5), and 14202 (§6).[1] They appear as *Ad petitionem* (§1, as 1 Comp. 3.27.1 (X–)), *Uxoratus* (§3, as 1 Comp. 3.28.8 = X 3.32.8), *Si hospitale* (§5) and *Si cum aliquo* (§6), as 2 Comp. 3.26.1 (X–) and 3.22.1 (X–).

The decretal was originally a rule that Alexander III provided for the Cruciferi in *c.*1169, a copy of which survives in a seventeenth-century history of the order, purportedly transcribed from an original in the Bolognese archives.[2] This copy is not identical to the rule that formed the basis for the decretal: it contains later interpolations, reflecting the order's expansion into a *congregatio* under a *magister* at Bologna later in the century, and omits sentences that are preserved in the decretal (§6 and the end of §5).[3]

An abbreviated version of the rule circulated as a decretal by the mid-1170s. It can first be found in Bologna, where Simon of Bisignano cited several of its statements as an *extravagante,* 'Ad petitionem', in his *Summa in Decretum* (1177×79).[4] Within a few years it was copied in England into several members of the early *Wigorniensis* Group, and extracts were taken for the *Appendix concilii Lateranensis,* an early systematic collection, as *Ad petitionem* (§1, 4–6) and *Uxoratus* (§3).

Largely overlooked by other English collections, the sections were received more enthusiastically on the continent via the *Appendix.*[5] The fuller text also arrived in Reims likely via

---

[1] Their relationship to one another has, until now, been uncertain, McLaughlin, 'Extravagantes', 169.

[2] *Storia dell'ordine dei Crociferi* (Treviso, Bibl. comunale, cod. 474, fol. 1). The rule is ed. 'Papst. in Venetien', 227–30. See, too, P. F. Kehr, ed., *Italia pontificia,* V. *Aemilia sive provincia Ravennas* (Berlin, 1911), 284–6; Baaken, 'Papsturkunden', 336.

[3] The integrity of the Bolognese rule seems never to have been challenged, despite its clear changes in tone and terminology. The early rule within it consists of simple statements of practice, directed to 'you', and addressing clerics and laity under a *maior prior;* in contrast, for example, the final section presents orders (*mandamus, prohibemus*) to brothers, subject to a *maior magister* and general chapter, it prefers technical detail, and stresses reverence and honour. The additions go beyond a change in register, transforming a rule to be read aloud into a constitution for a congregation. For similar reasons, a section of the rule (*Statuimus insuper . . . triginta vicibus decant*) may also contain later additions, in its liturgical feasts and more monastic focus on church. Several earlier phrases, missing from the decretal texts, may also be later enhancements.

[4] *Summa in Decretum,* ed. Aimone, citing §1 at C.20 q.4 c.1 v. *virgines;* §3 at C.27 q.2 c.22 v. *Si quis* and 25 v. *agatho;* §5 at C.18 q.2 c.12 v. *De monachis;* §6 at C.18 q.1 c.1 v. *statuendum.*

[5] The *Collectio Gilberti* included §6 under DE STATU REGULARIBUS and §5 under DE ECCLESIIS EDIFICANDIS: Heckel, 'Dekretalensammlungen', 203, 207; BL Harley 3834, fols 179v–180r, 181r. *Uxoratus* (§3) was known to the compiler of *Collectio Lipsiensis,* who made a reference to it in his long copy of *Ad petitionem* (15.1), placing *Uxoratus* itself at 58.9; the former reinserting §2, truncated (as from B) and after §3: Leipzig, Universitätsbibl. 975, fols 125v, 147r. See, too, *Collectio Bamburgensis* (15.1, 49.9); *Collectio Casselana* (25.1, 57.10); 1 Comp. 3.27.1 (X–); *CS,* pp. 98, 110. In England, it was included in the *Collectio Fontanensis,* the only monastic collection, at 1.13: Oxford, Bodl. Laud Misc. 527, fol. 26v; P. Landau, '*Collectio Fontanentis*', in Pennington and Eichbauer, eds, *Law as Profession and Practice,* 196 n.

an ancestor of the *Wigorniensis* Group and was used to form the *Collectio Brugensis* (1187/8).[6] *Brugensis* preserves our fullest copy of the original decretal. It suggests that the lost *Wigorniensis* ancestor included the longer text, perhaps in its circulating form, since it reflects, too, what was available to Stephen of Bisignano. The ancestor was the source *Brugensis* (omitting the address and the last phrase of §1) and perhaps for *Cheltenhamensis* (omitting §2). Deviations in the *Collectio Wigorniensis* are closer to those in the Bolognese rule and Bisignano's citations, suggesting it copied another circulating copy (omitting the first part of §3). See Figure A.1.

The edition here is based upon the earliest version of *Brugensis* (Vatican City, Ottob. Lat. 3027, fol. 43r–v) [A]. This is supplemented by that in *Collectio Wigorniensis* (BL Royal 10 A.ii, fol. 14r) [B], *Collectio Cheltenhamensis* (BL Egerton 2819, fols 54v–55r) [C] and *Appendix concilii Lateranensis* (5.9 and 27.5)[7] [D] and compared to the rule as published by Kehr [R₂]. It notes more substantial divergences, including word substitutions, but not minor scribal variations, such as word order. **BOLD CAPITALS** mark the titles of fragments, *italics* text in decretal copies missing from the surviving rule (R₂), and [square brackets] text in the rule that is omitted from the decretals.

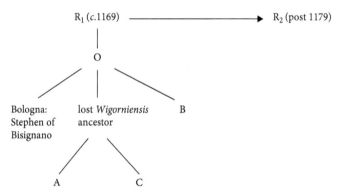

Figure A.1. Stemma for the lost decretal, *Ad petitionem* (O).

Alexander [episcopus seruus seruorum dei] dilectis filiis Girardo priori et fratribus iuxta disciplinam bone memorie Cleti uiuentibus[8] [salute et apostolicam benedictionem. Quod calcatis deo auctore...][9]

§1. AD uestram PETITIONEM regulam secundum quam uiuere debeatis, et omnipotenti deo seruire, duximus constituendam:[10] Inprimis[11] statuentes ut professionem maiori priori

---

[6] Duggan, 'New Case Law', 285–6. Another early continental collection, *Collectio Francofortana*, copied §§1–2 as *Ad petitionem*, under the title 'QUALITER PROFESSIO FIERI DEBEAT', BL Egerton 2901, fol. 46r.

[7] On which see Duggan, 'Appendix Concilii Lateranensis'; P. Crabbe, *Concilia omnia*, 3 vols (2nd ed. Cologne, 1551), II. 850, 900.

[8] From A (beginning Girardo) and D, which give 'Cleti' as 'electi'. Titles vary: INCIPIUNT DECRETALES EPISTOLAE A[LEX.] PAPAE III DE STATU RELIGIOSORUM ET DE EORUNDEM PRIUILEGIO QUORUM PRIMA DESTINATU EST GERARDO PRIORI ET FRATRIBUS (B, at opening of part II); GIRARDO PRIORI ET FRATRIBUS (C); ALEXANDER III. CRUCIATIS (1 Comp. 3.27.1).

[9] An opening section in R₂ notes that recipients wished to serve in a military habit and requested instruction in *regulares disciplinae*. It takes them, their houses, and possessions under papal protection.

[10] *instituendum* (C).

[11] *In primis id* (A); *Inprimo* (B); *In primis siquidem* (R₂).

omnes laici faciant, in manu eius se absque proprio uiuere[12] promittentes et continentiam quantum permiserit[13] diuina gratia seruare. Cui siquidem tam clerici quam laici, sicut proprio[14] magistro et animarum rectori, debitam in omnibus promittant obedientiam,[15] nec alicui inter uos professo liceat ad alium ordinem absque prioris sui licentia ullo modo transire, nisi forte ad religionem migrauerit artiorem. Nullus, absque prioris maioris licentia, hospitale audeat[16] facere. [Nullus qui sub rectore alicuius uestrorum hospitalium manet absque rectoris consilio in alium locum transmigrare presumat; quod si a prefato rectore se in aliquo grauari presenserit, tunc cum ipso eodem rectore aut cum alio fratre, quem rector mittendum elegerit, ad maiorem prepositum suam querimoniam deferat, ut quidquid illud fuerit, ipsius maioris prepositi iuditio legitime terminetur.] Nullus proprium habeat; si quid adquisierit suo rectori incunctanter assignet. [Nullus clericus siue laicus lineis uestimentis preter bracas utatur et nemo uestrum iaceat nisi uestitus.] Nullus uestrum alicui uobiscum esse uolenti crucem tribuat, sed per[17] medium annum si cognitus sit si incognitus per integrum annum[18] uobiscum *in probatione*[19] permaneat, et tunc maiori priori [a rectore hospitalis uel ab aliis duobus siue tribus fratribus] presentetur, ut ab ipso, non ab alio crucem suscipiat. §2. Eum uero[20] quem noueritis *debito* seruilis condition*is* astrictum absque permissione domini sui nullo modo in consortium uestrum recipiatis, et si quempiam[21] talem per ignorantiam receperitis, eum statim si a domino suo[22] fuerit repetitus, sibi[23] absque [ulla] contradictione reddatis, nisi forte ipsum[24] ex ignorantia fratrum et eius[25] a quo ordinatus est contigerit esse promotum. §3. *UXORATUS* autem sine licentia propriae uxoris inter uos nullatenus recipiatur, qua integre fame et opinionis ita existat,[26] quod nulla merito suspicio habeatur, eam ad secunda uota uelle migrare uel quod minus continenter debeat uiuere; que,[27] si prout dictum est talis extiterit,[28] marito eius[29] in consortio uestro recepto, ipsa publice in conspectu ecclesie[30] continentiam pro-fessa in domo propria cum filiis suis familiaque poterit permanere.[31] Si autem talis fuerit quae suspicione non careat, uoto continentie celebrato, a conuersatione secularium homi-num se remoueat, et in loco religioso deo seruitura[32] perpetuo commoretur.[33] Nullus uestrum aliquam mulierem tonsorare[34] audeat uel eam ad c*o*habitandum[35] secum assumat. §4. NEMO UESTRUM ALICUI coronam faciat in capite.[36] §5. SI HOSPITALEm domum *in aliquo loco* sine[37] oratorio feceritis, liberum uobis erit[38] absque conscientia[39] episcopi, in cuius parrochia fuerit, ipsam domum constituere.[40] *Quod si oratorium ibidem edificare*

---

[12] *uicturos* (D); *eius se* missing in B; *eius* missing in C.   [13] *promiserit* (B).
[14] Missing in B, C.   [15] *et reuerentiam et subiectionem exhibeant* (R₂).   [16] *audet* (B).
[17] *primo* (C).
[18] *unum annum integrum* (C); B supplies *uel integrum* for *si cognitus … annum.*
[19] A, B, C, D. The section ends in A after *permaneat.*
[20] *Eum … conditionis* missing in B. §2 omitted in D.   [21] *siquem* (B); *siquidem* (C).
[22] *suo* missing in C; *eum … repetitus* missing in B.   [23] Missing in C.
[24] *ipsum* missing in B; *ad sacros ordines* (R₂).   [25] *episcopi* (R₂).
[26] *extiterit* (R₂); *ita* missing in C.   [27] *Quod* (C).   [28] *existit* (C).   [29] *suo* (C).
[30] B omits *Uxoratus … ecclesie.*   [31] *remanere* (D).
[32] *in loco* [*solitario,* erased] *religioso seruitum* (B); *in loco religioso, ubi Deo seruiat* (D); *in loco ubi religiose deo seruiat* (R₂).
[33] *moretur* (D). *Uxoratus* (58.9) in *Collectio Lipsiensis* ends here.   [34] *tonsare* (B).
[35] *adchoabitandum* (C).
[36] Here, *Statuimus … pauperibus largiatur* (R₂), offers a detailed section on customs, touching on diet, liturgical calendar, and participation in divine offices, especially by the sick, as well as places and times of silence, and the portion for the poor after a brother's death.
[37] *in aliquo alio loco* (C); *Si hospitale in aliquo loco absque* (D); *absque* (R₂).   [38] *sit* (R₂).
[39] *licentia* (R₂).   [40] *construere. In singulis domibus vestris …* (R₂).

uolueritis, id absque licentia et assensu[41] *episcopi non faciatis, iustitia sua sibi in omnibus seruata.*[42] [In singulis domibus uestris septem fratres ad minus inter clericos et laicos ad dei seruitium commorentur.[43]] **§6. Sɪ cᴜᴍ ᴀʟɪᴏ** *uestrum, eo mortuo, pecunia inuenta fuerit, et in uita sua non patefecerit, nec ad ecclesiam nec ad hospitale sepeliatur, sed extra ciuitatem in campis deponatur.*[44]

---

[41] *consensu* (C). (B) ends at *non faciatis.*   [42] *reservata* (C).

[43] R$_2$ continues from here with provisions for governing the order and additional regulations. §6, part of the original rule, is missing from R$_2$.

[44] *Et cum aliquo* .... *ad hospitalem* ... *deportetur* (C).

Robert de Courson's
Hospital Decree (1213)

The papal legate promulgated a decree for leper-houses and for hospitals for the sick and pilgrims at his councils at Reims (July 1213), Paris (August 1213), and Rouen (March 1214). Early thirteenth-century copies of the decree for the latter two councils survive, to which their antiquarian editors supplied numbers and titles. The single decree at Paris [III.9 in Mansi] was divided into two at Rouen [II.39–40], but is otherwise largely identical.[1]

The Paris decree is edited here from Paris, Bibl. de l'Arsenal MS 769, fol. 118v (P), a thirteenth-century manuscript from the abbey of St Victor.[2] The Rouen decree is edited from the council's only manuscript copy, which is also thirteenth-century, from the monastery of Mont St Michel: Avranches, Bibl. mun. MS 149, fol. 5v (R).[3] Aside from its separation into two, the differences between the Rouen and Paris versions are largely scribal and are marked here using *italics* for what is missing from (R) and [square brackets] for what is missing from (P). Differences in words or word order in (R) are signalled in the footnotes.

§[4] De domibus leprosorum et hospitalibus infirmorum et peregrinorum salubri consilio statuimus: ut si facultates loci patiuntur quod ibidem manentes[5] [competenter] possint uiuere de com[m]uni, competens eis uiuendi regula statuatur, cuius substantia in tribus articulis maxime continetur, scilicet ut proprio renuntient, continentie uotum emittant, et suo prelato obedientiam fidelem et deuotam promittant; et habitu religioso non seculari utantur.

§[6] Cum autem pauci sani[7] possint multis infirmis competentius[8] ministrare, illud omnino indignum est ut numerus sanorum ibidem manentium excedat numerum infirmorum aut peregrinorum. Bona enim ex deuotione fidelium *ibidem*[9] collate non sunt sanorum usibus[10]

---

[1] Mansi XXII. 835–6, 913. Chapter 8, above, examines the decree and Robert's legation.

[2] There is a second manuscript, from the abbey of Anchin, which I have not yet been able to consult: Douai, Bibl. mun. MS 357, fols 156–66, for which see C. Dehaisnes, *Manuscrits de la bibliothèque de Douai* (Paris, 1878), 190–1.

[3] Entitled, 'Concilium magistri Roberti de Corcon <legati> apud Rothomagun celebratum, presentibus archiepiscopo Rothomagensi R. cum suis suffraganeis et aliis prelatis Normannie' (fol. 3v). The manuscript also contains the only surviving copies of two provincial councils of this period, of Rouen in 1223 and 1231, R. Kay, 'Mansi and Rouen', *Catholic Historical Review* 52:2 (1966), 170. On the manuscript: R. Kay, 'Romanus and Rouen: A Papal Legate's Tainted Visitation in 1227', *Annales de Normandie* 51:2 (2001), 111. A copy of a letter survives from Courson, as legate, to King John, on behalf of the abbot and convent: Kew, The National Archives, SC 1/1/17, dated Nov. 1212 (*sic*).

[4] Mansi XXII. 835–6, 913, supplies the title DE IIS QUI MANENT IN DOMIBUS LEPROSORUM ET HOSPITALIBUS, UT INFIRMIS ET PEREGRINIS MINISTRENT.

[5] *morantes* (R).

[6] Mansi XXII. 913 supplies the title (40) 'NE A MULTITUDINE SERVIENTIUM FACULTATES PAUPERIBUS DEPUTATAE ABSORBEANTUR; & QUI IN SERVIENTES NON RECIPIENDI'.

[7] *paucissimi* (R) for *pauci sani*.   [8] *multis infirmis possint competenter* (R).

[9] *domui* (R).   [10] *usibus sanorum* ~~collata~~ (R).

deputata sed potius infirmorum. Nec etiam illud sub silentio pretereundum est[11] quod quidam sani uiri et mulieres *et* matrimoni[al]i uinculo copulati, quandoque transferunt se ad tales domos, ut sub optentu[12] religionis possint iurisdictionem et potestatem eludere[13] secularium dominorum; qui tamen in domo religionis manentes, non minus, immo magis seculariter et delicate uiuunt, et operibus carnis uacant, quam *antea*[14] uacare consueuerant. Unde statuimus ut in habitu religionis religiose uiuant, uel de domibus eiciantur, ita tamen quod bona domui collata secum non absportent, ne de fraude sua commodum reportare uideantur.[15]

§Concerning houses of lepers and hospitals for the sick and for pilgrims we have established, through wholesome advice, that if the resources of the place allow those who dwell there to [capably] live a common life, a suitable rule should be established for them, which in substance should comprise most particularly three elements, namely that they should renounce any property of their own, should take a vow of continence, and they should promise faithful and devoted obedience to their prelate (head); and the habit of a religious not a secular should be used.

§Since moreover a few healthy persons should be able to care very capably for many sick people, it is entirely unfitting that the number of healthy dwelling there should exceed the number of the sick and pilgrims. For truly, the goods gathered there from the devotion of the faithful have not been assigned for the use of the healthy but rather for the infirm. Nor yet must it be passed by in silence that certain healthy men and women and those bound by the fetters of wedlock, sometimes bring themselves to such houses in order that under the canopy of religion they might be able to elude the jurisdiction and power of secular rulers; and although dwelling in a house of religion, they live not less but more secularly and luxuriously and have leisure for the fleshly pursuits in the way in which they were accustomed to enjoy them before. Whence we establish that they must live religiously in the dress of religion or be ejected from the houses, but in such a way that the goods gathered to the house should not be carried away with them, nor that they be thought to gain advantage from their fraud.

---

[11] *pretereundum est sub silentio* (R).   [12] *obtentu* (R).   [13] *elidere* (R).
[14] *umquam* (R).   [15] *uideantur commodum reportare* (R).

Bibliography

Primary Sources

Manuscripts

Avranches, Bibliothèque municipale, MS 149
Berlin, Staatsbibliothek, Preußischer Kulturbesitz, Cod. Phill. 1735
Cambridge, Corpus Christi College, MS 262
Cologny, Fondation Martin Bodmer, Cod. Bodmer 68
Dammarie-lès-Lys, Archives départementales de Seine-et-Marne, 11Hdt/A3
Einsiedeln, Stiftsbibliothek, Cod. 191(277)
Leipzig, Universitätsbibliothek, MS 975
London, British Library: Additional MSS 8602, 18460; Cotton Claudius A IV; Cotton
   Vespasian E XVII; Egerton 2819; Egerton 2901; Harley 3834; Royal 9 E VII; Royal 9
   E XIV; Royal 10 A II
   London, The National Archives, SC 1/1/7
Munich, Bayerische Staatsbibliothek: Clm 14006; Clm 14431; Clm 19413; Clm 28174; Clm
   29555/1
Oxford, Bodleian Library, Laud Misc. 527
Oxford, New College, MS 205
Paris, Bibliothèque de l'Arsenal, MS 769
Paris, Bibliothèque nationale de France: latin 523; latin 3259; latin 3892; latin 3904; latin
   4568; latin 4613; latin 10758; latin 14317; latin 14524; latin 15996; nouvelle acquisition
   latine 1632
St Gallen, Stiftsbibliothek: Cod. Sang. 196; Cod. Sang. 299; Cod. Sang. 397
Troyes, Bibliothèque municipal: MS 60; MS 192
Vatican City: Chig. F.IV.75; Vat. lat. 1367; Vat. lat. 1377; Ottob. lat. 3027
Wolfenbüttel, Herzog August Bibliothek, MS Blankenburg 130
York, Borthwick Institute, Archbishops Register 1A

Printed Sources

Acta Pontificum, ed. J. V. Pflugk–Harttung, 3 vols (Tübingen, 1880–6)
Acta Stephani Langton Cantuariensis episcopi, A.D. 1207–1228, ed. K. Major, Canterbury
   and York Society 50 (Oxford, 1950)
Actes et documents anciens intéressant la Belgique, ed. C. Duvivier (Brussels, 1898)
Actus pontificum Cenomannis in urbe degentium, ed. G. Busson and A. Ledru, Archives
   historiques du Maine 2 (Le Mans, 1901)
Die Admonitio generalis Karls des Großen, ed. H. Mordek, K. Zechiel-Eckes, and
   M. Glatthaar, MGH *Fontes iuris Germanici antiqui* XVI (Hanover, 2012)
Alcuin, *Epistolae*, ed. Ernst Dümmler, MGH *Epistolae* IV (Berlin, 1895), 1–481
Alexander III, *Epistulae et privilegia*, PL 200, cols 69–1320

Agobard of Lyon, *De dispensatione ecclesiasticarum rerum*, ed. L. van Acker, *Angobardi Lugdunensis opera omnia*, CCCM 52 (Turnhout, 1981), 119–42

Alger of Liège, *Liber de misericordia et justitia*, PL 180, cols 857–968

Anastasius IV, *Epistolae et privilegia*, PL 188, cols 989–1088

Ancient Laws and Institutes of England, ed. B. Thorpe, I (London, 1840)

Annales Laureschamenses, ed. G. H. Pertz, MGH *Scriptores* I (Hanover, 1826)

Annales regni Francorum inde ab a. 741 usque ad a. 829, ed. F. Kurze, MGH *Scriptores rerum Germanicarum* VI (Hanover, 1895)

The Annals of Saint-Bertin, ed. J. L. Nelson (Manchester, 1991)

Anselmi episcopi Lucensis Collectio canonum una cum collectione minore, ed. F. Thaner (Innsbruck, 1906–15; repr. 1965)

Astronomus, *Vita Hludowici imperatoris*, ed. E. Tremp, *Thegan, Die Taten Kaiser Ludwigs/ Astronomus, Das Leben Kaiser Ludwigs*, MGH *Scriptores rerum Germanicarum* LXIV (Hanover, 1995), 279–555

Astronomus, *Vita Hludowici imperatoris*, tr. T. F. X. Noble, *Charlemagne and Louis the Pious: The Lives by Einhard, Notker, Ermoldus, Thegan and the Astronomer* (University Park, PA, 2009), 226–302

Baluze, S., *Concilia Galliae Narbonensis* (Paris, 1668)

Benedict Levita, *False Capitularies*, ed. G. Schmitz, 10 December 2014, <http://www.benedictus.mgh.de/edition/edition.htm>

Bernard of Pavia, *Summa decretalium*, ed. E. A. T. Laspeyres (Regensburg, 1860; repr. Graz, 1956)

Bibliotheca Topographica Britannica, ed. J. Nichols, 8 vols (London, 1780–90)

Die Briefe des heiligen Bonifatius und Lullus, ed. M. Tangl, MGH *Epistolae selectae* I (Berlin, 1916)

Bonizo of Sutri, *Liber de vita christiana*, ed. E. Perels, Texte zur Geschichte des römischen und kanonischen Rechts im Mittelalter, I (Berlin, 1930)

The Book of St Gilbert, ed. R. Foreville and G. Keir (Oxford, 1987)

Burchard of Worms, *Decretum Libri XX*, PL 140, cols 537–1057

Cabaniss, A., tr., *Charlemagne's Cousins: Contemporary Lives of Adalard and Wala* (Syracuse, NY, 1967)

Calendar of Patent Rolls of Henry III, ed. H. C. Maxwell Lyte, 6 vols (London, 1901–13)

Die Canones-sammlungen zwischen Gratian und Bernhard von Pavia, ed. E. Friedberg (Leipzig, 1897; Graz, 1958)

Capitula episcoporum, ed. P. Brommer, R. Pokorny, and M. Stratmann, 4 vols, MGH *Capitula episcoporum* (Hanover, 1984–2005)

Capitularia regum Francorum, ed. A. Boretius and V. Krause, 2 vols, MGH *Capitularia* (Hanover, 1883–97)

Cartulaire de la commune de Fosses, ed. J. Borgnet (Namur, 1867)

Les cartulaires de la prévôté de Saint-Martin à Ypres précédés d'une esquisse historique sur la prévôté, ed. E. Feys and A. Nelis, 2 vols (Bruges, 1880–4)

Cartulaire de l'abbaye de Saint-Corneille de Compiègne, ed. É.-É. Morel, Société historique de Compiègne, III (Paris, 1977)

Cartulaire de l'église Nôtre-Dame du Paris, ed. M. Guérard, 4 vols (Paris, 1850)

Cartulaire de l'hôpital Saint-Jean de Bruxelles (actes des XIIe et XIIIe siècles), ed. P. Bonenfant (Brussels, 1953)

Cartulaire général de l'ordre des Hospitaliers de S. Jean de Jérusalem (1100–1310), ed. J. Delaville Le Roulx, 4 vols (Paris, 1894–1906)

Het cartularium van het O. L. Vrouw gasthuis te Ieper, II en III (Le cartulaire de l'hôpital Notre-Dame à Ypres), ed. O. Mus, Bijdragen tot de geschiedenis van de liefdadigheidsinstellingen te Ieper VII en VIII (Ypres, 1966)

The Cartulary of Countess Blanche of Champagne, ed. T. Evergates (Toronto, 2010)

Cassiodori senatoris variae, ed. T. Mommsen, MGH *Auctores antiquissimi* XII (Berlin, 1894)

Chapters of the Augustinian Canons, ed. H. E. Salter, Canterbury and York Society 29 (London, 1922)

Chartae Latinae Antiquiores: Facsimile-Edition of the Latin Charters, ed. G. Cavallo and G. Nicolaj, 2nd series, Ninth Century, Part 58, Italy 30 (Zurich, 2001)

The Chrodegang Rules: The Rules for the Common Life of the Secular Clergy from the Eighth and Ninth Centuries, Critical Texts with Translations and Commentary, ed. and tr. J. Bertram (Aldershot, 2005)

Chronica patriarcharum Gradensium, ed. G. Waitz, MGH *Scriptores rerum Langobardicarum et Italicarum* (Hanover, 1878), 392–7

The Chronicle and Historical Notes of Bernard Itier, ed. and tr. A. W. Lewis (Oxford, 2012)

The Chronicle of Bernard Itier, ed. and tr. A. W. Lewis (Oxford, 2012)

Chronique des abbés de Fontenelle (Saint-Wandrille): Texte établi, traduit et commenté, ed. F. P. Pradié, Les classiques de l'Histoire de France au Moyen Age 40 (Paris, 1999)

Codex Carolinus, ed. W. Gundlach, MGH *Epistulae* III (Berlin, 1892), 469–657

Codex diplomaticus cavensis, ed. M. Morcaldi, M. Schiani, and S. de Stefano, 12 vols (Naples, 1873–2015)

Codex Iustinianus, ed. P. Krüger, 13th ed., Corpus Iuris Civilis 2 (Berlin, 1963)

Codice diplomatico longobardo, I and II, ed. L. Schiaparelli, Fonti per la Storia d'Italia 62–3 (Rome, 1929–33)

Codice diplomatico sant'Ambrosiano delle carte dell'ottavo e nono secolo, ed. A. Fumagalli (Milan, 1805)

Codice diplomatico veronese: Dalla caduta dell'impero romano alla fine del periodo carolingio, ed. V. Fainelli, I (Venice, 1940)

Collectio Dacheriana, ed. J.-L. D'Achery, *Spicilegium sive collectio veterum aliquot scriptorum qui in Galliae bibliothecis delituerat*, I (Paris, 1723), 509–63

Compilatio nova decretalium domini Gregorii pape noni (Speyer, 1486)

Les conciles de la province de Tours: Concilia provinciae Turonensis (saec. XIII–XV), ed. J. Avril (Paris, 1987)

Concilia aevi Karolini (742–842), ed. A. Werminghoff, 2 vols, MGH *Concilia* II (Hanover and Leipzig, 1896)

Concilia aevi Merovingici, ed. F. Maassen, MGH *Concilia* I (Hanover, 1893)

Collectio Dionysio-Hardiana, ed. J. W. Cochlaeus (Mainz, 1525)

Concilia Galliae (314–506), ed. C. Munier, CCSL 148 (Turnhout, 1963)

Concilia Galliae (511–695), ed. C. de Clercq, CCSL 148A (Turnhout, 1963)

Concilia omnia tam generalia quam particularia..., ed. P. Crabbe, 3 vols (2nd ed. Cologne, 1551)

Concilia Rotomagensis provinciae, ed. P. Bessin (Rouen, 1717)

Conciliorum oecumenicorum generaliumque decreta, ed. G. Alberigo, A. Melloni et al., Corpus Christianorum, 2 vols (Turnhout, 2006–13)

Constitutiones mit der Glosse von Johannes Andreae (Speyer, 1481)

'Consuetudines Corbeienses', ed. J. Semmler, in K. Hallinger, ed., *Corpus Consuetudinum Monasticarum*, I (Siegburg, 1963), 355–422

Corpus iuris canonici, ed. E. Friedberg, 2 vols (Leipzig, 1879; repr. Graz, 1959)

Corpus iuris canonici, 3 parts (Rome, 1582)

Corpus of British Medieval Library Catalogues XIV: Hospitals, Towns and the Professions, ed. N. Ramsay and J. M. W. Willoughby (Oxford, 2009)

Councils and Synods: With Other Documents Relating to the English Church I, AD 871–1204, ed. D. Whitelock, M. Brett, and C. N. L. Brooke, 2 vols (Oxford, 1981)

Councils and Synods: With Other Documents Relating to the English Church II, AD 1205–1313, ed. F. M. Powicke and C. R. Cheney, 2 vols (Oxford, 1964)

The Coutumes de Beauvaisis *of Philippe de Beaumanoir*, tr. F. R. P. Akehurst (Philadelphia, 1992)

Cronache e statuti della città di Viterbo, ed. I. Ciampi (Florence, 1872)

Das Testament des Bischofs Berthramn von Le Mans vom 27 März 616, ed. M. Weidemann, Römisch-Germanisches Zentralmuseum Mainz, Forschungsinstitut für Vor- und Frühgeschichte Monographien 9 (Mainz, 1986)

Decrees of the Ecumenical Councils, ed. N. P. Tanner, II (Washington, DC, 1990)

Decretales Pseudo-Isidorianae et Capitula Angilramni, ed. P. Hinschius (Leipzig, 1863)

Decretum magistri Gratiani, ed. E. Friedberg, Corpus Iuris Canonici 1 (Leipzig, 1879)

Die Dekretalensammlung des Bernardus Compostellanus antiquus, ed. H. Singer, Sitzungsberichte der kaiserlichen Akademie der Wissenschaften in Wien, Phil.-Hist. Kl. 171.2 (Vienna, 1914)

Digesta, ed. T. Mommsen and P. Krueger, 16th ed., Corpus iuris civilis 1 (Berlin, 1954)

Diuersorum patrum sententie siue Collectio in LXXIV titulos digesta, ed. J. T. Gilchrist, Monumenta Iuris Canonici Series B: Corpus Collectionum 1 (Vatican City, 1973)

Documents Illustrating the Activities of the General and Provincial Chapters of the English Black Monks, 1215–1540, ed. W. A. Pantin, 3 vols, Camden 3rd ser. 45, 47, 54 (London, 1931–7)

'Documents relatifs á l'administration de l'hôpital capitulaire de Notre-Dame de Tournai du XIIe au XVe siècles', ed. J. Pycke, *Annales de la Société belge d'histoire des hôpitaux* 8 (1970), 3–53

Dugdale, W., *Monasticon Anglicanum*, 6 vols (London, 1846)

Durham Episcopal Charters, 1071–1152, ed. H. S. Offler, Surtees Society 179 (Gateshead, 1964)

Ehrle, F., 'Ein Bruchstück der Acten des Concils von Vienne', *Archiv für Literatur- und Kirchengeschichte des Mittelalters* 4 (1888), 361–470

Einhard, *Vita Karoli Magni*, ed. O. Holder-Egger, MGH *Scriptores rerum Germanicarum* XXV, 6th ed. (Hanover, 1911)

Epistolae Merovingici et Karolini aevi I–III, ed. E. Dümmler, MGH *Epistolae* III–V (Berlin, 1892–9)

Epistolae Romanorum pontificum genuinae et quae ad eos scriptae sunt a S. Hilaro usque ad Pelagium II, ed. A. Thiel, I (Brunsberg, 1868)

Eugenius II, *Epistula ad Bernardum Viennensem archiepiscopum*, PL 105, cols 643–4

Excerpta Valesiana, ed. J. Moreau and V. Velkov (Leipzig, 1968)

Florus of Lyon, *Capitula ex lege et canone collecta*, PL 119, cols 419–22

Foedera, conventiones, literae, et cujuscunque generis acta publica, inter reges Angliae, ed. T. Rymer, 3rd ed., I (London, 1745)

Formulae Imperiales e curia Ludovici Pii, ed. K. Zeumer, MGH *Formulae Merowingici et Karolini aevi* I (Hanover, 1886)

The Formularies of Angers and Marculf: Two Merovingian Legal Handbooks, tr. A. Rio, Translated Texts for Historians 46 (Liverpool, 2008)

Fredegard, *Chronica*, ed. B. Krusch, MGH *Scriptores rerum Merovingicarum* II (Hanover, 1888)

Geschichte des Bistums Le Mans von der Spätantike bis zur Karolingerzeit: Actus pontificum Cenomannis in urbe degentium und Gesta Aldrici, ed. M Weidemann, 3 vols, Römisch-Germanisches Zentralmuseum, Forschungsinstitut für Vor- und Frühgeschichte 56 (Mainz, 2000)

'Gesta domni Aldrici Cenomannicae urbis episcopi', in *Geschichte des Bistums Le Mans*, ed. M. Weidemann, I (Mainz, 2000)

Gesta episcoporum Neapolitanorum, ed. G. Waitz, MGH *Scriptores rerum Langobardicarum et Italicarum* (Hanover, 1878), 398–466

Gesta regis Henrici secundi Benedicti abbatis, ed. W. Stubbs, 2 vols, Rolls Series (London, 1867)

Goffredus Tranensis, *Summa super titulis decretalium* (Lyon, 1519; repr. Aalen, 1992)

Göller, E., 'Die Gravamina auf dem Konzil von Vienne und ihre literarische Überlieferung', in *Festgabe, enthaltend vornehmlich vorreformationsgeschichtlich Forschungen, Heinrich Finke* (Münster, 1904), 195–221

Gousset, T., ed., *Les actes de la province ecclésiastique de Reims*, 4 vols (Reims, 1842–4)

Gregorii I papae Registrum epistolarum, ed. P. Ewald and L. Hartmann, MGH *Epistolae* I–II (Berlin, 1887–91)

Hardouin, J., *Acta conciliorum et epistolae decretales ac constitutiones summorum pontificorum*, VII (Paris, 1714)

Henricus de Segusia, *Lectura sive Apparatus domini Hostiensis super quinq[ue] libris decretaliu[m]*, 2 vols (Strasbourg, 1512)

Henricus de Segusia, *Summa super titulis decretaliu[m]* (Venice, 1480)

Hinkmar von Reims, *Collectio de ecclesiis et capellis*, ed. M. Stratmann, MGH *Fontes iuris Germanici antiqui* XIV (Hanover, 1990)

Histoire de la ville de Montdidier, ed. V. de Beauville, 4 vols (Paris, 1857)

The Historia occidentalis of Jacques de Vitry: A Critical Edition, ed. J. F. Hinnebusch, Spicilegium Friburgense 17 (Fribourg, 1972)

Honorii III Romani pontificis opera omnia, ed. C. A. Horoy, Bibliotheca patristica medii aevi, 5 vols (Paris, 1879–82)

Hugh of Floreffe, *De B. Juetta sive Jutta, vidua reclusa, Hui in Belgio*, in *Acta Sanctorum*, 3rd ed., 70 vols (Paris, 1863–1940), II. 145–69

Innocent II, *Epistolae et privilegia*, PL 179, cols 53–658

Innocent III, *Elogio della carità (Libellus de Eleemosyna)*, ed. S. Fioramonti (Vatican City, 2001)

Innocent III, *Regestorum sive epistolarum libri XVI*, PL 214–16

Innocent IV, *Apparatus super quinque libros decretalium* (Venice, 1491)

Iohannis Beleth, *Summa de ecclesiasticis officiis*, ed. H. Douteil, CCCM 41A (Turnhout, 1976)

Iscrizioni delle chiese e degli altri edifici di Milano dal secolo VIII ai Giorni nostri, ed. V. Forcella (Milan, 1889)

Isidori Hispalensis Episcopi Etymologiarum sive Originum Libri XX, ed. W. M. Lindsay (Oxford, 1911)

Italia pontificia, V. Aemilia sive provincia Ravennas, ed. P. F. Kehr (Berlin, 1911)

Iuliani epitome Latina Novellarum Iustiniani, ed. G. F. Hänel (Leipzig, 1873; repr. Osnabrück, 1965)

Ivo of Chartres, *Decretum*, ed. M. Brett, 23 September 2015, <https://ivo-of-chartres.github.io/decretum.html>

Ivo of Chartres, *Epistulae, PL* 162, cols 9–504

James of Vitry, 'The Life of Mary of Oignies', tr. M. H. King, in A. B. Mulder-Bakker, ed., *Mary of Oignies: Mother of Salvation*, Medieval Women: Texts and Contexts 7 (Turnhout, 2006), 34–127

Jerome, *Ad Nepotianum*, ed. A. Cain, *Jerome and the Monastic Clergy: A Commentary on Letter 52 to Nepotian, with an Introduction, Text, and Translation*, Supplements to Vigiliae Christianae 119 (Leiden, 2013)

Jerome, *Epistolae, PL* 22, cols 325–1224

Julianus Pomerius, *De vita contemplativa, PL* 59, cols 415–520

Die Kanonessammlung des Kardinals Deusdedit, ed. V. W. von Glanvell (Paderborn, 1905)

Die Konzilien der karolingischen Teilreiche 843–859 (Concilia aevi Karolini 843–859), ed. W. Hartmann, MGH *Concilia* III (Hanover, 1984)

Die Konzilien der karolingischen Teilreiche 860–874 (Concilia aevi Karolini 860–872), ed. W. Hartmann, MGH *Concilia* IV (Hanover, 1988)

Die Konzilsordines des Früh- und Hochmittelalters, ed. H. Schneider, MGH *Ordines de celebrando concilio* I (Hanover, 1996)

Leges Langobardorum, ed. G. H. Pertz, MGH *Legum* IV (Hanover, 1868)

Leges Langobardorum, 643–866, ed. F. Beyerle, 2nd ed. (Witzenhausen, 1962)

'Legislatio Aquisgranensis', ed. J. Semmler, in K. Hallinger, ed., *Corpus Consuetudinum Monasticarum*, I (Siegburg, 1963)

The Letters of Gregory the Great, tr. J. R. C. Martyn, 3 vols (Toronto, 2004)

Lex romana canonice compta: Testo di leggi romano-canoniche del sec. IX, ed. C. G. Mor (Pavia, 1927)

Lex romana Visigothorum, ed. G. Haenel (Leipzig, 1849)

Lex Visigothorum, ed. K. Zeumer, MGH *Leges nationum Germanicarum* I (Hanover, 1902)

Liber censuum de l'Eglise romaine, ed. P. Fabre and L. Duchesne, 3 vols, Bibliothèque des écoles françaises d'Athènes et de Rome, 2e série 6 (Paris, 1889–1952)

Liber diurnus Romanorum pontificum, ed. H. Foerster (Berlin, 1958)

Liber extravagantium decretalium, ed. E. Freidberg, Corpus Iuris Canonici 2 (Leipzig, 1881)

Liber pontificalis, ed. L. Duchesne, *Le Liber pontificalis: Texte, introduction et commentaire*, 2 vols (Paris 1886–92)

Lucius II, *Epistolae et privilegia, PL* 179, cols 823–936

Marculfi Formularum: Libri Duo, ed. A. Uddholm (Uppsala, 1962)

Matthew Paris, *Chronica Majora*, ed. H. R. Luard, 7 vols (London, 1872–83)

Matthew Paris, 'Vita sancti Stephani archiepiscopi Cantuariensis', in *Ungedruckte Anglo-Normannische Geschichtsquellen*, ed. F. Liebermann (Strasbourg, 1879), 318–29

Memorials of the Church of SS Peter and Wilfrid, Ripon, ed. J. T. Fowler, I, Surtees Society 84 (Durham, 1882)

Memorie e documenti per servire all'istoria del Ducato di Lucca, ed. D. Barsocchini, V/2 (Lucca, 1837)

'Neue Kapitularien und Kapitulariensammlungen', ed. H. Mordek and G. Schmitz, *Deutsches Archiv fur Erforschung des Mittelalters* 43 (1987), 361–439, repr. Mordek, *Studien zur fränkischen Herrschergesetzgebung* (Frankfurt, 2000), 81–160

Novellae, ed. R. Schöll and W. Kroll, 6th ed., Corpus Iuris Civilis 3 (Berlin, 1959)

The Old English Version of the Enlarged Rule of Chrodegang: Edited Together with the Latin Text and an English Translation, ed. B. Langefeld, Münchner Universitätsschriften, Texte und Untersuchungen zur Englischen Philologie 26 (Frankfurt, 2004)

Œuvres de Rigord et de Guillaume le Breton, ed. H. F. Delaborde, 2 vols (Paris, 1882–5)

Papal Decretals Relating to the Diocese of Lincoln in the Twelfth Century, ed. and tr. W. Holtzmann and E. W. Kemp, Lincoln Record Society 47 (Hereford, 1954)

'Papsturkunden in Campanien', ed. P. Kehr, in *Nachrichten von der Königlichen Gesellschaft der Wissenschaften zu Göttingen: Phil.-hist. Klasse* (Göttingen, 1900), 286–344

Papsturkunden in England, ed. W. Holtzmann, 3 vols, Abhandlungen der Königlichen Gesellschaft der Wissenschaften zu Göttingen, Phil.-hist. Klasse, NS 25; Abhandlungen der Akademie der Wissenschaften in Göttingen, Phil.-hist. Klasse, 3rd ser. 14–15, 33 (Göttingen, 1930–52)

'Papsturkunden in Venetien. Bericht über die Forschungen L. Schiaparellis', ed. P. Kehr, *Nachrichten von der Königlichen Gesellschaft der Wissenschaften zu Göttingen: Phil.-hist. Klasse* (1899), 197–249

The Parliament Rolls of Medieval England, ed. C. Given-Wilson et al. (Leicester, 2005)

Paschasius Radbertus, *Vita sancti Adalhardi abbatis Corbeiensis*, PL 120, cols 1507–56

Passio Praeiecti episcopi et martyris Averni, ed. B. Krusch, MGH *Scriptores rerum Merovingicarum* V (Hanover, 1905), 212–48

Patrologiae cursus completus, seu bibliotheca universalis omnium ss. Patrum doctorum, scriptorumque ecclesiasticorum, Series Latina, ed. J.-P. Migne, 221 vols (Paris, 1844–64)

Paucapalea, *Summa des Paucapalea über das decretum Gratiani*, ed. J. F. von Schulte (Giessen, 1890)

Peter of les Vaux-de-Cernay, *The History of the Albigensian Crusade*, tr. W. A. Sibly and M. D. Sibly (Woodbridge, 1998)

Peter the Chanter, *Verbum adbreviatum: Textus conflatus*, ed. M. Boutry, CCCM 196 (Turnhout, 2004)

Polycarpus, *Die Sammlung 'Policarpus' des Kardinals Gregor von S. Grisogono*, ed. C. Erdmann, U. Horst, and H. Fuhrmann, MGH, accessed Aug. 2019, <http://www.mgh.de/datenbanken/leges/kanonessammlung-polycarp>

Quinque Compilationes Antiquae, ed. E. Friedberg (Leipzig, 1882; repr. Graz, 1956)

Reading Abbey Cartularies, ed. B. R. Kemp, 2 vols, Camden 4th ser. 31, 33 (London, 1986–7)

Regesta Pontificum Romanorum, ed. P. Jaffé, rev. S. Loewenfeld, F. Kaltenbrunner, and P. Ewald, 2nd ed., 2 vols (Leipzig, 1885–8)

Régestes de la Cité de Liège, ed. E. Fairon and J. Haust, 4 vols (Liège, 1933–40)

Regino of Prüm, *Libri duo de synodalibus causis et disciplinis ecclesiasticis*, ed. F. G. A. Wasserschleben (Leipzig, 1840; repr. Graz, 1964)

Das Register Gregors VII, ed. E. Caspar, 2 vols, MGH *Epistolae selectae* II (Berlin, 1920–3)

Les registres de Grégoire IX, ed. L. Auvray (Paris, 1896)

'Réglement d'ordre intérieur de l'hopital Notre-Dame à Ypres, en 1268', *Annales de la Société à l'Émulation pour l'étude de l'histoire et des Antiquités de la Flandre*, 2nd ser. 7 (1849), 247–54

Regulae expositae apud Antiochiam in encaeniis XXV, PL 67, cols 159–64

La règle du maître: introduction, texte, traduction et notes, ed. A. de Vogüé, 2 vols, Sources chrétiennes 105–6 (Paris, 1964)

Robert of Auxerre, *Chronicon*, ed. O. Holder-Egger, MGH *Scriptores* XXVI (Hanover, 1882), 219–87

Robert de Torigni, *Chronique*, ed. L. Delisle, 2 vols (Rouen, 1872)

Rufinus von Bologna, *Summa Decretorum*, ed. H. Singer (Paderborn, 1902; repr. 1963)

The Rule of Saint Benedict, ed. and tr. B. L. Venarde (Cambridge, MA, 2011)

Sacrorum conciliorum nova et amplissima collectio, ed. G. D. Mansi, 31 vols (Venice, 1758–98), repr. and cont. L. Petit and I. B. Martin, 60 vols (Paris, 1901–27)

Sacrosancta concilia, ed. P. Labbe and G. Cossartii, XIII (Venice, 1730),

Selected Letters of Pope Innocent III, ed. C. R. Cheney and W. H. Semple (London, 1953)

Das Sendhandbuch des Regino von Prüm, ed. F. W. H. Wasserschleben and W. Hartmann, Ausgewählte Quellen zur deutschen Geschichte des Mittelalters. Freiherr vom Stein-Gedächtnisausgabe, XLII (Darmstadt, 2004)

Sicardi Cremonensis episcopi Mitralis de officiis, ed. G. Sarbak and L. Weinrich, CCCM 228 (Turnhout, 2008)

Die 'Summa de ordine ecclesiastico': Eine römisch-rechtliche Quelle Benedicts, ed. G. Schmitz and M. Weber, 2004, <http://www.benedictus.mgh.de/quellen/summa.pdf>

The Summa Parisiensis on the Decretum Gratiani, ed. T. P. McLaughlin (Toronto, 1952)

Statuta capitulorum generalium ordinis Cisterciensis ab anno 1116 ad annum 1786, ed. J.-M. Canivez, 8 vols (Louvain, 1933–41)

Les Statuta ecclesiae antiqua, ed. C. Munier, Bibliothèque de l'Institut de Droit Canonique de l'Université de Strasbourg 5 (Paris, 1960)

Les statuts synodaux français du XIIIe siècle, 1. *Les statuts de Paris et le synodal de l'ouest*, ed. O. Pontal, Collection de documents inédits sur l'histoire de France 9 (Paris, 1971)

Stephan von Doornick (Étienne de Tournai), *Die summa über das Decretum Gratiani*, ed. J. F. von Schulte (Giessen, 1891; repr. 1965)

Summa in Decretum Simonis Bisinianensis, ed. P. V. Aimone (Fribourg, 2007)

'Texts on Hospitals: Translation of Jacques de Vitry, *Historia Occidentalis* 29, and Edition of Jacques de Vitry's Sermons to Hospitallers', ed. J. Bird, in P. Biller and J. Ziegler, eds, *Religion and Medicine in the Middle Ages* (York, 2001), 109–34

The Theodosian Code and Novels, and the Sirmondian Constitutions, tr. C. Pharr, T. S. Davidson, and M. R. Pharr (Princeton, 1952)

Theodosiani libri xvi cum constitutionibus sirmondianis et leges novellae ad Theodosianum pertinentes, ed. T. Mommsen and P. M. Meyer, 2 vols (Berlin, 1905)

Theophanes, *Chronographia*, ed. C. de Boor, 2 vols (Leipzig, 1885)

Thomas of Cantimpré, 'Supplement to James of Vitry's *Life of Mary of Oignies*', tr. H. Feiss, in A. B. Mulder-Bakker, ed., *Mary of Oignies: Mother of Salvation*, Medieval Women: Texts and Contexts 7 (Turnhout, 2006), 129–65

Thomas of Eccleston, 'Liber de adventu minorum in Angliam', in *Monumenta Franciscana*, ed. J. S. Brewer, Rolls Series (London, 1958), 3–72

Thomas of Monmouth, *The Life and Miracles of St William of Norwich*, ed. A. Jessop and M. R. James (Cambridge, 1896)

Le Traité 'De usura' de Robert de Courçon: Texte et traduction publiés avec une introduction, ed. G. LeFèvre, Travaux et mémoires de l'université de Lille 10, Mémoire 30 (Lille, 1902)

Die Urkunden der Merowinger, ed. C. Brühl, T. Kölzer, M. Hartmann, and A. Stieldorf, 2 vols, MGH *Diplomata* (Hanover, 2001)

Die Urkunden Lothars I und Lothars II, ed. T. Schieffer, MGH *Diplomata* (Berlin, 1966)

Vita Ansberti episcopi Rotomagensis, ed. W. Levison, MGH *Scriptores rerum Merovingicarum* V (Hanover, 1910), 613–41

Vita Walae, ed. G. H. Pertz, MGH *Scriptores* II (Hanover, 1829), 533–69

William Durant, *Tractatus de modo generalis concilii celebrandi* (Lyon, 1531)

The Works of the Emperor Julian, ed. and tr. W. C. Wright, 3 vols (London, 1923)

Secondary Sources

Airlie, S., '"For it is Written in the Law": Ansegis and the Writing of Carolingian Royal Authority', in S. Baxter, C. E. Karkov, J. L. Nelson, and D. Pelteret, eds, *Early Medieval Studies in Memory of Patrick Wormald* (Farnham, 2009), 219–36

Anderson, M., 'Mistranslations of Josephus and the Expansion of Public Charity in Late Antiquity', *Early Medieval Europe* 25:2 (2017), 139–61

Arnold, J., ed., *Oxford Handbook of Medieval Christianity* (Oxford, 2014)

Arnoux, M., *Des clercs au service de la réforme: Etudes et documents sur les chanoines réguliers de la province de Rouen* (Turnhout, 2000)

Atzeri, L. '*Submota conditione*: una questione terminologica nella prima legge contro gli apostati di Teodosio I', in K. Muscheler, ed., *Römische Jurisprudenz: Dogmatik, Überlieferung, Rezeption: Festschrift für Detlef Liebs zum 75. Geburtstag* (Berlin, 2011), 11–32

Austin, G., 'Bishops and Religious Law, 900–1050', in J. S. Ott and A. Trumbore Jones, eds, *The Bishop Reformed: Studies of Episcopal Power and Culture in the Central Middle Ages* (Aldershot, 2007), 40–57

Austin, G., 'Authority and the Canons in Burchard's Decretum and Ivo's Decretum', in M. Brett and K. G. Cushing, eds, *Readers, Texts and Compilers in the Earlier Middle Ages: Studies in Medieval Canon Law in Honour of Linda Fowler-Magerl* (Farnham, 2009), 35–58

Austin, G., *Shaping Church Law around the Year 1000: The Decretum of Burchard of Worms* (Farnham, 2009)

Avril, J., 'Le IIIe concile du Latran et les communautés de lépreux', *Revue Mabillon* 60 (1981), 21–76

Avril, J., *Le Gouvernement des Evêques et la vie religieuse dans le diocese d'Angers (1148–1240)*, 2 vols (Paris, 1985)

Avril, J., 'Le statut des maisons-dieu dans l'organisation ecclésiastique médiévale', in *Actes du 110e Congrès National des Sociétés savantes, Montpellier, 1er–5 avril 1985* (Paris, 1987), 285–97

Baaken, K., 'Papsturkunden für die Crociferi', in K. Herbers, H.-H. Kortüm, and C. Servatius, eds, *Ex ipsis rerum documentis: Beiträge zur Mediävistik: Festschrift für Harald Zimmermann zum 65. Geburtstag* (Sigmaringen, 1991), 335–43

Baldwin, J. W., *Masters, Princes, and Merchants: The Social Views of Peter the Chanter and his Circle*, 2 vols (Princeton, 1970)

Baldwin, J. W., *The Government of Philip Augustus: Foundations of French Royal Power in the Middle Ages* (Berkeley, CA, 1986)

Baldwin, J. W., 'Paris et Rome en 1215: Les réformes du IVe concile de Latran', *Journal des Savants* 1 (1997), 99–124

Balzaretti, R., 'The Politics of Property in Ninth-Century Milan: Familial Motives and Monastic Strategies in the Village of Inzago', *Mélanges de l'Ecole française de Rome Moyen Age* 111:2 (1999), 747–70

Barber, M., ed., *The Military Orders: Fighting for the Faith and Caring for the Sick* (Aldershot, 1994)

Barrow, J., 'Review Article: Chrodegang, his Rule and its Successors', *Early Medieval Europe* 14:2 (2006), 201–12

Barrow, J. 'Ideas and Applications of Reform', in T. F. X. Noble and J. M. H. Smith, eds, *Early Medieval Christianities c.600–c.1100*, Cambridge History of Christianity, III (Cambridge, 2008), 345–62

Barrow, J., *The Clergy in the Medieval World: Secular Clerics, their Families and Careers in North-Western Europe, c.800–c.1200* (Cambridge, 2015)

Baumann, D., *Stephen Langton: Erzbischof von Canterbury im England der Magna Carta (1207–1228)*, Studies in Medieval and Reformation Traditions 144 (Leiden, 2009)

Benson, R. L., 'Political Renovatio: Two Models from Roman Antiquity', in R. L. Benson and G. Constable, with C. D. Lanham, eds, *Renaissance and Renewal in the Twelfth Century* (Toronto, 1991), 339–86

Bériac, F., *Histoire des Lépreux au Moyen Age: Une société d'exclus* (Paris, 1988)

Bériou, N., and F.-O. Touati, *Voluntate dei leprosus: Les lépreux entre conversion et exclusion aux XIIème et XIIIème siècles* (Spoleto, 1991)

Berschin, W., *Greek Letters and the Latin Middle Ages: From Jerome to Nicholas of Cusa*, tr. J. C. Frakes (Washington, DC, 1988)

Bienvenu, J.-M., 'Pauvreté, misères et charité en Anjou aux XIe et XIIe siècles', *Le Moyen Age* 72 (1966), 387–424, and 73 (1967), 5–33, 189–216

Bienvenu, J.-M., 'Fondations charitables laiques au XIIe siècle: l'exemple de l'Anjou', in M. Mollat, ed., *Études sur l'histoire de la pauvreté (Moyen Age–XVIe siècle)*, 2 vols (Paris, 1974), II. 563–69

Bijsterveld, A.-J., 'The Medieval Gift as Agent of Social Bonding and Political Power: A Comparative Approach', in E. Cohen and M. de Jong, eds, *Medieval Transformations: Texts, Power, and Gifts in Context* (Leiden, 2001), 123–56

Bird, J., 'The Religious's Role in a Post-Fourth-Lateran World', in C. Muessig, ed., *Medieval Monastic Preaching* (Leiden, 1998), 209–29

Bird, J., 'Reform or Crusade? Anti-Usury and Crusade Preaching during the Pontificate of Innocent III', in J. C. Moore, ed., *Pope Innocent III and his World* (Aldershot, 1999), 165–85

Bird, J., 'Medicine for Body and Soul: Jacques de Vitry's Sermons to Hospitallers and their Charges', in P. Biller and J. Ziegler, eds, *Religion and Medicine in the Middle Ages* (York, 2001), 91–108

Bird, J., 'The Wheat and the Tares: Peter the Chanter's Circle and the Fama-Based Inquest Against Heresy and Criminal Sins, c.1198–1235', *Proceedings of the Twelfth International Congress of Medieval Canon Law: Washington DC: 1–7 August 2004*, MIC C, 13 (Vatican City, 2008), 763–856

Bischoff, B., 'Bücher am Hofe Ludwigs des Deutschen und die Privatbibliothek des Kanzlers Grimalt', in his *Mittelalterliche Studien: Ausgewählte Aufsätze zur Schriftkunde und Literaturgeschichte*, III (Stuttgart, 1981), 187–212

Bittermann, H. R., 'The Council of Chalcedon and Episcopal Jurisdiction', *Speculum* 13:2 (1938), 198–203

Blecker, M. P., 'Roman Law and "Consilium" in the Regula Magistri and the Rule of St Benedict', *Speculum* 47 (1972), 1–28

Blumenthal, U.-R., 'Conciliar Canons and Manuscripts: The Implications of their Transmission in the Eleventh Century', in *Proceedings of the Ninth International Congress of Medieval Canon Law, Munich, 13–18 July 1992*, MIC C, 10 (Vatican City, 1997), 357–79

Boeckl, C. M., *Images of Leprosy: Disease, Religion and Politics in European Art* (Kirksville, MO, 2011)

Bolton, B., 'Mulieres Sanctae', in D. Baker, ed., *Sanctity and Secularity: The Church and the World*, Studies in Church History 10 (Oxford, 1973), 77–95

Bolton, B., 'Fulk of Toulouse: The Escape that Failed', in D. Baker, ed., *Church, Society and Politics*, Studies in Church History 12 (Oxford, 1975), 83–93

Bolton, B., 'Hearts Not Purses? Innocent III's Attitude to Social Welfare', in E. Albu, ed., *Through the Eye of a Needle: Judeo-Christian Roots of Social Welfare* (Kirksville, MO, 1994), 123–45

Bolton, B., 'A Show with a Meaning: Innocent III's Approach to the Fourth Lateran Council, 1215', *Medieval History* 1 (1991), 53–67, repr. in her *Innocent III: Studies on Papal Authority and Pastoral Care* (Aldershot, 1995), 15–67

Bolton, B., 'Faithful to Whom? Jacques de Vitry and the French Bishops', *Revue Mabillon* NS 9 (1998), 53–72

Bolton, B., 'Thirteenth-Century Women Religious: Further Reflections on the Low Countries "Special Case"', in J. Dor, L. Johnson, and J. Wogan-Browne, eds, *New Trends in Feminine Spirituality: The Holy Women of Liège and their Impact* (Turnhout, 1999), 129–57

Bolton, B., 'Pastor Bonus: Matthew Paris's Life of Stephen Langton, Archbishop of Canterbury (1207–28)', *Nederlands Archief voor Kerkgeschiedenis* 84:1 (2004), 57–70

Bolton, B., 'The Absentee Lord? Alexander III and the Patrimony', in P. D. Clarke and A. Duggan, eds, *Pope Alexander III (1159–81): The Art of Survival* (Aldershot, 2010), 153–80

Bonenfant, P., *Hôpitaux et bienfaisance publique dans les anciens Pays-Bas des origines à la fin du XVIIIe siècle*, Annales de la Société Belge d'Histoire des Hôpitaux 3 (Brussels, 1965)

Bonenfant-Feytmans, A.-M., 'Les organisations hospitalières vues par Jacques de Vitry (1225)', *Annales de la Société Belge d'Histoire des Hôpitaux* 18 (1980), 19–45

Booker, C. M., *Past Convictions: The Penance of Louis the Pious and the Decline of the Carolingians* (Philadelphia PA, 2009)

Borgolte, M., 'Die Stiftungen des Mittelalters in rechts- und sozialhistorischer Sicht', *ZRG* 150 Kan. Abt. 74:1 (1988), 71–94

Borgolte, M., *Enzyklopädie des Stiftungswesens in Mittelalterlichen Gesellschaften*, I (Berlin, 2014)

Borgolte, M., 'Foundations "for the Salvation of the Soul": An Exception in World History?', *Medieval Worlds* 1 (2015), 86–105

Boshof, E., *Erzbischof Agobard von Lyon: Leben und Werk* (Vienna, 1969)

Boshof, E., 'Armenfürsorge im Frühmittelalter: Xenodochium, matricula, hospitale pauperum', *Vierteljahrschrift für Sozial- und Wirtschaftsgeschichte* 71:2 (1984), 153–74

Bottazzi, M., 'Tra papato e impero: L'uso dell'epigrafia nei secoli XI e XII a Viterbo', *Studi medievali*, 3rd ser. 47 (2006), 305–50

Boureau, A. 'Privilege in Medieval Societies from the Twelfth to the Fourteenth Centuries, or: How the Exception Proves the Rule', in P. Linehan and J. L. Nelson, eds, *The Medieval World* (London, 2001), 621–34

Bowman, J. A., 'Do Neo-Romans Curse? Law, Land and Ritual in the Midi (900–1100)', *Viator* 28 (1997), 1–32

Boyle, L. E., 'A Committee Stage at the Council of Vienne', in R. J. Castillo Lara, ed., *Studia in honorem emenentissimi cardinalis Alphonsi M. Stickler*, Studia et textus historiae iuris canonici 7 (Rome, 1992), 25–35

Brenner, E., *Leprosy and Charity in Medieval Rouen*, The Royal Historical Society's Studies in History, NS (Woodbridge, 2015)

Brett, M., 'Canon Law and Litigation: The Century before Gratian', in M. J. Franklin and C. Harper-Bill, eds, *Medieval Ecclesiastical Studies in Honour of Dorothy M. Owen* (Woodbridge, 1995), 21–40

Brett, M., and R. Somerville, 'The Transmission of the Council from 1130 to 1139', in J. Doran and D. J. Smith, eds, *Pope Innocent II (1130–43): The World vs. the City, Church, Faith and Culture in the Medieval West* (London, 2016), 226–71

Brodman, J. W., *Charity and Welfare: Hospitals and the Poor in Medieval Catalonia* (Philadelphia, PA, 1998)

Brodman, J. W., 'Religion and Discipline in the Hospitals of Thirteenth-Century France', in B. S. Bowers, ed., *The Medieval Hospital and Medical Practice* (Aldershot, 2007), 123–32

Brodman, J. W., *Charity and Religion in Medieval Europe* (Washington, DC, 2009)

Brody, S. N., *The Disease of the Soul: Leprosy in Medieval Literature* (Ithaca, NY, 1974)

Brooke, Z. N., *The English Church and the Papacy: From the Conquest to the Reign of John* (Cambridge, 1931)

Brown, P., *The Rise of Western Christendom: Triumph and Diversity, AD 200–1000*, 2nd ed. (Malden, MA, 1997)

Brown, P., *Poverty and Leadership in the Later Roman Empire* (Hanover, NH, 2002)

Brown, P. *Through the Eye of a Needle: Wealth, the Fall of Rome, and the Making of Christianity in the West, 350–550 AD* (Princeton, 2012)

Brown, P., 'From *Patriae Amator* to *Amator Pauperum* and Back Again: Social Imagination and Social Change in the West between Late Antiquity and the Early Middle Ages, ca. 300–600', in D. T. Rodgers, B. Raman, and H. Reimitz, eds, *Cultures in Motion* (Princeton, 2014), 87–106

Brown, T. S., 'Louis the Pious and the Papacy: A Ravenna Perspective', in P. Godman and R. Collins, eds, *Charlemagne's Heir: New Perspectives on the Reign of Louis the Pious (814–40)* (Oxford, 1990), 297–307

Brown, T. S., 'Lombard Religious Policy in the Late Sixth and Seventh Centuries: The Roman Dimension', in G. Ausendda, P. Delogu, and C. Wickham, eds, *The Langobards before the Frankish Conquest: An Ethnographic Perspective*, Studies in Historical Archaeoethnology (Woodbridge, 2009), 289–308

Brown, W. C., 'The *gesta municipalia* and the Public Validation of Documents in Frankish Europe', in W. C. Brown, M. Costambeys, M. Innes, and A. Kosto, eds, *Documentary Culture and the Laity in the Early Middle Ages* (Cambridge, 2013), 95–124

Bruck, E. F., *Über Römisches Recht im Rahmen der Kulturgeschichte* (Berlin, 1954)

Brundage, J. A., 'Teaching Canon Law', in J. Van Engen, ed., *Learning Institutionalized Teaching in the Medieval University* (Notre Dame, IN, 2000), 177–96

Brunner, K., ed., *Special Issue: Themenschwerpunkt Europäische Spitäler. Mitteilungen des Instituts für Österreichische Geschichtsforschung* 115:3–4 (2007)

Buckland, W. W., *A Text-Book of Roman Law: From Augustus to Justinian*, 3rd ed. (Cambridge, 1963)

Bullough, D. A., 'Leo, *qui apud Hlotharium magni loci habebatur*, et le gouvernement du Regnum Italiae à l'époque carolingienne', *Le Moyen Age* 67 (1961), 221–45

Bullough, D. A., '*Baiuli* in the Carolingian *regnum Langobardorum* and the Career of Abbot Waldo (d. 813)', *English Historical Review* 305 (1962), 625–37

Bulst, N., and K. H. Speiß, eds, *Sozialgeschichte mittelalterlicher Hospitäler* (Ostfildern, 2007)

Cabaniss, A., *Agobard of Lyons: Churchman and Critic* (Syracuse, NY, 1953)

Caille, J., *Hôpitaux et charité publique à Narbonne au Moyen Age de la fin du XIe à la fin du XVe siècle* (Toulouse, 1978)

Caron, P. G., 'L'evoluzione dalla *quarta pauperum* alla *pia fundatio* a scopo ospedaliero in alcuni testi della letteratura decretistica', *Il Diritto Ecclesiastico* 73 (1962), 137–59

Carrino, A., 'From the Criticism of Neo-Kantianism to Neo-Hegelianism in the Philosophy of Law', in E. Pattaro and C. Roversi, eds, *A Treatise of Legal Philosophy and General Jurisprudence XII: Legal Philosophy in the Twentieth Century: The Civil Law World I* (Berlin, 2016), 189–207

Cheney, C. R., *English Synodalia of the Thirteenth Century*, 2nd ed. (Oxford, 1968)

Cheney, M., 'The Council of Westminster 1175: New Light on an Old Source', in D. Baker, ed., *Sources and Methods of Ecclesiastical History*, Studies in Church History 11 (Oxford, 1975), 61–8

Chitwood, Z., 'The Proprietary Church and Monastery in Byzantium and the Eastern Christian World', *Viator* 47:3 (2016), 27–46

Chitwood, Z., 'Endowment Studies: Interdisciplinary Perspectives', *Endowment Studies* 1 (2017), 1–59

Chodorow, S., 'A Group of Decretals by Alexander III', in 'Three Notes on Decretal Letters', *Bulletin of Medieval Canon Law* NS 3 (1973), 51–5

Cipollone, G., 'Les Trinitaires: Fondation du XIIe siècle pour les captifs et pour les pauvres', in J. Dufour and H. Platelle, eds, *Fondations et œuvres charitables au Moyen Age* (Paris, 1999), 75–87

Cipollone, G., ed., *La liberazione dei 'captivi' tra Cristianità e Islam: Oltre la Crociata e il Gihād: Tolleranza e servizio umanitario*, Collectanea archivi Vaticani 46 (Vatican City, 2000)

Clarke, P. D., 'The Collection of Gilbertus and the French Glosses in Brussels, Bibliothèque royale, MS 1407–09, and an Early Recension of *Compilatio secunda*', *ZRG Kan. Abt.* 117 (Berlin, 2000), 132–84

Clarke, P. D., *The Interdict in the Thirteenth Century: A Question of Collective Guilt* (Oxford, 2007)

Clarke, P. D., and A. J. Duggan, eds, *Pope Alexander III (1159–81): The Art of Survival* (Aldershot, 2010)

Claussen, M. A., *The Reform of the Frankish Church: Chrodegang of Metz and the* Regula canonicorum *in the Eighth Century*, Cambridge Studies in Medieval Life and Thought, 4th ser. (Cambridge, 2004)

Clay, R. M., *The Mediaeval Hospitals of England* (London, 1909)

Coates, S., 'The Bishop as Benefactor and Civic Patron: Alcuin, York, and Episcopal Authority in Anglo-Saxon England', *Speculum* 71:3 (1996), 529–58

Cohen, M. R., *Poverty and Charity in the Jewish Community of Medieval Egypt* (Princeton, 2005)

Coing, H., 'Remarks on the History of Foundations and their Role in the Promotion of Learning', *Minerva* 19:2 (1981), 271–81

Conklin, G., 'Stephen of Tournai and the Development of *aequitas canonica*: The Theory and Practice of Law after Gratian', in S. Chodorow, ed., *Proceedings of the Eighth International Congress of Medieval Canon Law, San Diego, University of California at La Jolla, 21–27 August 1988*, MIC C, 9 (Vatican City, 1992), 369–86

Connolly, D. K., 'Imagined Pilgrimage in the Itinerary Maps of Matthew Paris', *The Art Bulletin* 81:4 (1999), 598–622

Constable, G., '*Nona et decima*: An Aspect of Carolingian Economy', *Speculum* 35 (1960), 224–50

Constable, G., 'Monks and Canons in Carolingian Gaul: The Case of Rigrannus of Le Mans', in A. C. Murray, ed., *After Rome's Fall: Narrators and Sources of Early Medieval History: Essays Presented to Walter Goffart* (Toronto, 1998), 120–36

Constable, G., 'The Fourth Lateran Council's Constitutions on Monasticism' in A. A. Larson and A. Massironi, eds, *The Fourth Lateran Council and the Development of Canon Law and the ius commune*, Ecclesia militans 7 (Turnhout, 2018), 147–57

Constantelos, D. J., *Byzantine Philanthropy and Social Welfare* (New Brunswick, NJ, 1968)

Corcoran, S., 'Hincmar and his Roman Legal Sources', in R. Stone and C. West, eds, *Hincmar of Rheims: Life and Work* (Manchester, 2015), 129–55

Corcoran, S., 'Roman Law in Ravenna', in J. Herrin and J. Nelson, eds, *Ravenna: Its Role in Earlier Medieval Change and Exchange* (London, 2016), 163–97

Corran, E., *Lying and Perjury in Medieval Practical Thought: A Study in the History of Casuistry* (Oxford, 2018)

Cossar, R., 'Lay Women in the Hospitals of Late Medieval Bergamo', *Florilegium* 21 (2004), 43–65

Costambeys, M., M. Innes, and S. MacLean, *The Carolingian World* (Cambridge, 2011)

Cox, R. W., 'Gratian (circa 12th Century)', in D. R. Brunstetter and C. O'Driscoll, eds, *Just War Thinkers: From Cicero to the 21st Century*, War, Conflict and Ethics Series (Abingdon, 2018), 34–49

Crislip, A. T., *From Monastery to Hospital: Christian Monasticism and the Transformation of Health Care in Late Antiquity* (Ann Arbor, MI, 2005)

Cubitt, C., 'Bishops and Councils in Late Saxon England: The Intersection of Secular and Ecclesiastical Law', in W. Hartmann, ed., *Recht und Gericht in Kirche und Welt um 900* (Munich, 2007), 151–68

Cullum, P. H., 'St Leonard's Hospital, York, in 1287', in D. Smith, ed., *The Church in Medieval York: Records Edited in Honour of Professor Barrie Dobson*, Borthwick Texts and Calendars 24 (York, 1999), 17–28

Curta, F., 'Merovingian and Carolingian Gift Giving', *Speculum* 81 (2006), 671–99

Cushing, K. G., *Papacy and Law in the Gregorian Revolution: The Canonistic Work of Anselm of Lucca* (Oxford, 1998)

Cushing, K. G., *Reform and the Papacy in the Eleventh Century: Spirituality and Social Change* (Manchester, 2005)

Dannenberg, L.-A., 'Charity and Law: The Juristic Implementation of a Core Monastic Principle', in G. Melville, ed., *Aspects of Charity Concern for one's Neighbour in Medieval vita religiosa* (Berlin, 2011), 11–28

Davis, A. J., *The Holy Bureaucrat: Eudes Rigaud and Religious Reform in Thirteenth-Century Normandy* (Ithaca, NY, 2006)

Davis, A. J., 'Preaching in Thirteenth-Century Hospitals', *Journal of Medieval History* 36:1 (2010), 72–89

de Beauvillé, V., *Histoire de la ville de Montdidier*, 4 vols (Paris, 1857)

de Clercq, C., *La législation religieuse franque: Étude sur les actes de conciles et les capitulaires, les statuts diocésains et les règles monastiques*, 2 vols (1936, 1958)

De Spiegeler, P., 'La Léproserie de Cornillon et la Cité de Liège (XIIᵉ–XVᵉ siècle)', *Annales de la Société belge d'histoire des hôpitaux* 18 (1980), 5–16

De Spiegeler, P., *Les hôpitaux et l'assistance à Liège (Xᵉ–XVᵉ siècles): Aspects institutionnels et sociaux* (Paris, 1987)

De Spiegeler, P., 'Les structures hospitalières de quelques villes mosanes du diocèse de Liège', in P. Montaubin, ed., *Hôpitaux et maladreries au Moyen Age: Espace et environnement* (Amiens, 2004), 101–12

Dehaisnes, C., *Manuscrits de la bibliothèque de Douai*, Catalogue général des manuscrits des bibliothèques publiques des départements 6 (Paris, 1878)

Delivré, F., 'The Foundations of Primatial Claims in the Western Church (Eleventh–Thirteenth Centuries)', *Journal of Ecclesiastical History* 59 (2008), 383–406

Depreux, P., 'The Development of Charters Confirming Exchange by the Royal Administration (Eighth–Tenth Centuries)', in K. Heidecker, ed., *Charters and the Use of the Written Word in Medieval Society* (Turnhout, 2000), 43–62

Depreux, P., '*Hincmar et la loi* Revisited: on Hincmar's use of Capitularies', in R. Stone and C. West, eds, *Hincmar of Rheims: Life and Work* (Manchester, 2015), 156–69

Depreux, P., 'The Penance of Attigny (822) and the Leadership of the Bishops in Amending Carolingian Society', in R. Meens, D. van Espelo, B. van den Hoven van Genderen, J. Raaijmakers, I. van Renswoude, and C. van Rhijn, eds, *Religious Franks: Religion and Power in the Frankish Kingdoms: Studies in Honour of Mayke de Jong* (Manchester, 2017), 370–85

Devisse, J., 'L'influence de Julien Pomère sur les clercs carolingiens [De la pauvreté au Ve et IXe siècles]', *Revue d'histoire de l'Église de France* 56:157 (1970), 285–95

Dey, H. W., '*Diaconiae, xenodochia, hospitalia* and Monasteries: "Social Security" and the Meaning of Monasticism', *Early Medieval Europe* 16 (2008), 398–422

Dickson, M. and C., 'Le cardinal Robert de Courson: Sa vie', *Archives: D'Histoire Doctrinale et Littéraire du Moyen Age* 9 (1934), 53–142

Didier, N., 'Henri de Suse en Angleterre (1236?–1244)', in *Studi in Onore di Vincenzo Arangio-Rviz nel XLV anno del suo insegnamento*, 4 vols (Naples, 1953), II. 333–51

Diem, A., 'The Carolingians and the *Regula Benedicti*', in R. Meens, D. van Espelo, B. van den Hoven van Genderen, J. Raaijmakers, I. van Renswoude, and C. van Rhijn, eds, *Religious Franks: Religion and Power in the Frankish Kingdoms: Studies in Honour of Mayke de Jong* (Manchester, 2017), 243–61

Dierkens, A., 'La Christianisation des campagnes de l'Empire de Louis le Pieux: L'Example du diocèse de Liège sous l'épiscopat de Walcaud (*c.*809–*c.*831)', in P. Godman and R. Collins, eds, *Charlemagne's Heir: New Perspectives on the Reign of Louis the Pious* (Oxford, 1990), 309–29

Dionisotti, A. C., 'Greek Grammars and Dictionaries in Carolingian Europe', in M. W. Herren, ed., *The Sacred Nectar of the Greeks: The Study of Greek in the West in the Early Middle Ages*, Kings College London Medieval Studies 2 (London, 1988), 1–56

Donohue Jr., C., 'The Dating of Alexander the Third's Marriage Decretals: Dauvillier Revisited After Fifty Years', *ZRG Kan. Abt.* 68 (1982), 70–124

Dor, J., L. Johnson, and J. Wogan-Browne, eds, *New Trends in Feminine Spirituality: The Holy Women of Liège and their Impact* (Turnhout, 1999)

Drossbach, G., 'Das Hospital—eine kirchenrechtliche Institution? (ca. 1150–ca. 1350)', *ZRG* 118 Kan. Abt. 87 (2001), 510–22

Drossbach, G., *Christliche caritas als Rechtsinstitut: Hospital und Orden von Santo Spirito in Sassia (1198-1378)* (Paderborn, 2005)

Drossbach, G., ed., *Hospitäler in Mittelalter und Früher Neuzeit: Frankreich, Deutschland und Italien. Eine vergleichende Geschichte/Hôpitaux au Moyen Age et aux Temps modernes: France, Allemagne et Italie, Une histoire comparée* (Oldenbourg, 2007)

Drossbach, G., 'Hospitäler in Patrimonium Petri', in M. Scheutz, A. Sommerlechner, H. Weigl, and A. S. Weiß, eds, *Europäisches Spitalwesen: Institutionelle Fürsorge in Mittelalter und Früher Neuzeit*, Mitteilungen des Instituts für Österreichische Geschichtsforschung, Ergänzungsband 51 (Vienna, 2008), 41–52, 91–104

Duff, P. W., *Personality in Roman Private Law* (Cambridge, 1938)

Duggan, A. J., 'Conciliar Law 1123-1215: The Legislation of the Four Lateran Councils', in W. Hartmann and K. Pennington, eds, *The History of Medieval Canon Law in the*

Classical Period, 1140–1234: From Gratian to the Decretals of Pope Gregory IX (Washington, DC, 2008), 318–66

Duggan, A. J., '*De consultationibus*: The Role of Episcopal Consultation in the Shaping of Canon Law in the Twelfth Century', in B. C. Brasington and K. G. Cushing, eds., *Bishops, Texts and the Use of Canon Law around 1100: Essays in Honour of Martin Brett* (Aldershot, 2008), 191–214

Duggan, A. J., 'Making Law or Not? The Function of Papal Decretals in the Twelfth Century', in P. Erdö and S. Szuromi, eds, *Proceedings of the Thirteenth International Congress of Medieval Canon Law, Esztergom, 3–8 August 2008*, MIC C, 14 (Vatican City, 2010), 41–70

Duggan, A. J., 'Master of the Decretals: A Reassessment of Alexander III's Contribution to Canon Law', in P. D. Clarke and A. Duggan, eds., *Pope Alexander III (1159–81): The Art of Survival* (Aldershot, 2010), 365–417

Duggan, A. J., '"Justinian's Laws, Not the Lord's": Eugenius III and the Learned Laws', in I. Fonnesberg-Schmidt and A. Jotischky, eds, *Pope Eugenius III (1145–1153): The First Cistercian Pope* (Amsterdam, 2018), 27–68

Duggan, C., 'English Canonists and the *Appendix concilii Lateranensis*', *Traditio* 18 (1962), 459–68

Duggan, C., *Twelfth-Century Decretal Collections and their Importance in English History* (London, 1963)

Duggan, C., 'The Reception of Canon Law in England in the Later-Twelfth Century', in S. Kuttner and J. J. Ryan, eds, *Proceedings of the Second International Congress of Medieval Canon Law, Boston College, 12–16 August 1963*, MIC C, 1 (Vatican City, 1965), 359–90, repr. in C. Duggan, *Canon Law in Medieval England: The Becket Dispute and Decretal Collections* (London, 1982), no. 11

Duggan, C., 'Decretals of Alexander III to England', in F. Liotta, ed., *Miscellanea Rolando Bandinelli, Papa Alessandro III* (Siena, 1986), 87–151, repr. in C. Duggan, *Decretals and the Creation of 'New Law' in the Twelfth Century: Judges, Judgements, Equity and Law* (Aldershot, 1998), no. 3

Duggan, C., 'English Secular Magnates in the Decretal Collections', in S. Chodorow, ed., *Proceedings of the Eighth International Congress of Medieval Canon Law, San Diego, University of California at La Jolla, 21–27 August 1988*, MIC C, 9 (Vatican City, 1992), 593–616

Duggan, C., 'Papal Judges Delegate and the Making of the "New Law" in the Twelfth Century', in T. N. Bisson, ed., *Cultures of Power: Lordship, Status and Process in Twelfth-Century Europe* (Philadelphia, PA, 1995), 172–99

Duggan, C., *Decretals and the Creation of 'New Law' in the Twelfth Century: Judges, Judgements, Equity and Law* (Aldershot, 1998)

Duggan, C., 'Decretal Collections from Gratian's *Decretum* to the *Compilationes antiquae*: The Making of the New Case Law', in W. Hartmann and K. Pennington, eds, *The History of Medieval Canon Law in the Classical Period, 1140–1234: From Gratian to the Decretals of Pope Gregory IX* (Washington, DC, 2008), 246–92

Dulfour, J., and H. Platelle, eds, *Fondations et œuvres charitables au Moyen Age: Actes du 121e congrés national des sociétés historique et scientifiques, section histoire médiévale et philologie* (Paris, 1999)

Durand, G., 'Richard de Gerberoy, évêque d'Amiens: Ce qu'on peut savoir de son œuvre littéraire', *Bibliothèque de l'école des chartes* 99 (1938), 268–96

du Plessis, P., 'Property', in D. Johnston, ed., *The Cambridge Companion to Roman Law* (Cambridge, 2015), 175–98

Ekonomou, A. J., *Byzantine Rome and the Greek Popes: Eastern Influences on Rome and the Papacy from Gregory the Great to Zacharias, A.D. 590–752* (Lanham, MD, 2007)

Elkins, S. K., *Holy Women of Twelfth-Century England* (Chapel Hill, NC, 1988)

Erdmann, C., and G. Laehrs, 'Ein karolingischer Konzilsbrief und der Fürstenspiegel Hincmars von Reims', *Neues Archiv der Gesellschaft für Ältere deutsche Geschichtskunde* 50 (1935), 106–34

Esders, S., *Römische Rechtstradition und merowingisches Königtum: Zum Rechtscharakter politischer Herrschaft in Burgund im 6. und 7. Jahrhundert* (Göttingen, 1997)

Esders, S., and S. Patzold, 'From Justinian to Louis the Pious: Inalienability of Church Property and the Sovereignty of a Ruler in the Ninth Century', in R. Meens, D. van Espelo, B. van den Hoven van Genderen, J. Raaijmakers, I. van Renswoude, and C. van Rhijn, eds, *Religious Franks: Religion and Power in the Frankish Kingdoms: Studies in Honour of Mayke de Jong* (Manchester, 2017), 386–408

Esders, S., and H. Reimitz, 'After Gundovald, before Pseudo-Isidore: Episcopal Jurisdiction, Clerical Privilege and the Uses of Roman Law in the Frankish Kingdoms', *Early Medieval Europe* 27:1 (2019), 85–111

Everett, N., 'Literacy and the Law in Lombard Government', *Early Medieval Europe* 9 (2000), 93–127

Everett, N., 'Lay Documents and Archives in Early Medieval Spain and Italy, c.400–700', in W. C. Brown, M. Costambeys, M. Innes, and A. Kosto, eds, *Documentary Culture and the Laity in the Early Middle Ages* (Cambridge, 2013), 63–94

Eyler, J., 'Introduction: Breaking Boundaries, Building Bridges', in J. Eyler, ed., *Disability in the Middle Ages: Reconsiderations and Reverberations* (Aldershot, 2010), 1–10

Farmer, S., 'The Leper in the Master Bedroom: Thinking Through a Thirteenth-Century Exemplum', in R. Voaden and D. Wolfthal, eds, Framing the Family: Narrative and Representation in the Medieval and Early Modern Periods (Tempe, AZ, 2005), 79–100

Fasolt, C., 'A New View of William Durant the Younger's "Tractatus de modo generalis concilii celebrandi"', *Traditio* 37 (1981), 291–324

Fasolt, C., *Council and Hierarchy: The Political Thought of William Durant the Younger*, Cambridge Studies in Medieval Life and Thought, 4th ser. (Cambridge, 1991)

Faulkner, T., *Law and Authority in the Early Middle Ages: The Frankish leges in the Carolingian Period*, Cambridge Studies in Medieval Life and Thought, 4th ser. (Cambridge, 2016)

Feenstra, R., 'Foundations in Continental Law since the 12th Century: The Legal Person Concept and Trust-Like Devices', in R. Helmholz and R. Zimmermann, eds, *Itinera Fiduciae: Trust and Treuhand in Historical Perspective*, Comparative Studies in Continental and Anglo-American Legal History 19 (Berlin, 1998), 305–26

Felten, F. J., *Äbte und Laienäbte im Frankenreich: Studie zum Verhältnis von Staat und Kirche im früheren Mittelalter*, Monographien zur Geschichte des Mittelalters 20 (Stuttgart, 1980)

Felten, F. J., 'Konzilsakten als Quellen für die Gesellschaftsgeschichte des westfränkischen Reiches um die Mitte des 9. Jahrhunderts', in *Proceedings of the Ninth International Congress of Medieval Canon Law, Munich, 13–18 July 1992*, MIC C, 10 (Vatican City, 1997), 339–56

Ferruolo, S. C., 'The Paris Statutes of 1215 Reconsidered', *History of Universities* 5 (1985), 1–14

Finn, R., *Almsgiving in the Later Roman Empire: Christian Promotion and Practice, 313–450* (Oxford, 2006)

Fiori, A., 'Roman Law Sources and Canonical Collections in the Early Middle Ages', *Bulletin of Medieval Canon Law* 34 (2017), 1–31

Fischer Drew, K., 'Another Look at the Origins of the Middle Ages: A Reassessment of the Role of the Germanic Kingdoms', *Speculum* 62:4 (1987), 803–12

Fontette, M., *Les religieuses à l'âge classique du droit canon: Recherches sur les structures juridiques des branches féminines des Ordres* (Paris, 1967)

Foreville, R., *Latran I, II, III et Latran IV*, Histoire des conciles oecuméniques 6 (Paris, 1965)

Foreville, R., *Le Pape Innocent III et la France*, Päpste und Papsttum 26 (Stuttgart, 1992)

Foreville, R., and J. R. de Pina, *Du premier Concile du Latran à l'avènement d'Innocent III*, Histoire de l'Église: Depuis les origins jusqu'à nos jours (Paris, 1944)

Forni, A., 'La "nouvelle prédication" des disciples de Foulques de Neuilly: intentions, techniques et réactions', in *Faire croire: Modalités de la diffusion et de la réception des messages religieux du XIIe au XVe siècle*, Collection de l'école française de Rome 51 (Rome, 1981), 19–37

Fouracre, P., 'Carolingian Justice: the Rhetoric of Improvement and Contexts of Abuse', in *La giustizia nell'alto medioevo (secoli v–viii)*, II. Settimane di Studio del centro Italiano di Studi sull' alto medioevo 42 (Spoleto, 1995), 771–803

Fouracre, P., 'Eternal Light and Earthly Needs: Practical Aspects of the Development of Frankish Immunities', in W. Davies and P. Fouracre, eds, *Property and Power in the Early Middle Ages* (Cambridge, 1995), 53–81

Fouracre, P., *The Age of Charles Martel* (London, 2000)

Fouracre, P., 'The Use of the Term *Beneficium* in Frankish Sources: A Society Based on Favours?', in W. Davies and P. Fouracre, eds, *The Languages of Gift in the Early Middle Ages* (Cambridge, 2010), 62–88

Frank, T., 'Spätmittelalterliche Hospitalreformen und Kanonistik', *Reti Medievali Rivista* 11 (2010), 1–40

Fuhrmann, H., 'The Pseudo-Isidorian Forgeries', in D. Jasper and H. Fuhrmann, eds, *Papal Letters in the Early Middle Ages* (Washington, DC, 2001), 135–95

Gadille, J., *Le diocèse de Lyon*, Histoire des diocèses de France 16 (Paris, 1983)

Gallagher, C., *Canon Law and the Christian Community: The Role of Law in the Church According to the Summa Aurea of Cardinal Hostiensis*, Analecta Gregoriana 208 (Rome, 1978)

Gallagher, C., *Church Law and Church Order in Rome and Byzantium: A Comparative Study* (Aldershot, 2002)

Ganshof, F. L., 'Jean Imbert, Les hôpitaux en droit canonique [compte-rendu]', *L'Antiquité Classique* 18:1 (1949), 214–15

Ganshof, F. L., *Recherches sur les capitulaires* (Paris, 1958)

Ganshof, F. L., 'Le droit romain dans les capitulaires et dans la collection d'Ansegise', *Ius Romanum Medii Aevi*, pt 1, 2b, *cc* alphabeta (Milan, 1969), 1–43

Ganshof, F. L., 'Charlemagne's Programme of Imperial Government', in F. L. Ganshof, *The Carolingians and Frankish Monarchy: Studies in Carolingian History*, tr. J. Sondheimer (London, 1971), 55–85

Ganz, D., *Corbie in the Carolingian Renaissance*, Beihefte der Francia 20 (Sigmaringen, 1990)

Ganz, D., 'The *Epitaphium Arsenii* and Opposition to Louis the Pious', in P. Godman and R. Collins, eds, *Charlemagne's Heir: New Perspectives on the Reign of Louis the Pious (814–840)* (Oxford, 1990), 537–50

Ganz, D., 'The Ideology of Sharing: Apostolic Community and Ecclesiastical Property in the Early Middle Ages', in W. Davies and P. Fouracre, eds, *Property and Power in the Early Middle Ages* (Cambridge, 1995), 17–30

García y García, A., 'The Fourth Lateran Council and the Canonists', in W. Hartmann and K. Pennington, eds, *The History of Medieval Canon Law in the Classical Period, 1140–1234: From Gratian to the Decretals of Pope Gregory IX* (Washington, DC, 2008), 367–78

Gaudemet, J., 'Survivances Romaines dans le droit de la monarchie Franque du Vème au Xème siècle', *Tijdschrift voor Rechtsgeschiedenis* 23 (1955), 149–206

Gaudemet, J., *Le gouvernement de l'église à l'époque classique IIe partie: Le gouvernement local*, Histoire du droit et des institutions de l'église en Occident 8:2 (Paris, 1979)

Gazzini, M., ed., *Studi confraternali: orientamenti, problemi, testimonianze* (Florence, 2009)

Gazzini, M., 'Le rete ospedaliera di Bobbio fra alto e basso medioevo', in E. Destefanis and P. Guglielmotti, *La diocesi di Bobbio: Formazione e sviluppi di un'istituzione millenaria* (Florence, 2015), 481–507

Gibbs, M., and J. Lang, *Bishops and Reform 1215–1272, with Special Reference to the Lateran Council of 1215* (Oxford, 1934)

Gilchrist, J. T., *Canon Law in the Age of Reform, 11th–12th Centuries* (Farnham, 1993)

Gilchrist, R., *Contemplation and Action: The Other Monasticism* (London, 1995)

Glendinning, R., 'Eros, Agape, and Rhetoric around 1200: Gervase of Melkley's *Ars poetica* and Gottfried von Strassburg's *Tristan*', *Speculum* 67:4 (1992), 892–925

Goffart, W., *The Le Mans Forgeries: A Chapter from the History of Church Property in the Ninth Century* (Cambridge, MA, 1966)

Goodson, C. J., *The Rome of Pope Paschal I: Papal Power, Urban Renovation, Church Rebuilding and Relic Translation, 817–824*, Cambridge Studies in Medieval Life and Thought, 4th ser. (Cambridge, 2010)

Görich, K., *Otto III: Romanus Saxonicus et Italicus: Kaiserlich Rompolitik und sächsische Historiographie* (Sigmaringen, 1993)

Goudriaan, K., 'Early Hospital Development in the Provinces of Holland, Zealand and Utrecht', in his *Piety in Practice and Print: Essays on the Late Medieval Religious Landscape*, ed. A. Dlabacová and A. Tervoort (Hilversum, 2016), 31–73

Gougaud, L., *Les Chrétientés celtiques* (Paris, 1911)

Grüttner, M., 'Der Lehrkörper 1918–1932', in R. vom Bruch and H.-E. Tenorth, eds, *Geschichte der Universität Unter den Linden 1810–2010*, II. *Die Berliner Universität zwischen den Weltkriegen 1918–1945*, ed. M. Grüttner (Berlin, 2012), 135–86

Guglielmi, N., 'Modos de marginalidad en la edad media: Extranjería, Pobreza, Enfermedad (A propósito de estatutos de hospitals y leproserias)', *Anales de Historia Antigua y Medieval* 16 (1971), 7–188

Halfond, G. I., *The Archaeology of Frankish Church Councils, AD 511–768* (Leiden, 2010)

Hanenburg, J. J. H. M., 'Decretals and Decretal Collections in the Second Half of the Twelfth Century', *Tijdschrift voor Rechtsgeschiedenis* 34:4 (1966), 552–99

Hanssens, S., 'De legatiereis van Robert van Courson in Vlaanderen en Henegouwen', in *Miscellanea historica in honorem Alberti de Meyer*, 2 vols (Louvain, 1946), I. 528–38

Harouel, J.-L., 'Un grand savant et administrateur: Jean Imbert (1919–1999)', *Tijdschrift voor rechtsgeschiedenis/Revue historique de droit français et étranger* 78:1 (2000), 1–11

Harries, J., 'The Background of the Code', in J. Harries and I. Wood, eds, *The Theodosian Code: Studies in the Imperial Law of Late Antiquity* (London, 1993), 1–16

Hartmann, W., 'Vetera et nova: Altes und neues Kirchenrecht in den Beschlüssen karolingischer Konzilien', *Annuarium Historiae Conciliorum* 15 (1983), 79–95

Hartmann, W., *Die Synoden der Karolingerzeit im Frankenreich und in Italien*, Konziliengeschichte A: Darstellungen (Paderborn, 1989)

Hartmann, W., and K. Pennington, eds, *The History of Medieval Canon Law in the Classical Period, 1140-1234: From Gratian to the Decretals of Pope Gregory IX* (Washington, DC, 2008)

Hausmann, F.-R., *'Deutsche Geisteswissenschaft' im zweiten Weltkrieg: Die 'Aktion Ritterbusch' (1940-1945)* (Dresden, 1998)

Heckel, M., 'Siegfried Reicke †', *ZRG* 89 *Kan. Abt.* 58 (1972), xi–xix

Hefele, C. J., *A History of the Councils of the Church from the Original Documents*, tr. W. R. Clark, 5 vols (Edinburgh, 1872–96)

Heinen, S., 'Pseudoisidor auf dem Konzil von Aachen im Jahr 836', in K. Ubl and D. Ziemann, eds, *Fälschung als Mittel der Politik? Pseudoisidor im Licht der neuen Forschung* (Wiesbaden, 2015), 97–126

Helmholz, R. H., 'The Law of Charity and the English Ecclesiastical Courts', in P. Hoskin, C. Brooke, and B. Dobson, eds, *The Foundations of Medieval Ecclesiastical History: Studies Presented to David Smith* (Woodbridge, 2005), 111–23

Henderson, J., *The Renaissance Hospital: Healing the Body and Healing the Soul* (London, 2006)

Henderson, J., P. Horden, and A. Pastore, eds., *The Impact of Hospitals 400–1500* (Bern, 2007)

Hennigan, P., *The Birth of a Legal Institution: The Formation of the Waqf in the Third-Century A.H. Hanafi Legal Discourse* (Leiden, 2004)

Hildebrandt, M. M., *The External School in Carolingian Society* (Leiden, 1992)

Hillner, J., 'Families, Patronage, and the Titular Churches of Rome, *c.*300–*c.*600', in K. Cooper and J. Hillner, eds, *Religion, Dynasty, and Patronage in Early Christian Rome, 300–900* (Cambridge, 2007), 225–61

Hoffmann, H., and R. Pokorny, *Das Dekret des Bischofs Burchard von Worms: Textstufen, Frühe Verbreitung, Vorlagen* (Munich, 1991)

Honoré, T., *Law in the Crisis of Empire, 379–455 AD: The Theodosian Dynasty and its Quaestors* (Oxford, 1998)

Horden, P., 'Religion as Medicine: Music in Medieval Hospitals', in P. Biller and J. Ziegler, eds, *Religion and Medicine in the Middle Ages* (York, 2001), 135–53

Horden, P., 'The Earliest Hospitals in Byzantium, Western Europe, and Islam', *Journal of Interdisciplinary History* 35:3 (2005), 361–89

Horden, P., 'A Non-Natural Environment: Medicine without Doctors and the Medieval European Hospital', in B. S. Bowers, ed., *The Medieval Hospital and Medical Practice* (Aldershot, 2007), 133–45

Horden, P., 'Poverty, Charity, and the Invention of the Hospital', in S. F. Johnson, ed., *The Oxford Handbook of Late Antiquity* (Oxford, 2012), 715–43

Hourlier, J., *L'âge classique (1140–1378): Les religieux*, Histoire du Droit des Institutions de l'Église en Occident 10 (Paris, 1974)

Hubert, É., 'Hôpitaux et espace urbain à Rome au Moyen Age', in P. Montaubin, ed., *Hôpitaux et maladreries au Moyen Âge: espace et environnement* (Amiens, 2004), 113–29

Huffman, J. P., '*Potens et Pauper*: Charity and Authority in Jurisdictional Disputes over the Poor in Medieval Cologne', in R. C. Figueira, ed., *Plenitude of Power: The Doctrines and Exercise of Authority in the Middle Ages* (Aldershot, 2006), 107–24

Humfress, C., 'Poverty and Roman Law', in M. Atkins and R. Osborne, eds, *Poverty in the Roman World* (Cambridge, 2006), 183–203

Humfress, C., 'Law and Custom under Rome', in A. Rio, ed., *Law, Custom, and Justice in Late Antiquity and the Early Middle Ages: Proceedings of the 2008 Byzantine Colloquium* (London, 2011), 23–47

Humphress, C., 'Telling Stories about (Roman) Law: Rules and Concepts in Legal Discourse', in P. Dresch and J. Scheele, eds, *Legalism: Rules and Categories* (Oxford, 2015), 79–104

Imbert, J., *Les hôpitaux en droit canonique (du décret de Gratien à la sécularisation de l'administration de l'Hôtel-Dieu de Paris en 1505)*, L'Eglise et l'Etat au Moyen Age 8 (Paris, 1947)

Imbert, J., 'Le régime juridique des établissements hospitaliers du Nord de la France au Moyen Age', *Revue du Nord* 29 (1947), 195–204

Imbert, J., 'Le droit romain dans les textes juridiques carolingiens', in *Studi in onore di Pietro de Francisci*, 4 vols (Milan, 1956), III. 61–7

Imbert, J., ed., *Histoire des hôpitaux en France* (Toulouse, 1982)

Imbert, J., 'Les conciles et les hôpitaux (IXᵉ siecle)', in J. Dufour and H. Platelle, eds, *Fondations et œuvres charitables au moyen âge* (Paris, 1999), 39–47

Innes, M., 'The Classical Tradition in the Carolingian Renaissance: Ninth-Century Encounters with Suetonius', *International Journal of the Classical Tradition* 3:3 (1997), 265–82

Innes, M., 'Kings, Monks and Patrons: Political Identities and the Abbey of Lorsch', in R. Le Jan, ed., *La royauté et les élites dans l'Europe carolingienne (du début du IXᵉ siècle aux environs de 920)* (Lille, 1998), 301–24

Innes, M., *State and Society in the Early Middle Ages: The Middle Rhine Valley, 400–1000*, Cambridge Studies in Medieval Life and Thought, 4ᵗʰ ser. (Cambridge, 2000)

Innes, M., 'Charlemagne's Government', in J. Story, ed., *Charlemagne: Empire and Society* (Manchester, 2005), 71–89

Innes, M., 'Charlemagne, Justice and Written Law' in A. Rio, ed., *Law, Custom, and Justice in Late Antiquity and the Early Middle Ages: Proceedings of the 2008 Byzantine Colloquium* (London, 2011), 155–203

Jankrift, K. P., 'Vieillir parmi les morts "vivants": La léproserie, hospice pour habitants non lépreux?', in B. Tabuteau, ed., *Lépreux et Sociabilité du Moyen Age aux Temps modernes* (Rouen, 2000), 31–8

Jasper, D., 'Papal Letters and Decretals Written from the Beginning through the Pontificate of Gregory the Great (to 604)', in D. Jasper and H. Fuhrmann, eds, *Papal Letters in the Early Middle Ages* (Washington, DC, 2001), 7–87

Jasper, D., 'Papal Letters of the Merovingian and Carolingian Periods', in D. Jasper and H. Fuhrmann, eds, *Papal Letters in the Early Middle Ages* (Washington, DC, 2001), 89–134

Johnston, D., 'Munificence and Municipia: Bequests to Towns in Classical Roman Law', *Journal of Roman Studies* 75 (1985), 105–25

Johnston, D., 'Trust and Trust-Like Devices in Roman Law', in R. Helmholz and R. Zimmermann, eds, *Itinera Fiduciae: Trust and Treuhand in Historical Perspective*, Comparative Studies in Continental and Anglo-American Legal History 19 (Berlin, 1998), 45–56

Jones, A. E., *Social Mobility in Late Antique Gaul: Strategies and Opportunities for the Non-Elite* (Cambridge, 2009)

Jones, A. W. 'Fulk of Neuilly, Innocent III, and the Preaching of the Fourth Crusade', *Comitatus: A Journal of Medieval and Renaissance Studies* 41 (2010), 119–48

Jong, M. de, 'Carolingian Monasticism: The Power of Prayer', in R. McKitterick, ed., *New Cambridge Medieval History*, II, *c.700–c.900* (Cambridge, 1995), 622–53

Jong, M. de, *In Samuel's Image: Child Oblation in the Early Medieval West* (Leiden, 1996)

Jong, M. de, 'Charlemagne's Church', in J. Story, ed., *Charlemagne: Empire and Society* (Manchester, 2005), 103–35

Jong, M. de, *The Penitential State: Authority and Atonement in the Age of Louis the Pious, 814–840* (Cambridge, 2009)

Jong, M. de, 'The State of the Church: *Ecclesia* and Early Medieval State Formation', in W. Pohl and V. Wieser, eds, *Der frühmittelalterliche Staat—Europäische Perspektive Forschungen zur Geschichte des Mittelalters* 16 (Vienna, 2009), 241–55

Jong, M. de, 'Paschasius Radbertus and Pseudo-Isidore: The Evidence of the *Epitaphium Arsenii*', in V. L. Garver and O. M. Phelan, eds, *Rome and Religion in the Medieval World: Studies in Honor of Thomas F. X. Noble* (Farnham, 2014), 149–72

Jong, M. de, 'The Empire that was Always Decaying: The Carolingians (800–888)', *Medieval Worlds* 2 (2015), 6–25

Jong, M. de, *Epitaph for an Era: Politics and Rhetoric in the Carolingian World* (Cambridge, 2019)

Jugnot, G., 'Deux fondations augustiniennes en faveur des pèlerins: Aubrac et Roncevaux', in M.-H. Vicaire, ed., *Assistance et charité*, Cahiers de Fanjeaux 13 (Toulouse, 1978), 321–41

Jürgasch, T., 'Christians and the Invention of Paganism in the Late Roman Empire', in M. R. Salzman, M. Sághy, and R. L. Testa, eds, *Pagans and Christians in Late Antique Rome: Conflict, Competition and Coexistence in the Fourth Century* (Cambridge, 2015), 115–38

Kaczynski, B. M., 'Some St. Gall Glosses on Greek Philanthropic Nomenclature', *Speculum* 58 (1983), 1008–17

Kaczynski, B. M., *Greek in the Carolingian Age: The St. Gall Manuscripts* (Cambridge, MA, 1988)

Kaiser, W., *Die Epitome Iuliani: Beiträge zum römischen Recht im frühen Mittelalter und zum byzantinischen Rechtsunterricht*, Studien zur europäischen Rechtsgeschichte 175 (Frankfurt am Main, 2004)

Kaiser, W., 'Justinian and the *Corpus Iuris Civilis*', in D. Johnston, ed., *The Cambridge Companion to Roman Law* (Cambridge, 2015), 119–48

Kantor, G., 'Property in Land in Roman Provinces', in G. Kantor, T. Lambert, and H. Skoda, eds, *Legalism: Property and Ownership* (Oxford, 2017), 55–74

Kasten, B., 'Erbrechtliche Verfügungen des 8. und 9. Jahrhunderts', *ZRG* 107 *Kan. Abt.* 76 (1990), 236–338

Kaufhold, H., 'Sources of Canon Law in the Eastern Churches', in W. Hartmann and K. Pennington, eds, *The History of Byzantine and Eastern Canon Law to 1500* (Washington, DC, 2012), 215–342

Kay, R., 'Mansi and Rouen: A Critique of the Conciliar Collections', *Catholic Historical Review* 52:2 (1966), 155–85

Kay, R., 'Romanus and Rouen: A Papal Legate's Tainted Visitation in 1227', *Annales de Normandie* 51:2 (2001), 111–19

Kearley, T. G., 'The Creation and Transmission of Justinian's Novels', *Law Library Journal* 102:3 (2010–11), 377–97

Kennedy, V. L., 'The Content of Courson's *Summa*', *Mediaeval Studies* 9 (1947), 81–107

Kéry, L., 'Ein neues Kapitel in der Geschichte des kirchlichen Strafrechts: Die Systematisierungsbemühungen des Bernhard von Pavia (†1213)', in W. P. Müller and

M. E. Sommar, eds, *Medieval Church Law and the Origins of the Western Legal Tradition: A Tribute to Kenneth Pennington* (Washington, DC, 2006), 229–51

Kéry, L., *Canonical Collections of the Early Middle Ages (ca. 400-1140): A Bibliographical Guide to the Manuscripts and Literature* (Washington DC, 2013)

Keyvanian, C., *Hospitals and Urbanism in Rome, 1200-1500* (Leiden, 2015)

Keyzer, W. de, 'Le léproserie Saint-Ladre de Mons et ses statuts de 1202', *Annales de la Société Belge D'histoire des Hôpitaux* 12 (1974), 3–18

Keyzer, W. de, 'L'évolution interne des léproseries à la charnière des XIIᵉ et XIIIᵉ siècles: Le cas de l'évêché de Cambrai', in B. Tabuteau, ed., *Lépreux et sociabilité du Moyen Age aux temps modernes* (Rouen, 2000), 13–20

Kletzer, C., 'Custom and Positivity: An Examination of the Philosophic Ground of the Hegel-Savigny Controversy', in A. Perreau-Saussine and J. B. Murphy, *The Nature of Customary Law* (Cambridge, 2007), 125–48

Klingshirn, W. E., *Caesarius of Arles: The Making of a Christian Community in Late Antique Gaul*, Cambridge Studies in Medieval Life and Thought, 4th ser. (Cambridge, 2004)

Knibbs, E., 'Ebo of Reims, Pseudo-Isidore, and the Date of the False Decretals', *Speculum* 92:1 (2017), 144–83

Knibbs, E., 'Pseudo-Isidore's Ennodius', *Deutsches Archiv für Erforschung des Mittelalters* 74 (2018), 1–52

Knowles, D., and R. N. Hadcock, *Medieval Religious Houses, England and Wales*, 2nd ed. (London, 1971)

Koziol, G., 'Christianizing Political Discourses', in J. H. Arnold, ed., *The Oxford Handbook of Medieval Christianity* (Oxford, 2014), 473–89

Kramer, R., 'Teaching Emperors: Transcending the Boundaries of Carolingian Monastic Communities', in E. Hovden, C. Lutter, and W. Pohl, eds, *Meanings of Community across Medieval Eurasia: Comparative Approaches* (Leiden, 2006), 309–37

Kramer, R., 'Order in the Church: Understanding Councils and Performing *ordines* in the Carolingian World', *Early Medieval Europe* 25:1 (2017), 54–69

Kramer, R., *Rethinking Authority in the Carolingian Empire* (Amsterdam, 2019)

Kramer, R., and C. Gantner, 'Lateran Thinking: Building an Idea of Rome in the Carolingian Empire', *Viator* 47:3 (2016), 1–26

Krautheimer, R., *Studies in Early Christian, Medieval and Renaissance Art* (New York, 1969)

Kuttner, S., *Repertorium der kanonistik (1140-1234): Prodromus corporis glossarum* I, Studi e testi 71 (Vatican City, 1937)

Kuttner, S., 'Bernardus Compostellanus Antiquus: A Study in the Glossators of the Canon Law', *Traditio* 1 (1943), 277–340

Kuttner, S., 'Some Considerations on the Role of Secular Law and Institutions in the History of Canon Law', in *Scritti di sociologia e politica in onore di Luigi Sturzo* II (Bologna, 1953), 351–62, repr. in S. Kuttner, *Studies in the History of Medieval Canon Law* (Aldershot, 1990), no. 6

Kuttner, S., 'Joannes Andreae and his *Novella* on the Decretals of Gregory XI: An Introduction', *Jurist* 24 (1964), 393–408

Kuttner, S., 'Raymond of Peñafort as Editor: The "Decretales" and "Constitutiones" of Gregory IX', *Bulletin of Medieval Canon Law* 12 (1982), 65–80, repr. in S. Kuttner, *Studies in the History of Medieval Canon Law*, no. 12

Kuttner, S., 'The Revival of Jurisprudence', in R. L. Benson, G. Constable, and C. D. Lanham, eds, *Renaissance and Renewal in the Twelfth Century* (Toronto, 1991), 299–323

Kuttner, S., and E. Rathbone, 'Anglo-Norman Canonists of the Twelfth Century: An Introductory Study', *Traditio* 7 (1949–51), 279–358

La Porte-du Theil, F. J. G., 'Notice et Extraits', in *Notices et extraits des manuscrits de la Bibliothèque nationale et autres bibliothèques*, VI (Paris, 1801)

Lacroix, M.-T., *L'Hôpital Saint-Nicholas du Bruille (Saint André) à Tournai de sa Fondation à sa mutation en Cloître (± 1230–1611)* (Louvain, 1977)

Laistner, M. L. W., 'Notes on Greek from the Lectures of a Ninth Century Monastery Teacher', *Bulletin of the John Rylands Library* 7 (1923), 421–56

Lalouette, J., 'Une laïcisation hospitalière menée tambour battant: L'exemple de Reims (1902–1903)', in Marie-Claude Dinet-Lecomte, ed., *Les hôpitaux, enjeux de pouvoir: France du Nord et Belgique (IVe–XXe siècle)*, Revue du Nord, hors série, Collection Histoire 22 (Lille, 2008), 247–64

Landau, P., *Jus patronatus: Studien zur Entwicklung des Patronats im Dekretalenrecht und der Kanonistik des 12. und 13. Jahrhunderts*, Forschungen zur kirchlichen Rechtsgeschichte und zum Kirchenrecht 12 (Cologne, 1975)

Landau, P., 'Die Entstehung der systematischen Dekretalensammlungen und die europäische Kanonistik des 12. Jahrhunderts', *ZRG* 96 *Kan. Abt.* 65 (1979), 120–48

Landau, P., 'Die Leprakranken im mittelalterlichen kanonischen Recht', in D. Schwab, D. Giesen, J. Listl, and H.-W. Strätz, eds, *Staat, Kirche, Wissenschaft in einer pluralistischen Gesellschaft: Festschrift zum 65. Geburtstag von Paul Mikat* (Berlin, 1989), 565–78

Landau, P., 'Bernardus Papiensis', in M. Stolleis, ed., *Juristen: Ein biographisches Lexikon*, 2nd ed. (Munich, 2001), 81–2

Landau, P., 'The Origins of Legal Science in England in the Twelfth Century: Lincoln, Oxford and the Career of Vacarius', in M. Brett and K. G. Cushing, eds, *Readers, Texts and Compilers in the Earlier Middle Ages: Studies in Medieval Canon Law in Honour of Linda Fowler-Magerl* (Farnham, 2009), 165–82

Landau, P., '*Collectio Fontanentis*: A Decretal Collection of the Twelfth Century for an English Cistercian Abbey', in K. Pennington and H. Eichbauer, eds, *Law as Profession and Practice in Medieval Europe: Essays in Honor of James A. Brundage* (Burlington, VT, 2011), 187–204

Lapidge, M., *Anglo-Latin Literature: 900–1066* (London, 1993)

Lapidge, M., *Hilduin of Saint-Denis: The* Passio S. Dionysii *in Prose and Verse*, Mittellateinische Studien und Texte 51 (Leiden, 2017)

Larson, A. A., 'Early Stages of Gratian's *Decretum* and the Second Lateran Council', *Bulletin of Medieval Canon Law* NS 27 (2007), 21–56

Larson, A. A., and A. Massironi, eds, *The Fourth Lateran Council and the Development of Canon Law and the* ius commune, Ecclesia militans 7 (Turnhout, 2018)

Le Blévec, D., 'Le rôle des femmes dans l'assistance et la charité', in E. Privat, ed., *La femme dans la vie religieuse du Languedoc*, Cahiers de Fanjeaux 23 (Toulouse, 1988), 171–90

Le Blévec, D., 'L'ordre canonial et hospitalier des Antonins', in *Le Monde des chanoines (XIe–XIVe s.)*, Cahiers de Fanjeaux 24 (Toulouse, 1989), 237–54

Le Blévec, D., 'Fondations et œuvres charitables au Moyen Age', in J. Dufour and H. Platelle, eds, *Fondations et œuvres charitables au Moyen Age* (Paris, 1999), 7–22

Le Blévec, D., *La part du pauvre: L'assistance dans les pays du Bas-Rhône du XIIe siècle au milieu du XVe siècle*, Collection de L'école française de Rome 265, 2 vols (Paris, 2000)

Le Bras, G., 'Les fondations privées du haut empire', in *Studi in onore di Salvatore Riccobono* (Palermo, 1936), III. 23–67

Le Clech-Charton, S., ed., *Les établissements hospitaliers en France du Moyen Age au XIXe siècle: Espaces, objets et populations* (Dijon, 2010)

Le Grand, Léon, 'Les béguines de Paris', *Mémoires de la Société de l'Histoire de Paris et de l'Ile-de-France* 20 (1893), 295–357

Le Grand, Léon, 'Les maisons-dieu: Leurs statuts au XIIIe siècle', *Revue des Questions Historiques* 60 (1896), 95–134

Le Grand, Léon, 'Les maisons-dieu: Leur régime intérieur au Moyen Age', *Revue des Questions Historiques* 63 (1898), 99–147

Le Grand, L., ed., *Statuts d'hôtels-dieu et de léproseries: recueil de textes du XIIe au XIVe siècle* (Paris, 1901)

Le Maho, J., 'Hospices et xenodochia du diocèse de Rouen à l'époque prénormande (VIe–IXe siècles)', in J. Dufour and H. Platelle, eds, *Fondations et œuvres charitables au Moyen Age* (Paris, 1999), 49–61

Lecler, J., *Le concile de Vienne 1311–1312*, Histoire des conciles œcuméniques 8 (Paris, 1964)

Lefevre, S., 'Les lépreux à Saint-Lazare de Paris aux XIIe–XIIIe siècles', in *Santé, médecine et assistance au Moyen Age: 110e congrès national des sociétés savantes, Montpellier 1985* (Paris, 1987), 399–409

Lesne, E., *Histoire de la propriété ecclésiastique en France*, 6 vols (Lille, 1910–43)

Lester, A. E., 'Cares beyond the Walls: Cistercian Nuns and the Care of Lepers in Twelfth- and Thirteenth-Century Northern France', in E. Jamroziak and J. Burton, eds, *Religious and Laity in Western Europe, 1000–1400: Interaction, Negotiation, and Power* (Turnhout, 2006), 197–224

Lester, A. E., *Creating Cistercian Nuns: The Women's Religious Movement and its Reform in Thirteenth-Century Champagne* (New York, 2011)

Levy, E., *West Roman Vulgar Law: The Law of Property* (Philadelphia, 1951)

Lewis, A., 'Slavery, Family, and Status', in D. Johnston, ed., *The Cambridge Companion to Roman Law* (Cambridge, 2015), 151–74

Leyser, K., *Communications and Power in Medieval Europe: The Carolingian and Ottonian Centuries*, ed. T. Reuter (London, 1994), 143–64

Liebs, D., 'Roman Law', in A. Cameron, B. Ward-Perkins, and M. Whitby, eds, *Cambridge Ancient History XIV: Late Antiquity: Empire and Successors, AC 425–600* (Cambridge, 2000), 238–59

Liebs, D., 'Roman Vulgar Law in Late Antiquity', in B. Sirks, ed., *Aspects of Law in Late Antiquity* (Oxford, 2008), 35–53

Linehan, P., 'Councils and Synods in Thirteenth-Century Castile and Aragon', in G. J. Cuming and D. Baker, eds, *Councils and Assemblies*, Studies in Church History 7 (Cambridge, 1971), 101–11

Little, L. K., *Benedictine Maledictions: Liturgical Cursing in Romanesque France* (Ithaca, NY, 1993)

Longère, J., ed., *Le troisième concile de Latran (1179): Sa place dans l'histoire* (Paris, 1982)

Longère, J., 'L'influence de Latran III sur quelques ouvrages de théologie morale', in J. Longère, ed., *Le troisième concile* (Paris, 1982), 91–110

Lunven, A., 'From *Plebs* to *Parochia*: The Perception of the Church in Space from the Ninth to the Twelfth Century (Dioceses of Rennes, Dol, and Saint-Malo)', in M. Cohen and F. Madeline, eds, *Space in the Medieval West: Places, Territories, and Imagined Geographies* (Farnham, 2014), 99–114

Lupoi, M., *The Origins of the European Legal Order*, tr. A. Belton (Cambridge, 2000)

Luttrell, A., 'The Earliest Hospitallers', in B. Z. Kedar, J. Riley-Smith, and R. Hiestand, eds, *Montjoie: Studies in Crusade History in Honour of Hans Eberhard Mayer* (Aldershot, 1997), 37–54

Lynch, J. H., *Simoniacal Entry into Religious Life from 1000 to 1260: A Social, Economic and Legal Study* (Columbus, OH, 1976)

Lynch, J. H., and P. C. Adamo, *The Medieval Church: A Brief History*, 2nd ed. (London, 2014)

McCormick Schoolman, E., 'Local Networks and Witness Subscriptions in Early Medieval Ravenna', *Viator* 44 (2013), 21–41

MacKay, D.-L., *Les hôpitaux et la charité à Paris au XIIIe siècle* (Paris, 1923)

McKeon, P. R., 'The Carolingian Councils of Savonnières (859) and Tusey (860) and their Background: A Study in the Ecclesiastical and Political History of the Ninth Century', *Revue Bénédictine*, 84 (1974), 75–110

McKitterick, R., *The Frankish Church and the Carolingian Reforms, 789–895* (London, 1977)

McKitterick, R., 'Some Carolingian Law Books and their Functions', in B. Tierney and P. Linehan, eds, *Authority and Power: Studies on Medieval Law and Government Presented to Walter Ullmann on his Seventieth Birthday* (Cambridge, 1980), 13–27

McKitterick, R., 'Knowledge of Canon Law in the Frankish Kingdoms before 789: The Manuscript Evidence', *Journal of Ecclesiastical History* 36 (1985), 97–117

McKitterick, R., *The Carolingians and the Written Word* (Cambridge, 1989)

McKitterick, R., *Charlemagne: The Formation of a European Identity* (Cambridge, 2008)

McKitterick, R., 'Charlemagne's *missi* and their Books', in S. Baxter, C. E. Karkov, J. L. Nelson, and D. Pelteret, eds, *Early Medieval Studies in Memory of Patrick Wormald* (Farnham, 2009), 253–67

Maclachlan, E. P., 'Liturgical Vessels and Implements', in T. J. Heffernan and E. A. Matter, eds, *The Liturgy of the Medieval Church* (Kalamazoo, MI, 2001), 369–429

MacLean, S. 'Legislation and Politics in Late Carolingian Italy: The Ravenna Constitutions', *Early Medieval Europe* 18 (2010), 394–416

Magnou-Nortier, E., 'Formes féminines de vie consacrée dans les pays du Midi jusqu'au début du XIIe siècle', in E. Privat, ed., *La femme dans la vie religieuse du Languedoc (VIIIe–XVe s.)*, Cahiers de Fanjeaux 23 (Toulouse, 1988), 193–216

Magnou-Nortier, E., 'The Enemies of the Peace: Reflections on a Vocabulary, 500–1100', in T. Head and R. Landes, eds, *The Peace of God: Social Violence and Religious Response in France around the Year 1000* (Ithaca, NY, 1992), 58–79

Makowski, E., *Canon Law and Cloistered Women: Periculoso and its Commentators, 1298–1545* (Washington, DC, 1997)

Makowski, E., *'A Pernicious Sort of Woman': Quasi-Religious Women and Canon Lawyers in the Later Middle Ages* (Washington, DC, 2005)

Maleczek, W., *Papst und Kardinalskolleg von 1191 bis 1216: Die Kardinäle unter Coelestin III. und Innocenz III.* (Vienna, 1984)

Marcombe, D., *Leper Knights: The Order of St Lazarus of Jerusalem in England, c.1150–1544* (Woodbridge, 2003)

Marec, Y., 'Le création de l'école d'infirmières de Rouen en 1900: Une laïcisation ou une modernisation des services hospitaliers?', in M.-C. Dinet-Lecomte, ed., *Les hôpitaux, enjeux de pouvoir: France du Nord et Belgique (IVe–XXe siècle)*, Revue du Nord, hors série, Collection Histoire 22 (Lille, 2008), 237–46

Maréchal, G., *De sociale en politieke gebondenheid van het Brugse hospitaalwezen in de Middeleeuwen*, Anciens pays et assemblées d'états 73 (Kortrijk-Heule, 1978)

Martin, H., *Catalogue des manuscrits de la bibliothèque de l'Arsenal*, II (Paris, 1886)

Meeder, S., 'Monte Cassino and Carolingian Politics around 800', in R. Meens, D. van Espelo, B. van den Hoven van Genderen, J. Raaijmakers, I. van Renswoude, and C. van Rhijn, eds, *Religious Franks: Religion and Power in the Frankish Kingdoms: Studies in Honour of Mayke de Jong* (Manchester, 2017), 279–95

Melve, L., 'Ecclesiastical Reform in Historiographical Context', *History Compass* 135 (2015), 213–21

Menache, S., *Clement V*, Cambridge Studies in Medieval Life and Thought, 4th ser. (Cambridge, 1998)

Merzbacher, F., 'Das Spital im Kanonischen Recht bis zum Tridentinum', *Archiv für Katholisches Kirchenrecht* 148 (1979), 72–92

Mesmin, S. C., 'Waleran, Count of Meulan and the Leper Hospital of S. Gilles de Pont-Audemer', *Annales de Normandie* 32:1 (1982), 3–19

Meyer, A., 'Organisierter Bettel und andere Finanzgeschäfte des Hospitals von Altopascio im 13. Jahrundert (mit Textedition)', in G. Drossbach, ed., *Mittelalter und Früher Neuzeit* (Oldenbourg, 2007), 55–105

Miller, D. H., 'The Roman Revolution of the Eighth Century: A Study of the Ideological Background of the Papal Separation from Byzantium and Alliance with the Franks', *Mediaeval Studies* 36 (1974), 79–133

Miller, T. S., 'The Knights of Saint John and the Hospitals of the Latin West', *Speculum* 53:4 (1978), 709–33

Miller, T. S., *The Birth of the Hospital in the Byzantine Empire* (Baltimore, MD, 1997)

Moddelmog, C., 'Stiftung oder Eigenkirche? Der Umgang mit Forschungskonzepten und die sächsischen Frauenklöster im 9. und 10. Jahrhundert', in F. Rexroth and W. Huschner, eds, *Gestiftete Zukunft im mittelalterlichen Europa: Festschrift für Michael Borgolte zum 60. Geburtstag* (Berlin, 2008), 215–43

Mollat, M., ed., *Études sur l'histoire de la pauvreté (Moyen Age–XVIe siècle)*, Publications de la Sorbonne, 'Etudes' 8, 2 vols (Paris, 1974)

Mollat, M., 'Hospitalité et assistance au début du XIIIe siècle', in D. Flood, ed., *Poverty in the Middle Ages*, Franziskanische Forschungen 27 (Werl, Westfalia, 1975), 37–51

Mollat, M., *Les pauvres au Moyen Age* (Paris, 1978)

Mollat, M., 'Complexité et ambiguité des institutions hospitalières: Les statuts d'hôpitaux (les modèles, leur diffusion et leur filiation)', in G. Politi, M. Rosa, and F. della Peruta, eds, *Timore e carità i poveri nell'Italia moderna: Atti del convegno 'Pauperismo e assistenza negli antichi stati italiani (Cremona, 28–30 marzo 1980)* (Cremona, 1982), 3–12

Mollat, M., 'Les premiers hôpitaux: VIe–XIe siècles', 'Floraison des fondations hospitalières (XIIe–XIIIe siècles)', 'Dans la perspective de l'Au-delà (XIVe–XVe siècles)', in J. Imbert, ed., *Histoire des hôpitaux en France* (Toulouse, 1982), 15–32, 35–66, 67–95

Mollat, M., and P. Tombeur, *Le concile de Vienne: Concordance, index, listes de fréquence, tables comparatives*, Conciles œcuméniques médiévaux 3 (Louvain-la-Neuve, 1978)

Montaubin, P., 'Le déménagement de l'Hôtel d'Amiens au XIIIe siècle', in P. Montaubin and J. Schwerdroffer, eds, *Hôpitaux et maladreries au Moyen Age: Espace et environnement* (Amiens, 2004), 51–85

Montaubin, P., 'Origine et mise en place des hôpitaux cathédraux de la province ecclésiastique de Reims, IVe–XIIIe siècle', in Marie-Claude Dinet-Lecomte, ed., *Les* hôpitaux, enjeux de pouvoir: France du Nord et Belgique (IVe–XXe siècle), Revue du Nord, hors série, Collection Histoire 22 (Lille, 2008), 13–46

Montaubin, P., 'Une tentative pontificale de reprise en main du Midi: La légation du cardinal Pietro Beneventano en 1214–1215', in Innocent III et le Midi, Cahiers de Fanjeaux 50 (2015), 391–418

Montaubin, P., and J. Schwerdroffer, eds, Hôpitaux et maladreries au Moyen Age: Espace et environnement: Actes du colloque international d'Amiens-Beauvais, 22, 23 et 24 novembre 2002 (Amiens, 2004)

Moore, J. C., Pope Innocent III (1160/1–1216): To Root up and to Plant (Leiden, 2003)

Moore, J. C., 'Pope Innocent III and Usury', in F. Andrews, C. Egger, and C. M. Rousseau, eds, Pope, Church and City: Essays in Honour of Brenda M. Bolton (Leiden, 2004), 59–75

Moore, M. E., 'The Ancient Fathers: Christian Antiquity, Patristics and Frankish Canon Law', Millennium: Jahrbuch zu Kultur und Geschichte des ersten Jahrtausends n. Chr./ Yearbook on the Culture and History of the First Millennium C.E. 7 (2010), 293–342

Moore, M. E., A Sacred Kingdom: Bishops and the Rise of Frankish Kingship, 300–850 (Washington, DC, 2011)

Moore, R. I., The Formation of a Persecuting Society, 2nd ed. (Oxford, 2007)

Mordek, H., Kirchenrecht und Reform im Frankenreich: Die Collectio Vetus Gallica, die älteste systematische Kanonessammlung des fränkischen Gallien, Beiträge zur Geschichte und Quellenkunde des Mittelalters 1 (Berlin, 1975)

Mordek, H., 'Karolingische Kapitularien', in H. Mordek, ed., Überlieferung und Geltung normativer Texte der frühen und hohen Mittelalters, Quellen und Forschungen zum Recht im Mittelalter 4 (Sigmaringen, 1986), 25–50, repr. in his, Studien zur fränkischen Herrschergesetzgebung: Aufsätze über Kapitularien und Kapitulariensammlungen ausgewählt zum 60. Geburtstag (Frankfurt am Main, 2000), 55–81

Mordek, H. 'Fränkische Kapitularien und Kapitulariensammlungen: Eine Einführung', in his Studien zur fränkischen Herrschergesetzgebung: Aufsätze über Kapitularien und Kapitulariensammlungen ausgewählt zum 60. Geburtstag (Frankfurt am Main, 2000), 1–53

Morey, A., and C. N. L. Brooke, Gilbert Foliot and his Letters, Cambridge Studies in Medieval Life and Thought NS 11 (Cambridge, 1965)

Morini, C., 'Xenodochium nelle glosse anglosassoni ai "Bella Parisiacae Urbis" di Abbone di St. Germain-des-Prés', Aevum 69 (1995), 347–55

Morris, R., 'The Problems of Property', in T. F. X. Noble and J. M. H. Smith, eds, Early Medieval Christianities c.600–c.1100: The Cambridge History of Christianity, III (Cambridge, 2008), 327–44

Müller, E., Das Konzil von Vienne, 1311–1312: Seine Quellen und seine Geschichte (Münster, 1934)

Müller, W. P., 'The Recovery of Justinian's Digest in the Middle Ages', Bulletin of Medieval Canon Law NS 20 (1990), 1–29

Mundy, J. H., 'Hospitals and Leproseries in Twelfth- and Early Thirteenth-Century Toulouse', in J. H. Mundy, R. W. Emery, and B. N. Nelson, eds, Essays in Medieval Life and Thought: Presented in Honor of Austin Patterson Evans (New York, 1965), 181–205

Mundy, J. H., Studies in the Ecclesiastical and Social History of Toulouse in the Age of the Cathars (Aldershot, 2006)

Munier, C., 'Droit canonique et droit romain d'après Gratien et les Décrétistes', in G. Le Bras, ed., Etudes d'histoire du droit canonique (Paris, 1965), II. 943–54

Neel, C. 'The Origins of the Beguines', in J. M. Bennet, E. A. Clark, J. F. O'Barr, B. A. Vilen, and S. Westphal-Wihl, eds, *Sisters and Workers in the Middle Ages* (Chicago, 1976), 240–60

Nelson, J. L., 'Legislation and Consensus in the Reign of Charles the Bald', in P. Wormald, ed., *Ideal and Reality in Frankish and Anglo-Saxon Society: Studies Presented to J. M. Wallace-Hadrill* (Oxford, 1983), 202–27

Nelson, J. L., 'Making Ends Meet: Wealth and Poverty in the Carolingian Church', *Studies in Church History* 24 (1987), 23–36

Nelson, J. L., 'The Last Years of Louis the Pious', in P. Godman and R. Collins, eds, *Charlemagne's Heir: New Perspectives on the Reign of Louis the Pious (814–840)* (Oxford, 1990), 147–59

Nelson, J. L., 'Literacy in Carolingian Government', in R. McKitterick, ed., *The Uses of Literacy in Early Mediaeval Government* (Cambridge, 1990), 258–96, repr. in J. L. Nelson, *The Frankish World 750–900* (London, 1996), 1–36

Nelson, J. L., '"Not Bishops' Bailiffs But Lords of the Earth": Charles the Bald and the Problem of Sovereignty', in D. Wood, ed., *The Church and Sovereignty: Essays in Honour of Michael Wilks*, Studies in Church History subsidia 9 (Oxford, 1991), 23–34

Nelson, J. L., 'The Intellectual in Politics: Context, Content and Authorship in the Capitulary of Coulaines, November 843', in L. Smith and B. Ward, eds, *Intellectual Life in the Middle Ages: Essays Presented to Margaret Gibson* (London, 1992), 1–14

Nelson, J. L., 'Kingship and Empire in the Carolingian World', in R. McKitterick, ed., *Carolingian Culture: Emulation and Innovation* (Cambridge, 1994), 52–87

Nelson, J. L., 'The Wary Widow', in W. Davies and P. Fouracre, eds, *Property and Power in the Early Middle Ages* (Cambridge, 1995), 82–113

Nelson, J. L., *The Frankish World 750–900* (London, 1996)

Nelson, J. L., 'Aachen as a Place of Power', in M. de Jong, F. Theuws, and C. Van Rhijn, eds, *Topographies of Power in the Early Middle Ages*, The Transformation of the Roman World 3 (Leiden, 2001), 217–41

Nelson, J. L., 'The Voice of Charlemagne', in R. Gameson and H. Leyser, eds, *Belief and Culture in the Middle Ages: Studies Presented to Henry Mayr-Harting* (Oxford, 2001), 76–88

Nelson, J. L., 'Law and its Applications', in T. F. X. Noble and J. M. H. Smith, eds, *Early Medieval Christianities, c.600–c.1100: The Cambridge History of Christianity* (Cambridge, 2008), 299–326

Nelson, J. L., 'Charlemagne and Ravenna', in J. Herrin and J. Nelson, eds, *Ravenna: Its Role in Earlier Medieval Change and Exchange* (London, 2016), 239–52

Nelson, J. L., 'Charlemagne and the Bishops', in R. Meens, D. van Espelo, B. van den Hoven van Genderen, J. Raaijmakers, I. van Renswoude, and C. van Rhijn, eds, *Religious Franks: Religion and Power in the Frankish Kingdoms: Studies in Honour of Mayke de Jong* (Manchester, 2017), 350–69

Nicholson, H., ed., *The Military Orders*, II. *Welfare and Warfare* (Aldershot, 1998)

Nicholson, H., *The Knights Hospitaller* (Woodbridge, 2001)

Niermeyer, J. F., *Mediae Latinitatis lexicon minus* (Leiden, 1976)

Noble, T. F. X., 'The Monastic Ideal as the Model for Empire: The Case of Louis the Pious', *Revue Bénédictine* 86 (1976), 235–50

Noble, T. F. X., 'The Place in Papal History of the Roman Synod of 826', *Church History* 45:4 (1976), 434–54

Noble, T. F. X., *The Republic of St Peter: The Birth of the Papal State, 680–825* (Philadelphia, PA, 1984)

Noble, T. F. X., 'The Declining Knowledge of Greek in Eighth- and Ninth-Century Papal Rome', *Byzantinische Zeitschrift* 78 (1985), 56–62

Noble, T. F. X., 'Topography, Celebration, and Power: The Making of a Papal Rome in the Eighth and Ninth Centuries', in M. de Jong and F. Theuws, eds, *Topographies of Power in the Early Middle Ages*, The Transformation of the Roman World 3 (Leiden, 2001), 45–91

Noble, T. F. X., 'Kings, Clergy and Dogma: The Settlement of Doctrinal Disputes in the Carolingian World', in S. Baxter, C. E. Karkov, J. L. Nelson, and D. Pelteret, eds, *Early Medieval Studies in Memory of Patrick Wormald* (Farnham, 2009), 237–52

Noonan, J. T., 'Gratian Slept Here: The Changing Identity of the Father of the Systematic Study of Canon Law', *Traditio* 35 (1979), 145–72

North, W. L., 'Polemic, Apathy, and Authorial Initiative in Gregorian Rome: The Curious Case of Bruno of Segni', *Haskins Society Journal* 10 (2001), 113–25

Omont, H., 'Glossarium Andegavense, MS 477 (461) de la bibliothèque d'Angers', *Bibliothèque de l'école des chartes* 59 (1898), 665–88

Orme, N., 'Clay, Rotha Mary (1878–1961)', Oxford Dictionary of National Biography (2004): doi: 10.1093/ref:odnb/61734

Orme, N., and M. Webster, *The English Hospital 1070–1570* (London, 1995)

Ortenberg West-Harling, V., 'The Church of Ravenna, Constantinople and Rome in the Seventh Century', in J. Herrin and J. Nelson, eds, *Ravenna: Its Role in Earlier Medieval Change and Exchange* (London, 2016), 199–210

Osheim, D. J., 'Conversion, *Conversi*, and the Christian Life in Late Medieval Tuscany', *Speculum* 58:2 (1983), 368–90

Pacaut, M., *Alexandre III: Etude sur la conception du pouvoir pontifical dans sa pensée et dans son œuvre*, L'Eglise et l'Etat au Moyen-Age 11 (Paris, 1956)

Pacini, G. P., 'Fra poveri e viandanti ai margini della città: Il "nuovo" ordine ospitaliero dei Crociferi fra secolo XII e XIII', Religiones novae, Quaderni di storia religiosa 2 (1995), 57–85

Pacini, G. P., 'I Crociferi e le comunità ospedaliere lungo le vie dei pellegrinaggi nel veneto medioevale secoli XII–XIV', in A. Rigon, ed., *I percorsi della fede e l'esperienza della carità nel Veneto medievale* (Padua, 2002), 155–72

Patetta, F., *Sull' introduzione in Italia della Collezione d'Ansegiso e sulla data del cosi detto Capitulare Mantuam Duplex attribuito all'anno 787* (Turin, 1890)

Patlagean, E., 'La pauvreté Byzantine au VIe siècle au temps de Justinien: aux origines d'un modèle politique', in M. Mollat, ed., *Études sur l'histoire de la pauvreté (Moyen Age–XVIe siècle)*, 2 vols (Paris, 1974), I. 59–81

Patzold, S., *Episcopus: Wissen über Bischöfe im Frankenreich des späten 8. bis frühen 10. Jahrhunderts*, Mittelalter-Forschungen 25 (Ostfildern, 2008)

Patzold, S., 'Capitularies in the Ottonian Realm', *Early Medieval Europe* 27:1 (2019), 112–32

Pennington, K., 'The Making of a Decretal Collection: The Genesis of *Compilatio tertia*', *Proceedings of the Fifth International Congress of Medieval Canon Law, Salamanca, 21–25 September 1976*, MIC C, 6 (Vatican City, 1980), 67–92, repr. in K. Pennington, *Popes, Canonists and Texts 1150–1550* (Aldershot, 1993), no. 8

Pennington, K., 'An Earlier Recension of Hostiensis's *Lectura* on the Decretals', *Bulletin of Medieval Canon Law* 17 (1987), 77–90, repr. in K. Pennington, *Popes, Canonists and Texts, 1150–1550* (Aldershot, 1993), no. 17

Pennington, K., 'Henricus de Segusio (Hostiensis)', in *Popes, Canonists and Texts 1150–1550* (Aldershot, 1993), no. 16, 1–12

Pennington, K., 'Decretal Collections 1190–1234', in W. Hartmann and K. Pennington, eds, *The History of Medieval Canon Law in the Classical Period, 1140–1234: From Gratian to the Decretals of Pope Gregory IX* (Washington, DC, 2008), 293–317

Pennington, K., 'The Decretalists 1190 to 1234', in W. Hartmann and K. Pennington, eds, *The History of Medieval Canon Law in the Classical Period, 1140–1234: From Gratian to the Decretals of Pope Gregory IX* (Washington, DC, 2008), 211–45

Pennington, K., 'Roman Law at the Papal Curia in the Early Twelfth Century', in U.-R. Blumenthal, A. Winroth, and P. Landau, eds, *Canon Law, Religion and Politics: Liber Amicorum Robert Somerville* (Washington, DC, 2012), 233–52

Peyroux, C., 'The Leper's Kiss', in S. Farmer and B. H. Rosenwein, eds, *Monks and Nuns, Saints and Outcasts: Religion in Medieval Society* (London, 2000), 173–88

Philipsborn, A., 'Der Fortschritt in der Entwicklung des byzantinischen Krankenhauswesens', *Byzantinische Zeitschrift* 54:2 (1961), 338–65

Pixton, P. B., *The German Episcopacy and the Implementation of the Decrees of the Fourth Lateran Council, 1216–1245: Watchmen on the Tower* (Leiden, 1994)

Plöchl, W. M. *Geschichte des Kirchenrechts: Das Kirchenrecht der abendländischen Christenheit 1055 bis 1517*, 3 vols (Vienna/Munich, 1953–69)

Pohl, W., 'Social Language, Identities and the Control of Discourse', in E. Chrysos and I. Wood, eds, *East and West: Modes of Communication: Proceedings from the First Plenary Conference at Merida*, The Transformation of the Roman World 5 (Leiden, 1999), 127–41

Pontal, O., *Histoire des conciles mérovingiens* (Paris, 1989)

Pontal, O., *Les conciles de la France Capétienne jusqu'en 1215* (Paris, 1995)

Pössel, C., 'Authors and Recipients of Carolingian Capitularies, 779–829', in R. Corradini, R. Meens, C. Pössel, and P. Shaw, eds., *Texts and Identities in the Early Middle Ages*, Forschungen zur Geschichte des Mittelalters 12, Denkschriften der phil.-hist. Klasse 344 (Vienna, 2006), 253–7

Pottage, A., 'Law after Anthropology: Object and Technique in Roman Law', *Theory, Culture and Society* 31 (2014), 147–66

Powell, J. M., *Anatomy of a Crusade, 1213–1221* (Philadelphia, PA, 1986)

Radding, C. M., and A. Ciaralli, *The Corpus Iuris Civilis in the Middle Ages: Manuscripts and Transmission from the Sixth Century to the Juristic Revival* (Leiden, 2007)

Ragab, A., *The Medieval Islamic Hospital: Medicine, Religion, and Charity* (Cambridge, 2015)

Rawcliffe, C., *Medicine for the Soul: The Life, Death and Resurrection of an English Medieval Hospital: St Giles Norwich, c.1249–1550* (Stroud, 1999)

Rawcliffe, C., 'Learning to Love the Leper: Aspects of Institutional Charity in Anglo-Norman England', *Anglo-Norman Studies* 23 (2001), 231–50

Rawcliffe, C., *Leprosy in Medieval England* (Woodbridge, 2006)

Rawcliffe, C., 'Christ the Physician Walks the Wards: Celestial Therapeutics in the Medieval Hospital', in M. P. Davies and A. Prescott, eds, *London and the Kingdom: Essays in Honour of Caroline M. Barron*, Harlaxton Medieval Studies 16 (Donington, 2008), 78–97

Reeves, A., *Religious Education in Thirteenth-Century England: The Creed and Articles of Faith* (Leiden, 2015)

Reicke, S., *Das deutsche Spital und sein Recht im Mittelalter, Erster Teil: Geschichte und Gestalt, Zweiter Teil: Das deutsche Spitalrecht*, 2 vols (Stuttgart, 1932)

Reicke, S., 'Antrittsrede des Hrn. Reicke', Jahrbuch der Preußischen Akademie der Wissenschaften: Jahrgang 1942 (Berlin, 1943), 163–5, with 'Erwiderung des Hrn. Heymann', 165–6

Reilly, D. J., 'Art', in M. B. Bruun, ed., *The Cambridge Companion to the Cistercian Order* (Cambridge, 2013), 125–39

Resl, B., 'Hospitals in Medieval England', in M. Scheutz, A. Sommerlechner, H. Weigl, and A. S. Weiß, eds, *Europäisches Spitalwesen: Institutionelle Fürsorge in Mittelalter und Früher Neuzeit*, Mitteilungen des Instituts für Österreichische Geschichtsforschung, Ergänzungsband 51 (Vienna, 2008), 41–52

Resl, B., 'Bequests for the Poor', M. Rubin, ed., *Medieval Christianity in Practice* (Princeton, 2009), 209–16

Reuter, T., and G. Silagi, eds, *Wortkonkordanz zum Decretum Gratiani*, 5 vols (Munich, 1990)

Reuter, T., '"Kirchenreform" und "Kirchenpolitik" im Zeitalter Karl Martells: Begriffe und Wirklichkeit', in J. Jarnut, U. Nonn, and M. Richter, eds, *Karl Martell in seiner Zeit*, Beihefte der Francia 37 (Sigmaringen, 1994), 35–59

Reuter, T., 'Assembly Politics in Western Europe from the Eighth Century to the Twelfth', in P. Linehan and J. L. Nelson, eds, *The Medieval World* (London, 2001), 432–50

Reynolds, R. E., 'Rites of Separation and Reconciliation in the Early Middle Ages', in *Segni e riti nella Chiesa altomedievale occidentale*, Settimane di studio del centro Italiano di studi sull'Alto Medioevo 33 (Spoleto, 1987), 405–33

Rhijn, C. van, *Shepherds of the Lord: Priests and Episcopal Statutes in the Carolingian Period* (Turnhout, 2007)

Rhijn, C. van, '"Et hoc considerat episcopus, ut ipsi presbyteri non sint idiothae": Carolingian Local *Correctio* and an Unknown Priests' Exam from the Early Ninth Century', in R. Meens, D. van Espelo, B. van den Hoven van Genderen, J. Raaijmakers, I. van Renswoude, and C. van Rhijn, eds, *Religious Franks: Religion and Power in the Frankish Kingdoms: Studies in Honour of Mayke de Jong* (Manchester, 2017), 162–80

Richards, J., *Sex, Dissidence and Damnation: Minority Groups in the Middle Ages* (London, 1990)

Riché, P., 'Le grec dans les centres de culture d'occident', in M. Herren with S. A. Brown, eds, *Sacred Nectar of the Greeks: The Study of Greek in the West in the Early Middle Ages*, King's College London Medieval Studies (London, 1988), 143–68

Rigon, A., 'Schole, confraternite e ospedali', in G. Andenna, ed., *Pensiero e sperimentazioni istituzionali nella 'Societas Christiana' (1046–1250)* (Milan, 2007), 407–27

Rio, A., 'Charters, Law Codes and Formulae: The Franks between Theory and Practice', in P. Fouracre and D. Ganz, eds, *Frankland: The Franks and the World of the Early Middle Ages: Essays in Honour of Dame Jinty Nelson* (Manchester, 2008), 7–27

Rio, A., *Legal Practice and the Written Word in the Early Middle Ages: Frankish Formulae c.500–1000*, Cambridge Studies in Medieval Life and Thought, 4th ser. (Cambridge, 2009)

Rio, A., 'Introduction', in A. Rio, ed., *Law, Custom, and Justice in Late Antiquity and the Early Middle Ages: Proceedings of the 2008 Byzantine Colloquium* (London, 2011), 1–22

Rio, A., 'Waltharius at Fontenoy? Epic Heroism and Carolingian Political Thought', *Viator* 46:2 (2015), 1–64

Risse, G. B., *Mending Bodies, Saving Souls: A History of Hospitals* (Oxford, 1999)

Rist, R., 'The Power of the Purse: Usury, Jews, and Crusaders, 1198–1245', in B. Bolton and C. Meed, eds, *Aspects of Power and Authority in the Middle Ages* (Turnhout, 2007), 197–213

Roach, L., 'Emperor Otto III and the End of Time', *Transactions of the Royal Historical Society*, 6th ser. 23 (2013), 75–102

Roach, L., *Kingship and Consent in Anglo-Saxon England, 871–978: Assemblies and the State in the Early Middle Ages*, Cambridge Studies in Medieval Life and Thought, 4th ser. (Cambridge, 2013)

Roberts, P., *Stephanus de Lingua-Tonante: Studies in the Sermons of Stephen Langton* (Toronto, 1968)

Rocca, E. N., *Il diritto ospedaliero nei suoi lineamenti storici*, Biblioteca della rivista di storia del diritto Italiano 20 (Milan, 1956)

Rolker, C., *Canon Law and the Letters of Ivo of Chartres*, Cambridge Studies in Medieval Life and Thought, 4th ser. (Cambridge, 2010)

Rolker, C. ed., *New Discourses in Medieval Canon Law Research: Challenging the Master Narrative*, Medieval Law and Practice 28 (Leiden, 2019)

Rosenwein, B. H., *To Be the Neighbor of Saint Peter: The Social Meaning of Cluny's Property, 909–1049* (Ithaca, NY, and London, 1993)

Rosenwein, B. H., *Negotiating Space: Power, Restraint and Privileges of Immunity in Early Medieval Europe* (New York, 1999)

Rosenwein, B. H., 'Property Transfers and the Church, Eighth to Eleventh Centuries: An Overview', *Mélanges de l'Ecole française de Rome: Moyen-Age* 111:2 (1999), 563–75

Rouche, M., 'La Matricule des Pauvres: Evolution d'une institution de charité du Bas Empire jusqu'à la fin du Haut Moyen Age', in M. Mollat, ed., *Études sur l'histoire de la pauvreté (Moyen Age-XVIe siècle)*, 2 vols (Paris, 1974), I. 83–110

Rouse, R. H., and M. A. Rouse, 'Ennodius in the Middle Ages: Adonics, Pseudo-Isidore, Cistercians, and the Schools', in J. R. Sweeney and S. Chodorow, eds, *Popes, Teachers and Canon Law in the Middle Ages* (Ithaca, NY, 1989), 91–113

Rubin, M., *Charity and Community in Medieval Cambridge*, Cambridge Studies in Medieval Life and Thought, 4th ser. (Cambridge, 1987)

Rubin, M., 'Development and Change in English Hospitals, 1100–1500', in L. Granshaw and R. Porter, eds, *The Hospital in History* (London, 1989), 41–59

Rubin, M., ed., *Medieval Christianity in Practice* (Princeton, 2009)

Sabapathy, J., 'Some Difficulties in Forming Persecuting Societies Before Lateran IV Canon 8: Robert of Courson Thinks about Communities and Inquisitions', in G. Melville and J. Helmrath, eds, *The Fourth Lateran Council: Institutional Reform and Spiritual Renewal* (Affalterbach, 2017), 175–200

Saint-Denis, A., *L'Hotel-Dieu de Laon 1150–1300: Institution hospitalière et société aux XIIe et XIIIe siècles* (Nancy, 1983)

Santangeli Valenzani, R., 'Pellegrini, Senatori e Papi: gli xenodochia a Roma tra il V e il IX secolo', *Rivista dell'Istituto Nazionale d'Archeologia e Storia dell'Arte* 19/20 (1996/7), 203–26

Sarris, P., *Economy and Society in the Age of Justinian* (Cambridge, 2006)

Sassier, Y., 'L'utilisation d'un concept romain aux temps carolingiens: La res publica aux IXe et Xe siècles', *Médiévales* 15 (1988), 17–29

Saunier, A., 'La trame hospitalière médiévale: Hiérarchie ou réseaux?', in P. Montaubin, ed., *Hôpitaux et maladreries au Moyen Age: Espace et environnement* (Amiens, 2004), 201–19

Sayers, J. E., *Papal Government and England during the Pontificate of Honorious III (1216–1227)*, Cambridge Studies in Medieval Life and Thought, 3rd ser. (Cambridge, 1984)

Schäpers, M., *Lothar I. (795–855) und das Frankenreich*, Rheinisches Archiv 159 (Cologne, 2018)

Scharf, J., 'Studien zu Smaragdus und Jonas', *Deutsches Archiv für Erforschung des Mittelalters* 17 (1961), 353–84

Scheutz, M., A. Sommerlechner, H. Weigl, and A. S. Weiß, 'Einleitung', in M. Scheutz, A. Sommerlechner, H. Weigl, and A. S. Weiß, eds, *Europäisches Spitalwesen: Institutionelle Fürsorge in Mittelalter und Früher Neuzeit*, Mitteilung des Instituts für Österreichische Geschichtsforschung, Ergänzungsband 51 (Vienna, 2008), 11–18

Scheutz, M., A. Sommerlechner, H. Weigl, and A. S. Weiß, eds, *Quellen zur europäischen Spitalgeschichte in Mittelalter und Früher Neuzeit*, Quelleneditionen des Instituts für Österreichische Geschichtsforschung 5 (Vienna, 2010)

Schmitz, G., 'Ansegis und Regino: Die Rezeption der Kapitularien in den Libri duo de synodalibus causis', *ZRG 150 Kan. Abt.* 74 (1988), 95–132

Schmitz, G., 'The Capitulary Legislation of Louis the Pious', in P. Godman and R. Collins, eds, *Charlemagne's Heir: New Perspectives on the Reign of Louis the Pious (814–840)* (Oxford, 1990), 425–36

Schmitz, G., 'Intelligente Schreiber: Beobachtungen aus Ansegis- und Kapitularienhandschriften', in H. Mordek, ed., *Papsttum, Kirche und Recht im Mittelalter: Festschrift für Horst Furhmann zum 65. Geburtstag* (Tübingen, 1991), 79–93

Schmitz, G., 'Einleitung', in his ed., *Collectio Capitularium Ansegisi*, MGH *Cap.* NS 1 (Hanover, 1996), 1–416

Schmitz, G., '... *pro utile firmiter tenenda sunt lege*: Bemerkungen zur Brauchbarkeit und zum Gebrauch der Kapitulariensammlung des Ansegis', in D. R. Bauer, R. Hiestand, B. Kasten, and S. Lorenz, eds, *Mönchtum—Kirche—Herrschaft, 750–1000: Josef Semmler zum 65. Geburtstag* (Sigmaringen, 1998), 213–29

Schmitz, G., 'Die Synode von Aachen 836 und Pseudoisidor', in P. Depreux and S. Esders, eds, *La productivité d'une crise: Le règne de Louis le Pieux (814–840) et la transformation de l'Empire Carolingien/Produktivität einer Krise: Die Regierungszeit Ludwigs des Frommen (814–840) und die Transformation des Karoloingischen Imperiums* (Ostfildern, 2018), 329–42

Schönfeld, Walther, 'Die Xenodochien in Italien und Frankreich im frühen Mittelalter', *ZRG 43 Kan. Abt.* 87 (1922), 1–54

Schramm, P. E., *Kaiser, Rom und Renovatio: Studien und Texte zur Geschichte des römischen Erneuerungsgedankens vom Ende des karolingischen Reiches bis zum Investiturstreit*, 2 vols (Berlin, 1929)

Schultheiss, K., 'Gender and the Limits of Anti-Clericalism: The Secularization of Hospital Nursing in France, 1880–1914', *French History* 12:3 (1998), 229–45

Siems, H., 'Von den piae causae zu den Xenodochien', in R. Helmholz and R. Zimmermann, eds, *Itinera Fiduciae: Trust and Treuhand in Historical Perspective*, Comparative Studies in Continental and Anglo-American Legal History 19 (Berlin, 1998), 57–83

Simons, W., *Cities of Ladies: Beguine Communities in the Medieval Low Countries, 1200–1565* (Philadelphia, 2001)

Sirks, J. B., 'Shifting Frontiers in the Law: Romans, Provincials and Barbarians', in R. Mathisen and H. Sivan, eds, *Shifting Frontiers in Late Antiquity: Papers from the First Interdisciplinary Conference on Late Antiquity, the University of Kansas, 1995* (Aldershot, 1996), 146–57

Smith, J. M. H., '"Emending Evil Ways and Praising God's Omnipotence": Einhard and the Uses of Roman Martyrs', in K. Mills and A. Grafton, eds, *Conversion in Late Antiquity and the Early Middle Ages: Seeing and Believing* (Rochester, 2003), 189–223

Sohm, R., *The Institutes: A Textbook of the History and System of Roman Private Law*, tr. J. C. Ledlie, 3rd ed. (Oxford, 1907)

Sommerlechner, A., 'Spitäler in Nord- und Mittelitalien vom 11. bis zum Beginn des 14. Jahrhunderts', in M. Scheutz, A. Sommerlechner, H. Weigl, and A. S. Weiß, eds, *Europäisches Spitalwesen: Institutionelle Fürsorge in Mittelalter und Früher Neuzeit*, Mitteilungen des Instituts für Österreichische Geschichtsforschung, Ergänzungsband 51 (Vienna, 2008), 105–34

Sotinel, C., 'The Church in the Roman Empire: Changes without Reform and Reforms without Change', in C. M. Bellitto and L. I. Hamilton, eds, *Reforming the Church before Modernity: Patterns, Problems, and Approaches* (Farnham, 2005), 155–71

Sotinel, C., 'Places of Christian Worship and their Sacralization in Late Antiquity', *Revue de l'histoire des religions* 222:4 (2005), 411–34, tr. in C. Sotinel, *Church and Society in Late Antique Italy and Beyond*, no. 12 (Farnham, 2010)

Southern, R. W., *Robert Grosseteste: The Growth of an English Mind in Medieval Europe* (Oxford, 1984)

Spiegel, G. M., *The Past as Text: The Theory and Practice of Medieval Historiography* (Baltimore, MD, 1999)

Stabler Miller, T., 'What's in a Name? Clerical Representations of Parisian Beguines (1200–1328)', *Journal of Medieval History* 33:1 (2007), 60–86

Stasolla, F. R., 'A proposito delle strutture assistenziali ecclesiastiche: gli xenodochi', *Archivio della Società romana di storia patria* 121 (1998), 5–45

Stathakopoulos, D., 'Discovering a Military Order of the Crusades: The Hospital of St. Sampson of Constantinople', *Viator* 37 (2006), 255–73

Stein, P., 'Vacarius and the Civil Law', in C. Brooke, D. Luscombe, G. Martin, and D. Owen, eds, *Church and Government in the Middle Ages: Essays Presented to C. R. Cheney on his 70th Birthday* (Cambridge, 1976), 119–37

Sternberg, T., *Orientalium more secutus: Räume und Institutionen der Caritas des 5. bis 7. Jahrhunderts in Gallien*, Jahrbuch für Antike und Christentum Ergänzungsband 16 (Münster, 1991)

Stolleis, M., *The Law under the Swastika: Studies on Legal History in Nazi Germany*, tr. T. Dunlap (Chicago, 1998)

Stolte, B. H., 'Law for Founders', in M. Mullett, ed., *Founders and Refounders of Byzantine Monasteries*, Belfast Byzantine Texts and Translations, 6:3 (Belfast, 2007), 121–39

Stolte, B. H., 'The Law of New Rome: Byzantine Law', in D. Johnston, ed., *The Cambridge Companion to Roman Law* (Cambridge, 2015), 355–73

Stone, R., 'Introduction: Hincmar's World', in R. Stone and C. West, eds, *Hincmar of Rheims: Life and Work* (Manchester, 2015), 1–43

Story, J., *Carolingian Connections: Anglo-Saxon England and Carolingian Francia, c.750–870* (Farnham, 2003)

Summerlin, D., 'Three Manuscripts Containing the Canons of the 1179 Lateran Council', *Bulletin of Medieval Canon Law* 30 (2013), 21–43

Summerlin, D., 'The Reception and Authority of Conciliar Canons in the Later-Twelfth Century: Alexander III's 1179 Lateran Canons and their Manuscript Context', *ZRG Kan. Abt.* 100 (2014), 112–31

Summerlin, D., 'Using the Canons of the Third Lateran Council of 1179', in P. Carmassi and G. Drossbach, eds, *Rechtshandschriften des deutschen Mittelalters, Produktionsorte und Importwege*, Wolfenbüttler Mittelalter-Studien 29 (Wiesbaden, 2015), 245–60

Summerlin, D., 'Papal Councils in the High Middle Ages', in A. Larson and K. Sisson, eds, *Companion to the Medieval Papacy*, Brill's Companions to the Christian Tradition 70 (Leiden, 2016), 174–96

Summerlin, D., 'Hubert Walter's Council of Westminster in 1200 and its Use of Alexander III's 1179 Lateran Council', in M. H. Eichbauer and D. Summerlin, eds, *Canon Law and Administration, 1000–1234*, Medieval Law and its Practice 26 (Leiden, 2018), 121–39

Sweetinburgh, S., *The Role of the Hospital in Medieval England: Gift-Giving and the Spiritual Economy* (Dublin, 2004)

Sydow, J., 'Kanonistische Fragen zur Geschichte des Spitals in Südwestdeutschland', *Historiches Jahrbuch* 83 (1964), 54–68

Sydow, J., 'Spital und Stadt in Kanonistik und Verfassungsgeschichte des 14. Jahrhunderts,' in Hans Patze, ed., *Der deutsche Territorialstaat im 14. Jahrhundert*, Vorträge u. Forschungen 13 (Sigmaringen, 1970–1), 175–95

Tabuteau, B., 'De l'expérience érémitique à la normalisation monastique: étude d'un processus de formation des léproseries aux XIIe–XIIIe siècles', in J. Dufour and H. Platelle, eds, *Fondations et œuvres charitables au Moyen Age* (Paris, 1999), 89–96

Taylor, A. L., *Epic Lives and Monasticism in the Middle Ages, 800–1050* (Cambridge, 2013)

Théry, J., 'A Heresy of State: Philip the Fair, the Trial of the "Perfidious Templars," and the Pontificalization of the French Monarchy', *Journal of Medieval Religious Cultures* 39:2 (2013), 117–48

Thomas, E., and C. Witschel, 'Constructing Reconstruction: Claim and Reality of Roman Rebuilding Inscriptions from the Latin West', *Papers of the British School at Rome* 60 (1992), 135–77

Thomas, J. P., *Private Religious Foundations in the Byzantine Empire* (Washington, DC, 1988)

Thomas, Y., 'La langue du droit romain, problèmes et methods', *Archives de la philosophie du droit* 19 (1974), 103–25

Thompson, S., 'The Problem of the Cistercian Nuns in the Twelfth and Early Thirteenth Centuries', in D. Baker, ed., *Medieval Women*, Studies in Church History, Subsidia 1 (Oxford, 1978), 227–52

Thompson, S., *Women Religious: The Founding of English Nunneries After the Norman Conquest* (Oxford, 1991)

Tierney, B., 'The Decretists and the "Deserving Poor"', *Comparative Studies in Society and History* 1:4 (1959), 360–73

Tierney, B., *Medieval Poor Law: A Sketch of Canonical Theory and its Application in England* (Berkeley, CA, 1959)

Tierney, B., 'Canon Law and Church Institutions in the Late Middle Ages', in P. Linehan, ed., *Proceedings of the Seventh International Congress of Medieval Canon Law, Cambridge, 23–27 July 1984*, MIC C, 8 (Vatican City, 1988), 49–69

Timmermann, J., 'Sharers in the Contemplative Virtue: Julianus Pomerius's Carolingian Audience', *Comitatus* 45 (2014), 1–45

Touati, F.-O., 'Les groupes de laïcs dans les hôpitaux et les léproseries au Moyen Age', in *Les Mouvances laïques des ordres religieux: Actes du troisième colloque international du CERCOR, Tournus, 17–20 juin 1992* (Saint-Étienne, 1996), 137–62

Touati, F.-O., *Archives de la lèpre: Atlas des léproseries entre Loire et Marne au Moyen Age*, Mémoires et documents d'histoire médiévale et de philologie 7 (Paris, 1996)

Touati, F.-O., *Maladie et société au Moyen Age: La leper, les lépreux et les léproseries dans la province ecclésiastique de Sens jusqu'an milieu du XIVe siècle*, Bibliothèque du Moyen Age 11 (Brussels, 1998)

Touati, F.-O., 'Un dossier à rouvrir: L'assistance au Moyen Age', in J. Dufour and H. Platelle, eds, *Fondations et œuvres charitables au Moyen Age* (Paris, 1999), 23–38

Touati, F.-O., 'La géographie hospitalière médiévale (Orient–Occident, IVe–XVIe siècles): des modèles aux réalités', in P. Montaubin, ed., *Hôpitaux et maladreries au Moyen Age: Espace et environnement: Actes du colloque international d'Amiens-Beauvais, 22, 23 et 24 novembre 2002* (Amiens, 2004), 7–20

Touati, F.-O., '"Aime et fais ce que tu veux": Les chanoines réguliers et la révolution de charité au Moyen Age', in M. Parisse, ed., *Les chanoines réguliers: Émergence et expansion (XIe–XIIIe siècles)* (Saint-Étienne, 2009), 159–210

Touati, F.-O., *Yves de Chartres (1040–1115): Aux origines de la révolution hospitalière médiévale* (Paris, 2017)

Townsend, W. T., 'Councils Held under Pope Symmachus', *Church History* 6:3 (1937), 233–59

Trump, D., 'Die Überlieferung des römischen Rechts in der Herrschaftszeit Karls des Kahlen: Ein Experiment', *Concilium medii aevi* 19 (2016), 71–86

Tsuda, T., 'Was hat Ansegis gesammelt? Über die zeitgenössische Wahrnehmung der Kapitularien in der Karolingerzeit', *Concilium aevi medii* 16 (2013), 209–31

Uhrmacher, M., 'Die Verbreitung von Leprosorien und Kriterien zu ihrer Klassifizierung unter räumlichen Aspekten: Das Beispiel der Rheinlande', in P. Montaubin, ed., *Hôpitaux et maladreries au Moyen Age: Espace et environnement* (Amiens, 2004), 159–78

Ullmann, W., *The Growth of Papal Government in the Middle Ages*, 2nd ed. (London, 1962)

Ullmann, W., 'Public Welfare and Social Legislation in the Early Medieval Councils', in G. J. Cuming and D. Baker, eds, *Councils and Assemblies, Studies in Church History* 7 (Cambridge, 1971), 1–39

Uyttebrouck, A., 'Hôpitaux pour lépreux ou couvents de lépreux? Réflexions sur le caractère des premières grandes léproseries de nos régions à leurs origines', *Annales de la Société belge d'histoire des hôpitaux* 10 (1972), 3–29

Vanderputten, S., 'Female Monasticism, Ecclesiastical Reform, and Regional Politics: The Northern Archdiocese of Reims, circa 1060–1120', *French Historical Studies* 36:3 (2013), 363–83

Vauchez, A., 'Assistance et charité en occident, XIIIe–XVe siècles', in V. B. Bagnoli, ed., *Domanda e consumi: Livelli e strutture (nei secoli XIII–XVIII)* (Florence, 1978), 151–62

Vessey, M., 'The Origins of the *Collectio Sirmondiana*: A New Look at the Evidence', in J. Harries and I. Wood, eds, *The Theodosian Code: Studies in the Imperial Law of Late Antiquity* (London, 1993), 178–99

Vogel, C., 'Les sanctions infligées aux laïcs et aux clercs par les conciles gallo-romains et mérovingiens', *Revue de droit canonique* 2 (1952), 5–29, 171–94, 311–28

von Heckel, R., 'Die Dekretalensammlungen des Gilbertus und Alanus nach den Weingartner Handschriften', *ZRG Kan. Abt.* 29 (1940), 116–357

Ward-Perkins, B., *From Classical Antiquity to the Middle Ages: Urban Public Building in Northern and Central Italy AD 300–850* (Oxford, 1984)

Watson, S., 'The Origins of the English Hospital', *Transactions of the Royal Historical Society* 6th ser. 16 (2006), 75–94

Watson, S., 'The Sources for English Hospitals 1100–1400', in M. Scheutz, A. Sommerlechner, H. Weigl, A. S. Weiß, eds, *Quellen zur europäischen Spitalgeschichte in Mittelalter und früher Neuzeit*, Quelleneditionen des Instituts für Österreichische Geschichtesforschung 5 (Vienna, 2010), 65–103

Watson, S., 'A Mother's Past and her Children's Futures: Female Inheritance, Family and Dynastic Hospitals in the Thirteenth Century', in C. Leyser and L. Smith, eds, *Motherhood, Religion, and Society in Medieval Europe, 400–1400* (Farnham, 2011), 213–50

Watson, S., 'Hospitals in the Middle Ages', in P. E. Szarmach, ed., Oxford Bibliographies in Medieval Studies (New York, June 2017) DOI: 10.1093/OBO/9780195396584-0233

Watt, J. A., 'The Theory of Papal Monarchy in the Thirteenth Century: The Contribution of the Canonists', *Traditio* 20 (1964), 179–317

Wei, I. P. *Intellectual Culture in Medieval Paris: Theologians and the University c.1100–1330* (Cambridge, 2012)

Weigand, R., 'The Development of the *Glossa ordinaria* to Gratian's *Decretum*', in W. Hartmann and K. Pennington, eds, *The History of Medieval Canon Law in the Classical Period, 1140–1234: From Gratian to the Decretals of Pope Gregory IX* (Washington, DC, 2008), 55–97

Weinrich, L., *Wala: Graf, Mönch und Rebell: Die Biographie eines Kardingers* (Lübeck-Hamburg, 1963)

Wemple, S. F., *Women in Frankish Society: Marriage and the Cloister, 500–900* (Philadelphia, PA, 1981)

Werner, K. F., '*Missus, marchio, comes*: Entre l'administration centrale et l'administration locale de l'Empire carolingien', in W. Paravinicini and K. F. Werner, eds, *Histoire comparée de l'administration (IVᵉ–XVIIIᵉ siècles): Actes du XIVᵉ colloque historique francoallemand Tours, 27 Mars–1 Avril 1977*, Beihefte der Francia IX (Zurich, 1980), 191–239

West, C., 'Lordship in Ninth-Century Francia: The Case of Bishop Hincmar of Laon and his Followers', *Past and Present* 226:1 (2005), 3–40

West, C., *Reframing the Feudal Revolution: Political and Social Transformation between Marne and Moselle, c.800–c.1100*, Cambridge Studies in Medieval Life and Thought, 4ᵗʰ ser. (Cambridge, 2013)

West, C., ed., Special issue: *Religious Exemption in Pre-Modern Eurasia, c.300–1300 CE, Medieval Worlds* 6 (2017)

White, S. D., *Custom, Kinship, and Gifts to the Saints: The* Laudatio Parentum *in Western France, 1050–1150*, Studies in Legal History (Chapel Hill, NC, 1988)

Wickham, C., 'Land Disputes and their Social Framework in Lombard-Carolingian Italy, 700–900', in W. Davies and P. Fouracre, eds, *The Settlement of Disputes in Early Medieval Europe* (Cambridge, 1986), 105–24

Wickham, C., *Early Medieval Italy: Central Power and Local Society 400–1000* (Ann Arbor, MI, 1989)

Wickham, C., 'Aristocratic Power in Eighth-Century Lombard Italy', in A. C. Murray, ed., *After Rome's Fall: Narrators and Sources of Early Medieval History: Essays Presented to Walter Goffart* (Toronto, 1998), 153–70

Wickham, C., 'Consensus and Assemblies in the Romano-Germanic Kingdoms: A Comparative Approach', in V. Epp and C. H. F. Meyer, eds, *Recht und Konsens im frühen Mittelalter*, Vorträge und Forschungen 82 (Ostfildern, 2017), 389–426

Wilks, M. J., 'Ecclesiastica and Regalia: Papal Investiture Policy from the Council of Guastalla to the First Lateran Council, 1106–23', in G. J. Cuming and D. Baker, eds, *Councils and Assemblies*, Studies in Church History 7 (Cambridge, 1971), 69–85

Wilks, M., 'Thesaurus Ecclesiae (Presidential Address)', in B. Sheils and D. Wood, eds, *The Church and Wealth*, Studies in Church History 24 (Cambridge, 1987), 15–45

Wilmart, A., 'L'admonition de Jonas au Roi Pépin et le florilège canonique d'Orléans', *Revue Bénédictine* 45 (1933), 214–33

Winroth, A., *The Making of Gratian's Decretum*, Cambridge Studies in Medieval Life and Thought, 4ᵗʰ ser. (Cambridge, 2000)

Winroth, A., 'Where Gratian Slept: The Life and Death of the Father of Canon Law', *ZRG Kan. Abt.* 99 (2013), 105–28

Wirbelauer, E., *Zwei Päpste in Rom. Der Konflikt zwischen Laurentius und Symmachus (498–514): Studien und Texte*, Quellen und Forschungen zur antiken Welt 16 (Munich, 1993)

Witt, R. G., *The Two Latin Cultures and the Foundation of Renaissance Humanism in Medieval Italy* (Cambridge, 2011)

Witters, W., 'Pauvres et pauvreté dans les coutumiers monastiques du Moyen Age', in M. Mollat, ed., *Études sur l'histoire de la pauvreté (Moyen Age–XVIᵉ siècle)*, 2 vols (Paris, 1974), I. 177–215

Wogan-Browne, J., and M.-E. Henneau, 'Liege, the Medieval "Woman Question", and the Question of Medieval Woman', in J. Dor, L. Johnson, and J. Wogan-Browne, eds, *New Trends in Feminine Spirituality: The Holy Women of Liège and their Impact* (Turnhout, 1999), 21–32

Wolf, K. B., *The Poverty of Riches: St Francis of Assisi Reconsidered* (Oxford, 2003)

Wood, I., 'Disputes in Late Fifth- and Sixth-Century Gaul: Some Problems', in W. Davies and P. Fouracre, eds, *The Settlement of Disputes in Early Medieval Europe* (Cambridge, 1986), 7–22

Wood, I., 'Saint Wandrille and its Historiography', in I. Wood and G. A. Loud, eds, *Church and Chronicle in the Middle Ages: Essays Presented to John Taylor* (London, 1991), 1–14

Wood, I., 'The Code in Merovingian Gaul', in J. Harries and I. Wood, eds, *The Theodosian Code: Studies in the Imperial Law of Late Antiquity* (London, 1993), 161–77

Wood, I., 'Reform and the Merovingian Church', in R. Meens, D. van Espelo, B. van den Hoven van Genderen, J. Raaijmakers, I. van Renswoude, and C. van Rhijn, eds, *Religious Franks: Religion and Power in the Frankish Kingdoms: Studies in Honour of Mayke de Jong* (Manchester, 2017), 95–111

Wood, S., *The Proprietary Church in the Medieval West* (Oxford, 2006)

Wormald, P., 'In Search of King Offa's "Law-Code"', in I. Wood and N. Lund, eds, *People and Places in Northern Europe 500–1600: Essays in Honour of Peter Hayes Sawyer* (Woodbridge, 1991), 25–46

Wormald, P., 'Lex Scripta and Verbum Regis: Legislation and Germanic Kingship from Euric to Cnut', in his *Legal Culture in the Early Medieval West: Law as Text, Image and Experience* (London, 1999), 1–43

Wormald, P., *The Making of English Law: King Alfred to the Twelfth Century, 1. Legislation and its Limits* (Oxford, 1999)

Wormald, P., 'The Leges Barbarorum: Law and Ethnicity in the Post-Roman West', in H.-W. Goetz, J. Jarnut, and W. Pohl, eds, *Regna and Gentes: The Relationship between Late Antique and Early Medieval Peoples and Kingdoms in the Transformation of the Roman World*, The Transformation of the Roman World 13 (Leiden, 2003), 21–53

Young, B. K., 'Autun and the *Civitas Aeduorum*: Maintaining and Transforming a Regional Identity in Late Antiquity', in T. S. Burns and J. W. Eadie, eds, *Urban Centers and Rural Contexts in Late Antiquity* (East Lansing, MI, 2001), 25–46

Young, S. E., *Scholarly Community at the Early University of Paris: Theologians, Education and Society, 1215–1248*, Cambridge Studies in Medieval Life and Thought, 4ᵗʰ ser. (Cambridge, 2014)

Zechiel-Eckes, K., 'Sur la tradition manuscrite des Capitula... De coertione Iudeorum ou Florus de Lyon au travail', *Revue Bénédictine* 107 (1997), 77–87

Zema, D. B., 'Economic Reorganization of the Roman See during the Gregorian Reform', *Studi Gregoriani* 1 (1947), 137–68

Ziegler, J., 'Secular Canonesses as Antecedents of the Beguines', *Studies in Medieval and Renaissance History* ns 13 (1992), 115–35

Zutshi, P., 'The Avignon Papacy', in M. Jones, ed., *The New Cambridge Medieval History*, VI. *c.1300–1415* (Cambridge, 2000), 651–73

Electronic Sources

Capitularia: Edition of the Frankish Capitularies, ed. K. Ubl and collaborators (Cologne, 2014–): <https://capitularia.uni-koeln.de/ ... >

Mischke, B. 'Manuscript of the Month January 2016: Wolfenbüttel Cod. Guelf. 130 Blank.': < ... en/blog/handschrift-des-monats-blankenb-130/> [acc. July 2019]

'Gotha, Forschungsbibliothek, Memb. I 84': < ... mss/gotha-flb-memb-i-84/> (acc. July 2019]

'Vercelli, Biblioteca Capitolare Eusebiana, CLXXIV': < ... mss/vercelli-bce-clxxiv/> [acc. July 2019]

Firey, A. dir., Carolingian Canon Law Project, <http://dx.doi.org/10.17613/M6P926>

Neveu, M. B., 'Notice sur la vie et les travaux de Jean Imbert', Academie des Sciences Morales et Politiques: séance du 25 novembre 2002: <https://www.asmp.fr/travaux/notices/imbert_neveu.htm#a> [acc. May 2018]

Pennington, K., Bio-Bibliographical Guide to Medieval and Early Modern Jurists, <http://amesfoundation.law.harvard.edu/BioBibCanonists/MainEntry_biobib2.php> [acc. June 2019]

Pennington, K. et al., Medieval and Early Modern Jurists: A Bio-Bibliographical Listing, <http://faculty.cua.edu/pennington/biobibl.htm> [acc. Aug. 2014]

Unpublished Secondary Sources

Satchell, M., 'The Emergence of Leper Houses in Medieval England, 1100–1250' (D.Phil. dissertation, University of Oxford, 1998)

Watson, S., 'Fundatio, Ordinatio, and Statuta: The Statutes and Constitutional Documents of English Hospitals to 1300' (D.Phil. dissertation, University of Oxford, 2004)

Index